THE ACTS OF THE
APOSTLES

THE ACTS OF THE
APOSTLES

What Really Happened in the Earliest Days of the Church

GERD LÜDEMANN
Assisted by Tom Hall

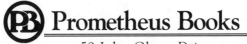 Prometheus Books

59 John Glenn Drive
Amherst, New York 14228-2197

Published 2005 by Prometheus Books

Inquiries should be addressed to
Prometheus Books
59 John Glenn Drive
Amherst, New York 14228–2197
VOICE: 716–691–0133, ext. 207
FAX: 716–564–2711
WWW.PROMETHEUSBOOKS.COM

09 08 07 06 05   5 4 3 2 1

Library of Congress Cataloging-in-Publication Data
Lüdemann, Gerd.
    [Frühe Christentum nach den Traditionen der Apostelgeschichte. English]
    The Acts of the Apostles : what really happened in the earliest days of the church / by Gerd Lüdemann.
        p. cm.
    Rev. ed. of: Early Christianity according to the traditions in Acts.
    Includes bibliographical references and index.
    ISBN 1–59102–301–7 (hardcover : alk. paper)
    1. Bible. N.T. Acts—Commentaries. 2. Bible. N.T. Acts—History of Biblical events. 3. Bible. N.T. Acts—History of contemporary events. 4. Church history—Primitive and early church, ca. 30–600. I. Title.

BS2625.53.L84 2005
226.6'067—dc22

2005007016

Printed in the United States on acid-free paper

CONTENTS

CHAPTER II

ACTS 8:4–15:35: THE SPREADING OF THE GOSPEL
IN THE GENTILE WORLD 115

CHAPTER III

CHAPTER IV

CHAPTER V
CHRONOLOGICAL CHART OF PAUL'S LIFE AND OF PRIMITIVE CHRISTIANITY FROM 30 TO 70 CE

CHAPTER VI
THE REAL VALUE OF LUKE'S ACCOUNT IN ACTS FOR PRIMITIVE CHRISTIANITY BETWEEN 30 AND 70 CE

CHAPTER VII
A BRIEF NARRATIVE OF PRIMITIVE CHRISTIANITY FROM 30 TO 70 CE

APPENDIX
ACTS OF THE APOSTLES AS A HISTORICAL SOURCE

SELECT BIBLIOGRAPHY

INDEX OF NEW TESTAMENT PASSAGES

INDEX OF MODERN AUTHORS

PREFACE

This book, a companion volume to *Jesus After 2000 Years* (Prometheus Books, 2001), seeks to establish the historical value of the words and deeds of Jesus' disciples and of Paul as they appear in the New Testament book of Acts just as the earlier study dealt with the sayings and actions of Jesus in the New Testament Gospels and in the Apocrypha. These two historical-critical assessments constitute a major part of the factual groundwork for a future *History of Primitive Christianity*.

As the specialist is well aware, many excellent and extensive commentaries on *The Acts of the Apostles* are already available in English.[1] I have no desire to write another one along the same lines and repeat what others have said many times. Rather, my goal is to focus on historical questions in order to discover what objective information can be gleaned from the text of Luke.[2] Surprisingly enough, such an agenda is missing in many contemporary commentaries though *"the major problem that confronts any interpreter of the Acts of the Apostles today is the historicity of the Lucan account."*[3] The results of my study should therefore be of interest not only to colleagues but also to lay Christians who are open to critical scholarship and also to the increasing number of people who—after disavowing established forms of Christianity—share a secular viewpoint. This book seeks to provide both groups and the general public with historical data that may satisfy a growing desire to know what really happened in the earliest days of the Christian church.

The precursor of the present study of Acts is my 1989 monograph, *Early Christianity According to the Traditions in Acts*, which was published by Fortress Press and translated from the German[4] by my friend John Bowden, to whom I express heartfelt gratitude. The present book represents a thorough revision and a restructuring of that text which may still be consulted for secondary literature and details of exegesis. At the same time the new volume aims at a less technical analysis of Acts and at a more detailed exposition of the current historical knowledge of Primitive Christianity[5] on the basis of Luke's narrative[6] and Paul's authentic letters.[7] In order to offer complete analyses, I have limited to a minimum the explicit discussion of secondary literature in the body of the text. Nonetheless, I have included discussions of important issues in the footnotes and in chapter endnotes. This has the advantage of maintaining the flow of thought in the running commentary.

In the final chapter I have drawn on the historically assured material to compose "A Brief Narrative of Primitive Christianity from 30 to 70 CE" that, like Luke's account in Acts, gives due attention to Paul. Reading it may be recommended as a way into the book and into the topic it addresses.

Silke Röthke, Frank Schleritt, Hemant Mehta, Walter Höfig, and Alf Özen have helped me at various stages in the preparation of the manuscript. Of utmost value have been the unstinting efforts of my good friend Tom Hall, who has not only improved my English but also functioned as a constant partner in a dialogue now documented in this book.

Gerd Lüdemann
Göttingen, Germany
December 31, 2004

NOTES

1. For detailed study I recommend the splendid commentaries by C. K. Barrett, *A Critical and Exegetical Commentary on the Acts of the Apostles,* 2 vols. (Edinburgh: T & T Clark, 1994–98), and Joseph A. Fitzmyer, *The Acts of the Apostles: A New Translation with Introduction and Commentary* (New York: Doubleday, 1998). Interestingly enough, both quite often circumvent hard historical questions and seem to opt *in dubio pro reo,* i.e., in favor of the author of Acts if the question is at best open. See the analyses below for details. In passing I may add that with both commentaries I consider the so-called Western text of Acts (codex D and other witnesses) a secondary albeit ancient version.

2. Throughout the book I am using the name "Luke" as the name of the author of

Luke-Acts though we probably do not know who actually wrote the two volumes. Church tradition from the second century ascribes the two volumes to Luke "the beloved physician" (Col. 4:14).

3. Fitzmyer, *Acts of the Apostles*, p. 124. Italics added.

4. Gerd Lüdemann, *Das frühe Christentum nach den Traditionen der Apostelgeschichte. Ein Kommentar* (Göttingen: Vandenhoeck & Ruprecht, 1987).

5. On the terminological question see my *Primitive Christianity: A Survey of Recent Studies and Some New Proposals* (London and New York: T & T Clark, 2003), pp. 1–2. As it turns out, scholars use "Early Christianity," "Earliest Christianity," and "Primitive Christianity" as synonyms, and my own work is no exception. Yet "Primitive Christianity" would be the most adequate term.

6. Now in progress is a project similar to that presented in this book. It is the work of the members of the Acts Seminar of Westar Institute, the parent organization of the Jesus Seminar. In his article "Introducing the Acts Seminar" in *The Fourth R* 13, no. 3 (May–June 2000), pp. 6–10, Dennis R. Smith makes the following reference to my 1989 study of Acts: "Determining the sources of Acts is a difficult endeavor. The most significant recent study is Gerd Lüdemann's *Early Christianity According to the Traditions in Acts*. He defines several sources in Acts with a great deal of confidence. But while Lüdemann's study is foundational, it is not the last word" (p. 8). Not only does this revision of my book indicate an implicit acceptance of Smith's statement, but I also remain in full agreement with the goals of Westar Institute, of which I am a Fellow, as well as those of the Acts Seminar. I sincerely hope and trust that our kindred projects will advance both scholarly and general knowledge of Primitive Christianity.

7. The minimal consensus is that the historical Paul wrote Romans, 1 Corinthians, 2 Corinthians, Philippians, Galatians, 1 Thessalonians, and Philemon.

INTRODUCTION
THE LAYOUT AND METHOD
OF THE ANALYSIS

To carry out the program described in the preface, I undertake an analysis of the whole of Acts in order to determine the historical value of the account, i.e., the degree to which the reports in Acts correspond to what really happened—as far as that can be established. In this respect it goes against the main thrust of modern scholarship, which is to delve into Acts (and the Gospel of Luke) primarily to discover the author's theology,[1] the purpose of his writing, and the "meaning" of the text.[2]

But since Acts also purports to be a historical account of early Christianity,[3] academic theology must constantly be concerned with its historical value,[4] especially in view of Luke's clear intention—allowing, of course, for the differences between ancient and modern canons of historiography—to provide historical reportage. Indeed, the opening verse of Acts points back to the introduction to his gospel, in which Luke claims to be engaged in critical historiography based on a thorough evaluation of available sources and certifies the accuracy of the result. In this introduction (Luke 1:1–4), which also functions as prologue to Luke-Acts, the author explicitly refers to previous accounts—some of which he implies are none too accurate in all respects—and vows to produce what we may term a reliable new critical edition. The opening words of Acts, "In the first book, Theophilus . . . ," constitute a commitment only a little short of guarantee that the same intention led him in his description of the mission and spread of Christianity in this second book. In effect he rendered obsolete the apologetic ecclesi-astical "histories" of the second century even before they appeared, and in doing so he left Paul far behind and in a sense anticipated Eusebius.[5]

Was Luke an eyewitness to any of the events he reports? The question is so fundamental that it must be addressed again. If he was, then Acts contains, like Paul's letters, primary source material; if not, it is secondary throughout. In the latter case its historical value cannot approach that of the letters unless its sources are explicit and verified. For Paul's reports of Primitive Christian history reflect a participating observer, and because they generally display literary integrity, their authority is qualitatively superior to that of Acts, in which all accounts would nec-essarily involve at least one unspecified remove from the events. This is not to overlook the sometimes tendentious or even self-serving nature of the epistolary genre; indeed, critical evaluation may show a secondary source to be more reli-able than a primary one. Still, if Luke is not an eyewitness, his reports cannot be accorded the same level of historical value as that granted to the authentic epis-tles. At least we would have to apply other tools and ask different questions in order to determine the value of Acts. I am in full agreement at this point with Colin Hemer when he writes, "The designation of Acts as 'secondary' is formally valid, but this does not answer the separate question of its trustworthiness as a source. Is Acts, 'secondary' as it is, trustworthy or not? 'Primary' sources them-selves are not exempt from error either, and certainly not from *Tendenz*. Until we reexamine the evidence specifically, the range of possible options remains open."[6]

By what criteria can we hope to resolve this problem? We could compare Paul's theology with Luke's—or, better yet that of the Paul he portrays in Acts. Then, if a notable difference appeared, we might dismiss the traditional notion that the author of Acts was for some time a close companion of Paul.

But this will not wash, because such differences (or misperceptions!) of sub-jective beliefs simply cannot be employed to solve historical questions. Although nobody denies that the Paul of Acts differs from the Paul of the letters, disso-nance between two portraits does not prove the veracity or error of either. For that matter, the apostle himself affirms that his theology was variously under-stood—and misunderstood—by his own contemporaries;[7] and in the subsequent period it was understood only superficially, if at all.[8] Thus we must not categor-ically rule out the possibility that the very un-Pauline theology of Luke's Paul has its origin in somebody close to the historical Paul.[9]

If the problem at hand must be solved using historical considerations, may one deny Luke's status as eyewitness on the grounds that he ignored major con-flicts attested by the letters? It has often been noted that he mentions neither Titus—a Gentile who was the subject of a dispute at the Jerusalem conference—

nor the several community crises that Paul himself refers to. This line of argument is suspect, however, because it demands the assumption that Luke must be completely neutral and utterly objective. Since it hardly requires a critical reading of Acts to recognize that the author is aware of events he does not report, his clearly intentional omission of such details as the delivery of the collection in chapter 21 and Paul's execution at the end of Acts can hardly be advanced as proof that he was not present at those events.[10]

That Luke was not a companion of Paul can be demonstrated only by the use of historical statements that uncover complete personal ignorance of Paul on the part of the author of Acts.

Let this be put to the test. One of the keystones of Pauline research is that the available sources establish beyond cavil the number of times Paul visited Jerusalem as a Christian. In Gal. 1:15–24 he gives his solemn oath (verse 20) that he was in Jerusalem only once (verse 18) between the time of his conversion (verses 15–16) and his attendance at the Jerusalem conference (2:1–10). Taken together, the reported unanimity concerning the collection (Gal. 2:10) and the history of the collection recorded in the letters (and thus subject to contemporary verification within the Pauline community) give powerful support to the contention that subsequent to the conference Paul returned to Jerusalem only on the occasion when he brought the collection.

Yet recently various scholars have objected to the view that Paul cannot have visited Jerusalem between his conversion and the conference. In order to substantiate their claim, they have adduced autobiographical literature of antiquity in which persuasion rather than truth is the overriding concern.[11] Yet what may be true for autobiographical literature in general cannot legitimately be assumed to hold in a specific case like that of Paul in his letter to the Galatians. Facing stiff opposition from within the Galatian communities he was writing to, Paul had no other choice than to be precise, the more so since he swears not to lie (Gal. 1:20).[12] Moreover, his adversaries who had invaded the Galatian churches *did* know how often Paul had really been in Jerusalem and would surely have told the members of the congregations if he had left out a journey.[13]

Thus an extra journey to Jerusalem between the trip to visit Cephas and the trip to participate in the Jerusalem conference fourteen years later must be excluded. The same is true for the time between the conference and Paul's final journey to Jerusalem, the more so since once he began gathering the collection, any suspension or delay would be fatal to the project. Rather, the gathering came *directly* after the agreement over the collection and was not a long-postponed operation, planned before Paul's founding of his communities and only now, several years later, being implemented. If indeed a direct connection could be established between the agreement he had made several years previously and the collection—in which case we could even speak of a "collection journey"—then we must exclude an intervening journey to Jerusalem with empty hands. Moreover, reasons of finance and organization tell against this "intermediate journey to Jerusalem." In other words, a probability bordering on certainty indicates that Paul went to Jerusalem only three times.[14]

In Acts, however, we find Paul making no fewer than five journeys to Jerusalem.[15] Granted that Luke is wont to create itineraries in order to contextualize the activities of Jesus and Paul (see pp. 393–94, below), it is all but impossible to imagine that a firsthand observer of a considerable number of the events described would have so gravely distorted the historical facts.

Further, it is strange that Luke did not report Paul's fundamental and decisive claim to be an apostle on equal footing with the apostles in Jerusalem. And last but not least, had Luke been a companion of Paul, one would expect him to have reported more about Paul's early days.

All in all, it is highly unlikely that Luke was an eyewitness to Paul's mission. The Paul encountered by his contemporaries has been supplanted by a more controllable and "user-friendly" persona whose lineaments are defined by the hopes and fears of a later period, and Christianity's earliest period is rendered by a far-from-unbiased author from a later generation.

Still, this issue may not be as important as it was for earlier scholars, for it will have relatively little impact on the analysis of individual passages. If the author was indeed an eyewitness to some of the reported events, he clearly was not present during all of Paul's missions, and it was not until decades later that he wrote Acts. In that case, his portrayal of what he witnessed could hardly be as vivid as one written earlier. Moreover, if we assume that he was using his personal itinerary record or a similar document from his own pen—which might be up to a quarter of a century old[16]—we would have to examine it as critically as if it did not stem from the author. In other words, the question of the author's personal knowledge of Paul no longer bears the great importance for the historicity of Acts that many scholars, myself included, used to think.[17]

I earlier observed that Luke knew more than he reported. Not only that, but he explicitly announces in the prologue to his gospel (Luke 1:1–4) that in writing about Jesus, he relied on the work of predecessors—work that he evidently used in both his volumes. That is to say, Luke wrote using traditions (for a definition see below, pp. 19–20). Where did these traditions come from? Who transmitted them to Luke? Can they be reconstructed? The question of the origin of the traditions in the portions of Acts that relate to Paul can have but one of three answers:

1. Luke knew and used only the letters of Paul.

2. Luke had before him none of Paul's letters, but only other traditions.
3. Luke used both the letters and extant traditions.

To deal with this matter, we must examine each of the possibilities. Turning initially to the first possibility and the first part of the third, let us seek to determine whether the author of Acts knew and used the letters of Paul.

Luke's familiarity with the letters of Paul is an old and well-founded hypothesis; the later one dates his work, especially Acts, the more compelling it becomes. As a member of the third Christian generation who also stands within the Pauline tradition (or else the detailed portrait of Paul is inexplicable) his knowledge of the existence of Pauline letters is almost certain.[18] Accordingly, the issue is not whether Luke *knew* the Pauline letters but whether he *used* them to compose his work.

Since his use of them can be attested only by sure traces of the epistles in Acts, we must look for parallel passages in Acts and the authentic epistles, and decide whether these can best be explained by the hypothesis that Luke used Paul.

Scholars have advanced several important reasons in support of the argument that Luke used Paul's letters:

(a) Except for Caesarea, Tarsus, Cyprus, Beroea, and Malta, all the places and areas that Acts identifies with the Apostle's activity are named in the Pauline corpus. Moreover, at one point Paul's itinerary reported in Acts bears a striking resemblance to one that can be reconstructed from the letters: Paul travels from Philippi via Thessalonica and Athens to Corinth (cf. Acts 16–18 with 1 Thess. 2–3).

> *Rebuttal:* Theories other than dependence can explain a considerable similarity of travel reports and mission locations.

(b) 2 Corinthians 11 and Acts 9 agree closely in their accounts of Paul's hairbreadth escape from Damascus; it is further noteworthy that both end with Paul being lowered from the city wall in a basket.

> *Rebuttal:* The objection made in this case is that one must suppose Luke to have omitted 2 Cor. 12:1–10 from his overall account in Acts. Such an omission would be almost incomprehensible had he made direct use of 2 Cor. 11:32–33.[19]

(c) For the most part, the names of Paul's colleagues mentioned in Acts match the information in Paul's letters.

Rebuttal: The names of Paul's colleagues were generally known in the Pauline communities; such a parallel hardly demonstrates reliance on Paul's letters.

(d) Literary dependence is suggested by individual passages like Acts 15:7–11 (cf. Gal. 2:6–16), Acts 19:21–22 (cf. Rom. 15:22–25) and Acts 26:17–18 (cf. Gal. 1:16); common terms like "destroy"[20] in Acts 9:21 (cf. Gal. 1:23) and "zealous"[21] in Acts 22:3 (cf. Gal. 1:14) are similarly suggestive.

Rebuttal: The use of the verb "to hear" in Gal. 1:13, 23 indicates that "destroy" was already part of the oral tradition (and the same may apply for "zealous"). The information in Acts 19:21–22 about Paul's trip could easily have come from oral reports, and thus can hardly be taken to demonstrate use of the letters. The same applies for Acts 15:7–11.[22]

(e) Luke 21:34–36 is dependent on 1 Thess. 5:1–11.[23]

Rebuttal: If 1 Thess. 5:1–11 derives from various elements of tradition,[24] it seems difficult not to accept the traditional view that Luke 21:34–36 uses similar elements of tradition. In it "Pauline echoes are I Thess. 5.3, 6; Rom. 13.13, where independent reference to pre-Pauline tradition is possible. Note also that in the Lord's Supper Luke (22.19–20) makes use of a tradition from the Pauline mission sphere, as Paul does in I Cor. 11.23–26."[25]

To be sure, the grounds cited indicate significant parallels, but not one rises to the level of compelling proof that Luke used Paul's letters. Of course it may be, as certain cases have already suggested, that an alternate hypothesis is more compelling. Could not Luke have employed traditions that he received from the Pauline mission fields—traditions in which were embedded items that came from a community's knowledge of the details from the letters? To test this possibility, I have in what follows presumed the "tradition hypothesis."

Although a lengthy discussion of why Luke might have avoided using Paul's letters is not appropriate here, it is clear that he knew at least some of them.[26] Nonetheless, the existence of various "heresy hypotheses" should be noted. The most recent is that of Walter Schmithals, who argues that Luke is doing battle with a form of hyper-Pauline Gnosticism that relied in part on Paul's letters. Thus some of his opponents' Pauline sources had become suspect for Luke as a result of his having encountered them in the process of debate with these knowledgeable heretics.[27] For a further explanation of this thesis, see below, pages 270–75 on Acts 20:17–38.

Others have offered the simple explanation that Luke may have avoided unnecessary use of Paul's letters because they were available to anyone, possibly even in a collection. Note that because of where it is placed in the canon, Acts can serve as an introduction to Paul's letters without creating any appreciable degree of repetition. In a like manner, Tacitus avoids including Seneca's last great discourse because "it has been given to the public in his own words" (*Annals* 15.63); and Sallust, no doubt for the same reason, omits a speech of Cicero against Catiline (*Cat* 31.6). Quite unlike Luke, however, these two authors announce their omissions.

If one repudiates Pauline derivation of the passages cited above, the parallels could be broadly explained by invoking "traditions," the age, origin, and content of which would then need to be defined further. In this context the term "tradition" must be interpreted as freely as possible in order not to prejudice the results: the discussion that follows understands "tradition" to include written sources, orally transmitted material, and general knowledge that was part of Luke's cultural environment.

With this in mind, the question of the historical value of Acts must also be reformulated. At the outset we should ask not about the historical value of Acts itself, but about that of the embedded traditions in Acts. If Luke did not participate in the events that he describes, the question of the historicity of Acts must yield to the quest for the historical value of its constituent traditions. Indeed, Luke's activity as a writer consists in linking traditions together, in composing a consecutive narrative on the basis of the traditions. It follows from this that the first task is to separate Luke's purpose from the traditions he reworked, and the next is to examine the historical value of his source materials.

My procedure is indebted to the form critical approach to Acts and follows the lead of Martin Dibelius, who cogently demonstrates that Luke freely adapted contemporary literature and historical accounts, which he adeptly marshaled and arranged to suit his narrative and thematic purposes—and highlighted the material with dramatic speeches. This leads, of course, to the recognition that historical reliability must be judged on a case by case basis, and will depend on the accuracy of Luke's sources.[28]

The analysis that follows divides Acts into series of texts. In the translation I have employed underlines, capitals, italics, and boldfaced type to stress key words and ideas, and thus foster a close reading of the text. Unless otherwise indicated italics denote Luke's editorial pen. One must always take into account, of course, that Luke's vocabulary, style, and agendas have been so effectually engrafted onto his sources as to give the entire text an undeniably Lukan flavor. Each block of text is then outlined. This serves a dual purpose: It recalls the content of the text, and it provides an initial insight into its structure and an inkling of the connection between the sentences and clauses, and thus of their intended meaning. Both of these issues are the theme of the subsequent section, which is an analysis of the *purpose* of the passage. In general, this involves two steps. The first is a short and necessarily less than comprehensive analysis of elements of Luke's language. Of course, linguistic features alone do not offer decisive proof that the author has created a specific passage but must be supplemented by other criteria. Therefore, next follows a discussion of the context of the passage and what it is that Luke seeks to convey.

In the case of each passage I shall next examine whether Luke has reworked *tradition.* Its existence may have been suggested in the analysis of Luke's purpose— by indications of tensions which do not derive from Luke's evident intention, for example, or by un-Lukan expressions. Nevertheless, the possibility of tradition must always be demonstrated separately. While we have particularly good reason for assuming traditions in Acts 16–21, the situation in Acts 1–5; 6–12; 21–28 is different; for traditions cannot be extracted from or controlled by a comparison with the letters of Paul (as they often can in Acts 16–21). This is true even if in individual sections (Acts 5; 8; 12) information from outside Luke can be used as comparative and/or corroborative material. Still, it is important to recognize that elements of tradition *can* be discovered as the basis of *individual* sections without resorting to broad-spectrum source theories. Obviously that does not exclude the possible existence of overlapping strands of sources, but as the detailed analyses will show, it does in part explain elements within them. Finally, I shall seek to reinforce the broad notion of "tradition" already mentioned—one that includes not only written sources but also oral reports and information that were generally available to Luke, including, of course, the results of his apparently wide reading.

After that—under the heading "Historical Elements"—each text analysis subjects the reconstructed traditions in that block to historical verification. In this pursuit Paul's letters often play a significant part in both specific matters of information and overall chronology. Historical questions are necessarily drawn from a hypothetically derived tradition, of course, and specific findings may accordingly be subjected to criticism and counterproposals. Nevertheless, simplistically challenging the commentary as overly reliant on hypotheses would involve a dubious and counterproductive generalization. For the alternative path, one that is too often followed, would be merely to restate—and thus tacitly affirm the historicity of—the Acts account. When the situation requires deciding which of two hypotheses better elucidates a passage, I shall therefore seek to offer either a choice based on the best evidence or an objective analysis of the data on which such a decision must depend. In spite of a full measure of amiability and due recognition of the imperfect nature of human knowledge, I cannot bring myself to concur with Stählin's assertion that in most cases the historicity of narrative elements in Acts is a wide-open question. His case is grievously undercut when his very next sentence reveals the reason for his apparent diffidence: He deplores the widespread scholarly skepticism about Luke's reports and offers in rebuttal the bland, insubstantial postulation that the overwhelming majority of Luke's reports probably reflect pretty closely the actual events.[29]

Last but not least, I separately address the question of the historical value of Luke's account.[30] For one thing, in his shaping of the tradition may be hidden valuable information that my analytic method has failed to evoke. For another, many scholars and laypersons still regard the Acts account as the authoritative source for information about Primitive Christianity. Therefore the issue of historicity must be addressed separately and forthrightly. Third, by focusing specifically on the historical value of Luke's narrative, I can encompass the possibility that Luke might after all have been a companion of Paul, and that his reports therefore deserve a critical evaluation on their own merits.

In examining Luke's account for its historical truth I am not dealing with concerns that are alien to the author, for he does claim—albeit from a different perspective than mine—to be concerned with the historical truth. Furthermore, searching for the historical truth was exactly the job that a historian of Luke's age and before was supposed to do. Note the comments by Lucian of Samosata,[31] a theorist from the second century who bases his judgment on Thucydides, promoting "him above all others as the paradigm of what a historian should be."[32]

How to Write History 41–42, 47

(41) That, then, is the sort of man the historian should be: fearless, incorruptible, free, a friend of free expression and the truth, intent, as the comic poet[33] says, on calling a fig a fig and a trough a trough, giving nothing to hatred or to friendship, sparing no one, showing neither pity nor shame nor obsequiousness, an impartial judge, well disposed to all men up to the point of not giving one side more than its due, in his books a stranger and a man without a country, independent, subject to no sovereign, not reckoning what this or that man will think, but stating the facts.[34] (42) Thucydides laid down this law very well: He distinguished virtue and vice in historical writing, when he saw Herodotus greatly admired to the point where his books were named after the Muses. For Thucydides says that he is writing a possession for evermore rather than a prize-essay

for the occasion, that he does not welcome fiction but is leaving to posterity the true account of what happened. He brings in, too, the question of usefulness and what is, surely, the purpose of sound history: that if ever again men find themselves in a like situation they may be able, he says, from a consideration of the records of the past to handle rightly what now confronts them.[35] (. . .) (47) As to the facts themselves, he should not assemble them at random, but only after much laborious and painstaking investigation. He should for preference be an eyewitness, but, if not, listen to those who tell the more impartial story, those whom one would suppose least likely to subtract from the facts or add to them out of favor or malice. When this happens let him show shrewdness and skill in putting together the more credible story. When he has collected all or most of the facts let him first make them into a series of notes, a body of material as yet with no beauty or continuity. Then, after arranging them into order, let him give it beauty and enhance it with the charms of expression, figure, and rhythm.[36]

Some would argue that since Luke places himself in the context of ancient historical writings he deserves to be measured on the basis of the ancient standards. Thus, even if some of his details are inaccurate, he adhered to contemporary standards of historiography by offering a broadly truthful account that was both thoughtful and entertaining, albeit marked here and there by romantic colorations and hyperbole of biblical rhetoric. Other scholars, however, insist that ancient canons of historicity differ so radically from those of today that any judgment must be invidious. Yet such urgings are irrelevant, deceptive, or as false as the occasionally advanced claim that the ancients were not concerned about false attribution of writings. Let me emphasize that the ancients who were educated enough were interested both in what really happened and in whether a document carried the correct name of the writer.[37] Thus my work on Acts is directly related to their interest and to the goal of modern enlightenment—and ultimately to Luke himself. Despite his glaring inaccuracies, he was without doubt the first Christian historian,[38] and he was part of the Greco-Roman tradition—a careful study of which indicates that historiography did not wait until the Enlightenment to become a self-conscious form of literary art. A number of Greek and Roman historians engaged in an ongoing discourse about historical truth.

My analyses do not even presuppose the impossibility of miracles. I am not taking what Colin Hemer has described as "an absolute position that miracles do not happen, and that *all* alleged instances must accordingly be either rejected or re-explained."[39] Yet I do both recognize and posit that the three-storied universe of the ancients is an outmoded concept and that anything in Acts and elsewhere that presupposes it must be rejected insofar as we are committed to dealing with representations of fact. For the rest, I examine every miracle story of Acts for its historical veracity and do not base my judgment on preconceived notions as to what can or cannot happen. One note of qualification is in order at this point, however: God or god should play no role in the historical investigation. The Acts of the Apostles must be investigated as all other religious or nonreligious texts are examined. And the rule that applies for historical science should also apply for theological science when it comes to the investigation of the historical records of Christianity. Such a presupposition that history has to be reconstructed as if God does not exist should find a common agreement among scholars of the twenty-first century.[40] Van Harvey has rightly said, "What we call historical inquiry is really the formalization by professional historians of our modern, Promethean desire to know, a desire that is actually rooted in everyday life. Historical reasoning is merely the formalization of one method that has, over time, proved to be our best guarantor of achieving this desire and of holding in check the special pleading, obscurantism, and tendentiousness that are omnipresent in human existence."[41] Following the lead of John Dominic Crossan I define "history" as follows, "*History is the past reconstructed interactively by the present through argued evidence in public discourse.* There are times we can get only alternative perspectives on the same event. (There are *always* alternative perspectives, even when we do not hear them.) But history as argued public reconstruction is necessary to reconstruct *our* past in order to project *our* future."[42]

Yet, for whatever reason, Christian scholars are sometimes chary about heeding this protocol in all respects. Instead, they resort to philosophical reflections destined to protect the believer against history. Two examples may suffice.[43] Ben Witherington remarks, "These stories [of Acts] will no doubt continue to create problems for some moderns who rule out in advance the supernatural, including supernatural events such as miracles, and dismiss all history writing that includes such tales as precritical and naive in character. I would suggest that such an a priori approach to miracles is equally uncritical and naive, not least because science has hardly begun to plumb the depth of what is and is not possible in our universe."[44] And Joseph A. Fitzmyer opines, "If one is philosophically convinced that miracles do not happen or that God does not so intervene in human history, then all such narratives immediately become unhistorical or nonhistorical. If, however, one accepts the possibility of such divine intervention, judgment is then open to their historical validation. Clearly, Luke reckoned with such possibility, for he did not hesitate to include such items in his narratives in Acts."[45]

> *Rebuttal:* We can reckon with the possibility of supernatural events only if the historical analysis of a specific case admits of no other explanation. At any rate, one ought not to begin with the assumption that miracles occur.

A NOTE ON THE SPEECHES IN ACTS

As to the speeches in Acts that encompass roughly 30 percent of the whole volume, I presuppose that Luke composed them, following a precept like that of Thucydides in *History of the Peloponnesian War* 1.22.1:

> As to the speeches that were made by different men, either when they were about to begin the war or when they were already engaged therein, it has been difficult to recall with strict accuracy the words actually spoken, both for me as regards that which I myself heard, and for those who from various other sources have brought me reports. Therefore the speeches are given in the language in which, as it seemed to me, the several speakers would express, on the subjects under consideration, the sentiments most befitting the occasion, though at the same time I have adhered as closely as possible to the general sense of what was actually said.[46]

Two things should be noted here. First, Thucydides contends that the speeches he reports represent what was said or what under the circumstances is most likely to have been said—not what he thinks ought to have been (or wishes had been) said. Second, historians of ancient Greece and Rome did not consider themselves free to weave the speeches of important figures (the only kind they would report) out of the thread of their own imaginations.[47]

While it remains a fact that Luke composed the speeches in Acts,[48] this does not exclude the possibility that he did so on the basis of traditional elements that can yet be determined. On the other hand, we would do well to recall that in his gospel (Luke 4:18–27) he created a keynote address of Jesus on the basis of the terse report he found in Mark 6:2. Clearly Luke was capable of fabricating a full-length speech.

THE TRADITIONS AVAILABLE TO LUKE IN ACTS

Having developed the layout of the present book, it is only proper that the reader should be made aware of my general conclusions about whence Luke derived the material of Acts—excluding such hardly debatable sources as the Gospel of Luke, the LXX, Luke's general reading (see p. 20 above), and his common knowledge.[49] I wish to emphasize that my findings are based on an intensive concern with the whole text of Acts and were written only toward the end of the preparation of the manuscript; for full awareness of method only follows the actual use of working methods. However, this is not to say that I went into this with little planning and only in retrospect decided what my methodology had been.[50]

(a) In Acts 15:40–21:36 Luke has had recourse to an itinerary that was fleshed out by several individual episodes.[51] This same source may have contained reports about Paul's early period (Acts 9) and even accounts of the Jerusalem conference (Acts 15). For the relationship of Acts 13–14 to the itinerary see page 174 below.

(b) Luke had access to at least a précis account of Paul's trial before Festus (Acts 25:6–12), along with information about Paul's transfer from Jerusalem to Caesarea, the charge lodged against him, his decision to appeal to the emperor on the basis of Roman citizenship, and so forth. Still, such a source is far more hypothetical than the one adduced above, since Paul's letters do not serve as controls. The following three assumptions likewise lack the advantage of epistolary verification.

(c) Written reports from the Hellenist groups (Acts 6–8; 11; possibly 13–14) were available to Luke.

(d) Luke also knew a number of stories about Peter that came to him in written or oral form (Acts 3; 5; 12).

(e) In Acts 1–5 Luke drew on a number of oral traditions that originated in the early period of the Jerusalem community and were relatively brief and specific in nature.

(f) Finally, since I have never discovered a thoroughly convincing hypothesis that covers all the "we-sections" (Acts 16:10–17; 20:5–15; 21:1–18; 27:1–28:16), I shall not take any assumptions or preconceptions into the process of analyzing them. The specific case of Acts 27, however, may show an at least partly satisfactory solution.[52]

NOTES

1. Yet there is a different assessment of the present situation by Beverly Roberts Gaventa, *The Acts of the Apostles* (Nashville, TN: Abingdon Press, 2003). She writes about her own commentary on Acts, "Generally speaking, however, readers will find this commentary absorbed with questions about Luke's theological perspective as it is conveyed in his narrative, as those questions have too often taken a backseat to what might be called the quest for the 'historical Acts of the Apostles'" (ibid., p. 59).

2. I have written *meaning* with quotation marks in order to indicate I am quite

familiar with the discussion of whether the purpose of a text is identical with its meaning. I shall not deal with that problem, however, because it is irrelevant for my study. Even at places of distinguished learning nowadays the quest for the historicity of Luke-Acts is not on the agenda; see François Bovon, *Studies in Early Christianity* (Tübingen: J. C. B. Mohr/Paul Siebeck, 2003), pp. 19–37 ("Studies in Luke-Acts: Retrospect and Prospect"). In this essay, though, the Harvard professor—despite his neglect of the historical question—advocates "a multiplicity of approaches" (p. 36).

   3. Cf. Acts 1:2–3 recapitulating Luke 1:1–4. Luke's preface "certainly has the vocabulary of a historical preface and easily fits within the frame of reference" (Gregory E. Sterling, *Historiography and Self-Definition: Josephos, Luke-Acts and Apologetic Historiography* [Leiden: E. J. Brill, 1992], p. 340). I assume that the author had Acts in mind when he wrote Luke 1:1–4 and that the two books complement each other. A different view is offered by M. C. Parsons and Richard I. Pervo, *Rethinking the Unity of Luke and Acts* (Minneapolis, MN: Fortress Press, 1993). The study by Loveday Alexander, *The Preface to Luke's Gospel: Literary Convention and Social Context in Luke 1.1–4 and Acts 1.1* (New York: Cambridge University Press, 1993), has provided a host of parallels from historical and scientific writings, the latter being closer to Luke-Acts than the former. As a result she suggests "that Luke is writing from within a Christian social context which is in significant respects like that of the hellenistic schools themselves" (p. 211). Yet that does not change the view that Luke was also a historical writer who wanted to give members of his communities the certainty that what they were taught actually happened. The problem with Luke is the discrepancy between what he set out to do and what he actually performed. When Luke "has discovered the redemptive significance of an event, he can go on to deduce from it the 'correct' chronology, which means, among other things, that he can begin to modify Mark" (Hans Conzelmann, *The Theology of St. Luke* [New York: Harper & Brothers, 1960]), p. 33.

   4. Cf. the account by C. K. Barrett, *Luke the Historian in Recent Study* (London: Epworth Press, 1961), which is still worth reading.

   5. See Philipp Vielhauer, "On the 'Paulinism' of Acts," in *Studies in Luke-Acts*, ed. Leander E. Keck and J. Louis Martyn (Philadelphia: Fortress Press, 1980): 47–48.

   6. Colin J. Hemer, *The Book of Acts in the Setting of Hellenistic History* (Tübingen: J. C. B. Mohr/Paul Siebeck, 1989), p. 15.

   7. See Rom. 3:8 and by contrast 1 Cor. 6:12; 8:1.

   8. See 2 Pet. 3:15–16.

   9. Vielhauer, "On the 'Paulinism' in Acts," p. 48: "The author of Acts is in his Christology pre-Pauline, in his natural theology, concept of the law, and eschatology, post-Pauline. He presents no specifically Pauline idea. His 'Paulinism' consists in his zeal for the worldwide Gentile mission and in his veneration for the greatest missionary to the Gentiles." Reacting to this statement, which had had an enormous influence on subsequent studies of Luke-Acts, Joseph A. Fitzmyer, *The Acts of the Apostles: A New Translation with Introduction and Commentary* (New York: Doubleday, 1998) retorts, "This is, however, a clearly exaggerated view of the differences between the theology of the Lucan Paul, as many writers have since pointed out. . . . Lucan theology, even Luke's interpreta-

tion of Paul's teaching may have to be regarded as a development beyond what is found in Paul's uncontested letters, but that does not mean that he has given us such a biased view of Paulinism as Vielhauer implies" (ibid., p. 147). See further Stanley E. Porter, *The Paul of Acts: Essays in Literary Criticism, Rhetoric, and Theology* (Tübingen: J. C. B. Mohr/Paul Siebeck, 1999), pp. 199–206.

10. The question of whether such "omissions" increase or decrease Luke's trustworthiness is, of course, another matter. See below, pp. 361–64, "The Real Value of Luke's Account in Acts for Primitive Christianity between 30 and 70 CE."

11. Charles H. Talbert, *Reading Luke-Acts in Its Mediterranean Milieu* (Leiden and Boston: Brill, 2003), pp. 205–206 refers to George Lyons, *Pauline Autobiography: Towards a New Understanding* (Atlanta: Scholars Press, 1985), and to Jack T. Sanders, "Paul's 'Autobiographical' Statements in Galatians 1–2," *Journal of Biblical Literature* 85 (1966): 335–43 to suggest that Paul's remarks in Gal. 1–2 should be considered suspect.

12. I realize that in ancient autobiographical literature persons made assurances of truthfulness while at the same time compromising veracity. Yet my argument with respect to Paul is based on the specificity of his situation.

13. On the Jerusalem origin of the opponents in Galatia see my *Opposition to Paul in Jewish Christianity* (Minneapolis, MN: Fortress Press, 1989), pp. 97–103.

14. See my *Paul, Apostle to the Gentiles: Studies in Chronology* (Philadelphia: Fortress Press, 1984), p. 37n51, 147–48.

15. Acts 9:26–30; 11:30; 15:4; 18:22; 21:15–17.

16. See Martin Hengel, *Between Jesus and Paul: Studies in the Earliest History of Christianity* (Philadelphia: Fortress Press, 1983), p. 127. Luke "may have written his two-volume work some twenty to twenty-five years later, perhaps referring back in the so-called 'source' to earlier notes which he had written himself. The gap in time can explain some obscurities and mistakes, and also his carelessness in narrative must be noted."

17. See my *Early Christianity According to the Traditions in Acts: A Commentary* (Minneapolis, MN: Fortress Press, 1989), p. 4.

18. See John Knox, "Acts and the Pauline Letter Corpus," in *Studies in Luke-Acts*, pp. 279–87.

19. Moreover, Acts 9:23–25 could go back to a tradition mediated by 2 Cor. 11:32–33. See below, p. 131.

20. In Greek, *porthein.*

21. In Greek, *zēlotēs.*

22. Despite William O. Walker, "Acts and the Pauline Corpus Revisited," in *Literary Studies in Luke-Acts: Essays in Honor of Joseph B. Tyson*, ed. Richard B. Thompson and Thomas E. Phillips (Macon, GA: Mercer University Press, 1998), pp. 77–86 (bibliog.). See now Heikki Leppä, *Luke's Critical Use of Galatians*, academic diss., University of Helsinki (Vantaa, 2002). He provides a valuable history of research at pp. 13–32 of his dissertation.

23. Lars Aejmelaeus, *Wachen vor dem Ende. Die Traditionsgeschichtlichen Wurzeln von 1 Thess 5:1–11 und Luk 21:34–36* (Helsinki: Kirjapaino Raamattutalo, 1985). Cf.

Aejmelaeus, *Die Rezeption der Paulusbriefe in der Miletrede (Apg 20:18-35)* (Helsinki: Suomalainen Tiedeakatemia, 1987).

24. Cf. Aejmelaeus, *Wachen vor dem Ende,* p. 136.

25. Gerd Lüdemann, *Jesus After 2000 Years: What He Really Said and Did* (Amherst, NY: Prometheus Books, 2001), p. 391.

26. Thus, e.g., Otto Bauernfeind, *Die Apostelgeschichte* (Tübingen: J. C. B. Mohr/Paul Siebeck, 1980), pp. 295–98.

27. See Walter Schmithals, *Die Apostelgeschichte des Lukas* (Zürich: Theologischer Verlag, 1982), p. 16.

28. Martin Dibelius, *Studies in the Acts of the Apostles* (London: SCM Press, 1956), p. 107.

29. Cf. Gustav Stählin, *Die Apostelgeschichte,* 7th ed. (Göttingen: Vandenhoeck & Ruprecht, 1980), p. 8.

30. My *Early Christianity According to the Traditions in Acts* did not address that question separately and was rightly criticized for it by I. Howard Marshall, *The Acts of the Apostles* (Sheffield: Sheffield Academic Press, 1992), pp. 87–88: "Lüdemann ignores the three possibilities: (a) that Luke had access to historical information which he inserted at the redactional stage; (b) that Luke's redactional concerns and the tradition could at times coincide (e.g. Luke and Peter may have shared some theological expressions or concepts); and (c) that material expressed in Lukan style may be simply tradition put in his own words or manner of expression rather than his own creation."

31. See Daniel Marguerat, *The First Christian Historian: Writing the "Acts of the Apostles"* (Cambridge and New York: Cambridge University Press, 2002), pp. 13–20.

32. W. J. McCoy, "In the Shadow of Thucydides," in *History, Literature, and Society in the Book of Acts,* ed. Ben Witherington III (Cambridge and New York: Cambridge University Press, 1996), p. 9.

33. Aristophanes or Menander. The latter is favored by Helene Homeyer, *Lukian: Wie man Geschichte schreiben soll* (Munich: Wilhelm Fink Verlag, 1965), pp. 251–52. Homeyer's commentary is worth consulting for the passages from Lucian quoted in the present volume and beyond.

34. In Greek, *ti pepraktai legôn.*

35. Lucian in eight volumes, VI. With an English translation by K. Kilburn, Loeb Classical Library (London: William Heinemann and Cambridge: Harvard University Press, 1959), pp. 57, 59. Chapter 42 is a free paraphrase of Thucydides 1.22.4: "And it may well be that the absence of the fabulous from my narrative will seem less pleasing to the ear; but whoever shall wish to have a clear view both of the events which have happened and of those will some day, in all human probability, happen again in the same or a similar way—for these to adjudge my history profitable will be enough for me. And, indeed, it has been composed, not as a prize-essay to be heard for the moment but as a possession for all time." (Translation from Thucydides, *History of the Peloponnesian War* in four volumes, I, books I and II with an English translation by Charles Foster Smith, Loeb Classical Library [London: William Heinemann and New York: G. P. Putnam's Sons, 1928], pp. 39, 41.)

36. Lucian in eight volumes, VI, p. 61. Chapter 47 is based on Thucydides 1.22.2–3:

"But as to the facts of the occurrences of the war, I have thought it my duty to give them, not as ascertained from any chance informant nor as seemed to me probable, but only after investigating with the greatest possible accuracy each detail, in the case both of the events in which I myself participated and of those regarding which I got my information from others. (3) And the endeavor to ascertain these facts was a laborious task, because those who were eye-witnesses of the several events did not give the same reports about the same things, but reports varying according to their championship of one side or the other, or according to their recollection" (ibid., p. 39).

37. I am touching the field of pseudepigraphy. See my *Die Intoleranz des Evangeliums. Erläutert an ausgewählten Schriften des Neuen Testaments* (Springe: zu Klampen, 2004), pp. 255–66, and the comprehensive history of research by Martina Janssen, *Unter falschem Namen. Eine kritische Forschungsbilanz frühchristlicher Pseudepigraphie* (Frankfurt: Peter Lang, 2003).

38. Robert L. Wilken, *The Myth of Christian Beginnings: History's Impact on Belief* (Garden City, NY: Doubleday, Anchor Books, 1972), pp. 33–51; Marguerat, *The First Christian Historian*, p. xi.

39. Hemer, *Book of Acts*, p. 438.

40. All this has less to do with a "materialistic worldview" than with common practice among professional historians. Here I go against Talbert, *Reading Luke-Acts*, pp. 215–16. On p. 215 he erroneously writes about my approach, "The materialistic worldview, represented by Lüdemann, dictates that the world was and is ruled by iron physical laws that not even God could or can bend."

41. Van A. Harvey, *The Historian and the Believer: The Morality of Historical Knowledge and Christian Belief* (Urbana and Chicago: University of Illinois Press, 1996), pp. xx–xxi.

42. John Dominic Crossan, *The Birth of Christianity: Discovering What Happened in the Years Immediately After the Execution of Jesus* (San Francisco: HarperSanFrancisco, 1998), p. 20.

43. I cite another example in an endnote since it is only indirectly related to Acts. John Meier writes concerning the historicity of the divine conception of Jesus that, "by itself, historical-critical research simply does not have the sources and tools available to reach a final decision on the historicity of the virginal conception as narrated by Matthew and Luke. One's acceptance or rejection of the doctrine will be largely influenced by one's philosophical and theological presuppositions, as well as the weight one gives Church teaching. Once again, we are reminded of the built-in limitations of historical criticism. It is a useful tool, provided we do not expect too much of it" (John P. Meier, *A Marginal Jew: Rethinking the Historical Jesus*, vol. 1, *The Roots of the Problem and the Person* [New York: Doubleday, 1991], p. 222). *Rebuttal:* The claim that Jesus had no human father is a historical judgment that can be verified or falsified. I suspect that Roman Catholic Church doctrine has made Meier write such sentences. Let me repeat here what I wrote a few years ago about Roman Catholic scholars like Meier: "[W]e also have to ask how we are to judge North American stars of exegesis like R. E. Brown . . . , J. A. Fitzmyer . . . and J. P. Meier . . . , who have occupied themselves with the birth of Jesus

from a virgin more thoroughly than most others and in the end have not felt able to contradict Roman Catholic dogma. Either they were too cowardly to do so, or they have allowed it to become second nature to live a spiritual ghetto existence, according to the principle 'when in doubt judge in favour of the church and its dogma.' . . . Has it not become clear that these scholars—like many of their Catholic colleagues in Germany—are simply apologists, whom one cannot trust to point the way?" (Gerd Lüdemann, *Virgin Birth? The Real Story of Mary and Her Son Jesus* (Harrisburg, PA: Trinity Press International, 1998), p. 141.

44. Ben Witherington III, *The Acts of the Apostles: A Socio-Rhetorical Commentary* (Grand Rapids, MI: William B. Eerdmans, 1998), pp. 223–24.

45. Fitzmyer, *Acts of the Apostles*, p. 126. Fitzmyer continues, "At any rate, there is no way to offer any proof of their historicity. (Needless to say, the fact that Acts forms part of the inspired New Testament does not make the Lucan account, narrated in the past tense, necessarily historical. Neither church teaching nor theologians have ever maintained that the necessary formal effect of inspiration is historicity.)." The latter statement calls for a critical comment. In the *Catechism of the Catholic Church* one reads, "The Church holds firmly that the four Gospels, whose *historicity* she unhesitatingly affirms, faithfully hands on what Jesus, the Son of God, while he lived among men, really did and taught for their eternal salvation, until the day when he was taken up" (*Catechism of the Catholic Church* [Washington, DC: United States Catholic Conference, 1994], p. 35 [126.1]). I wonder whether the same, according to Catholic doctrine, must not be true for what the Acts of the Apostles says that the apostles, including Paul, while they lived among men, really did and taught for their eternal salvation.

46. Translation with some modifications from Thucydides, *History of the Peloponnesian War* in four volumes, I, books I and II, with an English translation by Charles Foster Smith, Loeb Classical Library (London: William Heinemann and New York: G. P. Putnam's Sons, 1928), p. 39.

47. Cf. Charles William Fornara, *The Nature of History in Ancient Greece and Rome* (Berkeley: University of California Press, 1983), pp. 154–55.

48. "In their final form, however, the speeches are clearly Lucan compositions" (Fitzmyer, *Acts of the Apostles*, p. 105).

49. For the source theories put forward by a number of respected scholars, see also ibid., pp. 80–89.

50. Yet, "theory must follow not precede the practice" (D. C. Parker, *The Living Text of the Gospels* [Cambridge and New York: University Press, 1997], p. 7). Parker is a textual critic and rightly admonishes critics from other areas of biblical studies to follow his advice.

51. For a parallel cf. a journal used as a model by Xenophon for his *Anabasis* and on it see Rainer Nickel, *Xenophon* (Darmstadt: Wissenschaftliche Buchgesellschaft, 1979), pp. 85–86, 118.

52. Cf. Jürgen Wehnert, *Die Wir-Passagen der Apostelgeschichte: Ein lukanisches Stilmittel aus jüdischer Tradition* (Göttingen: Vandenhoeck & Ruprecht, 1989).

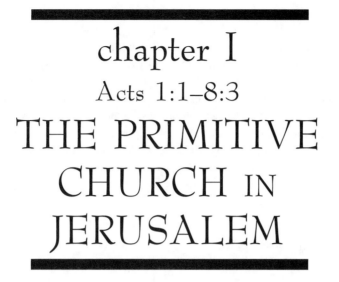

chapter I
Acts 1:1–8:3
THE PRIMITIVE CHURCH IN JERUSALEM

The work . . . begins with a conversation between the disciples and the Risen One who answers their most important question; that is, most important to the readers. Thereupon the author describes the real beginning of the first congregation through the sending of the Spirit at Pentecost, and the congregation's preaching which falls entirely to Peter. To be sure, several other apostles, like John and Matthias, are occasionally mentioned, but they remain shadows. Luke does not care to portray individual personalities, nor would the tradition have helped him to do so. The history of the early congregation makes up this first part, a quarter of the whole book.[1]

[1]
ACTS 1:1–8
RECAPITULATION; JESUS' WORDS AND ACTIONS OF FAREWELL

(1) *In the previous book,* Theophilus, *I have dealt with all that Jesus did and taught from the beginning,* (2) *until the day when he was taken up, after he had given commands through the Holy Spirit to the apostles whom he had chosen.* (3) To them he presented himself alive after his passion by many proofs, appearing to them during forty days *and speaking about the kingdom of God.* (4a) And while eating with them, (4b) he ordered them not to depart from Jerusalem, *but*

to wait for the promise of the Father, (4c) *which* [, he said,] *"you heard from me;* (5a) *for John baptized with water,* (5b) *but you will be baptized with the Holy Spirit not many days from now."* (6) *So when they had come together, they asked him,* "Lord, do you at this time restore the kingdom to Israel?" (7) *He said to them, "It is not for you to know times or seasons that the Father has established by his own authority.* (8) *But you will receive power when the Holy Spirit comes upon you, and you will be my witnesses in Jerusalem, and in all Judea and Samaria, and to the end of the earth."*

OUTLINE

1–2:   The prologue

3–8:   Jesus' farewell actions and words of commission

LUKE'S PURPOSE

Verses 1–2: This paragraph, ostensibly a dedication to one Theophilus,[2] introduces the second part of Luke-Acts and expressly speaks of "the previous book," that is, Luke's Gospel, whose content the author describes as Jesus' doings and teachings.[3] Here the commandments Jesus gives to his disciples/apostles before the ascension are at variance with those in Luke 24, unless one surmises Jesus had given them during the farewell meal.[4] The choosing alluded to in verse 2 was related in Luke 6:13, and is here referred to in preparation for the list that follows in verse 13.

Verse 3: "Forty days," which may derive from tradition (see below, p. 33), is nonetheless to be understood as part of the "fifty days" from which Pentecost (2:1) derives its name. No doubt Luke's aim in this specification is to help to account for the time between Passover, when Jesus died, and the Feast of Weeks, the first subsequent major Jewish festival, when the recently restored apostolate (1:26) announce to their fellow Jews the testimonial good news about their risen Lord.

Verse 4: "Eating together" (cf. 10:41) in verse 4a echoes Luke 24:41–43. The order in verse 4b not to leave Jerusalem points back to Luke 24:49, where the disciples are ordered to remain in the city until they are endowed with the power of the Most High. Indeed, verse 4c, "which you have heard from me," creates a flashback to the situation of Luke 24:49.

Verse 5: This speech of Jesus (or more accurately, "The Risen Christ") has two functions. Verse 5a points to a central event of the past, "John baptized with water" (Luke 3:16a), while 5b announces the imminent fulfillment of the Baptist's promise of the Holy Spirit (Luke 3:16b)—an event that will happen "not many days from now" and is duly reported in Acts 2. Thus in another echo of Luke 24:49, Jesus both reiterates a saying of John the Baptist and relates it to the present by connecting it with the outpouring of the Spirit in Acts 2. Note, moreover, that according to both passages the disciples are staying in Jerusalem, and that subsequently 11:16 looks back to the saying of Jesus in verse 5.

Verses 6–7: "Jesus" corrects an imminent expectation, brushing aside the question of whether the kingdom is coming immediately (cf. Luke 1:32–33; 24:21). Here the kingdom (verse 3b) is replaced by the Spirit, meaning that Jesus' preaching of the kingdom of God is to be interpreted in this spiritual, ecclesiological sense. In this way the time of Jesus' future coming (in Greek, *parousia*)—his imminent advent "with the sound of the trumpet of God" (1 Thess. 4:16)—is shifted into an indeterminate future (but not an uncertain one: see verse 11; 17:31). Thus the content of verse 8 receives emphasis (cf. Luke 24:47–48) in that the preaching of the gospel throughout the world is being represented beforehand and is, moreover, the work of the Spirit, whose coming has been prophesied in verse 7. Note also that the task of the apostles is there defined as being witnesses to Jesus (see p. 42 below). Paul will later take up their work (cf. 22:15; 26:16–18).

Verse 8: This verse contains the postulate and syllabus of Acts. Here the expression "to the end of the world"[5] denotes Rome[6] and prefigures the geographical sweep of Acts, which carries the reader from Jerusalem to Rome. Note how clearly 19:21 and 23:11 attest to Luke's interest in the capital of the Roman Empire. Oddly enough, Galilee receives no attention in Luke's syllabus. Indeed, no missionary activity is reported to occur in the home territory of Jesus and the disciples. Acts 9:31 will be the only place where Luke mentions Galilee[7] and points to the existence of Christian churches in that area.

THE TRADITIONS REWORKED BY LUKE

1. Jesus' presenting himself alive after his passion (verse 3a) and appearing over forty days (verse 3b) are juxtaposed in the report. The first idea matches the appearance of the exalted Jesus from heaven (1 Cor. 15:5)—reported to Paul after his "conversion"—and the second recalls reports found elsewhere about a particular period during which Jesus remained with his disciples after the resurrection.[8] The number "forty" is formulaic in biblical writing: Israel was forty years in the wilderness, Moses forty days and forty nights on Sinai (Exod. 24:18; 34:28), Elijah went forty days and forty nights to Mount Horeb (1 Kings 19:8), and Jesus spent forty days in the wilderness (Mark 1:13). Luke has connected concepts that he knew

from both oral and written traditions. The phrase "by many proofs" that seems to have been added to certify the actual presence of the exalted Jesus is uncertain in meaning. "Proof" (in Greek, *tekmerion*) is used only here in the New Testament and suits the means by which the risen Christ—whether still on earth or from heaven—demonstrated his real presence.[9]

2. The hope for the restoration of Israel's kingdom—resulting from the future coming of Jesus—is reflected in the question in verse 6, "Lord, do you at this time restore the kingdom to Israel?" As noted in the analysis of verses 6–7 above, Luke "corrects" this element of tradition by replacing "kingdom" with "Spirit."

HISTORICAL ELEMENTS

The account must be considered unhistorical in its present form, since Luke fails to mention the first appearances in Galilee, reports of which he knew from the Gospel of Mark, and which are reflected in Mark 16:7; Matt. 28:16; and John 21.

Historical and unhistorical details are mixed together in the individual traditions mentioned above:

(a) "Appearances"—in reality, "visions"—of the post-Easter Jesus must have taken place in Jerusalem (after those in Galilee). That can be said with certainty of the vision of James (1 Cor. 15:7a), since the Lord's brother joined the primitive community only at a *later* date, and the same must be true of the vision of all the apostles (1 Cor. 15:7b). Note also the "appearance" to more than five hundred brothers at one time (1 Cor. 15:6) as evidence for a tradition of Jerusalem appearances. In its earliest form, the tomb story (Mark 16:1–8) does not record any special Jerusalem appearance of Jesus to the women (in contrast to Matt. 28:9–10; John 20:14–18) and therefore cannot be utilized here.[10] On the other hand, the tradition of Jesus being with his disciples for forty days is unhistorical because it goes back to a later conception. Its creators wanted to stretch the time of communication on earth between Jesus and his disciples after the resurrection.

(b) Jewish Christians in Jerusalem may have shared the expectation of the imminent restoration of the kingdom to Israel through the future coming of Jesus. Otherwise it is difficult to explain why influential segments of Jewish Christianity remained for years in Jerusalem or continued to stress the theological significance of that city as the place of Jesus' soon-forthcoming advent in glory.[11] The belated and hesitant nature of their acceptance of the Gentile mission (Gal. 2:9) probably reflects the original expectation of a reestablishment of Israel that would accompany Jesus' return.

(c) Luke's narrative about the bestowal of the Spirit on the disciples is definitely unhistorical in the context of a mission command that includes Gentiles.

Indeed, the Gentile mission was hotly disputed in Primitive Christianity. While the Jerusalem apostles saw themselves engaged in a mission exclusively to the Jews, Paul and the Hellenists wrung the mission to the Gentiles as a sort of concession from the Jerusalem church.[12]

THE HISTORICAL VALUE OF LUKE'S ACCOUNTS

The historical value is nil. The resurrection of Jesus did not take place. The disciples had visionary experiences. By historicizing the objective correlative of inward events, Luke created an account that for centuries caused, and even to this day continues to cause, enormous confusion.[13]

[2]
ACTS 1:9–11
JESUS' ASCENSION

(9) And when he had said this, as they were **looking***, he was lifted up, and a cloud took him out of their sight. (10) And while they were gazing* into heaven *as he went, look, two men stood by them in white clothing. (11) They said, "Galilean men, why do you stand* **looking** into heaven*? This Jesus, who was taken up from you* into heaven*, will come in the same way as you saw him go* into heaven*."*

OUTLINE

9: Jesus lifted up in a cloud into heaven
10–11: Angelic interpretation of Jesus' ascension

LUKE'S PURPOSE

Verse 9: The use of the verb "to look" (in Greek, *blepein*) "places the Ascension in the same category of events as any other happening in the story of Jesus."[14] At the same time, God lifted up Jesus[15] and the clouds are evidence of God's presence.[16]

Verses 10–11: The fourfold repetition of "into heaven," underlined above, clearly indicates an editor's hand. The two men in white clothing (verse 10) recall the two men in shining garments in the tomb (Luke 24:4). The anticipation of Jesus' return (verse 11) probably derives from Luke and connects this passage with verses 6–7: imminent expectation expressed in verse 6 and rejected in verse 7 here becomes a distant expectation—not in resignation, but in hope.

THE TRADITIONS REWORKED BY LUKE

Underlying this is a tradition the form of which can no longer be ascertained. It reports the miraculous ascension of Jesus. Motifs belonging to this are "the cloud" and "two men in shining garments" (cf. Luke 24:4) as interpreters of the events. (A duplication of this tradition which has been worked over even more intensively by Luke appears in Luke 24:50–53.)[17] The tradition includes neither a chronological relation to Easter Day nor a connection with a particular place. The use of "Galilean [men]" as a form of address is not part of the tradition but derives from Luke (cf. 2:7).

HISTORICAL ELEMENTS

The ascension did not take place. It is related to a concept of space and time, according to which—given a three-storied view of the cosmos—rising upward within a cloud (Luke 24:51; Acts 1:11) was understood as assumption into heaven and an empty tomb was a sign of the removal of the dead.

THE HISTORICAL VALUE OF LUKE'S ACCOUNT

This statement concerning Luke's factually inaccurate assertion must be qualified with regard to two groups of scholars. (a) Moderately conservative scholars speak first of the symbolism of the ascension and then of the historicity of the event; one of them finally says, "What happened lies beyond simple literal description. It is in this kind of way that the story of the ascension of Jesus is best understood."[18] One would like to ask whether this was also the case with other ascension accounts from the ancient world. (b) However, it is wrong to go to the other extreme and agree with one modern scholar that "Anyone who interprets the happenings narrated by Luke . . . as a simple historical event does not take them 'literally' in Luke's sense. One takes narratives of this kind 'literally' only when one asks very carefully about the theological purposes of their author."[19] Clearly Luke's thinking was rooted in the conceptions of the time, and he really thought that Jesus ascended to heaven. His reason for that was the report of the empty tomb. That any "theological" significance of the ascension of Jesus can be maintained when the historical result is nil, I doubt very much; it is impossible to predicate rational discourse on an event that did not occur. To offer an argument from analogy, a decisive proof of the nonexistence of Jesus would certainly have negative consequence for the theological quest for Jesus.

[3]
ACTS 1:12–14
THE EARLIEST COMMUNITY

(12) *Then they returned to Jerusalem from the mount named "The Olive Grove," which lies near Jerusalem, a Sabbath day's journey away.* (13) *And when they had entered, they went to the upstairs room where they were staying,* Peter and John and James and Andrew, Philip and Thomas, Bartholomew and Matthew, James the son of Alphaeus and Simon the Zealot and Judas the son of James. (14) *All these were of one mind in devoting themselves to prayer, together with the women and Mary the mother of Jesus, and with his brothers.*

OUTLINE

12: The return of the apostles to Jerusalem
13–14: The apostles mentioned by name in the upstairs room along with the women, Jesus' mother, Mary, and his brothers

LUKE'S PURPOSE

Verse 12: This verse serves as a transition from the preceding account to the report that follows. The place of the ascension, "The Olive Grove" or Mount of Olives, and its distance from Jerusalem are mentioned in passing. Luke may be the source of both data, since the specification "a Sabbath day's journey" points to the mutual proximity of the several places near Jerusalem where the disciples are staying. Clearly Luke considers the Jerusalem theme particularly important here: Having witnessed Jesus' ascension near Jerusalem, the disciples then return *to* Jerusalem. For the designation "Mount of Olives" see Luke 19:29/Mark 11:1 (Matt. 21:1 omits Bethany). Knowing from Mark's account that the Mount of Olives and Bethany, if not different names for the same place, are close together, Luke changes the place-name from the one he employed earlier: In Luke

24:50–53 the setting of the ascension vision was Bethany. As biblical authors are wont to do, Luke includes the mountain motif in accounts of exaltations and transportations.

Verses 13–14: Luke describes in verse 14 the devout and prayerful[20] conduct of the first community in an idyllic way. "Persistent prayer is often the setting for major events in Lucan writings. Here the community's prayer of expectation (of the coming baptism with the Spirit) parallels that of Jesus before his baptism in Luke 3:21."[21] This portrait prepares for both the subsequent means of choosing a replacement for Judas and such subsequent idealizations of the earliest community as 4:32. The mention of women members of the first community may reflect Luke's editing, but does he refer to women followers of Jesus or wives of the apostles? Several considerations suggest that in verse 14 "with the women" (in Greek, *syn gynaixin)* is meant to denote the apostles' wives. Linguistic considerations strongly imply that the women were wives of the disciples. Had female followers of Jesus been intended,[22] customary Greek usage would call for placing the definite article before "women." Further, when Luke refers to Jesus' female followers in his Gospel, they are either named or more clearly delineated. The simple fact is that in Acts Luke so totally ignores the women who came from Galilee with Jesus that they are mentioned nowhere else in the book—that is, if indeed they are referred to here. If it is they whom we meet in verse 14, they appear simply to include the "women from Galilee" motif—at most for the sake of completeness. If, however, these are the wives of the apostles, verse 14 would picture a kind of "holy family of the earliest community" consisting of the kindred of the disciples and the kindred of the Lord, listed in a chiastic pattern: men (twelve apostles) and their wives; women (represented by Mary the mother of Jesus) and men (the brothers of Jesus). To the degree that this proposal is sustainable, Acts 1:14 could be viewed as analogous to the kinship patterns described in Luke 1–2—and possibly inspired by Luke's reading of Mark 6:1–6. Finally, on the basis of 1 Cor. 9:5 we may surmise that it was known in the communities that the apostles had wives; indeed, the reference to Peter's mother-in-law (Mark 1:30 par.) shows beyond cavil that the principal disciple had a wife. It follows clearly from the foregoing that the reference to Jesus' brothers[23] *derives* from Luke and simply fleshes out the overall picture that he seeks to project in verse 14.

THE TRADITIONS REWORKED BY LUKE

Verse 13: Two items call for a comment:

(a) Luke lists the apostles, but in a different order than that found in Luke

6:14–16. The most important difference is that Acts lists John second, whereas the Gospel has Andrew second and John third. This variance may be due to a narrative decision to have Peter and John appear in the present text as a pair (see chapters 3–5). Note also that in contradistinction to parallel reports in other gospels, Luke often places Peter and John together. For example, they are named in Luke 22:8, where Mark 14:13 says only "two of his disciples," and Matt. 26:17 simply "the disciples."[24] It should, of course, be noted that the list of the twelve in Mark 3:16–19 has "Thaddeus" in place of Luke's "Judas, brother of James" and "Simon the Canaanite" for Luke's "Simon the Zealot."

(b) It is possible that traditional information about the meeting place of the Jerusalem community underlies the expression "upstairs room" (in Greek, *hyperoon*).[25] On the other hand, 9:37, 39 and 20:8 raise the possibility that Luke has inserted it.

HISTORICAL ELEMENTS

Verse 13: Certainly the names of the disciples of Jesus are for the most part historical, the more so since the synoptic parallels that are independent of one another support most of them. Nonetheless, Jesus called them disciples, not apostles. Despite examples of ambiguous terminology in the synoptic gospels (see, for example, Mark 6:30 and 35; Matt. 10:1 and 2; Luke 6:13a and 13b), it was not until after the resurrection of Jesus—which was the interpretation of Jesus' death, but not a historical event—that the "Risen One" appointed the aforementioned disciples to be apostles (see Matt. 28:19). Paul's self-reported appointment to be an apostle was also attributed to the resurrected Jesus—although a number of the original apostles remained unconvinced.

THE HISTORICAL VALUE OF LUKE'S ACCOUNT

The narrated events did not occur. Luke's introduction of an idyllic element into the picture of the earliest community in Jerusalem is historically misleading. These people were expecting the return of Jesus from heaven at any moment and shared in that enthusiastic hope. Furthermore, it is out of the question that Jesus' brothers joined the community at such an early stage. Jesus' (natural) family considered him to be out of his mind.[26]

[4]
ACTS 1:15–26
JUDAS REPLACED BY MATTHIAS

(15) *In those days Peter stood up among the* <u>*brothers*</u>*—the company numbered about one hundred twenty in all—and said:* (16) *"*<u>*Brothers*</u>*, the Scripture had to be fulfilled, which the Holy Spirit spoke beforehand by the mouth of David concerning Judas, who became a guide to those who arrested Jesus.* (17) *For he was numbered among us and had received his portion in this ministry.*

(18) Now this man bought a field with the reward for his unrighteousness, and falling headlong he burst asunder in the middle and his intestines gushed out. (19a) *This became known to all the inhabitants of Jerusalem,* (19b) and the field came to be called in their language Akeldama, that is, the field of blood. (20) For it is written in the Book of Psalms, 'May his camp become desolate, and let there be no one to dwell in it;' and 'Let another take his office.' (21) *So it is necessary that one of the men who have accompanied us during all the time that the Lord Jesus went in and out among us,* (22) *beginning from his baptism by John until the day when he was taken up from us—that one of these men become with us a witness to his resurrection."*

(23) And they put forward two: Joseph *named* Barsabbas, who was also *known as* Justus, and Matthias. (24) *And they prayed and said, "You, Lord, who know the hearts of all, show which one of these two you have chosen* (25) *to take the place in this ministry and apostleship from which Judas turned aside to go to his own place."* (26) *And they cast lots for them, and the lot fell on Matthias, and he was numbered with the eleven apostles.*

OUTLINE

15: Introduction
16–22: Peter's sermon
23–26: Casting lots for the replacement of Judas

LUKE'S PURPOSE

Verse 15: "In those days"—a favorite phrase of Luke[27]—joins the preceding to the following episode. A thematic link is Luke's report of the harmonious prayer of the eleven apostles with other members of the congregation (verses 13–14), for it leads the reader to expect something in harmony with that report. The parenthetical element "about one hundred twenty" indicates a group far greater than the number of disciples given in verses 13–14 and therefore enumerates the whole community.

Verses 16–17: In defending the passion of Jesus, the earliest Christian tradition developed the idea of demonstrating the necessity of an event by reference to scripture.[28] Employing this motif, Luke assigns the "betrayal" by Judas to divine necessity.[29] Verse 20a takes up this prophecy (= Ps. 69:26 [LXX 68:25—not literally]). The remarks about the action of Judas (verses 16c–17) illustrate Luke 22:3, 47.

Verses 18–20: This passage is largely traditional (see below, p. 43); nevertheless, "this became known to all the inhabitants of Jerusalem" (verse 19a) reflects Luke's language (cf. 4:16; 9:42; 19:17). The end of verse 20 forms a transition to the choice; this part of the verse cites Ps. 109:8 (LXX 108:8) where, as in the present text, mention of a replacement appears in language that is literally the same except for "let take." Judas plays an important hortatory role in the broad scheme of Luke's two volumes. Having tempted Jesus (Luke 4:1–12), Satan had withdrawn "until the appointed hour" (Luke 4:13). That hour arrived when Satan "entered into Judas" (Luke 22:3) and made him Jesus' "betrayer." By chronicling Judas's fate to show what happens to instruments of Satan in the community, Luke admonishes his readers against allowing Satan any place in their lives. The deterministic interpretation of Ps. 69:26 does not go against this (see the references above to the divine necessity of an event).

Verse 21: The emphasis on divine necessity reinforces the idea of the previous verse and harks back to verse 16.

Verse 22: "Beginning from" is a typical Lukan idiom.[30] "Taken up" points back to 1:9 (cf. Luke 24:51). Verse 22 offers important evidence both for Luke's understanding of the role of John the Baptist in "salvation history" and for his conception of the office of apostle.

(a) John's central thematic importance is adduced in Acts 10:37 and 13:24–25. Both times his role and that of Jesus are distinguished, creating the impression that they represent two different epochs. Note also that in contrast to Mark 1:9, Luke's narrative places the imprisonment of John the Baptist (Luke 3:19–20) *before* the baptism of Jesus (Luke 3:21), thus making it seem that John did not perform the baptism. This sense of distinction is further intensified by Luke 16:16; here John clearly belongs to a period distinctly set apart from the time beginning after him ("from then on"). Conzelmann has concisely explained Luke's concept of John the Baptist: "John no longer marks the arrival of the new aeon, but the division between two epochs in the one continuous story, such as it is described in Luke xvi, 16. The eschatological event does not break out after John, but a new stage in the process of salvation is reached, John himself still belonging to the earlier of the two epochs which meet at this point."[31]

One doubts whether this theory can be applied without ado as Conzelmann opines. For in Acts 1:22 Jesus' baptism by John is the beginning of his own career, and sharing in this baptism is the qualification for the witnesses; therefore John here stands within the same time frame as Jesus. Besides, the clause "up to John" in Luke 16:16 may indicate either inclusion (he is part of the period of the law and the prophets) or exclusion (he is not part of this period). For these two reasons one cannot definitively attach John the Baptist to one period or the other. He seems to belong to both.

(b) To be an apostle one must first have been with Jesus during the whole time from his baptism (Luke 3:21) to his ascension: It is noteworthy that Luke omits the flight of the disciples reported in Mark 14:50, and in Luke 23:49 tells us that all Jesus' acquaintances are witnesses to the crucifixion. An apostle also must have been—by divine determination—a witness of his resurrection (verse 22). Since the number of apostles is evidently restricted to twelve, both this limitation and the stated criteria implicitly exclude Paul (but see Acts 14:4, 14). The subsequent election of Matthias restores the apostolate to its full complement of twelve before the outpouring of the Spirit. Note, however, that the death of James the son of Zebedee in Acts 12 fails to occasion any mention of a substitute! If we follow Luke's scenario, the apostolic era ends with chapter 12; James (12:17)—the brother of Jesus—along with the presbyters (15:2, 4, 6, 22–23; 21:18) takes their place.

Verse 23: "Named" (see on 8:10) and "known" reflect Luke's language.

Verse 24: The prayer motif in verse 24 derives from Luke (cf. earlier 1:14 and later the community prayer in 4:24–30).

Verse 25: This echoes verses 17–18 by repeating the phrase "in this ministry." The mention of a particular, defined apostleship underlines Luke's concept of the twelve apostles (see on 1:22). The method of selecting somebody by lot for religious or social purposes is often mentioned in the Old Testament[32] and was widely used among Greeks and Romans.[33]

Verse 26: The replacement is successfully achieved. The Twelve are reconstituted.

THE TRADITIONS REWORKED BY LUKE

Judas

"As does Matthew in his story of Judas's death so Luke relates Judas's dereliction in God's providence: what Judas has done was foreseen by Scripture of old. Luke associates Ps 69:26 and Ps 109:8 with Judas' defection. The implication is that God's providence will provide a replacement for him among the Twelve."[34] The name Judas Iscariot—the man from Karioth—and his membership in the circle of the Twelve (Mark 14:10)[35] derive from tradition. The same judgment applies for his "delivering up" (or "handing over") of Jesus—an action that does not necessarily suggest a betrayal. Note that Paul refers to "the night when he was delivered up" (1 Cor. 11:23). Undoubtedly the narrative of the death of Judas (verses 18–20) in Peter's speech (verses 16–22) goes back to tradition. Further important narratives of Judas's end appear in Matt. 27:1–10[36] and in a fragment from Bishop Papias of Hierapolis[37] from the second century.[38] Matthew's version differs from the Acts and Papias versions in reporting Judas's repentance, his return of the money, and his suicide.[39] It is impossible to reconstruct or even posit a specific story of the death of Judas on the basis of the three versions. What we have are only elements of tradition: a horrible death, a field as the place of death, and an elaboration from passages in Psalms.

The Twelve—The Apostles

In this section the titles of Jesus' followers as the Twelve, the twelve apostles, and/or simply apostles also derive from tradition. For the notion of the twelve apostles see Mark 6:7, 30. The Twelve are recipients of an "appearance" in 1 Cor. 15:5, and appear in the lists of the Twelve in Mark 3:16–19; Matt. 10:2–4; Luke 6:14–16; and Acts 6:2. The term "apostles" is in 1 Cor. 15:7 as an element of tradition, and again in Gal. 1:19—in both cases as a designation of the important figures in Jerusalem. The term "disciples" as names of Jesus' followers is broader—see Mark 6:1; Matt. 10:24–25; and Luke 6:17—and is applied to the same persons. Luke uses it in the book of Acts in 6:1 for the first time. Even though sometimes used interchangeably by the gospel writers (see, e.g., Luke 9:1–2, 10, 14), the two terms should be distinguished: A disciple is a pupil or follower; an apostle is one who is sent out to teach and preach, to spread the good news.

Joseph Barsabbas and Matthias

The names of the two candidates, Joseph Barsabbas and Matthias (verse 23), most likely derive from tradition. Yet we have no way to tell whether the casting of lots was part of a pre-Lukan story.

HISTORICAL ELEMENTS

(a) The concept and the creation of a group of twelve goes back to the historical Jesus.[40] The existence of a group of twelve in the earliest period of the first community is attested by 1 Cor. 15:5. Paul mentions it here only because he is repeating the tradition that he had handed on in his sermon when the Corinthian community was founded. He himself has no personal knowledge of the Twelve as such. Certainly during his first visit to Jerusalem he meets Cephas, the dominant member of the community. But apparently a group officially designated as apostles at that time formed the leadership of the Jerusalem community (cf. Gal. 1:19), and this may have contained at least some of the Twelve. Apart from 1 Cor. 15:5 we find traces of the tradition about the Twelve in Gospel lists that are probably independent of one another (Mark 3:16–19/Matt. 10:2–4/Luke 6:14–16), and in the Q-derived logion Matt. 19:28/Luke 22:28–30. In this last case, we have the traditional Jewish concept of exalted leaders who will sit on thrones in future glory and judge the twelve tribes of Israel. But in that case "the Twelve" as an expression "was not a purely numerical designation of twelve individual personalities, but signified the group of the representatives of the twelve tribes in the end time."[41] It is thus an abstract entity.

Whoever suggests that this group was founded after Easter runs into chronological problems. In that case it was Peter who would have organized the group of twelve in Galilee or Jerusalem. Very soon—too soon to be true—it was replaced by the Jerusalem apostolate, a group of disciples who "saw" the resurrected Christ (1 Cor. 15:7).

A considerable body of scholarship, relying on 1 Cor. 15:5, has energetically denied that Judas was one of the Twelve. Had he been, it is argued, Paul or his tradition would have spoken of an appearance of Jesus to the Eleven,[42] for after the betrayal and his subsequent suicide, Judas would no longer have been one of the Twelve. By this line of reasoning, the appearance to the Twelve reported in 1 Cor. 15:5 shows that Judas was not one of them. But such arguments are not convincing because, as noted above, the Twelve is a corporate entity. In the absence of one member, the group continued and the vacancy was not necessarily filled immediately. Beside that, it is entirely possible that by the time the tradition Paul uses was formed, the replacement had been made and the group was once again literally "the Twelve."

In support of Judas's historicity, it should be noted that the pre-Markan tradition reflected in Mark 14:10 understood Judas to be one of the Twelve (see also Mark 14:20, 43). Thus—as further confirmed by the foregoing—Judas's membership in the Twelve is historically probable, as is the group's existence in the period before Easter.

(b) The remarks made above about the traditions of the name of Judas Iskarioth and his membership in the circle of the Twelve are historical because—as I hardly need point out—nobody would have made Judas a member of the Twelve after Easter. His role in connection with Jesus' arrest and execution was too offensive to have been fabricated by Christian believers.

(c) The reconstruction of the traditions surrounding Judas's death has brought out the fragmentary character of the tradition. Apart from his death in connection with Jesus' arrest and crucifixion little can be said with certainty.

(d) As for the "betrayal" of Jesus by Judas one has to keep in mind that the Primitive Christian tradition that is reflected in Mark 14:18 used Psalm 41:10 to make Jesus foretell this "betrayal." While this is certainly unhistorical, the "betrayal" is certainly not. Yet one must not make the "betrayal" as narrow as it is understood in the gospels of the New Testament. Rather we should assume as the historical kernel of the "betrayal" that some undetermined action taken by a member of the Twelve—Judas Iskarioth—played a decisive role in the arrest and death of Jesus.[43]

Matthias

Concerning the election of Matthias, not only do we lack historical certainty, inasmuch as no other records corroborate the event, but, as indicated above, it was not necessary—as Luke thinks—for the full membership of the Twelve to be filled immediately. Furthermore, we should recall the evidence of a rapid diminution in the perceived importance of the Twelve. Finally, one faces the difficulty of explaining how the election of Matthias would have become fixed in the tradition had the continuity of the Twelve been of short duration. While I therefore incline to reject the historicity of the election of Matthias, I do not assign the same degree of historical doubt to the existence of the disciples Matthias and Joseph.

The Historical Value of Luke's Account

The historical worth of Luke's account is nil. Neither was there a lot cast to replace Judas nor did Peter deliver a sermon on the necessity of doing so.[44] The setting of Peter's speech and the choice of Matthias are foggy, as is the number of 120 disciples in verse 15.

[5]
ACTS 2:1–13
THE COMING OF THE HOLY SPIRIT AT PENTECOST

(1) *And* when the day of Pentecost was fulfilled, they were all together in one place. (2) *And* suddenly there came from heaven a sound like a mighty rushing wind, *and* it filled the entire house where they were sitting. (3) *And* what seemed to be tongues as of fire spread among them *and* rested on each one of them. (4) *And* they were all filled with the Holy Spirit *and* began to **speak** in *other* tongues as the Spirit gave them to declare boldly.

(5) <u>But</u> there were dwelling in Jerusalem Jews, devout men from every nation under heaven. (6) And hearing this noise, a large crowd of them gathered, and they were bewildered, because each one heard them **speak** in his own language. (7) <u>But</u> they were amazed and astonished, saying, "Are not all these who are **speaking** Galileans? (8) And how is it that we hear, each of us in his own native language? (9) Parthians and Medes and Elamites and residents of Mesopotamia, Judea and Cappadocia, Pontus and Asia, (10) Phrygia and Pamphylia, Egypt and the parts of Libya belonging to Cyrene, and visitors from Rome, (11) both Jews and proselytes, Cretans and Arabians—we hear them **speaking** in our own tongues of the mighty works of God." (12) <u>But</u> all of them were amazed and perplexed, saying to one another, 'What does this mean?' (13) <u>But</u> others mocking said, "They are filled with sweet new wine."

OUTLINE

1–4: The glossolalia of the disciples assembled in a house in Jerusalem on the first Pentecost
    1: Details of time and place
    2–4: The glossolalia through the descent of the Spirit
5–13: The language miracle
    5: The presence of Jews from every nation under heaven in Jerusalem
    6–13: The language miracle and the reaction of the Jews

LUKE'S PURPOSE

The text can be divided into two parts: Verses 1–4 describe speaking in tongues, while verses 5–13 report a linguistic miracle.[45]

Verses 1–4: This section reflects numerous elements typical of Luke's language and style. Note, for example, the use of "and," seven times in a row (marked by italics). The manner of expression in verses 2–3 is reminiscent of descriptions of the Sinai theophany.[46] Note Philo,[47] *Decalogue 46* (on Exod. 19:16–25): "Then from the midst of the fire that streamed from heaven there [emanated] a voice . . . for the flame became articulate speech in the language familiar to the audience, and so clearly and distinctly were the words formed by it that they seemed to see rather than hear them." Philo's stress on the interconnection of fire, voice, and language is particularly striking in its close parallel with Luke's account of Pentecost in Acts 2:1–4. "But in Philo there is no suggestion either of a miracle in tongues or of a multilingual proclamation of Torah."[48] And finally Luke's indication of time, "Pentecost" (verse 1), fits this complex of Sinai motifs if indeed, as many scholars agree, Pentecost was in his time understood as "a festival celebrating the making of the covenant."[49]

The unit of text culminates in the sentence of verse 4b: "And they began to speak in other tongues (in Greek, *heterais glossais*) as the Spirit empowered them." The context indicates that the phrase "other tongues" refers to the fact that those present could understand the Spirit-filled disciples, as made clear in verse 11: "We hear them speaking in our own tongues (in Greek, *tais hêmeterais glossais*) of the wonderful works of God."[50] Thus verse 4 is the expression of a language miracle, and its context is developed in the narrative in the following verses.

Another observation shows that Luke indeed shaped the text under review: Verses 2 and 3 have an almost completely parallel construction:

A: And suddenly there came from heaven a sound
A1:   And divided tongues appeared to them
B: like a mighty rushing wind
B1:   as of fire
C: and it filled the whole house where they were sitting
C1:   and it sat on each one of them.

Verses 5–13: This section also contains elements of Luke's language and style. The frequent use of "and" (in Greek, *kai*) in verses 1–4 is replaced by the use of the Greek *de*, rendered in the text by "but" and indicated by underlining. Furthermore, it is skillfully connected to the previous unit. Verse 6 points back to verse 2: "noise" recalls "sound." Verses 6, 8, 11 take up verse 4 and show that the event is a language miracle. A list of the various peoples is framed within the unit of verses 5–13 by "we hear" in verses 8 and 11.[51] The contrasting reactions of the hearers described in verses 12 and 13 are in accordance with Luke's narrative style.[52]

THE PURPOSE OF VERSES 1–13 IN THE CONTEXT

With the account of the receiving of the Spirit, the promise Jesus made in 1:8 is fulfilled.[53] It is no coincidence that the ensuing speech of Peter (verses 14–40) begins with this theme (verses 17–18). From now on the receiving of the Spirit is constitutive for being a Christian.[54] However, its specific effects must still be defined in each case.

In addition to describing the receiving of the Spirit, it seems to be Luke's purpose to depict the Pentecost event as a language miracle. On the very day the Christian religion is founded, the Holy Spirit equips the members of this new movement with the languages of all other peoples! This undoubtedly expresses Luke's conviction of the universal nature of Christianity. Still, the universal preaching of the gospel does not yet include the Gentile mission, since here the audiences are Diaspora Jews, who only with some difficulty can be considered representatives of the nations of the world.[55]

THE TRADITIONS REWORKED BY LUKE

The two above sections made it clear that the present text is a self-contained unit. The following analysis will first demonstrate the discontinuities in the passage, and then attempt to identify the elements of tradition that they reveal.

1. The event depicted in verses 1–4 takes place in a house (verse 2), but the sequel (verses 5–13) evidently occurs in the open air.

2. Verses 9–11 interrupt the argument and likely go back to a source. That the list of peoples nevertheless fits very well in verses 5–13 may well be an indication of Luke's editorial work.

The disparity between verses 1–4 and 5–13 to which I have drawn attention can be intensified at one point. Verse 4 says that the disciples spoke "in other tongues." If we regard "other" as an edit, then speaking in tongues, i.e., an example of glossolalia, which we know from 1 Cor. 14, would surface as the kernel of the tradition.[56] In that case the tradition contained in verses 1–4 (and possibly verse 13) reports an ecstatic experience of a group of disciples meeting in someone's house, and it was Luke who first interpreted this tradition as a language miracle in order to prepare the reader for the idea of the worldwide mission. The evidence that Luke probably no longer knew the nature of the original glossolalia supports this suggestion. In Acts 19:6 he identifies it with prophecy (cf. 10:46). This makes "the synthesis with the language miracle easier."[57] In framing an analysis of the tradition, then, it is necessary to make a distinction between glossolalia (verses 1–4) and language miracle (verses 5–13).

Glossolalia is generally an incomprehensible ecstatic speech. Of the Corinthian glossolalia in particular, it can be said with certainty that it was not speaking in foreign languages. It had to be translated,[58] not because it was a foreign language but because it was incomprehensible.[59] In Paul's worldview, it was the language of the angels.[60]

In analyzing the tradition of the language miracle (verses 5–13), close attention should be paid to a later rabbinic legend about a language miracle at Sinai, in which the voice of God divided itself into seventy world languages and the law was made known to all nations.[61] "This means that there are striking points of contact between Sinai and a miracle in foreign tongues—something that was certainly useful for Luke's purposes."[62]

By way of summary, the two traditions that can be extracted are the story of the ecstasy of the disciples in a Jerusalem house (perhaps verse 13 also belongs to this), and the list of peoples. The language miracle is not an independent tradition, but a composition of Luke on the basis of knowledge of the Sinai tradition; his interest in the language miracle is evident from his adoption of the list of peoples.

The possibility that the language miracle is the bedrock of the tradition[63] is remote. In that case one would have to assume that the report of the glossolalia had already become attached at the level of tradition. Yet as was demonstrated above, Luke no longer had any idea of it. Therefore the proposal would be based on a second-degree hypothesis.

HISTORICAL ELEMENTS

At various times it has been suggested that "Pentecost" should be identified with the "appearance to more than five hundred brothers at once" that Paul adduces in 1 Cor. 15:6 in order to underscore the actuality of Christ's appearance. Hans Conzelmann has objected to this: "The development from a christophany (sc. like 1 Cor. 15:5) to this theophany (sc. like Acts 2) is really not conceivable, because in the older version of the Easter christophany the Spirit is not mentioned."[64]

Yet, in all likelihood, Luke introduced the features of a theophany into the story of Acts 2, where the theme of the glossolalia constitutes the kernel of the tradition. I therefore regard it as likely that the report of an appearance of Christ to more than five hundred brothers has a causal connection with the tradition behind 2:1–4. As for Conzelmann's observation that the older version of Easter christophany does not mention the Spirit, one has to keep in mind that for Paul, our earliest witness, at least a partial equivalence of Christ and the Spirit existed from the start.[65]

THE HISTORICAL VALUE OF LUKE'S ACCOUNT

Notwithstanding the many incorrect details listed above, Luke's idea that at the beginning of the Christian church there was some sort of group experience involving a large group of people is probably correct. That fits in with the historical record in that an "appearance" to more than five hundred brothers at one time led to a decisive breakthrough. It was not until this event that "Christianity" went public in Jerusalem. Yet the very nature of such a large-scale ecstatic experience surely seems to exclude the idyllic picture that Luke draws throughout in the first chapters of the book of Acts of the primitive community.

[6]
ACTS 2:14–36
PETER'S SERMON AT PENTECOST

(14a) *Now Peter, standing with the eleven, lifted up his voice and boldly declared to them,*

(14b) *"Men of Judea and all who dwell in Jerusalem, let this be known to you, and give ear to my words. (15) These (men) are not drunk, as you suppose, since it is only the third hour of the day. (16) But this is what was uttered through the prophet Joel:*

(17) *'And in the last days it shall be, God declares, that I will pour out my Spirit on all flesh, and your sons and your daughters shall* prophesy, *and your young men shall see visions, and your old men shall dream dreams; (18) even on my male servants and my female servants in those days I will pour out my Spirit, and they shall* prophesy. *(19) And I will show wonders in the heavens above and signs on the earth below: blood, and fire, and smoking mist. (20) The sun shall be turned into darkness and the moon into blood before the day of the Lord comes, the great and magnificent day. (21) And it shall come to pass that everyone who calls upon the name of the Lord shall be saved.'*

(22a) *Men of Israel, hear these words: (22b) Jesus of Nazareth, a man attested to you by God with mighty works and wonders and signs that God did through him among you, as you yourselves know*—(23) *this* [man], *who was delivered up by the determinate plan and foreknowledge of God, you crucified and killed by the hands of lawless men.* (24) Him God raised up, having loosed the pangs of death, because it was not possible that he should be held in its power. (25) *For* **David** *says concerning him, 'I saw the Lord always before me, for he is on my right hand, that I may not be shaken.* (26) *Therefore my heart was glad, and my tongue rejoiced; my flesh also shall dwell in hope.* (27) *For you will not abandon my soul to Hades, or let your Holy One see* <u>decay</u>. (28) *You have made known to me the paths of life; you will fill me with gladness by your presence.'*

(29) *Brothers, I can confidently tell you that the patriarch* **David** *both died and was buried, and his tomb is with us to this day.* (30) *Being therefore a prophet, and knowing that God had sworn with an oath to him that he would set one of his descendants on his throne,* (31) *he foresaw and spoke about the resurrection of the Christ, that he was not abandoned to Hades, nor did his flesh see* <u>decay</u>. (32) *This Jesus God raised up, and of that we all are witnesses.* (33) *Being thus exalted at the right hand of God, and having received from the Father the promise of the Holy Spirit, he has poured out upon us what you are now seeing and hearing.* (34) For **David** did not ascend into the heavens, but he himself says, 'The Lord said to my Lord, "Sit at my right hand, (35) until I make your enemies your footstool."' (36) *Therefore let all the house of Israel know for certain that God has made him both Lord and Christ, this Jesus whom you crucified."*

OUTLINE

14a: Note of framework

14b–15: Introduction

16–21: Quotation from scripture (Joel 3:1–5) to explain the situation

22–24, 32–33: Proclamation concerning death and resurrection of Jesus

25–31, 34–35: Quotation from scripture (Ps. 16:8–11) to connect Jesus with David

36: Culmination of Peter's exposition with a testimony

LUKE'S PURPOSE

Verse 14–15: "Peter" catches the hearer's attention (verse 14) and in verse 15 rejects the misunderstanding of the event reflected in verse 13. The third hour is 9 AM.

Verse 16: This is an introductory formula to indicate that what just happened is a fulfillment of Joel's prophecy.

Verses 17–18: This is the first part of the quotation from Joel.[66] As noted this passage is preceded by a refutation of the assumption that those who are seized by the Spirit are drunk: It is only the third hour. Luke uses theme of misunderstanding on the part of the hearers also in 3:12 and 14:15 as a literary device. The verb "to declare boldly" (verse 14a) is picked up from verse 4[67] and thus shows that Peter's speech belongs with what has gone before. Note that it is not foreigners who raise the charge of drunkenness, but local Jews who are not affected by the Pentecost event. The jeering claim that the people are drunk serves to add life to the story and to further the action by expanding on what may well have been part of the basic Pentecost tradition (verse 13). It is not Luke's interpretation of the Pentecost experience.

Verses 19–20: After a prophetic characterization of the church as being governed in the present by the Spirit in verses 17–18 a prophesy, again based on scripture, leads the way from the present to an apocalyptic future. It matches the scheme in Luke 21:5–36 that itself is based on Mark 13:1–37.

Verse 21: Now the speech addresses the present, and "Peter" comes to the point of the quotation: "Anyone who calls on the name of the Lord (i.e. Jesus) will be saved." In other words, the Christian offer of salvation is universal, and clearly this portion of the Joel quotation prepares the way for Peter's proclamation about the significance of Jesus' death and resurrection (verses 22b–24).

Verse 22: Cast in parallel to verse 14a, verse 22a begins the second portion of Peter's address and represents an editorial division. In verse 22b the mention of the "mighty works and wonders and signs" points back to the Gospel of Luke where the miracles of the prophet Jesus foster the right understanding of Christ.

Verse 23: In conformity with Luke's theology, the passion occurs according to God's plan.[68] This matches Luke 23:18–25 where the Jews bring about the condemnation of Jesus by the Romans. Note also the variation in the statements about the passion in Acts 3:15; 4:10; 5:30; 7:52; 10:39.

Verse 24: By raising Jesus up—to quote freely the German Acts scholar Gustav Stählin—God has forced death to surrender Jesus. Note that the conception of the death of Jesus as a positive act of salvation (see 20:28) is remote from this.[69] In this way God's plan, which is described more closely in the following verses, materializes.

Verses 25–31: The quotation in verses 25–28 exactly matches the LXX (Ps. 16 [15]: 8–11). Verse 31, the conclusion, takes up verse 27. The exegetical train of thought runs as follows: David himself long ago envisioned the person of the Messiah Jesus, whose soul would not remain in Hades and whose body would not be delivered over to decay. Using this quotation again in a sermon he places in the mouth of Paul at Pisidian Antioch (13:35–36), Luke makes clear the difference between David and Jesus in this matter. Thus he has provided the scriptural proof for verse 24. "David" as the putative author of Psalm 16:10 (LXX 15:10) asserts the necessity of the incorruptible nature of Jesus' body: "For you will not abandon my soul to Hades, nor let your Holy One see decay." Luke's reason for citing this verse is that David was speaking about the Messiah, whom Luke equates with Jesus, the one to whom God had allegedly promised that neither would his soul remain in Hades nor his body decay. By having "Paul" later use the same text in a sermon, Luke underscores the special character of Jesus' incorruptible body, and he clarifies the difference between David and Jesus by making Paul continue: "For David, after he had served the counsel of God in his own generation, fell asleep, and was laid with his fathers and saw decay. But he whom God raised up saw no decay" (13:36–37).

Verses 32–33: Therefore God has raised Jesus from the dead—an occurrence to which the apostles are witnesses—and indeed to a place at his own right hand. This elevation of Jesus shows that the Father has tendered on his behalf the bestowal of the Holy Spirit that, as Peter's hearers know from the Pentecost event, he has poured out upon them. Luke thus harks back to 1:4 and explains the command therein that the disciples are to await the promise of the Father (i.e., the outpouring of the Holy Spirit) that they received from Jesus.

Verses 34–35: These verses offer the scriptural proof—here adducing Psalm 110:1 (LXX: 109:1—following the pattern of verses 25–31); however, the argument is that since God did not fulfill the prophecy in David, the scripture must have had someone else in mind. And since Christ represents the fulfillment of the prophecy, it was clearly he whom the scripture announced.

Verse 36: This verse, addressed to the hearers, serves both to conclude the speech and to prepare for the question interjected in verse 37; such an interruption is clearly a literary device (cf. 10:44). For "what shall we do?" cf. Luke 3:10, 12, 14 (note the context of repentance as in Acts 2:37).

THE TRADITIONS REWORKED BY LUKE

Two particular elements of the speech probably existed in Luke's source(s):

1. The use of Joel 3:5 in verse 21. In Rom. 10:13 Paul used this passage; in both cases Christians as a group are characterized as "those who call on the name of the Lord." As the apparently spontaneous use of this expression in 1 Cor. 1:2 suggests, Joel 3:5 may some while earlier have been adopted as an integral element of the Christ-proclamation.

2. The use in verses 34–35 of Ps. 110 (LXX 109) in a christological context

is, as the parallels in 1 Cor. 15:25, Mark 12:36, etc., demonstrate, part of the tradition. It may well be that "loosed the pangs of death" (verse 24), when found in connection with the saying about the resurrection (ibid.), also reflects tradition.[70]

HISTORICAL ELEMENTS

1. Immediately following the death of Jesus and the appearances, Peter began to play a determining role in what was soon to become the Jerusalem community (see 1 Cor. 15:5).

2. Very early in the development of the Christian community, Joel 3:5 became a familiar proof text.

3. Ps. 110 (LXX 109) was being employed very early on in discussions about the significance of Christ.

THE HISTORICAL VALUE OF LUKE'S ACCOUNT

The Pentecost account found in Acts is certainly unhistorical. That on the first day of Pentecost Peter delivered any such speech in Jerusalem is quite out of the question.[71] It should be noted that "Peter" is using the Greek translation of the Old Testament and not the Hebrew text, while clearly the historical Peter—as well as the other disciples and Jesus himself—would have cited the Hebrew scriptures, and in all likelihood from memory, since it is almost certain that none of them could either read or write.[72] What Christianity has long considered a supremely inspiring and edifying inaugural event we must now recognize as a product of Luke's consummate literary artistry.

[7]
ACTS 2:37–41
REACTION TO PETER'S SERMON AT PENTECOST

(37) *Now when they heard this they were cut to the heart, and said to Peter and the rest of the apostles, "Brothers, what shall we do?" (38) And Peter said to them, "Repent, and be **baptized** every one of you in the name of Jesus Christ for the forgiveness of your sins, and you will receive the gift of the Holy Spirit. (39) For to you is the promise and to your children and to all who are far away, everyone whom the Lord our God calls to himself." (40) And with many other words he testified and exhorted them, saying, "Save yourselves from this corrupt*

generation." (41) *So those who received his word were* **baptized**, *and there were added that day about three thousand souls.*

OUTLINE

37: Reaction of the audience with a question
38: Call to repentance and baptism, which leads to receiving the Holy Spirit
39: Reassurance of the hearers
40: Conclusion of Peter's sermon
41: Note of success

LUKE'S PURPOSE

Verse 38: Peter's answer—really the conclusion of his speech—illustrates Luke's view of what becoming a Christian entails: repentance, baptism for the forgiveness of sins, and the bestowing of Holy Spirit.

Verse 39: This shows Luke's hand, for here he completes his echo of Joel 3:5 by alluding to verse 3:5b—which was dropped from Peter's speech at verse 21—and also takes up Isa. 57:19. By thus doubly emphasizing that the mission to the Gentiles must be zealously preserved, Luke has linked this verse to Peter's speech.

Verse 40: It is Luke who has Peter address the crowd "with many other words." This literary device "gives the author freedom to record those words of the speaker which fit in with the author's plan, but at the same time to indicate to the reader that these words do not exhaust what the speaker said."[73] The warning with which it closes, "save yourselves from this corrupt generation" (verse 40b), clearly reflects, "shall be saved"—the closing phrase of the Joel quotation in verse 21.

Verse 41: Verse 41a is related both substantively and formally to 4:4, 8:12, and 18:8; verse 41b similarly resembles 2:47b, 4:4, 5:14, 6:7, 11:24b, 12:24, and 16:5. The number 3000 is intended to emphasize the prodigious nature of the occurrence, the more so since the number of believers has increased dramatically since 1:15 ("about 120"). Both here and later when Luke speaks of multitudes, he is giving way to the same predilection that leads him to employ the Sanhedrin, or the Proconsul and his staff, or a king, or even the exalted company on the Areopagus, as an audience for the apostles in order to emphasize that "this has not been done in a corner" (26:26). This conviction colors the account he gives of the first mission. One can hardly deny, however, that Luke loves the dramatic effect of multitudes of converts.

THE HISTORICAL VALUE OF LUKE'S ACCOUNT

Luke gives a totally misleading impression of the spreading of the Gospel in Jerusalem. For one thing, Jerusalem at the time of Jesus was a city of about twenty-five thousand inhabitants.[74] It would be strange indeed if on a single day more than 10 percent of the whole population came to accept Jesus as the Messiah. Another difficulty arises when one tries to imagine baptizing three thousand people on the same day: Where and how and by whom would those baptisms have been performed? Luke's narrative theory leads us to neglect the historical evidence that the Hellenists and Paul were responsible for the expansion of Christianity—outside of Jerusalem. When a good while later Luke has James talk to Paul about the tens of thousands of believers in Jerusalem (21:20), we at last know beyond all question how to read the fantastic Lukan numbers of Christians in Jerusalem. It therefore comes as a great surprise that very learned scholars up to this day prefer not to contest the veracity of Luke's account. Note, for example, Barrett: "Who baptized these 3,000 is not stated. There is no reason to doubt that considerable numbers adopted the Christian position, convinced at least that something out of the ordinary had occurred and willing to accept the latest messianic claim."[75] "In this verse Luke gives an idealized picture of the earliest church—idealized but not for that reason necessarily misleading. . . . There is no ground for doubting the outline of Luke's account; if he had not given it we should doubtless have conjectured something of the kind. The question at whose answer we can only guess is the relation between the things the Christians *did* and that which constituted their existence as Christians."[76]

> *Rebuttal:* Yes, and doubtless we would have imagined without being prompted that new converts were so eager to join this heterodox community that it required one baptism every fifteen seconds during a twelve-hour day to gather them all into the fold—and that such amazingly effective crowd management somehow reflected the essence of the new faith.

[8]
ACTS 2:42–47
THE FELLOWSHIP OF THE BELIEVERS

(42) And they **devoted much time** to the apostles' teaching and fellowship, to the **breaking of bread**, *and to prayer.*

(43) *And all felt a sense of awe, and many wonders and signs came about through the apostles.*

(44) *And all who believed were together and had all things in common.* (45) *And they sold their possessions and property and shared the proceeds with any who had need.* (46) *And day-by-day,* **devoting much time** *to being in the temple together and* **breaking bread** *in their homes, they received their food with glad and generous hearts,* (47a) *praising God and finding favor with all the people.*

(47b) *And day-by-day the Lord added to their number those who were being saved.*

OUTLINE

42: The role of the community
43: The role of the apostles
44–47a: The role of the community (continued)
47b: Summary

LUKE'S PURPOSE

This section is a summary from Luke's pen with parallels in 4:32–37 and 5:12–16. "In each case there is a coherent account, into which some detail, often derived from another major summary, has been inserted."[77] The verses refer (a) to what has been reported previously, and (b) to what will follow.

(a) Verse 42 is related to 1:14 (and 2:46). Compare "wonders, signs" (verse 43) with verses 19, 22; "by the apostles" (verse 43) with verse 37; verse 46a is related to 1:14a; verse 47b ("added") to verse 41. For "together" in verse 44 see 2:1.

(b) Verse 43a is related to 5:5b and 5:11; verse 43b to 5:12a; verses 44–45 to 4:32 and 4:34–35. Verse 46a is related to 5:12b; verse 47a to 4:33, and 5:13b; verse 47b to 5:14.

Here Luke throws a highly favorable light on the primitive church of Jerusalem. He presents a utopian portrait of the Jerusalem community, and at the same time recalls Greek ethical ideals.[78] Since the summaries also contain elements of admonition (see below, pp. 73–77 on 4:32–37), they serve an important hortatory function for Luke. The expression "those being saved" in verse 47b echoes the last phrase of Joel 3:5 quoted in 2:21.

THE TRADITIONS REWORKED BY LUKE

Verse 42: Elements of this may go back to tradition. Indeed, "fellowship" (in Greek, *koinônia*) does not appear elsewhere in Luke-Acts, and verse 42 is partly taken up again in verse 46 (see the underlining and italics in the translation). Such thematic duplication within the summary is unusual and does not appear in the other summaries. Here Luke has apparently included information from a tradition that reported the fellowship of the first Christians, their eating together, and their instruction by the apostles. Luke, like Paul (Rom. 12:12–13), is using hortatory traditions from the Pauline mission sphere and retroactively transferring them to the Jerusalem community.

Verse 45: The traditional basis of the statement about selling possessions is suggested by reports like 4:36–37 and 5:1–10 that clearly came down to Luke from such a source.

HISTORICAL ELEMENTS

Verses 42–43: Instruction by the apostles may have a historical kernel. Note that in Gal. 1:17 Paul refers to those who were apostles before him in Jerusalem. This allows us to conclude that they had a leading role in the early period of the Jerusalem community and beyond.

Verse 46: The meeting places are the homes of individual members of the Jesus community like the Mary who is mentioned in Acts 12:12.

THE HISTORICAL VALUE OF LUKE'S ACCOUNT

The idealization of the earliest community by Luke leads to a great deal of confusion among both the general public and the scholarly guild. Luke's introduction of the idea of a golden age into the history of the church has had a tremendous impact on later Christian generations and served any number of clever Christian bishops as a weapon against heretics. Yet we actually know very little about the earliest community in Jerusalem, and therefore the assertions we can contest greatly outnumber those we are able to defend historically. That there was dissent among the followers of Jesus in Jerusalem almost from the very beginning is clearly demonstrated by the rise of the Hellenists (see below, pp. 94–96). And recently agreement has been growing that from the earliest times Christian belief and practice were far more diverse than we see in this summary picture of the church.

Luke reports in verse 46 and elsewhere (Acts 3–5; 21:26) that members of the primitive Jerusalem community including the apostles (and later Paul) spent much time in the Temple. He has kept secret, though, that the reason for doing so was their self-identification with the new Temple that they believed would replace the old on the very same site. As Dunn suggests, for example, what appeared to be devotion to the Temple itself could well reflect a conviction that it would, in accordance with Mal. 3:1, be the site of Jesus' return.[79] Many of them had either observed or taken part in Jesus' so-called cleansing of the Temple (Mark 11:15–19), which is commonly understood to have been a symbolic act calling for the abolition of the temple cult. Yet the ultimate aim of his protest may have been neither cult reform nor preventing further profanation of the Temple, but God's establishment of an eschatological "Temple." Not only did Jesus direct his action against the whole Temple operation, but also he based it on a vision of a different kind of Temple—various other prophetic concepts of which can be found in earlier Judaism.[80] We see another reflection of Jesus' attack on the Temple in the account of his trial, when in Mark 14:58, antagonistic (and probably suborned) witnesses testify against him: "We heard him say, 'I will destroy this Temple that is made with hands, and in three days I will build another, not made with hands.'" In all likelihood this logion about the Temple derives from Jesus, especially since verse 57 explicitly labels it false testimony[81] and thus blunts, indeed obscures, the point of Jesus' radical preaching.[82] Luke's idyll of the pious, quiet, harmonious community in Jerusalem papers over the existence of intense, imminent expectation.

[9]
ACTS 3:1–10
THE HEALING OF THE LAME BEGGAR

(1) Now Peter and John went up to the temple at the hour of prayer, the ninth hour.

(2) Now a man who had been born a cripple was carried there every day and laid at the gate of the temple called Beautiful to beg ALMS from those entering the temple. (3) When he saw Peter *and John* about to go into the temple, he asked to <u>receive</u> alms. (4) *And Peter gazed at him, as did John, and said, "Look at us."* (5) And he fixed his attention on them, expecting to <u>receive</u> something from him. (6) But Peter said, *"Silver or gold I have none; but what I have, that I give to you. In the name of Jesus Christ of Nazareth, rise up and* **walk!**" (7a) And he took him by the right hand and raised him up, (7b) and *immediately* his feet and ankles

grew strong. (8) *And leaping up, he stood, and began to **walk**, and he entered the temple with them, **walking** and leaping and **praising God**.* (9) And all the people saw him **walking** and **praising God**, (10) and recognized him as the one who sat for ALMS at the Beautiful Gate of the temple. And they were filled with wonder and amazement at what had happened to him.

OUTLINE

> 1: Introduction
> 2–3: Exposition
> 4–7: Healing
> 8: Demonstration
> 9–10: Effect on the people

LUKE'S PURPOSE

Luke has purposely placed this miracle story here. "It is thus the first explicit example of the 'many wonders and signs wrought through the apostles' (2:43) and another example of Joel's words quoted in 2:19. Indirectly, it gives further proof of God's accreditation of Jesus himself (2:22), as the healing power of his name awakens faith in him."[83]

Verse 1: It is typical of Luke that the apostles—as Jews who are loyal to the law—observe the hours of prayer. For the indication of the time of prayer, "around the ninth hour," which is 3 PM, see 10:3, 30.[84] Bringing John into the story here and in verses 3, 4, etc. (see also 8:14) is a Lukan touch: Note that John remains a mere bystander—to the extent that Luke uses singular verbs in verse 4 ("said") and verse 7 ("raised up"). The reason for bringing him onstage at this point is that later on Luke will need two witnesses before the Supreme Council (4:13). Moreover, he has—as Luke 22:8 shows[85]—a preference for pairs of missionaries.

Verses 2–3: These verses contain the exposition of the miracle story. No one who was lame (or blind) was allowed to participate in temple worship.[86]

Verses 4–5: Verse 4 derives from Luke. Verse 5 belongs (along with verses 2–3) to the traditional description of the situation. The editorial suture would thus be "receive" (end of verse 3 and verse 5).

Verse 6: The phrase "I have no silver or gold" may refer explicitly to the relinquishment of possessions described in 2:44–45, but surely one notes the groundwork being laid for 4:32 and will hear an echo in a later speech by Paul

(20:33). "Peter does not beg the exalted Jesus for healing, but releases the very power of healing through utterance of the name of Jesus Christ."[87] Thus, this story has a magical touch like all the other narratives that refer to the name of Jesus.[88] Barrett's claim that the present story along with that in chapter 19 belongs to "Luke's great anti-magical passages"[89] must therefore be rejected. It seems to me that Barrett is trying to rewrite first-century modalities of perception so as to make the story less embarrassing to modern critical readers. He apparently overlooks the truth of the statement that your magic is my miracle (see below, p. 117).

Verse 7: Through the channel of the touch "the miraculous powers of the healer stream forth over the sick man."[90] Luke likes to use the adverb "immediately" (in Greek, *parachrêma*) to dramatize the occurrence of miracles.[91]

Verse 8: When the healed man praises God, one naturally recalls 2:47, which reported the same action by the community. Because both this and the report that the man "entered the Temple with them" prepare for verse 11 with its obviously redactional transition, we are justified in attributing this entire verse to Luke.

Verses 9–10: These verses both have traces of Luke's editorial work. "Praising God" is a redundant link to verse 8, which, as noted above, echoes 2:47.

THE TRADITIONS REWORKED BY LUKE

The section contains a complete miracle story with a unified style. It demonstrates the elements typical of the Synoptic performance of such events:

(a) A defining of the situation (a beggar lame from birth, 3:2–3, 5); (b) a verbal command (3:4, 6); (c) the curative or restorative action (3:7a); (d) the result effected (3:7b); (e) the response of the witnesses (3:10). In all likelihood this account recounts a story about Peter's miraculous cure of a lame man that found its way to Luke from a source in Jerusalem.

To one intent on analyzing the tradition, this story offers illuminating parallels—especially with Acts 14:8–10 (healing of a lame man in Lystra by Paul) and Luke 5:17–26 (Jesus heals a lame man). This healing story and that found in Luke 5:17–26 (which is rooted in Mark 2:1–12) probably reflect similar events, but the present account contains so many textual similarities to Acts 14:8–10 that a cognate relationship between the two must be assumed (cf. the detailed comparison with 14:8–10 on pp. 178–79 below). It is also noteworthy that while faith is made an explicit and indeed essential element in both 14:9 and Luke 5:20, it receives no mention and plays no apparent role in Acts 3:1–10. Accordingly, 3:16 must be seen as a Lukan addition that can be traced to the Second Evangelist via Mark 2:5.

Since the healing stories in Acts 3 and 14 are so formally and linguistically similar, one must have been the source of the other. The miracle by Peter is likely the original version, lacking as it does any mention of faith (a fact that weakens any argument that Luke "borrowed" Acts 14 and Acts 3 from Mark 2). Also supporting the primacy of the story involving Peter is the detail of the "Beautiful Gate" and the fact that this gate cannot be assigned a location.[92] A further indication of a traditional basis for this story is the mention of "the hall of Solomon" in the transitional verse 11. At any rate, the locus of the story is Jerusalem. Two possibilities exist for when and where the tradition took shape: (a) in Jerusalem during the first ten years after Jesus' crucifixion, when Peter was the leader of the community and probably also did "miracles" there (see the commentary on 5:1–10), and (b) almost any place at a later time, when Peter was still considered one of the leading figures of Primitive Christianity. In the latter case Luke would have supplied the place-name "Beautiful Gate."

HISTORICAL ELEMENTS

Like all miracle stories in Acts and in the canonical gospels, the narrative of the healing of the lame man in verses 1–10 can be explained by the desire to make Jesus and his apostles into carriers of divine power among wretched people in need of help. So many similar miracle stories appear in the first-century cultural environment of Christianity and earlier in the Old Testament that we must decide against the historicity of the present miracle, the more so since according to present day medical judgment the immediate (instant) healing of one lame from childhood is all but unthinkable. (The same judgment, of course, applies to all the other miracle stories in Acts and the gospels.) Let me here repeat that my statement is not based on a preconceived notion that miracles are impossible. I would suggest, however, that bringing "God" or supernatural occurrences into the picture is an insurmountable hindrance to critical study.[93] Historical work must orient itself to reconstructing what really happened without in advance excluding events that transcend causality—if indeed such a reconstruction can be made on the basis of the available evidence. Still, one must obviously exclude such eccentric or bizarre positions as the belief that the earth is located at the center of the universe.

Be that as it may, the story surely reflects the existence of a community—either in Jerusalem or elsewhere—whose members attributed extraordinary results and perhaps even miracles to Peter's activity in Jerusalem.

THE HISTORICAL VALUE OF LUKE'S ACCOUNT

Luke presents the healing of the lame beggar as the first instance of the "many wonders and signs" that the apostles brought about (2:43). He thus reinforces his own description of the ascendant and irresistible church of Jesus Christ. Yet he has become a victim of self-deception, because the earliest phase of the primitive church was different. One can hardly explain the real rise of what became later Christianity if the original Jerusalem church was as powerful as Luke depicts it. One would have expected it to have a greater impact on future Christianity. Instead, after 70 CE it disappeared and the Ebionites, as its descendants, were labeled heretical a century afterward.[94]

[10]
ACTS 3:11–26
PETER'S SPEECH IN SOLOMON'S PORTICO

(11) *While he still clung to Peter and John, all the people ran together to them in the portico called Solomon's, utterly astonished.*

(12a) *But when Peter saw it, he addressed the people:*

(12b) *"Men of Israel, why do you wonder at this, and why do you stare at us as though by our own power or piety we have made him walk?* (13a) *The God of Abraham, the God of Isaac, and the God of Jacob, the God of our fathers, glorified his **SERVANT** Jesus,* (13b) *whom you both handed over and **denied** in the presence of Pilate, even when he had decided to dismiss him.* (14) *You **denied** the Holy and Righteous One, and asked that a murderer be granted to you,* (15a) *the author of life you killed,* (15b) *whom God raised from the dead. To this we are witnesses.* (16) *And on the ground of faith in his name, this [man] whom you see and know, his name has made strong; indeed the faith that comes through it has given him back to perfect soundness in the presence of you all.*

(17) *Now, brothers, I know full well that you acted in ignorance, as did also your rulers;* (18) *but what God proclaimed beforehand by the mouth of all the **prophets**, that his Messiah would suffer, he thus fulfilled.* (19) *Repent therefore, and turn to him so that your sins may be blotted out,* (20) *that seasons of refreshing may come from the presence of the Lord, and that he may send the Christ appointed for you, Jesus,* (21) *whom the heaven must receive until the time of universal restoration about which God spoke by the mouth of his holy **prophets** long ago.* (22) *Moses said, "A **prophet** shall the Lord God raise up for*

you like me from your brothers. You must heed him in whatever he tells you. (23) *And it shall be that every soul who does not listen to that **prophet** shall be cast out from the people."* (24) *And all the **prophets**, from the time of Samuel and those who came after him, as many as have spoken, also proclaimed these days.* (25) You are the sons of the **prophets** and of the covenant that God made with your fathers, saying to Abraham, "And in your offspring shall all the families of the earth be <u>blessed</u>." (26) *To you first God sent his **SERVANT**, when he raised him up, to <u>bless</u> you, if you turn each one of you away from your malicious acts."*

OUTLINE

> 11: Transition: The lame man with Peter and John in the hall of
>   Solomon; the amazement of the people
> 12a: Introduction to Peter's speech
> 12b–26: Peter's speech
>   12b–13a: The miracle as a work of God
>   13b–18: Proclamation of the death and resurrection of Jesus
>   19–21: The call to repentance and the eschatological prospect
>   22–26: The fulfillment of prophecy

LUKE'S PURPOSE

Verse 11: A transition links the foregoing miracle story with the speech by Peter. "Astonished" takes up "wonder" (verse 10). The subsequent events take place in the hall of Solomon, which Luke evidently understands to be part of the Temple complex and to have the "Beautiful Gate" of verse 2 as an entrance.

Verse 12a: "When he saw the people" connects the sermon to follow with verse 11.

Verses 12b–15a: The address "men of Israel" in verse 12b matches 2:22a. Just as 2:15 does for the Pentecost speech, verse 12b forbids a misunderstanding after the address. Even more clearly than 2:23, verses 13–15a point back to Luke 23:16, 18–25. "Servant of God" (verse 13) occurs as a title for Jesus also in verse 26; 4:27, 30; elsewhere in the New Testament it appears only as a quotation from Isa. 42:1 in Matt. 12:18.

Verse 15b: Like 2:24, this half-verse emphasizing that God raised Jesus from the dead—which stands in contrast to the killing of Jesus by the Jews in the previous verse—adds the Lukan theme of witness to it (see 2:32 and p. 42 on 1:22 for the twelve apostles as witnesses).

Verse 16: This badly crafted sentence contains a contrived reference to the miracle story. And while Luke adds that in the absence of faith, no miracle can occur, we find no mention of faith of the person who is healed,[95] but only of Peter's and John's "who, believing in the power of Jesus' name, were able to cure the lame beggar."[96] The awkward formulation seems to show Luke's difficulties in shaping the tradition to his theology (cf. the miracle stories in the Gospel which are interpreted in terms of the concept of faith in 5:20; 7:9, 50; 8:48; 18:42).

Verse 17: "Now" is a sign of division (see on 20:22, 25). Luke commonly combines this ignorance motif with references to the passion.[97]

Verse 18: Luke's theology understands Christ's suffering to have been a fulfillment of the scriptures (see Luke 24:26–27, etc); further prophetic testimony appears in verses 21b and 24.

Verse 19: This Lukan call for repentance assures that following it will lead to God's forgiveness of sins (see earlier 2:38).

Verses 20–21: Notwithstanding two traditional elements in these verses,[98] Luke has given them a specific meaning. Despite their killing of Jesus, the Jews have been granted a further opportunity for repentance before the final coming of Jesus; not only was Christ's suffering announced by the scriptures, but so also were the proclamations he delivered between the resurrection and his ascension[99] and the final coming itself ("the time of universal restoration," verse 21); thus everything is part of the salvation history foretold by scripture. Verse 21 seems to indicate a delay of Jesus' future coming. Despite this delay, it will take place on the appointed day; see 1:7). Note that the foretelling by the prophets of Christ's suffering (verse 18b) and the promised "time of universal restoration" (verse 21b) create the context for the call to repentance and the eschatological promise.

Verses 22–26: In contrast to the prospect in verses 20–21, this section offers a retrospective commentary on the earthly Jesus, involving further scriptural proof and yet another admonition to repent. Verses 22–24 are a unit that includes a citation (Deut. 18:18–19) attesting to Moses as one of the prophets and the contemporary relevance of prophecy. Accordingly, Moses must be one of the prophets mentioned in verses 18 and 21 whose proclamation refers to "these days" (verse 24). Gen 22:18 (LXX) probably stands behind verse 25. In addition to several minor details, Luke has altered "all the nations of the earth" to read "all the families of the earth." Since the present audience is exclusively Jewish, this change was necessary, for throughout Acts the "the nations" refers to Gentiles, while "families" includes the Jews. By including the specification "first" in verse 26, Luke asserts the preeminence of their status relative to the blessing, and thus has altered the quotation to adapt it to Peter's sermon to Jews.

It is important to note the essential similitude of Peter's speeches in Acts 2 and 3:

1. The Joel quotation in 2:21 promised grace to those who call upon the Lord's name, while 3:23 threatens those who reject the message with destruction. And despite the contrast in their contents, the parallel structure of 2:21 ("and it shall be" + offer of salvation) and 3:23 ("and it shall be" + threat) suggests that 3:23 represents an intentional echo of 2:21.

2. Acts 2 shows the fruit of repentance to be the gift of the Holy Spirit (verses 33–34, esp. 38); in Acts 3 its consummation is the second coming of Jesus (verses 19–21).

3. Both speeches employ scriptural proof in arguing that Joel and the other prophets spoke of the present time. In short, one could reasonably propose that the two speeches of Peter are in effect one extended oration.

THE TRADITIONS REWORKED BY LUKE

Verse 25: The interpretation of the seed of Abraham in terms of Jesus (verse 25) had earlier appeared in Gal. 3:16. Three explanations for this can be plausibly argued: (a) Paul and Luke go back quite independently to a single tradition. (b) Luke is using Gal. 3:16. (c) Luke is employing a tradition from the Pauline mission literature that ultimately derives from Gal. 3:16.

HISTORICAL ELEMENTS

Verse 25: The tradition of the christological interpretation of Gen. 22:18 derives from a time before Luke. Since it is based on the LXX, it betokens a Greek-speaking community. How old it is taken to be depends on one's preference from among the three possibilities mentioned in the previous section. In my view it should be the third.

THE HISTORICAL VALUE OF LUKE'S ACCOUNT

Peter has never delivered a speech like this in Jerusalem. See my further comments on Acts 2 above, page 54.

[11]
ACTS 4:1–22
PETER AND JOHN BEFORE THE HIGH COUNCIL

(1a) *And as they were speaking to the people,* (1b) *the priests and the captain of the temple and the Sadducees came upon them,* (2) *greatly annoyed because they taught the people and proclaimed in Jesus the resurrection from the dead.* (3) *And they laid hands on them and put them in custody until the next day. For it was already evening.*

(4) *But many of those who had heard the word believed, in number totaling about five thousand men.*

(5) *On the next day their rulers, elders, and scribes gathered together in Jerusalem,* (6) *with Annas the high priest and Caiaphas and John and Alexander, and all who belonged to the high priestly family.* (7) *And having set the two in their middle, they inquired, "By what power or by what name did you do this?"*

(8) *Then Peter, filled with the Holy Spirit, said to them, "Rulers of the people and elders,* (9) *if today we are being examined concerning a good deed done to a crippled man, and by what means this man has been healed,* (10) *let it be known to all of you and to all the people of Israel that it was in the **NAME** of Jesus Christ the Nazorean, whom you crucified and whom God raised from the dead. Through that **NAME** this man stands before you well.* (11) This Jesus is the stone rejected by you—the builders—that has become the head of the corner. (12) *And in none other is there salvation, for there is no other **NAME** under heaven which is given to men by which we must be saved."*

(13) *Now when they saw the boldness of Peter and John, and perceived them to be uneducated, ordinary men, they were astonished. They recognized them as former companions of Jesus.* (14) *Yet seeing the man who was healed standing beside them, they had nothing to say in opposition.* (15) *But when they had commanded them to leave the high council, they conferred with one another,* (16) *saying, "What shall we do with these men? For that a notable sign has been performed through them is evident to all the inhabitants of Jerusalem, and we cannot deny it.* (17) *But in order that it may spread no further among the people, let us forbid them with **threats** ever again to use this **NAME** in talking to anyone."* (18) *So they called them and charged them not to speak out or teach at all in the **NAME** of Jesus.* (19) *But Peter and John answered them, "Whether it is right before God to listen to you rather than to God, you must judge,* (20) *for we cannot but declare what we have seen and heard."* (21) *And when they had further **threatened** them, they let them go, seeing no way to punish them; after*

all, everyone was praising God for what had happened, (22) since the man on whom this sign of healing was performed was more than forty years old.

OUTLINE

1–3: Imprisonment of Peter and John in the evening by the priests, the captain of the temple and the Sadducees

4: The great success of the sermon: the community grows to five thousand members

5–22: Before the high council

5–7: Peter and John taken the next morning before the council and their authority questioned

8–12: Peter's witness

13–22: Peter and John forbidden to preach, but refuse to obey; the apostles set free because of the people praising God for the healing of a man lame from birth

LUKE'S PURPOSE

The foregoing action reaches a crisis. Following the healing of the lame man and Peter's sermon to the people, opposition arises, and the apostles are put into prison.

Verses 1–3: Although Peter gave the foregoing speech alone (3:12), verse 1a attributes it to both apostles. This passage sets the scene for the subsequent trial by reporting the outrage of the Temple authorities when they discover Peter and John evangelizing the crowd. Luke glosses over the point that only the Sadducees should have been offended by the apostles' preaching the resurrection of the dead (verse 2b, cf. 23:6).

Verse 4: The stunning increase of the Jerusalem church continues: first 120 (1:15), then 3,000 (2:41), and now 5,000 men join the community. Since nowhere in Acts does "men" (in Greek, *andres*) include women,[100] the number must be even higher. At the time of Paul's last visit, Jewish believers number in the tens of thousands (21:20).

Verses 5–7: This introduces the hearing. The question, "By what power or by what name did you do this?" points back to 3:12, 16 (cf. 3:6), and requires the apostles to make the speech that follows. The reader, of course, knows already what Peter will say.

Verses 8–12: After the introduction (verse 8), verses 9–12 connect the miracle reported in chapter 3 with the proclamation of Christ. Verses 9–10 refer to the healing story; note the following verbatim parallels to the previous narratives: "let it be known" (= 2:14); "in the name of Jesus Christ the Nazorean" (= 3:6); "whom you crucified" (= 2:36); "whom God has raised from the dead" (= 3:15). In addition, the reference to Ps. 118:22 adduces proof from scripture not yet employed in Acts, but may involve a deliberate echo of the report in Luke 20:17/Mark 12:10–11. As mentioned above, verse 11 cites Ps. 118:22 to give scriptural proof for the proclamation. Verse 12 reiterates a key motif of the address: The name of Jesus is the modality by which people are saved. For Luke, as the example of the crippled man has shown, any distinction between physical and spiritual healing is fallacious. "Miracles are manifestations of the future salvation in the present if received by faith (cf. Luke 17:11–19)."[101]

Verse 13: The climax comes when the apostles repudiate the ban on their preaching as unconscionable and impossible for them to obey. The appearance of "boldness" as a keyword in verse 13 as well as verses 29 and 31 indicates Luke's insistence that Christian proclamation is not subject to Jewish intervention. (Analogous to this is his report in 28:30 that even while imprisoned Paul was "not hindered" from preaching in Rome.) The all but incredible report that only now do the accusers recognize Jesus' relationship to the apostles is as clearly a fictional contrivance (cf. 4:1–2) as the surprise registered upon discovering the lack of education shown by these troublemakers (verse 13a). Obviously their untutored status stands in tension with the spiritual eloquence of Peter, and the discovery of their tie to Jesus further raises the dramatic pitch until suddenly the accusers see what is really a stake.

Verse 14: The report that they had "nothing to say in opposition," which may well reflect Luke 21:15, links the present scene to 3:1–10, and in suggesting their frustration sets the scene for the action to be taken against the apostles. By his very presence beside the apostles, the formerly lame man calls down upon them the ire of the Jewish authorities.

Verses 15–16: Verse 16 reminds the reader that the present deliberations— at which the apostles are not present (note verse 15)—have stemmed from the healing miracle, and gives Luke a chance place the insight he intends for the reader into both the minds and the mouths of the Jewish authorities. Of course he couches it in his language: Through the apostles a clear sign has been given to all the inhabitants of Jerusalem.

Verses 17–18: The prohibition against preaching is, of course, issued only so the apostles will have an opportunity to flout it. "To declare," echoes 2:4, 14.

Verses 19–20: "Whether it is right before God to listen to you rather than to God, you must judge" (verse 19; cf. 5:29) alludes to Socrates: Under similar circumstances he similarly challenged his judges: "I will obey the god rather than you."[102] Not only does Luke thus attest to his Greek readers his own Hellenistic education, but he also validates the Jerusalem mission. On verse 20 see 10:39.

Verse 21: This corroborates verses 17–18 by reiterating that the Jewish authorities are unable to keep the gospel message from being spread.

Verse 22: This concludes the scene that began in 3:1 by reemphasizing the wonderful nature of the healing: The man had been lame for more than forty years before his miraculous healing!

THE TRADITIONS REWORKED BY LUKE

Verse 11: Ps. 118:22 is an element of earliest Christian apologetic against the Jews: See Mark 12:10–11 par.; 1 Pet. 2:4–7.[103]

HISTORICAL ELEMENTS

Verse 11: Although the apologetic use of Ps. 118:22 predates Acts, this interpretation cannot be convincingly attributed to Peter.

THE HISTORICAL VALUE OF LUKE'S ACCOUNT

Verse 4: While hardly any New Testament critic today defends the historicity of Peter's speech in Acts 4, many a scholar has tried—at least indirectly—to lend credence to the large number of converts. Thus I. H. Marshall opines, "Luke's figure for the size of the church may include Christians from the country districts as well as the city."[104] Wolfgang Reinhardt reasons, "Since there is . . . no convincing theological interpretation of the figures 'about 3,000' and '(about) 5,000,' one will instead have to accept that Luke was dependent on a reliable transmission of these figures."[105] C. K. Barrett surprisingly writes,

> Only in chs. 2 and 4 are large specific numbers of converts recorded. It is of course highly unlikely that in the first hours and weeks of the church's life anything like precise statistics were kept; it is, however, fair to note that only here (in ground covered by Acts) it is likely that such large accessions of believers took place, for only in Jerusalem (Galilee is in Acts surprisingly neglected) would there be found considerable numbers of people who had some idea of, and sympathy with, what Jesus stood for, and needed only such impetus as the events of Pentecost and a supernatural healing could give to bring them over the boundary into the company of believers; and whatever judgment is reached

regarding the historicity of these events there can be no doubt that the time was marked by a good deal of religious excitement.[106]

Rebuttal: All of these judgments—given Luke's tendency and the size of the population of Jerusalem of less than 30,000—may well strike the critical observer as lacking in objective supporting data; indeed, they often seem less like scholarly conclusions than wishful attempts to validate traditional texts.[107]

[12]
ACTS 4:23–31
THE PRAYER OF THE COMMUNITY AFTER THE RETURN OF PETER AND JOHN

(23) *When they were released, they went to the members of their community and reported what the chief priests and the elders had said to them.* (24a) *And when they heard it, they lifted their voices together to God and said,*

(24b) *"Sovereign Lord, who made the heaven and the earth and the sea and everything in them,* (25a) *who by the mouth of our father David, your servant, said by the Holy Spirit,* (25b) *'Why do the Gentiles rage, and the peoples plot in vain?* (26) *The kings of the earth have set themselves, and the rulers have* **gathered together***, against the Lord and against his Anointed'*—(27) *they were* **gathered together** *truly in this city against your holy servant Jesus, whom you anointed, both Herod and Pontius Pilate, along with the Gentiles and the peoples of Israel,* (28) *to do whatever your hand and your plan had predestined to take place.* (29) *And now, Lord,* look upon their threats and grant to your servants to continue to speak your word with all boldness, (30) *while you stretch out your hand to heal, and signs and wonders are performed through the name of your holy servant Jesus."*

(31) *And when they had prayed, the place in which they were gathered together was shaken, and they were all filled with the Holy Spirit and continued to speak the word of God with boldness.*

OUTLINE

23–24a: The return of Peter and John; prayerful reaction of the assembled
         community
24b–30: Prayer of the community
    31: Summary report: earthquake, coming of the Holy Spirit,
         preaching of the word of God with boldness

LUKE'S PURPOSE

Verses 23–24a: This is a narrative link joining the previous unit to verses
24b–30, the report of the community prayer.

Verses 24b–25a: "Lord" in verse 24b is an address to God which elsewhere
occurs in the New Testament in the prayer of Simeon (Luke 2:29) and at Rev.
6:10. The conception of God the creator of heaven and earth and sea comes from
the Old Testament. The original text of verse 25a cannot be reconstructed.[108]

Verses 25b–26: The verbatim quote of Ps. 2:1–2 is from LXX, and therefore
indicates Luke's hand.

Verse 27: The phrase "they were gathered together" which comes from the
quotation in verse 26 introduces the interpretation. Judging from his passion narrative, it is evident that Luke intends a specific understanding of three of the
named groups in the quotation (Gentiles, peoples, kings, rulers): "kings" points to
Herod Antipas, "rulers" to Pilate, and "peoples" to Israel. Given this hermeneutic
pattern, the fourth term, "Gentiles," can easily be supposed to refer to the Roman
soldiers. Although verse 27 contains an allusion to Luke 23:12, "the general tone
is different from that of Luke's passion narrative. There Pilate is exonerated in an
apologetic manner, whereas here, in line with Luke's fundamental view of salvation history, Pilate's guilt is stressed."[109] *Both* approaches are due to Luke. For
"your servant" (also in verse 30) see the commentary on 3:13.

Verse 28: Both the language and the content are typical of the Evangelist:
Both "your hand" and "your plan" (Luke 7:30; Acts 2:23; 13:36; 20:27) are his
expressions, and the idea of God's predetermined will originates with him.

Verse 29: The prayer turns back to the present distress of the community:
"and now" is a Lukan transitional phrase; in the New Testament it occurs elsewhere only in 5:38; 20:32; 27:22 (note also 17:30; 20:22, 25). Also Lukan is
"boldness," a clear echo of verse 13. This prayer invites God's attention to the
threats of the Jewish authorities reported in verses 17, 21.

Verse 30: This refers to the healing and the wondrous deeds that have been carried out in Jesus' name since chapter 2. Later, by way of summary, 5:12 and 6:8 report the fulfillment of the prayer's petition.

Verse 31: This verse describes God's acknowledgment of the prayer; because it includes a shaking of the place and all members of the community are filled with the Holy Spirit, the event amounts to a sort of second Pentecost. "The end of the episode shows that the Christians have thus with God's help defeated the attempt to stifle their mission. At the same time, however, the way is paved for the coming narrative of the new persecution."[110] And once again the boldness of the apostles (cf. verses 13, 29) is affirmed.

THE TRADITIONS REWORKED BY LUKE

Verses 24b–30: The often advanced theory that here we find recorded part of an old community prayer[111] is to be repudiated on the basis of style; what we see here is not so much prayer as exegesis of Ps. 2:1–2. Clearly the prayer is patterned on the Hebrew Bible and other Jewish scriptures,[112] but that hardly indicates that it antedates Luke.

HISTORICAL ELEMENTS

Verses 25b–26: The historical locus of insinuating Ps. 2:1–2 into the passion narrative can no longer be established.

THE HISTORICAL VALUE OF LUKE'S ACCOUNT

The historical worth is nil. The Jerusalem community never spoke the prayer of this passage, not even after the release of Peter and John, if for no other reason than because their arrest never happened. By creating this idealized scenario, Luke has contributed to the sacred myth of Christian origins with the consequences that I have outlined earlier (see above, p. 54).

A Note on Luke's General Knowledge in Acts 3–4:31

Since the narrative *details* of Acts 3–4:31 are historically worthless, the narrative framework can hardly be based on accurate historical foundations. Therefore the negative result of the historical analysis of the traditions in Acts 3–4:31 casts serious doubts on the reliability of Luke's "knowledge" of the first years of the Christian church in Jerusalem. It has been suggested that the missionary activity

of the Jerusalem community shortly after the crucifixion of Jesus must have sufficiently alarmed Sadducean circles (cf. the action of the Sadducee Ananus
against James in 62 CE),[113] that they would at least have considered action
against the church.[114] Yet we have very little solid indication of any significant
missionary activity. In short, it is evident that *Luke himself fabricated the scenario in Acts 3–4 on the basis of the Gospel of Mark.*

[13]
ACTS 4:32–37
SUMMARY DESCRIPTION OF THE CONGREGATION'S LIFE;
BARNABAS'S DONATION

(32) Now the whole fellowship of believers was of one heart and soul, and no
one claimed any possession as his _own_, but they held everything in common.

(33a) And with great power the **apostles** gave witness to the resurrection of
the Lord Jesus, (33b) and great grace was upon them all.

(34a) There was not even any impoverished among them, (34b) for as many
as were _owners_ of lands or houses sold them and brought the proceeds of the sale
(35) *and laid it at the **apostles' feet**, and it was distributed to each as any had need.*

(36) But Joseph, who was named *by the **apostles*** Barnabas (which means
son of encouragement), a Levite, a Cypriote by birth, (37) since he _owned_ a piece
of land, sold it, and brought the money and *laid it at the **apostles' feet**.*

OUTLINE

32: The unity of the community

33: An aside: the testimony of the apostles to the resurrection and
the grace that rests on all of them

34–35: The selling of possessions, pooling of resources, and distribution of
common property by the apostles according to individual needs

36–37: The example of Barnabas

LUKE'S PURPOSE

Verse 32: This verse emphasizes the oneness of the community. "Those who
believed" and "everything in common" point back to 2:44b. Verse 32b ("no one

claimed any possession as his own") makes it plain that individuals retained the right of use of possessions, but ceded to the community their rights of ownership, with the result that "they held everything in common." To characterize the earliest community, Luke here combines the biblical expression "one heart and one soul" (cf. Deut. 6:6) with Greek ideals.[115] It should be noted, however, that sharing with those of a different social class is a characteristically Jewish ideal, and one little in evidence among Greeks; therefore, we here have a synthesis that points beyond Luke's use of literary knowledge to a Jewish-Christian adaptation of a Greek ideal.

Verse 33: This brief intermission in Luke's portrait of the primitive community exhibits his apologetic agenda in emphasizing the relation between the power of the apostles' testimony and Jesus' resurrection (cf. 1:22).[116] Verse 33b once again lays stress on the divine grace that empowered the whole community, a theme that enables a smooth return to the operational description of the earliest community that commenced in verse 32 and will resume in verse 34.

Verses 34a: The remark that "there was not even any impoverished among them" which may be based on Deut. 15:4a ("there will be no impoverished among you") is the reason for the statement in verse 33b that great grace had come upon the Christians. That verse 34a picks up the train of thought from verse 32 after the interruption—if verse 33 is not a reflection of different sources, but rather of Luke's desire to portray both the operational principles of the community and the special calling of the apostles.

Verses 34b–35: This at first seems to assert the community's total repudiation of personal possessions and thus to impugn the accuracy of verse 32. We now read that believers sold both their real and personal property and handed over the proceeds to the apostles, who then saw to the needs of everyone. But this does not mean that people totally divested themselves of their possessions. As suggested under verse 32, Luke is at pains to differentiate surrender of possessions (verses 34–35) from resignation of the individual right to possessions (verse 32). Be that as it may, he is not as concerned with the details of the arrangement as he is with defining the principle of providing "as any had need" (verse 35, cf. 2:45). His ultimate purpose is to show that the community realized both Old Testament and Greek ideals (cf. above on verse 32). No doubt Luke's intention is clarified in verses 35 and 37, when he reports that Barnabas and the other followers gave the money they realized from the sale of property to the apostles, who used it for the benefit of the community. The use of the phrase "laid at their feet" here and its repetition in 5:2 suggest Luke's editorial hand.

These two positive and the following two negative examples indicate Luke's concern: Now we have those with possessions selling them for the benefit of the poor, whereas earlier (in 2:45) the apostles have the task of distribution. Here we see an important element of "Luke's concrete social utopia,"[117] according to which those with possessions undertake such renunciation that there are neither rich nor needy in the community. For his own church,

> Luke has a concrete social goal in view: an equal distribution of property within the community. He is far from offering a political program for a comprehensive redistribution of property throughout society. He does, however, have a program, but it is for the Christian community. In his picture of the first Christian community in Jerusalem, he formulates his own utopian vision of a Christian community that is characterized by material and social equality.[118]

The clause "as any had need" in verse 35b corresponds word for word with 2:45c and once again reflects the thrust of Luke's idealistic construct mentioned just above. In paradigmatic fashion Luke projects what he expects of his community back to the time of the first community.

Verses 36–37: These verses "present the correct information out of which the ideal picture of the community sharing was developed. The following episode, however, does not fit well with the ideal."[119] "By the apostles" certainly derives from Luke. The meaning of Barnabas is not "son of encouragement" but rather "son of Nebo."[120] So far in Acts the Jerusalem perspective is still dominant. Here, as later in 11:22, Luke assigns Barnabas to Jerusalem. For the phrase "lay at the apostles' feet," cf. 4:35; 5:2.

THE TRADITIONS REWORKED BY LUKE

Verses 32–35: For the elements of "tradition" in the summary description, see the comments on 2:42–47, pages 57–58 above.

Verses 36–37: Luke must have known a tradition—whether oral or written—that Barnabas had sold a field to sustain the Jerusalem community. The reason for assuming this is that the Lukan framework generalizes, while the information about the sale of one field is specific and is in tension with the framework. Similarly the designation of his origin, "a native of Cyprus," is an element of tradition. It means either that Barnabas comes from Cyprus (cf. 15:39, where Barnabas and Mark travel to Cyprus), or that his family originated there (cf. 11:20; 21:16, Mnason the Cypriot).

HISTORICAL ELEMENTS

There can be little doubt about the historicity of Barnabas's sale of a field in support of the Jerusalem community. Paul's letters make it clear that the Jerusalem community long depended on the support of Gentile Christians. Barnabas's action may likewise have been a gift of love, but when this donation was made is uncertain. It might belong in the early period, though it could reflect events after the conference—at the time of the collection taken up by the Antiochene and Pauline communities (see 1 Cor. 16:1–2; Acts 11:29–30)—that were editorially transferred to the earlier period.

THE HISTORICAL VALUE OF LUKE'S ACCOUNT

Luke continues the painting of the earliest community against a golden foil. By reporting Barnabas's action, he undermines his own picture of a community holding everything in common after a total surrender of possessions by all the members of the Jerusalem fellowship. Thus, even though he again misleads his readers by painting an idyllic picture of the earliest community, by applying the tools of the historical-critical method, we discover that we owe to him a decisive insight into an important reality of the earliest community in Jerusalem.

The following remark by Fitzmyer is misleading: "Nothing is said about how long common ownership of property was so practiced, or even how widespread it was among Christians."[121]

Rebuttal: Luke unambiguously reports that the whole Jerusalem community practiced it in the golden early days. To be sure, we are not told how long this Edenic situation lasted; but in view of the phrases "*whole* fellowship," "*no one* claimed any," and "*everything* in common" (verse 32), the clear implication that Luke limits the pervasiveness of communal sharing must be seen as a bald and willful misrepresentation.

[14]
ACTS 5:1–11
ANANIAS AND SAPPHIRA

(1) But a *man named* Ananias, with his wife Sapphira, sold a piece of property, (2) and with his wife's knowledge he <u>put aside for</u> himself part of the proceeds and brought only the remainder of it and laid it *at the apostles' feet.*

(3) Then Peter said, "Ananias, how has Satan possessed you to lie to the Holy Spirit and <u>to put aside</u> for yourself some of the proceeds of the land? (4) *While it remained unsold, did it not remain your own? And after it was sold, was*

it not at your disposal? Whatever led you to contrive this deed in your heart? You have not lied to men but to God."

(5) When Ananias heard these words, **he fell down and breathed his last**. *And great fear came upon all who heard of it*. (6) The younger men rose and wrapped him up and carried him out and buried him.

(7) *About three hours later his wife came in, not knowing what had happened. (8) And Peter said to her, "Tell me whether you sold the land for such and such a price." And she said, "Yes, that was the price."*

(9) *Then Peter said to her, "How can you have agreed to test the Spirit of the Lord? Look, the feet of those who have buried your husband are at the door, and now they will carry you out."*

(10) *Immediately* **she fell down** *at his feet* **and breathed her last**. *When the young men came in they found her dead, and they carried her out and buried her beside her husband.* (11) *And great fear came* upon the whole church and *upon all who heard of these things.*

OUTLINE

1–2: Exposition: The sale of a piece of land and the retention of part of the proceeds by Ananias and Sapphira

3–6: The questioning and punishment of Ananias

7–10: The questioning and punishment of Sapphira

11: The impression on the church and all who heard of it

LUKE'S PURPOSE

Verses 1–2: The phrase "a man named" derives from Luke. "He sold a piece of property" is a link to 4:37, where the same verb is used for Barnabas's sale of the field. Luke employs the phrase "at the apostles' feet" earlier in 4:35, 37 thus indicating that 5:1–10 along with 4:32–37[122] deal with the same issue.

Verses 3–6: "Holy Spirit" in verse 3 derives from Luke, because the "Holy Spirit" plays a major role in his work. Verse 4 is thoroughly Lukan in style and content. Its literary form renders it clearly exceptional, and its obvious purpose is to serve as an explanation for readers. It denies the formerly enunciated obligation to renounce possessions by emphasizing the voluntary nature of both the sale and the transfer of funds. Note also that verse 4c, "You have not lied to men but to God," anticipates both Peter's saying in 5:29 and Gamaliel's advice in 5:38–39, both of which go back to Luke. And, as in 4c, both stress the idea that one's primary commitment is to God. The note at verse 6 about the burial of Ananias (cf. later verse 10) fits in with Jewish burial customs.[123] Sapphira could not be told about her husband's death because Luke still needed her for the next unit.

Verses 7–10: In all likelihood Luke has composed this episode on the model of the previous one (verses 3–6) to increase the story's dramatic effect and drive home the point made there.[124] In verse 8 Peter asks whether the contribution given was the whole amount. Since Peter's question in verse 8—whether the whole amount of the sale had been handed over—is clearly a ploy (he has already learned it had not), its evident purpose is to recapitulate verses 2–3 and thereby reinforce the enormity of the embezzlement. Sapphira's collapse at Peter's feet (verse 10) is yet another employment of a rhetorical device—cf. "at the apostles' feet" (4:35, 37; 5:2)—that must obviously be attributed to the author.

Verse 11: In view of 8:1 and 9:31, Luke has deliberately chosen the term "church" (in Greek, *ekklesia*) as a designation of the individual Jerusalem community. Verse 5b has been repeated with the addition of "the whole church." One is tempted to conclude that Luke addressed 4:32–5:11 to his own community. Certainly in the account at hand "church" denotes the Jerusalem community, but for the reader it potentially includes the whole church, including Luke's congregation.

Acts 5:1–11 is clearly tied together with 4:32–37, for after 4:34, 36–37, Luke is here depicting a third case in which the gain of property sold is laid at the apostles' feet (verse 2). The example of Ananias and Sapphira is a display of what would conceivably happen to those who defy the Holy Spirit. Yet while the present story does not contain direct instructions for Luke's community, but a didactic example from the earliest Christian period, it shows that Luke's paramount concern is not the total renunciation of property that leads to a "communism of love," but genuine dedication to God—or at very least not trying to deceive him. Ananias and Sapphira receive punishment not for failing to renounce all their possessions or for making only a portion of them available to the community, but for the deceitful nature of their actions and the venal disposition thus displayed. By presenting a specimen of conduct that is detrimental to the community, Luke puts the exemplary behavior of Barnabas and the community into the right perspective.

THE TRADITIONS REWORKED BY LUKE

In the editorial process Luke did not simply add verse 4, but reshaped the whole story. The names Ananias and Peter come from a tradition, as does the death of Ananias caused by God's action in response to Peter's denunciation of him for breaking a rule of the Christian community. The verb in verses 2 and 3, "to put aside" (for oneself)—in Greek, *nosphizein*—is relatively uncommon, appearing elsewhere in biblical writings only in Josh. 7:1, 2 Macc. 4:32, and Titus 2:10. The similarity of circumstances suggests that it might come from the story of Achan (Josh. 7:1), who stole property devoted to God and thus under ban, for this would comport with its use in early Jewish-Christian circles intending that very allusion. Overall, the story corresponds to Jewish rule miracles. "In the Jewish rule miracles the issue is almost always one of life or death. Breaches of the law lead to death, observance of the law preserves from death. The law does not chastise; it kills. This seems to us archaic and inhuman, especially in the case of unimportant transgressions but is a sign of great seriousness about the observance of the divine will: in the presence of God the issue is one of life and death."[125]

Therefore we may reasonably hypothesize that the tradition reflected a punitive rule miracle. But if so, it is not a simple matter to specify the rule Ananias broke. Luke offers the contextual indication that the crime is a form of embezzlement; other than that, one can adduce only the breaking of rules that a community has defined as sacred. While money management may well have been the issue, the details need not have been as Luke portrays them. It should also be noted that a number of early Christian parallels report offences against sacred law.[126] See, for example, 1 Cor. 3:16–17: "Do you not know that you are God's temple and that God's Spirit dwells in you? If any one destroys God's temple, God will destroy him. For God's temple is holy, and that temple you are." Another example appears in 1 Cor. 5:13b when, at the end of a section concerned with the community, Paul writes, "Cast out the evil one from your midst." The use of this citation of Deut. 17:7[127] is surely indicative of the nature of the traditions that informed Acts 5.[128]

In the case reported in 1 Cor. 5:1–5, Paul was dealing with incest. His decision was that the offender be consigned to Satan (cf. the involvement of Satan in Acts 5:3): thus while his flesh might be destroyed, his spirit would be saved at the judgment (1 Cor. 5:5b). But the tradition that Luke employed in Acts 5:1–11 seems to have had no interest in the sinner's future fate, nor are we given to understand that Peter remanded him to Satan. Nevertheless the resolution of the problem is the same: A "holy" man carries out the prescription of sacred law so as to cause a sinner's death. Peter's place in the tradition is thus powerfully implied.

HISTORICAL ELEMENTS

There can be little doubt that the tradition originated during the earliest period of the Jerusalem community under the leadership of Peter. The parallel to 1 Cor. 5 strongly suggests that a similar event gave rise to this account: One of the community, having violated sacred law, was anathematized and ostracized by the leader of the community. Whether in the actual case the malefactor died is far from certain, but according to sacred law he should have. Thus the "heightening of the event to the point at which it becomes a judgment of God with fatal consequences" may accord with the "rules of popular tradition."[129] Finally, let me emphasize once again that the exact nature of Ananias's "sin" in the original tradition is no longer clear.

The result of my analysis must be defended against an apologetic comment of Barrett. He writes,

> What was the origin of the story? Did Peter in fact strike dead two unsatisfactory church members? Judas (1.18) and Herod (12.23) died unhappy deaths; Paul struck blind Elymas, the magus of the proconsul Sergius Paulus (13.11); and there is nothing more miraculous in striking dead than in raising the dead (e.g., 9.32–43). There are OT parallels, notably Lev. 10.1–5. The difference and the difficulty are moral as well as rational, but are mitigated by the fact that Peter is not actually said to have caused, or even to have willed, the two deaths. . . . (H)e foretells her [Sapphira's] death, but foretelling is not willing, and with Ananias he did not even go so far.[130]

Rebuttal: The excessively defensive nature of this last commentary glosses over two things that should be clear to any careful exegete. The specific manner of foretelling Sapphira's death is tantamount to a death sentence: "Look, the feet of those who have buried your husband are at the door, and now they will carry you out." (One can almost hear the line from *Macbeth* spoken by Banquo's assassin: "Let it come down!") As concerns Ananias's fate, Peter had no need to predict it since he in effect pronounced it: "You lied to God!" Can we seriously imagine that Luke's readers were the sorts who would understand such an imprecation to be merely an objective assessment of the situation—or who would expect a just God so recently and flagrantly insulted to overrule Peter's condemnation in a sudden outburst of compassion?

The Historical Value of Luke's Account

Fitzmyer's exegesis of the present passage represents an approach to Acts that many of his Christian colleagues share. While not flatly denying the historicity of the account and thus leaving it open as a possibility, Fitzmyer stresses the theological point the text makes. This tale, then, is "the main incident in Acts that raises questions about the historical value of the Lucan narrative as a whole."[131] Later Fitzmyer continues,

Say what one will about such precedents in the OT, in contemporary Judaism, or the Greco-Roman world, the story of Ananias and Sapphira reveals how evil and deception finally manifest themselves among God's new people and disrupt the idyllic existence that Luke has so far depicted. Whether one can determine anything about the historicity of the incident, whether it be folkloric or legendary, it effectively teaches the lesson that Luke wants to achieve by incorporating it into his account of the early days of the Christian community: The "fear" that Luke says came upon the whole church as a result (5:11) of the deception has to be understood as salutary fear.[132]

Rebuttal: This is all very well, but it sidesteps the basic question of historicity. The answer, of course, is that the story as presented by Luke is fiction. It would be a refreshing and salutary change of tactics if in such cases Christian scholars would bite the bullet and admit the obvious.

[15]
ACTS 5:12–16
MANY SIGNS AND WONDERS DONE

(12a) *By the hands of the apostles many signs and wonders were regularly done among the* _people_. (12b) *And all of them used to meet by common consent in Solomon's Colonnade.* (13a) *No others dared to join them,* (13b) *but the* _people_ *held them in high esteem.* (14) *And more were added as believers in the Lord, a* **multitude** *both of men and women.* (15a) *As a result they would even carry the sick out into the streets and lay them on cots and mats,* (15b) *so that as Peter came by at least his shadow might fall on some of them.* (16) *And there also came together a* **multitude** *from the towns around Jerusalem, bringing the sick and those afflicted with unclean spirits, all of whom were healed.*

OUTLINE

12a: Signs and wonders done by the apostles
12b: Peaceful Temple attendance of Christians in the hall of Solomon
13: People's attitude toward the Christians
14: The continuing growth of the community
15–16: Healings by Peter's shadow and healing of the sick from all the environs of Jerusalem

LUKE'S PURPOSE

This passage ascribes miraculous power to the apostles and witnesses a continuing growth of the Christian community via conversions. In its description of
miracles performed by the apostles, this last extended summary in Acts goes well
beyond all the previous summaries. Tensions are evident: Verses 12a and 12b
have no natural connection, nor do verses 13a and 13b. Verse 13a says that non-
members did not dare to join in community activities, but verse 13b blithely
informs us that this same group of people thought very highly of them. To be sure
this does not necessarily involve a conflict, for one may admire a group yet
shrink from joining it, but a more serious conflict appears to exist between verses
13 and 14. According to the former verse none dared join, but according to the
latter verse many joined. Perhaps we are to assume that what people cannot do,
God can! The puzzling beginning of verse 15, "as a result," apparently connects
it to verse 12a, since it is quite out of place in the present context. One might suspect that incongruent sources or traditions have been ineptly combined, but neither the language nor the overall content gives any hint of this.[133]

Verse 12a: This echoes 2:19, 22, 43; 4:30 and thus once again states the miracles of the apostles in summary form.

Verse 12b: "By common consent" again reflects Luke's theology. Fre-
quenting Solomon's hall is another way of expressing the idea of the Christian
unanimity symbolized by their custom of gathering in the Temple—something
already reported in 2:46. As previously mentioned in 3:1, Luke pictures
Solomon's hall as part of the Temple.

Verse 13: The fear attributed to the populace recalls 5:1–11; see esp. verse
11b: "Great fear fell upon all who heard of it." The high regard for the Christians,
while it clashes here, is taken up in the next episode (see esp. verse 26).

Verse 14: Luke frequently refers to both men and women. The report of the
community's continued rapid growth is a logical sequel to the positive public
attitude mentioned in verse 13.

Verse 15: Here we discover the results of the situation described in verses
12–14. Luke omitted from his gospel the report found in 15a, which is clearly
modeled on Mark 6:56, but he uses it here. The note about Peter's miraculous
shadow at verse 15b—a surely intended parallel to the account involving Paul's
handkerchiefs in 19:12—again praises Peter's control of magical powers.

Verse 16: This verse amounts to yet another report—though an indirect
one—of the spread of the good news both spiritually and bodily among large
numbers of people in the towns and the countryside around Jerusalem. As he
does explicitly in Luke 6:17, the author may here imply supplicants coming from

all the cities of Judea to the capital to seek healing for their sick and strongly appeals to the reader's imagination. It seems evident that Luke is here preparing the way for the next chapter's report that the gospel has spread to Hellenists— those "outside" the original Jewish-Christian community (6:1; cf. 1:8).

THE TRADITIONS REWORKED BY LUKE

Verse 15b: The story of Peter's healing shadow reflects tradition and is the peak of ascribing supernatural powers to the prince of the apostles. As such it stands at the end of a constantly developing tradition destined to glorify a leader of the church.

HISTORICAL ELEMENTS

Verse 15b: If only because of the evident history of the tradition, claiming authenticity for the legend of Peter's healing shadow is quite out of the question.

THE HISTORICAL VALUE OF LUKE'S ACCOUNT

Verses 12a, 15–16: By making not only Peter but also other apostles perform the miracles, by bringing throngs of outsiders to Jerusalem, and by claiming that all the sick were healed, Luke once again loses sight of the real situation in Jerusalem and again commits a serious blunder that many people have imagined to be historically accurate.

Verse 15b: Concerning the healing power of Peter's shadow, Howard Marshall opines,

> The idea that shadows had magical powers, both beneficent and malevolent, was current in the ancient world and explains the motivation of the people. Similar beliefs about Paul's powers are attested in 19:12. Luke relates this detail as a special proof of Peter's reputation among the people; he was regarded as having exceptional healing powers. Whether, however, Peter or Luke would have shared the superstitions [sic!] which the people undoubtedly showed is another matter.[134]

Rebuttal: That is nothing more than a cunning but desperate attempt to defend the historicity of the story while at the same time distinguishing Christian faith from superstitious magic. Indeed, your magic is my miracle.

[16]
ACTS 5:17–42
THE APOSTLES ARRESTED AND FREED

(17) *But the high priest rose up, and all who were with him (that is, the party of the Sadducees), and filled with jealousy* (18) *they laid hands on the apostles and put them in the public prison.*

(19) But during the night an angel of the Lord opened the prison doors and brought them out, and said, (20) "Go and stand in the temple and speak to the people all the words of this life." (21a) And when they heard this, they entered the temple about daybreak and taught.

(21b) **Now when** *the high priest* **came,** *and those who were with him, they called together the high council and all the senate of the sons of Israel and sent to the prison to have them brought.* (22) **Now when** *the officers* **came,** *they did not find them in the jail, so they returned and reported,* (23) *"We found the prison securely locked and the guards standing at the doors, but when we opened them we found no one inside."* (24) *But when the captain of the temple and the chief priests heard these words, they were greatly perplexed about them,* [*wondering*] *what this would lead to.* (25) **Now when** *someone* **came** *and told them, "Look! The men whom you put in jail are standing in the temple and teaching the people,"* (26) *then the captain went with the officers and brought them, but not by force, for they were afraid of being stoned by the people.* (27a) *And when they had brought them, they set them before the council.*

(27b) *And the high priest questioned them,* (28) *saying, "We strictly charged you not to teach in this name, yet here you have filled Jerusalem with your teaching, and you intend to bring this man's blood upon us."*

(29) *But Peter and the apostles answered, "One must obey God rather than men.* (30a) *The God of our fathers raised Jesus,* (30b) *on whom you laid violent hands by hanging him on a tree.* (31) *God exalted him at his right hand as leader and savior, to give repentance to Israel and forgiveness of sins.* (32) *And we are witnesses to these things, and so is the Holy Spirit, whom God has given to those who obey him."*

(33) *When they heard this, they were enraged and wanted to slay them.*

(34) *But there stood up in the council* a Pharisee *named* Gamaliel, *a teacher of the law held in honor by all the people, and he gave orders to put the men outside for a little while.* (35) *And he said to them, "Men of Israel, take care what you are about to do with these men.* (36) *For before these days Theudas rose up, claiming to be somebody, to whom a number of men, about four hundred,*

attached themselves. He was slain, and all who were duped by him were dispersed and came to nothing. (37) After him Judas the Galilean rose up in the days of the census and drew away some of the people after him. He too perished, and all who followed him were scattered. (38) *And now, I tell you, keep away from these men and let them alone, for if this plan or this undertaking is of man, it will fail;* (39a) *but if it is of God, you will not be able to overthrow them. You might even be found opposing God!"*

(39b) *So they took his advice,* (40) *and when they had called in the apostles, they had them flogged and charged them not to speak in the name of Jesus, and let them go.*

(41) *Then they left the council chamber, rejoicing that they were counted worthy to suffer dishonor for the name.* (42) *And all day long, in the temple and from house to house, they did not cease teaching and preaching Jesus as the Christ.*

OUTLINE

17–18: Exposition: Arrest of the apostles by the High Priest and the Sadducees
19–21a: Miracle of their deliverance accompanied by a command to witness
21b–27a: Events leading to legal procedures against the apostles
27b–40: Legal hearing
    27b–28: Charge of the High Priest
    29–32: Peter's speech of defense
    33: Furious reaction of the high council
    34–39b: Gamaliel's speech
    39c–40: Reaction of the high council. Punishment and release of the apostles
41–42: Joy of the apostles over suffering in Jesus' name and continuation of the preaching in the temple

LUKE'S PURPOSE

This episode takes up the theme of Acts 3–4 using different events. Angered and offended at the proclamation of Jesus as Messiah, the Jewish authorities attempt to silence the apostles, who then continue to preach with renewed confidence (cf. esp. 4:18–20).

Verses 17–18: The section attributes the arrest of the apostles to the "jealousy" of the Jewish authorities, an animus that results especially from the extraordinary popular success of the apostles. Note the similarity to 4:2, where the Sadducees were outraged that the apostles were teaching the people. The report of their jailing at 5:18 likewise closely matches that in 4:3.

Verse 19: The note about the freeing of the apostles from prison by an angel has no parallel in Acts 4, but similar wondrous liberations occur in 12:4–10 and 16:23–34. It should be noted, however, that the present account of their freeing lacks color and drama in comparison to those in chapters 12 and 16. At best it offers a generic report of a miraculous release that Luke introduced into the narrative context here in order to demonstrate once again God's steadfast support of the apostles. Yet the sequel is strangely silent about the miraculous release; indeed, throughout the hearing no reference whatever is made to the ban reported in 4:18 that forbade teaching in Jesus' name. The miraculous release story, then, does not penetrate to the narrative level, but remains on the surface of an authorial monologue.

Verses 20–21a: For the temple as the place of the activity of the apostles see above, page 59.

Verses 21b–26: This section establishes the setting of the judicial transaction. The Jewish authorities are informed of what has happened. Concerning the Jewish leaders' anxiety about the people, see 4:21.

Verse 27: Here Luke has constructed the beginning of the hearing proper.

Verse 28: This verse clearly derives from Luke, since it is based on 4:18. The failure of the apostles to observe the ban on teaching in Jesus' name (verse 28a), indeed their persistence in filling Jerusalem with Christian teaching (verse 28b) is the essential charge; to this is added the allegation that they sought to blame the Sanhedrin for Jesus' death. The latter assertion not only heightens the narrative tension, but also calls the reader's attention to the ultimate consequences of the council's proceedings: Besides the present action against the apostles, the Sanhedrin is indirectly responsible for the killing of Jesus, and on both counts is subject to God's punishment.

Verse 29: Cf. "one must obey God rather than men," with 4:19, "Is it right before God to listen to you rather than to God?"

Verse 30: Verse 30b depicts the Jewish leaders as the ones who have crucified Jesus (cf. 2:23; 3:14–15). Note also its verbatim correspondence to 10:39b and the allusion to Deut. 21:22–23 (LXX). Although it originally referred to hanging up a dead body after stoning, this passage could, even in the pre-Christian period, refer to crucifixion. The allusion is likely due to Luke's own pondering over the death of Jesus (cf. Luke 23:39 [Mark differs]) and could ultimately derive from Gal. 3:13.

Verse 31: The notion that the exalted Jesus can cause repentance to take place and the forgiveness to be granted is not thus expressed elsewhere in Acts. The present phrasing most likely derives from Luke, however, for he often uses repentance and forgiveness as a pair; furthermore, verse 31 corresponds in content to 2:33: The Jesus who is exalted to the right hand of God pours out the Holy Spirit as a gift.

Verse 32: Verse 32a, the apostles' witness, goes back to Luke; note the same statement in 2:32; 3:15 (along with a creedal statement on Jesus). The phrase "these things" refers to the "saving" acts of God (resurrection, ascension, the offer of repentance through Jesus). The conception in verse 32b that the Holy Spirit is a further independent witness alongside the apostles appears only here in Luke. Granted, "the juxtaposition of the testimony of the apostles and of the Spirit is explained by 2:32–39 and Luke 24:48–49,"[135] but this correspondence of elements hardly rises to the level of a parallel in either of the passages mentioned.

Verse 33: As in 7:54 the effect of the testimony of the apostles is described. "Luke imagines the Sanhedrin as an assembly swept away by an irresistible passion."[136] See further on 23:6.

Verses 34–39: This section must be understood in terms of Luke's apologetic intentions. Moreover, verse 34 corresponds to 4:15: In both cases the apostles must leave the room before the discussion. Gamaliel's advice in verses 38–39 contains Luke's apologetic program.[137] That the Christian plan is "from God" has of course long been clear to the readers. Indeed, by his miraculous intervention on behalf of the two apostles, God has made clear that that the proclamation of the apostles represents his cause. Here Luke makes the Pharisees resemble the Christians, since both, in contrast to the Sadducees, teach the resurrection from the dead (see 23:6–9). Therefore the Sadducees appear as enemies and persecutors of the Christians. Gamaliel's advice is supported by two historical examples, the rebellions of Theudas and Judas. In this passage, though, they certainly derive from Luke, who has anachronistically juxtaposed them.

Theudas entered public life at the time of the procurator Fadus (44–46 CE).[138] According to Luke this occurred before Gamaliel's speech and even before the census (6 BCE). Luke's Gamaliel further says that Judas the Galilean appeared during the time of the census, *after* Theudas. There has been an attempt to exonerate Luke from this mistake by postulating the existence of another Theudas who was not known to Josephus. Not only is the name Theudas extremely rare, however, but the reference to Theudas in Acts 5 is meaningful only if, like Judas, he initiated an important movement. In that case, however, it is unlikely that Josephus would have overlooked that Theudas.[139]

Luke uses Gamaliel's speech as an occasion for providing historical allusions. But if these are recognized as Luke's additions, the presence of Gamaliel at this point must also be attributed to him—even though the mediating role of the "Hillelite" Gamaliel accords well the words of advice he offers here. Nevertheless, the Lukan portrait of Gamaliel is undermined—at least at the narrative level—by the evidence that Gamaliel's pupil, Paul, did not seem disposed to exhibit the tolerance attributed to his teacher. Our conclusion must be that the person and speech of Gamaliel at this point are Luke's creation.

Verse 40: This verse relies for language on 5:28 and 4:18. It is extraordinary that despite the assent of the Sanhedrin to Gamaliel's advice, the apostles are flogged. This tension can best be explained in terms of the redaction. The suffering of the apostles serves as a model for the time of Luke (see also the next verses 41–42).

Verses 41–42: In language and content these verses derive wholly from Luke. They depict once again the roots of the earliest Christian community in Judaism—note the preaching in the Temple—but then describe it in terms of the situation of the contemporary Lukan church and Christian existence (ca. 85 CE or later) by invoking the theme of suffering, the necessity of which in 14:22 is here retroactively described as a joy.

To sum up, apart from the miraculous release described in verse 19, the passage under discussion is a variation on Acts 3–4. There the apostles Peter and John are arrested because of their miracles and preaching, brought before the supreme council, but set free after a warning for lack of sufficient legal grounds. Luke goes a step beyond this in chapter 5 by having *all* the apostles arrested by the Jewish authorities because of their successful activity, but miraculously released by God, who can intervene on behalf of his missionaries at any time. In the course of another action undertaken by the high council it is shown that no human prohibition can effectively oppose the divinely willed proclamation of the apostles in the name of Jesus Christ. Gamaliel stresses programmatically that nobody *opposing God* can defeat the Christian cause—a message directed at Luke's readers. The scene ends with an indirect look at the apostles' suffering and their constant proclamation of the Good News.

THE TRADITIONS REWORKED BY LUKE

Verses 19–21a: It is to serve his theological agenda, then, that Luke has inserted a miraculous liberation similar to the release stories in Acts 12 and 16. This is not in its original context, nor is it subsequently referred to. Comparison with Acts 12, Acts 16, and non-Christian parallels (see below, p. 216) indicates that the action was composed entirely by Luke, while the details of the liberation miracle derive from tradition.

Verse 34: The person of Gamaliel either was known to Luke from the tradition on Paul's pre-Christian period (22:3) or was part of his general knowledge.

Verses 36–37: The information about Theudas and Judas derives from Luke's reading or from oral information.[140]

HISTORICAL ELEMENTS

Verses 19–21a: Luke himself has woven the elements of the tradition of a miraculous release into this passage. They have nothing to do with a historical nucleus.

Verses 38–39: Occasionally, scholars claim a historical nucleus in Gamaliel's advice.[141] Yet the clearly Lukan context of verses 38–39 and the impossibility of historically verifying "Gamaliel's advice" from rabbinic writings suggest that the verses are Luke's creation.

THE HISTORICAL VALUE OF LUKE'S ACCOUNT

Not a single verse of Luke's account corresponds to events in Jerusalem after the formation of the Christian community there. Luke relates a totally fictitious story in order to establish a theological point: The message about Jesus Christ is unstoppable because it is from God.

Verses 36–37: Yet some modern scholars are unwilling to describe Luke's chronological confusion as what it clearly is: a blunder. Fitzmyer offers a classic example showing that apologetic criticism willy-nilly bogs down. He writes,

> Many attempts have been made to explain this confusion. Some have maintained that there was another rebel named Theudas in the last days of Herod the Great (37–4 B.C.); but no real evidence supports such a claim. There is little likelihood that Luke was dependent on Josephus and his way of referring to the two incidents, so that one cannot so explain the confusion. . . . Whatever one says about Gamaliel's speech, one has to live with it in the present form, despite the confusion it causes. We have no real answer as to why Luke so composed it, but as Hemer (*Book of Acts*, 163) has put it, "one such slip on his [Luke's] part would not entitle us to argue for his general unreliability. The fact that Luke's background information can so often be corroborated may suggest that it is wiser to leave this particular matter open rather than to condemn Luke of a blunder."[142]

Colin J. Hemer, to whom Fitzmyer refers as an authority in exegetical matters, suggests how Luke may have known Gamaliel's advice—from Saul/Paul himself! Hemer writes,

It may be doubted whether Paul was of age to be a member of the Sanhedrin, but likely enough in any case that he received an account from Gamaliel himself at a time when his mind was much exercised over the new teaching. He had apparently been close to Gamaliel, and his teacher's reaction would have made its mark. And Luke, we suppose, was later close to Paul. Such a reconstruction can only be inferential and speculative, but it is plausible. It might be Paul's first latent imprint on the narrative.[143]

Rebuttal: It is passing strange that Paul did not heed his teacher's advice. As Richard I. Pervo quips, he "had apparently slept through Gamaliel's lecture on not persecuting new movements."[144] Once again wishful thinking has led a loyal defender of a no doubt well-intentioned myth to advance supposition as argument when no evidence could be found.

[17]
ACTS 6:1–15
THE APPOINTMENT OF THE SEVEN AND THE ATTACK ON STEPHEN[145]

(1) *Now in those days when the disciples were growing in number, the Hellenists made a complaint against the Hebrews because their widows were neglected in the daily distribution.*

(2) And the twelve *called the body of the disciples and said, "It is not right that we should neglect the word of God in order to wait on tables.* (3) *Therefore, brothers, pick out from among you* seven men *of good reputation, full of the Spirit and of wisdom, whom we may appoint to this duty.* (4) *But we will devote ourselves to prayer and to the ministry of the word."* (5) *And what they said pleased the whole body,* and they chose Stephen, *a man full of faith and of the Holy Spirit,* and Philip, and Prochorus, and Nicanor, and Timon, and Parmenas, and Nicolaos, a proselyte of Antioch. (6) These they presented before the apostles, *and they prayed and laid their hands on them.*

(7) *And the word of God continued to spread; and the number of the disciples multiplied greatly in Jerusalem, and very many of the priests were obedient to the faith.*

(8) *And Stephen, full of grace and power, did great wonders and signs among the people.*

(9) Then some members of the so-called Synagogue of the Freedmen com-

prising Cyrenians and Alexandrians, and people from Cilicia and Asia, came forward and disputed with Stephen. (10) But they could not hold their own against his *wisdom and the Spirit* with which he spoke. (11) Then they secretly instigated certain men, who said, "We have heard him speak blasphemous words against Moses and God." (12) And they stirred up the people and the elders and the scribes, and they came upon him and seized him and brought him before the council, (13) and produced false witnesses who said, "This man is forever saying things against this holy place and the law; (14) for we have heard him say, 'This Jesus of Nazareth will destroy this place, and will alter the customs handed down to us by Moses.'"

(15) *And gazing at him, all who sat in the council saw that his face was like the face of an angel.*

OUTLINE

    1: Exposition: The problem of neglect of the Hellenistic widows
  2–6: Solution of the conflict: the choice of the Seven
    7: Summary and note about priests joining the community
    8: Summary description of the miracles of Stephen among the people
 9–14: Two charges against Stephen
          9–10: The unsuccessful attack by the members of the Hellenist communities by means of disputations
       11–14: The attack by false witnesses, its impact on the people, the elders, and the scribes, and the proceedings before the Sanhedrin
   15: Description of Stephen's face

LUKE'S PURPOSE

Chapter 6 introduces a new section in Acts. The account begins with the report in 6:1 of dissension within the community and its resolution by the appointment of deacons in 6:5–6. This continues the description of the communal organization of the congregation found in 2:44–45 and 4:32–5:11. But now—after the preparatory remarks in 5:16—the mission that had previously been limited to Jerusalem reaches out to the surrounding areas through the preaching of the Hellenists. This section (6:1–8:3) focuses on the person of Stephen, as 8:4–40 does on the figure of Philip.

Verse 1: The conflict reported here is intrinsically plausible. Many pious

Jews settled in Jerusalem in the evening of their lives in order to be buried in the holy city. Therefore the care of their widows was a problem that no doubt arose relatively often. However, Luke creates an artificial conflict. Since members of the Jerusalem community were probably part of the Jewish community's care of the poor,[146] a conflict of the sort Luke describes was unlikely to occur. We shall have to ask later what real conflict Luke has thus camouflaged.

Verses 2–3: Two groups are pictured in conflict: the leaders of the community—here the Twelve—and the full assembly. The leaders summon the body and make proposals to it. The description of the task of the Seven, to see to the care of the widows, uses a phrase that recalls the summaries in 2:45 and 4:35. While it was said there that the apostles (!) distributed the resources of the earliest community ("as any had need"), from now on the Seven (and no longer the apostles) will see to this task.

Verse 4: This reflects the Lukan notion that the Twelve were concerned with prayer and preaching the word (see 2:42; 4:29, and for the expression "ministry of the word" see Luke 1:2: The eyewitnesses as the servants of the Word means the twelve apostles).

Verse 5: Luke points back to verse 2. The proposal made by the Twelve, the leaders of the community, meets with the agreement of the body of disciples, the full assembly. Luke is likely to be responsible for the order of the list in verse 5, but the names come from tradition. He puts Stephen at the head, for he will soon be the focus of events. Nor is it accidental that Philip occupies second place, as he will be the major figure throughout Acts 8. The name of the proselyte Nicolaos, who occupies the last place, goes back to tradition, but his position at the end is due to redaction. Thereby Luke shows that he knows the difference between a born Jew and a proselyte.

Verse 6: Luke adds the prayer and the laying-on of hands. The latter also appears in 13:3, and represents the entrusting of someone with a special task.

Verse 7: This is a Lukan summary. By echoing verse 1 as well as 2:41, 47, and 4:4, verse 7a stresses the constant and rapid growth in the community. In verse 7b the report that many priests had joined the community indicates a further development, since previously only ordinary Jewish people had become Christians.

Verse 8: This verse, deriving from Luke in terms of language, is a transition to the following episode. Stephen is not depicted "serving food" but speaking in public, nor in "serving the word," but being effective through miracles.

Verses 9–14: Verse 9 is a kind of prelude to the conflict that follows and that ends in Stephen's death. In verse 10 Luke points back to verse 3, and this links verses 1–7 to verses 8–15. The parallel between verse 10 and Luke 21:15—where

Jesus promises his disciples to give them "a mouth and wisdom, which none of your adversaries will be able to withstand or contradict"—shows that the author of Acts sees Jesus' promise realized in the trial of Stephen. After the failure of the first attack against Stephen, verse 11 introduces a second, and verse 12 describes its success. Even "the people," who hitherto sided with the Hellenists (cf. also verse 8), are influenced, as are also—less surprisingly—the elders and scribes, who had already been involved in actions against the earliest Jerusalem community (Acts 4; 5). Verse 13 says explicitly that the witnesses were false, whereas in verse 11 they were still described neutrally as "men." And even though the accusations in verses 11 and 13 differ (verse 11 speaks of blasphemy against Moses and God; verse 13 mentions attacks on the temple and the law), Luke presents the statement made by the men/false witnesses as wrong in any case.

Verse 15: This verse, in language colored by Luke, is an anticipatory image he has somewhat awkwardly inserted between 6:14 and 7:1. "The sequel to this remark is 7:55–56."[147]

THE TRADITIONS REWORKED BY LUKE

Verse 1: On the underlying conflict between the Hellenists and the Hebrews, which Luke tries to tone down, see below, pages 95 and 105. In addition, the abrupt introduction of the dispute between the Hebrews and the Hellenists suggests the employment of tradition.

Verse 5: The bedrock tradition is the list of the Seven. That all of them have Greek names makes their Greek origin clear: Stephen, Philip, Prochorus, Nicanor, Timon, Parmenas, and Nicolaos. The sacred number "seven" was undoubtedly part of the tradition. The echo of this passage in 21:8 (where Philip is called one of the Seven) need not tell against this.

Verse 9: This verse reflects the tradition that one or more such communities existed in Jerusalem. Available evidence points to at least eleven such synagogues in Rome.[148]

Verse 10: Stephen is portrayed as a preacher, quite a different role from that assigned to him in verse 2. One need not give deep thought to Luke's account before asking whether the daily care for the widows could have improved at all under such conditions. It follows from this that the understanding of Stephen in verse 10 is quite different from that in verses 1–7. Therefore despite the Lukan peculiarities of language indicated in the translation by italics, verse 10 seems to have a traditional nucleus.

Verses 11–14: This piece reflects elements of Stephen's preaching at the level of tradition.

HISTORICAL ELEMENTS

There is a certain consensus among scholars that the Hellenists are Greek-speaking Jews and the Hebrews Aramaic-speaking Jews of Jerusalem.[149] This consensus is based on both the narrower and wider contexts of Acts 6. The Seven have Greek names (verse 5) in contrast to the predominantly Semitic names of the twelve apostles (only Andrew and Philip are exceptions here). Further, Luke uses only one word etymologically related to "Hebrew," the noun *Hebraios*, which commonly connotes a linguistic grouping. See the phrase "in the Hebrew language"[150] in Acts 21:40.[151] Although some controversy no doubt arose between the parties of the Hebrews and the Hellenists in the early period of the primitive community, no information about the nature of the dispute is available on the basis of the tradition contained in verses 1–6. In view of the causal connection between the traditions behind verse 7 and verses 8–15, one can make a reasoned guess at how the conflict was triggered: Aramaic-speaking Christians who were strict observers of the law fell out with Greek-speaking Christians over the question of law, and linguistic and cultural differences added a further element to the dispute. This falling out must have taken place in the earliest period of the primitive community in Jerusalem, since Paul was already persecuting members of this Hellenist group outside Jerusalem, yet no longer found them in Jerusalem during his first visit.

Verses 11–14: According to verse 11 Stephen spoke against Moses and God, i.e., he criticized the law. Furthermore, according to verse 14 he invoked Jesus to criticize the Temple and the law. Obviously, however, the formulaic charge that Jesus will alter the customs handed down by Moses does not mean total abrogation of the law. (Such a step was not to be expected unless a Jew deliberately became a Greek, something very unlikely in the case of Stephen.) Regardless of what the future tense means in verse 14, we must cautiously conclude that Stephen disparaged the law and the Temple, and that on the basis of God's will as revealed in or taught by Jesus he announced the destruction of the Temple and censured at least some significant points of the law.

A Note on Hellenistic Jewish Communities in Jerusalem

The presence in Jerusalem of the groups named in verse 9 has a good deal to be said for it historically. It can be supported by the following evidence: A Greek inscription found in Jerusalem shortly before the First World War indicated, among other things, that the synagogue had been built by the priest and synagogue president Theodotus, son of Vettenus, and that a guest house and water supply for pilgrims had been connected with it. Perhaps this inscription is a reference to the *Libertini* (a Latin loanword that denotes freed Jews) mentioned in verse 9. The father of Theodotus has a Roman name, Vettenus, which he may have adopted after being freed because he owed his freedom to a Roman member of the *gens Vettena*. In that case his family may have belonged to the synagogue of the *Libertini* in Jerusalem.[152]

A Note on the Place of the Dispute over Stephen

It is historically improbable that all the Hellenistic Jews mentioned in verse 9 were, as Luke suggests, involved in the dispute with Stephen. Rather, the controversy must have arisen in one Hellenistic synagogue to which Stephen belonged. The issue was that Stephen, a preacher filled with the Spirit, had a critical attitude toward the Law of Moses, a posture at which his opponents took offence. As is common in such cases, the quarrel was initially verbal and then became physical. (How remote Luke already is from the historical Stephen is evident from the fact that in verse 13a he presents the information about Stephen's criticism of the law as untrue.) We may assume that Stephen combined faith in Christ with an understanding of the law in a way that was unacceptable to the members of the Hellenistic synagogue. At any rate, it was considered blasphemous and led to the action hinted at in verse 12 and described in Acts 7:57–58. Stephen's view of the law led not only to a fatal dispute in the Hellenistic synagogue(s) but also, as 6:1–2 indirectly depicts, to a split in Primitive Christianity.

THE HISTORICAL VALUE OF LUKE'S ACCOUNT

Luke's account is problematic if not contradictory, because the care of the widows was not related to the dispute over the law. Fortunately, as in other cases, he has retained in his narrative enough traditional elements to allow us to reconstruct the most likely course of events.

[18]
ACTS 7:1–53
STEPHEN'S SPEECH

(1) And the high priest asked, "Are these things so?"

(2) And Stephen said: "Brothers and fathers, listen. The God of glory

appeared to _our father_ Abraham when he was in Mesopotamia, before he lived in Haran, (3) and said to him, 'Go out from your **land** and from your kindred and go into the **land** that I will show you.' (4) Then he went out from the **land** of the Chaldeans and settled in Haran. And after his father died, [God] resettled him from there into this **land** in which you are now living. (5) Yet he gave him no inheritance in it, not even a foot's length, but promised to give it to him as a possession and to his offspring after him, though he had no child. (6) But God spoke to this effect—'His offspring will be sojourners in a **land** belonging to others, who will enslave them and afflict them for four hundred years. (7) And the nation to which they shall be in bondage I will judge,' God said, 'and after that they shall come out and worship me in this place.' (8a) And he gave him the covenant of circumcision.

(8b) And so Abraham fathered Isaac, and circumcised him on the eighth day, and Isaac [fathered] Jacob, and Jacob [fathered] the twelve patriarchs.

(9) And the patriarchs, jealous of Joseph, sold him into Egypt; but God was with him (10) and rescued him out of all his afflictions and gave him favor and wisdom before Pharaoh, king of Egypt; and he made him ruler over Egypt and over all his household. (11) Now there came a famine throughout all Egypt and Canaan, and great affliction, and _our fathers_ could find no food. (12) But when Jacob heard that there was grain in Egypt, he sent out _our fathers_ a first time. (13) And at the second time Joseph made himself known to his brothers, and Joseph's family became known to Pharaoh. (14) And Joseph sent and summoned Jacob, his father, and all his kindred, seventy-five persons in all. (15) And Jacob went down into Egypt, and he died, he and _our fathers_, (16) and they were carried back to Shechem and laid in the tomb that Abraham had bought for a sum of silver from the sons of Hamor in Shechem.

(17) But as the time of the promise drew near, which God had pledged to Abraham, the people grew and multiplied in Egypt (18) until there arose over Egypt another king who did not know Joseph. (19) This [king] cleverly abused our people, forcing _our fathers_ to expose their infants so that they would die. (20) At this time **MOSES** was born; and he was handsome in God's sight. And he was brought up for three months in his father's house. (21) But when he was exposed, Pharaoh's daughter adopted him and brought him up as her own son. (22) And **MOSES** was instructed in all the wisdom of the Egyptians, and he was mighty in his words and deeds. (23) But when he was _forty years_ old, it came into his heart to visit his brothers, the sons of Israel. (24) And seeing one of them being wronged, he came to his aid and avenged him by striking down the Egyptian. (25) He supposed that his brothers would understand that God was rescuing them by his hand, but they did not understand. (26) And on the following day he appeared

to them as they were quarreling and tried to reconcile them, saying, 'Men, you are brothers. Why do you wrong each other?' (27) But the man who was wronging his neighbor thrust him aside, saying, 'Who made you a ruler and a judge over us? (28) Do you want to kill me as you killed the Egyptian yesterday?' (29) And **MOSES** fled at this saying and became an exile in the land of Midian, where he fathered two sons. (30) Now when *forty years* were fulfilled, an angel appeared to him in the wilderness of Mount Sinai, in a flame of fire in a bush. (31) And when **MOSES** saw it, he was amazed at the sight, and as he drew near to look, there came the voice of the Lord: (32) 'I am the God of your fathers, the God of Abraham and of Isaac and of Jacob.' And **MOSES** trembled and did not dare to look. (33) Then the Lord said to him, 'Take off the sandals from your feet, for the place where you are standing is holy ground. (34) I have surely seen the affliction of my people who are in Egypt, and have heard their groaning, and I have come down to deliver them. And now come, I will send you to Egypt.'

(35) **This MOSES**, whom they denied, saying, 'Who made you a ruler and a judge?'—**this** [man] God sent as both ruler and redeemer by the hand of the angel who appeared to him in the bush. (36) **This** man led them out, performing wonders and signs in Egypt and at the Red Sea and in the wilderness for *forty years*. (37) **This** is the **MOSES** who said to the Israelites, 'God will raise up for you a prophet like me from your brothers.' (38) **This** is the one who was in the congregation in the wilderness with the angel who spoke to him at Mount Sinai, and with _our fathers_. He received the living words of God to pass on to us.

(39) _Our fathers_ refused to obey him, but thrust him aside, and in their hearts they turned to Egypt, (40) saying to Aaron, 'Make for us gods who will go before us. As for **this MOSES** who led us out from the land of Egypt, we do not know what has become of him.' (41) And they made a calf in those days, and offered a sacrifice to the idol and rejoiced in the works of their hands. (42) But God turned away and gave them over to worship the host of heaven, as it is written in the book of the prophets: 'Did you bring to me slain beasts and sacrifices, during the forty years in the wilderness, O house of Israel? (43) And you took up the tent of Moloch and the star of your god Rephan, the images that you made to worship; and I will send you into exile beyond Babylon.'

(44) _Our fathers_ had the tent of witness in the wilderness, just as he who spoke to **MOSES** directed him to make it, according to the pattern that he had seen. (45) This _our fathers_ in turn brought in with Joshua when they dispossessed the nations that God drove out before _our fathers_. So it was until the days of David, (46) who found favor in the sight of God and asked to find a dwelling place for the house of Jacob. (47) But Solomon built a house for him. (48) Yet the Most High does not dwell in houses made by hands, as the prophet says, (49)

'Heaven is my throne, and the earth my footstool. What kind of house will you build for me?', says the Lord, 'or what is the place of my rest? (50) Did not my hand make all these things?'

(51) *YOU* stiff-necked people, uncircumcised in heart and ears; *YOU* always resist the Holy Spirit, just as *YOUR FATHERS* did. (52) Which of the prophets did not *YOUR FATHERS* persecute? And they killed those who announced beforehand the coming of the Righteous One, of whom *YOU have become betrayers and murderers*, (53) [YOU] who received the law by ordinances of angels, and did not keep it."

OUTLINE

1: Transition to the speech
2–38: The history of Israel from Abraham to Moses
    2–8a: The Abraham story
    8b: Transitional note: from Isaac to the twelve patriarchs
    9–16: The Joseph story
    17–38: The Moses story
39–50: Israel's apostasy: idolatry and building of the Temple
    39–43: Idolatry
    44–50: Building of the Temple
        44–47: The tent of meeting and the building of the Temple for the house of Jacob
        48–50: Polemic against the view that God dwells in the Temple
51–53: The guilt of Israel

LUKE'S PURPOSE AND THE TRADITIONS REWORKED BY HIM

Luke's primary aim here is to paint a portrait of Stephen. To do so, he pictures his hero arraigned and standing before the Sanhedrin in Jerusalem, and permitted full scope in delivering what is clearly one of the keynote speeches in Acts. To be sure, his extended history lesson *cum* polemic fails to respond to the high priest's question, "Is this so?" (verse 1); nevertheless, it is in its own way responsive to the charges lodged by the bribed witnesses hired by diaspora Jews who had moved to Jerusalem. Thus this episode begins with the hatching of a despicable plot against this noble exemplar of the Christian community, the outstanding member of the "seven men of good reputation, full the Spirit and of wisdom" (6:3); its purpose, however, extends beyond both story telling and character portrayal.

Verse 1: This is a transition.

Verses 2–8: Verse 2a is obviously a Lukan creation, since the introduction to Stephen's speech shows a verbatim correspondence with the start of Paul's speech in 22:1. Luke has also strayed from the biblical account (Gen. 11:28–12:1) in verses 2–4, for he has God appearing to Abraham in Mesopotamia before he traveled to Haran. Verse 4 then reports his departure from Chaldaea to dwell in Haran. Mesopotamia, however, is generally understood to lie between Chaldaea and Haran. Either Luke's geography is faulty, or he is relying on conflicting traditions—or both. Also noteworthy is the heavy stress he lays on place names, chronology, and movement even though he gets it wrong! Since the speech is not historical, Stephen's allusion to fictitious listeners at the end of verse 4 ("this land in which you are now living") is certainly Luke's creation. Verse 8b establishes the descent of Joseph, next to be discussed, from Abraham.

Verses 9–16: Here the repetition of "our fathers" in verses 11–12 addresses the fictitious audience just as it did in verse 4. "Abraham" in verses 16 and 17 establishes a link with verses 2–8a.

Verses 17–38: This biographical sketch of Moses follows the pentateuchal schematic division into three forty-year periods (cf. verses 23, 30, 36), and can be seen as a Lukan synopsis for the benefit of his readers—not the least because Stephen's contemporaries in Jerusalem would hardly have needed to be told what they already well knew. Verses 20–23 employ the same tripartite scheme that we find in Luke's outline of Paul's life (see, e.g., 22:3). Identifying Moses as "mighty in words and deeds" hardly sits well with Ex. 4:10, where Moses tells the Lord that he is "slow of speech and of tongue," but is identical with Luke's description of Jesus in his gospel: Jesus was "a man, a prophet, mighty in deed and word before God and before the whole people" (Luke 24:19). Clearly the author is creating a parallel between the two figures, one that we see again in verses 35–36, which are also Lukan. Both the content and vocabulary of verse 25 have a decidedly Lukan flavor, and what he says here of Moses is elsewhere characteristic of Jesus: His salvific work also went unrecognized (see 3:17; 4:10–12, and the comments on verses 20–23). The Moses-Jesus typology evident in verses 20–23 is repeated in "ruler" (of Moses, verse 35); cf. "author" (of Jesus) in Acts 3:15; 5:31. Similarly, "redeemer" (of Moses, verse 35) recalls "about to redeem Israel" (of Jesus, Luke 24:21), and miracles are attributed to Moses (verse 36) as they are to Jesus and the apostles (5:12). In verse 37 (as before in 3:22) we have Deut. 18:15 adduced as a christological argument.

Verses 39–43: "Our fathers" (note "our father Abraham" in verse 2) appears also in verses 11, 12, 15, 19, 38, 44, 45. In verses 39–41 Luke alludes to Israel's first episode of idolatry (the golden calf) and intensifies the point in verses 42–43; note that in his citation of Amos 5:25–27 (LXX) Luke changes "Damascus" to "Babylon" in order to make the prophecy conform to the Babylonian exile.

Verses 44–47: Lukan language is evident throughout this section. "Tent of witness" in verse 44 echoes "tent of Moloch" in verse 43, and effects a rather awkward transition by referring to a second tent, "the tent of witness," that the Israelites took with them in the wilderness and that was the forerunner of the Temple.

Assuming that Luke shaped Stephen's speech, one is quite amazed at Stephen's criticism of the Temple that depicts it as a product of apostasy. For Luke relates Primitive Christianity closely to the Temple in that the first Christians meet there daily for prayer[153] and Jesus begins his activity in the holy city of Jerusalem in the temple.[154] Moreover, during his last visit to Jerusalem Paul agrees to participate in a ceremony in the Temple.[155]

Verses 48–50: By means of this polemic against the idea of the Temple as God's dwelling place (cf. 17:24), Luke liberates Christianity—and especially Gentile Christians—from the Temple, and, by implication, from the necessity of following Jewish law and practices.

Verses 51–53: These verses constitute an arraignment of Israel. It is noteworthy that there is no call to repentance, a typical element of other mission sermons in Acts. Israel's history is epitomized as rebellion against God: "You always resist the Holy Spirit, just as your fathers did" (verse 51). The point is that the present guilt of the Jews, highlighted by their betrayal (cf. Luke 6:16) and murder of the righteous one (verse 52), corresponds to the behavior of their fathers. Therefore he now speaks of "your fathers" while in verses 11–50 he usually referred to "our fathers." The Jews had failed, as Luke would have it, to observe the law that came from God through the ministration of angels (verse 53—cf. verse 38 and Gal. 3:19). The covenant of circumcision (verse 8a), which assured the promise of salvation, has been nullified by what amounts to a rejection of Moses, and hence of the promise whose fulfillment the law embodied (verse 17).

A Note on the Special Way Luke Shaped Stephen's Speech

Of the many sermons in Acts, this speech is the longest and marks a turning point in both the narrative and the thematic structure of the book. In the person of the first Christian martyr, Luke makes it unforgettably if not painfully clear that despite Christianity's Old Testament roots (*"our* fathers"), those condemned by Stephen, the authorities who personally represent Judaism, have always resisted the Holy Spirit (verse 51), and thus are no longer the true Israel, but have forfeited that title to the Christian community. The separation of Jews and Christians, a theme absent from the first five chapters of Acts, has been narratively foreshadowed.

Luke relates individual themes of the speech to the accusation: Note for example the assertion that the Jews had not observed the law although God willed it (verses 38, 53) or the statement that Solomon had built a temple for Jacob (!) (verse 47). Luke artfully demonstrates the falsity of the charges that Stephen had derogated the law and the temple (6:11, 13–14, and recall the editorial transition in verse 1) by employing individual themes to respond to the accusations. He has Stephen show that it was not he, but the Jews who had made a mockery of the law (verses 38, 53) and that Solomon had built the Temple for all the people of Jacob.

Beyond that, Stephen's speech serves Luke as a way to set forth his concept of the true nature of piety, a subject he deals with at greater length in 17:22–31. Furthermore, by limiting the relevance of the Temple to Judaism, Luke has used Stephen both to elucidate and provide justification for his own vision of salvation history.

Probably no one unifying aim or concept shaped Stephen's speech. To be sure, verses 2–38 form a unit with the thematic pattern "promise—oppression in Egypt—fulfillment by Moses"; and the idolatry of Israel (verses 39–43) follows both narratively and thematically. But verses 44–50 amount to a digressive and oblique sort of transition, and verses 51–53 conclude the defense by returning to the accusation and making a countercharge. This is not the place to decide how much of Stephen's speech derives from tradition, but the following passages may well have served as sources, since surely Luke knew at least some of them: Deut. 6:20–24; 26:5–9; Josh. 24:2–13; Neh. 9:6–31; Jth. 5:6–18; 1 Macc. 2:52–60; Ps. 78; 105; 106; 136; Wisd. of Sol. 10; Wisd. 44–50; 3 Macc. 2:2–12; 4 Ezra 3:4–36.

HISTORICAL ELEMENTS

First of all, it is difficult to assign any appreciable weight to the observation by Fitzmyer that

> No matter how one judges the historicity of the speech of Stephen, in its present Lucan form it records an invaluable first-century testimony about the way some Christians had begun to consider the relation of the Christian church to contemporary Judaism. Even though it is put on the lips of Stephen, it reveals how some Jewish Christians were trying to interpret the Christ-event in light of their traditional biblical religion and esteem for the law of Moses.[156]

Rebuttal: In its present form the speech is not a unit; as Dibelius notes, verses 2–34 have no discernible purpose, inasmuch as they contain nothing more than a synopsis of Israelite history.[157] Fitzmyer's reflections, then, however insightful their commentary on early Christianity may seem, are in the long run pointless insofar as we are interested in the authenticity of the Lukan report. To say that what may well be a piece of fiction nonetheless reflects the writer's perspective does very little to alter its fictional character.

The Historical Value of Luke's Account

In having Stephen deliver an anti-Jewish sermon, Luke seeks to deal with problems that existed in his own communities. "At the time when Luke wrote, the Jews were the Christians' mighty and irreconcilable enemies."[158] Stephen never delivered such a speech or elements of it in Jerusalem prior to his martydom or on any other occasion.

[19]
Acts 7:54–8:3
The Stoning of Stephen and Its Consequences

(54) *Now when they heard these things they were infuriated, and they ground their teeth against him.*

(55) *But he, full of the Holy Spirit, gazed into heaven and saw the glory of God, and Jesus* standing at God's right hand; *(56) and he said, "Look, I see the heavens opened, and the Son of Man* standing at God's right hand."

(57) But they CRIED WITH A LOUD VOICE and stopped their ears and rushed together upon him. (58) Then they cast him out of the city and **stoned** him; *and the witnesses laid down their clothes at the feet of a young man named Saul.* (59) And they **stoned** Stephen, *while he was saying in invocation, "Lord Jesus, receive my spirit."* (60) *And he knelt down* and CRIED WITH A LOUD VOICE, "Lord, do not hold this sin against them." And when he had said this, he died.

(8:1a) *And Saul entirely approved of his murder.* (1b) And there arose on that day a great persecution against the community in Jerusalem; and they were *all* scattered abroad throughout the regions of Judea and Samaria, except the apostles. (2) And devout men buried Stephen, and made great lamentation over him. (3) But Saul sought to destroy the community; for he entered house after house, dragging out men and women, and sending them to prison.

OUTLINE

54: The high court's reaction to Stephen's speech
55–56: Stephen's vision
57–60: The stoning of Stephen
8:1a: Saul's approval of the murder of Stephen
1b–3: The persecution of the Jerusalem church
    1b: The expulsion of all but the
    apostles
    2: The burial of Stephen
    3: The persecution of the church by Saul

LUKE'S PURPOSE

Verses 55–56: Luke has shaped both the account of the vision in verse 55 and its depiction in verse 56 by Stephen, for the verses evidently depend on Luke 22:69: "From now on the Son of Man will sit at the right hand of the power of God." Note that in adapting Mark 14:62 to his passion account, Luke has omitted "you will see" from the Markan text he used; his purpose was to show that the vision of the exalted Christ was not—as Mark 14:62 suggests it would be—granted to adversaries. Here, therefore, the vision is granted only to Stephen, the believing witness.

Verses 57–60: Verse 57 contains elements of Lukan language: "They cried with a loud voice" corresponds to the same expression in verse 60 (note capitals). Employing Saul to oversee the garments of the executors is Luke's way of linking Stephen's martyrdom with the subsequent story of Paul. The great missionary is introduced in the lowly role of a bystander. As is obvious from the repetition of "stoned" (set in bold), verse 59a picks up the story that was interrupted by verse 58a. The account of Stephen's death (verses 59b, 60b) bears such a close resemblance to that of Jesus' death (Luke 23, verses 46 and 34 respectively), that it is undoubtedly redactional. Also noteworthy is that Luke 23:46 ("Father, into your hands I commend my spirit") is an almost verbatim transcription of Ps. 30:6 (LXX), commonly employed in Judaism as an evening prayer. In Stephen's case, of course, the exclamation ("Lord Jesus, receive my spirit") is intended to indicate that he had seen the Risen One. For the introductory phrase "he knelt down" in verse 60a see Luke 22:41 (diff. Mark 14:35); Acts 9:40; 20:36. The author has thus created yet another parallel between the two martyrdoms of Stephen and Jesus. The crying out also recalls the last word of Jesus at Luke 23:46, as does the petition earlier alluded to, "Lord, do not hold this sin against them," which all but repeats Luke 23:34: "Father, forgive them, for they know not what they do."[159]

Verse [8:] 1a: This is certainly Luke's creation; not only does he want to involve Saul in the execution, but it completes the narrative action begun in verse 58 with Saul guarding people's clothes, continues in verse 1a with his satisfaction at the killing of Stephen, and culminates in verse 8:3 by depicting him as a rabid vigilante.

Verses 1b–2: The account of Stephen's burial by devout men corresponds to Jesus' burial by a "good and just" Jew, Joseph of Arimathea.[160] "Luke makes no attempt to indicate that they were believers."[161]

Verse 3: Saul's participation in the persecution as opposed to his onlooker's role in verse 1a adds greater emphasis to his involvement and thus prepares for the subsequent story of his conversion. Note the way in which verse 3 is picked up in 9:1–2.

THE TRADITIONS REWORKED BY LUKE AND ITS HISTORICAL ELEMENTS

The passages concerning the Hellenists and Stephen that have thus far been analyzed are the result of such a thorough reworking by Luke that a clean separation of redaction from tradition was impossible. Rather, here and there, one can recover traditional elements. Therefore it seems more useful to deal with the tradition underlying these texts by means of a summary, while simultaneously discussing the historical question.

A Note on the Execution of Stephen as the Result of a Riot

As 6:12b–14; 7:1; 7:58b show, Luke attempted to make Stephen's trial and execution look like an orderly procedure carried out by the high council. Yet, Luke's account lacks any sentence and Stephen is stoned without a verdict. In the absence of any indication of participation by the Sanhedrin, the stoning is all but certainly an act of mob justice. Moreover, the high council was unable to carry out capital sentences—only the Roman occupying force could. The key fact bears repeating once again: Since the record shows no legal proceeding against him, Stephen must have fallen victim to mob action.

From this we must further conclude that the tradition has been completely overlaid by Lukan language and shaping, particularly in the scene of the riot in verse 57. Stoning remains possible as a manner of his death, as lynch law often made use of it.[162]

A Note on the Expulsion of the Hellenists

At this point it needs to be asked whether 6:8–15 (the drumhead action initiated by the Hellenistic Jews) and 7:54–8:1a (the condemnation and execution of Stephen) are causally related. Since verse 54 does not mention of the name "Stephen"—which one would have expected after such a long sermon (7:1–53)—a direct connection between the two sections seems likely. Underlying Acts 6–7, then, is an account of the criticism of the Temple and law by Stephen and the Hellenists leading to a popular uprising with serious consequences for both: Stephen was killed and his followers had to leave Jerusalem.

THE HISTORICAL VALUE OF LUKE'S ACCOUNT

By connecting Paul with the murder of Stephen, Luke has invented a historical myth which, though clearly lacking historical validity, has had enormous influence. Let me emphasize that Paul neither participated in the execution of Stephen nor persecuted Hellenists in Jerusalem. Those reports have their origin in Luke's wish to connect the future hero of his work with the origin of the new religion in Jerusalem. The historical Paul would no doubt have been thunderstruck at such falsification—after all, he was "unknown personally to the churches of Christ in Judea,"[163]—as would the Damascus community whose members Paul persecuted. Amazing things happen when those who portray the past allow their personal agendas to inform their accounts—why, even the dead can be raised from their graves!

NOTES

1. Ernst Haenchen, "The Book of Acts as Source Material for the History of Early Christianity," in *Studies in Luke-Acts*, ed. Leander E. Keck and J. Louis Martyn (Philadelphia: Fortress Press, 1980), p. 259.

2. Cf. Luke 1:3. Perhaps Theophilus—as addressee of both volumes—"had to attend to the distribution of the two writings" (Martin Dibelius, *Studies in the Acts of the Apostles* [London: SCM Press, 1956], p. 135).

3. See Luke 5:15; 6:18; 9:11; cf. 24:19.

4. Luke 24:41–43.

5. Cf. Isa. 49:6.

6. Cf. Psalms of Solomon 8:15: God "brought someone [Pompey] from the end of the earth, one who attacks in strength; he declared war against Jerusalem, and her land."

7. Yet cf. Acts 1:11; 2:7; 5:37.

8. "Eighteen months" (Gnostics in Irenaeus, *Against all Heresies* 1.3.2 and the Ophites [ibid., 1.30.14]); "545 days" (*Martyrdom and Ascension of Isaiah* 9:16); "550 days" (*Apocryphon of James*, NHC I.2; p. 2.19–20).

9. Cf. the "proofs" in Mark 16:9–20 and Luke 24:13–40.

10. For details see my *The Resurrection of Christ: A Historical Inquiry* (Amherst, NY: Prometheus Books, 2004).

11. See Rom. 11:26.

12. For details see my *Paul: The Founder of Christianity* (Amherst, NY: Prometheus Books, 2002).

13. See my *Resurrection of Christ*, pp. 189–208.

14. C. K. Barrett, *The Acts of the Apostles*, 2 vols. (Edinburgh: T & T Clark, 1994–98), 1:81.

15. "He [Jesus] was lifted up" is *passivum divinum*.

16. See Exod. 16:10; 19:9; 24:15–18; 33:7–11; Ezek. 10:3–4; Ps. 18:12; Dan. 7:13; Mark 9:7; 1 Thess. 4:17; Rev. 11:12.

17. See my *Resurrection of Christ*, pp. 113–14.

18. I. Howard Marshall, *The Acts of the Apostles: An Introduction and Commentary* (Grand Rapids, MI: Wm. B. Eerdmans, 1980), p. 60.

19. Gerhard Lohfink, *Die Himmelfahrt Jesu: Untersuchungen zu den Himmelfahrts- und Erhöhungstexten bei Lukas* (Munich: Kösel Verlag, 1971), p. 250.

20. Cf. Rom. 12:12; Col. 4:2.

21. Joseph A. Fitzmyer, *The Acts of the Apostles: A New Translation with Introduction and Commentary* (New York: Doubleday, 1998), p. 215.

22. Thus, representing the majority opinion, ibid., p. 215.

23. Ibid., p. 216, in all seriousness is thinking not of "(natural) brothers" but of "relatives," though nobody would question the meaning of "(natural) brothers" for the Greek word *adelphos*—except that the Roman Catholic Church, because of the dogma of Mary's enduring virginity, excluded "(natural) brothers." See my *Virgin Birth? The Real Story of Mary and Her Son Jesus* (Harrisburg, PA: Trinity Press International, 1998), pp. 10–14.

24. So also in Luke 8:51 (Mark 5:37: "Peter, James, John"); and in Luke 9:28 (Mark 9:2/Matt. 17:1: "Peter, James, John").

25. Cf. Acts 12:12.

26. Mark 3:21.

27. Luke 1:39; 2:1; 4:2; 5:35; 6:12; 23:7; 24:18; Acts 6:1; 7:41; 9:37; 11:27.

28. See, e.g., Mark 14:21, 49. For the details see Martin Dibelius, *From Tradition to Gospel* (New York: Charles Scribner's Sons, 1934), pp. 178–218.

29. Cf. also the remarks by Hans Conzelmann, *The Theology of St. Luke* (New York: Harper & Brothers, 1960), pp. 153–54, on divine necessity in Luke-Acts.

30. See Luke 23:5; 24:27, 47; Acts 8:35; 10:37 (elsewhere in the New Testament only in Matt. 20:8; John 8:9).

31. Conzelmann, *Theology of St. Luke,* pp. 22–23.

32. 1 Chron. 25:8–9; 26:13, etc.

33. Barrett, *Acts of the Apostles*, 1:104.

34. Fitzmyer, *Acts of the Apostles*, p. 220.

35. Matt. 26:14 and Luke 22:3 repeat Mark's information.

36. Matt. 27:1–10: (1) "When morning came, all the chief priests and the elders of the people took a decision on Jesus to kill him; (2) and they bound him and led him away and delivered him to Pilate the governor. (3) When Judas, who had delivered him up, saw that he was condemned, he repented and brought back the thirty pieces of silver to the chief priests and the elders, (4) and said, 'I have sinned, in that I have delivered up innocent blood.' But they said, 'What is that to us? See to it yourself.' (5) And he threw down the pieces of silver in the temple, departed, went out and hanged himself. (6) But the chief priests took the pieces of silver and said, 'It is not lawful to put them into the treasury, since they are blood money.' (7) So they took a decision and bought with them the potter's field, to bury strangers in. (8) Therefore that field is called the Field of Blood to the present day. (9) Then was fulfilled what is spoken by the prophet Jeremiah, who says, 'And they took the thirty pieces of silver, the price of him on whom a price had been set by some of the sons of Israel, (10) and they gave them for the potter's field, as the Lord commanded me.'"

37. Cf. Kirsopp Lake, "The Death of Judas," in *The Beginnings of Christianity*, ed. F. J. Foakes Jackson and Kirsopp Lake, pt. 1, 5 vols. (London and New York: Macmillan, 1920–33), 5:22–30. Papias's version of Judas's death has been preserved partially by Apollinarius of Laodicea. The content is that "Judas, having become so swollen in flesh that he could not pass when a wagon was easily coming by, was struck by the wagon, and all his inwards emptied out" (Fitzmyer, *Acts of the Apostles*, p. 224).

38. For details see my *Early Christianity According to the Traditions in Acts: A Commentary* (Philadelphia: Fortress Press, 1989), p. 34.

39. See my *Jesus After 2000 Years: What He Really Said and Did* (Amherst, NY: Prometheus Books, 2001), pp. 244–45.

40. For a summary statement see my *The Great Deception: And What Jesus Really Said and Did* (Amherst, NY: Prometheus Books, 1999), pp. 102–103.

41. Joachim Jeremias, *New Testament Theology*, vol. 1, *The Proclamation of Jesus* (Philadelphia: Fortress Press, 1971), p. 234.

42. Thus some secondary textual witnesses.

43. See the monograph by William Klassen, *Judas: Betrayer or Friend of Jesus?* (Minneapolis: Fortress Press, 1996).

44. Differently—along with many others—Fitzmyer, *Acts of the Apostles*, p. 125: Luke's account "that Peter summoned the Early Christians to reconstitute the Twelve" is "substantially historical."

45. For the following see my *Resurrection of Christ*, pp. 78–85.

46. See Exod. 19:16–19; Num. 11:25; Deut. 4:11.

47. Philo was a Jewish philosopher in Alexandria who wrote before Luke and who was an older contemporary of the apostle Paul.

48. Barrett, *Acts of the Apostles*, 1:121.

49. Hans Conzelmann, *Acts of the Apostles: A Commentary on the Acts of the Apostles* (Philadelphia: Fortress Press, 1987), p. 16.

50. Cf. verses 6, 8.

51. On the list of peoples see my *Early Christianity According to the Traditions in Acts*, pp. 40–41.

52. See Acts 17:32; 28:24.

53. Cf. Luke 24:49.

54. Cf. Acts 8:14–24; 19:1–7.

55. According to Acts 4:36 (cf. 11:20) the Levite Barnabas is "a native of Cyprus" (in Greek, *Kyprios tô genei*); cf. also in Acts 2:5 "from every nation" (in Greek, *apo pantos ethnous*) and in Acts 2:8 "the [his] own language" (in Greek, *tê idia dialektô*).

56. See the commentaries and Christopher Forbes, *Prophecy and Inspired Speech in Early Christianity and Its Hellenistic Environment* (Tübingen: J. C. B. Mohr/Paul Siebeck, 1995). Cf. my evaluation in *Primitive Christianity: A Survey of Recent Studies and Some New Proposals* (Edinburgh and New York: T & T Clark, 2003), pp. 102–103.

57. Conzelmann, *Acts of the Apostles*, p. 15.

58. 1 Cor. 14:5.

59. Cf. 1 Cor. 14:19, 23.

60. 1 Cor. 13:1; cf. 2 Cor. 12:4.

61. Cf. Gen. 10:1–31.

62. Hans-Josef Klauck, *Magic and Paganism in Early Christianity: The World of the Acts of the Apostles* (Edinburgh: T & T Clark, 2000), p. 8.

63. Thus apparently Conzelmann, *Acts of the Apostles*, p. 16.

64. Ibid.

65. See Rom. 8:9–11: (9) "But you are not in the flesh, you are in the Spirit, *if* the Spirit of God really **dwells in you**. *If* someone does not possess the Spirit of Christ, he does not belong to him. (10) But *if* Christ **(dwells) in you**, then although the body is a dead thing because of sin, yet the spirit is life itself because of righteousness. (11) *If* the Spirit of him who raised Jesus from the dead **dwells in you**, he who raised Jesus from the dead will give life to your mortal bodies also through his Spirit which **dwells in you**." See my *Resurrection of Christ*, p. 79.

66. For the slight divergences between the Joel quotation (LXX) in verses 17–18 and 19–21 and the present section in Acts see my *Early Christianity According to the Traditions in Acts*, pp. 44–45.

67. The verb "to declare boldly" (in Greek, *apophtheggesthai*) occurs in only one other passage in the New Testament, Acts 26:25. Cf. 4:18.

68. Conzelmann, *Theology of St. Luke*, pp. 151–53.

69. Note that Luke in his Gospel does not adopt the ransom saying of Mark 10:45 but reformulates it in a different context (Luke 22:27).

70. Note the correspondence with Polycarp's letter to the Philippians 1:2: I rejoiced "that the steadfast root of your faith which was famed from primitive times abides until now and bears fruit unto our Lord Jesus Christ, who endured to face even death for our sins, whom God raised, having loosed the pangs of Hades; on whom, though you did not see him, you believe with joy unutterable and full of glory." (In all likelihood Bishop Polycarp of Smyrna was unfamiliar with Acts.)

71. Differently—along with many Acts scholars—Fitzmyer, *Acts of the Apostles*, p. 125: Luke's account that Peter "addressed Jews assembled in Jerusalem for the first feast after Jesus' death and burial" is "substantially historical."

72. For the general situation in Roman Palestine see Catherine Hezser, *Jewish Literacy in Roman Palestine* (Tübingen: J. C. B. Mohr/Paul Siebeck, 2001).

73. Dibelius, *Studies in the Acts of the Apostles*, p. 178.

74. See Joachim Jeremias, *Jerusalem in the Time of Jesus: An Investigation into Economic and Social Conditions during the New Testament Period* (Philadelphia: Fortress Press, 1969). Jeremias's calculation "results in a population of about 20,000 inside the city walls at the time of Jesus, and 5,000 to 10,000 outside. This figure, of from 25–30,000, must be the upper limit" (p. 84).

75. Barrett, *Acts of the Apostles*, 1:162.

76. Ibid., p. 166.

77. Fitzmyer, *Acts of the Apostles*, p. 268. Fitzmyer explains ibid., "In this case, the coherent account is found in vv 42, 46–47a; the insert, in vv 43–45. Verse 43 corresponds to 5:11–12a; vv. 44–45 are a summary of 4:32, 34–35."

78. See the examples below, n. 115.

79. See James D. G. Dunn, *The Acts of the Apostles* (Valley Forge, PA: Trinity Press International, 1996), p. 36.

80. Isa. 60:1–14; Mic. 4:1–2a; Hag. 2:6–9; 1 Enoch 90:28–29.

81. Cf. Acts 6:15, where the author has relocated it—probably to tone it down.

82. See below, p. 366.

83. Fitzmyer, *Acts of the Apostles*, p. 276.

84. For the sixth hour as the time of prayer see Acts 10:9.

85. Mark 14:13 differs.

86. See Lev. 21:18; 2 Sam. 5:8.

87. Haenchen, *Acts of the Apostles*, p. 200.

88. See Acts 3:16; 4:10, 12, 17, 18, 30. Cf. 4:7.

89. Barrett, *Acts of the Apostles*, 1:182.

90. Ibid.

91. See Luke 1:64; 4:39; 8:44, 47, 55; 13:13; 18:43; Acts 5:10; 12:23; 13:11.

92. Cf. Martin Hengel, *Between Jesus and Paul: Studies in the Earliest History of Christianity* (Philadelphia: Fortress Press, 1983), pp. 103–104.

93. See the "Layout and Method of the Analysis" above, pp. 13–30, on "miracles," p. 23.

94. See my *Paul: The Founder of Christianity* (Amherst, NY: Prometheus Books, 2002), pp. 88–91; *Heretics: The Other Side of Early Christianity* (Louisville, KY: Westminster John Knox Press, 1996), pp. 52–60.

95. However, there may be an indirect reference to the beggar's faith in his praise of God (3:8–9).

96. Fitzmyer, *Acts of the Apostles*, p. 286.

97. Cf. Luke 23:34 (if original); Acts 13:27.

98. The traditional elements are the terms "refreshing" (in Greek, *anapsyxis*) and "restoration" (in Greek, *apakatastasis*) both of which occur only here in the New Testament. "Seasons of refreshing" (verse 20) and "time of universal restoration" (verse 21) seem to explain each other, the former indicating that the latter—the final salvation through the second coming of Jesus—has arrived. Yet apart from the two traditional terms as a whole I see no pre-Lukan tradition in these verses, and the exhortation in verse 19 that the Jews convert so that the end may come may be explained as due to the setting of the speech in the context of Acts.

99. Luke 24:44–47.

100. Several times "men" is coupled with "women" (in Greek, *gynaikes*). See Acts 5:14; 8:3, 12; 9:2; 17:12; 22:4.

101. Gerhard Krodel, *Acts* (Minneapolis, MN: Augsburg Publishing House, 1986), p. 111.

102. Plato *Apology* 29d.

103. See Barnabas Lindars, *New Testament Apologetic* (London: SCM Press, 1973), pp. 169–86.

104. I. Howard Marshall, *The Acts of the Apostles: An Introduction and Commentary* (Grand Rapids, MI: Wm. B. Eerdmans, 1980), p. 99.

105. Wolfgang Reinhardt, "The Population Size of Jerusalem and the Numerical Growth of the Jerusalem Church," in *The Book of Acts in Its First Century Setting*, vol. 4, *The Book of Acts in Its Palestinian Setting,* ed. Richard Bauckham (Grand Rapids, MI: Wm. B. Eerdmans, 1995), p. 265.

106. Barrett, *Acts of the Apostles*, 1:222

107. See above, n. 74, the judgment by Jeremias, *Jerusalem at the Time of Jesus.*

108. The restoration of the original text at this point seems as impossible as the attempt is in vain to explain the origin of the corrupt text. Haenchen, *Acts of the Apostles,* p. 226n3, thinks that two later additions have crept into verse 25a: "of our father" (in Greek, *tou patros hêmon*) and "by the Holy Spirit" (in Greek, *dia pneumatos hagiou*).

109. Haenchen, *Acts of the Apostles*, p. 229.

110. Ibid.

111. Thus Roloff, *Apostelgeschichte*, p. 85.

112. Isa. 37:16–20; Tob. 3:11–15; 8:5–7.

113. Josephus *Jewish Antiquities* 20.199–203. See the analysis in my *Heretics*, pp. 49–52.

114. See Roloff, *Apostelgeschichte*, p. 80.

115. For "everything in common" cf. the maxim, "Friends' goods are common property," Aristotle *Nicomachean Ethics* 9.8.2. This ideal probably goes back as far as Pythagoras; see Diogenes Laertius 10.11 and Timaeus, ibid., 8.10.

116. According to Fitzmyer, *Acts of the Apostles*, p. 313, Luke "expresses abstractly the testimony borne to 'the resurrection' of the Lord, which no one really witnessed. . . . He means that the apostles bear witness to the risen Christ who has appeared to them alive (1:3)." That amounts to splitting hairs because Luke clearly assumes the factuality of Jesus' resurrection.

117. Thus a headline in the book by Luise Schottroff and Wolfgang Stegemann, *Jesus and the Hope of the Poor* (Maryknoll, NY: Orbis Books, 1986), p. 116.

118. Ibid., p. 116. Schottroff and Stegemann consider the description "communism based on love" as misleading. "For while Luke gives ambiguous description of communal ownership (e.g., *panta koina* ["everything in common"]), his meaning is clear: Private property benefited the entire community. Possessors of property (lands and houses) sold it and gave the proceeds to the apostles. The money was then given to those who needed it, so that there was now no one in need in the community (Acts 4:34f)" (ibid., p. 119).

119. Conzelmann, *Acts of the Apostles*, p. 36.

120. Ibid.

121. Fitzmyer, *Acts of the Apostles*, p. 313.

122. Cf. later a variant reading of the same clause in 5:10.

123. Cf. Tob. 1:17; 2:3–4, 7.

124. Or the two episodes together constitute a negative illustration of 4:32–37. For a different result see Robert M. Price, *The Widow Traditions in Luke-Acts: A Feminist Critical Scrutiny* (Atlanta: Scholars Press, 1997), p. 219: "(I)t was originally only Sapphira, not Ananias, who was blasted like a fig tree. As the story now reads, she is indeed superfluous—so why is she there at all? She stands at the side, having been *shoved* aside, from an earlier position of centrality. Originally, then, Ananias had no role in this story at all."

125. Gerd Theissen, *The Miracle Stories of the Early Christian Tradition* (Edinburgh: T & T Clark, 1983), p. 110.

126. See Ernst Käsemann, *New Testament Questions of Today* (London: SCM Press, 1969), pp. 66–81 ("Sentences of Holy Law in the New Testament").

127. Cf. Deut. 19:19; 21:21; 22:21, 24.

128. Cf. further 1 Cor. 14:38; Gal. 1:9.

129. Roloff, *Apostelgeschichte*, p. 93. For the historicity of a cursing which results in death, see the examples in Harold Remus, *Pagan-Christian Conflict over Miracle in the Second Century* (Cambridge, MA: Philadelphia Patristic Foundation, 1983), pp. 93–94.

130. Barrett, *Acts of the Apostles*, 1:262.

131. Fitzmyer, *Acts of the Apostles*, p. 317.

132. Ibid, p. 320.

133. Textual critical comment: The Jerusalem Bible places verse 12a after verse 14.

134. Marshall, *Acts of the Apostles*, pp. 15–16.

135. Conzelmann, *Acts of the Apostles*, p. 42.

136. Haenchen, *Acts of the Apostles*, p. 251.

137. See Conzelmann, *Acts of the Apostles*, p. 43.

138. See Josephus *Jewish Antiquities* 20.97–99.

139. The reason that F. F. Bruce, *The Acts of the Apostles*, 2nd ed. (Grand Rapids, MI: Wm. B. Eerdmans, 1973), gives for the historicity of a second Theudas is insufficient. He cites Origen *Contra Celsum* 1.57, where it is said, "Among the Jews there was one Theudas before the birth of Jesus." He differentiates this Theudas from the one mentioned by Josephus (p. 147). This argument is faulty, since in this passage Origen is using Acts, as is apparent from his reference to Simon the magician in 1.57 (cf. Acts 8) and also from his reference to Judas (Acts 5). Thus, Acts has created the order "Theudas, then Judas." Origen concludes that Theudas was active in the pre-Christian era on the basis of Acts

5:37, where it is said that Judas arose in the days of the census, i.e., at the time of the birth of Jesus but *after* the time of Theudas. In order to avoid the above conclusions one would have to assume "that Origen had access to additional information about the Jews under Tiberius, which he might have gotten from Philo of Alexandria" (Rainer Riesner, *Paul's Early Period: Chronology, Mission, Strategy* [Grand Rapids, MI: Wm. B. Eerdmans, 1998], p. 332). Yet that is idle speculation rooted in the wish to relieve Luke of a blunder.

140. For this question see Dibelius, *Studies in the Acts of the Apostles*, pp. 186–87.

141. See my *Early Christianity According to the Traditions in Acts*, pp. 72–73 for details.

142. Fitzmyer, *Acts of the Apostles*, p. 334.

143. Hemer, *Book of Acts*, p. 343n72.

144. Richard I. Pervo, *Profit with Delight: The Literary Genre of the Acts of the Apostles* (Philadelphia: Fortress Press, 1997), p. 60.

145. For the exegesis of Acts 6:1–15 I have used material from my *Paul: The Founder of Christianity*, pp. 260–66, which is based on my *Early Christianity According to the Traditions in Acts*, pp. 73–85.

146. See my *Early Christianity According to the Traditions in Acts*, pp. 74–76.

147. Fitzmyer, *Acts of the Apostles*, p. 360.

148. See Harry J. Leon, *The Jews of Ancient Rome* (Philadelphia: Jewish Publication Society of America, 1960), pp. 135–66.

149. Martin Hengel, *Between Jesus and Paul: Studies in the Earliest History of Christianity* (Philadelphia: Fortress Press, 1983), pp. 1–29, 129–56.

150. In Greek, *Hebraidi dialektô*.

151. Cf. John 5:2; 19:13, 17, 20.

152. See Fitzmyer, *Acts of the Apostles*, p. 357 for a discussion with bibliography.

153. Luke 24:53; Acts 2:46; 5:42.

154. Luke 2:22–39, 41–51; 4:9.

155. Acts 21:26–27.

156. Fitzmyer, *Acts of the Apostles*, pp. 367–68.

157. Dibelius, *Studies in the Acts of the Apostles*, p. 167.

158. Haenchen, *Acts of the Apostles*, p. 290.

159. It is possible though that Luke 23:34 may have been inserted into the Gospel of Luke later.

160. Luke 23:50–51.

161. Dunn, *Acts of the Apostles*, p. 106. Dunn continues, "And inserting the account as he does, after the church being scattered by persecution, suggests that he did not expect his readers to identify them as Christians. We might of course ask, Why not the Apostles? Here again it is hard to avoid the impression that Stephen had been left to stew in his own juice, and that none of the believers so respected by the people felt able to stand with him at the last" (ibid.).

162. See Philo *On the Special Laws* 1.54–57.

163. Gal. 1:22.

chapter II

Acts 8:4–15:35

THE SPREADING OF THE GOSPEL IN THE GENTILE WORLD

Although the situation may appear desperate when the entire early congregation with the exception of the apostles is driven from Jerusalem, this part ends with the ultimate recognition of the Gentile mission free of the Torah. By alternately portraying events within and outside Jerusalem, this portion of Acts integrates the local history of the early church and the beginning of the worldwide mission to the Gentiles.[1]

[20]

ACTS 8:4–25

THE DEFEAT OF SIMON "THE MAGICIAN" BY PHILIP
AND PETER'S INTERVENTION

(4) Now those who were scattered went about preaching the word.

(5) Philip *came down* to the city of Samaria, and *proclaimed the Christ* to them. (6) And the crowds with one accord *gave heed to* what Philip said, when they heard him and saw the **signs** which he did. (7) *For unclean spirits came out of many who were possessed, crying out with a loud voice; and many paralyzed and crippled folk were cured.* (8) *So there was much joy in the city.*

(9) But there was a man *called* Simon who had previously practiced **_magic_** in the city and amazed the nation of Samaria, pretending to be someone great.

(10) They all *gave heed to* him, from the least to the greatest, saying, "This man is that power *of God which is called* Great." (11) And they gave heed to him, because for a long time he had FASCINATED them with his **_magic_**.

(12) *But when they believed Philip as he preached about the kingdom of God and the **NAME** of Jesus Christ, they were baptized, both men and women.* (13) *Even Simon himself believed, and after having been baptized he continued with Philip. And seeing **signs** and powers [working wonders] performed, he was FASCINATED.*

(14) *Now when the apostles at Jerusalem heard that Samaria had received the word of God, they sent to them Peter and John,* (15) *who went down there and **prayed** for them so they might receive the **Holy Spirit**.* (16) *For until then the Spirit had not fallen on any of them, but they had only been baptized in the **NAME** of the Lord Jesus.* (17) *Then they laid their hands on them and they received the **Holy Spirit**.* (18) *Now when Simon saw that the Spirit was given through the laying on of the apostles' hands, he offered them money,* (19) *saying, "Give me also this power, that any one I lay my hands on may receive the **Holy Spirit**."* (20) *But Peter said to him, "May your silver perish with you, because you thought that you could obtain the gift of God with money!* (21) *You have no share nor rights in this, for your heart is not right before God.* (22) *Repent therefore of this wickedness of yours, and **pray** to the Lord that, if possible, the thought of your heart may be forgiven you.* (23) *For I see that you are in bondage to bitterness and enslaved by sin."* (24) *And Simon answered, "**Pray** for me to the Lord, that nothing of what you have said may come upon me."*

(25) *And so, after giving their testimony and speaking the word of the Lord, they returned to Jerusalem, preaching the gospel to many villages of the Samaritans.*

OUTLINE

4: Generalized note about the travel and preaching of the expelled Hellenists
5–8: Philip's successful preaching in Samaria
9–13: Philip defeats Simon Magus
9–11: The past history: Simon's previous activity in Samaria
12–13: The success of Philip's mission; Simon's conversion and baptism
14–24: Peter and John in Samaria
14–17: The Holy Spirit bestowed through Peter and John
18–24: Simon repudiated by Peter
25: Return of Peter and John to Jerusalem

LUKE'S PURPOSE

Verse 4: This is a brief note of transition. It has a close parallel in 11:19 (on this see below, p. 150). Luke summarizes Philip's activity as "preaching the word." Identical with this is the statement in verse 5 that he proclaimed Christ to the people of Samaria.

Verses 5–8: This section—based on tradition but shaped by Luke's language—summarizes Philip's successful missionary work in Samaria that included exorcisms and cures of physical ailments.

Verses 9–11: Describing Simon's activity in Samaria, these verses refer to the period before Philip's coming, which one needs to know so as to understand what follows. At verse 10 Luke's hand (identified in the translation by italics) is visible in the qualification of the "Great Power" by "of God"[2] and by the addition of "which is called."[3]

Verses 12–13: Luke demonstrates that the Christian miracle worker and preacher Philip is superior to Simon. "The narrative is structured in such a way that it is evident that Philip's miracle-working is much more impressive than Simon's."[4] Verse 12 is a link to verses 5–8. Philip's preaching about the kingdom of God recalls Jesus preaching about the same subject.[5] "What the risen Christ spent teaching his apostles when he appeared to them (1:3) now becomes part of the Christian message borne abroad by Jesus' disciples."[6] Verse 13 contains a word play on "power" (in Greek, *dynamis*). Simon, himself the great power (of God), is fascinated with the powers that Philip demonstrated. No wonder that he himself got baptized—thus declaring himself to be inferior to Philip and his message. In other words, the magic by which Simon had previously fascinated the people in Samaria is overshadowed by the spiritual power of Philip. As a scientific theologian I take "powers"—those causing miracles—to be the equivalent of "magic," the more so since "in polemical writing, your magic is my miracle, and vice versa."[7] Yet for Luke the believer, the "source of the power [was] crucial. It determined whether an act was magic or miracle. If the source of a powerful act was God, then it was legitimate and valid; if the very same act was performed through the power of another source then it was regarded as magic and invalid."[8] Thus Luke clearly degrades Simon by labeling him a magician, though the story as such reveals Philip rather than Simon to be a magician, especially since Simon's "magical" activities—in contrast to the ones performed by Philip—are nowhere described.[9]

Verses 14–17: The Christians in Samaria receive the Holy Spirit, for the Jerusalem apostles endorse the Samaria mission. By this means Peter and John are "smuggled into" the story of Philip (on this see further below, p. 119). The separation of baptism and the imparting of the Holy Spirit is artificial and done for the sole purpose of bringing the Jerusalem apostles into the story. Elsewhere in Luke-Acts baptism and bestowal of the Holy Spirit coincide (see, for example, 2:38; 10:44–48).

Verses 18–24: This section addresses the problem raised by verses 5–13. Did the convert Simon remain a member of the Christian congregation? Its Lukan character follows from content and context. The negative use of the topic of money finds an analogy in 5:1–11 (and see 24:24–26). The notion that money does not guarantee salvation (verses 18–19) can also be found in Peter's remark in 3:6: "Silver and gold have I none, but what I have, I give to you: In the name of Jesus Christ the Nazarene, walk!" The whole thrust of verses 18–24 leads to the conclusion that the Holy Spirit is a gift of grace and cannot be purchased.[10] At the end of the story, one question remains open. Since Luke does not indicate Peter's response to Simon's plea not to let Peter's curse come upon him (verse 24), what happens to Simon? "If the curse remained on Simon, I would expect Luke to have told his audience of the dreadful result, as he did in the cases of Judas and of Ananias and Sapphira. The silence suggests to me that the curse was lifted. The fact that Peter calls on Simon to repent and to 'pray to the Lord' (8.22) offers a way out that was not offered to Judas or to the couple in Acts 5. It is not said explicitly that Simon repented, but that is implied in his request for Peter to 'pray to the Lord' for him."[11] What we have here, then, may be Luke's offer to rival groups to rejoin the Christian community.

Verse 25: Luke's narrative framework makes Peter and John return to Jerusalem. Having preached the word of the Lord (cf. 4:29; 6:2) in the city of Samaria (verse 5), during their return they also tell the good news in many villages of Samaria. This completes the second part of 1:8, where the Twelve were told that they would be the witnesses of Jesus not only in Jerusalem and Judea, but also in Samaria. Since in Luke's opinion the mission of the Hellenist Philip was not fully valid, two of the Jerusalem apostles had to carry out a mission in Samaria.

THE TRADITIONS REWORKED BY LUKE

Verses 5–8: The basis of this report is either a written account or oral traditions concerning the spirit-filled activity in Samaria of the preacher Philip, one of the seven Hellenists.

Verses 9–13: Here Luke has summarized an ingredient of the early Christian tradition about Simon, who, as early as the middle of the second century, was regarded as the first heretic and a Gnostic.[12] In verse 10b an authentic Simonian tradition seems to surface. After subtracting Luke's additions we find a confession of Simon's followers acknowledging him to be the Great Power. Since elsewhere in Early Christian and Jewish literature "power" is synonymous with "god,"[13] the conclusion must be drawn that Simon's adherents worshipped him as (the highest) God. According to the tradition behind verses 9–13, they were not a negligible group. This inference is based on verse 10a ("they all gave heed to him [Simon], from the least to the greatest") and on the statement that sometime before the arrival of Philip, Simon had already been active in Samaria. Of course, the precise location of Simon's activity can no longer be ascertained. Luke erroneously speaks of *the* city of Samaria (verse 5), as if there were no other cities in Samaria, while Justin mentions Gittha.[14] He further reports that Simon had a considerable following in Samaria a century later, "Almost all the Samaritans, but also a few among other nations, confess him as the first god and worship him."[15] This statement has been called "an excessive exaggeration"[16]— a claim that would seem difficult to justify, for Justin himself came from Flavia Neapolis (Shechem) in Samaria and thus could speak from personal knowledge. If the great importance of Simonian religion in Samaria around the middle of the second century is a fact, then it lends indirect support to the related statement in verse 10a, which pertains to conditions a century earlier.

I suggest that the tradition of Simon Magus underlying this section stems from Hellenist circles reporting the encounter between the supporters of Simonian and Christian religions. It is important to realize that the Hellenists were, as the story shows, confronted with other competing religions almost from the start, and were doubtless exposed to all sorts of religious ideas, doctrines, and symbols.

Verses 14–24: This section—as was shown in the previous section—is a composition of Luke, the more so since he clearly added Peter and John to verses 14–17 in order to enforce a Jerusalem perspective.[17] Yet his creation of verses 14–24 does not mean that Luke has not used any tradition. It is likely that at verse 22 the author of Acts has inserted a reference to the consort of Simon Magus, in the expression "thought of your heart" (in Greek, *epinoia tês sarkos sou*).[18] *Epinoia* occurs only at this place in the whole New Testament and is a technical term for the feminine partner in Simonian gnosis, as we know from second-century sources. The use of *epinoia* at this point in Acts is perhaps best explained by assuming that Luke is referring ironically to Simon's female consort, the embodiment of Simon's confusion and the root of his heresy. In the story in Acts, Luke disparages the *epinoia* as material aspiration. Simon wants to buy the Holy Spirit in order to go into the business of dispensing it for profit, and Peter attributes this aspiration to Simon's *epinoia tês kardias*.[19]

Verse 25: See on verses 14–24.

HISTORICAL ELEMENTS

The missionary work in Samaria performed by the Hellenist Philip is historical. It took place in the 30s, after the expulsion of the Hellenists from Jerusalem on the occasion of the martyrdom of Stephen. However, it is not completely clear whether it was addressed to the Samarians (the Gentile population of Samaria)[20] or the Samaritans (members of the religious community) who had their sanctuary on Mount Gerizim. As Simon Magus in all probability appeared among the Gentile population of Samaria and was worshipped there as an avatar of the god Zeus, it is likely that Philip also preached among that same population. However, this does not rule out a mission among the Samaritans.

Similarly, the clash of the Hellenists with adherents of the Simonian religion in Samaria can clearly claim historicity. Anyone who set foot there inevitably encountered Simon's adherents, since at least up to the middle of the second century he had a large following in Samaria (see above, p. 119). This throws light on the details of the Hellenist mission in Samaria.

THE HISTORICAL VALUE OF LUKE'S ACCOUNT

Luke has made Simon into a magician and has introduced a sharp separation between magic and religion. His narrative, though, allows us to conclude that magic played an important part in the spread of the Christian religion. It is instructive to recall the affirmations about the power of the name of Jesus in the healing stories found in Acts 3–4 and to note that Luke does not scruple to claim that Philip overpowered Simon and that the latter had himself baptized. Not only was he quite successful in persuading ancient readers with these clearly propagandist claims, but a number of modern scholars continue to dumbfound careful and unbiased readers by believing him.[21]

[21]
ACTS 8:26–40
PHILIP AND THE CONVERSION OF THE ETHIOPIAN EUNUCH

(26) But an angel of the Lord said to Philip, "Rise and go south to the road that leads down *from Jerusalem to Gaza.*" *This is a desert road.* (27) And he rose and went. *And look,* an Ethiopian, a eunuch, a minister of Candace the queen of the

Ethiopians, in charge of all her treasure, *had come to Jerusalem to worship* (28) *and was returning*; seated in his carriage, *he was reading the prophet Isaiah.*

(29) But the Spirit said to Philip, "Go up and join the carriage." (30) So Philip ran up to him, and heard him reading Isaiah the prophet and asked, "Do you understand what you are reading?" (31) And he said, "How can I, unless some one guides me?" And he invited Philip to come up and sit with him. (32) *The passage of the scripture he was reading was this: "As a sheep led to the slaughter or a lamb before its shearer is dumb, so he opens not his mouth.* (33) *In his humiliation justice was denied to him. Who will ever talk about his descendants? For his life is taken up from the earth."* (34) *And the eunuch said to Philip, "Tell me, please, who is it that the prophet is speaking about here, himself or someone else?"* (35) *Then Philip opened his mouth, and starting with this passage, he **preached** about Jesus to him.*

(36) As they went along the road they came to some water, and the eunuch said, "Look, here is water! *What is to prevent my being baptized?"*[22] (38) And he ordered the carriage to stop, and they both descended into the water, Philip and the eunuch, and he baptized him.

(39a) And when they came up out of the water, the Spirit of the Lord snatched Philip away; and the eunuch saw him no more, (39b) *for he went on his way rejoicing.*

(40) *But Philip was found at Azotus, and passing on he **preached** in all the towns until he reached Caesarea.*

Outline

26–28:   Dual exposition
29–35:   Philip interprets Scripture and preaches about Jesus to the eunuch
36 and 38:   Philip baptizes the eunuch
39:   Divine transportation of Philip after performing the baptism; joyful return of the eunuch
40:   Philip in Azotus (Ashdod). After preaching the gospel, arrival of Philip in Caesarea

Luke's Purpose

Verse 26: The angel motif in derives from Luke.[23] The expression "from Jerusalem to Gaza" reflects Luke's Jerusalem perspective. "This is a desert road" is an editorial explanation[24] that refers to the road between Jerusalem and Gaza.

Verses 27–28: The phrase that the eunuch had come to Jerusalem to worship (verse 27) "implies that he was a Jew or at least a proselyte coming from the diaspora."[25] The reference to the prophet Isaiah in verse 28 (as well as the later reported quotation of Isa. 53:7–8 in verses 32–33) comes from the author. In Luke 4:17–18 the Evangelist similarly expands Mark 6 with a prophetic testimony from Isaiah and puts it on the lips of Jesus.

Verses 29–35: Verses 32–34 derive from the Evangelist and, like Luke 4:18–19, are Isaiah testimonies understood as pointing to Christ. By contrast the traditional story that Luke edited is about Philip's *proclamation* of Jesus, as verse 35 shows.

Verses 36–38: For the expression in verse 36, "What is to prevent my being baptized?" see the nearly identical expression in 10:47 (cf. 11:17). Verse 38 shows that the eunuch was traveling in the company of others.

Verse 39: The motif of rejoicing derives from Luke.[26] The sentence "for he (the eunuch) went on his way rejoicing" (verse 39b) seems to be in tension with verse 39a. At any rate, the action of the Spirit of the Lord—and not the eunuch's departure in joy—is the reason why he no longer saw Philip.

Verse 40: This is a pragmatic supplement to inform the reader where Philip will be later, in Caesarea (21:8).

THE TRADITIONS REWORKED BY LUKE

If we extract from the text the features that certainly flow from Luke's pen, we are left with the following elements of tradition: "An Ethiopian, a eunuch, a minister of Candace the queen of the Ethiopians, in charge of all her treasure" (verse 27); "and they both descended into the water, Philip and the eunuch, and he baptized him" (verse 38); "when they came up out of the water, the Spirit of the Lord snatched Philip away; and the eunuch saw him no more" (verse 39).

Since the elements of the tradition are fragmentary a form-critical classification does not seem to be possible. These difficulties notwithstanding, some conclusions can possibly be drawn: (a) The story circulated independently because it played no role in the rest of Acts. (b) A distinct sense of the legendary arises from the blending of personal, miraculous, and edifying elements. Parallels between this story and 1 Kings 18 and 2 Kings 2 can be noted.[27] (c) Perhaps in circles of the Hellenists the story was seen as fulfillment of Old Testament prophecies.[28]

HISTORICAL ELEMENTS

The tradition, although no doubt based on legend, ultimately reflects an event, the "conversion" of an Ethiopian eunuch,[29] that must have been one of the notable successes of Philip in particular and the Hellenists in general. Such a possibility inheres in what we know about the Hellenists, while the detailed nature of the traditional elements found in Acts 8 (Ethiopian, eunuch) and the lack of consistency with respect to Acts 10 render the foregoing conclusion probable. The chronological setting must be the early 30s.

THE HISTORICAL VALUE OF LUKE'S ACCOUNT

With this story Luke adds a second report about Philip to his narrative about the Hellenist mission outside Jerusalem. Remarkably enough, he does not mention a bestowal of the Spirit on the eunuch, though as concerns verse 39 an ancient codex contains a secondary reading to that effect. Apparently Luke could not imagine that the eunuch received the Holy Spirit, and in this way Luke remained faithful to his precept—evident in the first story about Philip (8:5–25)—not to connect the bestowing of the Spirit with the preaching of the Hellenists and to suppress any reports to this effect. In this respect, he is the representative of an institutionalized church that does not allow other forms of Christianity to flourish beside it and hence can portray such toleration only by distorting the historical facts. Nevertheless, he reports enough to allow us to restore a picture of what the Hellenists really thought about themselves. That the possession of the Spirit is one of the main features of the Hellenist tradition follows not only from the stories about Stephen and Philip, but can also be demonstrated on the basis of a later report about Philip's daughters in Acts 21:8–9, a passage that seems to be historically accurate (see below, p. 282).

[22]
ACTS 9:1–19A
THE CONVERSION AND HEALING OF SAUL

(1) *But Saul, still breathing threats and murder against the disciples of the Lord, went to the high priest* (2) *and requested from him letters to the synagogues at Damascus, so that if he found any belonging to the Way, men or women, he might*

bring them bound to Jerusalem. (3) *But as he went on his way* he approached Damascus, and suddenly a light from heaven flashed around him. (4) And falling to the ground he heard a voice saying to him, *"Saul, Saul, why are you perse-cuting me?"* (5) *And he said, "Who are you, Lord?"* And he said, *"I am Jesus, whom you are persecuting.* (6) But rise and go into the city, and you will be told what you are to do."* (7) The men who were traveling with him stood speechless, hearing the voice but seeing no one. (8) But Saul rose from the ground, and although his eyes were open, he saw nothing. So they led him by the hand and brought him into Damascus. (9) And *for three days* he was without sight, and nei-ther ate nor drank.

(10a) But there was a disciple at Damascus *named* Ananias. (10b) The Lord said to him in a vision, "Ananias." And he said, "Here I am, Lord." (11) And the Lord [said] to him, "Rise and go to the street called Straight, and at the house of Judas look for a man of Tarsus *named* Saul, for *look*, he is praying, (12) and he has seen in a vision a man *named* Ananias come in and lay his hands on him so that he might regain his sight." (13) *But Ananias answered, "Lord, I have heard from many about this man, how much evil he has done to your saints at Jerusalem.* (14) *And here he has authority from the chief priests to bind all who call on your name."* (15) *But the Lord said to him, "Go, for he is a chosen instru-ment of mine to bear my name before the Gentiles and kings and the children of Israel.* (16) *For I will show him how much he must suffer for the sake of my name."* (17) So Ananias departed and went into the house. And *laying his hands* on him he said, "Brother Saul, the Lord Jesus who appeared to you on the road by which you came has sent me so that you may regain your sight and be *filled with the Holy Spirit."* (18) And *immediately* something like scales fell from his eyes, and he regained his sight. Then he *rose* and was baptized; (19a) and taking food, he was strengthened.

OUTLINE

   1–2: Saul the persecutor
   3–9: The appearance of Christ to Saul near Damascus
   10–19a: Ananias's vision of Christ and the commission; he carries it out

LUKE'S PURPOSE

Verses 1–2: Both the content and linguistic particularities indicate that these verses are an expository introduction created by Luke. The author's clear purpose is to link previous reports—Saul's involvement in Stephen's death (7:58; 8:1a) and his persecution of the Jerusalem community (8:3)—with a story about the persecutor's miraculous conversion. Luke sets this event on the road from Jerusalem to Damascus, where—we are told—Saul is traveling under the aegis of the high priest to arrest any Christians he can find and take them to Jerusalem. Thus he highlights the contrast between the rabid persecutor and the submissive convert.

Verses 3–9: For further insight into Luke's purpose, one does well to compare the parallel conversion accounts found here and in Acts 22 and 26. The present report appears in the third person singular, while the two later accounts are in the first person singular. In 22:3–16 Paul describes the event to fellow-Jews in the course of a speech given in the temple; in 26:4–5, 9–18 he is addressing Agrippa, Festus, and Bernice. The form and content of both speeches are clearly apologetic. By way of corroborating this assertion, I offer the following summary of the detailed comparison in my earlier study of Acts.[30]

There is a causal connection among the three accounts. At the level of Luke's editing, the second account presupposes the first (see 22:12), just as the third version can be understood as an abbreviation of the two previous ones. In this latter the contrast between Paul's pre-Christian and Christian periods is heightened (note the elaboration of Paul's activity as a persecutor, 26:10–11), and the conversion of Acts 9 is understood as a call to the Gentile mission. The account in chapter 22 occupies an intermediate position; in it theme of the Gentile mission is indicated by the immediate context (22:17–21).

In view of the many correspondences, the difference between 9:7 (Saul's companions heard the voice) and 22:9 (Saul's companions did not hear a voice) should not be interpreted in terms of different sources. However, we can hardly regard the difference as carelessness on Luke's part, since in interrupting the dialogue between Jesus and Saul, 22:9 deliberately points back to 9:7 (note the alternation between hearing and seeing); here readers are given an additional piece of information about the conversion of Saul. The question left open in 9:7, whether Saul's companions had seen a light, is thus answered in the affirmative. (9:7 had denied only that the companions had seen anyone—i.e., Jesus.) Moreover, the statement in 22:9 that Saul's companions had not heard a voice sounds like a Lukan correction of the pre-Lukan statement to the contrary in 9:7. Here Luke wants to exclude the possibility that Saul's companions were privy to a revelation that was reserved solely for Saul.

The above statement that the third version is an abbreviation of the first two is not intended, of course, as a conclusive demonstration that individual motifs in it are not original or that the tradition that underlies all three reports was the story of a conversion or a call. Furthermore, it is uncertain whether Ananias was part of this tradition.

Verses 4–6: Luke has shaped verses 4b–6—an appearance dialogue which has Old Testament analogies, the typical form of which is tripartite: (a) Address or call; (b) Response in the form of a question; (c) Self-introduction and charge. A similar scheme occurs in other contexts shaped by the Evangelist: 9:10–11; 10:3–5. Two further points strengthen this assumption: First, the omission of verses 4b–6 would not affect the action; second, Luke's fondness for using dialogue in constructing an event. Another typically Lukan trait shows up in verse 4, where the duplication "Saul, Saul" corresponds to the repeated address in Luke 8:24 (Mark differs); 10:41; and 22:31.

Verses 10–12: Yet another of the Evangelist's favorite literary devices appears in verse 10b, where a divine decision is announced in a vision (in Greek, *horama*). In the analysis of Luke's editorial work, it is important to note carefully the context of verses 10c–16. Luke has reported this event in a form parallel to both the preceding story of Philip and the Ethiopian eunuch (8:26–40) and the following account of Cornelius (10:1–11:18): in all three cases he establishes a narrative nexus between the actions of two people. And despite the variant detail that here Saul's vision (though not Ananias's) is implied rather than given narrative form (9:12), in both this and the Cornelius story the connection is effected by duplicate visions. By contrast, 8:26–40 reports a divine appearance only to Philip, who is thereby directed to the eunuch. And quite unlike the second figure in the later narratives—Ananias in Acts 9 and Peter in Acts 10–11—the eunuch has no visionary experience. Thus it appears likely that the three stories not only belong together, but also were so structured and arranged as to lead toward a climax. Hence one is justified in suspecting that Luke placed Ananias's vision in the account in order to make that episode fit better into the overall narrative complex. This tentative conclusion is further strengthened by the fact that Christ's appearance to Saul (9:3–4) is surely out of place in the story-telling genre that is characteristic of chapters 8 and 10–11—though to be sure, 9:12 shows that Luke wants us to see it as a seamless fit. The introduction of the house of Judas in verse 11 may go back to Luke. He is typically interested in "lodging"[31] and has therefore elaborated the story with local Damascus coloring.

Verses 13–14: This is a retrospect on 8:3.

Verses 15–16: These verses derive from Luke, as is evident from language but especially content: The stress on the primacy and prestige of God's name strongly suggests redaction. Any number of instances in Acts show that "the whole realization of faith is linked with the concept of the name"[32] and the power of the divine name, it has been suggested, can be described as "the specifically Lukan way of depicting the presence of Christ."[33] (See, for example, 3:16; 4:12; 8:12.) Here we also find the by now familiar Lukan contrast between Jews and

Gentiles, and along with this the characterization of Paul as confessor—even to Israel—and as sufferer, although he was first and foremost a missionary. In Luke, the necessity of suffering commonly serves as a periphrasis for the divine plan, and while many take verse 15 to allude to Saul's missionary activity, what we see here in fact is the first appearance of the theme of suffering. Since the Greek phrase, *bastazein to onoma enôpion tinos*, does not mean "carry the name to someone" but "bear the name before someone," the topic of suffering is at hand—as verse 16 will shortly confirm. Yet the circumstances of Paul's suffering are hardly ever described in Acts; instead, he overcomes all the difficulties. Note also that verse 15—as a matter of course—shows Paul to be among the great figures of this world.[34]

Verse 17–19a: Verse 17 continues the story of Ananias's commission to heal Saul (verse 12); the cure involves the additional benefit of being filled with Holy Spirit. Verses 17 and 18 seem to clash inasmuch as Saul's baptism is reported to occur subsequent to the bestowing of the Holy Spirit. Verse 19a concludes the episode.

THE TRADITIONS REWORKED BY LUKE

Verses 3–9: With redacted portions set aside, one can delineate the following as traditional elements: (a) Saul, the persecutor of Christians, approaches Damascus. (b) A dazzling light shines from heaven, prostrating Saul (and apparently blinding him). (c) Saul's companions also hear the words addressed to him, and lead him (blinded?) to Damascus. When thus reconstructed, the tradition can be recognized as a legend describing God's punishment of one who has scorned his will.[35] To be sure, reconstruction of tradition by subtraction can never be entirely secure. One cannot, for example, eliminate the possibility that verses 4b–6—though certainly Lukan as we find them—are not rooted in tradition. Here, at least, such a suspicion could approach likelihood, seeing that at the level of tradition the voice in verse 7 is clearly the same one that has spoken to Saul. And in all honesty one cannot summarily reject the possibility that Luke has deleted elements from the tradition he received. Any decision concerning what substitutions may be appropriate is likely to alter the definition of form. Let it be noted here that when subsequently I shall speak of a "christophany," two things should be kept in mind: First, verses 3–9 are not about visions like those in 9:10–19a; 10–11; and second, the subject of the event before Damascus is the persecuted Christ. Such a classification allows the story to be regarded as a conversion or call.

One could further ask whether the kernel of the tradition in Acts 9:3–9 originates in Damascus and goes on to identify the jubilant cry in, "He who once per-secuted us now proclaims the faith that he tried to destroy,"[36] as the starting point. Yet one should not attempt at too narrow a delineation of the development of the tradition because the difficulties referred to earlier remain.

Verses 10–19a: That the disciple Ananias must derive from tradition is all but certified by the negative characterization of others of the same name (5:1–10; 23:2), for Luke would not have chosen this name to add to the tradition, which likely included his residence in Damascus as well as his healing—and perhaps baptizing (9:18)—of Paul there. If these elements were not inherent parts of a tra-dition that included the reports underlying verses 3–9, then Luke must have con-nected the two strands.

HISTORICAL ELEMENTS

Verses 3–9: The tradition reflected in verses 3–9 agrees with Paul's letters in asserting that a signal and specific event turned the erstwhile persecutor into a proclaimer, Christ's archenemy into his most fervent disciple (see Gal. 1). It would also be difficult to deny that the conversion experience occurred in or near Damascus. By recording in Gal. 1:17 that after his conversion he went to Arabia and then returned to Damascus, Paul thereby indicates that city as either the spe-cific or approximate locus of his conversion.

The tradition also follows Paul's epistolary claim of Christ's appearance to him: note the Easter language in his report of seeing the Lord (1 Cor. 9:1–2, cf. John 20:18, 24) and the account in 1 Cor. 15:8 of Jesus' appearing to him (cf. Luke 24:34; 1 Cor. 15:3–7). These two passages indicate a single event: 1 Cor. 9:1 records Paul's actual perception of Jesus; 1 Cor. 15:8 is a later corroboration of the event. To be sure, a remarkable difference separates Acts 9:3–9 from 1 Cor. 9:1–2 and 15:8: Acts does not report a visual perception of the Lord, but only that Paul hears his words (verses 4b–6, a detail that may or may not be traditional) and falls to the ground following a great light from heaven. But in spite of the failure of verses 3–9 to indicate that Saul saw the Lord, we should make note of both 9:17c, where Ananias describes the heavenly light as Jesus appearing (in Greek, *ophtheis*) to Saul (cf. 26:19), and 9:7, where the failure of Saul's companions to see anyone implies that Saul did see someone—i.e., Jesus. It is doubtful, then, whether the tradition behind 9:3–9 and the letters of Paul stand in direct conflict as concerns the nature of Jesus' appearance, for both accounts attest that Paul saw the Lord.

Other differences may seem insuperable. For example, although Paul makes it emphatic that the Damascene christophany marked the beginning of his missionary career (see esp. Gal 1:15), this fact does not appear in Acts 9, because there the central issue is that Jesus has overcome the one who persecuted his followers. But we must recall that Paul's about-face from persecutor to propagandist involved such a fundamental realignment of a far-reaching force diagram that what Luke narrated in Acts 9 and 26—two stories with different focal points—may in fact have taken place within a relatively short time—with Acts 22 coming in the middle, as noted earlier. In short, it may be that Acts 9 and 26 represent two different aspects or ramifications of a single crucial event.

Verses 10–19a: Concerning the historicity of Ananias and his role in Saul's transformation, the available evidence will not support any final judgment. Be that as it may, one may not properly cite Gal. 1:12 as evidence that Paul's revelation cannot have involved a human source. Surely the ministering role of Ananias does not put in question the extraordinary character of Paul's conversion and call.[37] Elsewhere (1 Cor. 11:23–25) Paul could quote a tradition about the Eucharist—which more or less matches the accounts of the Synoptics—and still claim that he had received this very account from the "Lord."

THE HISTORICAL VALUE OF LUKE'S ACCOUNT

Verses 1–2: No historical support can be adduced for Paul's journey from Jerusalem to Damascus on the warrant of the high priest in order to arrest Christians there and bring them back to Jerusalem. In fact, the jurisdiction of the high court did not extend as far as Damascus, but was limited to Judea.[38] "Luke's report that Paul, the Pharisee and pupil of the scribes, had acted as a judge on behalf of the synagogues and along with others had passed sentences of death (Acts 22.4; 26.10; cf. 9.1), is an exaggerated piece of elaboration."[39] Moreover, according to 22:19 (cf. 26:11) Paul inflicts only synagogue punishments.

Verses 3–9: I said above that only after examining the historical considerations would it be possible to essay some final comments as to whether the tradition narrates a conversion or a call. It is now clear that the most important result of the historical reconstruction is the discovery of a tradition essentially in agreement with Paul's own testimony. It reports a christophany and depicts the circumstances that go with it—with conversion being an all-but-inherent aspect. Certainly no call to mission can be found in Acts 9. But given the many other parallels between tradition and Paul, we can *ex hypothesi* attribute its absence to the editor Luke, since in his overall plan Paul's mission has not yet emerged as a theme. In all likelihood Luke deliberately interpreted the tradition of Paul's calling (see Acts 22 and 26) as a conversion story and purposely included it in a series of three conversion accounts (8:26–40; 9:1–19a; 10:1–11:18). Thus the tradition of the "Damascus event" that Luke received was a call story that essentially corresponded with Paul's own testimony. Luke has told it three times to suit as many literary purposes, and in Acts 9 removes it one stage further from historical truth by interpreting the call as a conversion.

[23]
ACTS 9:19B–31
SAUL FROM DAMASCUS TO JERUSALEM

(19b) *He stayed some time with the* DISCIPLES *in Damascus. (20) Soon he was proclaiming Jesus in the synagogues, saying, "This is the Son of God." (21) And all who heard were amazed, and said, "Is not this the man who was in Jerusalem trying to destroy those who called on this name? Did he not come here for the sole purpose of arresting them and taking them bound before the chief priests?" (22) But Saul increased all the more in strength, and confounded the Jews who lived in Damascus by demonstrating that Jesus is the Christ. (23) When many days had passed, the Jews plotted to kill him, (24) but their plot became known to Saul.* They were watching the gates day and night, **to murder him;** (25) but his DISCIPLES took him by night and let him down over the wall, lowering him in a basket.

(26) *And when he had reached Jerusalem he tried to join the* DISCIPLES; *and they were all afraid of him, for they did not believe that he was a* DISCIPLE. *(27) But Barnabas took him and brought him to the apostles, and related to them how on the road he* (Saul) *had seen the Lord, who spoke to him, and how at Damascus he had* preached boldly in the name of *Jesus. (28) So he went in and out among them in Jerusalem,* preaching boldly in the name of *the Lord.* (29) And he spoke and disputed against the Hellenists; but they were seeking **to murder him**. (30) *And when the brothers learned of it, they escorted him to Caesarea,* and sent him off to Tarsus.

(31) *So the church throughout all Judea and Galilee and Samaria had peace and was being built up. And walking in the fear of the Lord and in the comfort of the Holy Spirit, it multiplied.*

OUTLINE

LUKE'S PURPOSE

Verses 19b–25: Verses 19b–20 seem entirely redactional. The indeterminate "several days" in verse 19b and Paul's "Jews first" approach (a repeated pattern in Acts) both suggest Luke's presence. Saul's proclamation that "Jesus is the Son of God" seems either an indirect citing of Gal. 1:16 based on general knowledge existing within the community tradition or—and this is a considerably less likely alternative—he uses his knowledge of Pauline tradition in order to sound Pauline (cf. similarly 13:38–39; 20:28). Verse 21a exhibits typically Lukan language, and verse 21b restates previous direct narration (8:1, 3; 9:1, 14) in the form of a question; by choosing the previously unused verb "to destroy" (in Greek, *porthein*), the writer indicates his knowledge of Pauline tradition (cf. Gal. 1:13, 23). The end of verse 21 is a clear echo of 9:2. The redactional nature of verse 22 is evident from its description of Paul's preaching (Jesus is the Christ—cf. 18:5, 28) and his initial appeal—in accordance with Luke's pattern—to the Jews of Damascus. The description of the action plan against Paul (verse 23) derives from the Evangelist (cf. 20:3, 19). Concerning verses 24b–25 see below, page 132.

Verse 26: The narrator provides Paul with such a sudden translation that it seems as if the basket that lowered him from the Damascus wall deposited him in Jerusalem. From Jerusalem to Damascus as the crow flies is about 125 miles. Luke has created Saul's determination to associate with the disciples in Jerusalem after his conversion because he and his church view the Jerusalem community as the fountainhead of salvation history. The disciples' fear of Saul (like that of Ananias earlier) is sufficiently credible to justify the insertion of an intermediary.

Verse 27: The later tradition of the Paul-Barnabas partnership (Acts 13–14) may have suggested to Luke Barnabas's introduction of Saul to the Jerusalem community (note the parallel in 11:25–26). This purported collaboration may derive from Luke's inclination to create historical narrative, for in subsequent chapters the two are missionary partners. This verse also employs Barnabas as a handy narrator to summarize the previously reported conversion of Saul (verses 3–9) and his evangelizing in Damascus (verse 20).

Verse 28: Saul not only talks with the apostles in Jerusalem but also preaches there and debates with the Hellenists. What he previously did by himself in Damascus, he is now doing—in the exalted company of the Twelve—in Jerusalem.

Verse 29: The new apostle steps into the role that resulted from Stephen's death, and accordingly the Hellenistic Jews plot to murder Saul—just as they had done with Stephen (6:11–14), and as the Jews of Damascus had planned to murder Saul (verse 23). The similarity of this oft-repeated motif to what we find in Luke 19:47 is inescapable.

Verse 30: The plot against Saul reported in the previous verse requires sending him to safety in Tarsus.

Verse 31: This obviously Lukan summary offers a running assessment of the developing situation. The persecutor having been converted, the tide of persecution has ebbed; and the followers of Jesus, no longer confined to Jerusalem (cf. 5:11), now live in peace in Judea, Samaria, and Galilee, observing the will of God and strengthened by the Holy Spirit. The sequence "Judea, Galilee, Samaria" suggests the possibility of a geographical misapprehension on Luke's part, but it may reflect his notion of their importance. Note the reverse sequence at Luke 17:11 describing the journey of Jesus, who "went through"[40] Samaria and Galilee" to Jerusalem.[41]

THE TRADITIONS REWORKED BY LUKE

Verses 19b–20: Although Paul's preaching in Damascus almost certainly comes from tradition, such an assumption cannot find direct support in this text, for it shows Lukan influence throughout, and is clearly generated by historical considerations (see below, p. 133).

Verses 24–25: That the flight from Damascus comes from the tradition is evident *first* from source-critical considerations: Verses 23–24a consist of a general exposition that reports a plan to murder Paul. The seam between verse 24a and verse 24b is clearly marked by the shift from general to specific reporting. *Second*, the reconstructed tradition bears a strong likeness to Paul's autobiographical statement in 2 Cor. 11:32–33: "At Damascus, the ethnarch of King Aretas guarded the city of Damascus in order to seize me, (33) but I was let down in a basket through a window in the wall <u>and escaped his hands</u>."

The two texts, Acts 9:23–25 and 2 Cor. 11:32–33, have an amazing similarity and break off with the lowering of Paul down "through" an opening in the wall, leaving aside the Pauline note of success in verse 33b (underlined in the above translation), which has no parallel in Acts. Luke is clearly using tradition at this point. It must have been as brief as 2 Cor. 11:32–33. If Luke had known a longer story, he would hardly have presented such a compact version. We must still recall, however, that the Jews as persecutors of Paul in this narrative derive from Luke. As to the origin of the tradition that Luke inserted here, two possibilities exist: (a) it ultimately stems from Paul's own oral account; (b)—which is more likely—it originates from 2 Cor. 11:32–33. "What is shared with 2 Corinthians derives from a piece of Pauline tradition whose basis is nothing other than 2 Cor. 11:32–32."[42] In the churches where Paul's letters were read, "a secondary oral tradition developed that had Pauline biography as its principal subject."[43]

Verses 26–30: While verse 29 derives from Luke, the travel note in verse 30 is too specific not to reflect tradition.

Verse 31: It is remarkable to find a report of communities in Galilee about which Luke makes neither previous nor subsequent mention in Acts. While it is all but impossible to decide whether Luke knew of traditions from the area of Galilee, his suppression of the Galilean resurrection tradition (Luke 24:6) makes it clear that had he known them he could hardly have made use of them.

HISTORICAL ELEMENTS

Verses 19b–25: The traditions herein contained corroborate Paul's own report of the need to escape from Damascus. The necessity reflects pressure from the ethnarch of King Aretas IV of Damascus. This functionary, who held power from 9 BCE to 39 CE, was not the governor, but the head of the Nabataeans, an ethnic group in the city of Damascus. Robert Jewett notwithstanding,[44] the action delineated cannot be connected with a political rule of the Nabataeans over Damascus between 37 and 39 CE, for that control never existed.[45] Why action was taken against Paul is not clear. Perhaps Paul's preaching to the gentile sympathizers of Judaism led to turbulence, as it did in his later career. One should also consider Paul's evangelising in Nabataean territory in Arabia (Gal. 1:17), an effort that preceded his stay in Damascus. The ethnarch's animus could have stemmed from this earlier mission by Paul, for in all likelihood its outreach included the Nabataeans living in Damascus.

The action directed against Paul by the ethnarch cannot properly be used to corroborate Luke's repeated accounts of Paul's persecution by Jews. Attributing the interference by the Nabataean ethnarch to the prompting of the Jews would be an unwarranted harmonization. That Paul would not omit any role of the Jews in the persecution in order to spare them follows from the immediate context of 2 Cor. 11:32–33. In verse 24 he points out that he received "five times from the hands of the Jews the forty lashes less one."[46]

Verses 26–29: The historical setting for Luke's narrative is Paul's first visit to Jerusalem to visit Cephas. This sojourn lasted only two weeks (Gal 1:18) and led to the acknowledgment of Paul as a "brother" and a missionary among the Gentiles. (Gal 2:7–8 goes back to Paul's first Jerusalem visit as a Christian and must be distinguished from Gal 2:9—the agreement reached at the Jerusalem conference fourteen years later between Paul and Barnabas and the "pillar" apostles.)[47]

Verse 30: The report of Paul's journey from Jerusalem toward Tarsus is historical. It agrees with Paul's own statement that after visiting Cephas he proceeded to visit Syria and Cilicia. Tarsus was located in Cilicia, and after 44 CE

Syria and Cilicia comprised a single province. Gal. 1:21, written around 52 CE (see below, p. 359), may simply reflect Paul's use of contemporary terminology.

THE HISTORICAL VALUE OF LUKE'S ACCOUNT

Verses 23–25: The above analysis has demonstrated that it was Luke who portrayed the Jews as instigators of the attack on Paul and that the real persecutor of the apostles was the ethnarch of Aretas. This clear result notwithstanding, interpreters have tried to rehabilitate Luke's opinion. Laurence Welborn outlines some details,

> Through this opening in the wall, a swarm of anti-Jewish phantasies have found entree into Christian accounts of the early life of Paul. The Jews, it is said, bribed the ethnarch of Aretas with money. The ethnarch was intimidated by the size and power of the Jewish community in Damascus. The Jews are pictured standing with the soldiers in the gates, ready to point their finger at their kinsman. A little psychologizing supplies the Jews with motives: they were bewildered and disappointed at the apostasy of the Pharisee and persecutor; they felt resentment over the success of his proselytising in the synagogues of Damascus.[48]

It seems that Lukan true believers, once they have assimilated and internalized his programmatic scheme of Jewish plots and assaults against the apostle, are extremely loath to accept—however persuasive the evidence—the notion of a plan of capture that reflects a different source and motive.

[24]
ACTS 9:32–43
TWO MIRACLES OF PETER

(32) Now as Peter *went through all* [the areas], he came down also to the SAINTS who lived at Lydda. (33) There he found a man *named* Aeneas, bedridden for eight years, *who was* paralyzed. (34) And Peter said to him, "Aeneas, Jesus Christ heals you; rise and make your own bed." And *immediately* he rose. (35) *And all the residents of Lydda and the Sharon saw him, and they turned to the Lord.*

(36) Now there was in Joppa a disciple *named* Tabitha, which, translated, means Dorcas. *She was full of good works and acts of alms.* (37) *In those days* she became ill and died, and when they had washed her, they laid her in an upper room. (38) And as Lydda is near Joppa, the disciples, hearing that Peter was

there, sent two men to him, urging him, "Please come to us without delay." (39) So Peter rose and went with them. And when he arrived, they *took* him to the upper room. *All* the <u>widows</u> stood beside him wailing and showing tunics and other garments that Dorcas had been making while she was with them. (40) But Peter had all go out, and *knelt down and prayed*; and *turning* to the body he said, "Tabitha, *arise.*" And she opened her eyes, *and when she saw Peter she sat up.* (41) And he gave her his hand and raised her up. Then calling the SAINTS and <u>widows</u>, he presented her alive. (42) **And it became known throughout all Joppa, and many believed in the Lord.** (43) *And he stayed in Joppa for many days with one Simon, a tanner.*

OUTLINE

32–35: Peter's healing of Aeneas in Lydda
36–42: Peter's resurrection of Tabitha in Joppa

LUKE'S PURPOSE

The narrative setting of these two miracle stories is Peter's progress to Caesarea; the events showcase him as a representative of the twelve apostles who carries on the tradition of Jesus' words, deeds, and miracles—not by his own power but through that of Jesus Christ (9:34). Concurrently, Luke uses this "inspection tour" (verse 32) to establish the bond that relates the believers of Lydda and Joppa to the mother community in Jerusalem (cf. 8:4).

Verse 32: The verb "to go through" (in Greek, *dierchesthai*) appears in 8:4; 19:1. No doubt "all" is a Lukan touch as well, for it probably points back to the previous verse. The "saints" in Lydda (see later verse 41) are members of the local community (cf. 9:1). For Luke the word means the same as "disciple" (cf. verse 38).

Verses 33–34: For Lukan language see the italicized phrases. The announcement, "Aeneas, Jesus Christ heals you," likely derives from Luke's desire to stress the source of the healing. Peter's subsequent word of command in verse 34 corresponds to 14:10 and Luke 5:24.

Verse 35: That *all* the inhabitants of the plain of Sharon saw the cured Aeneas is as great an exaggeration as that they were all converted.

Verses 36–37: The expression "alms" corresponds to 10:2 and is a favorite word of Luke's. Moreover the description of Tabitha (for the name see below, p. 136, on verse 40)—that she is full of good works—and the subsequent reference to the clothing that she made for others (verse 39c) stem from the Evangelist. By listing the details of her charitable work Luke shows that she is worthy of the miracle.[49]

Verse 38: This effects the transition between the two miracle stories, linking them by noting the nearness the two cities, Peter's stay in Lydda, and the embassy of the two men. Since Joppa lies only about twelve miles from Lydda, the note in verse 38 accurately reflects the geography of the region.[50]

Verses 39–40: For Lukan edits see the italicized phrases in the translation. Both the kneeling down (cf. Luke 22:41 [Mark differs]; Acts 7:60; 20:36; 21:5) and the prayer motif in verse 40 derive from the Evangelist. "She/he sat up" (in Greek, *anekathisen*) precisely matches Luke 7:15.

Verse 41: For the phrase at the end of the verse, "he presented her alive," cf. 1:3.

Verse 42: The conclusion of the first story forms a striking parallel to verse 35 (the ending of the second story). No doubt Luke purposely created the likeness between the final sentences of these stories so as to impress the reader with the similarity of the events (see the boldface print in the translation).

One cannot help but recognize here the influence of resurrection narratives found in the Hebrew Bible—see 1 Kings 17:17–24 and 2 Kings 4:32–37 for verses 36–42 (cf. similarly Luke 7:15). No doubt Luke's narrative format comes from his reading of the Bible rather than from tradition. Naturally, that renders the task of recreating the tradition itself both more difficult and less certain.

Verse 43: "This verse sets up a transition to the next story: Instead of returning to Lydda, which he had left so hastily, Peter stays on in Joppa, where the messengers of Cornelius will find him."[51]

THE TRADITIONS REWORKED BY LUKE

Verses 33–35: In the process of editing a miracle narrative Luke has considerably compressed it. The story is devoid of a specific situational context (verse 32 provides only general narrative framework) and lacks a true conclusion: That is to say verse 35 does not follow the typical miracle story format because it omits the *effect on the observer*, and passes directly from the miracle itself to the consequences.[52] The narrative seems to represent a faint echo of Mark's account of the healing of the palsied man (Mark 2:1–12 parr.).

Verses 36–42: This account strikes one as a particularly well-crafted miracle story. It economically introduces the person of Tabitha, certifies her death, and brings on stage both the miracle worker and the weeping widows, whose demeanor provides a contrast to his devout actions. In accordance with formal proprieties, the miracle worker's command is followed by the resurrection (verse 40), and the following verse completes the formula by offering the demonstration of the miracle. All these factors, in addition to its "once upon a time" opening phrase, suggest that this may have come to Luke as a "free-standing" story. An interesting parallel can be seen in Jesus' reviving of Jairus's daughter (Mark 5). According to Wellhausen, "Tabitha recalls the Talitha in Mark 5.41; vv. 39, 40 so correspond with Mark 5.40, 41 that we cannot think the two stories independent of each other."[53] Furthermore, since both accounts tell of wailing women or widows, Wellhausen's case is strengthened to the degree that we are justified in reaching the tentative conclusion that the two narratives had entered the stream of tradition before Luke's time. However, Luke's account may simply be an adaptation of the story he found in Mark 5. (Note that in Luke 8:53–54—which is based on Mark 5:40–41—the Third Evangelist omitted the details he included in the present Acts story.)[54]

Verse 43: Because of its specific detail, one may consider the note of Peter's lodging in Joppa at the house of Simon the Tanner to be traditional. Yet the names of people, places, and occupations do not guarantee the reliability of reports in Acts any more than those in the Third and Fourth Gospels.[55] Also worthy of note is Luke's interest in lodging places, and that in Luke 8:41 the evangelist has "invented" the name of the person who remains anonymous in Mark 5:22.[56] The conclusion to be drawn is that the specific information given by Luke in verse 43 need not go back to tradition.

Historical Elements

Both accounts find their historical setting in a sojourn by Peter in Lydda and Joppa, two cities so notably Jewish as to suggest that Peter's missionary journey is an example of his preaching among the Jews, the previous endorsement of which is attested in Gal 2:7, but which must have followed Paul's visit to Cephas reported in Gal 1:18. Accordingly, we may safely place Peter's travel to Lydda and Joppa, and perhaps his founding of communities there, somewhere between Paul's visit to Cephas (35 CE) and the conference (48 CE).

Verses 36–42: Furthermore it is a fact that miracle traditions are attached to leading figures of early Christianity, the more so since the "Risen One" promised the disciples that they would perform miracles.[57] Nevertheless, whether the miracle traditions arose in the places where Luke sets the events they report is uncertain; an authorial reassignment to venues of his choosing is not impossible. Still, some lost connection between Aeneas and Peter may once have existed; and the same can be said, though with less certainty, of Tabitha.[58]

Verse 43: We have no way of historically confirming Peter's stay with Simon the tanner, or, indeed, that of Paul with Judas in the Straight Street (cf. 9:11).

THE HISTORICAL VALUE OF LUKE'S ACCOUNT

For one thing, neither of the two "miracles" actually occurred; both show such strong traces of secondary development that not even the kernel of a miracle remains visible. For another, the two stories were intended to show how Christianity spread. According to Luke, a miracle leads to mass conversions reminiscent of those reported in 4:4. Haenchen's analysis is sound: "The first miracle having converted the entire plain of Sharon, there remains for the second, though it is a far greater miracle, only its effect on the citizens of Joppa. And so, if we put the data together, the whole of the country west of the Jordan, from Ashdod northward almost as far as Caesarea, has now become Christian."[59] Only someone far removed from the area could believe such fairy tales—whose sole purpose, after all, was to edify existing Christian communities and to spread the gospel among the uneducated. And while Luke had, to be sure, read similar tales in Mark's gospel, reporting such things again and again as factual events causes one to wonder about his intellectual integrity. After all, he is also the author of Luke 1:1–4.

[25]
ACTS 10:1–48
CORNELIUS'S CONVERSION AND PETER

(1) Now a man at Caesarea *named* Cornelius, a centurion of what was known as the Italian Cohort, (2)—*a **devout** man who feared God with all his household, gave alms generously to the [Jewish] people, and prayed to God continually*—(3) saw clearly in a vision about the ninth hour of the day an angel of God come in and say to him, "Cornelius." (4) And he gazed at him in terror and said, "What is it, Lord?" And he said to him, "Your prayers and your alms have ascended as a memorial before God. (5) And now send men to Joppa and bring one Simon called Peter. (6) He is *lodging* with one Simon, a tanner, whose house is by the seaside." (7) When the angel who spoke to him had departed, he called two of his servants and a **devout** soldier from among those who attended him, (8) and having related everything to them, he sent them to Joppa.

(9) But on the next day, as they were on their journey and approaching the city, Peter went up on the housetop *to pray, about the sixth hour.* (10) And he

became hungry and wanted [something] to eat, but while they were preparing it, he fell into a trance (11) and *saw* the heavens opened and a vessel like a great sheet *descending*, being let down by its four corners upon the earth. (12) In it were every kind of four footed and crawling beast of the earth and birds of the air. (13) And there came a voice to him: "Rise, Peter; kill and eat." (14) But Peter said, "By no means, Lord; for I have never eaten anything common or unclean." (15) And *a voice* came to him again a second time, "What God has made clean, do not call common." (16) This happened *three times*, and the vessel *was taken up* at once to heaven.

(17) *And even as Peter was puzzling over what the vision that he had seen might mean, look, the men who were sent by Cornelius, having made inquiry for Simon's house, stood at the gate* (18) *and called out to inquire whether Simon called Peter was lodging there.* (19) *And while Peter was yet pondering the vision, the Spirit said to him, "Look, three men are asking for you.* (20) *Rise and go down and accompany them without hesitation, for I have sent them."* (21) *And Peter went down to the men and said, "Look, I am the one you are asking for. What is the reason for your coming?"* (22a) *And they said, "Cornelius, a centurion, an upright and God-fearing man, who is well spoken of by all the nation of the Jews, was directed by a holy angel to send for you to come to his house* (22b) *and to hear what you have to say."* (23a) *So he invited them in to be his guests.*

(23b) *The next day he rose and went away with them, and some of the brothers from Joppa accompanied him.* (24) *And on the following day they entered Caesarea. Cornelius was expecting them and had called together his relatives and close friends.* (25) *When Peter entered, Cornelius met him and fell down at his feet and worshipped him.* (26) *But Peter lifted him up, saying, "Stand up; I too am a man."* (27) *And as he talked with him, he went in and found many gathered.* (28) *And he said to them, "You yourselves know how unlawful it is for a Jew to associate with or approach a Gentile, but God has shown me that I should not call any person common or unclean.* (29) *So when I was sent for, I came without objection. I ask then why you sent for me."*

(30) *And Cornelius said, "Four days ago, about this hour, I was praying in my house at the ninth hour, and look, a man stood before me in bright clothing* (31) *and said, 'Cornelius, your prayer has been heard and your alms have been remembered before God.* (32) *Send therefore to Joppa and ask for Simon who is called Peter. He is lodging in the house of Simon, a tanner, by the sea.'* (33) *So I immediately sent for you, and you have been kind enough to come. Now therefore we are all here present before God to hear all that you have been commanded by the Lord."*

(34) *So Peter opened his mouth and said: "Truly I understand that God*

shows no partiality, (35) *but in every nation anyone who reveres him and does what is right is acceptable to him. (36) As for the word that he sent to Israel, preaching good news of peace through Jesus Christ, he is Lord of all. (37) You yourselves know what happened throughout all Judea, beginning from Galilee after the baptism that John proclaimed:* (38) *how God anointed Jesus of Nazareth with the Holy Spirit and with power, how he went about doing good and healing all who were oppressed by the devil, for God was with him. (39) And we are witnesses of all that he did both in the country of the Jews and in Jerusalem. Him they put to death by hanging him on a tree,* (40) *but God raised him on the third day and made him to appear,* (41) *not to all the people but to those of us who had been chosen by God as witnesses, who ate and drank with him after he rose from the* **dead**. (42) *And he commanded us to preach to the people and to testify that he is the one appointed by God to be judge of the living and the* **dead**. (43) *To him all the prophets bear witness that everyone who believes in him receives forgiveness of sins through his name."*

(44) *While Peter was still saying these things, the Holy Spirit fell on all who were listening to the word. (45) And* the circumcised believers *who had come with Peter were amazed, because the gift of the Holy Spirit was poured out on the Gentiles also. (46) For they heard them speaking in tongues and extolling God. Then Peter declared,* (47) *"Can anyone withhold water for baptizing these people, who have received the Holy Spirit just as we have?"* (48) *And he commanded them to be baptized in the name of Jesus Christ. Then they asked him to remain for some days.*

OUTLINE

1–8: Cornelius's vision and obedience
9–16: Peter's vision
17–23: Encounter between Cornelius's messengers and Peter
24–48: The events in Cornelius's house in Caesarea

LUKE'S PURPOSE

A Note on the Cornelius Story and the Narrative about the Centurion from Capernaum

At the outset (verses 1–18) this narrative vividly recalls Luke's rendition of the cure of the centurion's slave (Luke 7:1–10 par. Matt. 8:5–13). For Matthew the centurion is merely a Gentile who approaches Jesus in such humility and trust that his slave is cured. Luke 7:2–5 also identifies him as a Gentile, but emphasizes his Jewish sympathies: The Jewish elders entreat Jesus on the grounds of his love for the Jews and the synagogue he built for them. Cornelius in Acts 10 is similarly portrayed: While a Gentile, he is a God-fearer, generous in alms and faithful in prayer. A further similarity is that both supplicants send messengers to the healer's residence (Luke 7:3/Acts 10:7–8). Matthew, on the other hand, adds an undoubtedly original feature to the story (Matt. 8:6, cf. Luke 7:6) that Jesus should not bother to go into the centurion's house. To be sure Luke 7:1–10 and Acts 10 differ in a fundamental respect, for one account is a miracle story (the centurion's servant is healed) and the other reports a conversion. Though the two do not necessarily represent a duplication, this thesis remains attractive,[60] the more so since numerous close parallels indicate that in Acts 10 Luke's hand has been freely applied.

Verse 1: It matches Luke's apologetic concerns that the first Gentile convert is a Roman officer; the historically doubtful note that Cornelius belonged to the Italian cohort (see below, p. 145) adds cogency to this observation.[61]

Verse 2: Luke describes the centurion in much the same way he portrays others he wishes the reader to see as worthy of divine favor.[62] Cornelius's continual prayer is obviously an exaggeration; surely junior officers of the Roman legions had to give most of their time to the performance of military duties.[63] For "fear God" see page 173 on 13:43; for the house formula see page 216 on 16:15.

Verses 3–6: The specifications of time likely derive from Luke; cf. the references to the Jewish times of prayer in Luke 1:10; Acts 3:1; 10:9, 30. For vision dialogues (verses 3b–6) cf. 9:4–5. Cornelius's question in verse 4 matches that of Saul in 9:5. Verses 5–6 pick up 9:43 (Peter with Simon the Tanner).

Verses 7–8: God's command must be obeyed. Note that one of Cornelius's servants is, like his commander, a devout soldier.

Verses 9–16: This fanciful account is indelibly stamped by Luke's language. The description of Peter's vision has an obvious purpose: to show that religious definitions of foods as pure or impure no longer obtain. When Peter later adduces this vision (verse 28), he interprets it as an indication that social contacts between Jews and Gentiles are now permissible, i.e., Gentiles are no longer unclean. Clearly Luke invests Peter's vision with far-reaching metaphor: The repudiation of dietary taboos both practically and religiously implies the end of social restrictions between Gentiles and Jews; hereafter full fellowship will be the rule among followers of the Way—as Luke will demonstrate in the Pauline part of Acts, chapters 16–28.

Verses 17–21: Linguistically, the description of puzzlement (verse 17a) recalls 5:34. Verses 17b–18 exhibit Luke's linkage of the Peter and the Cornelius stories by placing Cornelius's messengers at the door. Peter's perplexity in verse 19a harks back to verse 17a; note in particular the echo of the keyword "vision." It is noteworthy that in verses 19b–20 the Spirit addresses Peter again, but on a topic not related to the former vision. Verse 21 depicts Peter's obedience to the demand of the Spirit.

Verses 22–23a: Verse 22a is a narrative summary of the vision reported in verses 1–8. Verse 22b anticipates the explicit divine instructions (verse 28) that spell out what was carefully implied in verses 10–16. The lodging motif found in verses 18 and 23a (and earlier in verse 6) is typical of the author of Luke-Acts.[64]

Verses 23b–24: The trip from Joppa to Caesarea (verse 23b) not only sets up the encounter between Peter and Cornelius, but by including the Jewish believers in the action (cf. 10:45), it also sets the stage for an ensuing debate (11:1–18). Verse 24 prepares the next scene.

Verses 25–27: Cornelius goes out to greet his visitor, and then ushers him in to meet the company gathered there.

Verses 28–29: Here we have Luke's interpretation of Peter's vision: No longer are there Jew and Greek, no longer can anyone be labeled clean.

Verses 30–33: This speech by Cornelius repeats verses 1–8, and verse 33b in turn paves the way for Peter's speech (verses 34–43): The whole household of Cornelius is eager to receive the Lord's message from Peter.

Verses 34–35: This is essentially a footnote to the previous story, for surely Cornelius is the paradigm of those who—whatever their nationality—have earned God's favor by revering him and living righteously. As a god-fearer and liberal almsgiver (10:2, 22), he exemplified the criteria.

Verses 36–43: Verse 36, which may contain an echo of Luke 2:10–14, shows enough syntactic difficulty that it may be corrupt.[65] But its intent seems relatively clear insofar as it forms a unit with verses 34–35: as the prince and messenger of peace, Jesus has become Lord of all—including those of the nations (verses 34–35). Thus verse 36 both thematically summarizes the foregoing events and provides a segue to the following section (verses 37–43). Some have argued that the phrase "you yourselves know" (verse 36) should be understood to reflect a pre-Lukan tradition,[66] since the address it introduces is hardly relevant to the situation and would have little or no meaning for Cornelius and his household. Nevertheless, since the readers of Luke-Acts are the real audience of this speech, it would be hasty to derive the existence of a tradition from this evidence alone. Indeed, other considerations point to Luke as the creator of Peter's Caesarea speech at verses 37–43. The feature that it contains much more information about the life of the historical Jesus than Peter divulges elsewhere may be due to the

Gentile audience which Luke takes into account. Also conveniently appropriate to the situation is the absence of specific Old Testament quotations with which his speeches in Acts 2 and 3 are amply endowed: Luke is clearly accommodating the style and content of the exhortation to an audience representing both Judaism and the Gentile world. Perhaps that explains the limited use of scriptural testimony (verse 43), whereas "Gentile sermons" in Acts (14:15–17; 17:22–31) are free of scriptural allusions.

Verses 44–48: From these verses we discover Luke's view of what results when Gentiles accept the gospel. The scene is much like that of Pentecost: The Spirit comes upon all Peter's hearers, they speak in tongues (verse 46), and they receive baptism. The discontinuity in verse 44 is a Lukan device; Peter has said all that needs to be said, and it is necessary to prepare for the climax of the episode. The reaction of the Jewish believers (verse 45) when they see the Spirit poured out upon the Gentiles[67] sets the stage for Peter's forthcoming explanation to the Jerusalem community of the full import of the Cornelius episode. That the baptism follows the receiving of the Spirit (verses 47–48) does not represent an inherent contradiction with Luke's theology—which envisions the bestowal of the Spirit after baptism (cf. 8:16; 19:5–6)—for narrative considerations have called for a reversal of events here, just as they did in 9:17–18.

THE TRADITIONS REWORKED BY LUKE

The foregoing analysis attests the high degree to which Lukan language and content have colored the entire Cornelius episode; indeed, nearly every verse bears the imprint of Luke's narrative style and theology. Still we can, as I have suggested, find our way back to traditions Luke has drawn upon. For example, by epitomizing the significance of the vision (all people are equal), verses 19b–20 (the instruction of the Spirit) render the previous report of the vision all but unnecessary, little more than a dramatic flourish. Nor is it clear why, *after* Peter's vision, the Spirit must offer further direction, for the instructions delivered by the heavenly voice were hardly ambiguous (10:15; 11:9). The best explanation seems to be that verses 10–16 go back to a tradition that Luke has introduced into this context (for the reasons, see pp. 141, 144 above). Verses 17 (Peter's puzzlement) and 19a (his reflection on the vision) have served to reduce the tension between verses 10–16 and verse 19. Luke is also responsible for verses 27–29a, which center on Peter's allusion (verse 28) to the vision of verses 10–16.

Seeing how Luke has shaped the Cornelius story, then, we can reasonably suppose that the Cornelius narrative was founded upon the following traditions:

1. Luke had heard about the conversion of a Gentile Roman officer in Cae-

sarea. (Whether his name was Cornelius we do not know; the centurion of Capernaum is anonymous.) Everything else was added at a later stage—by Luke or his source: an angel prompting Cornelius, Peter's sojourn in Joppa, his instruction by a heavenly voice, his acceptance of Cornelius' invitation, his preaching to Cornelius and his household, and their baptismal receipt of the Holy Spirit. The nub of this story corresponds to that of the Ethiopian eunuch (8:26–39).

2. The vision in 10:10–16 goes back to tradition. By its repudiation of dietary restrictions it creates a new norm for Christian practice. Luke no doubt wisely inserted it into this context, which already contains the theme of Gentiles and Jews. If included along with the tradition(s) underlying the "incident at Antioch" (Gal. 2:11–14), it would be out of place, since in that city eating with Gentiles was already a common practice. Associating the vision with Peter at this point is most likely a redactional touch; therefore, we may hypothesize that 10:10–16 originated in a Hellenistic Jewish Christianity that had nullified Jewish dietary restrictions (cf. Mark 7:15; Rom.14:14).

A Note on "The Circumcised Believers"(verse 45)

"The circumcised believers" (in Greek, *hoi ek peritomês pistoi*) or, in other places, "the circumcised" (*hoi ek peritomês*)[68] is a common way of designating Jewish Christians who strictly observe the law. Luke may have learned the term from Gal. 2:12, but it more likely came to him as part of a tradition (note also Col. 4:11, and see further Titus 1:10—though in the latter case those addressed are probably not Jewish Christians but Jews). In any case, Luke shows his considerable narrative skill in working this tradition-based term into his narrative at this useful juncture.

HISTORICAL ELEMENTS

Verses 1–8: The historical core of the clearly legendary tradition of the "conversion" of a Roman officer in Caesarea is the success of unknown Hellenistic missionaries and not Peter's role in converting a Gentile named Cornelius. Gal. 2:7 leaves no question but that during the 30s Peter had taken the new faith exclusively to Jews, and the report of his preaching in Lydda and Joppa corroborate Paul's attestation. Of course Peter, like Jesus, may well have gained the interest of non-Jews, who could understandably have been attracted by a Jewish movement that was beginning to reach out proselytize Gentiles as well. Also relevant to this point is the high regard he apparently found among those of another primarily Gentile community (see 1 Cor. 1:12) and also in the Roman church. But that does not justify postulating the conversion of a gentile Roman centurion by Peter. "The conversion of Cornelius is for the author the fundamental case of a Gentile conversion which is validated by a vision from God and therefore, later, in 15.7, regarded as a test case."[69]

As noted earlier, the historical nub of the tradition is most reasonably located in the period between Paul's early visit to Cephas and the Jerusalem conference; i.e., sometime between 35 and 48 CE, and more specifically after his escape from Agrippa I around 43 CE. (See below, pp. 154–63, on Acts 12.) It was then that Peter moved outside Jerusalem.

Verses 10–16: The tradition may reflect the historical self-justification of a Jewish-Christian community that felt the necessity of dispensing with Jewish food laws. Who received the vision or where cannot be determined.

THE HISTORICAL VALUE OF LUKE'S ACCOUNT

Verse 1: It is an error to place the Italian cohort in Caesarea in the thirties, since that contingent was formed in 69 CE and operated only in Syria.[70] Undoubtedly Luke has bent the facts in order to provide a context in world history for the people and events of his account.[71] Hengel considers it profitless to raise this objection, arguing that Luke's location of this unit "may be an anachronism but need not necessarily be so. Auxiliary cohorts could be posted anywhere in the Roman Empire according to need, cf. Josephus, *Antt* 19, 364–6."[72] But present knowledge of the composition and deployment of the cohorts all but obviates the possibility that a troop composed of Roman citizens from Italy would have been posted to Caesarea in 40 CE.[73] Despite his well-known erudition and judgment, Hengel's insistence on our scanty "knowledge of Roman troops in Syria and Palestine,"[74] does not materially weaken a conclusion based on currently available knowledge.

A Note on Luke's Depiction of Persons from the Roman Military

It is amazing what an important role Roman military personnel play in Luke-Acts. According to Hans von Campenhausen, "Till about A.D. 175, there were, as far as we can tell, no Christian soldiers, and, therefore, no actual questions that called for the attention of Christians. . . . From the end of the second century, however, it became more and more frequent for soldiers to come into contact with the Christian mission and to be converted. Could they, then, as Christians, remain in their former calling?'[75] In Luke 3:10–14—a passage clearly composed by the Evangelist[76]—John the Baptist addresses publicans and soldiers, two supporting pillars of the Roman Empire. Upon their question what they should do the Baptist urges them to carry out their profession conscientiously. And as if this were not enough, Luke makes a Roman centurion the first Christian from the Hellenistic Roman Gentile world. All this "shows how far ahead he (Luke) is of his time and what a special standpoint he has to adopt in it."[77] This preparation for the positive role of Roman military personal in Luke's church and beyond corresponds to the positive "portrayal of Roman soldiers in connection with the trial and execution of Jesus. . . . Comparison with the report by Mark makes Luke's tendency clear, namely to make the Roman soldiers seem relatively uninvolved. . . . Here Luke has so toned down the negative action of the soldiers which he found in his sources that he can depict them in a markedly positive way in the arrest of Paul in Jerusalem and the subsequent negotiations. . . . So in Luke's account, Paul's arrest by the Roman army seems virtually to be a protective measure in a threatening situation."[78] And once again historical truth comes in a distant second to the evangelist's zeal in promoting his ecclesiastical program.

[26]
ACTS 11:1–18
PETER IN JERUSALEM: THE AFTERMATH OF CORNELIUS'S
CONVERSION

(1) *Now the apostles and the brothers who were throughout Judea heard that the Gentiles also had received the word of God. (2) But when Peter came up to Jerusalem, the circumcised [believers] disputed with him, saying, (3) "You went to uncircumcised men and ate with them." (4) But Peter offered them a detailed and orderly explanation: (5) "I was in the city of Joppa praying, and in a trance I saw a vision, a vessel descending—like a great sheet let down by four corners— from heaven, and it came down to me. (6) Looking at it closely, I observed and saw the four-footed beasts of the earth, and the wild and crawling beasts, and birds of the air. (7) And I heard a voice saying to me, 'Rise, Peter; kill and eat.' (8) But I said, 'By no means, Lord; for nothing common or unclean has ever entered my mouth.' (9) But a voice answered a second time from heaven, 'What God has made clean, do not call common.' (10) This happened three times, and all was drawn up again into heaven. (11) And look, immediately three men arrived at the house in which we were, sent to me from Caesarea. (12) And the*

Spirit told me to go with them, making no distinction. These six brothers also accompanied me, and we entered the man's house. (13) *And he told us how he had seen the angel stand in his house and say, 'Send to Joppa and bring Simon called Peter,* (14) *who will declare to you a message by which you will be saved, you and all your household.'* (15) *As I began to speak, the Holy Spirit fell on them just as on us at the beginning.* (16) *And I remembered the word of the Lord, how he said, 'John baptized with water, but you will be baptized with the Holy Spirit.'* (17) *If then God gave the same gift to them as he gave to us when we believed in the Lord Jesus Christ, who was I that I could stand in God's way?"* (18) *When they heard these things they fell silent. And they glorified God, saying, "Then to the Gentiles also God has given repentance that leads to life."*

OUTLINE

1: The Jerusalem apostles and brothers in Judea hear that the Gentiles have accepted the word

2–3: (When Peter is in Jerusalem) Jewish-Christian objections to Peter's dealings with non-Jews

4–17: Peter's speech (retrospect on chapter 10)

18: Reaction of the hearers: praise of God

LUKE'S PURPOSE

Verse 1: The phrase "the Gentiles have accepted the word of God" recalls 8:14, "Samaria has accepted the word of God." In both cases the news will impel the Jerusalem believers to a critical decision.

Verses 2–3: The key words in the chastisement by the members of the circumcision party, "You **went to** uncircumcised people and **ate with** them," point back to 10:27 and/or 10:48. The theme of eating may further allude to 10:10–16. Thus verses 2–3 focus the reader's attention on what is Luke's primary concern In the following section.

Verses 4–17: By recapitulating the previous events, Luke highlights and emphasizes them. "The report does not schematically repeat all that has been said before; this would only weary the reader."[79] Interesting minor alterations appear: In the case of 11:13–14/10:5, 32, the earlier passages fail to note that Peter's speech has as its intent the salvation of Cornelius and his household; and in 11:15 the coming of the Spirit is placed at the beginning—since here it is a descriptive detail, not the result of an exhortation—rather than forming a climax (as in

10:44) so as better to show its effect on what followed. One should not, however, be led to suppose Luke's reliance on different sources. As Martin Dibelius has aptly explained: "A speech can obviously be regarded by the author as an assertion or addition which does not necessarily affect the course of the narrative."[80] The first of the two variations noted (11:13–14/10:5, 32) is a matter of narrative style. "The legend itself does not at this point disclose what is to be the outcome, so tension arises when, in the retelling of the story, both the message and the ultimate purpose of the angel's appearance are included."[81] As previously in 10:45–46, verses 15–16 again adduce the similarity of the Gentile Christian experience with the Pentecost event.

By way of summary, we may safely agree with Dibelius concerning Luke's understanding of the significance of the Cornelius story.

> Luke wanted to show how the will of God was made known to Peter in the conversion of Cornelius; it was because of this same will that the Gentiles were called, and just how this came about Luke proposed to relate immediately afterwards (11.20f) in several examples concerning (named) people in Antioch. Here, however, the classic example was to be described the decisive first manifestation of this will. This is how Luke regards the story of Cornelius, and as such he makes Peter quote it[82] . . . and James. . . .[83] Therefore, right at the beginning of the story of Cornelius, God must speak words of authority to Peter, telling him to go to the Gentiles.[84]

Acts 15:7 is dramatic evidence of the important role this story plays in preparing for the resolution of subsequent conflicts. Even apart from its protracted and repetitive narrative line, Luke stresses this episode's importance by placing it at the end of a series of three conversion stories and by creating an effective coordination of individuals and events by the use of visions.

THE TRADITIONS REWORKED BY LUKE AND ITS HISTORICAL ELEMENTS

This section contains neither traditional nor historical elements.

THE HISTORICAL VALUE OF LUKE'S ACCOUNT

Luke quite purposely told the Cornelius story in such great detail—no doubt to achieve the highest possible degree of verisimilitude and thematic impact. He knew that the participants in the Jerusalem conference were divided over the mission to the Gentiles, and commissioning Paul to that task was a compromise hesitantly accepted—if indeed it was—by a powerful group within the Jerusalem community.

Therefore, we can see how bold a fabrication was the story of the centurion Cornelius. To claim that at the turning point in the history of the Christian mission stands one man alone—Peter, a tool in the hands of God—is as dramatically compelling as it is untrue.

Yet despite Luke's obvious concern in reproducing the story of Cornelius, Haenchen would have it otherwise: "He has told it in such a way that it can be understood only from the standpoint of its theological meaning. Thus viewed, even those parts which otherwise appear odd and fragmentary lose their strangeness, and the effect of the whole is marvelously rounded and self-contained."[85] In view of the kind of fairy tale Luke asks us to believe, this is nonsensical talk.

[27]
ACTS 11:19–30
THE CHURCH AT ANTIOCH

(19) *Now those who had been scattered because of the persecution that arose over Stephen traveled* as far as Phoenicia and Cyprus and Antioch, *addressing the word* to none except Jews. (20) But there were some natives of Cyprus and Cyrene among them, and these, when they arrived at Antioch, began to address the Greeks as well, *preaching the **LORD** Jesus.* (21) *And the hand of the **LORD** was with them, **and a great number who believed turned to the LORD**.*

(22) *The news reached the ears of the church in Jerusalem, and they sent Barnabas to Antioch.* (23) *When he arrived and saw the divine grace at work, he rejoiced and exhorted them all to remain faithful to the **LORD** with steadfast purpose*; (24) *for he was a good man, full of the Holy Spirit and of faith. **And a large company was added to the LORD**.*

(25) So Barnabas went to Tarsus and looked for Saul; (26a) and when he had found him, he brought him to Antioch. For a whole year they met with the church, and taught a large company of people.

(26b) It was at Antioch that the disciples were for the first time called Christians.

(27) Now *in those days* prophets came down from Jerusalem to Antioch. (28) And one of them *named* Agabus stood up and foretold by the Spirit that there would be a great famine over all the world (this took place in the days of Claudius). (29) So the disciples determined, everyone according to his ability, to send relief to the brothers living in Judea. (30) And they did so, sending it to the elders by the hand of Barnabas and Saul.

OUTLINE

19–21: Spread of the preaching of the gospel to Antioch. Notice of success

22–24: (After this event is noted by the Jerusalem community) sending of Barnabas to Antioch. Notice of success

25–26a: Barnabas brings Saul from Tarsus to Antioch. They work together there for a year

26b: Passing remark about the origin of the name "Christians"

27–30: Prophecy of a general famine by Agabus and the taking of a collection from Antioch to Jerusalem by Barnabas and Saul

LUKE'S PURPOSE

Verses 19–21: Verse 19a literally matches 8:4a, which in turn refers to 8:1. The verse is not a continuation of the interrupted statement 8:4a but a link to it. Luke wants to describe the continuation of the mission of the Hellenists, whose external stimulus was the killing of Stephen in 7:54–8:1a. To cite Julius Wellhausen freely, after the delayed intermezzo of Paul's conversion, and after Peter's missionary journey, a contradiction to that of Philip, Luke refers back to chapter 8. In verses 19b–20 the phrases "address the word"[86] and "preach the Lord Jesus"[87] derive from Luke. Verse 19b points out that the Hellenists originally turned only to Jews, whereas according to verse 20 the Hellenists addressed Gentiles[88] also. Underlying verses 19–20 is the pattern "to the Jews first—then to the Gentiles" which also holds for Luke's Paul.[89] For the other Lukan features in this section, see the words and phrases printed in italics.

Verses 22–24: This section's derivation from Luke is evident from its language and content. Note that as in other cases the Jerusalem community intervenes when a decisive change is about to occur. This is especially true when 11:22–24 is compared with 8:14–24: Both passages are intended to show Jerusalem's sanction of the Hellenists' outreach and to attest the unity of the two groups within the earliest community. In fact, the danger of a split was very real, as is suggested by the suspicious independence with which the narratives about the Hellenists and Peter run side by side in Acts 6–12.

Verses 25–26a: Here Luke introduces the soon-to-be hero of his book and has him brought by Barnabas from Tarsus to Antioch.

Verse 26b: In the course of his summary report, Luke introduces an interesting detail about the emergence of the name "Christian," but rather than being part of the narrative, it occurs at the author-reader level. Obviously the historical accuracy of the information in verse 26b depends at least in part on the trustworthiness of the narrative to which verse 26b belongs. Therefore we must carefully examine it by next asking whether any tradition is contained in the account that we have so far analyzed only with an eye to Luke's purpose.

Verses 27–28: "In those days" is a broad expression of time often employed by Luke for joining episodes.[90] The famine extends over the whole world as did Quirinius's census according to Luke 2:1–2. In other words, in both passages the Evangelist is extrapolating sweeping statements from local phenomena. Many famines marked the reign of Claudius, but they were as limited as the census. It is possible that Luke generalized from a famine in Judea that seems to have taken place between 46 and 48 CE.[91] Luke's report of a famine prophesied by Agabus during the reign of Claudius reflects the author's unflagging commitment to embedding the chronicle of salvation in the events of secular history.[92]

Verses 29–30: These verses attest the solidarity of Antioch's satellite church with Jerusalem community; its members send Barnabas and Saul to Jerusalem with money to relieve the suffering of fellow believers. (As often in Acts, Judea is a synecdoche for Jerusalem.) As both the content and the context suggest, Luke is almost certainly the source of this relief mission. The gathering and delivery of the collection bespeak the solidarity of Antioch and Jerusalem, a relationship appropriate to their mutual involvement in salvation history—a process that here is forwarded by the Antiochene community through the future torchbearers, Barnabas and Saul/Paul, whose commissioning is reported in the emphatically positioned final phrase of the section.

THE TRADITIONS REWORKED BY LUKE

Looking at 11:19–30 as a whole we come to recognize that a relatively large number of facts are set side by side with little or no specific narrative context. This increases our suspicion that Luke has condensed a number of traditional pieces and consolidated them using some links of his own making.

Verses 19–21, 22–23: The report of the Hellenist mission to Phoenicia, Cyprus, and Antioch is part of the tradition, since here we have concrete information without a bias. The sources about the mission on *Cyprus* were probably reports about Barnabas—a Greek-speaking Jewish Christian active in the Antioch community (verse 22; cf. Acts 13:1)—on which Luke drew for his information in verse 19. Since Luke garnered the majority of his material from *Antioch* (cf. later verse 26b and 13:1–3; 15:1–2, etc.), he had to include a mention of that city here at the end, all the more since from 13:1 on Antioch will come into the foreground of the narrative. Verses 22–23 reflect a tradition concerning Barnabas's activity in

Antioch (cf. 13:1–2). From this we recognize that linking Barnabas and Jerusalem (cf. earlier 4:36; 9:37) is Luke's doing: Verse 24 fails to recall that in verse 22b the Jerusalem community sent him for no apparent reason to Antioch. Thus the tradition-based link between Barnabas and Antioch is evident.

Verse 20: The note about the mission to the Gentiles is from tradition, since it does not fit into Luke's view of history. But it indicates that the Hellenists were the first to inaugurate a Gentile mission; it was not, as Luke claims in chapters 10–11, Peter with his conversion of Cornelius.

Verses 25–26a: Tarsus as the place of Paul's stay is confirmed by 11:30. The activity of Barnabas and Paul in Antioch for the period of a year is probably part of the tradition, since it is a specific unmotivated report in a context containing miscellaneous fragments of tradition.

Verse 26b: The information about the origin of the name "Christian" in Antioch probably goes back to an isolated piece of information that Luke has inserted here; a less likely possibility is that it was part of the source that goes back to the Hellenists.

Verses 27–29: Since verse 27 contains an interesting detail about the activity of prophets in Jerusalem and Antioch, it might reflect tradition, although the only specific information we have appears in the next verse. The prophet Agabus (verse 28) also appears in 21:10, where he prophesies Paul's end. If his appearance stems from the Evangelist, his original place in the tradition may be in the context of 11:27–30. In that case his prophecy would relate at the level of tradition to a famine in Judea under Claudius. But more probable is the opposite assumption, that he derives from the source about Paul's last visit to Jerusalem.[93] The information about a collection (in Greek, *diakonia*) for Jerusalem appears only at this place in Acts, whereas it recurs often in Paul—where it is designated with the same Greek noun.[94] For that reason the note about the collection for Jerusalem is a piece tradition directly connected with an account about Paul's collection trip to Jerusalem.

Verse 30: The journey made by Barnabas and Paul to Jerusalem appears elsewhere in Acts only in 15:1–4, and in Paul in Gal. 2:1. One can decide whether at the level of tradition it relates to taking a collection to Jerusalem only on the basis of historical considerations.

HISTORICAL ELEMENTS

The traditions behind verses 19–30, namely that the Hellenists began the missions to the Gentiles on Cyprus, in Phoenicia, and at Antioch, are without doubt historical. Their origins probably lie in the middle 30s.

A Note on the Origin of the Name "Christians" (in Greek, Christianoi)

The ending –*anoi* is a Latinism and denotes the supporters of a person (Pompeians, Herodians, etc.). In the second century names of sects were formed in an analogous way (Valentinians, Simonians, etc.). For this reason it is uncertain whether the name Christians denotes *political* followers of Christ, but tradition is surely correct in reporting that the name "Christian," like the above parallels, was a term used by outsiders. In other words, the name does not derive from the program of the group concerned, but is a term probably assigned by political authorities seeking to classify it, or by rival groups intent on defining boundaries. Soon, however, Christians adopted the name, probably because it aptly reflected their primary concern. Only two generations later Bishop Ignatius of Antioch, the very place where this designation first arose, in a letter to the Magnesians not only spoke of "Christianity" (in Greek, *Christianismos*) as a matter of course, but triumphantly proclaimed: "For Christianity did not base its faith on Judaism, but Judaism on Christianity" (10:3).[95] Accordingly, one may conclude that the name "Christians" reported in Acts 11:26b derives from outsiders in Antioch, and that it did not take long for the people thus described to adopt that name. Thus Mark 9:41 speaks of those who belong to Christ, which may already reflect the name "Christians."

A Note on the Cooperation of Paul and Barnabas

The tradition that for a considerable period of time Paul and Barnabas worked together in the Antiochene mission has a high degree of probability. We find Barnabas and Paul together at Antioch during the incident at Antioch (Gal. 2:11–14); Paul and Barnabas went together to Jerusalem (Gal. 2:1) when the Jerusalem conference took place; and they were put in charge of the mission to the Gentiles (Gal. 2:9). Last but not least, 1 Cor. 9:6 adduces their previous partnership.

On the basis of a Pauline chronology reconstructed on the sole basis of the letters[96] we must at this point reject a journey of Paul and Barnabas to Jerusalem in order to deliver a collection. Moreover, Luke used the traditional material underlying Acts 21 (see p. 280 below) to create the collection motif and, probably, the prophet Agabus. It is striking that throughout Acts 15–21 we find no mention of the collection. The journey of Barnabas and Paul may have come from one or more elements of the traditions dealing with the Jerusalem conference—material that he could easily duplicate here.

Not to be ruled out is the somewhat more tenuous possibility that what we have here represents a historically reliable tradition telling of a gift by the community at Antioch for the relief of their Jerusalem brethren. After all, Paul committed himself at the conference to gathering financial support for the Jerusalem community, and Barnabas similarly pledged the support of the Antiochene community.[97] The tradition thus envisaged would have reflected the Antioch community's taking up a collection for the relief of the Jerusalem church.

THE HISTORICAL VALUE OF LUKE'S ACCOUNT

This section confirms what has been said previously on more than one occasion. Luke used valuable historical material but in nearly every detail changed the facts in order to support his preconceived agendas and interpretations. He subordinates the Hellenists to Jerusalem, changes the chronology to suit his notion of the history of salvation, and even ascribes the beginning of the Gentile mission to Peter. If we did not have the Paul's letters, Luke's twisting of the historical record would almost surely have gone unnoticed.

[28]
ACTS 12:1–25
HEROD'S PERSECUTION OF THE JERUSALEM CHURCH;
PETER'S IMPRISONMENT AND MIRACULOUS ESCAPE

(1) *Around that time* **Herod the king** *laid hands on* some from the church in order to mistreat them. (2) He killed James the brother of John by the sword, (3) *and when he saw that it pleased* **THE JEWS**, he proceeded to arrest Peter also. This was during the days of Unleavened Bread. (4) *And when he had seized him, he put him in prison, delivering him over to four squads of soldiers to guard him, intending after the Passover to bring him out to the people.* (5a) So Peter was kept in prison, (5b) *but earnest PRAYER for him was made to God by the church.*

(6a) *On the very night when* **Herod** *was about to bring him out,* (6b) Peter was sleeping between two soldiers, bound with two chains, and sentries before the door were guarding the prison. (7a) And look, an ___angel___ of the Lord stood next to him, and a light shone in the cell. (7b) *He tapped Peter on the side and woke him, saying, "Get up quickly." And the chains fell from his hands.* (8) And the ___angel___ said to him, "Dress yourself and put on your sandals." And he did so. And he said to him, "Wrap your cloak around you and follow me." (9a) And he went out and followed him. (9b) *He did not know that what was being done by the* ***angel*** *was real, but thought he was seeing a vision.* (10) When they had passed the first sentinel and the second, they came to the iron-gate leading into the city. It opened for them of its own accord, and they went out and went along one street, and immediately the ***angel*** left him. (11) *When Peter came to himself, he said, "Now I am sure that the Lord has sent his* ***angel*** *and rescued me from the hand of Herod and from all that the people of* ***THE JEWS*** *were expecting."*

(12) When he realized this, he went to the house of Mary, the mother of John whose other name was Mark, where *many* were gathered together and were praying. (13) And when he knocked at the door of the gateway, a servant girl *named* Rhoda came to answer. (14) *Recognizing* Peter's voice, in her *joy* she did not open the gate but ran in and *reported* that Peter was standing at the gate. (15) They *said to* her, "You are out of your mind." But she kept insisting that it was so, and they kept saying, "It is his ***angel!***" (16) But Peter continued knocking, and when they opened, they saw him and were *amazed*. (17a) But *motioning* to them with his hand to be silent, (17b) he *described* to them how the Lord had brought him out of the prison. (17c) *And he said, "Tell this to James and to the brothers."* (17d) Then he departed and went to another place.

(18) *Now when day came, there was no little disturbance among the soldiers over what had become of Peter.* (19) *And after* **Herod** *searched for him and did not find him, he examined the sentries and ordered their execution. Then he went down from Judea to Caesarea and spent time there.*

(20) Now **Herod** was angry with the people of Tyre and Sidon, and they came to him in a body, and having won over Blastus, the king's chamberlain, they sought reconciliation, because their country depended on the king's country for food. (21) On an appointed day **Herod** put on his royal robes, took his seat upon the throne, and delivered an oration to them. (22) And the people were shouting, "The voice of a god, and not of a man!" (23) Immediately an ***angel*** of the Lord struck him down, because he did not give God the glory, and he was eaten by worms and breathed his last.

(24) *But the word of God increased and multiplied.* (25) *And after the completion of their service to Jerusalem Barnabas and Saul returned [to Antioch], bringing with them John, whose other name was Mark.*

OUTLINE

1–2: Execution of James the son of Zebedee on the orders of Herod
3–17: Imprisonment and release of Peter. He leaves Jerusalem

18–19: Execution of Peter's sentries on the order of Herod
20–23: Death of Herod in Caesarea
24–25: Summary. Return of Barnabas and Saul from Jerusalem to Antioch

LUKE'S PURPOSE

This chapter is in effect a parenthetical continuation of the previous episode. Barnabas and Saul, the bearers of the collection there reported as being sent from Antioch to Jerusalem, are in that latter city during the persecution—though they are not incorporated into the story—and return to Antioch soon after Peter's release and his strangely ambiguous departure to "another place" (verse 17d). This typically Markan technique of interweaving stories—in this case inserting a new incident between the sending and the return of messengers (cf. Mark 6:7–13, 30, par. Luke 9:1–6, 10)—may be Luke's model for this scene.

By again and again employing this theme of the release of apostles/missionaries (see also 4:1–22; 5:17–42; 16:19–40), Luke intends to emphasize his conviction that nothing can thwart God's plan of salvation. Like the summary notes in 9:31 and elsewhere, verse 24 once again assures the reader that the word of the Lord will overcome all its enemies. Luke's editorial pen can be recognized in the following examples.

Verses 1–2: The note "around that time" in verse 1 has a parallel in 19:23 and Luke 13:1; the verb "to lay on hands" also appears elsewhere in Luke-Acts.[98] "Herod the king" is Agrippa I, the grandson of Herod the Great.[99] He lived from 10 BCE to 44 CE.[100] The name Luke uses for Agrippa, Herod, is nowhere else documented. Obviously he has chosen the name Herod here to designate Agrippa I "as another persecutor in the Church's Judaean history, following Herod, Herod Antipas, Herodias and the Herodians, who figure as persecutors in the Gospel stories."[101] The wording of his actions "conveys the impression of a summary execution."[102] Yet only in verse 2 does concrete action surface. I am therefore inclined to consider the king's actions against "some from the church" as a generalization on the basis of the concrete information in verse 2; here it serves to increase the danger to the church, and after that to narrate the liberation from the danger by God or his angel.

Verse 3: "Hitherto Acts has presented the Jewish people as well-disposed to the Christians, and only the Sadducean leaders as hostile."[103] Luke probably created the clause, "When he saw that it pleased the Jews," in order effect a smooth transition to the subsequent attack on one of the community's leading figures. Thus verse 11 works together with verse 3 in identifying both Herod and the Jewish people as Peter's enemies. The changed perception of the people is as unhistorical as it is unexplained; it shows Luke's hand in shaping the story. Indeed, when James the brother of Jesus was attacked two decades later, that action was sufficiently unpopular that the responsible official, Ananus, was removed from power.[104] James's execution (verse 2) and the attack on Peter (verse 3) recall the hostility against Stephen (Acts 6–7). Indeed, both in Jerusalem[105] and in the Diaspora[106] we find a uniformly negative portrait of the Jerusalem populace. That no one replaces James indicates the end of a chapter in salvation history: The era of the earliest community is over, and those who will carry the mission to the Gentiles are now taking the stage.

Verses 4–5b: Verse 4 is an editorial anticipation of the following narrative. The exaggerated size of the military guard and the intention to have a dramatic public presentation (even though it never occurs) prepare for the statements in the subsequent story about the guarding of Peter by the soldiers (verses 5–6) and the anticipated presentation (verse 6). In verse 5b Luke gives the impression that fervent prayer of the community will contribute to the miraculous release of Peter. Since in verses 12 and 17 the community had not yet fully assembled for prayer, this half-verse is surely Luke's insertion.

Verses 6–7: Mentioning Herod (verse 6a) echoes verse 1 to keep him at the center of the story. For the formulations in verse 7a, see Luke 2:9. In verse 7b the Greek word *pataxas* (here meaning "tapped") has no doubt been chosen to serve as a contextual variant to *epataxen* ("struck down") at verse 23. In both cases the Greek verb "to strike" shows an angel of the Lord carrying out the rescue or the punishment.

Verse 8: "The angel even directs the stages by which Peter gets dressed. The Apostle simply does as he is told."[107]

Verses 9–11: Peter's bewilderment in verse 9b is resolved in the editorial verse 11. Since the event—which Peter experiences as a vision—is incredible yet presented as true, verse 9b also derives from Luke. Peter's eventual recognition of the "reality" of the event is pictured in verse 11: "Now I am sure that the Lord has sent his angel and rescued me from the hand of Herod and from all that the people of the Jews were expecting." (What he recognizes as "real" has obviously been adapted from verse 9b.) The negative portrayal of Herod and the Jewish people comports with the above comment on verse 3. The use of direct quotation makes the scene livelier and emphasizes the significance of Peter's insight.[108]

Verses 12–17: The Evangelist's language permeates this section. Moreover, he has clearly added John Mark to verse 12 in order to prepare for verse 25, and has created the artistic composition of the recognition scene in verses 13–16 on the basis of a simpler report. Finally, he has inserted verse 17c ("Tell this to James and to the brothers") by way of introducing the new leader of the Jerusalem Christian community—a purpose that does not become clear until chapter 21.

Verses 18–19: The section as a whole derives from Luke. The litotes in verse 18, "no little," occurs frequently in Luke. For the formulation "there was no little disturbance" see 19:23. In verse 19 the note about the execution of the negligent sentries derives wholly from Luke, for just as he stresses the miracle that freed Peter, he also highlights Herod's cruelty. Verse 19b clears the stage for the next episode.

Verses 20–23: Luke has included a tradition depicting Agrippa's death in such a way as to show it as God's punishment for his persecution of the earliest community.

Verses 24–25: The summary in verse 24 shows the continuous and widespread dissemination of God's word even in the face of persecution. With the return of Barnabas and Saul to Antioch (verse 25, cf. 11:30), and after a brief episode with Barnabas and a report of the Jerusalem conference, Paul takes up his starring role for the rest of the book. Having John Mark accompany him was somewhat awkwardly anticipated in verse 12.

THE TRADITIONS REWORKED BY LUKE

Verses 1–2: Luke has taken the report of the killing of James the son of Zebedee on the orders of Agrippa I from a tradition. It is impossible to decide whether he abbreviated an extended report about a martyrdom or whether the news of the death of James under Agrippa I had come down to him without further description.

It is often suggested that verses 1–2 and Mark 10:38–39 are directly related.[109] Since Eduard Schwartz[110] there should no longer be any room for doubt that this passage reflects the violent deaths of John and James, the sons of Zebedee. (It was standard practice among the earliest Christians to assign retroactively to Jesus predictions of events.)[111] In the view of Eduard Schwartz, Zebedee's two sons were martyred under Agrippa I, but Luke purposely omitted John from Acts 12. If true, this would be significant for our knowledge of Primitive Christianity; it would provide a *terminus ad quem* for the Jerusalem conference. Since Paul (Gal. 2:9) places John son of Zebedee at that gathering, it must be dated before 44, and not, as some would have it, around 48. Unfortunately for that theory, however, Gal. 2:9 itself tells against it, for it mentions only John, and that, taken together with the tradition in Acts 12:2, suggests the death of James. By noting that in Gal. 2:9 (in contrast with Gal. 1:19) Paul no longer feels it necessary to point out that James is the Lord's brother, we are impelled to the same assumption. Last of all, it is difficult to construct a convincing reason for the omission of John's name from Acts 12:2. Therefore, however attractive Eduard Schwartz's proposal on Acts 12:2 may be, it must at last be seen as improbable, and so must the notion of a direct connection between Mark 10:38–39 and Acts 12:2.[112]

Verses 3–17: The previous analysis showed that verses 3–4, 5b–6a, 9b, 11, and 17c derive from Luke; the account of Rhoda's recognition (verses 13–16) also shows Lukan trademarks. That a tradition may be thus delineated by subtraction becomes eminently likely in view of the following considerations.

(a) Although motifs typical of Hellenistic miraculous release stories—like fetters falling off (verse 7) and doors opening by themselves (verse 10)—do not prove the existence of a tradition, they are strongly suggestive of such a presence.

(b) It is not difficult to identify the probable beginning and the end of the tradition. Since verse 4 provides an anticipatory situation, verse 5a must be the beginning. Verse 17d can be clearly recognized as the concluding element in Luke's source: surely no narrator as creative as Luke would end a section on such an insignificant note (in Acts 15 Peter is again in Jerusalem), yet it suits well with a story that lacks both interest in details and even a reference to the miraculous release.

(c) The extensive use of local color in verse 10, the wealth of personal details lavished on the portraits of Rhoda the maid and Mary, and the specification of Mary's house as the place where the Christians meet add up to a strong argument for tradition.

The apparent tradition we have thus discerned behind verses 12:5–17 contains Peter's imprisonment in Jerusalem, his miraculous release, the amazement of the believers who had gathered to pray in Mary's house, and Peter's departure from the city. A form critical analysis would surely note the parallel to typical pattern of miraculous release stories. But this hardly exhausts the possibilities, for the tradition was probably based on a simpler kind of recognition scene. (Though one might prefer to discover two different traditions in the miraculous release and the recognition, such an attempt will involve more difficulties than the above assumption.) Jerusalem Christians may well have created this tradition out of their recognition and awe at the "miraculous" release from prison of Peter, the disciple of the Lord. As for Peter's command in verse 17c to tell "James and the brothers" about his liberation, the message reflects Luke's knowledge of James' special role in the structure of the Jerusalem church (cf. 1 Cor 15:7), especially since so far James has played no role in the Acts account.

Verses 20–23: This piece is based on a tradition that told about the death of Agrippa I. A conflict of some sort having arisen between him and the people of Tyre and Sidon, the latter solicited the good offices of the chamberlain Blastus as mediator. We are given no further details about the settlement, but are informed that Agrippa, dressed in royal finery, delivered a speech (presumably to the people of Sidon and Tyre), upon hearing which the people exclaimed, "[That is] the voice of a god, and not of a man." Because Agrippa accepted their praise instead of assigning the glory to God, an angel of the Lord struck him dead, and worms ate his corpse.

That here we have a tradition worked over by Luke is evident from the many details it contains, from the difference between the reason for Agrippa's death given by the tradition and that suggested in Acts 12:1 (Agrippa's persecution of the church) and from Josephus's parallel account of the death of Agrippa.[113] The Acts version seems to be an epitome of Josephus's story, but Luke's redaction blurs such details as the position of Blastus and the role of the royal robes and fails to demonstrate any connection between Agrippa's controversy with the people of Sidon and Tyre and his speech. In both cases, however, death is the penalty for accepting divine accolades. In this concurrence we see the Jewish origin of the tradition.[114] "Both accounts report that the flattering crowd deified Agrippa. That is, his sin was not a solicitation of deification but rather only the failure to reject it."[115] That Agrippa died from an infestation of worms (Acts 12:23) or that violent pains in his entrails preceded his demise (Josephus) are two variations on the widespread theme that a horrible death was the fate of those who despise God (cf. Acts 1:18). Yet note that Josephus is friendlier to Agrippa than Luke is.[116]

HISTORICAL ELEMENTS

Verses 1–2: The killing of James the son of Zebedee on the orders of Agrippa I,[117] who was king from 41 to 44 CE, is probably historical. James was no longer alive at the conference a few years later, for otherwise he would have been mentioned in Paul's account in Gal. 2:9. And since Mark 10:38–39 contains an ex post facto prophecy of the martyrdom of James and his brother John, it is natural to make Agrippa responsible for the killing of James.[118] Concerning the reason for Agrippa's persecuting the Christians, Martin Hengel has pointed out that the king "sought above all to secure and keep the good will of the Sadducean priestly party of the nobility who were the political leaders."[119] Given this situation, it made sense for Agrippa to attack a group that focused so much on the resurrection of its leader who himself had questioned the significance of the present Temple.[120]

Verses 3–17: Any judgment as to the historical value of the story of Peter's miraculous release depends in large measure on the historicity of Agrippa's complicity in James's death. While one must emphasize that the historical standing of the miraculous release is denied by the story itself, it is still eminently reasonable to accept the historical core that Agrippa had Peter arrested. Such an assumption is well supported by Agrippa's recent execution of James, for at that time Peter was among the leaders of the Jerusalem community. The legend seems also to contain the historical nucleus that Peter left Jerusalem. This alone would explain why some years later James the brother of Jesus represented the earliest community at the conference and Peter was his subordinate.[121]

In order to leave Jerusalem at all, Peter obviously had to be released from prison. It is not surprising that scholars differ over how he was set free—that is, when the question is even raised: Some argue that the issue cannot be resolved inasmuch as verses 7–10 bear such a strong tincture of the ancient miraculous release stereotype. Roloff, however, conjectures "that the apostle managed to escape from prison in dramatic circumstances and that afterwards the group around Mary and her son John Mark supported him in his secret departure from Jerusalem."[122] While that proposal unfortunately begins with nothing more than a demythologized paraphrase of the account in Acts, its second part represents as good a guess as any. It also possible that once he recognized the outrage caused by James's execution, Agrippa had Peter released. Yet we simply do not know.

That the Jerusalem community included Mary and her maid Rhoda and that Mary had a house in the city are very likely historical. Yet that does not mean that Mary's house is a house church of the Hellenists in Jerusalem.[123]

Verses 20–23: Although Agrippa's reported conflict with the citizens of Tyre and Sidon lacks corroboration, we know from the Hebrew Bible (1 Kings 5:23; Ezek. 27:17) that Phoenicia's economy had long been partially dependent on Palestine, a situation that could well be reflected in verse 20.[124] We therefore have some warrant for supposing the reported conflict, the desire for peace, and the mediating role of Agrippa's chamberlain to be historical. The tradition about Agrippa's death in Caesarea is corroborated by Josephus's report, however skeptical we may be of the legendary details of both accounts.

THE HISTORICAL VALUE OF LUKE'S ACCOUNT

The moral of Luke's history writing is that prayer can achieve great things, even the liberation of a prisoner from a heavily guarded jail. For God's plans are inexorable and they provide for keeping the elect safe just as they do for the elimination of enemies. Yet when even the elect get killed—and it is certainly one of the qualities of Luke's historical writing that occasionally he reports such facts—he usually prefers neither to focus on it nor to embellish it.

To be blunt, the course of events that Luke relates in Acts 12 with respect to Peter's liberation did not happen as he claims. No angel led Peter out of the prison and no chains fell from his hands. By telling an edifying story about the total victory of God over a ruthless enemy of the church, Luke has again introduced theology at the expense of history.

The following quote from a scholarly commentary on Acts shows what difficulty a "believing" theologian faces if he or she takes the text of Acts at face value:

The person who believes in the reality of the supernatural will not find it difficult to accept this story as it stands, along with other, similar stories in the bible
and Christian history. In this particular instance there is no element in the story
which forbids such a view of it.[125]

To this it should, of course, be added that many other "miracles" reported in
Acts require critical scholars to deny their historicity when so compelled by
analysis of the texts. It is *not* a question of belief in the reality of the supernatural. See further above, pages 22–23.

Martin Hengel's suggestion concerning the liberation of Peter deserves special note because it reveals the degree to which even a famous historian of
Judaism and Primitive Christianity can be led astray. He writes,

Could an action by the anti-Herodian and anti-Sadducean opposition, say from
Pharisaic circles, underlie this "liberation" (quite apart from the narrative elaboration)? The "angel" who freed Peter appears in the narrative as a young man
[one cannot discover where—GL] whom Peter did not know and [who] did not
introduce himself to him, but disappeared again quickly into the darkness of the
night. At that time—and later, at the time of the execution of James [the brother
of Jesus in 62 CE]—there were evidently Pharisees who were well disposed
towards Christians (cf. Acts 15.5) and who wanted to put an and to this demonstration of power by Agrippa I and the clientele of the high-priestly nobility for
religious and political reasons. The whole narrative has very earthly features,
like the powerful blow with which Peter is awoken and the precise orders that
he has to get ready to travel quickly. In this case all the typological echoes and
Old Testament allusions that the commentators introduce lead in the wrong
direction. Was this "liberation" perhaps a successful action on the part of the
(Pharisaic?) opponents and of the high-priestly and Herodian party, which
wanted to prevent a further spectacular "judicial" murder of a Christian?[126]

Rebuttal: This is the worst sort of example of a scholar historicizing myth.
To be able to do so, he has to ignore the specific texts. For one thing, the note
about the Pharisees as members of the community at Acts 15:5 is clearly
Luke's fabrication; for another, the person who leads Peter out of the prison
is never called "young man" but always "angel" (verses 7–11: five times).
Hengel's diatribes against other scholars are wont to lead him overboard.[127]
Unfortunately, his extraordinary erudition has not prevented his exegesis
from being vulnerable to criticism at many points. It might be great fun to
concoct the story of a nocturnal undercover operation—especially when it
can be dramatically interwoven with a bit of cloak-and-dagger intrigue about
an internal revolt by wise, upright, and nobly motivated members of a

repressive regime. (Dare one think of it as a tongue-in-cheek Judeo-Roman Watergate with chains instead of tape?) And no doubt imagination is a fine thing; but when impressed into service by belief to take the place of critical scholarship, it is soon revealed as a sad travesty of both.

[29]
ACTS 13:1–12
BARNABAS AND SAUL ON CYPRUS

(1) Now there were at Antioch in the local church prophets and teachers: Barnabas, Simeon who was called Niger, Lucius of Cyrene, Manaen, who had been brought up together with Herod the tetrarch, and Saul. (2) While they were worshipping the Lord and _fasting_, the Holy Spirit said, "Set apart for me Barnabas and Saul for the work to which I have called them." (3) Then after _fasting_ and _praying_ they laid their hands on them and sent them off.

(4) So, being sent out by the **Holy Spirit**, they went down to Seleucia, and from there they sailed to Cyprus. (5) When they arrived at Salamis, _they proclaimed the word of God in the synagogues of the Jews._ And they had John to assist them.

(6) When they had gone through the whole island as far as Paphos, they came upon a certain MAGICIAN, a Jewish false prophet _named_ Bar-Jesus. (7) He was with the proconsul, Sergius Paulus, _a man of intelligence, who summoned_ Barnabas and Saul and _sought to hear the word of God._ (8) But Elymas the MAGICIAN—_for that is the meaning of his name—opposed them, seeking to turn the proconsul away from the faith._ (9) _But_ Saul, _who was also called_ Paul, _filled with the **Holy Spirit**, looked intently at him_ (10) _and said, "You son of the devil, you enemy of all righteousness, full of all deceit and villainy, will you not stop making crooked the straight paths of the Lord?_ (11) _And now, look, the hand of the Lord is upon you, and you will be blind and unable to see the sun for a certain period." Immediately mist and darkness fell upon him, and he groped about for someone to lead him by the hand._ (12) _Then the proconsul believed, when he saw what had occurred, for he was astonished at the teaching about the Lord._

OUTLINE

1–3: The sending out of Barnabas and Saul by order of the Holy Spirit
4–5: Journey of Barnabas and Paul from Antioch via Seleucia to Cyprus
and the preaching in the synagogues of Salamis
6–12: Successful appearance before the proconsul Sergius Paulus in
Paphos and the defeat of the magician Bar-Jesus Elymas

LUKE'S PURPOSE

Verses 1–3: Luke has purposely placed Barnabas at the head of the list and Saul
at its end in order to highlight the following chapter's two protagonists. The other
three persons, since they are unknown to the reader, are assigned further identifying details. The notion that the Holy Spirit is capable of speech derives from
Luke (see 8:29; 10:19). For verse 3 see 6:6; both passages report hands being laid
on a particular group with prayer, but here fasting is added. Both practices will
appear in the commissioning of elders in 14:23, a passage that is clearly redactional (cf. Luke 2:37). The parallel between verse 3 (which uses the verb "to fast"
[in Greek, *nêsteuein*) and 14:23 (in which the noun "fasting" [in Greek, *nêsteia*]
appears) allows us to conclude that verse 3 goes back to Luke, especially since
it picks up the verb "to fast" of verse 2 (see the underlining).

Verses 4–5: The note in verse 4 about Barnabas and Saul being sent out by
the Holy Spirit echoes verse 2, in which the Holy Spirit commissioned them.
Verse 5a reflects Luke's scheme of going first to the Jews; the "word of God" as
the content of preaching appears elsewhere three times in this chapter (verses 7c,
44, 46). The use of the plural "synagogues" in referring to Jewish meeting places
indicates that verse 5 is a summary.

Verses 6–12: Lukan language colors this passage (see the italics in the translation). Luke describes Bar-Jesus first as a sorcerer who is in control of powers.
"But these powers are the false powers with which man should have no truck:
powers opposed to god yet subordinate to God. And so Luke's proof of the superiority of Christianity over magic lies in his demonstrating that the former with
its invocation of the name of Christ is more powerful. Secondly, Bar-Jesus is
called a 'false prophet.'[128] A prophet who speaks against the Christian kerygma
is *ipso facto* a false prophet." Verse 8b is Luke's explanation that magician (in
Greek, *magos*) is a translation of Elymas. He considers Bar-Jesus and Elymas to
be the same person and attests "son of the devil" (verse 10) as the opposite of
Bar-Jesus, which means son of Jesus/Joshua. It should also be noted that the

introduction of Paul's name in verse 9 parallels that of Peter's name in Luke 6:14: Luke's hand is clearly indicated by his previously exclusive use of "Saul" to refer to the apostle who subsequently is always "Paul." In all likelihood Luke associates this change of name with the Sergius Paulus because employing the apostle's Roman name is appropriate now that the mission to the Gentiles has begun.[129] One can hardly regard the correspondence of this name change to that from Bar-Jesus to Elymas as historical coincidence.

A brief analysis of Luke's narrative structure will demonstrate even more clearly than heretofore the evident fact of Luke's editorial hand. For one thing, the story has been stripped of its exposition and conclusion. And after Paul and Barnabas encounter the magician/false prophet (verse 6), the confrontational exchange that one would reasonably expect fails to occur. Rather, immediately following the introduction of the "false prophet" (verse 6b), we find at his side another new figure, Sergius Paulus (verse 7a), who asks to hear the word of God from the two missionaries. Then, of all things, the aforementioned Bar-Jesus is reintroduced as Elymas, but the identity of Bar-Jesus with Elymas is not made clear. When Bar-Jesus Elymas seeks to prevent Sergius Paulus from adopting the true faith offered by the two missionaries, Paul calls down upon the wretch a solemn curse that renders him blind for a "certain period." Though this blinding can hardly be called a "teaching about the Lord," the proconsul became a believer,[130] astonished, i.e., captivated, by the "teaching about the Lord." (The latter key expression picks up the "word of God" in verse 7.) Yet it remains strange that Luke does not report the proconsul's baptism since this ritual existed from the very beginning of the Christian mission.[131] (For an explanation see below, p. 168.)

Luke thus accomplishes two goals: He adduces the inherent connection between spreading God's word and demonstrations of his power (here a punitive miracle), and at the same time stresses the importance of Christian teaching and distinguishes it from magic—lest such a misunderstanding arise from the effect of Paul's curse. These observations make it evident that either Luke has radically dismembered a traditional story, or he has inserted notes into a story that was seriously lacking in details.[132] At any event the author is once again intent (as he was in chapter 8) to distinguish between Christianity and rival religious persuasions. Accordingly, he brands Bar-Jesus Elymas (as he did Simon "Magus") by making him a magician—and note his demotion to the status of false prophet in verse 6. (For the connection between magic and being a Jew see 16:20–21; 19:13). By limiting the period of Elymas's blindness, Luke apparently holds open, as he previously did in chapter 8, the possibility that other rivals may be converted.

Distinguishing Christians from enemies is not, of course, Luke's sole purpose. He is also interested in the person of Sergius Paulus, whose conversion to Christianity is truly extraordinary; since here it is no mere centurion like Cornelius in Acts 10, but a Roman proconsul who accepts the faith, we are justified in seeing Lukan apologetic at work. Had the convert's high rank appeared in the tradition, Luke would surely have gone a step further and reported the official's baptism and, no doubt, an outpouring of the Spirit.

It is fitting to conclude my redaction analysis of Acts 13:1–12 with Haenchen's comment:

> Luke's story . . . serves several purposes. First, it shows that at the outset of the Pauline mission the highest Roman authority of a province, the proconsul, "came to faith." What better *apologia* for Christianity could there be? There are many passages ahead that will confirm that Luke, especially in the second half of Acts, wanted to present such an apologia. But we could also refer back to the story of Cornelius: the first Gentile convert was actually a Roman officer. Second—and this is especially important in the Lucan design—Paul's feat enables the real hero, to whom only a modest role has hitherto been assigned, to step forward into the first place.[133]

THE TRADITIONS REWORKED BY LUKE

Verse 1: The five persons' names and the place name (Antioch) are part of the tradition. This conclusion is confirmed by the detailed descriptions of Symeon, Lucius, and Manaen, as well as by the fact that Acts elsewhere depicts prophets as itinerant (11:27–28; 21:10). One cannot be sure, however, that the list of five came to Luke in its present form, for his interference is clear from the position of Barnabas and Saul.[134] To be sure, the number five is unexpected, and the designation of the individuals as "prophets and teachers" may be part of the tradition, for we can no longer decide who are teachers and who are prophets.[135] We do not find teachers elsewhere in Luke, but the teacher-prophet connection is evident in Didache 13:10–12, even more in 15:1, and (together with apostles) appears in 1 Cor. 12:28—which certainly derives from tradition, and may well come from Antioch.[136] The connection of fasting (verse 42) with "worshipping the Lord" goes back to tradition. It should be noted that the latter phrase is best translated "serving the Lord," for while it includes prayer, it has a broader significance. The active presence in Antioch of both prophets and teachers means that we are to assume a relatively settled community (though Agabus is a different matter).

Verses 2–5: Whether the sending out of Barnabas and Saul was part of the tradition, and whether they mark the beginning of a continuous source are issues that must wait until after the completion of the analysis of Acts 13–14.[137]

Verses 6–12: The tradition probably does not indicate Paul's mission on Cyprus; it is a Lukan creation cobbled together from such traditional elements as Barnabas's Cypriot origin, his mission on Cyprus with John Mark, and the joint activities of Barnabas and Paul. The names Saul and Paul (verse 9) derive from tradition, as does the report in verse 6 that the apostle took John Mark with him, though neither "Paul" nor "Mark" were originally part of the story. Both the names and the actions of Sergius Paulus and Bar-Jesus Elymas at verses 6–8 come from the tradition; in view of the name Bar-Jesus, the latter's Jewish origin may stem from tradition and his two names may refer to a single person.[138] It should be stressed, however, that at the level of tradition Sergius Paulus and Bar-Jesus Elymas do not play interrelated roles.

HISTORICAL ELEMENTS

Verse 1: In all likelihood historical facts stand behind the tradition, certainly to the extent that the five persons named served the Antioch community as prophets and/or teachers, though clearly they were subject to reassignment by the Spirit at any time. This movement from settled ministry to itinerant mission and back again comports with Paul's later career: Although he travels widely, he often settles in his communities for considerable periods of time.

Verses 2–8: That Sergius Paulus was an actual person who lived on Cyprus, and that his retainers included a prophet Bar-Jesus Elymas are probably to be accepted, though Acts provides the only evidence linking [a proconsul] Sergius Paulus with Cyprus.[139] That we have numerous examples of associations between members of the Roman nobility and astrologers, magicians, and philosophers is worth noting—witness, for instance, Tiberius's close connection with the astrologer Thrasyllus.[140] Be all that as it may, we have no way of dating these persons. The superfluous "unable to see the sun" in verse 10 could be Luke's way of hinting that a customary activity of Bar-Jesus Elymas was trafficking in observations of Helios.[141] If so, we might wish to see here an analogue to the quizzical allusion to Simon's "thought" (in Greek, *epinoia*) in 8:22.

The double name Saul/Paul that tradition assigns to the apostle may well be historically reliable.[142] The Graecized form of *Sha'ul* is an entirely plausible name for the Benjaminite (Phil 3:5) whose famous forebear was King Saul (1 Sam. 9:1). The Roman name Paul, which the apostle uses in his letters, is obviously historical, since it appears in the letters. It is, furthermore, rare in the East.

Because Luke is the source of Paul's Cyprus mission, the notion that the apostle adopted the name Paul[143] only after his encounter with the Roman pro-consul Sergius Paulus is improbable—unless, of course, a no longer discoverable tradition underlies the redaction. And, as noted above, Sergius Paulus cannot be placed on Cyprus. See also page 302 below on the name Paul.

As we have them in the present context, traditional reports about a shared mission by Barnabas and John Mark are not historical; they are derivatives of the historical mission conducted on Cyprus by Barnabas and John Mark (see 15:39).

THE HISTORICAL VALUE OF LUKE'S ACCOUNT

Verse 12: Luke's report of the conversion of the proconsul Sergius Paulus has found at least partial credence among scholars. Thus Fitzmyer defends it[144] and so does Markus Öhler in his mammoth volume on Barnabas,[145] adding the speculation that Sergius Paulus gave them letters of recommendation to help them in their travel.[146] Kirsopp Lake and Henry Joel Cadbury are not credulous with respect to Luke's story of the conversion of Sergius Paulus, yet they explain Luke's report about it by assuming a misunderstanding on his part. He "may have mistaken courtesy for con-version."[147] Ben Witherington writes, "Certainly, the proconsul responded posi-tively to the message, and apparently also to the miracle. Probably it is best to take the verb in question as an inceptive aorist—the proconsul 'began to believe' at this juncture."[148] What can be said about Simon Magus applies to the proconsul also. Yet "Luke does not see him as truly or fully converted."[149]

Surely Luke knows what he is doing when he so casually reports the conver-sion of Sergius Paulus—or, as Wengst puts it,

> so drily and does not develop it further. As a historical fact the conversion of a proconsul would have had quite a different influence in forming tradition. For Luke the apologetic aim which he can thus already pursue "at the beginning of the Pauline mission" is an important one. The fact that he can actually conceive of a conversion of a proconsul is even more amazing than the story he tells about the centurion Cornelius. He is more restrained when it comes to the procurator Felix and King Agrippa. But at any rate the one has a "rather accu-rate" knowledge of Christianity and is further instructed by Paul (24.22, 24) and the other exclaims, "You almost persuade me to become a Christian" (26.28). The almost matter-of-course way in which according to 9.15 Luke shows Paul among the great of this world belongs in the same context.[150]

Paul never converted Sergius Paulus, the proconsul of Cyprus, for the simple reason that these two individuals never crossed each other's path. Whatever may have been the specific nature and content of his sources, the simple fact is that

Luke has combined and transmuted them into an inspiring but fundamentally fictitious account. It seems equally clear that since his aim was the furtherance of what he considered to be God's plan for the salvation of mankind, he suffered no pangs of conscience over this nobly motivated deception.

[30]
ACTS 13:13–52
PAUL AND BARNABAS IN ANTIOCH OF PISIDIA

(13) Setting sail from Paphos, Paul and those about him came to Perga in Pamphylia. But John left them and returned to Jerusalem. (14a) *Now they passed on from Perga and came to Pisidian Antioch.* (14b) And on the Sabbath day they went into the synagogue and sat down. (15) *After the reading from the Law and the Prophets, the rulers of the synagogue sent a message to them, saying, "Brothers, if you have any word of exhortation for the people, speak."*

(16) *So Paul stood up, and motioning with his hand said:*

*"Men of Israel and you **who fear God**, listen. (17) The God of this people of Israel chose our fathers and made the people great during their stay in the land of Egypt, and with uplifted arm he led them out of it. (18) And for about* <u>*forty years*</u> *he bore with them in the wilderness. (19) And after destroying seven nations in the land of Canaan, he gave them their land as an inheritance (20) for about 450 years. And after that he gave them judges until Samuel the prophet. (21) Then they asked for a king, and God gave them Saul the son of Kish, a man of the tribe of Benjamin, for* <u>*forty years*</u>*. (22) And when he had removed him, he raised up David to be their king, to whom he bore witness and said, 'I have found David the son of Jesse, a man after my heart, who shall do all my will.' (23) Of this man's offspring according to promise God has brought to Israel a savior, Jesus. (24) Before his coming, John had proclaimed a baptism of repentance to all the people of Israel. (25) And as John was fulfilling his course, he said, 'What do you suppose that I am? I am not he. No, but look, after me there comes one, the sandals of whose feet I am not worthy to untie.'*

*(26) BROTHERS, sons of the family of Abraham, and those among you **who fear God**, to us the message of this salvation has been sent. (27) For the inhabitants of Jerusalem and their rulers, knowing neither him nor the voices of the prophets read out every Sabbath, fulfilled them by condemning him. (28) And though they found in him no guilt worthy of death, they asked Pilate to have him executed. (29) And when they had brought about all that was written of him, they*

took him down from the tree and laid him in a tomb. (30) *But God* **raised** *him from the dead.* (31) *He appeared for many days to those who had come up with him from Galilee to Jerusalem, who are his witnesses to the people.* (32) *And we bring you the good news that what God promised to the fathers,* (33) this he has fulfilled to us their children by **raising** Jesus, as also it is written in the second Psalm, 'You are my Son, today I have begotten you.' (34) And as for the fact that he **raised** him from the dead, no more to return to <u>decay</u>, he has spoken in this way, 'I will give you the holy and sure blessings of David.' (35) Therefore he says also in another psalm, 'You will not let your Holy One see <u>decay</u>.' (36a) *For David, after he had served the counsel of God in his own generation,* (36b) *fell asleep and was laid with his fathers and saw* <u>*decay*</u>, (37) *but he whom God* **raised** *up saw no* <u>*decay*</u>.

(38) *Let it be known to you therefore, BROTHERS, that through this man forgiveness of sins is proclaimed to you. Through him everyone who believes is set free from all those sins* (39) *from which you could not be exonerated by the law of Moses.* (40) *Beware, therefore, lest what is said in the Prophets should come about:* (41) *'Look, you scoffers, be astounded and perish; for I am doing a work in your days, a work that you will not believe, even if someone tells it to you.'"*

(42) *As they went out, the people begged that these things might be told them the next Sabbath.* (43) *And after the meeting of the synagogue broke up, many Jews and devout converts to Judaism followed Paul and Barnabas, who, as they spoke with them, urged them to continue in the grace of God.*

(44) *The next Sabbath almost the whole city gathered to hear the* **word of God**. (45) *But when the Jews saw the crowds, they were filled with jealousy and began to contradict what was spoken by Paul, reviling him.* (46) *And Paul and Barnabas spoke out boldly, saying, "It was necessary that the* **word of God** *be spoken first to you. Since you thrust it aside and judge yourselves unworthy of eternal life, look, we are turning to the Gentiles.* (47) *For so the Lord has commanded us, saying, 'I have made you a light for the Gentiles, that you may bring salvation to the ends of the earth.'"*

(48) *And when the Gentiles heard this, they began rejoicing and glorifying the* **word of God**, *and as many as had been destined for eternal life believed.* (49) *And the* **word of the Lord** *spread throughout the whole region.* (50) *But the Jews incited the devout women of high standing and the leading men of the city, stirred up persecution against Paul and Barnabas, and drove them out of their district.* (51) *But they shook off the dust from their feet against them and* went to Iconium. (52) *And the disciples were filled with joy and with the Holy Spirit.*

OUTLINE

13–14a: Journey from Paphos via Perga to Pisidian Antioch. John Mark leaves
14b–15: Paul and Barnabas in the synagogue at Antioch
16–41: Paul's speech
42–43: Success of the sermon among Jews and proselytes
44–52: (On the next Sabbath) Crowds come but the Jews resist. Paul and Barnabas turn to the Gentiles

LUKE'S PURPOSE

Verses 13–14a: The phrase "those about Paul" (in Greek, *hoi peri Paulon*), implies Paul's preeminence—since Barnabas is tacitly defined as Paul's follower—and thus further emphasizes the growing importance of Paul from verse 9 onward. John Mark's departure (verse 13b) is, as it were, necessitated by verse 5c.

Verses 14b–15: The initial visit to the synagogue is part and parcel of Luke's redactional pattern. Verse 15 correctly indicates that a sermon might be delivered subsequent to readings from the Torah and the prophets. Luke erroneously speaks of rulers of the synagogue; there was only one at a time (see the comments on 18:8, 17 below, p. 239).

Verses 16–41: Paul's speech in Pisidian Antioch shows a structural parallel with Jesus' inaugural sermon in Nazareth in Luke 4:16–30: In both cases they stand almost programmatically at the beginning of the protagonist's activities. Ernst Haenchen has given the following apt descriptions:

> Paul with one stroke becomes that great missionary whose image survived in the Church so much more forcefully than his theology. Luke does not hesitate to invent a long speech and put it in his mouth. It is intended (as distinct from the Areopagus speech, addressed to pagans) to show how Paul spoke to a synagogue audience. And that, according to Luke, is how Paul's mission almost invariably began.[151]
>
> Both the sermon and the resultant events are ideal and typical occurrences clothing in historical dress a host of similar crises constantly recurring. The whole Pauline mission—as Luke and his age saw it—is compressed and epitomized in this scene.[152]

In what follows I shall discuss only what clearly derives from Luke.

Verse 16: The gesture of the speaker is similarly described in 12:17; 21:40; 26:1.

Verse 17: "As in Stephen's speech, only more briefly, the orator begins by outlining the history of salvation from the time of the fathers."[153]

Verse 23: For Jesus as Son of David see (apart from the genealogies in Matt. 1 and Luke 3), Luke 1:32–33; 18:38–39; 20:44; Acts 2:31. In addition see Rom. 1:3 as pre-Pauline feature of Jesus as son of David, and Mark 12:35–37 as evidence that at least some Christians disputed that Christ was the son of David.[154]

Verses 24–25: The role of John the Baptist in the history of salvation was already touched upon in 1:22. (See the exegesis above, p. 41, for details.)

Verse 26: The address "brothers" introduces a new section (see later on verse 38).

Verses 27–28: The content of these verses matches the preaching of Peter as related in 3:17–18. This "testifies not to the theological unity of the preaching of the real Peter and the real Paul, but to the composition of both speeches by Luke, whose own theology here again becomes visible."[155] At Luke 23:4 and Acts 3:13 Pilate recognizes Jesus' innocence; here the Jews do the same. "The responsibility for this alteration may be placed . . . not on some divergent tradition, but on Luke's desire for condensation of expression and grammatical simplicity."[156]

Verse 29: While the beginning of this verse corresponds to Luke 2:39—the rounding off of the story of the infant Jesus' "purification" at the Temple—the second part reports his burial; narrative compression thus serves to fill in the time between death and resurrection (cf. 1 Cor. 15:4a). Note that it is the Jews who handle Jesus' burial, and not Joseph of Arimathea.[157]

Verse 30: Cf. 3:15; 5:30; 10:40.

Verse 31: This verse recalls the first chapter of Acts: "for many days" takes up the "forty days" (1:3); for "his witnesses" see 1:22.

Verse 32: Cf. 26:6.

Verses 33–35: See above, pages 52–53, on 2:27.

Verses 36–37: Verse 36a: Cf. Luke 7:30; Acts 2:23; 20:27.[158] Verses 36b–37 match 2:29–31 (note the keyword "decay").

Verses 38–39: The theological term "forgiveness of sins" has occurred frequently in Peter's speeches (2:38; 5:31; 10:43). The content of these two verses is striking, because—as later in the Miletus speech (20:18–35)—Luke's Paul here employs terminology from the letters of the historical Paul by saying, "Let it be known to you therefore, brothers, that through this man forgiveness of sins is proclaimed to you. Through him everyone who believes is justified from everything from which you could not be justified by the Law of Moses." This is not to say that Luke "understood" Paul's doctrine of justification, for he fails to formulate the contrast between righteousness by faith and righteousness by works. Those unfamiliar with the relevant Pauline doctrines could hardly discern them from this oblique summary. These objections notwithstanding, verses 38–39 are clearly an attempt by Luke to lend a feeling of authenticity to Paul's first extended sermon in Acts, an oration that afforded Luke an opportunity to demonstrate his familiarity with Paul's preaching.

By way of relating this sermon at Antioch to other Pauline speeches, let me point out that the commencement of each of the three major journeys originating from Antioch offers the opportunity for an extended speech: on this occasion to the Jews of Pisidian Antioch, on the second to the Gentiles (chapter 17), and on the third to the Christians (chapter 20).

Verses 42–43: These two verses appear to comprise a doublet, for each begins with a similar chronological note ("going out"/"when the assembly broke up") and reports the audience's reaction to Paul's sermon (request for further contact with Paul and Barnabas). On the other hand, this apparent duplication can be ascribed to Luke's editing by seeing verse 42 as a general introduction and verse 43 as a more specific conclusion (note the implied benediction in the closing exhortation). Many Jews and devout converts,[159] we are told, were persuaded by the missionaries and were admonished, as noted above, to remain in a state of grace. This positive portrayal of some Antiochene Jews stands in sharp contrast to subsequent events.

The next section, extending from verse 44 to 52, derives entirely from Luke. It amounts to a narrative expression of his oft-repeated scheme of having the Jews reject the gospel message, with the necessary result that Paul and Barnabas seek converts among the Gentiles.

Verse 44: For the phrase "the whole city" cf. 21:30; 19:27; "word of God" is also used at verses 5, 7, 44, 46. Luke shows no concern that the whole city could not possibly be seated in the synagogue. He "abandons all realism of presentation for the sake of depicting Paul as a great orator and successful missionary."[160]

Verses 45–46: In its content the negative characterization of the Jews in verse 45 is typical of Luke[161] as is verse 46 in addressing the preaching to them first.[162] In the same verse, though, Luke introduces his idea of the Gentile mission. "Acts has so far (apart from the solitary conversion of Sergius Paulus) said nothing of a Pauline mission directed to the Gentiles."[163]

Verse 47: The Gentile mission is scripturally urged, not historically based; its supposed inspiration—Isa. 49:6—points here to Gentiles, but in Luke 2:32 to Jesus.

Verse 48–49: In content verse 48 provides a means of extending the previous two verses, the first of which is a standard Lukan summary notice and appears, as is typical of the evangelist, at the end of a scene that reports a successful mission.

Verse 50: Prominent women and leading citizens are a Lukan motif (cf. 17:12); the same can be said of Jewish persecution of Christian preachers (verse 45; 17:5, etc.).

Verse 51: When Paul and Barnabas shake the dust from their feet in response to their rejection by the Jews, the obvious analogue is Jesus' instruction to his disciples (Luke 10:11) that Luke found in Q. The theme of the Spirit derives from Luke. The entire verse is "an edifying Lucan conclusion, which with the word *mathethai* reminds the reader that a Christian community has arisen in Pisidian Antioch."[164]

THE TRADITIONS REWORKED BY LUKE

Verses 13–14, 50–51: Points along Paul's way—Perga (verse 13), Antioch (verse 14), and Iconium (verse 51)—may go back to tradition, along with the names of the missionaries Barnabas and Paul.[165] See, for example, the "Acts of Paul" (almost certainly from an independent source), which reports Paul's missionary activity in Iconium and Antioch.[166] The persecution in Antioch (verse 50) may likewise reflect tradition, but the view that it is Luke's insertion gains support from the reference in 2 Tim. 3:11 to "persecutions, my sufferings which I experienced in Antioch, in Iconium, in Lystra." If the author of 2 Tim. 3:11 did not know Acts 13:50,[167] a single tradition no doubt informed the two passages.

Verses 33–35: The quotation from Isa. 55:3 in verse 34 is so garbled as to be nearly unrecognizable. Perhaps it came to Luke already connected with the following citation of Ps. 16:10—for which see also 2:27.

HISTORICAL ELEMENTS

That Barnabas and Paul traveled to Perga, Antioch, and Iconium reflects a tradition quite lacking in support from Paul's letters. They allow us to infer only a mission to Syria and Cilicia directly following his first journey to Jerusalem (Gal. 1:21). To be sure, though, this evidence cannot eliminate all possibility of such a mission, because Paul's letters do not provide an exhaustive itinerary of his travels. Nonetheless, by combining the reliable data we have, it is possible to suppose the historicity of this mission in southern Galatia.

Further support for this comes from the high degree of likelihood that the traditional account of Paul's collaboration with Barnabas (see Gal. 2:1, 13; 1 Cor. 9:6) is historically sound. It is also noteworthy that southern Galatia lies along the route from Syria and Cilicia to Greece. Last of all, it is highly understandable that following the mission to Syria and Cilicia, in which Barnabas accompanied Paul, the two would undertake this Galatian venture.

Verses 33–35: This passage is of no help in attempting to date the tradition. Like the resurrection tradition (verse 30–31, see p. 52 above on 2:24), it offers no more than a glimpse into the faith of first-century Hellenistic-Christian communities.

THE HISTORICAL VALUE OF LUKE'S ACCOUNT

"Of a popular tradition or of an itinerary, such as comes to light in later chapters, there is here no trace. Luke here has created, admittedly not ex nihilo; but on the basis of the Christian preaching of his own time and its experiences with Jews and Gentiles he has composed a kind of abridgment of Pauline missionary history. The characteristic foreshortening of times and distances in Acts is also connected with this. The vast plateau and ranges of Asia Minor shrink; Perga, Antioch, and Iconium seem to lie side by side in neighbourly fashion; and it appears as if all that happened in Antioch is compressed into a week."[168]

[31]
ACTS 14:1–7
THE FOUNDING OF THE COMMUNITY AT ICONIUM BY PAUL AND BARNABAS

(1) *And it came to pass that in Iconium they entered together into the synagogue of the Jews and spoke in such a way that a great number of both Jews and Greeks believed. (2) But the disbelieving Jews stirred up and poisoned the minds of the Gentiles against the brothers. (3a) So for a long time they remained [there], (3b) speaking boldly for the Lord, (3c) who bore witness to the word of his grace, (3d) granting signs and wonders to be done by their hands. (4) But the multitude of the city was divided; some sided with the Jews and some with the apostles. (5) But when an attempt was initiated by both Gentiles and Jews, with their rulers, to mistreat them and to stone them, (6) they learned of it and fled to Lystra and Derbe, cities of Lycaonia, and to the surrounding country, (7) and there they preached the gospel.*

OUTLINE

1: Successful preaching in the synagogue of Iconium
2: Disbelieving Jews stir up the Gentiles
3: Paul's missionary work in Iconium followed by signs and wonders
4: The population is divided, siding with either the Jews or the apostles

5–7:   A plan by both Gentiles and Jews to stone Paul and Barnabas
leads to their flight to Lystra, Derbe, and their environs, and
preaching there

LUKE'S PURPOSE

This section exhibits both a highly schematic nature and a confused style.

Verse 1: Verse 1a employs the Lukan scheme of going to the Jews first. The
generalized report in verse 1b that the preaching in the synagogue induced a large
number of Jews and Greeks to become believers is similar to what is said in 18:4.
Cf. also the formula "Jews and Greeks," 19:10, 17; 20:21.

Verse 2: Cf. 13:45.

Verse 3: This brief summary, like that in verse 1, describes the success of the
preaching: Signs and wonders flowed from the work of Paul and Barnabas. The
verse is Lukan in both language and content. Verse 3b almost exactly matches
20:32. Verse 3c–d corresponds to the summary of the healing in 5:12; cf. 19:11.
Strangely enough, though, the content of verse 3 appears incompatible with that
of verse 2, which seems to deny the possibility of such a success as we find
reported here.

Verse 4: This summarizes the report so far: The populace is divided as noted
in verse 1b; some adhere to the (hostile) Jews, the others support the apostles.[169]

Many a scholar[170] has explained "apostles" to be the reflection of a source.
While it is true that apostles are primarily the leaders of the Jerusalem congregation "evidently *apostoloi* can also be used of those who preach the gospel among
the Gentiles. That the term is not used later in connection with Paul accords with
Lukan terminology; Paul now only appears as an individual, but Luke always
speaks of *apostoloi* in the plural."[171]

Verses 5–6: The description of the plan of the pagan mob with the Jews and
their leaders to maltreat the missionaries prepares the way for verse 19.[172]

Verse 7: The content of the proclamation is a necessary element of the narrative.

THE TRADITIONS REWORKED BY LUKE AND HISTORICAL ELEMENTS

No tradition can be discerned. In the words of Ernst Haenchen,

> Luke was here trying to formulate some particular content, based on the overall
> picture of Paul's missionary experiences, with which to give body and sub-
> stance to a stage of the journey that was known by him by name alone.[173]

Later Haenchen continues,

> The fact that that the missionaries are unable to stay in Iconium, but are eventually obliged to flee, exemplifies the affliction inseparable from being or becoming a Christian.[174]

The narrative itself contains no historical elements that can be related to a specific place, situation, or time.

THE HISTORICAL VALUE OF LUKE'S ACCOUNT

Luke is presenting theology and shows no concern for facts. Again Haenchen offers an apt observation:

> (T)he passage has a theological value of its own: the great number of Jews and Gentiles converted in Iconium certifies—which is why Luke mentions it—the power of the Lord. When the reader further hears of the many wonders, he must feel that they are also part of God's "witness" to the Christian proclamation. But the mention of these miracles is important in another respect: when in what follows a special miracle is recounted, the reader knows that it is not an isolated event, an exceptional case, but a link in a long chain.[175]

True enough, but what I miss here is a remonstrance by Haenchen against fabricating such long chains of incredibly incredible miracles.

[32]
ACTS 14:8–20A
PAUL AND BARNABAS AT LYSTRA

(8) *And at Lystra there was a man sitting who could not use his feet. He was crippled from birth and had never walked.* (9) *He listened to Paul speaking. And Paul, gazing at him and seeing that he had faith to be saved,* (10) *said in a loud voice, "Stand upright on your feet."* And he sprang up and began walking. (11) *And when the crowds saw what Paul had done, they lifted up their voices, shouting in Lycaonian, "The gods have come down to us in the likeness of men!"* (12) *And they called Barnabas "Zeus," and Paul "Hermes," because he was the chief speaker.* (13) *And the priest of Zeus, whose temple was at the entrance to the city, brought oxen and garlands to the gates and wanted to offer sacrifice with the*

crowds. (14) But when the apostles Barnabas and Paul heard of it, they tore their garments and rushed out into the crowd, crying out, (15) "Men, why are you doing this? We also are human beings like you, and we bring you good news, that you should turn from these vain things to the living God, who made the heaven and the earth and the sea and all that is in them. (16) In past generations he allowed all the nations to walk in their own ways. (17) Yet he did not leave himself without witness, for he did good by giving you rains from heaven and fruitful seasons, satisfying your hearts with food and gladness." (18) Even with these words they scarcely restrained the people from offering sacrifice to them. (19) But Jews came from Antioch and Iconium, and having persuaded the crowds, they stoned Paul and dragged him out of the city, supposing that he was dead. (20a) But when the disciples gathered about him, he rose up and entered the city.

OUTLINE

8–10: Healing of a lame man in Lystra by Paul

11–13: Reaction of the people of Lystra: They seek to offer sacrifices to Barnabas and Paul as Zeus and Hermes

14–17: Speech of Paul and Barnabas denying any special status

18: Despite this denial, the people nearly succeed in their purpose

19–20a: Stoning of Paul in Lystra by the people at the incitement of Jews from Antioch and Iconium

LUKE'S PURPOSE

Verses 8–10: The beginning of the story emphasizes the seriousness of the illness (verse 8) so as to prepare the greatness of the ensuing miracle (verses 9–10). This account of the healing of a lame man closely approximates that in 3:2–8, a story that of late has been held up as an example of the "typical style of miracle stories."[176] But "typical style" hardly does justice to the many close verbal similarities displayed by the two accounts:

1. "A man, crippled from birth" (verse 8/3:2).
2. The miracle worker gazes at the lame man (verse 9/3:4).
3. The lame man leaps up and walks around (verse 10/3:8).
4. Both contain the motif of faith. In 14:9 it appears as an integral part of the story, whereas in Acts 3 it is included in an interpretative framework (verse 16).

These close verbal parallels and the striking similarity of other miracles performed by Peter and Paul authorize us to conclude that the present healing story is a Lukan creation developed on the model of the account in Acts 3. He has two purposes in mind: One is to draw yet another parallel between Paul and Peter, and the other—evident in the fact that the outcome of the miracle (verses 11–13) segues to preaching to the Gentiles (verses 15–17)—is to distinguish between faith in the one God and idolatry.

Verses 11–13: Here the narration grows directly out of the previous episode: Paul's miracle leads the people to see Barnabas and Paul as incarnations of Zeus and Hermes. Since the Lystrans employ the local dialect in identifying Barnabas and Paul with pagan gods, the missionaries can raise objections only when they recognize the significance of the ensuing events.[177] Luke exploits the dramatic potential of this delayed reaction by creating the vivid scene in verse 13 and by drawing a detailed distinction between Christian preaching and the worship of idols (verses 15–17). This in turn allows the inhabitants of Lystra to abjure such useless idols as Zeus and Hermes and turn to the living God.

It is quite reasonable to wonder whether the remarkable scenario of Paul and Barnabas being worshipped as Zeus and Hermes could possibly derive from Luke, for it bears an indirect but discernible likeness to the legend reproduced by Ovid,[178] in which Jupiter/Zeus and Mercury/Hermes visit an elderly couple named Philemon and Baucis. Moreover, in this same locale Zeus and Hermes appear together on inscriptions.[179] Most likely, Luke has again exploited literary themes to fabricate an impressive story thus demonstrating his literary sophistication and skill.

Another incident parallel to Paul being mistaken for Hermes is the case of Egyptian priests taking Moses to be Hermes in Artapanus's history of Moses. Alexander Polyhistor in Eusebius cites Artapanus (third to second century BCE) thus:

> This Mousaeus was the teacher of Orpheus. As a grown man he bestowed many useful benefits on mankind, for he invented boats and devices for stone construction and the Egyptian arms and the implements for drawing water and for warfare, and philosophy. Further he divided the state into 36 nomes [districts] and appointed for each of the nomes the god to be worshiped, and for the priests the sacred letters, and that they should be cats and dogs and ibises. He also allotted a choice area to the priests. He did all these things for the sake of maintaining the monarchy firm for Chenephres, for formerly the masses were disorganized and would at one time expel kings, at others appoint them, often the same people but sometimes others. On account of these things Moses was loved by the masses, and was deemed worthy of godlike honor by the priests and called Hermes, on account of the interpretation of sacred letters.[180]

To be sure, the name Hermes is differently interpreted in the two stories. Ascribing Egyptian cultural achievements to Moses and thus relating him to Hermes is a far cry from designating Paul as Hermes because he is the primary spokesman of a pair of traveling healers. Nonetheless the common depiction of Moses and Paul as miracle workers provides a powerful link between the two stories.

> (Cf. Artapanus:) The king of the Egyptians learned of Moses' presence, summoned him and asked for what purpose he had come. He responded that the master of the universe had ordered him to release the Jews. When the king heard this, he confined him in prison. But when night came, all the doors of the prison opened of themselves, and some of the guards died, while others were relaxed by sleep and their weapons were broken. Moses came out and went to the royal chambers. He found the doors open and went in. There, since the guards were relaxed, he woke the king. The latter was astonished at what had happened and bade Moses to say the name of the god who had sent him, mocking him. But he bent forward and pronounced it into his ear. When the king heard it, he fell down speechless but revived when taken hold of by Moses.[181]

It is undeniable that Paul's healing of the lame man in Acts 14 closely resembles Moses' miracles. Note also the similarity to the miraculous release in Acts 12:6–10 and 16:25–26.

The net result of all this evidence is that we have compelling reason to conclude that Luke drew heavily on literary models in the process of creating his dramatic account of Paul/Hermes and Barnabas/Zeus in Lycaconia. It may be noteworthy that Ovid's companion story was set in Phrygia, which abuts Lycaonia. Only with the greatest difficulty, then, can one assign to coincidence Luke's use at this particular point of knowledge he had gained from reading—especially in view of the way he works local color into such passages as 17:16–34 and 19:23–40.

Verses 14–16: In verse 14 the apostles (cf. verse 4) "tear their clothes as a sign of horror and blasphemy."[182] The emphasis that we see in verse 16 on the humanity of the apostles appears also in 10:26.

Verse 17: Cf. 17:24–25

Verse 18: This verse harks back to verse 13 in which a priest led the people in seeking to make sacrifices to Barnabas and Paul, whose speech—which according to Luke they *both* delivered—barely persuaded the crowd not to commit this blasphemy.[183]

Verses 19–20a: This section doubtless goes back to the Evangelist, since once again hostile Jews stir up the crowd (cf. 14:2 and 14:5) to the point of seeking to harm the missionaries. Here, however, the situation becomes even worse, for Jews and Gentiles join together and in fact do stone Paul; the plan reported in 14:5 is now executed. Thus we see a Lukan narrative bridge that reaches all the way from 14:2 via 14:5 to 14:19–20. In view of the inherent difficulty of combining the worship of Barnabas and Paul and the Jewish persecution motif in a single narrative scheme, it would seem mean-spirited to complain too strenuously about the sudden shifts in loyalty and point of view that Luke has used to move the story along.

THE TRADITIONS REWORKED BY LUKE

Verses 8–14: Roloff makes the following case for assuming tradition in the present section:

> The figure of Barnabas may have stood at the center of the piece of tradition. He is the central figure who is regarded by the people as the father of the gods, Zeus, whereas Paul is clearly subordinate to him in verse 12; cf. verse 14. (The explanation that Luke finds for this is completely artificial. . . .) Presumably here we have a Barnabas legend set in Antioch. In it Barnabas is portrayed as the great missionary, who in an exemplary way withstands typical situations of the Gentile mission.[184]

Yet various factors undermine such a theory. The role of Hermes fits Paul because he does the speaking. That Luke appears to attribute a "superior" position to Barnabas reflects a misapprehension that stems from the author's insertion of literary material gleaned from his wide reading.

Verses 19–20a: In all likelihood this section is rooted in a tradition; the following reasons may be adduced: (a) These verses are readily detachable from the surrounding events. (b) Highly awkward transitions are apparent between verses 18 and 19, as well as between verse 20a and 20b. Furthermore, the mention of "disciples" in verse 20 is problematic in view of the lack of any previous mention of a community having been established in Lystra.[185] (c) Paul stands alone at center stage, while Barnabas has been relegated to the wings. (d) A parallel passage appears in 2 Tim. 3:11, a verse that also contains the same itinerary as the one found in Acts 13–14.

Luke had earlier employed this tradition when he had Paul and Barnabas flee from Iconium to Lystra to escape stoning, and previously when they were expelled from Antioch. 2 Tim. 3:11 makes it clear that the tradition was related to Paul, and told of his trials and tribulations in Antioch, Iconium, and Lystra—as well as reporting a near-fatal stoning in Lystra. Even the most thorough analysis of the tradition, however, will not determine who initiated the stoning (see further below, p. 183). The addition of Barnabas to the story in 13:50 and 14:5 appears to be the work of Luke. If attacks on Paul at the places mentioned can be regarded as part of the tradition, the way stations of Antioch, Iconium, and Lystra are similarly assured, as may also Derbe, which is closely connected with Lystra (14:6; cf. 14:20).

At this point we must consider whether the rest of the Acts 14 itinerary may have come from the tradition: Paul and Barnabas travel from Iconium to Lystra and Derbe and their environs (verse 6), then back to Lystra, Iconium, and Antioch (verse 21); in verses 24–26 they pass through Pisidia, Pamphylia, Perga, and Attalia, from where they return to Antioch.

But here we should recall what was pointed out in the previous section—that the return to Antioch takes us back to 13:1–2, and indicates the intrusion of Luke the editor. Accordingly that journey cannot be part of the tradition. And although one may wonder why a redactor could be interested in having Paul and Barnabas pass twice through Antioch (13:14/14:21), Iconium (13:51/14:21), and Lystra (14:6/14:21, see also Derbe [14:6/14:20]), it is noteworthy that the return journey was the occasion for appointing presbyters (verse 23) and conferring blessings. This chronological separation of events that have relevance for Luke's present situation affords them dramatic importance, since they arise out of a special visit, and extra action, by the missionaries. Therefore we should not suppose that the tradition reflected in this chapter indicated further travels of Paul (and Barnabas) beyond those places mentioned at the beginning (Antioch, Iconium, Lystra, and Derbe).

Our analysis of the tradition reflected in Acts 14, therefore, argues against the likelihood of a single source underlying Acts 13–14.

HISTORICAL ELEMENTS

The tradition behind verses 19–20a appears to have considerable historical validity since, even though he neglects to mention the place, Paul himself reports being stoned (2 Cor. 11:25). The tradition in Acts 14:19–20a therefore seems to indicate the historical location of the dangerous assault Paul suffered in Lystra, during the course of a mission in the mid 30s to various cities of southern Galatia (Derbe, Lystra, Iconium, and Antioch) as part of his activity in Syria and Cilicia (Gal. 1:21).[186] Earlier, on pages 180–81, we deferred a decision as to whether it was Jews or Gentiles who attacked Paul. Since Jews exercised the penalty of stoning as part of an orderly legal process, most scholars who have taken this scene to be at all historical[187] have simply assumed—often tacitly—the Jewish initiation of the stoning in 14:19–20. But important objections can be made: (a)

Jewish stoning was conducted outside the city, as we see in 7:58 (though one might object to this point on the grounds of 2 Chron. 24:21—the stoning of Zechariah in the temple, cf. 2 Chron. 10:18). (b) In Jewish law and practice stoning was a death penalty, and except for this instance no one is reported to have survived it. (c) Stoning was a form of lynch law widely employed in pagan antiquity.[188] (d) In this text Jewish animus against Paul is Luke's creation. Taking all things together, then, one can make a strong argument that Paul's "stoning" in Lystra was the result of a riot by the city's Gentile inhabitants. Whether the actual incident was a failed attempt at stoning or whether Paul may have escaped from a mob who were throwing stones at him, such a proposal has the double advantage of comporting with 2 Cor. 11:25 and lending historical color to Paul's laconic report there.

By way of anticipating the outcome of the forthcoming analysis of Acts 16:1–5, let it be noted that Paul probably converted Timothy in Lystra and there won him over as a fellow worker, and from there the two of them went on through southern Galatia and northward through Phrygia (cf. Acts 16:6, a passage which clearly has a direct relationship to chapter 14). The mention of Timothy in 2 Cor. 1:19 (cf. 1 Thess. 1:1; 3:1–6) in connection with the founding mission in Greece suggests that this stoning could have occurred during Paul's first journey to southern Galatia.

THE HISTORICAL VALUE OF LUKE'S ACCOUNT

Concerning Luke's explanation that Paul is identified with Hermes because he is the one who does the talking, Ernst Haenchen notes that the role of spokesman

> has in Hellenism another meaning than in our story: Hermes is "the one who does the talking" as the messenger of the gods, who conveys the orders, for example of Zeus their king. That Zeus quietly sits by and Hermes speaks for him is a conception alien to Hellenistic mythology. The identification of Paul with Hermes (and hence of Barnabas with Zeus) is thus strictly speaking not justified by reference to this particular trait of Hermes. . . . The healing of the cripple was admittedly a great miracle. But surely not so great as to persuade the Lycaonians that their very gods stood in their midst. If two Jewish exorcists heal a cripple, they may reasonably be regarded as great magicians, but no more.[189]

Haenchen later continues,

> Here we have not a historical report, but a story devised for edification. . . . It is indeed merely right to acknowledge that in applying to Luke the yardstick of the

modern historian we do him an injustice. For he lived in the tranquil conviction that the history of the apostolic mission was essentially a triumphant procession (albeit interrupted by occasional reverses) and therefore must be recounted as such.[190]

These "words from the wise" should suffice to epitomize the nonhistorical nature of Luke's evangelical romance about the perils of Paul[191] in southern Galatia.

[33]
ACTS 14:20B–28
THE RETURN OF PAUL AND BARNABAS TO ANTIOCH, THE STARTING POINT OF THEIR JOURNEY

(20b) And *on the next day* he went on with Barnabas to Derbe. (21) *When they had preached the gospel to that city* and had made *many* disciples, *they returned to* Lystra and to Iconium and to Antioch, (22) *strengthening the souls of the disciples, encouraging them to continue in the faith, and saying, "Through many tribulations we must enter the kingdom of God." (23) And when they had appointed elders for them in every church, with prayer and fasting they committed them to the Lord in whom they had believed.*

(24) Then they passed through Pisidia and came to Pamphylia. (25) And when they had spoken the word in Perga, they went down to Attalia, (26) and from there they sailed to Antioch, where they had been commended to the grace of God for the work that they had performed. (27) And when they arrived and gathered the church together, they declared all that God had done with them, and how he had opened a door of faith to the Gentiles. (28) And they remained no little time with the disciples.

OUTLINE

20b–23: From Derbe to Pisidian Antioch
24–28: From Pisidia back to Antioch at the Orontes

LUKE'S PURPOSE

Verse 20b: The phrase "on the next day" is typical of Luke.[192]

Verses 21–22: These verses are predominantly Lukan in language.[193] However, the verb "to make disciples" (in Greek, *matheteuein*) occurs only here in Luke-Acts (elsewhere in the New Testament only in Matt. 13:52; 27:57; 28:19), but in connection with the typically Lukan adjective "many" (in Greek, *hikanoi*) and the verb "to return" (in Greek, *hypostrephein*). The verb "to strengthen" (in Greek, *episterizein*) in verse 22 appears only there and in 15:32, each time in an ecclesiological context. The whole verse is focused on Luke's church and deals with Christian life that according to Luke is marked at least partly by "tribulation."

Verse 23: In this description of the appointment of elders, Luke portrays the ecclesiastical structure of his time—and imagines it to have existed in Paul's day.

Verses 24–26: Although these travel notes are fraught with Lukan language, it is still possible that the information was derived from tradition. Verse 26 reports the return of Barnabas and Paul to Antioch, "from where they had been commended to the grace of God for the work that they had performed" and thus completes the saga begun in 13:1–3.

Verse 27: This sanguine summary of the journey ("[God] had opened a door of faith to the Gentiles") will play an important part in the debate in Jerusalem in the next chapter.

Verse 28: This verse "creates one of the Luke's pauses."[194]

THE TRADITIONS REWORKED BY LUKE

Verses 20b–21 contain a traditional list of way stations: Derbe, Lystra, Iconium, and Antioch.

HISTORICAL ELEMENTS AND THE HISTORICAL VALUE OF LUKE'S ACCOUNT

On Derbe, Lystra, and Iconium as places of the missionary activity of Paul and Barnabas see the comments above, pages 174–75, on the historical elements behind 13:13–52.

As noted above, the return to Antioch and the itinerary in 14:24–25 bear the stamp of redaction; the historical substrate of this report may be Barnabas's return to Antioch alone. Only Paul's letters allow us to reconstruct the real chronological place of the missionary activity of Paul reflected in verses 20b–21. It took place about 35 CE after his trip to Syria and Cilicia (Gal. 1:21). See below, page 360.

[34]
ACTS 15:1–29
THE JERUSALEM CONFERENCE AND ITS RESULT

(1) *But some men came down from Judea and were teaching the brothers,* "Unless you are circumcised according to the custom of Moses, you cannot be saved." (2a) *And after Paul and Barnabas had no small dissension and debate with them,* (2b) Paul and Barnabas *and some of the others were appointed* to go up to Jerusalem *to the apostles and the elders about this question.*

(3) *So, being sent on their way by the church, they passed through both Phoenicia and Samaria, describing in detail the conversion of the Gentiles, and brought great joy to all the brothers.* (4) *When they came to Jerusalem, they were welcomed by the church and the apostles and the elders, and they declared all that God had done with them.* (5) But some believers who belonged to the party of the Pharisees rose up and said, "It is necessary to circumcise them and to order them to keep the law of Moses."

(6) The apostles and the elders gathered together to look into this matter. (7) *And after there had been much debate, Peter stood up and said to them,* "Brothers, you know that in ancient days God made a choice among you, that by my mouth the Gentiles should hear the word of the gospel and believe. (8) *And God, who knows the heart, has given testimony, giving them the Holy Spirit just as to us,* (9) *and in cleansing their hearts by faith, he has canceled all distinction between us and them.* (10) Now, therefore, why do you put God to the test by placing a yoke on the neck of the disciples that neither our fathers nor we have been able to bear? (11) Rather, we believe that we shall be saved by the grace of the Lord Jesus, just as they do."

(12) And the whole multitude <u>fell silent,</u> and they listened to Barnabas and Paul *as they related what signs and wonders God had done through them among the Gentiles.*

(13) *After they <u>fell silent,</u> James replied,* "Brothers, listen to me. *(14) Simeon has related how God first concerned himself with winning from among the Gentiles a people for his name. (15) And with this the words of the prophets agree, just as it is written, (16)* "After this I will return, and I will rebuild the tent of

David that has fallen; its ruins I will rebuild and restore it, (17) that the rest of human beings may seek the Lord, and all the nations who are called by my name, says the Lord, who makes these things (18) known from of old."

(19) Therefore my judgment is that we should not cause difficulty for Gentiles who turn to God, (20) but should write to them to abstain from the things polluted by idols, and from fornication, and from what has been strangled, and from blood. (21) For Moses has for many generations had in every city those who proclaim him, for he is read every Sabbath in the synagogues."

(22) *Then it **seemed best to** the apostles and the elders, with the whole church, to choose men from among them and send them to Antioch with Paul and Barnabas. They sent* Judas *called* Barsabbas, *and* Silas, *leading men among the brothers,* (23) *with the following letter: "The brothers, both the apostles and the elders, to the brothers of the Gentiles in Antioch and Syria and Cilicia, greetings.* (24) *Since we have heard that some persons have gone out from us and troubled you with words, unsettling your minds, although we gave them no instructions,* (25) *it has **seemed best to** us, having come to one accord, to choose men and send them to you with our beloved Barnabas and Paul,* (26) *men who have risked their lives for the sake of our Lord Jesus Christ.* (27) *We have therefore sent Judas and Silas, who themselves will tell you the same things by word of mouth.* (28) *For it has **seemed best to** the Holy Spirit and to us to lay on you no greater burden than these requirements:* (29) *that you abstain from what has been sacrificed to idols, and from blood, and from what has been strangled, and from fornication. If you keep yourselves from these, you will do well. Farewell."*

OUTLINE

1–3:   Christians in Judea insist on circumcision of Gentile converts; Paul and Barnabas sent from Antioch to Jerusalem; their journey through Phoenicia and Samaria

4–29: The Jerusalem conference

      4–6:   From the reception in Jerusalem to the assembly

      7–11: Peter's speech

      12:    Summary note about the report by Paul and Barnabas

      13–21: James's speech

      22–29: Sending of Paul and Barnabas together with Judas Barsabbas and Silas to Antioch with a letter

LUKE'S PURPOSE

Verses 1–3: The content of verses 1–3 constitutes an exposition of the primary problem that is "resolved" in what follows. Indeed, individual clauses bear a striking resemblance to those in both the preceding and subsequent context:

Verse 1: "Unless you are circumcised according to the custom of Moses" matches verse 5, "it is necessary to circumcise them and to charge them to keep the law of Moses" (cf. verse 24).

Verse 2a: "And after Paul and Barnabas had no small dissension and debate with them" matches verse 7, "And after there had been much debate. . . ."

Verse 2b: "to the apostles and elders to Jerusalem because of this disputed question" matches verse 6, "The apostles and elders gathered together to consider this matter."

Verse 4: That this verse so neatly fits into the context is a sure indication of its Lukan derivation. Not only does "By the church and the apostles and the elders" anticipate verse 22, "The apostles and the elders, with the whole church," but "And they declared all that God had done with them" both echoes 14:27, "They declared all that God had done with them" and is echoed in 15:12, "as they related what signs and wonders God had done through them among the Gentiles."

Verse 5: This repeats the demand for circumcision of the Gentiles (verse 3) that occasioned the sending of Barnabas and Paul from Antioch to Jerusalem. Now it is made once again in Jerusalem by Pharisaic Christians. Luke deems it desirable to specify once again the key problem at issue in the subsequent passage.

Verse 6: The convocation of apostles and elders sets the scene for the following speech and its endorsement of the work of Paul and Barnabas. Once again Luke's probably anachronistic description of the Jerusalem church is evident.[195] Verse 6 should not be construed as Luke's description of a meeting of "insiders"; verse 12 clearly assumes the same audience, and refers to it as "the whole assembly."

Verses 7–9: Verse 7a is a Lukan introduction to the speech by Peter that follows in verses 7b–11. Verses 7b–9 in effect summarize the narrative in chapters 10–11. Verse 7b makes it seem that the Cornelius episode occurred long ago—"in ancient days." Verse 8 is a reminder that the Spirit has already come upon the Gentiles in the person of Cornelius. Verse 9 interprets Peter's vision in chapter 10:9–16.

Verses 10–11: These verses challenge the listeners to accept the consequences of the Cornelius story and drive home the implications of the issue now under discussion: Luke's confession in verse 11 ("we believe that we shall be saved by the grace of the Lord Jesus") shows Luke's strongly Pauline inclinations, as did earlier 13:38–39.

Verse 12: The reference to the preceding context (14:27) shows that this verse derives from Luke. Although a basis in tradition cannot be absolutely rejected, the tension between the Lukan term "multitude" and "apostles, elders" (verse 6) is probably not inherent in the tradition, but more likely arises from careless narration on Luke's part.[196] The signs and wonders that characterize Paul's journey in Acts 13–14 justify the mission to the Gentiles. According to Luke, the God who acted in signs and wonders to rescue Israel from bondage in Egypt has acted with the same power among the Gentiles.

Verse 13: This is the introduction to James's speech to which "study of the speeches in Acts has unfortunately paid little attention."[197]

Verse 14: James's use of Peter's other name (Simeon) is deliberately archaic. His allusion to Peter's just-completed speech entails at least an indirect reference to the Cornelius story. The use of "a people from the nations"[198] evokes a similar echo, and at the same time anticipates verses 16–18, where its full implications are spelled out.

Verses 15–18: Verse 15 is simply Luke's introduction to verses 16–18, which comprise a conflated quotation from the LXX text of Amos 9:11–12 with small differences (the MT is anti-universalistic) and Isa. 45:21, which has little or no bearing on the necessity of Gentile Christians to observe Torah; its inclusion may perhaps be attributed to its gratifying support of Luke's ecclesiology. The newly defined people of God include both Jews (verse 16) and Gentiles (verse 17); indeed, verse 17a sees the Gentile mission as essential for the restoration of Israel.[199]

Verses 19–21: Verse 19 at first seems to constitute a general acceptance of Gentiles, but verse 20 limits this by the "conditions" of the Apostolic Decree (which is repeated in verse 29 and 21:25).[200] It gives cultic[201] stipulations that are derived from Leviticus 17–18.[202] They "had to do with those ritual prohibitions which enabled the Jew to live together with gentile Christians."[203] Verse 21 justifies the restriction of the Apostolic Decree implying that the holiness code of Leviticus 17–18 is generally known.

Verses 22–29: These verses are Lukan throughout. Note the repetition of "it seemed best to us" in verses 22, 25, 28 and that the letter (verses 23–29) reiterates the decree in verse 20 and is strongly reminiscent of the prologue to Luke's gospel (1:1–4) in structure and syntax. See further 23:26–30 as another example of Luke's creation of a "letter" to be incorporated in the account.

A Note on the Function of Chapter 15 in the Framework of Acts

Redactional analysis of Acts 10–11, 15 provides the following sketch of Luke's program: God revealed to Peter that Gentiles are hereafter to be admitted into full membership of the people of God, provided only that they fulfill the demands of the Apostolic Decree. Acts 15 thus marks the transition from proselytizing efforts conducted under the aegis of the Antiochene community to a fully independent mission conducted by Paul. In the interest of Luke's salvation history, the Jerusalem church legitimates the apostle's career before its proper start.

THE TRADITIONS REWORKED BY LUKE

Although the extensive Lukan redaction noted above frustrates any hope of identifying a single integrated source for chapter 15, it would be all but unthinkable to deny Luke's considerable reliance on traditions, either oral or written or both. Such a conclusion applies both to the scriptural citations in verses 16–18—which must have been embedded in the source, since they clash with the context[204]—and to the course of the conference. For one thing, the events can be reconstructed from Galatians 2; and since Luke was not an eyewitness, the strong parallels between Acts 15 and Paul's account—the participants, the agreement, the question of circumcision, etc.—only the presence of tradition is left to explain the situation. Further support for a basis in tradition comes from the specific details included: the list of names—Paul, Barnabas, Peter, James, Judas, and Silas; the precise description of the dispute; and finally the "solution" created by the decree.

To the degree that the above observations establish tradition as the probable basis of Acts 15 and at the same time offer two valid criteria for the reconstruction of the tradition—namely concreteness and, more important, agreement with the events of the conference that we can reconstruct from Galatians 2—then it is proper to reemphasize that only discrete elements of tradition can be identified. In my view they are—apart from verses 16–18—the following:

1. Barnabas and Paul travel to Jerusalem together (the departure from Antioch comes from the Lukan framework).

2. In Jerusalem the local Jewish Christians negotiate with Barnabas and Paul concerning the Gentile mission.

3. Separate convocations involve the community (verse 12) and the group of apostles (verse 6). Luke conflates the two even while indicating negotiations by different bodies.

4. Parties in both Jerusalem (verse 5) and Antioch (verse 1) demand circumcision of the Gentile Christians.

5. General approval is accorded the mission to the Gentiles (verses 10–11, 19).

6. Gentile Christians residing in Syria and Cilicia are required only to conform to the provisions of the Apostolic Decree.

7. Judas Barsabbas likely served as part of a delegation to Antioch. The link between him and Silas originated with Luke (see below on 15:40).

HISTORICAL ELEMENTS

Verses 16–18: The practice of using Old Testament quotations dealing with a "mission to the Gentiles" must have begun in a Greek-speaking community somewhere in the general area of Luke's church. In that community the purpose was to defend and perpetuate an existing practice. Greater chronological or geographical precision is impossible. The quotations clearly do not derive from the historical James.[205]

The close agreement between Gal. 2:2–10 and tradition elements related to the conference suggests that the two accounts reflect the same event, the Jerusalem conference. The following agreements between Gal. 2:1–10 and the elements of tradition mentioned lend compelling support to such a conclusion.

1. Barnabas and Paul travel together to Jerusalem (Acts 15:2/Gal. 2:1).

2. They participate in a conference about proselytizing Gentiles (Acts 15:12/Gal. 2:1, 9).

3. The conference involves both community sessions (Gal. 2:2a/Acts 15:12) and small group conclaves (Gal. 2:2b, 7/Acts 15:6). In describing the small group, Paul names people of note (Gal. 2:9); the tradition behind Acts 15:6 mentions "the apostles."

4. Conservative believers call for the circumcision of Gentile Christians; in Gal. 2:4–5 they are termed "the false brothers"; in Acts 15:5, "Christian Pharisees."

5. The demands that occasioned the conference and those put forward at it were essentially the same.[206]

6. According to both accounts the conference fully recognized the Gentile mission (Acts 15:10–11, 19; Gal. 2:9).

7. While Paul's account makes no direct mention of the Apostolic Decree, it may allude to that edict or a similar regulation in the statement, "Those of note laid nothing *additional* upon me" (Gal. 2:6d). It may well be that the decree (or some similar protocol) applied primarily to the mixed community of Antioch represented by Barnabas, whereas Paul's predominantly Gentile-Christian communities were little if at all affected.[207] If in fact Barnabas returned to Antioch following the conference, perhaps he and Judas carried the rule for mixed communities to the fellowship there.

All in all, then, a high degree of historical reliability attaches to the elements of tradition underlying Acts 15:1–29.

THE HISTORICAL VALUE OF LUKE'S ACCOUNT

Because the narrative in Acts 15 commonly passes for a reliable account of the Jerusalem conference, it now behooves us to throw in stark relief the differences between Luke's account and the best possible reconstruction of events that we can manage on the basis of Galatians 2 and the traditions underlying Acts 15:

1. Peter never delivered a speech like that in verses 7–11 because according to Gal. 2:12 he pulled back from table fellowship with Gentile Christians. This verdict holds true even if we take some variability in Peter's character into account, because Peter in this speech is depicted as a student of Paul.

2. Contrary to what Paul says in Galatians 2, according to Luke he is sent to Jerusalem as a delegate, and like Barnabas had only a spectator's role at the conference.

3. Luke in effect predates the conference with a view to legitimating the Pauline mission before it actually began. (Acts 13–14 is in effect a prototype.) This does not mean that Luke knew the date of the conference, but he could hardly have broken into his account of the Pauline mission to place the "council" in the same chronological context as Acts 18:22—where it probably belongs.

4. In the interest of church unity, Luke so thoroughly suppressed criticisms and reproofs that they are nearly unrecognizable. He also suppresses—both here and elsewhere in Acts—the presence of Titus, the Gentile Christian whose circumcision was a matter of dispute at the conference. Last, he goes so far as to separate the collection agreement from the account of the conference, and subsequently from that of Paul's last journey to Jerusalem (Acts 21); since Paul had regarded the collection as a symbol of unity (see Rom. 15:27), its mention would have implied a church in danger of schism. Therefore Luke pushed the collection ahead to 11:27–30.

5. By pouring sacred oil on troubled waters, Luke makes it seem that the conflict ended with the Jerusalem conference, but the letters of Paul tell another tale.[208] Indeed, dissension continued on into the second century and beyond.[209]

[35]
ACTS 15:30–35
THE RETURN OF PAUL AND BARNABAS FROM JERUSALEM TO ANTIOCH

(30) *So when they were sent off, they went down to Antioch, and having gathered the congregation together, they delivered the letter.* (31) *And when they had read it, they rejoiced because of its encouragement.* (32) *And* Judas and Silas, who were themselves prophets, *encouraged and strengthened the brothers with many words.* (33) *And after spending some time, they were sent off in peace by the*

brothers to those who had sent them.[210] (35) *But Paul and Barnabas remained in Antioch, teaching and preaching the word of the Lord along with many others.*

OUTLINE

30:   Letter delivered in Antioch

31:   The joy of those who read the letter

32–33:   Activity of Judas and Silas in Antioch; they are sent back to Jerusalem

35:   Activity of Paul and Barnabas in Antioch

LUKE'S PURPOSE

The language of this section has a Lukan stamp. The information that Judas and Silas are prophets (verse 32) recalls 13:1, as does the note that Paul and Barnabas had worked in Antioch (verse 35). Judas and Silas are sent back to Jerusalem where they belong (verse 27). Luke has created this section as a transition in order to connect the account of the Jerusalem conference with the following report on the start of Paul's independent mission.

Sections on the tradition and any historical elements are missing here because the whole section is entirely due to Luke.

NOTES

1. Cf. Ernst Haenchen, "The Book of Acts as Source Material for the History of Early Christianity," in *Studies in Luke-Acts*, ed. Leander E. Keck and J. Louis Martyn (Philadelphia: Fortress Press, 1980), p. 259.

2. Similarly the Third Evangelist adds "of God" to "power" in Luke 22:69, thereby correcting Mark 14:62 which he had in front of him.

3. Cf. Luke 10:39; Acts 10:1.

4. Andy M. Reimer, *Miracle and Magic: A Study in the Acts of the Apostles and the Life of Apollonius of Tyana* (Sheffield: Sheffield Academic Press, 2002), p. 94.

5. Luke 4:43; 8:1; cf. 16:16.

6. Joseph A. Fitzmyer, *The Acts of the Apostles: A New Translation with Introduction and Commentary* (New York: Doubleday, 1998), p. 405.

7. Robert M. Grant, *Gnosticism and Early Christianity,* rev. ed. (New York: Harper & Row, Torchbooks, 1966), p. 93. See the comments on this phrase by Reimer, *Miracle and Magic*, pp. 8–9.

8. Rick Strelan, *Strange Acts: Studies in the Cultural World of the Acts of the Apostles* (Berlin: Walter de Gruyter, 2004), p. 29.

9. See Stephen Haar, *Simon Magus: The First Gnostic?* (Berlin: Walter de Gruyter, 2003), p. 158. Haar's learned attempt to understand magic in Acts 8 not as the "doubtful dealings of some charlatan" but from within "the ancient tradition of wisdom" (ibid., p. 295; cf. Matt. 2:1) has not convinced me, the more so since "magic" is being used in a negative way in Acts 13:6, 8.

10. See further on this Acts 2:38; 10:45; 11:17.

11. Strelan, *Strange Acts*, p. 215.

12. In *1 Apol.* 26:3, written around 155 CE, the church father Justin mentions the following tenets of Simon's followers: (1) Simon is the "first god" (in Greek, *prôtos theos*); and (2) Helen, who traveled around with Simon and had previously dwelt in a bordello, is the first thought (in Greek, *prôtê ennoia*) generated by Simon. Despite the often-repeated view that Justin's report does not presuppose Gnostic teachings by Simon (thus recently Fitzmyer, *Acts of the Apostles*, p. 403), the opposite must be understood to be the case. For Gnostics, the "first thought" of the "first god" had in all likelihood generated the universe and, after having been degraded, had to be rescued by the "first god." Consequently, "in what Justin's Simonian informants told him they were alluding to their whole myth of creation, fall, and redemption" (Grant, *Gnosticism and Early Christianity*, p. 74). Note that Justin had composed a (now lost) work against all heresies to which he refers in *1 Apol.* 26:8. It began with Simon and included Menander along with Marcion. The likelihood that it contained the description of a full-blown Gnostic myth on Simon's part strengthens the viewpoint that *1 Apol.* 26:3 was an abbreviation of such a myth. Contra Gerd Theissen, "Simon Magus—die Entwicklung seines Bildes vom Charismatiker zum gnostischen Erlöser. Ein Beitrag zur Frühgeschichte der Gnosis," in *Religionsgeschichte des Neuen Testaments*, ed. Axel von Dobbeler, Kurt Erlemann, and Roman Heiligenthal (Tübingen: Francke Verlag, 2000), pp. 407–32.

13. See Mark 14:62; Gospel of Peter 5:19; Eusebius *Ecclesiastical History* 2.23.13; and the survey in my *Untersuchungen zur simonianischen Gnosis* (Göttingen: Vandenhoeck & Ruprecht, 1975), pp. 45–46.

14. Justin 1 *Apol.* 26:2.

15. Justin 1 *Apol.* 26:3.

16. Martin Hengel, *Between Jesus and Paul: Studies in the Earliest History of Christianity* (Philadelphia: Fortress Press, 1983), p. 207n133.

17. For a critique of suggestions that it is not a conflict between Simon and Philip but between Simon and Peter that underlies the tradition in Acts 8, see the illuminating remarks by Christopher R. Matthews, *Philip: Apostle and Evangelist* (Leiden: Brill, 2002), pp. 61–64.

18. C. K. Barrett, *The Acts of the Apostles*, 2 vols. (Edinburgh: T & T Clark, 1994–98), 1:416, sees it differently: He writes, "The *heart* is evidently here regarded as the seat of thought where purposes are entertained and plans made. . . . It can hardly be mere coincidence that Justin, writing (1 *Apol.* 26) of Simon as father of heresy, says that Helena, who accompanied Simon, was called *prote ennoia* and that Hippolytus (*Refutatio* 6.19) similarly speaks of her as *epinoia*. It does not follow that the historical Simon devel-

oped a gnostic system in which *ennoia* or *epinoia* played a part, or that this was personified by Helena, or for that matter that Simon had as a partner a woman called Helena. The process may have gone the other way: *epinoia,* met with in the text of Acts, was a good gnostic-sounding term, and Peter himself alleged that Simon had in his heart an *epinoia*; and the orthodox would be glad to find—or invent—an illicit relationship as a stick with which to beat the proto-gnostic." *Rebuttal:* There is no evidence that the orthodox read Acts 8 in such a way. To give one example, Bishop Irenaeus (*Against All Heresies* 1.23.1) transcribes Acts 8:4–25 before giving a catalogue of heretics. Yet, he omits verse 24, Simon's request to the apostles to pray for him.

19. Yet Friedrich Avemarie, *Die Tauferzählungen der Apostelgeschichte: Theologie und Geschichte* (Tübingen: J. C. B. Mohr/Paul Siebeck, 2002) thinks that "a secret hint in Acts to Ennoia-Helen does not make any sense, for it is only Simon who is being blamed in 8:20–23" (p. 226n79). However, since *epinoia* indeed is Simon's thought, the logic of Avemarie's argument is rather doubtful. Let me hasten to add that it is equally doubtful that the historical Simon ever received Christian baptism (contra Avemarie, *Tauferzählungen,* pp. 343–54). Acts 8:13 is clearly redactional and Simon's baptism is needed in order to demonstrate Philip's superiority over Simon. This polemical aim should not be translated into a factual statement. Equally unsatisfactory is Christoph Markschies's treatment of the story of Simon in Acts 8. He remarks: "If the author of the New Testament Acts is not concealing anything important (and we have no occasion to assume this), the 'Simonian system' came into being only after the death of Simon who was merely a magician, and also after the New Testament book was written" (*Gnosis* [London: SCM Press, 2003], p. 75). Markschies seems to be almost relieved that Simon "was merely a magician" without realizing that Luke had good reason to dismiss Simon as a mere magician in order to make him compete with Philip. Let me note in passing that Luke did not mention Peter's wife, though we know that he was married. Likewise he had no reason to mention Simon's Helen if indeed she was simply Simon's companion.

20. See Jürgen Zangenberg, "*Dynamis tou theou*. Das religionsgeschichtliche Profil des Simon Magus aus Sebaste," in Dobbeler, Erlemann, and Heiligenthal, *Religionsgeschichte des Neuen Testaments*, pp. 519–40.

21. See the thesis of Avemarie, *Die Tauferzählungen der Apostelgeschichte* (evaluated above, n. 19) that indeed Simon was baptized (verse 13). See further my *Primitive Christianity: A Survey of Recent Studies and Some New Proposals* (Edinburgh and New York: T & T. Clark, 2003), pp. 15–16 and below, p. 168 on Acts 13:12.

22. Verse 37 ("And Philip said, "If you believe with all your heart, you may." And he replied, "I believe that Jesus Christ is the Son of God") does not belong to the original text but was added later. "The motive of this scribal addition . . . was to remove the difficulty felt at the sudden, almost unprepared, baptism of the eunuch. The addition, which was known to Irenaeus, may give a second-century formula of interrogation before Baptism . . . which was still performed simply in the name of Jesus and not in the threefold name of the Trinity, Matt. xxviii.19" (C. S. C. Williams. *A Commentary on the Acts of the Apostles* [New York: Harper & Brothers Publishers, 1957], p. 120). See also Friedrich Wilhelm

Horn, "Apg 8,37, der Westliche Text und die frühchristliche Tauftheologie," in *The Book of Acts as Church History: Text, Textual Traditions and Ancient Interpretations*, ed. Tobias Nicklas and Michael Tilly (Berlin and New York: Walter de Gruyter, 2003), pp. 225–39.

23. Luke 1:11–25, 26–28; 2:8–20; Acts 5:19–20; 12:6–17.

24. Cf. Acts 16:12b; 17:21; 23:8.

25. Fitzmyer, *Acts of the Apostles*, p. 412.

26. Acts 5:41; 13:48; cf. 16:34.

27. Matthews, *Philip: Apostle and Evangelist*, p. 82. Matthews, ibid., also notes parallels between the present story and Luke 24:13–35. Matthews concludes "that when writing 1:8, Luke had the Philip traditions that now appear in Acts in mind, with the story of the Ethiopian functioning as an illustration of Isa. 49:6. In the end the combination of motifs centering on Ethiopia in Acts 8:26–40 and the undisputed identification of Ethiopia as the 'end of the earth' in Greco-Roman literary and ethno-geographic sources are decisive" (p. 74).

28. See Isa. 56:3b–5: "Let no eunuch say, 'I am nothing but a barren tree.' (4) For thus says the Lord: 'To the eunuchs who keep my Sabbaths, who choose the things that please me and hold fast my covenant, (5) I will give in my house and within my walls a monument and a name better than sons and daughters; I will give them an everlasting name that shall never be effaced.'" Cf. by contrast Deut. 23:1: "He whose testicles are crushed or whose male member is cut off shall not enter the assembly of the Lord."

29. "After this episode we hear no more of the Ethiopian eunuch. Presumably he continues on his journey, returns home, and spreads the good news there about Jesus the Christ, but the beginnings of Christianity in Nubia and Ethiopia cannot be traced back earlier than the fourth century" (Fitzmyer, *Acts of the Apostles*, p. 411).

30. See my *Early Christianity According to the Traditions in Acts: A Commentary* (Minneapolis, MN: Fortress Press, 1989), pp. 107–10.

31. Cf. Acts 16:14–15; 21:8, 16; 28:7, 16, 23, 30.

32. Hans Conzelmann, *The Theology of St. Luke* (New York: Harper & Brothers, 1960), p. 178n1.

33. Ibid., p. 178.

34. See later in Acts Paul's conversation with and speech before King Agrippa II (25:23–26:29).

35. There are examples in Wilhelm Nestle, *Griechische Studien* (Aaalen: Scientia Verlag, 1968), pp. 567–98.

36. Gal. 1:23.

37. Differently, Robert M. Price, *The Widow Traditions in Luke-Acts: A Feminist-Critical Scrutiny* (Atlanta: Scholars Press, 1997). According to Price, Ananias is a "fabrication since the Apostle himself denies that he was taught the gospel by any human agent (Galatians 1:1, 11–12)" (p. 220).

38. Against this, one should not adduce the "letter" from the Roman consul Lucius to King Ptolemy which is preserved in 1 Macc. 15:16–21. Lucius reports the renewal of the alliance and friendship between the Romans and the Jews which has just taken place (under the high priest Simon) and in verse 21 asks Ptolemy: "If therefore any traitors have escaped from their country to you, hand them over to Simon the high priest, that he may punish

them according to their law." But Lucius does not mention synagogues, as does Acts 9:1–2, but non-Jewish authorities to whom the Jews had escaped and—quite apart from the very open question of the authenticity of the writing—it is uncertain whether the order was still in force two hundred years later. See also Conzelmann, *Acts of the Apostles*, p. 71.

39. Martin Hengel, *Acts and the History of Earliest Christianity* (Philadelphia: Fortress Press, 1980), p. 74.

40. In Greek, *dia meson*.

41. Cf. Conzelmann, *Theology of St. Luke*, pp. 68–69. For a rebuttal see Hengel, *Between Jesus and Paul*, pp. 97–100—which I do not find always convincing.

42. Laurence L. Welborn, "Paul's Flight from Damascus: Sources and Evidence for an Historical Evaluation," in *Historische Wahrheit und theologische Wissenschaft*, ed. Alf Özen (Frankfurt: Peter Lang, 1996), p. 54.

43. Ibid., p. 57.

44. Robert Jewett, *A Chronology of Paul's Life* (Philadelphia: Fortress Press, 1982), pp. 30–33.

45. See the full analysis by Welborn, "Paul's Flight from Damascus," pp. 40–53.

46. Ibid., p. 59.

47. See my *Paul: The Founder of Christianity* (Amherst, NY: Prometheus Books, 2002), pp. 32–33, 40–44.

48. Welborn, "Paul's Flight from Damascus," pp. 58–59. For references see ibid.

49. Cf. Luke 7:2–5; Acts 10:2, 4.

50. Cf. rightly Hengel, *Between Jesus and Paul*, pp. 116–17.

51. Haenchen, *Acts of the Apostles*, p. 340.

52. Correctly, Gottfried Schille, *Die Apostelgeschichte des Lukas* (Berlin: Evangelische Verlagsanstalt, 1983), p. 238.

53. Julius Wellhausen, "Kritische Analyse der Apostelgeschichte," *Abhandlungen der Gesellschaft der Wissenschaften zu Göttingen—Philologisch-historische Klasse* n.s. 15, no. 2 (1914), p. 19.

54. See Jürgen Wehnert, "Das Markus-Evangelium als Quelle der Apostelgeschichte," in Özen, *Historische Wahrheit und theologische Wissenschaft*, pp. 31–32.

55. The tendency of the synoptic and the Primitive Christian tradition in the process of transmission is to add names at a later stage.

56. Perhaps even more suggestive is that the details play a key part in the succeeding story. Without them, the angel could not very well have sent Cornelius's messengers to Peter (10:5–6); "by the seaside" would hardly have provided sufficient directions.

57. Mark 6:7, 13; 16:17–18; Matt. 10:8; Luke 10:17.

58. Price, *The Widow Traditions,* suggests that Tabitha "is one of the women who [are] widows in 1 Timothy 5:16. She was not on the church roll herself, since she was self-sufficient and wealthy enough, like the later mistresses of widow houses, to support others not so fortunate" (p. 197). That is a bold thesis. Yet, it would account for the many widows in the text.

59. Haenchen, *Acts of the Apostles*, p. 341.

60. Note how Luke has freely used Mark 6 so as to put the mission to the Gentiles on Jesus' lips (Luke 4:25–27).

61. "It was Peter who first baptized a Gentile, and the Jerusalem congregation subsequently endorsed this decision and adopted it for its own. . . . Another peculiarity of the story is that the first Gentile to become a Christian should have been a Roman citizen, indeed a Roman officer. . . . (I)t fits admirably with all those passages in Acts which show the Christian Church on good terms with the Roman authorities. This passage amply illustrates the deep interpenetration in Luke's mind of a theological concern—the attempt to secure for the Church the toleration of the Roman State" (Haenchen, *Acts of the Apostles*, p. 360).

62. Cf. Luke 1:6 (Zechariah and Elisabeth); 2:25 (Symeon); 2:37 (Hannah); Acts 9:36 (Tabitha).

63. See Haenchen, *Acts of the Apostles*, p. 346.

64. See Henry J. Cadbury, "Lexical Notes on Acts III," *Journal of Biblical Literature* 45 (1926): 305–22.

65. See the commentaries ad loc.

66. See, e.g., Dibelius, *Studies in the Acts of the Apostles*, p. 111n5.

67. For "gift of the Holy Spirit" see 2:38.

68. See on this Edward Earle Ellis, *Prophecy and Hermeneutic* (Tübingen: J. C. B. Mohr/Paul Siebeck, 1978), pp. 116–28.

69. Dibelius, *Studies in the Acts of the Apostles*, p. 106.

70. Emil Schürer, *The History of the Jewish People in the Age of Jesus Christ (175 B.C.–A.D. 135)*, 3 vols., rev. and ed. Geza Vermes, Fergus Millar, and Matthew Black (Edinburgh: T. & T. Clark, 1973–87), 1:365.

71. Further examples appear in my *Paul, Apostle to the Gentiles*, p. 19.

72. Hengel, *Between Jesus and Paul*, p. 203n111.

73. See Schürer, *History of the Jewish People*, 1:365.

74. Hengel, *Between Jesus and Paul*, p. 203n111.

75. Hans von Campenhausen, "Christians and Military Service in the Early Church," in von Campenhausen, *Tradition and Life in the Church: Essays and Lectures in Church History* (Philadelphia: Fortress Press, 1968), pp. 162–63.

76. See my *Jesus After 2000 Years: What He Really Said and Did* (Amherst, NY: Prometheus Books, 2001), p. 277.

77. Klaus Wengst, *Pax Romana and the Peace of Jesus Christ* (London: SCM Press, 1987), pp. 90–91.

78. Ibid., p. 91.

79. Haenchen, *Acts of the Apostles*, p. 355.

80. Dibelius, *Studies in the Acts of the Apostles*, p. 110.

81. Ibid.

82. Acts 15:7.

83. Acts 15:14.

84. Dibelius, *Studies in the Acts of the Apostles*, pp. 117–18.

85. Haenchen, *Acts of the Apostles*, p. 357.

86. Cf. Acts 4:29, 31; 8:25; 13:46; 14:25; 16:6, 32.

87. Cf. similarly Acts 5:42.

88. Some important ancient texts read "Hellenists"—which would mean "Greek-speaking Jews"—instead of "Gentiles," but the context clearly excludes this.

89. See Acts 13:5, 14; 14:1; 16:13; 17:1–2, 10, 17.

90. Cf. Luke 23:7 and Luke 1:39; 6:12; 24:18; Acts 1:15; 6:1.

91. Josephus *Jewish Antiquities* 20.51.101. In addition to the famine in Judea mentioned above, the following famines are known to have occurred during the reign of Claudius: a famine in Rome at the beginning of Claudius's reign; a famine in Greece in 49; and another famine in Rome in 51. See Schürer, *The History of the Jewish People*, 1: 457n8.

92. See my *Paul, Apostle to the Gentiles*, p. 19.

93. See my *Opposition to Paul in Jewish Christianity* (Minneapolis, MN: Fortress Press, 1989), pp. 55–56.

94. 1 Cor. 16:15; 2 Cor. 8:4; 9:1–13; Rom. 15:31.

95. See also the occurrence of the name "Christians" along with the term "the third race" in the fragments that have survived from *The Preaching of Peter* (early second century). See the English translation in Montague Rhodes James, *The Apocryphal New Testament, Being the Apocryphal Gospels, Acts, Epistles, and Apocalypses* (Oxford: Clarendon Press, 1924), p. 17. The passage in question is from Clement of Alexandria *Stromateis* 6.5.39.

96. Lüdemann, *Paul, Apostle to the Gentiles*, pp. 13–14.

97. Cf. Gal 2:10 and the commentary ibid., pp. 77–80.

98. Luke 20:19; 21:12; Acts 4:3; 5:18; 21:27.

99. See Matt. 2:1.

100. See the monograph by Daniel R. Schwartz, *Agrippa I: The Last King of Judaea* (Tübingen: J. C. B. Mohr/Paul Siebeck, 1990).

101. Ibid., p. 120.

102. Haenchen, *Acts of the Apostles*, p. 382.

103. Ibid.

104. Josephus *Jewish Antiquities* 20.197–203, Cf. my *Heretics: The Other Side of Early Christianity* (Louisville, KY: Westminster John Knox Press, 1996), pp. 49–51.

105. See Acts 9:29; 21:27, 30, 36; 22:22; 23:12, 20–21.

106. See Acts 13:45, 50.

107. Haenchen, *Acts of the Apostles,* p. 383.

108. Cf. similarly Acts 25:12; 26:32.

109. Cf. Mark 10:38–39: Upon the request of the Zebedees John and James to sit in Jesus' glory—in heaven—one at his right hand and one at his left, Jesus says in verse 38, "You do not know what you ask. Can you drink the cup that I drink, or be baptized with the baptism with which I shall be baptized?" (39) And they said to him, "We can." And Jesus said to them, "The cup that I drink you will drink, and with the baptism with which I shall be baptized, you will be baptized."

110. See Eduard Schwartz, *Zum Neuen Testament und frühen Christentum: Gesammelte Schriften*, vol. 5 (Berlin: Walter de Gruyter, 1963), pp. 48–50.

111. Mark 8:31/9:31/10:33–34 (Jesus' death and resurrection); Mark 14:18 (the handing over of Jesus); Mark 14:30 (Peter's denial of Jesus).

112. See the full discussion by Schwartz, *Agrippa I*, pp. 209–12.

113. Josephus *Jewish Antiquities* 19.343–50: "After the completion of his third year of his reign over the whole of Judaea, Agrippa came to the city of Caesarea, which had previously been called Strato's Tower. Here he celebrated spectacles in honour of Caesar, knowing that these had been instituted as a kind of festival on behalf of Caesar's well-being. For this occasion there were gathered a large number of men who held office or had advanced to some rank in the kingdom. On the second day of the spectacles, clad in a garment woven completely of silver so that its texture was indeed wondrous, he entered the theatre at daybreak. There the silver, illumined by the touch of the first rays of the sun, was wondrously radiant and by its glitter inspired fear and awe in those who gazed intently upon it. Straightway his flatterers raised their voices from various directions—though hardly for his good—addressing him as a god. 'May you be propitious to us,' they added, 'and if we have hitherto feared you as a man, yet henceforth we agree that you are more than mortal in your being.' The king did not rebuke them nor did he reject their flattery as impious. But shortly thereafter he looked up and saw an owl perched on a rope over his head. At once, recognizing this as a harbinger of woes just as it had once been of good tidings, he felt a stab of pain in his heart. He was also gripped in his stomach by an ache that he felt everywhere at once and that was intense from the start. Leaping up, he said to his friends: 'I, a god in your eyes, am now bidden to lay down my life, for fate brings immediate refutation of the lying words lately addressed to me. I, who was called immortal by you, am now under sentence of death. But I must accept my lot as God wills it. In fact I have lived in no ordinary fashion but in the grand style that is hailed as true bliss.' Even as he was speaking these words, he was overcome by more intense pain. . . . The king as he lay in his lofty bedchamber and looked down on the people as they fell prostrate, was not dry-eyed himself. Exhausted after five straight days by the pain in his abdomen, he departed his life in the fifty-fourth year of his life and the seventh of his reign." (trans. Louis H. Feldman, Loeb Classical Library, Josephus IX, 1969, pp. 377–81.)

114. See 2 Macc. 9:5.

115. Schwartz, *Agrippa I*, p. 147.

116. Ibid.

117. For whom see Schwartz, *Agrippa I*; Schürer, *History of the Jewish People*, 1:442–54.

118. See my *Opposition to Paul*, p. 45.

119. Martin Hengel and Anna Maria Schwemer, *Paul Between Damascus and Antioch: The Unknown Years* (Louisville, KY: Westminster John Knox Press, 1997), p. 249.

120. See Schwartz, *Agrippa I*, pp. 117–18. Schwartz thinks that Agrippa persecuted the community for political reasons: "Now it is interesting that Peter and the sons of Zebedee were known as the 'zealots' among the apostles. Peter is reported to have wounded the high priest's son with his sword (see esp. John 18:10), and his nickname, appropriately, was 'Barjona' (= brigand, ruffian—Matthew 16:17). Similarly the sons of Zebedee are reported once to have wanted to call down heavenly fire upon a Samaritan village (Luke 9:54), a temperament, which earned them the nickname 'sons of thunder' (Mark 3:17). It is reasonable to suppose, therefore, that Agrippa arrested them for reasons

of state. It is possible, for example, that they were involved in disturbances, just as other Christians have been, shortly before, in Rome. Such an assumption—as opposed to the one linking the persecution to the opening of the Church to Gentiles—would explain, moreover, Luke's silence about the reason for the persecution. For he attempts, as consistently, as he can, to hide all evidence that the Church, or its representatives, were ever really in conflict with the State" (p. 123). Against this Hengel/Schwemer, *Paul Between Damascus and Antioch,* p. 247, rightly point out that the Romans never took action against the Christians at such an early time whereas they did intervene against other "prophets" like Theudas or the "Egyptian" who threatened the political order.

121. See my *Opposition to Paul,* pp. 44–63.

122. See Jürgen Roloff, *Die Apostelgeschichte* (Göttingen: Vandenhoeck & Ruprecht, 1981), p. 187.

123. Thus Elisabeth Schüssler Fiorenza, *In Memory of Her: A Feminist Theological Reconstruction of Christian Origins* (New York: Crossroad, 1983), p. 166.

124. For this see Alfred Wikenhauser, *Die Apostelgeschichte und ihr Geschichtswert* (Münster: Aschendorff, 1921), p. 323.

125. I. Howard Marshall, *The Acts of the Apostles: An Introduction and Commentary* (Grand Rapids, MI: Wm. B. Eerdmans, 1980), p. 209.

126. Hengel/Schwemer, *Paul Between Damascus and Antioch,* p. 470n1315.

127. For example, he writes about the analysis of Acts 18:1–23 presented in my *Paul, Apostle to the Gentiles,* pp. 141–94: "I can only regard his [Lüdemann's] attempt at criticism of Luke as a failure all down the line and add that deep insights into other disputed areas of earliest Christian history are hardly to be expected from an author who deals so violently with clear statements in the sources" (ibid., p. 476n1361). Other students of Hengel have taken up that sort of vulgar tone and have totally condemned my approach to the Lukan texts. See Claus-Jürgen Thornton, *Der Zeuge des Zeugen: Lukas als Historiker der Paulusreisen* (Tübingen: J. C. B. Mohr/Paul Siebeck, 1991). Lüdemann's "madness apparently has method" (". . . hat der Wahnsinn offenbar Methode") (ibid., p. 202n3). A little later he comments on my analysis of the edict of Claudius against the Jews, "Das ist Betrug" (That is deception) (ibid.). On Thornton's naive theological stance see my *Heretics: The Other Side of Early Christianity* (Louisville, KY: Westminster John Knox Press, 1996), pp. 263–64n235.

128. Haenchen, *Acts of the Apostles,* p. 398.

129. See Henry J. Cadbury, *The Making of Luke-Acts* (New York: Macmillan, 1927), p. 225.

130. In Greek, *episteusen.* Note that Luke in the same way—without giving the object of belief—at Acts 8:13 describes Simon's conversion.

131. Avemarie, *Die Tauferzählungen der Apostelgeschichte,* p. 401.

132. See below, pp. 166–67.

133. Haenchen, *Acts of the Apostles,* p. 403.

134. See above, p. 164.

135. Adolf von Harnack, *Die Mission und Ausbreitung des Christentums in den ersten drei Jahrhunderten,* 4th ed., 2 vols. (Leipzig: J. C. Hinrichs, 1924), 1:349n2

thought that the particle sequence *te . . . kai, kai . . . te* made it probable that the first three persons were prophets and the last two teachers. Rebuttal: The framework "Barnabas-Saul" derives from Luke.

136. See also Eph. 4:11, and for the analysis of further examples from early Christianity see Harnack, ibid., 1:332–79.

137. See below, p. 185.

138. Dibelius, *Studies in the Acts of the Apostles*, p. 16, differs.

139. See the analysis of Kirsopp Lake, "The Chronology of Acts," in *The Beginnings of Christianity*, 5:455–59. See further Riesner, *Paul's Early Period*, p. 146.

140. See Arthur Darby Nock, "Paul and the Magus," in *The Beginnings of Christianity*, 5:183–84.

141. See *Papyri Graecae Magicae* III, 198ff. (prayer to Helios); for the phenomenon of prophecy/magic see David Aune, *Prophecy in Early Christianity and the Ancient Mediterranean World* (Grand Rapids, MI: Wm. B. Eerdmans, 1983), pp. 23–48.

142. Harry J. Leon, *The Jews of Ancient Rome* (Philadelphia: Jewish Publication Society, 1960), p. 107, cites twelve examples of Semitic/Latin dual names from Roman Judaism.

143. Hermann Dessau, "Der Name des Apostels Paulus," *Hermes* 45 (1910): 347–68.

144. Fitzmyer, *Acts of the Apostles*, pp. 503–504.

145. Markus Öhler, *Barnabas: Die historische Person und ihre Rezeption in der Apostelgeschichte* (Tübingen: J. C. B. Mohr/Paul Siebeck, 2003), p. 291n97.

146. Ibid., p. 291.

147. Kirsopp Lake and Henry J. Cadbury, in *The Beginnings of Christianity*, 4:147.

148. Ben Witherington III, *The Acts of the Apostles: A Socio-Rhetorical Commentary* (Grand Rapids, MI: Wm. B. Eerdmans, 1998), p. 403.

149. Ibid.

150. Wengst, *Pax Romana*, p. 101.

151. Haenchen, *Acts of the Apostles*, p. 145.

152. Ibid., p. 417.

153. Ibid., p. 408.

154. See my *Jesus After 2000 Years*, pp. 86–87.

155. Haenchen, *Acts of the Apostles*, p. 410.

156. Ibid.

157. See further my *The Resurrection of Christ: A Historical Inquiry* (Amherst, NY: Prometheus Books, 2004), pp. 59–62.

158. For God's plan (verse 36) see Conzelmann, *Theology of St. Luke*, pp. 151–53.

159. For the so-called god-fearers and their relationship to the proselytes see my *Early Christianity According to the Traditions in Acts*, pp. 155–56.

160. Haenchen, *Acts of the Apostles*, p. 414.

161. Cf. 17:5; 18:6, etc.

162. Cf. 14:1; 16:13; 17:1, 10, 17; 18:4, 19; 19:8.

163. Haenchen, *Acts of the Apostles*, p. 414.

164. Ibid., p. 415.

165. Paphos (verses 6, 13) is no longer part of the tradition. Moreover one could not travel by ship from Paphos to Perga, as Luke presupposes.

166. See *New Testament Apocrypha,* revised edition of the Collection initiated by Edgar Hennecke and ed. Wilhelm Schneemelcher, English translation ed. R. McL. Wilson, vol. 2, *Writings Related to the Apostles, Apocalypses, and Related Subjects* (Louisville, KY: Westminster John Knox Press, 1992), pp. 220, 238–39.

167. Pace Burton Scott Easton, *The Pastoral Epistles* (New York: C. Scribner's Sons, 1947), who claims that 2 Tim. 3:11 is the first certain quotation of Acts in Christian literature (p. 67).

168. Haenchen, *Acts of the Apostles,* p. 418.

169. Cf. the similar formulation "some . . . others . . ." in Acts 17:32, 28:24.

170. Emphatically Roloff, *Apostelgeschichte,* p. 211.

171. Andreas Lindemann, *Paulus im ältesten Christentum. Das Bild des Apostels und die Rezeption paulinischer Theologie bis Marcion* (Tübingen: J. C. B. Mohr/Paul Siebeck, 1979), p. 62.

172. See Haenchen, *Acts of Apostles,* p. 421.

173. Ibid., p. 422.

174. Ibid., p. 423.

175. Ibid.

176. Conzelmann, *Acts of the Apostles,* p. 109.

177. See Henry J. Cadbury, *The Book of Acts in History* (New York: Harper & Brothers, 1955), pp. 21–22.

178. *Metamorphoses* 8.620–774.

179. See the commentaries.

180. Translation following James H. Charlesworth, ed., *The Old Testament Pseudepigrapha,* vol. 2, *Expansions of the "Old Testament" and Legends, Wisdom and Philosophical Literature, Prayers, Psalms, and Odes, Fragments of Lost Judeo-Hellenistic Works* (New York: Doubleday, 1985), pp. 898–99 (John J. Collins).

181. Ibid., p. 901.

182. Haenchen, *Acts of the Apostles,* p. 428.

183. On this point, see Acts 12:23.

184. Roloff, *Apostelgeschichte,* p. 213.

185. See ibid., p. 214.

186. See the chronological chart below, p. 358.

187. See, e.g., Gustav Stählin, *Die Apostelgeschichte* (Göttingen: Vandenhoeck & Ruprecht, 1980), p. 195; Marshall, *Acts of the Apostles,* p. 239.

188. See, e.g., Apuleius *Met.* 1.10.1; 2.27.4; 10.6.3.

189. Haenchen, *Acts of the Apostles,* p. 432.

190. Ibid., p. 434.

191. "Perils of Paul" is an allusion to the famous melodramatic tradition of "The Perils of Pauline"—featuring the heroine tied to railroad tracks by the mustachioed villain.

192. Ten times in Acts (but never in the Gospel of Luke!) and only seven times elsewhere in the gospels of Matthew (once), Mark (once), and John (five times).

193. For the terminology of the preaching see Conzelmann, *Theology of St. Luke*, p. 221; in particular a comparison with 8:25, 40 is instructive.

194. Ibid.

195. Strangely enough Roloff, *Apostelgeschichte,* regards Luke's account of the composition of the earliest Jerusalem community as "solid historical information" (p. 224).

196. Dibelius, *Studies in the Acts of the Apostles*, p. 95n6.

197. Richard Bauckham, "James and the Gentiles (Acts 15.13–21)," in *History, Literature, and Society in the Book of Acts*, ed. Ben Witherington III (Cambridge and New York: Cambridge University Press, 1996): 155 (154–84).

198. Cf. Jacque Dupont, "Un peuple d'entre les nations (Actes 15.14)," *New Testament Studies* 31 (1985): 321–35.

199. "The one is therefore meant to produce the other; the restoration is aimed at bringing in the Gentiles. So we should probably explain Luke's meaning like this: the true Israel will be achieved only when the Gentiles are brought into the community of the people of God. But that means that there is only one *laos* [people]; this is at the same time the *laos* which was gathered together from the Jews after Pentecost and the *laos* from the Gentiles to be added in the subsequent period" (Gerhard Lohfink, *Die Sammlung Israels* [Munich: Kösel Verlag, 1975]), p. 59–60).

200. See Kirsopp Lake "The Apostolic Council of Jerusalem," in *The Beginnings of Christianity*, 5:195–212, and now the comprehensive study by Jürgen Wehnert, *Die Reinheit des christlichen Gottesvolkes aus Juden und Heiden: Studien zum historischen und theologischen Hintergrund des sogenannten Aposteldekrets* (Göttingen: Vandenhoeck & Ruprecht, 1997).

201. The transmission of the decree in the Western text contains ethical conditions, which derive from cultic stipulations and hardly vice versa. It omits "what is strangled" and adds the negative form of the Golden Rule. Besides, "abstaining from blood" is understood as "not shedding blood"—and thus not as a dietary but as an ethical code.

202. Lev. 17:8 deals with things sacrificed to idols; 18:6–30 with fornication; 17:15 with strangled food (meat from animals which have not been slaughtered ritually); and 17:10–14 with eating any blood.

203. Conzelmann, *Acts of the Apostles*, p. 119.

204. See above, p. 189.

205. Differently, Bauckham, "James and the Gentiles," p. 184: The "probability that the substance of James' speech derives from a source close to James is high."

206. See my *Paul, Apostle to the Gentiles*, pp. 64–75.

207. See ibid., pp. 64–71 for the question touched on here.

208. See my *Opposition to Paul*, pp. 64–115.

209. Ibid., pp. 117–97.

210. Verse 34 reads, "But it seemed good to Silas to remain there." The best manuscripts do not contain it and most critics consider the verse secondary. "The scribes were so influenced by vs. 40 that they overlooked that Paul could have sent for Silas again after the latter's return to Jerusalem" (Williams, *Commentary on the Acts of the Apostles*, p. 186).

chapter III

Acts 15:36–21:36

PAUL'S MISSIONARY JOURNEY STARTING AND ENDING IN JERUSALEM

T he primary focus of this portion of Acts is Paul's mission, which is presented as a single and rather extensive journey covering twice the distance between Palestine and Greece.

[36]
ACTS 15:36–16:5
AFTER SEPARATING FROM BARNABAS, PAUL REVISITS
THE TERRITORY OF THE PREVIOUS MISSION

(15:36) *And after some days* Paul *said to* Barnabas, "Let us return and visit the brothers *in every city* where we *proclaimed the word of the Lord*, and see how they are." (37) Now Barnabas wanted to take with them John *called* Mark. (38) But Paul thought it best not to take with them one who had deserted them in Pamphylia and refused to share in their work. (39a) And there arose a sharp disagreement, so that they *separated* from each other. (39b) Barnabas took Mark with him and sailed away to Cyprus, (40) but Paul chose Silas and departed, *having been commended by the brothers to the grace of the Lord.* (41) And he went through Syria and Cilicia, *strengthening the churches.* (16:1a) Paul came also to Derbe and to Lystra.

(1b) A disciple *named* Timothy was there, the son of a believing Jewish woman and a <u>Greek</u> father. (2) He was *well spoken of* by the brothers at Lystra and Iconium. (3) This [man] Paul wanted to go with him, and he took him and circumcised him because of the Jews who were in those places, for they all knew that his father was a <u>Greek</u>.

(4) *As they went on their way through the cities, they delivered to them for observance the decisions that had been reached by the apostles and elders who were in Jerusalem.*

(5) *So the churches were strengthened in the faith, and they increased in numbers daily.*

OUTLINE

15:36–39a: After proposal by Paul to Barnabas to visit the communities founded earlier, the two argue

39b–16:1a: Barnabas takes John Mark with him to Cyprus; Paul takes Silas to Syria and Cilicia and comes from Derbe to Lystra

1b–3:   Paul circumcises Timothy and takes him along (from Lystra)

4:    The Apostolic Decree is delivered to the communities they visit

5.   Resulting growth in strength of faith and numbers of members in the communities

LUKE'S PURPOSE

Verses [15:] 36–41: Luke's report of Paul's separation from Barnabas is called for because hereafter the Pauline mission will have no use for a member of the Antioch congregation, especially since in the previous chapter Paul had emerged as the chief spokesperson. The source of the dispute was John Mark's desertion of Paul and Barnabas during their missionary activity in Pamphylia (13:13). The possibility of redaction is also signaled by the observation that it was Paul, and not Barnabas, who received a farewell blessing from the brothers in Antioch (verse 40); and the note about Silas in this same verse—if he is the Silas who earlier accompanied Judas Barsabbas (15:22, 27, 32–33)—raises a serious problem. Having returned to Jerusalem, he can hardly be Paul's companion now, as verse 40 claims. The best explanation is to consider his appearance in verses 22, 27, 32–33 as redactional, and in verse 40 as an element of tradition. That once again Luke has been careless remains an alternative possibility.

Verse [16:] 1a: Paul's journey to Derbe and Lystra is a Lukan doublet of 14:6–7, 20–21. Luke has Paul return to these cities after the conference so as not to picture Timothy as his companion until the independent Pauline mission has begun. This likely suggests Luke's understanding that Timothy played a significant role in Paul's independent mission.

Verses 1b–3: Luke makes explicit in verse 3 the reason Paul had Timothy circumcised: The mission he planned would take them among Jews who knew that Timothy's father was Greek. As those Jews presumably would, so Luke evidently supposes that his Gentile father means that Timothy is a Gentile; but since Luke's Paul must have none but Jews as fellow workers for his mission among Jews,[1] he has to make his colleague a Jew by circumcision. Luke's pragmatic imagination here controls the action: It provides "the main reason that Luke gives, the advantage that Paul would gain in having a circumcised Jewish Christian collaborator when he would be dealing with Jews in the area."[2] Here at least, Luke is clearly hedging on the promises made by Peter and James (15:9, 19) that Gentile Christians need not be circumcised. While this report in effect protects Paul from future attacks (cf. 21:21), the value of such immunity is purely theoretical, because Luke's church is not engaged in an effort to convert Jews (see below, pp. 345–46).

Verse 4: Here we have a reference to the decisions of the Jerusalem conference and an indication that its actions to promote church unity and continuity were being implemented. We should note that according to this report the Apostolic Decree was communicated only to those communities that predated the conference. Verse 1a specifically mentions Derbe and Lystra, but by Luke's understanding one could surely add Pisidian Antioch and Iconium (along with the Christians of Antioch and Syria/Cilicia; see 15:23) to the list of those affected by the decree—and therefore to be included in Paul's travels. Luke does not later trouble himself to report delivery of the decree to communities founded after the conference because while that edict was an element in salvation history, its significance for Luke's community was tenuous at best. "With the story of Timothy and the report of the delivery of the *dogmata* of the Apostles and elders, it is evident that the mission now beginning is undertaken in complete concord with the Jewish Christians of Jerusalem. Luke thus sees the Pauline mission, which from now on becomes his real theme, as harmoniously integrated into the total work of the Church."[3]

Verse 5: In following the pattern of 6:7 and 9:31, this short summary echoes those passages.[4] The increase of the Christian congregations in both spiritual intensity and numbers is basic to Luke's description of the Apostolic Age.

THE TRADITIONS REWORKED BY LUKE

Verses [15:] 36–41: Paul's separation from Barnabas (verse 39), his journey with Silas to Syria and Cilicia (verse 41, cf. Gal. 1:21), and the departure of Barnabas and Mark to Cyprus (verse 39; cf. 13:4, 13) are all founded on tradition.

Verse 16:1a: Probably dependent on tradition are the en route visits to Derbe and Lystra, though their causal connection to similar itinerary reports in chapter 14 suggest that Luke has created a doublet.

Verses 1b–3: The story about Timothy also reflects tradition. Note that Silas is kept offstage until his adventitious reappearance in 16:19, whereupon Timothy disappears until his sudden return to the narrative in 17:14–15. The tradition has probably provided the following elements: Timothy's arrival from Lystra and/or Iconium (verse 2), his mixed parentage (Jewish mother, Gentile father), and the acquaintanceship between Paul and the Christian Timothy.[5]

Paul's circumcision of Timothy is no doubt another datum from the tradition. Such an action may have been prompted by his mother's Jewishness, for while rabbinic law usually assumes paternal assignment of status, the mother is determinant in the case of a mixed marriage.

Although this rabbinic legal view was not formulated until the second century CE,[6] in all likelihood it was already part of a decision or rule handed down by the rabbis to be the authoritative interpretation of the written or oral Torah—a *halachah* (from the Hebrew, "to walk").[7] If such a circumcision was reflected in the tradition underlying 16:3, it was surely appropriate under the law. Haenchen, however, argues that Luke took the datum of Timothy's circumcision from a tradition dependent on Gal. 5:11, a passage apparently responding to rumors that even as a Christian Paul taught circumcision: "Here then Luke has not . . . tendentiously replaced the truth known to him by a patchwork of his own; rather was he the victim of an unreliable tradition."[8]

HISTORICAL ELEMENTS

Verses [15:] 36–39: The tradition is probably correct in reporting Paul's separation from the Antioch community; still, one cannot posit a connection between this and the incident at Antioch (Gal. 2:11–14).[9] Besides, a no longer definable conflict over principle has been redactionally assigned to the personal sphere—note that Paul's real opponents at Antioch were James's people, not Barnabas. Verses 40–41 probably reflect Paul's departure for Syria and Cilicia after the Cephas visit reported in Gal. 1:18.[10] One is tempted to accept the statement in the tradition that Silvanus[11] was Paul's companion, for that would suggest that Paul got to know Silvanus during the visit of Cephas.

Verse [16:] 1a: Without doubt Paul's journey through Derbe and Lystra (and Iconium and Antioch) is historical; these were the accustomed way stations on the land route from Syria/Cilicia to Ephesus.

Verse 1b: Likewise historical is Paul's association with Timothy, but contrary to Luke's report it was Paul himself who converted Timothy. In 1 Cor. 4:17 he writes, "Therefore I have sent to you Timothy, who is my beloved and faithful child in the Lord." In that same context, verse 14, Paul also refers to the Corinthians as his beloved children inasmuch as he has given birth to them through the gospel. The same therefore applies to Timothy. This conversion must have taken place while Paul was on the way to Greece, for there Timothy, Silvanus, and Paul were among those who conducted the mission that marked the origin of the Corinthian community.[12] Assuming the correctness of the chronology below, pages 357–60, Timothy's conversion (against Acts) occurred *before* the conference, and thus during Paul's first visit to Lystra.[13]

Many scholars—both early and recent—have rejected the historicity of the circumcision of Timothy on the basis of relevant passages in Paul's letter to the Galatians that stress the irrelevance of circumcision and reject its necessity for Gentile Christians.[14] Yet since Timothy came from a mixed marriage, with his mother being Jewish, by rabbinic law Timothy *was* a Jew. Therefore Paul could very well circumcise Timothy as a Jewish colleague. This would not have been at odds with baptism, because according to Paul "everyone should remain in the calling in which he was called" (1 Cor. 7:20). In the case of Timothy, this would mean remaining Jewish.[15] While it should be stressed that Luke's stated reason (that the Jews knew he had a Gentile father) is inaccurate, and while—contrary to Acts—Timothy was circumcised not considerably after he became a Christian but at the time of his conversion and quite possibly before he was baptized, the reported circumcision is no doubt historical.

THE HISTORICAL VALUE OF LUKE'S ACCOUNT

Verse [15:] 39a: It is noteworthy that Luke at least recognizes the existence of dissent in the earliest church, but he never delves into the precise nature of the conflict. Moreover, a disagreement over whether to include someone in a missionary team can hardly be the reason for the permanent estrangement of two who were once such close colleagues.

Verses [16:] 1–5: First, Luke falsely presupposes a planned mission by Paul among the Jews; second, he does not scruple to present Timothy as a Gentile whom Paul thinks he must circumcise; third, he chooses not to tell that Paul was the one who converted Timothy. Last, Luke places the meeting between Paul and Timothy too late.[16]

[37]
ACTS 16:6–10
PAUL'S CALL TO MACEDONIA

(6) *And they went through the region of* Phrygia and Galatia, *prevented by the Holy Spirit from speaking the word in Asia.* (7) *And when they had come to* Mysia, *they attempted to go into* Bithynia, *but the Spirit of Jesus did not let them.* (8) *So, passing by Mysia, they went down to* Troas. (9) *And a vision was seen by Paul in the night: a man of Macedonia stood there appealing to him, saying, "Come over to Macedonia and help us."* (10) *And when Paul had seen the vision, immediately we sought to go on into Macedonia, concluding that God had called us to preach the gospel to them.*

OUTLINE

6–8: Zigzag journey from Phrygia to Troas

9–10: Paul's vision of the Macedonian and the intention to go to Macedonia

LUKE'S PURPOSE

Luke has framed this account using language and style typical of his work. See especially the direct speech in verse 9b. The first person plural in verse 10 ("*we* sought") seems to be an awkward reflection of the "us" at the end of verse 9. The likely (or is it intended?) response of Luke's readers to this anchorless "we" is that "they quite instinctively felt drawn into the fellowship of this missionary group and experienced its destiny as their own."[17]

Verses 6–8: The instrumentality of the Holy Spirit (verse 6) or the Spirit of Jesus (verse 8) is a Lukan touch; once again he seeks to demonstrate the divine guidance of salvation history.

Verses 9–10: Luke has also composed the dream vision (verse 9)[18] in order to signify the special nature of the transition from Asia to Europe. No doubt the zigzag journey related in verses 6–8 is intended to accentuate by contrast the firm decision to pass straight over into Macedonia in supposed conformance with God's plan.

THE TRADITIONS REWORKED BY LUKE

Verses 6–8: The place names "Phrygia and the land of Galatia" appear once again in 18:23, but in reverse order; this and the unrealistically zigzag nature of the journey—along with three obviously redactional injunctions by the Holy Spirit— suggest that Luke has selectively reported elements of the tradition, leaving a fragmentary itinerary[19] with the stages "Phrygia, Galatia, Mysia, Troas."

Verses 9–10: The tradition may have indicated the significance of shifting the mission to Macedonia, for the passage distinguishes this from moves in other directions. Luke has created a dramatic scene to highlight the importance of this redirection.

HISTORICAL ELEMENTS

Verses 6–8: The places recorded in the tradition (Phrygian, land of Galatia) are real enough, but Luke has located them anachronistically. Both tradition and history assign them to Paul's journey before the Jerusalem conference: through Syria, Cilicia, and southern Galatia (Derbe, Lystra, Iconium) to north Galatia and from there by Troas to Macedonia. Nevertheless, Paul's mission in Troas seems to belong to a later period (2 Cor. 2:12/Acts 20:6).

Verses 9–10: It was said above that the tradition may have hinted at the importance of the move to Macedonia for Paul. This is supported by his own words in Phil. 4:15, "You . . . know that in the beginning of the gospel (in Greek, *en archê tou euaggeliou*) when I set out from Macedonia, no church entered into partnership with me." One should, of course, freely render "in the beginning of the gospel" as "in the early days of my proclamation of the gospel."[20] This would be an indication that the real beginning of Paul's missionary career stemmed from his preaching in Macedonia—that is, Philippi and Thessalonica.[21] The editorial work in verses 9–10 notwithstanding, the section under review shows the great importance Paul and his coworkers ascribed to the expansion of their missionary activity to Europe.[22] This took place in the late 30s CE.[23]

THE HISTORICAL VALUE OF LUKE'S ACCOUNT

By placing Paul's move to Macedonia subsequent to the Jerusalem Conference—and thus one decade too late—Luke conveys a totally misleading impression of this mission. To be sure, he has again preserved traditions that aid us in reconstructing the circumstances and the time of Paul's early mission in Greece; nevertheless, that we are obliged to rely on Paul's letters in order to set the record straight and expose what can only be termed a willful (self-)deception springing from a theological agenda must count heavily against Luke's reliability in historical matters.

[38]
ACTS 16:11–40
PAUL AND SILAS IN PHILIPPI

(11) So, *setting sail* from Troas, we *ran a straight course* to Samothrace, and the following day to Neapolis, (12a) and from there to Philippi, (12b) *which is a city of the first district of Macedonia and a Roman colony.* (12c) We remained in this city several days.

(13) And on the Sabbath day we went outside the gate to the riverside, where we supposed there was a *place of prayer*, and we sat down *and spoke to the women who had come together.* (14) And a woman *named* Lydia, from the city of Thyatira, a seller of purple cloth, a worshiper of God, was listening. The Lord opened her heart to pay attention to what was said by Paul. (15) And after she was baptized, and her household as well, she urged us, saying, "If you have judged me to be a believer in the Lord, come to my house and stay." And she prevailed upon us.

(16a) One day as we went to the *place of prayer* we met a slave girl (16b) who had an oracular spirit and brought her LORDS much gain by fortune telling. (17) She followed Paul and us, crying out, "These men are servants of the Most High God, who proclaim to you the way of salvation." (18a) And this she kept this up for many days, (18b) until Paul, who could stand it no longer, turned and said to the spirit, "I command you in the name of Jesus Christ to **go out** of her." And it did **go out** that very hour.

(19) But when her LORDS saw that their hope of gain was **gone out**, they seized Paul and Silas and dragged them into the marketplace before the rulers. (20) They brought them to the magistrates, saying, "These men are Jews, and they are disturbing our city. (21) They advocate customs that are not lawful for

us as Roman citizens to accept or practice." (22) The crowd joined in attacking them, and the magistrates tore their clothes off them and gave orders to beat them with rods. (23) And when they had inflicted many blows upon them, they threw them into prison, ordering the jailer to keep them safely. (24) Having received this order, he put them into the inner prison and secured their feet in the stocks.

(25) About midnight Paul and Silas were praying and singing hymns to God, and the prisoners were listening to them, (26) Suddenly there was a great earthquake, so that the foundations of the prison were shaken. And immediately all the doors were opened, and everyone's bonds were loosened. (27) When the jailer woke and saw that the prison doors were open, he drew his sword and was about to kill himself, supposing that the prisoners had escaped. (28) But Paul cried with a loud voice, "Do not harm yourself, for we are all here." (29) And the jailer called for lights and rushed in, and trembling with fear he fell down before Paul and Silas. (30) *Then he brought them out and said, "LORDS, what must I do to be saved?"* (31) *And they said, "Believe in the Lord Jesus, and you will be saved, you and your household."* (32) *And they spoke the word of the Lord to him together with all in his house.* (33) *And he took them the same hour of the night and washed their wounds; and he was baptized immediately, he and all his family.* (34) *Then he brought them up into his house and set food before them. And he rejoiced along with his entire household that he had believed in God.*

(35) But when it was day, the magistrates sent the police, saying, "Let those men go." (36) And the jailer reported these words to Paul, saying, "The magistrates have sent to let you go. Therefore come out now and go in peace." (37) But Paul said to them, "They have beaten us publicly, without a trial, men who are Roman citizens, and have thrown us into prison; and are they now going to release us secretly? No! Let them come and escort us out themselves." (38) The officers reported these words to the magistrates, and they were afraid when they heard that they were Roman citizens. (39) So they came and apologized to them. And they led them outside and asked them to leave the city. (40a) But having gone out of the prison,

(40b) they went to Lydia. And having seen the brothers, they encouraged them and departed.

OUTLINE

25–34: Their miraculous deliverance and conversion of the warder

35–40a: Official release

40b: Farewell to Lydia and the brothers

LUKE'S PURPOSE

Verses 11–12a: Luke is fond of the verb "to set sail."[24] "To run a straight course" occurs in only one other place in the New Testament: Acts 21:1.

Verse 12b: The original version is disputed. The reading of ancient codices ("which is the first city in the district of Macedonia") hardly makes sense, because Macedonia was not a "district." Rather the *province* of Macedonia was divided into four districts, in each of which the "first" city was the capital. Yet Philippi, as a colony, was neither a provincial nor a district capital.[25] Therefore in the translation of verse 12b I have—following the majority view among scholars—emended the text to correctly describe Philippi as a colony and a city in the first district of Macedonia. Although this explanation of Philippi's special political status is the only such example in Luke's writings, note his occasional insertion of parenthetical explanations: 8:26; 13:8; 17:21. These offerings could reflect either Luke's personal knowledge or the tradition he is using.[26]

Verses 13–15: Going to the place of prayer (verse 13) derives from Luke's scheme of having Paul make his initial approach to the Jews, but the term "place of prayer," used only here in Acts, is noteworthy. Also worth recalling here is the special role of women in Luke's writings.[27]

Verses 16–18: The beginning of verse 16 marks a break in the narrative, for the succeeding episode is introduced by a clearly Lukan transition ("One day as we went to the place of prayer . . .") and is only tenuously linked to the preceding story of Lydia by means of the keyword *proseuchê* ("place of prayer"), a term that takes us back to before the Lydia story, which also began at a "place of prayer." Furthermore, the information that the possessed girl "kept this up for many days" (verse 18a) confuses the narrative chronology because it is in tension with verse 16a: one would expect Paul to drive out the evil spirit (verse 18b) right away, not after many days. As Haenchen observes, "The story shows the reader two things: First, that the truth of the gospel has been confirmed also by the supernatural acknowledgement of the spirit-world, and second, that Paul through the exorcism in the name of Jesus is plainly superior to the spirits."[28]

Verses 19–24: Paul's successful exorcism triggers a violent reaction by the girl's owners.[29] They drag Paul before the city officials in the marketplace. Yet their accusations (verses 20–21) are unrelated to Paul's exorcism. It is not until verse 37 that Luke's purpose becomes evident.

Verses 25–29: The story of the miraculous release derives from tradition—not as an independent circulating story about Paul's release from a prison in Philippi but as a "reading fruit" on the part of Luke. It is the third prison escape scene in Acts and resembles those recorded in chapters 5 and 12. In all the passages God sets the Christian missionaries free; here in Acts 16 the narrative is developed in a particularly miraculous manner, and adds a conversion story (verses 30–34). The supernatural deed of God through the apostles thus clearly bolsters their mission.

Verses 30–34: This section shows Luke at work. The dialogue (verses 30–32) is typical of Luke's way of arranging scenes. The jailer's question, "Lords (in Greek, *kyrioi*), what shall I do to be saved," picks up "Lords" in verse 19 (there it is the possessed girl's masters).[30] Still, the scene retains its focuses on what is to Luke the overriding issue of conversion/salvation. Paul's answer in verse 31, "You and your house will be saved," is redactional, as was Peter's corresponding assurance in the Cornelius story (11:14). The word "house" (verse 34) points back to Lydia's invitation to her house in verse 15. The content of the sermon (verse 32) and the jailer's ministrations to the preachers (verse 33) reflect Luke's purpose. The phraseology "they spoke the word of the Lord" (verse 32) and the words "received" and "immediately" in verse 33 are certainly Lukan. The same can be said of "believed" in verse 34. On the motif of rejoicing, see 8:39.

Verses 35–40a: Here the main action is resumed, but with no note of the miraculous release. Verse 37 at last lets us see what Luke was setting the stage for in verse 20. Silas and Paul are Romans: despite the stereotypical association of Jews with magic[31]—a linkage twice made elsewhere in Acts[32]—Silas and Paul are not Jews. Those who truly practice magic are the accusers, the "Lords" of verses 16 and 19. That the magistrates order the release of Paul and Silas, apologetically escort them from the prison, and fawningly request them to leave the city (verses 35–39) all serve to vindicate the missionaries the eyes of Luke's Roman readers.[33]

Verse 40b: When Paul and Silas once again enter Lydia's house, a link to verse 15 brings the Philippi story full circle to a close.

THE TRADITIONS REWORKED BY LUKE

Verses 11–12a: Because of the chronicle-like style, we may safely assume these verses come from a tradition.

Verses 13–15: The odd phrasing of verse 13, "where we *supposed* there was a place of prayer," may reflect an eyewitness report.[34] Because it appears in Acts only in this episode, the term "place of prayer" (in Greek, *proseuchê*) suggests tradition, as do the name of Lydia and the details of her origin and baptism. Because of its echo in verse 31, the motif of "household" (verse 15) is likely a Lukan touch, though it is widely seen to reflect tradition—and elsewhere does come from reliable tradition.[35]

Verses 16–18: Luke adapted the healing story from tradition. On stylistic grounds we can identify its ending with the statement, "And it [the Spirit] did go out that very hour"; one cannot, however, discover its exact beginning. But in spite of that hiatus and the missing elements of demonstration and concluding chorus, the structure suggests that we have what was once a complete exorcism story.

Verses 19–24: The note about Roman authorities beating Paul and Silas with rods (verses 22–23) goes back to tradition. For one thing, it stands in tension with Luke's positive view of the Romans; for another, strong historical reasons suggest its factuality at this point (see below, p. 217).

Verses 25–29: This account of a prison escape—along with those in chapters 5 and 12—has many parallels in Jewish and Hellenistic narratives. Their function is religious propaganda, namely to depict a new religion's victory over all opposition. "The apparent home of this type was the Dionysiac tradition. So appealing was it that proponents of other religions, including Jews and Christians, made similar demonstrations of the vindicating power of their gods, and storytellers and novelists transformed them for their purposes. The Dionysiac tales, best known through the *Bacchae* of Euripides, reflect no interest in legal vindication, set as they are in the mythical past. Resistance to the mission is *theomachia* (obstinate flouting of a god), and such opposition receives its just due."[36] Probably Luke has added Paul and Silas to an ancient miraculous release story of that sort which was known to him.

Verse 37: Paul's Roman citizenship is not an element of the traditions that informed this section, but it may have appeared in other traditions that Luke had in hand and found useful to use at this point.[37]

HISTORICAL ELEMENTS

Verses 11–12a: The way stations are certainly historical. Paul himself speaks in Phil. 4:15–16 of the beginnings of the mission in Philippi. The places that he does not explicitly mention there—"Troas, Samothrace, and Neapolis"—are natural stops on the route to Philippi, and Paul must have passed through them.

Verses 13–15: That the person Lydia and her placement in Philippi are historical is supported both by her name and the information that she deals in purple fabrics. That being the case, her baptism and her hospitality are also no doubt historical. Since *proseuchê* denotes a synagogue (or some equivalent place of prayer),[38] it is highly unlikely "that only women were there,"[39] and we must no doubt assign that datum to Luke's editing.[40] The river would seem to be the Gangitis, which runs about a mile west of the city; it would of course have provided water for ritual washings. The best way of explaining these elements of tradition that appear in verse 13 (synagogue/place of prayer, river) is to understand them as historical facts that derive from Paul's first mission in Philippi. This chronological setting is all but certain in view of verses 14–15, which reflect Paul's foundation mission to Philippi.

Verses 16–18: The historical accuracy of the traditions underlying this passage is far from certain. While it is undeniable that Rom. 15:18–19 and 2 Cor. 12:12 unambiguously attribute "miracles" to Paul, one cannot demonstrate the causal connection of the present tradition with a Pauline miracle. Besides, a "miracle" that Paul reportedly performed elsewhere could have given rise to the tradition of a miracle in Philippi.

Verses 22–23: The report that the Romans maltreated Paul and Silas corresponds to Paul's own account in 1 Thess. 2:2 of his and Silas's suffering in Philippi. While 1 Thess. 2:2 unfortunately offers no further details of their punishment, the two stories seem to be directly connected. Furthermore, in 2 Cor. 11:25 Paul tells us he was on three occasions beaten with rods—straight metal strips used in Roman floggings.

Verses 25–29: The circumstances of the delivery from prison are pure fiction and have many analogies in the Jewish and Hellenistic world (see above, p. 216) Nevertheless, according to a recent commentator on Acts, "The existence of fictional parallels to details of the story cannot disprove it, and it is hard to see why the story of the earthquake should have been invented if there were not a basis of truth in it."[41] The logic behind this verdict is puzzling. For one thing, Luke often created scenes, and invented for Jesus and John the Baptist words that had no basis in tradition.[42] For another, it is unsatisfactory, to say the least, to glibly describe the parallels to verses 25–29 as "fictional" while upholding historicity for the present scene. Still and all, based on the tradition in verses 22–23, we can affirm that Paul and Silas were physically abused in the process of and/or subsequent to an arrest. Accordingly, verses 25–29 preserve a historical nucleus, and contain an essentially accurate account (enhanced, of course with miraculous features) of the release of Paul and Silas after maltreatment—as 1 Thess. 2:2 attests.

THE HISTORICAL VALUE OF LUKE'S ACCOUNT

In his report of events at Philippi, Luke has beclouded some facts with miraculous tales in order to make a theological point. "From a happy beginning it [the report] leads into a situation of hopeless distress and danger. But God proves stronger than the afflictions and uses them to serve his own purposes—how could one then despair? Luke has recounted this narrative that his readers might gather strength from it."[43]

Yet, the story of the converted jailer and the liberation of Paul and Silas from prison is fraught with incredible elements. Ernst Haenchen has brilliantly listed them thus: A jailer "who, seeing the doors open in an earthquake, at once wants to take his life, without so much as a glance at the cells, is a very unlikely sort of person. As if that were not enough, Paul in his cell knows what the jailer is about to do."[44] Furthermore, how could the keeper of the prison possibly "know who is calling to him from the cell (even if such shout were audible in his bedroom)? Above all, how does he know that the earthquake is the answer to Paul and Silas's hymn? To the reader it is obvious, but the jailer was asleep (v. 27—he was the only one in the whole jail who slept)."[45]

Here is the concluding sentence of the analysis of this episode by Haenchen, who like nobody else before him has skillfully demonstrated the many contradictions of the story. In the end, he comes to the author's defense:

> The author's freedom, which we encounter here, is strange to the modern reader. But it did not occur to any of the great Roman historians simply to say "how it actually happened." They all wanted to inform, influence and motivate. Luke would not have broken the tradition of great Roman historical writing (how far he knew it and used it as a model is another question) when he narrated the history of the mission in Philippi in his own fashion. The difference between *facta* and *ficta* has not been the same in all ages.[46]

Rebuttal: That summation is far too apologetic, yet at the same time typical of Haenchen's commentaries on Acts—in which he regularly and thoroughly debunks the historical value of Luke's account and almost simultaneously comes to the Evangelist's theological defense. To say that the great Roman historians did not write what actually happened does not mean—as Haenchen seems to imply—that they could write almost anything. History in its broadest sense may well be, as Napoleon observed, a myth we have agreed upon; but to deconstruct one such work of fiction while at the same time excusing its author's literary eccentricities on account of his apologetic agenda or because he may have entertained now outmoded criteria of truth is a dubious strategy. To paraphrase a contextually appropriate adage, such a methodology smacks of expropriating Petrine wealth in the cause of supplying a Pauline shortfall.

[39]
ACTS 17:1–15
PAUL AND SILAS IN THESSALONICA AND BEROEA

(1) Now when they had passed through Amphipolis and Apollonia, they came to Thessalonica, *where there was a synagogue of the Jews*. (2) *And Paul went in, as was his custom, and on three Sabbath days he reasoned with them from the Scriptures*, (3a) *explaining and expounding that it was necessary for the Christ to suffer and to rise from the dead, and (saying), "This Jesus, whom I proclaim to you, is the Christ."* (4) *And some of them were persuaded and joined Paul and Silas, as did a great multitude of the devout Greeks and not a few of the leading women*. (5) *But the Jews were jealous, and taking some wicked men of the rabble, they formed a mob, set the city in an uproar, and attacked the house of Jason, seeking to bring them out to the popular assembly*. (6a) And when they could not find them, they dragged Jason and some of the brothers before the city authorities, (6b) shouting, "These men who have turned the world upside down have come here also, (7) and Jason has received them, and they are all acting against the decrees of Caesar, saying that there is another king, Jesus." (8) And they unsettled the people and the city authorities, who heard these things. (9) And when they had taken bail from Jason and the rest, they let them go.

(10) The brothers immediately sent Paul and Silas away by night to Beroea, *and upon arriving they went into the synagogue*. (11) *Now these Jews were more receptive than those in Thessalonica, and they received the word eagerly, examining the Scriptures daily to see if these things were so*. (12) *Many of them therefore believed, together with not a few Greek women of high standing as well as men*. (13) *But when the Jews from Thessalonica learned that the word of God was being proclaimed by Paul at Beroea also, they came there too, inciting and stirring up the crowds*. (14) Then the brothers immediately sent Paul off on his way to the sea, but Silas and Timothy remained there. (15) Those who escorted Paul accompanied him as far as Athens and then returned, bearing instructions for Silas and Timothy to join him as soon as possible.

OUTLINE

   1: Journey by Amphipolis and Apollonia to Thessalonica
  2–3: Witnessing for Christ in the synagogue
   4: Partial success among Jews, god-fearers, and wives of the well-to-do

5–9: The unsuccessful attack of the Jews of Thessalonica aimed at Paul and Silas; accusations against Jason and other brothers

10–12: After escaping to Beroea Paul and Silas successfully preach the word among the Jews and among the well-to-do women and men in Beroea

13: Incitement against Paul by the Jews from Thessalonica

14–15: Paul's escape to Athens

LUKE'S PURPOSE

While portions of this section are based on tradition, the report of Paul and Silas's activities in Thessalonica and Beroea (verses 1–15) shows considerable Lukan shaping. The missions in Thessalonica (verses 2–9) and Beroea (verses 10b–12) are much alike in structure: The mission begins in the synagogue; the "sermon" is based on scripture; those converted are similarly identified (note especially the well-to-do women); and persecution follows the promulgation of he word. Moreover, the two narratives are neatly meshed: Verse 11 contrasts with verse 5, and the angry Jews from Thessalonica in verse 5 reappear in verse 13. And the section as a whole is strongly contextualized: Not only does verse 1a continue the narrative of 16:40, but also verse 15 announces the setting of the following action, Athens.[47]

Verse 1: The first part of this verse is a travel note; the second prepares for verse 2.

Verses 2–3: Luke has composed these two verses without relying on any tradition. Thus the sermon to the Jews derives from his scheme of making Paul and the other missionaries approach the Jews first (verse 2). The note that Paul reasoned with the Jews on *three* Sabbaths reflects the fact that "three" is a favorite number of Luke's. Also Lukan is the sermon message that the Christ had to suffer in accordance with the scriptures and rose again on the third day (verse 3a).[48] Verse 3b, like 1:4, is a redactional transition from third person narrative to direct speech in the first person.

Verse 4: The announcement of Jewish converts is schematic. For the significance of the reported conversion of a large number of Gentiles, see below, page 234. Parallels in 13:50 and 17:12 (see below) indicate that the conversion of the wives of the wealthy is to be assigned to the author.

Verse 5: The rebellion of the local Jews against Paul (verse 5) is an oft-repeated Lukan scenario. The unusually clumsy introduction of Jason—not as a person, but as the adjunct to a house—suggests the careless insertion of traditional material into a schematic account. The description of the public uproar is clearly like that in 19:29, 32.

Verses 6–9: The charge of creating unrest (verses 6b–7, cf. 16:20; 24:5) is so formulated that the reader can reject it out of hand as invalid.[49] For the piling up of charges against Paul, see the multiple accusations leveled by the Jews against Jesus in Luke 23:2–3 and esp. verse 5—a catalogue from which Mark differs.

Verse 10: Entering the synagogue derives from Luke's pattern of having Christian missionaries approach the Jews first (cf. verse 2).

Verses 11–12: "They" (here referring to Jews receptive to Paul's message) is a verbal—though not a referential—echo of "they" in verse 10, where it denotes Paul and Silas. The phrases "received the word"[50] and "if these things were so,"[51] as well as the understatement "not a few" (cf. verse 4) reveal the author at work. Validating the Christian message by recourse to scripture is a well-attested Lukan theme. Both verses are variants of verse 4 (see the above prefatory comments on verses 1–15), where the positive response of the Jews in Beroea is set in narrative contrast to the negative attitude of those in Thessalonica. The entire passage demonstrates Luke's narrative artistry. Note, for instance, his use of contextual variation in reporting the conversion of the wives of the leading citizens (cf. verses 12 and 4).

THE TRADITIONS REWORKED BY LUKE

Verse 1a: This part of the verse reflects a tradition about Paul's itinerary.

Verse 4: Although the account of Paul's success in preaching among the Gentiles also comes from tradition, its specific formulation could well indicate the presence of redaction.[52] Available historical data (see below, p. 223) suggest a traditional source undergirding verse 4.

Verses 5–9: The assumption that this section is also based on tradition rests on narrative tensions in the text. For one thing, the content exhibits little connection with the preceding events. For another, we find no explicit mention of Paul and Silas (note that in these verses they appear only as "them" (verses 5, 6a, and 7a; cf. verse 7a). In verse 9, however, "them" refers to Jason—who, as was noted earlier, makes an abrupt entrance—and the other recent converts. In short, Luke connects Paul and Silas with the scene only obliquely. Other elements in the content give further support to the finding that tradition stands behind verse 5–9:

1. Despite its plural subject in the context, the verb "to form a mob" (in Greek, *ochlopoiein*) in verse 5 is singular.

2. Jason is so abruptly introduced (note the similar introductions of Sosthenes in 18:17 and Alexander in 19:33) that at first we cannot tell whether Jason is a member of the community or simply a provider of lodgings. From the context we may assume the former, and may indeed suspect that he is identical with the Jason of Rom. 16:21.

3. The formula "to bring out before the popular assembly" (in Greek, *proagein eis ton dêmon*) found in verse 5 is taken by itself a specifically juridical term.[53]

4. The identity of the instigators of the uproar against the Christians remains strangely vague. Throughout most of the section grammatical evidence points to the Jews, though in verses 8 and 9 "they" are apparently a citizen mob and/or the city councilors who demand the payment of bail. In other words, by introducing the Jews as troublemakers Luke has obscured the real source of (and reason for?) the uproar.

5. The "city authorities" (in Greek, *politarchas*) in verse 8 indicate tradition:

> The term Politarch was principally, although not exclusively, used to designate the non-Roman chief civil magistrates of various Macedonian cities. The title is known not only from its mention here in Acts, but from numerous inscriptions as well. . . . The Politarchate was an annual magistracy, but was iterative. It could also be held simultaneously with other offices. The Politarchs were recruited from wealthier classes and functioned as the magistracy to which the task of administration and police duties fell. Thus the Politarchs were responsible for the maintenance of order in the city and for the surveillance, control and eventual prosecution of troublemakers. [54]

6. The phrase "to take security" or "to require bail" (in Greek, *lambanein to hikanon*) seems too specific not to go back to tradition, though Luke may (also?) have used it as a novelistic device.

While these six individual elements are still not enough to constitute a coherent story, they surely offer us the outlines of a tradition: Jason, a Thessalonian Christian, and a number of other Christians were harassed by their fellow citizens, hauled before the popular assembly, and after posting bail were released by one of the politarchs.

That leaves several points unsettled: (a) Did the tradition include a gathering in Jason's house? (b) Exactly what role did the crowd play? (c) What charges were leveled against Jason and the other believers? (In Luke's eyes, both charges mentioned in verses 6b–7 would make good sense; see above p. 220.)

For the mission in Beroea and the itineraries of Silas and Timothy see below, page 223.

HISTORICAL ELEMENTS

Verse 1a: Although Luke has the chronological context awry (see below, pp. 211–12), Paul's journey from Amphipolos and Apollonia to Thessalonica is undoubtedly historical. On his foundation mission to the Greek communities, he followed the via Egnatia from Philippi Via Amphipolis and Apollonia to Thessalonica—and the next stop along the way was Beroea.

Verse 2: Luke gives the impression that Paul remained in Thessalonica only three or four weeks. In fact, his stay was much longer, because while he was there he maintained himself—with frequent support form Philippi (Phil. 4:16)—lest he be a burden on anyone (1 Thess. 2:9).

Verse 4: The findings in Paul's letter to the Thessalonians (= 1 Thessalonians)[55] support the historicity of the report about converting many Gentiles. For one thing, Paul emphasizes in 1:9 that the Gentile Thessalonians had "turned to God from idols." For another, in 1:8 the apostle writes—addressing the former Gentile Thessalonians—that not only "the word of the Lord sounded forth from you in Macedonia and Achaia, but your faith in God has gone forth everywhere."

Verses 5–9: One must similarly conclude that the uproar over Jason is historical, for 1 Thess. 2:14 refers to the harassment of Gentile Christians there by their fellow citizens. In order to quell a public uproar, the authorities hauled a man named Jason and other Christians (was it from his house or in the course of a community gathering or riot?) before a public tribunal on indeterminate charges. The report of a suspension of charges upon payment of bail suggests the story's reliability. The above considerations indicate that this story could be a more complete version of the allusion in 1 Thessalonians, though to be sure, the events may have taken place at a later time.

Verse 10: Sending Paul and Silas to Beroea no doubt accurately reflects the existence of a Christian community there, though Paul never mentions it. The tradition in Acts 20:4 identifies this city as the home of Sopater/Sosipatros, one of Paul's companions named in Rom. 16:21. In all likelihood this was one of the Macedonian communities that contributed to the collection (see 2 Cor. 8:1–2).

Verses 14–15: This report about Timothy and Silas conflicts with Paul's account in 1 Thess. 3:2, according to which Timothy was sent from Athens to Thessalonica, and subsequently rejoined Paul in Corinth. Contrary to verse 14, then, he must have accompanied Paul to Athens (though the report in 18:5 agrees on the reunion in Corinth). Since Paul's reports naturally take precedence over those in Acts, it is probably safe to assume that Paul sent Silas back from Athens to Thessalonica, and that the mission of Timothy and Silas was to build up the Macedonian communities. They may also have brought financial support to Paul from Philippi (2 Cor. 11:9; Phil. 4:16).[56]

Why does Acts disagree with Paul on the movements of Timothy and Silas? Conzelmann[57] thinks it reflects Luke's tendency to simplify things. But that overlooks the possibility of a tendentious or schematic purpose on the author's part. I suspect that Luke preemptively changed the itineraries of Paul's companions in order to give Paul a solo role in the section on Athens.

THE HISTORICAL VALUE OF LUKE'S ACCOUNT

Luke again repeatedly blames the Jews (here, those of Thessalonica and Beroea) for attacks on Paul. Indeed, in the farewell speech to the presbyters of Ephesus at Miletus, Luke has Paul characterize plots of the Jews as something that constantly threatened his missionary work (20:19). Yet despite verse 5 the antagonists in Thessalonica were not Jews but, according to Paul's own witness in 1 Thess. 2:14, the general citizenry of Thessalonica.[58] Notice should also be taken of the lack of Jewish opposition in 16:11–40 and 17:16–34. Furthermore, in 9:23–24, one other place where we can check the veracity of Luke against the primary witness of Paul's letters, it was not the Jews who plotted against the apostle but the ethnarch of Aretas (see 2 Cor. 11:32–33). One is therefore justified in taking a skeptical view of Luke's reports about the Jews as persecutors of Paul and the other Christians. His schematic generalization of the unbelieving Jews as the principal troublemakers and persecutors involves a distortion of reality.

It is nonetheless true that Paul himself reports having received the Jewish punishment of forty lashes less one at the hand of his fellow Jews five times (2 Cor. 11:24), and in 1 Thess. 2:15 he quotes a tradition about the persecution of Jewish Christians by their fellow Jews in Judea.[59] As Klaus Wengst remarks aptly,

> We can easily understand how the Christian mission which appeared in the synagogues of the diaspora would lead to disputes there. That would be all the more likely to happen if it were particularly successful among the god-fearers, who were more or less firm members of the synagogue, acknowledged its ethical monotheism and observed certain ritual rules, but were not prepared to become full members of the Jewish community by accepting circumcision. . . . The Christian mission did away with this barrier. . . . So we can see how Jews would want to dissociate themselves from Christian missionaries and occasionally even denounce them to the authorities as troublemakers before they had official attention drawn to themselves by unrest. Luke for his part now turns the tables on the Jews: they did not keep to the religious questions which were the issue but denounced the Christian mission as political, thereby provoking unrest. However, by its schematic generalization this accusation becomes a distortion of reality.[60]

Surely this incisive explanation of "the action on the ground" helps us to understand better the political and religious dynamics at play in the Gentile mission field and better to appreciate the degree to which the author is rewriting history to suit his own purposes.

[40]
ACTS 17:16–34
PAUL IN ATHENS

(16) While Paul was waiting for them [Silas and Timothy] at Athens, *his spirit grew angry within him as he saw that the city was full of idols.* (17) *So he argued in the synagogue with the Jews and the God-fearers, and in the market place every day with casual passersby.* (18) Some of the Epicurean and Stoic philosophers also debated with him. And some said, "What is this babbler trying to say?" Others said, "He seems to be a proclaimer of *strange* divinities"—because he preached about Jesus and the Resurrection. (19) And they *took* him and brought him to the Areopagus, saying, "May we know what this new teaching is that you propound? (20) *For you are introducing ideas that sound strange to us; we wish to know therefore what they mean."*

(21) *Now all the Athenians and the foreigners who lived there spent their time in nothing except telling or hearing something new.*

(22) So Paul, standing in the middle of the Areopagus, said: "Men of Athens, I perceive that in all respects you are uncommonly religious. (23) For as I passed along, admiring your sacred monuments, I found among them an altar bearing the inscription, 'To an unknown god.' Now then, that which you worship but do not know—this is what I proclaim to you. (24) The God who made the world and everything in it, being Lord of heaven and earth, does not live in shrines made by man, (25) nor is he served by human hands, as though he needed anything, since he himself gives to all men life and breath and everything. (26) And he made from one (person) every nation of men to live on all the face of the earth, having determined their allotted periods and the boundaries of their habitation, (27) in order that they should seek God, and in the hope that they would feel their way toward him and at last find him. Yet he is not far from each one of us, (28) for "In him we live and move and have our being"; as even some of your poets have said, "We, too, are his offspring."

(29) Being then descended from God, we ought not to think that the Deity is like gold, or silver, or stone, a representation created by the art and imagination of man. (30) Although God overlooked the times of ignorance, he now commands all men everywhere to repent, (31) because he has fixed a day on which he will judge the world in righteousness by a man whom he has appointed, and of this he has given assurance to all men by raising him from the dead."

(32) Now when they heard of the resurrection of the dead, some scoffed; but others said, "We will hear you again on this." (33) So *Paul went out from among*

them. (34) But some men *joined* him and became believers, among them Dionysius the Areopagite and a woman *called* Damaris *and others with them.*

OUTLINE

16–20: Paul's arrival in Athens and encounter with the philosophers
        16a: Travel note
        16b: Paul's anger at the idols in the city
       17–18: Paul in the synagogue and in the marketplace;
                reaction of the Stoics and Epicureans
       19–20: Paul on/before the Areopagus. Content of his teaching
    21: Explanation about the Athenians for the reader
22–31: Paul's speech on/before the Areopagus
       22–23: Introduction
       24–25: I. God the creator needs no temple
       26–27: II. The seasons and limits given by God's creative impulse,
                his allotment of eras and boundaries, as well as the
                intended human response and hoped-for enlightenment
       28–29: III. The affinity of human beings to God
       30–31: IV. The possibility of repentance and the judgment to
                come
32–34: Reaction of the audience: Some reject Paul and some join him

LUKE'S PURPOSE

Verse 16: This transitional verse tells of Paul's anger over the idols in Athens and
prepares for verse 23.

    Verse 17: Once again we see Luke's scheme of having Paul approach the
Jews first, but in striking contrast to other passages we are told that almost *at
the same time* Paul debated with Jews in the synagogue and with Gentiles in the
market place.

    Verse 18: As in 19:23–40, this verse employs local coloring in setting the
scene. Clearly this is a literary creation in which the contrast between philosophical schools serves little other purpose than to create a milieu—unless it is to
evoke a parallel to Socrates, who argued with the representatives of philosophical schools, who accused him of introducing new gods. And like Socrates, Paul
speaks in the market place to everyone, and is seen to be introducing new gods.
As he later does in verse 32, Luke here sets up a contrast between two groups of

listeners; in this case all are shown to be unreceptive to Paul's preaching (cf. 2:12–13; 28:24). When Luke identifies the subject of Paul's proclamation as "Jesus and the Resurrection," he probably alludes to a Gentile misunderstanding of Christian preaching: they take it to mean "Jesus and the Anastasis," a divine couple. But that is exactly what Luke intended.[61]

Verses 19–20: Luke mentions the famous place of judgment in Athens in order to produce a worthy scene for Paul's speech. "Areopagus" could mean the hill of Ares, but this would be far too small for the scene. The other possible meaning of the term is the Athenian council, and this is more likely Luke's intent, a conclusion that is suggested by the expressions "in the middle" (verse 22; cf. verse 33), "took him" (verse 19), and "the Areopagite" (verse 34). But far from being placed on trial, Paul is invited to give an account of the new teaching (verse 19). Furthermore, his address is more a homily than a defense, and verse 21 indicates that curiosity motivated the Athenians more than accusatory zeal. And once again we see the author at work when we find in verse 20 the complaint that Paul is introducing strange teachings. This obviously picks up verse 18 in which Paul "seems to be a proclaimer of strange divinities," and echoes the accusation against Socrates that he was introducing "new demons."[62] Only the charge of leading the youth astray is absent.

Verse 21: This verse, which adduces the proverbial curiosity of the Athenians, is clearly directed to the reader.[63] Demosthenes had admonished them three hundred years earlier, "Instead of guarding your liberties, you are forever gadding about and looking for news."[64] Including this theme lends a further touch of local color to the scene.

Verses 22–31: This set piece serves as the theological explanation of the note about "preaching" in verse 18. If we except the brief expostulation in 14:15–17, it contains the only discourse in Acts that is addressed to Gentiles. It begins with a *captatio benevolentiae* (verse 22), an oft-repeated praise of Athens as the most pious city in Greece because of its many cultic images and festivals. We may also see Luke's hand in the inscription on the altar (verse 23). It is patterned after a type of inscription known (despite the lack of archaeological evidence) to have existed in Athens; but those referred to unknown gods. Luke has served his monotheistic agenda by replacing the plural with the singular.

At the redactional level the speech shows its (i.e., Luke's) concern to imply previous knowledge of the Christian God by means of the theme of an affinity between God and the works of creation. The first part of verse 28 is an echo of a poem of Epimenides the Cretan, the second part—a stock quotation in Stoic circles—stems from Aratus (b. 310 BCE). Luke is far from suggesting that this discourse was typical of sermons to Gentiles, since it was not a sermon. As with all the declamations in Acts, however, one must ask to what degree this one represents homiletic forms in Luke's time.

Although some have argued that the Areopagus speech reflects a post-Lukan revision of Acts, its many parallels in the Lukan opus suggest its originality. I shall list a number of these parallels following the sequence of the speech in addition to singular features of the speech, which are printed in italics:

- God the creator (verse 24)—cf. 4:24; 14:15.
- God is Lord (verse 24)—cf. 10:36, "He is the Lord of all."
- God does not dwell in temples (verse 24)—cf. 7:48.
- *God is not served by human worship because he does not need anything (verse 25).*
- God is the giver of being and of all gifts (verse 25)—cf. 14:17.
- Descent of all beings from one ancestor (verse 26)—cf. Jesus' descent from Adam in Luke 3:23–38.
- God guides the history of the nations (verse 26)—cf. 14:16.
- Human responsibility for finding God (verse 27)—cf. 14:15, 17.
- God is near to every human being (verse 27)—cf. 10:35.
- *Pantheism (verse 28).*
- *Divine race of humankind (verses 28–29).*
- *Idols are forbidden—because they are nonsensical (verse 29).*
- The previous ignorance of all men, which God has heretofore overlooked (verse 30)—cf. 14:16 (see further 3:17; 13:27)—must now give way to.
- A new revelation of God that is being offered to all men (verse 30)—cf. Luke 2:10 (the whole people).
- The new preaching begins with repentance (verse 30)—cf. Acts 2:38; 3:19; 13:24; 20:21; 26:20.
- The coming judgment (verse 31)—cf. 24:25.
- The man appointed (verse 31)—cf. 10:42.
- The resurrection of Christ (verse 31)—cf. Luke 24; often in Acts.

Of these eighteen points only four are not attested in Luke-Acts, but they are the characteristic features of a speech that Paul (alias Luke) would deliver to Gentiles in this solemn didactic discourse, and they further develop Luke's own ideas.

Verses 32–34: For verses 32–33 see the comments above on verse 18; both groups in the audience have reservations about Paul's preaching (see 2:12). For verse 33 see Luke 4:30; verse 34 has Lukan linguistic coloring.

THE TRADITIONS REWORKED BY LUKE

Verse 16a: The arrival of Paul in Athens from Thessalonica as reported in verse 16a reflects tradition (cf. 1 Thess. 3:1).

Verses 22–31: We can discover three different motifs in the Areopagus speech: creation (verses 24–26a, 27–28), preservation (verse 26b), and redemption (verse 31). The same scheme of motifs occurs in missionary (or propaganda) literature of Hellenistic Judaism as well as in Jewish and early Christian writings.[65] The frequency of this structural pattern in tradition suggests that we should not take the combination of the three themes in the Areopagus speech as Luke's theological conception. Rather, the pattern of the address is probably not Luke's creation, but a model he knew from missionary practice. Therefore we are led to assume a traditional basis of the Areopagus speech on the basis of a history-of-religions comparison.

Verses 32–34: The name of Dionysius the Areopagite probably comes from a tradition that also enabled Luke to place Paul before the Areopagus. The logic would run as follows: If Dionysius was converted when an Areopagite, then Paul must have appeared before the Areopagus. That the name of Damaris was also part of the tradition is supported by the consideration that Damaris—not elsewhere instanced as a woman's name—does not fit in the context of a speech before the Areopagus. Neither a pious Jewish woman nor a woman in the community would appear in public with men. And it must again be reiterated that these traditional elements are not necessarily related to a specific occasion, but only in general terms to Athens.

HISTORICAL ELEMENTS

Verse 16a: Paul's journey from Thessalonica to Athens during the founding mission of communities in Macedonia and Achaia is historical.[66]

Verses 22–31: It should be stressed that Paul occasionally employs *the scheme of motifs* of the Areopagus speech, a pattern rooted in tradition as well as evident in the formulation of 1 Thess. 1:9–10 and Rom. 1:18–2:10.

A summary of Paul's founding proclamation appears in 1 Thess. 1:9b–10: "You turned to God from idols, to serve a living and true God, (10) and to wait expectantly for the appearance from heaven of his Son Jesus, whom he raised from the dead, Jesus our deliverer from the wrath to come." Note how the list of motifs in Paul's letter to the Romans parallels this summary of the Apostle's missionary preaching: Creation (Rom. 1:20, 25), knowledge of God (1:19–20), worship of God (1:23, 25), repentance (2:4), judgment (2:5–6, 8), and salvation (2:7,

10). By way of qualification it must be conceded that the theme of preservation does not appear explicitly either in 1 Thess. 1:9–10 or in Rom. 1:18–2:10, but it is presupposed as an extension of remarks of creation. And of course there are noteworthy *differences* between Paul's epistolary message and the tradition of the Areopagus speech. The latter has two proofs for the knowledge of God by natural man: first, from the works of creation (17:24–25), second, from affinity to God (17:28–29). The first appears in Paul only as a lost possibility[67] while the latter seems to lack congruity with his view of human alienation from God.[68]

As just noted, the two proofs for the knowledge of God would seem to be inconceivable in Paul, while the preservation theme might be understood as a corollary of the topic of creation. On the other hand, one is entitled to wonder whether Paul might not occasionally depart from his negative view of the human condition in order to win Greeks to the Gospel. In any case, one should avoid adopting an unalterable position on what he could or could not have said, and take into account Paul's flexibility in seeking to be "all things to all men."[69]

Furthermore, not only must the parallels between 1 Thess. 1:9–10 and the tradition behind Acts 17 be kept in mind, but it is also safe to assume that in Athens Paul tried to convert Gentiles. True, his missionary activity did not begin with a reference to the unknown God, for an altar so dedicated did not exist. Be that as it may, it is safe to assume that during his stay in Athens Paul addressed to the Gentiles at least one speech the essence of which may be preserved in the Areopagus speech Luke attributes to him. Since this was a *type* of speech, a causal relationship between the tradition behind Acts 17 and Paul's epistolary sermons cannot be established with certainty.

Yet, one should not adduce 1 Cor. 2:1–5, where Paul disclaims all "persuasive words of wisdom" (verse 4), as proof that Paul could never have said anything like that in his speech in Athens. As noted above, Paul was able to summon up a considerable degree of flexibility, and delivered himself of a number of contradictory opinions. Still, the content of 1 Cor. 2:1–5 seems to reflect his experience in Athens (see below, pp. 231–32).

One can imagine any number of possible places for such a "sermon" as Luke sets before the Areopagus: the synagogue (where many Gentiles attended services), the market place, a street-corner, and even Paul's workshop or outside his living quarters. Nor is it reasonable to suggest that Paul delivered only one sermon, and that at the time of the founding of the community. We should rather imagine several appeals—addressed to different groups, but each containing the themes enumerated above.

Verse 34: Although Damaris and Dionysius the Areopagite are likely to have been historical persons, they do not belong in the story of the founding mission. For in 1 Cor. 16:15 Paul designates as "the first fruits of Achaea" (the region in which Athens was situated) the household of Stephanas—who when Paul was writing, was serving in Corinth, but whom Paul did not meet during his stay at Athens. Besides, it is doubtful that Paul had any notable missionary success in Athens, for an Athenian community plays no recognizable role in his missionary plans, his journeys, or the collection for the Jerusalem church. Indeed, we find no attestation of a Christian community in Athens until around 179 CE.[70]

One further point deserves notice here: Athens is the only place in which Paul preached without prompting a *persecution*. Some explain this on the basis of apologetics: The educated Gentiles of Athens dispute but do not turn violent. Furthermore, they suggest, the absence of the theme of persecution here can be explained by the fact that in this chapter Paul turns exclusively to the Gentiles— at which it seems only fair to point out that Jews do appear in verse 17a. Be that as it may, the historical record shows that except in this case, Gentiles did in fact initiate persecutions against the Pauline communities[71] and it was they who caused Paul serious trouble in Ephesus.[72] I would suggest, therefore, that the absence of a persecution theme in Acts 17 is an argument *in favor of* the existence of at least a modicum of solid historical information in the narrative.

THE HISTORICAL VALUE OF LUKE'S ACCOUNT

Although Luke clearly implies that Paul did not succeed in founding a community at Athens, he does not focus on the failure. Rather he places a long, bombastic speech on Paul's lips and associates him with one of the greatest philosophers that Athens had ever seen. Thereby he clearly falsifies history and obliges us to deconstruct this masquerade before we can even begin to get the facts straight. In view of this I think it only appropriate to dig deeper and consider what marks must have been left on Paul's soul by a defeat of the sort he suffered there.

When he founded the community in Corinth a few weeks later, he said some very negative things about the Greeks' search for wisdom—a modality that, in its extreme form, he had just encountered in Athens. An accurate reflection of Paul's first visit in Corinth may be found in the epitome of his founding mission, namely

1 Cor. 2:1–5

When I came to you, brothers, I did not come proclaiming to you the testimony about God with preeminent eloquence or *wisdom*. (2) For I decided to know nothing among you except Jesus Christ and him crucified. (3) And I was with you in weakness and in much fear and trembling; (4) and my speech and my message were not in persuasive words of *wisdom*, but in manifestation of Spirit and <u>power</u>, (5) that your faith might not depend on men's *wisdom* but on God's <u>power</u>.

For Paul it is clear why human wisdom is doomed to failure. He writes in

1 Cor. 1:17–25

Christ did not send me to baptize, but to preach the gospel, and not with eloquent *wisdom* lest the cross of Christ be emptied. (18) For the word of the cross
is **folly** to those who are perishing, but to us who are being saved it is God's
power. (19) For it is written, "I will destroy the *wisdom* of the wise, and the
cleverness of the clever I will set aside." (20) Where is the *wise* man? Where is
the scribe? Where is the debater of this age? Has not God made the world's
wisdom **folly**? (21) For since, in God's *wisdom* the world did not know God
through *wisdom,* God chose through the **folly** of what we preach to save those
who believe. (22) For Jews demand signs and Greeks seek *wisdom,* (23) but we
preach Christ crucified, a stumbling block to Jews and **folly** to Gentiles; (24) but
to those who are called, both Jews and Greeks, Christ, God's power and God's
wisdom. (25) For God's **folly** is *wiser* than men, and God's weakness is stronger
than men.

The upshot of this is very clear: Paul demonizes wisdom insofar as it does
not agree with his own faith. As we know from another passage in 1 Corinthians,
the Apostle does know another wisdom that is hidden and, indeed, can be equated
with Christ himself (cf. verse 24 above and 1 Cor. 2:6–8). But that wisdom is
closely connected with mystery and revelation and not with reason. Thus in the
end Paul suffered what Gilbert Murray almost a century ago called a failure of
nerve.[73] Like so many of his contemporaries he became an apostate to the Greek
heritage in which he and other Hellenistic Jews had been nurtured. Certainly the
advocacy of the risen and the returning Christ in Thessalonica (see 1 Thess.
1:9–10) shows that religious enthusiasm had taken precedence over reason, at
least once Paul had become a Christian. Then came the experience of Athens.
Having lost this argument, he may very well have felt himself driven to the conclusion that God was calling him to serve by preaching this divine folly. We can
see the effect of this in 1 Corinthians. From now on Paul sold Christianity as a
mystery religion that satisfied his and his converts' needs for hidden wisdom and
divine folly. That made him immune against any objection and allowed him to
continue his missionary zeal among the Greeks. The incipient dialogue between
Christianity and Greek philosophy was over for a long time.[74]

[41]
ACTS 18:1–17
PAUL IN CORINTH

(1) After this he left Athens and went to Corinth. (2) There he found a Jew *called* Aquila, a native of Pontus, who had recently come from Italy with his wife Priscilla, because Claudius had issued an edict that *all* Jews should leave Rome. And he approached them; (3) and, because he was of the same trade, made his home with them, and they worked together, for by trade they were tentmakers.

(4) And he argued in the synagogue every Sabbath, and sought to persuade Jews and Greeks.

(5) Then Silas and Timothy came down from Macedonia, and Paul devoted himself entirely to preaching, *testifying to the Jews that the Christ was Jesus.* (6) *And when they opposed him and resorted to abuse, he shook out his garments and said to them, "Your blood be on your* heads! I am innocent; from now on I shall go to the Gentiles." (7) *So he withdrew from there* and went to the house of a worshipper of God *called* Titius Justus, who lived next door to the synagogue. (8) Crispus, the ruler of the synagogue, now became a believer in the Lord along with all his household; and many of the Corinthians listened and believed, and were baptized.

(9) One night in a vision the Lord said to Paul, "Do not be afraid, but speak and do not be silent; (10) for I am with you, and no one shall attempt to do you harm; for there are many in this city who are my people."

(11) So he settled there for a year and six months, *teaching the word of God among them.*

(12) *But when* Gallio was proconsul of Achaia, *the Jews made a concerted attack on Paul and brought him before the* <u>tribunal</u>, (13) *saying, "This man is persuading men to worship God in ways that are against the **law**."* (14) *Paul was about to open his mouth, when Gallio said to the Jews, "If it had been a question of wrongdoing or vicious crime, I would not hesitate to attend to you, Jews; (15) but since it is a matter of questions about words and names and your own **law**, you may see to it yourselves; I have no mind to be a judge of these matters."* (16) *And he drove them from the* <u>tribunal</u>. (17) *And they all seized* Sosthenes, the ruler of the synagogue, *and beat him in front of the* <u>tribunal</u>. *But Gallio paid no attention to this.*

OUTLINE

1:   From Athens to Corinth

2–3: Paul works together with Aquila and Priscilla

4: Paul argues every Sabbath in the synagogue

5–8: Arrival of Silas and Timothy from Macedonia leads to an intensified missionary work by Paul

9–10: The Lord speaks in a vision to Paul

11: Note of length of stay in Corinth (eighteen months)

12–17: The Jews drag Paul before the tribunal of proconsul Gallio

LUKE'S PURPOSE

Verses 1–3: "All the Jews" in verse 2 is an exaggerated statement.[75] It matches Luke's general scheme of joining the history of salvation with profane history.[76] He had once before related the emperor Claudius to salvation history (11:28).

Verse 4: This verse exemplifies Luke's motif that Paul addresses himself to the Jews first. In anticipation of the next unit, verses 5–8, it identifies the two groups whom Paul addresses: Jews and Gentiles.

Verses 5–8: Verse 5 describes in Lukan language Paul's intensified missionary activity. The content of the testimony that "the Christ was Jesus" derives from Luke, being directed as in other passages[77] at the Jews. Typically, they resort to repudiation and charges of blasphemy, to which Paul responds (verse 6) with the symbolic action of shaking off his clothes,[78] and having declared his innocence of any wrongdoing, breaks off all contact with them. By invoking the blood and responsibility motif, Luke's Paul echoes various passages from the Hebrew Bible;[79] he disavows any responsibility for the failure of his fellow Jews to accept Jesus as the Messiah; and in turning to Gentiles, Paul does not repudiate his commission, but repeats the course he followed in Pisidian Antioch (13:46). Verses 7–8 then describe the success of the Gentile mission in Corinth.

Verses 9–10: "Vision" is a common Lukan narrative device[80] by means of which the assurance of the Lord (here = Christ) intensifies the drama of the scene. In this case it serves a double purpose, since it not only explains the long duration of Paul's stay in Corinth (verse 11, "eighteen months"), but also illustrates the significance of the Corinthian community in Luke's time. Furthermore, by foretelling that Paul will not undergo any harm in Corinth, the visionary promise of Christ provides a transition to the subsequent episode before Gallio.

Verses 12–17: The accusation that Paul "is persuading men to worship God in ways that are against the law" (verse 13) refers to the Jewish law, not Roman statutes—as Gallio's answer in verses 14–15 shows. Since during his last visit to Jerusalem Paul is confronted with similar Jewish charges,[81] the present accusation may be seen as a forerunner of the later theme. Historically, then, it does not belong here and therefore likely derives from Luke. Indeed, the whole scene before Gallio is not even the report of a trial. Rather, it is an intentional presentation of a nontrial, indeed an explication of why such a proceeding is illegitimate. Even a cursory reading reveals the absence of any conversation between Paul and Gallio. The only exchange is between the Jews and Gallio, who by refusing to accept the Jewish charge shows himself unwilling to interfere in the controversy between Jews and Christians, and thus a model statesman.[82] For Luke, the vicarious beating of the ruler of the synagogue, Sosthenes (verse 17), constitutes an ironic punishment of the Corinthian Jews for their attack on Paul and also provides a bit of comic relief, the more so since the beating goes unpunished (verse 18).

THE TRADITIONS REWORKED BY LUKE

Before reconstructing the traditions that Luke reworked, let me make a point that is all too commonly overlooked in studies of Acts. Though Luke often reports more than one visit by Paul to a given locality, only one account presents detailed information about the apostle's activity there, while any other visit is painted in broad strokes. The following catalogue lists the detailed reports first, followed by those of a general nature:

> Lystra (14:8-20; cf. 14:21 and 16:1–3);
> Philippi (16:12–40; cf. the two visits in 20:2, 3–6);
> Thessalonica (Acts 17:1–10; cf. 20:2);
> Ephesus (19:1–20:1; cf. 18:19–21).

His treatment of Corinth (18:1–17; cf. 20:2–3) follows the same pattern. It is unlikely that local traditions to which Luke had access described only one *specific visit*. He seems rather to have gathered various reports relating Paul's several visits to a given locality and combined them into a single account. In 18:1–17 five pieces of traditions can be identified:

> (a) Paul travels from Athens to Corinth (verse 1).
> (b) In Corinth Paul meets Aquila and Priscilla—who as Jews had to leave because of the edict of Claudius—and works with them (verses 2–3).
> (c) Paul's preaches the gospel in Corinth (verses 5–8).
> (d) Paul stays in Corinth for eighteen months (verse 11).
> (e) Incidents involving Gallio and Sosthenes (verses 12–17).

HISTORICAL ELEMENTS

Absolute dates

Verse 2: The date of the expulsion of the Jews from Rome is usually set in 49 CE. The Roman biographer Suetonius (early second century CE) writes: "Claudius expelled the Jews from Rome who were exceedingly riotous because of the instigator Chrestus."[83] The expulsion of the Jews by Claudius is also reported in verse 2. But the date 49 CE rests on the information supplied by the church father Orosius (from 417–418 CE), who derived it by subtracting the eighteen months found in verse 11 from the dates of Gallio's term in office—which could be determined from archival records. Hence it is certainly secondary.[84]

The Roman historian Dio Cassius, on the other hand, reports an imperial command regarding the Jews for the year 41 CE. He writes:

> As for the Jews, who had again increased so greatly that by reason of their multitude it would have been hard without raising a tumult to bar them from the city, he did not drive them out, but ordered them, while continuing their traditional mode of life, not to hold meetings.[85]

The wording of the passage seems to indicate that Dio Cassius has relied on a tradition that was also available to Suetonius, but which he has corrected: Here I refer to Dio Cassius's denial that Claudius expelled (all) the Jews.

As for the relationship of the data from Suetonius and Dio Cassius, one must point out that Suetonius's language can be interpreted to mean that only those Jews who rioted were driven out. In this case Dio's statement offers no contradiction, since he denies only that there was a general expulsion like the one under Tiberius.[86] Only if one tries to combine Acts' statement about the expulsion of *all* the Jews from Rome with Suetonius's account does the date of the expulsion becomes problematic.[87]

The historical kernel of these reports is no doubt the following: In 41 CE, Claudius issued a decree regarding the Jews; it pertained to the disturbances that had arisen in a synagogue and had involved Chrestus. The decree entailed the expulsion of those Jews who had been directly involved in the disturbances. One may, therefore, conclude that the tradition in acts 18:2–3 could very well derive from Paul's first visit to Corinth around 41 CE. This date fits in well with the chronology developed solely on the basis of the letters.

Verses 12–17: From the Gallio inscription we know that the proconsul held office in 51–52 CE.[88] With the date of the first visit in Corinth set (verse 1), it is readily apparent that Paul's second or third visit could well have occurred during Gallio's tenure.

Individual pieces of tradition with a historical value

Verse 1: Paul's trip from Athens to Corinth took place during his first missionary effort in Greece. This is clearly shown by 1 Thess. 2–3.

Verses 2–3: Two of Paul's letters reflect his close association with Aquila and Priscilla. First, 1 Cor. 16:8 notes their presence with Paul in Ephesus, and verse 19 extends their greetings to the Corinthian congregation. Thus it seems certain that they were personally acquainted with the members of that church, and likely that they had met Paul during his founding visit to that city. Later in Rom. 16:3 it is Paul who sends greetings to them. So the couple was in Rome when Paul composed his letter to the Christian congregation in the capitol of the Empire. A quite reasonable explanation of the couple's presence in Rome at this time is that after having been expelled in the year 41 CE they returned to Rome at the end of Claudius's reign (41–54 CE). All this renders it plausible that Paul met them in Corinth in 41.

Paul further mentions the couple in 1 Cor. 16:19, where they send greetings to the Corinthians "together with the church in their house." This permits the thesis that they were personally acquainted with the members of the Corinthian community. Since at the time of the writing of 1 Cor. 16 they are with Paul in Ephesus (see verse 8), it is most probable that they made Paul's acquaintance during his founding visit in Corinth. The phrase "together with the church in their house" affords us a glimpse of the couple's economic status. Whether the expression "the church in their house" should be understood as referring to a congregation that met in their house or to their household as a congregation,[89] it is clear that the couple is affluent. Thus we established as probable not only the tradition that Paul met Priscilla and Aquila in Corinth, but also the information preserved in Acts 18 that Paul worked for them in Corinth. That Paul performed manual labor in Corinth is firmly attested by his own words.[90] The affluence of the couple allowed them to employ others, among whom Paul should be counted, especially in view of the fact that Pricilla and Aquila would see in him a (Jewish) Christian comrade. This also implies that they were already Christians when they came to Corinth.[91] While the letters do not verify the additional report in Acts that they were tentmakers, this information comports with the statement that they practiced the same trade as Paul.

In Rom. 16:4, Paul gives the couple special praise for aiding him (literally, they "risked their necks" for his life). We may therefore suppose that this deed was connected with the dangers that Paul encountered in the vicinity of Ephesus.[92] This assistance and their mention in 1 Cor. 16:19 presuppose that they were in Ephesus until shortly before Paul's third and final visit to Corinth. Since Paul wrote Romans during that visit, the couple's emigration to Rome must have occurred not long before the composition of this letter. Their return to their old residence would have had great importance for Paul's missionary plans.

Verse 5: The arrival of Silas and Timothy from Macedonia occurred during Paul's founding visit to Corinth, for this datum corresponds exactly with 1 Thess. 3:6 (Timothy's arrival in Corinth from Thessalonica), 2 Cor. 1:19 (Paul, Silvanus and Timothy's activity during the founding mission in Corinth, cf. 2 Cor. 11:9), and the salutation from Paul, Silvanus, and Timothy in the first verse of 1 Thessalonians, which was composed in Corinth. That Timothy and Paul did not arrive in Corinth at the same time is evident from 1 Thess. 3:6, which indicates that Paul was already present in Corinth when Timothy came from Thessalonica. Thus, not only is the order of events in the first part of Acts 18 shown to be correct (first Paul worked with Pricilla and Aquila, *then* Timothy arrived), but the chapter also correctly places Timothy and Silas in Corinth during the foundation visit. Further, the statement that Timothy arrived in Corinth from Macedonia comports with 1 Thess. 3:6, which says that Timothy came to Paul in Corinth from Thessalonica—which was the capital of the Roman province of Macedonia.

Since Paul's own statements in 2 Cor. 11:8–9 indicate that he received money from the Philippians during his initial mission to Corinth,[93] Timothy was very likely part of the delegation that brought him the funds. Paul's statement at 1 Thess. 3:1–2 that he had sent Timothy to Thessalonica from Athens does not contradict this view, for Timothy could well have planned to make an excursion to Philippi during his visit to Thessalonica. The Lukan flavoring of the report in Acts 18:5 (that Paul "devoted himself entirely to preaching" after the arrival of Timothy and Silas from Macedonia) could be a redacted form of a tradition on the arrival of Timothy that included a monetary gift from the Philippian congregation. The circumstances and purpose of the monetary gift from Philippi, however, receive new illumination when we combine Paul's letters and Acts at this point: Timothy apparently played an active role in gathering this gift, and its purpose was evidently to relieve Paul from the necessity of daily work so that he could devote himself to the proclamation of the gospel. Thus the statement here formulated in Lukan idiom, "Paul devoted himself entirely to preaching," does preserve a kernel of historical truth.

Verse 8: Also, since 1 Cor. 1:14 mentions Crispus, the third element of tradition indicated above (on verses 5–8), with its reference to Crispus in verse 8, also derives from the first visit to Corinth. In 1 Cor. 1:14, Paul even remarks that contrary to his custom of not baptizing, he baptized Crispus and Gaius (who is not mentioned in Acts). In view of the context of this statement in 1 Corinthians, this baptism could have occurred only during the founding visit. While the tradition in Acts does not explicitly say that Paul baptized Crispus, it nevertheless also reports that Crispus' conversion and baptism occurred during the founding visit. This point of agreement speaks strongly in favor of the antiquity and reliability of the tradition about Crispus in Acts.

Verses 12–17:

Gallio

Though the above analysis excludes a report of a trial against Paul before Gallio, I assume that a reference to Gallio must have been part of a tradition concerning Paul's activity in Corinth. Such an assumption follows from the reconstruction of a chronology that is solely based on Paul's authentic letters. Indeed, the chronology does include a stay in Corinth at the time of Gallio's tenure as a proconsul of Achaia from 51 to 52 CE.[94] Yet any such judicial hearing occurred not during the foundation of the community but—if at all—on the occasion of a later visit of Paul. Since no tradition about a hearing or trial before Gallio can be recovered, one may doubt that anything of that sort ever took place, the more so since Paul did not say a single word in order to be rehabilitated.

Sosthenes

Since synagogues—despite Acts 13:5—normally had but one "ruler" at a time,[95] the identification of Sosthenes as head of the synagogue reflects a tradition differing in chronological setting from the one naming Crispus as the synagogue official who joined Paul and became a Christian. Unless Sosthenes was made ruler of the synagogue immediately after Crispus had joined Paul, the two probably represent different Pauline visits to Corinth. But since Luke was not an eyewitness in Corinth and had to rely on variant traditions—one of which associated Sosthenes with a visit of Paul to Corinth, and another Crispus—it is better not to assume that Sosthenes immediately replaced Crispus. Instead, Sosthenes seems to reflect the time of Gallio's tenure as proconsul, especially since they appear in the same scene.

Finally, the Sosthenes named in 1 Cor. 1:1 as the cosender of the letter is unlikely to be the same person as the ruler of the synagogue in Corinth. Yet a final decision cannot be made.

THE HISTORICAL VALUE OF LUKE'S ACCOUNT

In no other section of Acts has Luke preserved so many historically accurate details. Yet by attributing them to *a single* stay in Corinth, and by incorrectly setting them after the Jerusalem conference, he has for nearly two millennia misled scholars. Fortunately, a critical reading of Paul's authentic letters provides us with the means to get the facts straight.

Furthermore, one result of the analysis deserves to be repeated here. Paul never faced a trial or a hearing before Gallio, nor did these two individuals ever see each other. Obviously, therefore, the Jews did not drag Paul before Gallio's tribunal.

A final note: One should not try to reconstruct a historical kernel of a trial by assuming that Gallio shared the anti-Jewish attitude of his brother Seneca and then go on to speculate, as Riesner has done, that "the account in Acts completely concurs with this: Although Gallio does indeed confirm the Jewish right as a *religio legitima* to regulate its own affairs (Acts 18:15), he demonstrates anything but special sympathy (Acts 18:16), and does not even concern himself with anti-semitic assaults (Acts 18:17). . . . The historical background remains credible even if Luke has undeniably subjected the scene to literary stylizations."[96]

> *Rebuttal:* For one thing, in this scene there are no anti-Semitic undertones in Gallio's behavior. For another, this historicizing exegesis neither gets Paul back into the scene nor explains why he is given nothing to say. Historically speaking, it is inconceivable that Paul did not have anything to say. To that degree, at least, Luke has yet again given us not history, but a tendentious set piece.

[42]

ACTS 18:18–23

PAUL'S TRIP FROM EPHESUS VIA JERUSALEM TO ANTIOCH, GALATIA, AND PHRYGIA

(18a) *After this, Paul stayed many days longer and then took leave of the brothers and* set sail for Syria, and with him Priscilla and Aquila. (18b) At Cenchreae he had his hair cut, for he was under a vow. (19) And when they came to Ephesus, *he left them there, but he himself went into the synagogue and reasoned with the Jews.* (20) *When they asked him to stay for a longer period, he declined.* (21) *But on taking leave of them he said, "I will return to you if God wills,"* and then he put out to sea from Ephesus.

(22) When he had landed at Caesarea, he went up and greeted the church, and then went down to Antioch. (23a) After spending some time there, he departed (23b) and went *from place to place* throughout the region of Galatia and Phrygia, (23c) *strengthening all the disciples.*

OUTLINE

18–19a: Paul's journey from Corinth to Ephesus
19b–21a: Paul preaches in the synagogue at Ephesus
21b–23: Journey by Paul through Palestine to Antioch; his strengthening of the disciples in Phrygia and Galatia

LUKE'S PURPOSE

Verses 18–19a: The language of verse 18a derives from Luke. The designation "Syria" (cf. 20:3; 21:3) anticipates either the journey to Palestine or its extension as far as Antioch, which in turn becomes the starting point (18:23) of his subsequent journey. A noticeable discontinuity in verse 18b indicates that Luke is stitching together existing material. Syntactically, it seems most reasonable to see "Aquila" as the subject of "had his hair cut," in which case Aquila would because of a vow have had his hair shorn in Cenchreae, one of the two ports of Corinth. But the remark is contextually out of place and lacks an authentic setting. Rather than view verse 18b as the only extant fragment of a source telling of an oath by Aquila, we should seriously consider whether Luke might not be assigning the haircut to Paul. "A (Nazarite) vow counted as a meritorious work; one could be released from it only at the Temple."[97] Since Paul plans to travel to Jerusalem,[98] having his hair cut in keeping with such a vow makes good sense: while traveling to Jerusalem (i.e., to the Temple) Paul demonstrates his faithfulness to Jewish practice (cf. 21:23–24). In that case, the apparently ambiguous location of "had (his) hair cut" could be explained with little difficulty. Indeed, a literal rendering of the Greek all but eliminates the problem: "Paul … set sail for Syria and with him Priscilla and Aquila having had shorn in Cenchreae his head. ..." Obviously, placing "having had (his) hair cut" immediately after "Syria" would have made the phrase "and with him Priscilla and Aquila" very awkward grammatically. It should also be noted that having the couple accompany Paul on the trip to Ephesus may be Luke's idea, since in 18:24–28 he places them there. Historical considerations, though, make it more likely that the trip reflects tradition.

Verses 19b–21a: This passage clearly reflects Luke's style in both content and form. The sentence "he left them there (in Ephesus) but he himself went into a synagogue" (verse 19) could almost be taken to suggest that the synagogue is somewhere other than Ephesus.[99] But the departure from Ephesus reported in verse 21 shows that this was not intended, as does Paul's anticipated return in that same verse ("if God wills")—a return that occurs in 19:1. After "if God wills," Paul's itinerary is continued with his departure from Ephesus. The redactional nature of verses 19b–21a evidenced by a literary-critical analysis is corroborated by the presence of the Lukan pattern of going to the Jews first when Paul's initial colloquy (verse 19b) takes place in the synagogue. Note also that while verse 21 anticipates Paul's return, 19:1, which reports it, speaks only of his "arrival," as though it were his first time there. Accordingly, the redaction in verses 19b–21a stands in tension with the tradition-derived material in verses 18, 19a, 21b–23.

The reason for Luke's composition of 18:19b–21a is made clear by the following text (verses 24–28), for here we see indicated the presence of Christians in Ephesus before Paul's arrival. In short, Luke's purpose in this scene is to make Paul "the first Christian preacher in the city."[100]

Verses 21b–23: The phrases "from place to place" in verse 23b as well as "strengthening all the disciples" in verse 23c derive from Luke.

THE TRADITIONS REWORKED BY LUKE

Verses 21b–23: This passage poses great problems for interpreters because it is so brief. In my view the summary character of this travel report, which involves a straight line distance of more than twelve hundred miles, suggests the adoption of tradition, especially since it is hard to see why Luke should for no apparent reason have created such an extensive journey and then have offered such a sketchy description. Throughout, the report gives the impression of being an epitome whose details are known only to its creator.[101] The other possibility, namely that Luke himself "took scattered reports and from them fashioned a journey,"[102] has little traction because such a journey has no apparent place in Luke's narrative or his overall scheme. A trip that is clearly Luke's creation, Paul's so-called second journey to Jerusalem (11:27–30; 12:25) is very different from 18:22 not only in that it has a clear purpose, but because it evinces none of the characteristics of an epitome. In the present case, then, it appears that Luke has used an itinerary of a journey from Greece to Jerusalem.

HISTORICAL ELEMENTS

A summation of Paul's own testimonies suggests that he undertook a journey to Jerusalem from Greece the stages and sequence of which correspond to those in Acts 18.[103] To this degree the present tradition is historically valid; however, the chronological context in which it is set raises serious objections. It presupposes that Paul—in the middle of his journey for the collection—made a detour to Palestine. This would have been extremely arduous, given the distance of over 1200 miles as the crow flies, especially since he then resumed the collection in his communities. That scenario must be ruled out.[104] But the historical worth of the tradition underlying the journey in Acts 18–19 is clear if we place it in the historical context that can be reconstructed from Paul's letters. In that case it is an admirable account of the journey from Greece to Palestine that Paul undertook to attend the Jerusalem conference (Galatians 2). Assuming that some such hypothesis is correct, there are two possible routes:

(a) Since Paul traveled from Caesarea directly to Jerusalem (verse 22b), Titus must have gone with him on his trip from Greece; and since we know from Gal. 2:1 Paul and Barnabas traveled to Jerusalem, they must have met somewhere, though the place is no longer discoverable. (Nevertheless, we can at least exclude the possibility that Barnabas journeyed with Paul from Greece or Ephesus to Palestine.) The advantage of this is that the individual stopovers we find reported in verses 21–23 correspond with the itinerary that we derive from the letters of Paul.[105] The disadvantage is the position of Barnabas.

(b) Perhaps Titus accompanied Paul from Greece to Caesarea and on to Antioch, from where these two and Barnabas proceeded to Jerusalem for the conference. This suggestion has several advantages: (1) It corresponds to the travel account in verses 21–23 in depicting a journey to Antioch. (2) It portrays Barnabas as having a meaningful place in Paul's journey, since shortly before the conference he was apparently in Antioch (15:1–3; Gal 2:13), from where (in this case) he accompanied Paul to Jerusalem. (3) This hypothesis would indicate a plausible relation between the episode at Antioch and the conference, since that episode would then provide the occasion for that meeting.[106] This theory is weakened by the fact that verse 23 fails to indicate a journey from Antioch to Jerusalem, and that verse 22b ("he greeted the church") would have to be regarded as an editorial note—an anticipation of a later journey from Antioch to Jerusalem that is not described. It is possible, however, to set aside these two difficulties on the grounds that Luke is in the habit of arranging the movements of his characters in *a straight line*. Rather than report Paul's journey to Arabia (Gal. 1:17), for example, he keeps him in Damascus (9:19–22). Nor does he make note of Paul's intervening visit to Corinth.[107]

THE HISTORICAL VALUE OF LUKE'S ACCOUNT

For dogmatic reasons Luke has shifted forward the original chronological setting of Paul's second Jerusalem visit. Yet the Pauline letters allow us to correct the Acts narrative on this point, i.e., to reject a journey to Palestine between the conference and Paul's last visit. Except for these first-person documentary reports, though, Luke would have been wholly successful. Indeed, his account is still widely accepted, for many scholars defend his report at this point by postulating a journey to Jerusalem between the conference visit and the final visit bearing the collection. Or they posit a journey to the community at Antioch in Syria while dismissing the visit to Jerusalem as Luke's creation. In either case they uncritically take Luke's account at face value in accepting a detail with significant consequences for the reconstruction of the apostle's life.[108]

Let me first quote a few examples which come from scholars who think that Acts 18:22 is historical. I start with those who regard the Jerusalem visit as a historical fact.

Paul Walaskay writes,

> From Cenchreae the three missionaries sailed to Ephesus where they parted company. Priscilla and Aquila remained in Ephesus while Paul went on to Jerusalem (v. 19). These travel verses are quite terse. Luke inserts parenthetically that Paul visited the synagogue in Ephesus before departing for Jerusalem, and he merely "greeted the church" in Jerusalem before returning to his mission headquarters in Antioch. Luke's record of Paul's second missionary journey has come to an abrupt ending.[109]

Joseph A. Fitzmyer holds this view:

> Once again we see in this episode Paul carefully planning his missionary endeavor. He not only continues his work among the Corinthians after having been haled into court, but seeks to bring this phase of his activity to an end, as he leaves Corinth to return to Antioch in Syria. He makes a vow in Corinth, and though we are not told what relevance that has to his missionary work, he fulfills part of the obligation entailed by it by having his hair cut off in Cenchreae (18:18). He is dutiful in his obligation to God in that, having made the vow, he carries through with it. His journey back to Antioch includes also a visit to the church in Jerusalem, a visit that suits his character as a Jewish Christian.[110]

James D. G. Dunn offers the following reflections:

Despite his awareness of Paul's unpopularity in Jerusalem (9.29; 21.21, 27–36), Luke passes over the visit [to Jerusalem] in almost embarrassed silence—"having gone up and greeted the church (Jerusalem itself is not mentioned), he went down to Antioch." Mention of the visit to Antioch is almost as brief: beyond the fact that "Paul spent some time there" nothing more is said. Luke was presumably content thus to reaffirm the impression that the threads linking Paul's mission to the mother churches of Syria remain unbroken. Nothing more need be said. The minimalist reports, however, intrigue historians, who tend either to dispute whether the visits took place or to build them up into something more significant. But Luke clearly thought them of little importance (a brief interlude in the Aegean mission). This may be simply because for Paul they were intended as visits of reconciliation for the earlier breach (see Introduction to 15.30–41); whereas for Luke, since he had passed over that breach in silence, there was nothing else of substance he could report.

A decision to return to his main focus of mission in the Aegean by land would be understandable as it allowed further visits to the churches of his earlier mission from Antioch (13.14–14.23; 15.41–16.5), ensuring their solidarity with the developing Pauline mission. Paul had probably written to the Galatians by now and the visit would consolidate his position among them and allow him to set in hand what became one of his principal preoccupations in the latter phase of the Aegean mission—the collection for the poor among the saints in Jerusalem (Rom. 15.25; I Cor. 16.1; II Cor. 8–9). This may have been sparked by such a visit to Jerusalem, which had made Paul aware of the poverty of the church there. And the churches in Galatia are mentioned as among the first to be given instruction about it (I Cor. 16.). Of all this and the long days of travel covered in these verses Luke says nothing, content to summarize the purpose of the land journey by one of his standard phrases (14.22; 15.32, 41).[111]

Other scholars, while rejecting a visit to Jerusalem by Paul at this time in his career, still accept the Acts account that the apostle undertook a lengthy journey from Greece to Antioch between the conference and his final visit to Jerusalem.

Thus Ernst Haenchen writes,

The visit to Jerusalem involved the greatest danger for Paul. Paul had no great collection to deliver there, as is the case in Chapter 21. What should he be doing now in Jerusalem, where the encounter in Antioch[112] had certainly not been forgotten? But Luke did not know anything about this encounter. That deadly danger threatened in Jerusalem is a motif which is first introduced in Chapter 20. According to Luke's conviction Paul was on excellent terms with the community in Jerusalem. . . . Hence from the viewpoint of Acts a Pauline visit is quite reasonable, while from our knowledge of the situation it would have been a sense-less risk. . . . In reality Paul will have wanted to go to Antioch in order, after his great missionary success, to bind relations with the congregation still closer."[113]

Luke Timothy Johnson would have it that

> Paul's obvious destination was Antioch, the Church which had sponsored his mission and which was truly his homebase. Why does Luke, even so hurriedly, have Paul "go up" to greet the Church? For one reason only: to assert his con-tinuing fidelity to the original apostolic community.[114]

Gerhard Krodel has aptly summarized the main objections to the theory that Acts 18 be used to posit a trip of Paul from Greece to Palestine and back *after* the Jerusalem conference. He deserves to have the last word in this section: "It would be difficult to fit this lengthy time-consuming journey of Acts 18:21–23 into our chronology of Paul, remembering that travel by sea or crossing the Taurus mountains was not possible from November to mid-March, and dan-gerous in the month before or after. It would be equally difficult to find a reason for a visit of Paul to Jerusalem. The collection had not been completed and Paul was eager to get to Rome (Rom. 1:13; 15:29)."[115] Unfortunately this sober assessment of the problem of Acts 18:22 is a lone voice in the desert of Acts credulity. Indeed, no other section in Acts demonstrates so drastically how modern scholars continue to be hoodwinked by Luke's literary endowments.

[43]
ACTS 18:24–28
APOLLOS IN EPHESUS

(24) *Now* a Jew *named* Apollos, a native of Alexandria, came to Ephesus. He was an eloquent man, being powerful in the Scriptures. (25) He had been instructed in **the way of the Lord**. And being fervent in spirit, *he spoke and* taught <u>accurately</u> *the things concerning Jesus, though he knew only the baptism of John.* (26a) *He began to speak boldly in the synagogue,* (26b) *but when* Priscilla and Aquila *heard him, they took him and <u>more accurately</u> explained to him* **the way of God**.
(27a) And when he wished to cross to Achaia, the brothers encouraged him and wrote to the disciples to welcome him. (27b) *When he arrived,* he greatly helped those who through grace had believed, (28) for he powerfully refuted the Jews in public, showing by the Scriptures that the Christ was Jesus.

OUTLINE

24–26: Apollos's missionary work in Ephesus. He receives advanced instruction by Aquila and Priscilla

27–28: Apollos's trip to Achaia and his theological activity among the Jews

LUKE'S PURPOSE

Verses 24–25: Luke deliberately introduces Apollos as a "semi-Christian." Though he was instructed in the way of the Lord and taught accurately about Jesus,[116] "he knew only the baptism of John." This implies that his faith was deficient—as becomes clear in the next section 19:1–7. Here Luke introduces twelve disciples of John the Baptist who had not received the Holy Spirit because they had received only John's baptism. Since that is also true for Apollos, Luke is tacitly suggesting that in spite of his fervent and accurate evangelism, he has not received the bestowal of the Holy Spirit. Thus Luke says the same about Apollos as about Philip in chapter 8. In that case it was the Jerusalem apostles, in this case the Lukan Paul, who must intervene to impart the Holy Spirit.

Verse 26: Verse 26a contains Luke's well-known scheme of having his heroes approach the synagogue first. In verse 26b Aquila and Priscilla give Apollos full instruction. Luke emphasizes this by deliberately picking up from verse 25 "the way of the Lord" and "accurately." By explaining the way of God *more accurately* to Apollos they introduce him to full Christianity. Luke seeks to unite Apollos with Christianity properly understood, for in his view it was inherently impossible for a missionary to have worked independently even though in harmony with the apostolic Church—of which Paul was, in Luke's view, an extended arm. Therefore Luke felt it necessary to incorporate Apollos into the apostolic fellowship. Yet he has great difficulty in suppressing pre-Pauline tradition that showed Apollos from Ephesus to be an independent Christian teacher.[117]

Verses 27–28: The phrase "when he arrived" (verse 27b) goes back to Luke, for along with Apollos's refutation of the Jews in verse 28, it is another example of Luke's "to the Jews first" motif. The essence of Apollos's argument— "showing by the Scriptures that the Christ was Jesus"—is Lukan (cf. above on 18:5). Luke moves Apollos to Achaia (Corinth) because in the next section he wants to reserve Ephesus to Paul alone.

THE TRADITIONS REWORKED BY LUKE

Luke shapes the character of the Alexandrian Jew Apollos in accordance with the tension between his dogmatic purpose and the traditional material it reworks. Apparently this Christian charismatic (see verse 25: "fervent in the Spirit"—cf. Rom. 12:11) had strong ties to the Christian community of Ephesus. This community, already extant in Ephesus when Paul arrived and clearly indicated in "the brothers" (verse 27) who encouraged Apollos to go to Achaea (i.e., Corinth; see on 19:1), is also to be seen as part of this tradition.

HISTORICAL ELEMENTS

According to the abovementioned tradition, Paul was not the founder of the Ephesian church, a proposition that Paul's letters indirectly confirm.[118] For one thing, 1 Cor. 16:8–9 gives one the sense that Paul does not feel entirely at home in Ephesus. For another, unlike the churches Paul founded in Galatia, Achaia, and Macedonia, the Ephesian brotherhood did not join in the collection.[119]

Verse 24: The Pauline letters make it clear that Apollos collaborated with Paul in Ephesus (1 Cor. 16:12) and was known to the community in Corinth where, after Paul left Ephesus, he carried out a successful missionary effort. Indeed, Paul wrote that while he had planted the crop, it was Apollos who nurtured it (1 Cor. 3:6). More than that, one of the rival parties in Corinth called itself by Apollos's name (1 Cor. 1:12). And we learn that from Corinth Apollos went on to Ephesus, where for a time he found himself unable to decide whether to return straightaway to Corinth, as at least some of the Corinthian community wished him to do (1 Cor. 16:12).

The tradition that characterized Apollos as "fervent in the Spirit" could well be historically accurate, since 1 Corinthians corroborates the report and permits us thereby to infer a close association between him and the Corinthian enthusiasts. Apollos, then, was an early Christian pneumatic, similar in type to Stephen, Philip, the pneumatics at Corinth, and the itinerant preachers and healers reflected by the tradition that told of Jesus sending out his disciples.[120]

That this inspired teacher in Ephesus was a native of Alexandria suggests the possibility that a Christian community existed in Alexandria within a decade or two of Jesus' death.

THE HISTORICAL VALUE OF LUKE'S ACCOUNT

Luke did not see any contradiction in saying that Apollos had accurate knowledge about Jesus but later attained a more accurate view, especially since he has Apollos speak boldly in the synagogue (verse 26a) in the same way as the other representatives of Lukan Christianity. Yet these "declarations really cancel each other out. Either Apollos taught inaccurately in which case further instruction was possible and meaningful; or he taught accurately, which means that further instruction was unnecessary."[121] Here we have another example of Luke including material only to "neutralize" it by giving it a totally different thrust. Fortunately, since the elements of tradition that he includes are only superficially reworked, we are able to determine pretty accurately the content of the report as it came to him.

It would be a mistake to follow the lead of a recent commentator and, as he proposes, use Luke's account for historical reconstruction:

> The obvious question to ask about this text is why Priscilla and Aquila had not baptized Apollos, or at least why Luke did not care to record the event if they had and he knew about it. It is possible . . . that they might have thought it unnecessary, since he already had the Holy Spirit. It may also be that they thought that John's baptism was valid as a foreshadowing of Christian baptism, and perhaps Apollos had undergone that baptism. It is interesting that we have no evidence that the Twelve ever received Christian baptism, and it is even more interesting that Paul not only seems to imply that not all of his converts were baptized but also that he was glad, under the circumstances in Corinth, that this was the case (see 1 Cor. 1:14–17).[122]

Rebuttal: (a) Luke carefully avoids stating that Apollos had received the Holy Spirit. (b) In his letter to the Romans, Paul seems to assume that *all* members of the church were baptized[123] (c) The apostle does not imply that not all of his converts had been baptized; he simply says that he has personally baptized only a few. (For an explanation see above, pp. 238–39.)

It seems apparent that in the tradition(s) relating to Apollos, Luke had the makings of an edifying tale of dedicated believers rescuing a well-intentioned but improperly indoctrinated sympathetic spirit from the error of his ways. But he also had a hot potato in his hand, for he is dealing with the story of an effective preacher of the Way who lacks proper credentials, let alone official ordination. After juggling the toasty tuber from hand to hand for a while, he manages a successful resolution of the situation, but the juggling is noticeable.

[44]

ACTS 19:1–7

PAUL AND THE DISCIPLES OF JOHN THE BAPTIST IN EPHESUS

(1) *Now while Apollos was at Corinth, Paul passed through the interior of the country and came to Ephesus. There he found* some disciples, (2) *and he said to them, "Did you receive the Holy Spirit when you became believers?" And they said, "No, we have not even heard that there is a Holy Spirit." (3) And he said, "Into what then were you baptized?" They said, "Into* John's baptism." (4) *And Paul said, "John baptized with the baptism of repentance, telling the people to believe in the one who was to come after him, that is, Jesus." (5) On hearing this, they were baptized in the name of the Lord Jesus. (6) And when Paul had laid his hands on them, the Holy Spirit came on them, and they began speaking in tongues and prophesying. (7) There were about twelve men in all.*

OUTLINE

1: Apollos in Corinth; Paul finds disciples of John the Baptist in Ephesus

2–4: Conversation about the Holy Spirit and baptism

5–6: After baptism and after Paul has laid his hands on them the disciples of John receive the Holy Spirit speaking in tongues

7: Number baptized

LUKE'S PURPPOSE

Ernst Käsemann once remarked about the present text that if taken as an isolated passage it is "the despair of the exegete. Almost every sentence presents its own difficulties and the whole section gives the impression of being contradictory and untrustworthy."[124]

Verse 1: This brief transition connects what follows to the preceding episode (18:24–28). Apollos, now properly informed by Aquila and Priscilla, has moved to Corinth, and Paul arrives in Ephesus. (Luke thus avoids any encounter between them.) This verse takes up Paul's itinerary from where it left off in 18:23: Passing through Galatia and Phrygia in Asia Minor, he returns, as planned (18:21), to Ephesus.

Verses 2–4: Luke must be the source of the question that Paul asks John's disciples about whether they received the Spirit, for it assumes a necessary connection between baptism and Spirit that these disciples—in their still unenlightened condition—would not even imagine. "The peculiar expression 'baptized into John's baptism' results from Luke's concern to avoid speaking about a baptism in John's *name*."[125] Luke's corrective hand is evident also in verse 4, for here, by having John the Baptist call for faith in *Jesus*, he makes unambiguous what is only hinted at in Luke 3:16.[126] It should be noted, however, that Acts 13:24–25 conforms to the synoptic pattern in having John the Baptist preach a baptism of repentance while at the same time—as precursor—announcing the future coming of Jesus.

Verses 5–6: The previous verse set the stage for this baptism of the Johannine disciples in Jesus' name. The report in verse 6 about speaking in tongues obviously harks back to the story of Pentecost (Acts 2).

Verse 7: The expressions "about" as well as "twelve men" represent Luke's editorial work. For his numerical specifications, see the commentary on the number "seven" in 19:14.

The clear parallels between 19:1–7 and 18:24–28 must be assigned to the author. Both Apollos and the Ephesian disciples know only "the baptism of John" and in each case this doctrinal/spiritual weakness must be cured—in the one case by more accurate information, in the other by baptism and receiving the Holy Spirit. By setting these accounts in parallel, Luke conveys the impression that through instruction alone Apollos received the Holy Spirit, and thus reinforces his point that non-Pauline forms of Christianity must both conform to the teaching and gain the sanction of either the Jerusalem apostles[127] or Paul.

THE TRADITIONS REWORKED BY LUKE

That disciples of John were still to be found in the post-Easter period,[128] and that they came in contact with disciples of Jesus, may have been reported by the tradition; nonetheless, it is highly doubtful that either the *conversion* of the former or their connection to Ephesus were elements of that information. Rather, since Luke has no specific interest in disciples of John, I conclude that he found it expedient to use Ephesus as the setting of the story in order to establish the inferiority of Apollos to Paul. (Unlike Apollos, the properly baptized disciples of John whose faith was similar to that of Apollos received the Holy Spirit through Paul's intervention.) Except for Luke's redactional change that portrays John the Baptist calling for belief in Jesus, the message contained in 19:4 must be part of the tradition, for it appears in Q, but was not part of the tradition relating to the disciples of John.

HISTORICAL ELEMENTS

The probable historical core of the tradition tells of a group of John the Baptist's disciples who encountered Christian groups.[129] If, however, the contact between disciples of John and a Christian group is a Lukan creation, the authentic portion of the tradition indicated only the existence of a group of John's disciples. That the first could be true is suggested by the Johannine community's demotion of John the Baptist[130] and a later account in the Pseudo-Clementine Recognitions 1:54, 60.[131] In any case, two historical judgments are certain: First, "John's followers survived his death, were still known as an independent group"[132] and second, "John's teaching was not predicated upon either the arrival of Jesus or a future Spirit-immersion."[133]

THE HISTORICAL VALUE OF LUKE'S ACCOUNT

Haenchen has succinctly revealed the contradictory nature of Luke's account and writes,

> This incomplete Christianity . . . which reveals itself as such for these twelve men, helped Luke now to depict the incompleteness of Apollos' Christianity more concretely. Of course, Luke formulates this with extraordinary caution. He does not say, "Apollos had received only the baptism of John"—in that case, Aquila would have had to baptize him again as Paul had to do with the twelve men. And that the well-known missionary Apollos had first received Christian baptism from Aquila would have been a falsification that Luke did not want to write. So he helped himself with the expression "knowing only the baptism of John"—as if it dealt with a defect in the teaching, which could be corrected by instruction.[134]

Moreover, by way of pointing out Luke's ideological theology of history, he continues as follows:

> Its characteristic feature is this: it reads back into the past as an historical reality the postulate of an *Una sancta* grounded on the apostolic fellowship and then, conversely, uses this postulate to validate the claims of the orthodox Church of his own times. Luke has overpainted and re-shaped history in order to defend the *Una sancta apostolica* against the assaults of Gnostics and other heretics of his day. We can only understand him as an historian, if we have first understood him as a theologian. As a theologian he can only be understood from his doctrine of a legitimate Church.[135]

What Haenchen's critique fails to mention is Luke's irresponsible manipulation of the facts. Indeed, it is first and foremost Luke's constant twisting of real history in the interest of theological orthodoxy that subverts his ingenuous claim (Luke 1:1–4) to be a trustworthy historian.

[45]
ACTS 19:8–22
PAUL'S SUCCESSFUL MINISTRY IN EPHESUS

(8) *And he entered the synagogue and for three months spoke boldly, reasoning and persuading about the kingdom of God.* (9) *But when some became stubborn and continued in unbelief, speaking evil of the Way before the congregation, he withdrew from them and took the disciples with him,* reasoning daily in the lecture hall of Tyrannus. (10) This continued for two years, *so that all the residents of Asia heard the word of the Lord, both Jews and Greeks.*

(11) *And God was doing extraordinary miracles by the hands of Paul,* (12) *so that even handkerchiefs or aprons that had touched his skin were carried away to the sick, and their diseases left them and the evil spirits came out of them.*

(13) *Then some of the itinerant Jewish exorcists undertook to invoke the name of the Lord Jesus over those who had evil spirits, saying, "I adjure you by the Jesus, whom Paul proclaims."* (14) *Seven* sons of a Jewish high priest named Sceva were doing this. (15) But the evil spirit answered them, "Jesus I know, and Paul I recognize, but who are you?" (16) And the man with *the evil spirit* sprang at them, overpowered them, and thrashed all of them so violently that that they fled out of that house naked and *wounded.*

(17a) *This became known to all the residents of Ephesus, both Jews and Greeks;* (17b) *and fear fell upon them all, and the name of the Lord Jesus was extolled.* (18) *Also many of those who became believers confessed their former [occult] practices,* (19) *and a number of them who had practiced magic brought their books together and burned them in the sight of all. When they calculated the value of these books, they found it came to fifty thousand pieces of silver.* (20) *So the word of the Lord continued to increase and prevail mightily.*

(21) *When these things had been accomplished, Paul resolved in the Spirit to pass through* Macedonia and Achaia and go to Jerusalem, *saying, "After I have been there, I must also see* Rome." (22) And having sent into Macedonia *two of his helpers,* Timothy and Erastus, *he himself stayed in Asia for a while.*

OUTLINE

8–10: After doing missionary work in the synagogue for three months Paul leaves and does the same for two years in the school of Tyrannus

11–12: Summary: Paul the miracle worker

13–16: The failure of the Jewish exorcists

17–20: The effect on the local magicians. Voluntary burning of the magical books

21–22: Paul's travel plans

LUKE'S PURPOSE

Verse 8: Once again Luke trundles out his scheme of having Paul approach the Jews first, though in fact this is a renewed effort on his part (see 18:19) and it eventually alienates them. The period of time during which Paul preached to the Jews also derives from Luke: "three" is one of his favorite numbers. The phrase "persuading about the kingdom of God" further indicates his authorial hand, for he alone in the New Testament relates the term "kingdom" to reports of preaching (cf. 8:12). Note other striking parallels to this verse in chapter 28, verses 23 and 31.

Verses 9–10: We see an editorial stereotype in verse 9 when Paul abandons the Jews because of their rejection of his message. For "Way" see below on verse 23. The remark "all the residents of Asia heard the word of the Lord" is a typically Lukan exaggeration, and "Jews and Gentiles" (verses 10, 17, etc.) as the target of the missionary work is also found in 18:4.

Verses 11–12: These verses "provide (on the basis of hearsay about handkerchiefs and aprons) a succinct picture of Paul the miracle worker, a picture from a later time.[136] This note serves as the preparation for an episode: The miracle worker is contrasted to those who have no real power."[137]

Verses 13–16: Verse 13 is Luke's introduction to the next event.[138] That the language derives from Luke is clear if only from the verb "to undertake" (in the New Testament only in Luke-Acts).[139] The mention of Paul in the usurped formula of invocation almost surely stems from the author, as the demon's answer in verse 15 strongly implies. The number "seven" in verse 14 may go back to Luke. "Evil spirit" in verse 15 is found only in the Gospel of Luke[140] except for Matt. 12:45 (which—as Luke 11:26 shows—reflects Q). Similarly verse 16 features Lukan language: "to wound," like "wounds" (Luke 10:34), occurs nowhere else in the New Testament except in the third Gospel.[141]

Verses 17–20: These verses smack of redaction throughout, especially since they report the salutary conclusion of the preceding action. Verse 17a seems to do more than make explicit reference to verses 13–16: it could even be seen as something of a choral conclusion, and as such it could well have been attached to verses 13–16. Verse 17b ("and fear fell upon them all, and the name of the Lord Jesus was extolled") corresponds to 2:43; and note that verse 20 ("so the word of the Lord continued to increase and prevail mightily") parallels 2:47. In spite of its clearly comic elements, Luke is at pains to assign religious significance to the foregoing episode in order once again to drive home the point (see especially verses 18–19) that Christian power—and only Christian power—can overcome the forces of evil.

Verses 21–22: These verses display several specifically Lukan features. Not only does Paul's projected trek recall the beginning of Jesus' final journey as reported in Luke 9:51, but both the vocabulary and the theological concepts reflect the Third Evangelist. Concerning this last matter, note the motif of sending out in pairs (cf. below, p. 256) and the divine necessity for Paul to see Rome—though for the time being, he must remain in Asia.

THE TRADITIONS REWORKED BY LUKE

Verses 9–10: The datum that Paul taught for two years in Tyrannus's lecture hall most likely comes from tradition. The place reference means a building (not a group of people) and the name Trophimus designates its owner.

Verses 13–16: This story must have originated either as a burlesque legend or as a joke. As was clear in the case of the previous section (see on verses 10–12 above), Luke has adapted the language and content of the passage to his purposes. He did not invent this episode, however; rather, he all but surely took it from his knowledge of pagan literature. Dibelius is surely correct in proposing that while the underlying tradition had entertainment value, it lacked any religious or personal interest.

> The evil spirit will not be driven out by unauthorised exorcists, who have simply borrowed a formula which they have heard used by genuine exorcists – this is the sense of the story, told in a strain which is not without its comic element. It is not clear whether the misused formula was ever a Christian one, for the anecdote is embedded in a summary passage (19.11–13, 17–19), so that we no longer have the beginning of it. We have no description of the details of the incident and it is only at the end, and rather surprisingly, that we hear anything of the house in which the story takes place. Even if the incantation had been Christian in the first place, the story was certainly not fashioned by Christian interests.[142]

Note that it is criteria of content rather than of language that point to a traditional basis for verses 13–16.

Verses 21–22: The detailed nature of the planned itinerary indicates derivation from tradition, though as editor Luke has taken it upon himself to ascribe the scheme to Paul. The names Timothy and Erastus also come from tradition.[143]

HISTORICAL ELEMENTS

Verses 9–10: It could well be true that Paul worked for two years in Ephesus,[144] and since the indicated place is linked with a reliable indication of time, one may reasonably suspect that it, too, has historical validity. "Lecture hall" may refer to the private auditorium of the orator Tyrannus—that he used for instruction and rented to Paul for the latter's missionary activity. Such information helps us envision Paul's general modus operandi, and particularly that in Ephesus.

Verses 13–16: The above form-critical considerations suffice to certify the nonhistorical nature of the story.

Verses 21–22: The historicity of the contemplated itinerary can be accepted inasmuch as Paul himself reports in 1 Cor. 16:5 his intention to travel through Macedonia and on to Achaia (Corinth). The extension of that journey to Jerusalem (verse 21) is under contemplation only in 1 Cor. 16:4, and it is not until some years later that we hear of a plan to go to Rome (Rom. 1:13), at a time when Paul was fully determined to undertake the journey to Jerusalem (Rom. 15:25). Clearly, the travel plan Luke derived from tradition has been so editorially compressed as to compromise its accuracy. As a matter of fact, Paul sent Timothy—and possibly Erastus with him—to Macedonia and on to Corinth (1 Cor. 16:10; 4:17). To be sure, it was unusual in antiquity for people to travel alone, but Luke's predilection for sending people out in pairs,[145] together with Paul's silence on the matter, suggest that the apostle did indeed journey alone.

THE HISTORICAL VALUE OF LUKE'S ACCOUNT

Although Haenchen has written extensively about the nonhistoricity of the scene, he fails to take the logical next step, which is to accuse Luke of deceiving his readers for propagandist purposes. Regarding verses 13–16 he reasons,

> Elsewhere exorcists are not in the habit of appearing in groups—it would diminish not only their earnings and their authority but also their effectiveness. A High Priest by the name of Sceva (this is probably the Latin Scaeva) did not exist. . . . Luke has not signified any doubt about the authenticity of this High

Priest. He would have defeated his own purpose and the story would be worthless if only a few rogues had been beaten up by a demon. If on the other hand highly respected Jewish exorcists, sons of an actual High Priest, had experienced such a fiasco, then what Luke wanted to bring before the eyes of his readers with this story would be palpably clear: so powerful was the success of Paul that the great Jewish exorcists had themselves to take over the *onoma* which he invoked if . . . they wanted to remain "competitive." But even more, this attempt now reveals that no one is able to imitate Paul.[146]

With respect to verses 19–20 Haenchen remarks,

Of these many one-time magicians who have become Christians a large number now bring their books of magic for public burning, and it is calculated that in the process a value equivalent to 50,000 days' wages goes up in the flames. These Christians—they are only a portion of those "many" who have meddled with magic—must have had astonishing resources at their disposal—if we could trust the report historically. Only this is precisely what we may not do. In reality Luke only wants to show how magic lost ground through the activity of Paul (= Christianity), and according to his technique of narration he clothes this statement in the garb of an impressive scene. . . . Luke however expresses it positively: "So the Word of the Lord grew powerful and became stronger and stronger." The Word "of the Lord" is none other than the mission church itself, for which an abstraction like "Christianity" had not yet been invented.[147]

In full agreement with Haenchen's historical analysis I now go one step further and conclude that the present episode is another example of Luke's historical "method"—namely, complete and unabashed freedom to invent stories in the service of theological purposes. Religious enthusiasm seems to be at work here, proceeding almost methodologically to tailor useful facts to suit a preconceived purpose—and, as usual, at the expense of truth.

[46]
ACTS 19:23–40
A RIOT OF THE SILVERSMITHS OF EPHESUS AGAINST PAUL

(23) *About that time there arose no little disturbance concerning the Way.* (24) For a man *named* Demetrius, a silversmith, who made silver shrines of Artemis, brought *no little business* to the craftsmen. (25) These he gathered together, with the workmen in similar trades, and said, "Men, you know that our prosperity depends

on this business. (26a) *You also see and hear that not only in Ephesus but also in almost all of Asia this Paul has persuaded and turned away* a great many *people,* (26b) *saying that gods made with hands are not gods.* (27) And there is danger not only that this trade of ours may come into disrepute but also that the temple of the great goddess Artemis may be counted as nothing, and that she may even be deposed from her magnificence, she whom all Asia and the world worship."

(28) When they heard this they were enraged and were crying out, "Great is Artemis of the Ephesians!" (29a) *So the city was in an uproar, and they rushed together into the theater,* (29b) *dragging with them Gaius and Aristarchus, Macedonians who were Paul's travel companions.* (30) *But when Paul wished to go in among the crowd, the disciples would not let him.* (31) *And even some Asiarchs* [provincial officials] *who were friendly with him sent word to him, urging him not to venture into the theater.*

(32) Now some cried out one thing, some another, for the assembly was in chaos, and most of them had no idea why they had come together. (33) Some of the throng prompted Alexander, whom the Jews had put forward. And Alexander, motioning with his hand, wanted to make a defense to the crowd. (34) But when they recognized that he was a Jew, for about two hours they all cried out in chorus, "Great is Artemis of the Ephesians!"

(35) And when the town clerk had quieted the throng, he said, "Men of Ephesus, who is there who does not know that the city of the Ephesians is the guardian of the temple of the great Artemis, and of the sacred stone that fell from the sky? (36) Seeing then that these things cannot be denied, you ought to be quiet and do nothing rash. (37) For you have brought these men here who are neither temple robbers nor blasphemers of our goddess. (38) If therefore Demetrius and the craftsmen with him have a complaint against anyone, the courts are open, and there are proconsuls. Let them bring legal action. (39) But if you seek anything further, it must be settled in the regular assembly. (40a) For we really are in danger of being charged with rioting today, since we have no explanation to offer for this commotion." (40b) And when he had said these things, he dismissed the assembly.

OUTLINE

32–34:   Chaos in the gathering
35–40:   Soothing speech by the town clerk

LUKE'S PURPOSE

Verse 23: "About that time" is a Lukan introductory formula. The Lukan litotes "no little" (cf. 17:4, 12) is repeated in verse 24. "Way" as a technical term for Christianity derives from Luke.[148] Since previous mentions of the Way (plus the genitive) appear in 16:17 ("way of salvation"), 18:25 ("way of the Lord"), and 18:26 ("way of God"), the absolute use of "Way" may be echoing those. First and foremost, of course, verse 23 is Luke's introduction to the following episode, which tells of a bitter attack on this Christian "Way."

Verses 24–26: The protagonist Demetrius is introduced; he introduces the theme of "business" that previously appeared in 16:16. There the source of profit was a female soothsayer; here it is the production of silver temples honoring Artemis. Demetrius's assertion that Paul's influence has spread to most of Asia and seduced many people (verse 26a) is a Lukan exaggeration. The hearsay report of Paul's sermon against gods made with hands (verse 26b) harks back to 17:29, where in speaking before the Areopagus the apostle issued a similar diatribe against idols.

Verse 27: Now Demetrius intensifies the supposed threat that Paul poses to the economy by suggesting that he will bring the sanctuary of Artemis into disrepute— even though all Asia and people throughout the world worship Artemis! (Note that he contradicts his earlier claim in verse 26 that most of Asia has been led astray.)

Verses 28–29a: The whipped-up, emotional reaction of the craftsmen culminates in a chanted acclamation of Artemis. Luke's dramatic exaggeration spreads the craftsmen's uproar to the whole city (verse 29a).

Verses 29b–31: The height of the riot finds Paul's companions Gaius and Aristarchus dragged into the theater (verse 29b), but except for an oblique reference in verse 37 they disappear from the narrative. One suspects that Luke may have artificially placed them in the story in order to add both substance and drama to the introductory remark (verse 23) that identifies the Christian proclamation as the source of the conflict. Verses 30–31 strengthen that suspicion. When the hero finally takes the stage, he of course seeks to join the action, but the disciples, and even some friendly Asiarchs manage to deter him. "When they believe him to be in danger, these great men, who in all probability will also have had obligations in the state cult, have nothing more urgent to do than to warn the Christian missionary."[149] Since Paul and his friends thereupon disappear from the narrative, one must conclude that he has taken the advice of the brothers and the friendly officials. (The literary technique of keeping the main actor off the scene corresponds to that employed in Luke 7:1–10 [diff. Q].)[150] Following this insertion, which effectively removes Paul and his friends from the danger of the mob, verse 32 will return to the events in the theater (note this keyword in verse 29 and at the end of verse 31). All of this lends further support to the conclusion earlier drawn from the analysis of verse 29 that Paul's companions, and indeed Paul himself, have been editorially inserted into a story about a riot in Ephesus in order to further establish that imbroglio (note verse 23) as the result of a dispute over Christian preaching.

Whatever one may see as the overall significance of the pericope, the specific role assigned to the provincial officials reveals a secondary purpose of Luke. The Asiarchs,[151] who represented the leading families of the Roman province of Asia, were representatives and high priests of the confederation of Asian cities, and their half-religious, half-political function during a one-year tenure in office, was to keep Asia loyal—and subservient—to the Roman state. This confederation of officials—charged among other things with maintaining the cult of the reigning emperor and the goddess Roma—oversaw temple worship throughout the province. In view of this role, Luke's apologetic intent is obvious when he has them intervene on Paul's behalf: He is promoting the notion that important representatives of the religious and political life of the empire were on Paul's side. Why these officials intervened, it should be noted, is not mentioned; Luke merely alludes in passing to friendly relations between them and Paul (verse 31). Such an assertion is unique,[152] but its thrust is clear: Paul's friendly—dare I say "collegial"?—standing with men of such cultic and political eminence places the leading representative of Christianity on the level of highly placed representatives of the Roman state.

Verse 32: Luke's narrative artistry is the source of the details of the riot; see for instance 21:34, which has some verbatim correspondences. Calling the gathering an "assembly"[153] may reflect the technique of variation: this term also appears in verses 39–40, but verses 30, 33 have "crowd,"[154] while the word of choice is "throng"[155] in verses 33, 35. Luke also characterizes the riot variously as "disturbance"[156] (verse 23), "confusion"[157] (verse 29), "rioting"[158] (verse 40), and "commotion"[159] (verse 40).

Verse 33: This verse is difficult to understand: "Some of the throng prompted Alexander, whom the Jews had put forward. And Alexander, motioning with his hand, wanted to make a defense to the crowd." This probably means that the Jews felt threatened by the riot—though Paul occasioned it and "up to this point not a word against the Jews has been reported"[160]—and hoped that Alexander would dissociate them from Christianity's representative, i.e., Paul.

Verse 34: When the crowd recognizes Alexander to be a Jew, they commence a second outburst in support of Artemis (cf. verse 28). The extraordinary assertion that it was sustained for two hours raises still further the dramatic intensity of the scene. That animosity caused by Paul is redirected at a Jew suggests that here we may have a soft echo of the Gallio episode (18:12–17), for there, too, popular anger fell on a Jew after the Paul was conveniently removed from the scene.

Verses 35–36: By referring at verse 35 to the city as "the guardian of the temple of the great Artemis,"[161] the town clerk justifies the demand for peace and prudence made in verse 36.[162]

Verse 37: This allusion to the charges against Paul's two companions (verse 29) stresses that they are neither temple robbers nor blasphemers, and thereby undercuts the validity of the indictment—though lacking such indemnification, the Jew Alexander remains under accusation.

Verse 38: In referring to Demetrius's speech (verses 25–27), the town clerk alludes to a situation that he cannot have known about, since Demetrius made his speech to a closed gathering. Inasmuch as the scenario is manufactured, therefore, the details can hardly be taken at face value. It is further worth noting that Demetrius himself has been removed from the scene, leaving the crowd unaware of why it has gathered (verse 32). Nevertheless the speaker's appeal is cogent and well informed.

Verse 39: "Regular assembly"[163]—a meeting governed by the law—picks up "assembly"[164] at verse 32, where the noun designates an irregular gathering of people. Just as Demetrius's speech caused the riot, so the town clerk's timely expostulation defuses the situation by its appeal both to the vanity and to the common sense of the people, and its careful omission of any explicit claims as to the innocence of the accused—whose innocence he briefly and obliquely establishes in verse 37. The craftsmen are exhorted to place any real complaints before the courts, and the Ephesians are commended to the popular assemblies.

Verse 40: Since the town clerk's strategy is to deny any real grounds for the riot, it ends with a warning not to incur a charge of sedition. By reasserting the lack of justification for the ill-advised brouhaha, verse 40b concludes the story of a mob scene that, far from harming Christianity, allowed the author to create a rousing defense of the new religion against any possible charge of sedition.

THE TRADITIONS REWORKED BY LUKE

Like the account in 17:16–34, this story exhibits a considerable amount of local coloring: Note, for example, (1) the silversmith Demetrius, who makes souvenirs of the temple of Artemis; (2) the cult of Artemis in Ephesus, which indeed was world famous, and the temple itself, among the seven wonders of the ancient world; (3) the theater of Ephesus; (4) the quick-witted town clerk; (5) the city visualized as the guardian of the temple of Artemis. It goes without saying that the aforementioned local coloring cannot be used to establish any traditional story. Moreover, the setting of Acts at this point seems to be anachronistic; it was not until the end of the first century that Ephesus became known as the guardian of the temple of Artemis.[165]

The above analysis of the redaction indicates the artificial insertion of Paul and two of Paul's companions (both of whose names are from tradition) into an account of a riot in Ephesus.[166] This editorial inclusion gave the story a Christian flavor, and thereby enabled it to depict a conflict over the "Way" (verse 23). "The famous riot at Ephesus is the showcase exhibit of social disorder. This justly famous passage gains high praise for its verisimilitude. There are many good parallels in novels."[167]

The result of my analysis[168] excludes any possibility that the tradition may be related to the founding of the Ephesian congregation or to a critical moment in the community's life. Nor is Weiser's suggestion that Aristarchus (verse 29) appeared in a pre-Lukan tradition[169] persuasive, since that verse represents an editorial insertion. Weiser also adduces Philemon 24 to propose a close relationship between Aristarchus and Paul during the apostle's imprisonment in Ephesus (see 2 Cor. 1:8–9) and further assumes that the Demetrius episode is directly related to Paul's imprisonment in Ephesus. Among the problems involved in the above contentions is that Philemon 24 does *not* refer to Aristarchus (as it does to Epaphras) as a fellow prisoner, but rather identifies him (along with Mark, Demas, and Luke) as a fellow worker. Weiser in vain attempts to salvage his case by concluding that the tradition specifically focused on Aristarchus.

HISTORICAL ELEMENTS

Verses 23–40: Paul himself seems to attest to three occasions of mortal danger in Ephesus: He fought against "animals" (1 Cor. 15:32), he was prostrated by an unspecified condition (2 Cor. 1:8–9), and something occurred in or near Ephesus that caused Priscilla and Aquila to have "risked their necks" for him. This latter situation may be the incident mentioned in 2 Cor. 1:8, but none of these three (or two) events can be identified with or related to Luke's account,[170] to say nothing of a report he found in the tradition—if there was one. "Even if Luke had known of this event, he would not have concluded his description of Paul's missionary activity with it. The harmonious development ought not to end on so shrill a dissonance."[171]

Verse 29: The names of Paul's companions, Gaius and Aristarchus, who are both from Macedonia, certainly designate historical persons. The name Gaius does not derive from Acts 20:4 since there we hear about a Gaius *from Derbe*. Yet, we have no way to relate Gaius and Aristarchus to Ephesus.[172]

THE HISTORICAL VALUE OF LUKE'S ACCOUNT

The traditions underlying Acts offer little historical substance by which to determine the events of Paul's life during his stay in Ephesus.[173] Richard Pervo incisively summarizes the historical problem raised by Luke's account thus:

> [O]ne must still ask why Luke, who has devoted so little space to Paul's pastoral and missionary work in this, one of his most important centers, spends twenty verses on a spectacular display of fireworks, the net effect of which is to deflect attention from the serious trouble into which Paul got at Ephesus. The use of a similar ploy at Jerusalem two chapters later (chap. 21) supports the contention that this obscurity is due to Luke. If early church history must be seen through a glass darkly, that is in part due to this "historian's" fondness for smokescreens rather than mirrors.[174]

Haenchen has well described the intellectual effrontery (my expression, not Haenchen's) of Luke for presenting his readers with an allegedly historical account of the opposition to Paul in Ephesus:

> If we take the Demetrius story as an historical account and place this incident under close scrutiny, we find a regular tangle of difficulties. . . . Rather do we assume in the first place with Luke that Paul really threatened the existence of the Artemis cult by his missionary activity. But then we ought properly to expect all the circles interested in it to join in an action against Paul, and foremost all of the priesthood of the temple (which for that matter was at the same time a major bank with far-reaching connections and exercised the power of a large sum of capital!) and the city authorities. But no, Demetrius is allowed to make the running alone. He—yes, what does he really have in mind? Does he want to carry through an edict of expulsion against Paul or a lynching? It is not clear? Demetrius mobilizes his guild and leads a kind of popular assembly into the theatre. But then the inconceivable happens: nothing more is heard of him. How can a man who is presented as so good an organizer veil himself in silence at the very moment when—before an enthusiastic public—he ought to come out with a concrete proposal? Instead he lets the time expire unused, and not only he but his guild associates also.
> Just as incomprehensible is the attitude of the Asiarchs. They have the duty of advancing the cult of Caesar (and the goddess Roma). In spite of this, when they hear about the riot, their first thought is Paul's safety. Here we must con-

sider that these Asiarchs do not all live together. Do they all react in the same manner? Or do they immediately call a council? Be that as it may: they are fortunate that this messenger still meets with Paul, because the disciples restrained him! And Paul follows their advice.[175]

In light of the brilliant historical deconstruction of the present passage by Haenchen, it strikes me as odd—to say the least—that on the basis of Acts 19:31 Fitzmyer continues to insist on a "friendship" relationship between the Asiarchs and Paul. He writes, "Luke's mention of the Asiarchs implies the good relationship that existed between them and Paul and cannot simply be written off 'as highly unlikely.'"[176] Surely Fitzmyer errs, for those elected to preserve and promote the imperial cult (and thus no doubt among its staunchest supporters) could hardly have been personally well disposed to an obvious rival for men's hearts and minds who dismissed veneration of any but the one true God as idol worship.[177] Luke is not the only one whose will to believe leads him badly astray.

[47]
ACTS 20:1–16
PAUL'S JOURNEY TO GREECE, MACEDONIA, AND TROAS; THE RAISING OF EUTYCHUS; FROM TROAS TO MILETUS

(1) After the uproar ceased, Paul *sent for the disciples*, and after encouraging them, he said farewell and *departed for* Macedonia. (2) When he had gone through those regions and had given them much encouragement, he came to Greece. (3) There he spent *three* months, and *when a plot was made against him by the Jews* as he was about to set sail for Syria, he decided to return through Macedonia. (4) Sopater the son of Pyrrhus from Beroea accompanied him, along with Aristarchus and Secundus from Thessalonica, Gaius of Derbe, Timothy, and Tychicus and Trophimus from Asia. (5) These went on ahead and were waiting for us at Troas, (6) but we sailed away from Philippi *after the days of Unleavened Bread*, and in five days we joined them at Troas, where we stayed for seven days.
(7) *On the first day of the week, when we were gathered together to break bread, Paul talked with them, and since he intended to depart the next day, he continued talking until midnight.* (8) *A large number of* lamps was in the upstairs room where we were gathered, (9) and a young man *named* Eutychus sat on the window-ledge, and being heavy with sleep, as Paul's address continued for a long time, he was overcome with sleep and fell from the third story and was

taken up for dead. (10) But Paul went down and bent over him, and taking him in his arms, said, "Do not be alarmed, for his life is in him." (11) *Then Paul went back up and after he had broken bread and eaten, he continued to converse with them until daybreak; and then departed.* (12) Meanwhile, they took the youth away alive, and were not a little relieved.

(13) We went ahead to the ship and set sail for Assos, intending to take Paul aboard there, for so he had arranged, intending himself to go by land. (14) And when he met us at Assos, we took him on board and went to Mitylene. (15) And sailing from there we came the following day opposite Chios; the next day we touched at Samos, and the day after that we went to Miletus. (16) For Paul had decided to sail past Ephesus, so that he might not have to spend time in Asia, *for he was eager to be at Jerusalem, if possible, on the day of Pentecost.*

OUTLINE

1–3: Journeys of Paul and harassment by the Jews
4–5: List of Paul's companions and their journey to Troas
  6: Journey by Paul and his companions, described as "we," from Philippi to Troas
7–12: Revival of the youth Eutychus
13–16: Travel notes: from Troas to Miletus

LUKE'S PURPOSE

Verses 1–3: This section displays Lukan linguistic characteristics. Verses 1–2 report the itinerary Paul planned in 19:21: He travels through Macedonia and then on to Greece. The account of a Jewish plot against Paul (verse 3) is an oft-repeated Lukan element.

Verses 4–5: See below.

Verse 6: It is probably a Lukan creation that the departure followed the days of unleavened bread; incorporating Jewish feasts as an indication of time is a common practice of his.

Verses 7–12: As a seam is evident in verse 7 (those indicated by "them" appear from nowhere) Luke's hand is revealed; he apparently refers to a gathering of the Christian community in Troas. Since this same verse also anticipates future events, the long-winded sermon and conversation and next morning's departure, it must go back to Luke—especially since it also introduces the tradition beginning in verse 8. Typical Lukan locutions in verse 8 are "a large number of" and "named," and "we" is surely his since it clashes with "they (took)" in verse 12. Verse 11 is certainly out of place at this point, because it stands between Paul's reassurance (verse 10) and action and relief of the audience (verse 12). Still, the author must have had a specific reason for repeating the Eucharist motif ("breaking bread") found in the introduction (verse 7). It may well have been a way of incorporating this story—an understandable motive, because he lacked any traditions that related to Troas, and had given no other account of the city (cf. 16:8). Another thing this story accomplishes is to create a parallel between Paul's "resuscitation" of Eutychus and Peter's raising of Tabitha in 9:36–42. Nor is the profane character of this story a valid objection, for that simply reflects the distinctive character of the tradition—one that Luke may have adopted with little more change than inserting Paul and his companions (cf. 19:23–40). In short, the miracle story enables Luke to establish a correspondence between Paul and Peter on the apologetically useful grounds that they both have the miraculous power to raise people from the dead.[178]

Verses 13–16: Here it appears that only the haste indicated by verse 16 is Luke's work (see verse 6 and the above remarks thereon). Note that upon Paul's arrival in Jerusalem (21:17), we find no mention of this desire. Not only that, but the sense of haste (earlier implied in verse 1) stands in sharp contrast with Paul's next action: He summons the Ephesian elders to a meeting in Miletus (verse 17), necessitating a much greater delay than if he had spoken with them in Ephesus. "It would have taken at least five days for the Ephesians to reach Miletus (the distance from Miletus to Ephesus is about thirty kilometers by air; the distance by land was considerably greater). Samos would have been a more convenient meeting place."[179] But Luke's thematic repertoire includes both haste and delay; no doubt employing them in combination (the motive of haste frustrated by elements of delay) effectively depicts the martyr's voluntary yet inexorable path to the executioner. One can hardly help visualizing the "Gethsemane" episode (Luke 22:39–46) along the same lines.

THE TRADITIONS REWORKED BY LUKE

Verses 1–3: Luke's relatively minor editorial rearrangement of the travel information does not alter the fact that it is ultimately based on tradition (see the analysis of 19:21). That Paul did not sail from Achaea to Syria but took the land route via Macedonia stands as an accurate expansion of 19:21 and comports with the detailed itinerary in verses 13–16.

Verses 4–5: The names of Paul's companions certainly come from tradition, as does likely their journey to Troas, since it too is both precise and unbiased reportage.

Verse 6: The same can be said of the journey from Philippi to Troas made by Paul and those subsumed under the heading "we."

Verses 7–12: This episode displays numerous peculiarities. Dibelius assesses the situation effectively:

> The mood of the story is as secular as possible; this is seen particularly in the rationalised description of the miracle. We should expect Eutychus to be dead after his fall from the window, then everything that follows would be a great miracle. But the storyteller leaves open the question as to whether it is a miracle: "he was taken up as dead." Paul throws himself on him and embraces him. It is not made clear whether this happens in order to conjure the soul or to examine the unconscious boy; we are left equally uncertain as to whether Paul is seen as a worker of miracles or a doctor: "his life is still in him" . . . the skeptical reader is intended to be interested by the very fact that the matter remains unexplained: "they brought the boy alive" . . . The secular manner of telling the story, to which, in some sense, even the lamps in the room belong, is in accordance with the secular conclusion; only the occasion of the accident and the height of the fall are described: there is no edifying motif, neither is there any mention of prayer before the boy is restored to life, nor of praise to God afterwards. The whole account concludes: "they were not a little comforted." Dismay now gives way to peace of mind.[180]

Dibelius concludes from this that the story is not Luke's.

> This non-devotional style can certainly not be attributed to the author; indeed, he has introduced a certain Christian interest into the framing of the story and has taken the incident as a miracle (and not as a good diagnosis) by Paul. Thus we are dealing with what was originally a secular anecdote, probably containing a humorous undertone. Although the room was brightly lit, the boy fell asleep: the length of the speech was the reason! But the speaker made good the harm he had caused. How he did it we do not know. It is improbable that Christians with a literary education would have told of one of Paul's deeds in this style. I should prefer to assume that a current anecdote has come to be applied to Paul, that Luke found it in this form and introduced it into his narrative.[181]

We can follow Dibelius's characterization of the Eutychus anecdote even if, despite his suggestion, it was Luke who transferred the story to Paul (see below).

What, indeed, is the nature of the tradition Luke has placed here? Had such an anecdote already been assigned to Paul before Luke found it?[182] Or did it come to him as an isolated legend about Paul in general circulation,[183] a miracle story,[184] or a sort of missionary legend?[185] Except for Dibelius's theory, I find all these proposals unsatisfactory because they tend to ignore the secular character of the narrative, and too readily include the presence of *Paul* in the story at the traditional level. The difficulties fall away if we understand that Luke adapted the account from his secular reading and gave it the christianized "spin" indicated above.[186]

Verses 13–16: The simple and unembellished nature of these travel notes all but surely points to their derivation from tradition.

> It is inconceivable that Luke should have included insignificant and unimportant places in his account of the journey if he had not had a description of the route at his disposal. In support of this we may quote the mention of Attalia in 14.25 . . . , of Samothrace and Neapolis (16.11), Amphipolis and Apollonia (17.1), Caesarea and, probably, Jerusalem (18.22). The sentence in 20.13,14 which is completely unimportant for both the story of the mission and for the biography of Paul belongs here also.[187]

Conzelmann[188] challenges this hypothesis on the grounds that a mere list of points defining a journey likely indicates not the use of a source, but an authorial construction; and this alone would explain why the route first went through Miletus. Against Conzelmann, this hypothesis does not really explain the insignificant statement of verses 13–14: "We went ahead to the ship and set sail for Assos, intending to take Paul aboard there, for so he had arranged, intending himself to go by land. (14) And when he met us at Assos, we took him on board and went to Mitylene." Dibelius's hypothesis is the better one.

HISTORICAL ELEMENTS

Verses 1–3: Although Paul did make a trip from Ephesus to Corinth via Macedonia (see the remarks on 19:21), one is justified in doubting tradition that Paul chose the roundabout route through Macedonia and Asia Minor on his final journey to Jerusalem. Even granting all the gaps in our knowledge, if Rom. 15:25 is correct that Paul has the collection from Macedonia and Achaia with him in Corinth, he would most likely sail directly from Corinth to Palestine. If so, we may reasonably suppose that the tradition-based itinerary found in verses 1–3 represents Paul's journey en route to Palestine-Syria and the Jerusalem conference (see above, pp. 240–46 on 18:22). To be sure, it is possible that unreported factors necessitated a detour through Macedonia and Asia Minor; and if that were the case, verses 1–3 would correctly describe Paul's last journey to Jerusalem.

Verses 4–6: According to a fairly broad consensus, the list in verse 4 identifies the delegates and the communities that brought the collection. This agreement appeals to 1 Cor. 16:3 and 2 Cor. 8:19, for these passages indicate that the participating communities of Macedonia and Achaia would provide members to bring the collection. But any attempt to match these names with those bearing the collection is frustrated by the omission from 20:4 of names of representatives from Corinth and Philippi, communities we know to have participated in the collection. Therefore, it seems illegitimate to associate this list with the collection.[189] Rather, the list indicates those companions who supported Paul's missionary activity in and around Troas (cf. 2 Cor. 2:13). To say more would be to convey less.

Verses 7–12: While previous remarks demonstrate beyond cavil that the Eutychus episode is unhistorical, the datum "on the first day of the week" (verse 7) is historically valuable, since it may be the earliest evidence of Sunday being celebrated as the Christian sabbath.[190] From this it is clear that in verse 11 Luke considers "to break bread" (in Greek, *klasai arton*) to refer to the eucharist.

Verses 13–16: A tradition is the source of the journey of Paul and his companions from Troas either to Miletus or Ephesus, from where Paul continues on to Palestine-Syria; for an analysis of the historicity of such a journey, see above, page 268, on verses 1–3.

The Historical Value of Luke's Account

Verses 1–5: Whereas Luke is silent about the collection and withholds from the reader that the real reason for his journey to Jerusalem is to deliver it to the community there, Paul himself is explicit in this regard:

Rom. 15:25–31

(25) But now, I say, I go unto Jerusalem, ministering unto the saints. (26) For Macedonia and Achaia have been pleased to make a certain contribution for the poor among the saints at Jerusalem. (27) They were pleased to do so, and indeed they owe it to them; for if the Gentiles have come to share in their spiritual things, they ought also to aid them in material things. (28) Therefore, when I have accomplished this, and have delivered to them what has been collected, I will return to you before setting out for Spain. (29) And I know that when I come to you, I shall come in the fullness of the blessing of Christ. (30) Now I beseech you by our Lord Jesus Christ, and by the love of the Spirit, that you join me in earnest prayer to God on my behalf (31) that I may be saved form the unbelievers in Judea, and that my efforts on behalf of Jerusalem may be acceptable to the saints.

Verse 6: Luke gives the impression that Paul avoided Ephesus for lack of time and because of his pious wish to spend Pentecost at Jerusalem. The Pauline letters tell a different story. According to 2 Cor. 1:8–10 Paul had barely escaped death in Ephesus. It does not take much imagination to assume that from that time on he had to avoid Ephesus in order not to endanger his life again. In addition, it is noteworthy that Luke makes no further mention of Paul's eagerness to be in Jerusalem by Pentecost. Hence we must consider that motive to have been inserted by Luke as an external reason for Paul's hurry. Once again Luke suppresses an unpleasant reality to protect his hero's image.[191]

Verses 7–12: By sketching here once again "the miraculous power of the Apostle departing from his work, who now hastens irresistibly toward the humiliation of his imprisonment"[192] Luke again falsifies the facts. Still one wonders whether in this case Haenchen has been somewhat mesmerized into adopting apologetic rhetoric; for had the apostle been all that preoccupied with hastening to fulfill his destiny, he might not have spoken at such length as to put people to sleep. It is one thing to incorporate an old legend to improve the image of one's protagonist; it is another to recognize that candy is being distributed and at the same time apply to it a coating of fudge. Would Haenchen have us believe that a miracle actually occurred? Does he suppose that Paul had foreknowledge of what awaited him in Jerusalem? On this point, see the final comment in the following section, pages 274–75. It is not only Luke of whom we must sometimes be wary.

[48]
ACTS 20:17–38
PAUL'S FAREWELL SPEECH TO THE ELDERS OF EPHESUS
IN MILETUS

(17) Now from Miletus he sent to Ephesus *and summoned the elders of the church.* (18a) *And when they came to him, he said to them:*

(18b) *"You yourselves know how I lived among you the whole time from the first day that I set foot in Asia,* (19) *serving the Lord with all humility and with tears, enduring trials occasioned by the plots of the Jews;* (20) *how **I did not shrink from declaring to you** anything that was profitable, or from teaching you in public and from house to house,* (21) *testifying both to Jews and to Greeks of repentance toward God and of faith in our Lord Jesus Christ.* (22) ***NOW THEN**, I am going to Jerusalem, compelled by the Spirit, not knowing what will happen to me there,* (23) *except that the Holy Spirit testifies to me in every city that imprisonment and afflictions await me.* (24) *But I do not account my life of any value nor as precious to myself, if only I may finish my course and the ministry* *that I received from the Lord Jesus, to testify to the good news of God's grace.* (25) **NOW THEN,** *I know that none of you among whom I have gone about preaching the kingdom will see my face again.* (26) *Therefore I testify to you this day that I am innocent of the blood of all of you,* (27) **for I did not shrink from declaring to you** *the whole purpose of God.* (28) *Pay careful attention to yourselves and to all the flock, of which the Holy Spirit has made you overseers, to care for the church of God, which he obtained by the blood of his own Son.* (29) *I know that after my departure fierce wolves will come in among you, not sparing the flock;* (30) *and from among your own selves will arise men speaking twisted things, to draw away the disciples after them.* (31) *Therefore be alert, remembering that for three years I did not cease night or day to admonish everyone with tears.* (32) **AND NOW** *I commend you to God and to the word of his grace, which is able to build you up and to give you the inheritance among all those who are sanctified.* (33) *I coveted no one's silver or gold or apparel.* (34) *You yourselves know that these hands ministered to my necessities and to those who were with me.* (35) *In all things I have shown you that by working hard in this way we must help the weak and remember the words of the Lord Jesus, how he himself said, 'It is more blessed to give than to receive.'"*

(36) *And when he had said these things, he knelt down and prayed with them all.* (37) *And there was much weeping on the part of all; they embraced Paul and kissed him,* (38) *being saddened most of all by his statement that they would never see him again. Then they accompanied him to the ship.*

OUTLINE

17–18a: Paul summons the presbyters of Ephesus from Miletus
18b–35: Farewell discourse in Miletus
    18b–27: Paul's conduct in the past and future
    28–35: Exhortation
36–38: Farewell scene

LUKE'S PURPOSE

Not only is this the only address in Acts that Paul directs to Christians, but it is also striking in that it foresees the situation after his death. Accordingly the speech may be seen as addressed in considerable part to Luke's church. By so describing the Miletus speech, I have, of course, characterized it as a literary creation by Luke. As to genre, it is a farewell discourse and/or personal testament. For its milieu in the Hebrew Bible and Judaism, see Josh. 23; 1 Sam. 12; 1 Macc. 2:49–68.

Verses 17–18a: The existence of elders reflects the constitution of Luke's church.[193]

Verses 18b–21: Verse 18b alludes to 18:19. The reference to Paul's "trials" in verse 19 echoes Jesus' "trials."[194] The plottings of the Jews against Paul reflect Luke's fixed idea (cf. 20:3). Verse 20 closely resembles verse 27 (for the construction, see 10:47). In verse 21 the "testifying" theme (see verses 23, 24, 26) and the categories "Jews-Gentiles" (see on 18:4) derive from Luke.

Verses 22–25: "Now then" (in Greek, *kai nyn*) in verses 22 and 25, as well as "and now" (*kai ta nyn*) in verse 32, are Lukan division markers. The theme of the Spirit in verses 22–23 recalls 19:21. "Course" in verse 24 reflects Luke's concept of Paul's activity—indeed of his life—as a journey.[195] Luke himself has coined the phrase "to preach the kingdom" (verse 25).[196]

Verses 26–28: Paul's protestation of innocence in verse 26 has its unmistakable antecedent in 18:6, and verse 27 is to all intents and purposes a paraphrase of verse 20. Verse 28 reiterates the Lukan theme of the Spirit noted as recently as verses 22–23.

Verses 29–30: This is an *after the event* prophecy of what happened following Paul's death. "Adversaries" appeared from outside and inside the congregation (see further below, p. 273). The situation resembles that of the Pastoral letters.[197]

Verses 31–35: Verse 31 adds the two years and three months of 19:8, 10. The expression "word of grace" (verse 32) matches 14:3 verbatim, and verse 32b appears with minor modifications in 26:18. Verse 33 strikingly recalls Peter's repudiation of wealth in 3:6, and once again enunciates the parallel between him and Paul. Thus Paul was not interested in the property of others. Verses 34–35a follow up on this: Paul worked for his own living and for his companions' welfare. Verse 35b is a thematic paraphrase of teachings of Jesus found in the synoptic gospels, but its specific content is not to be found, not even in Luke's Gospel. Our historian has created a fictitious citation of Jesus and placed it in Paul's mouth.

Verses 36–38: In verse 36 both the prayer motif and the kneeling in prayer derive from Luke (cf. 21:5) as are the echo of verse 25 (they would not see him again) and the solemn escort in verse 38 (cf. 21:5). See also in 21:10–14 the prophecy of Agabus and Paul's reaction to it.

Result: In the Miletus speech Luke has not only created for the Paul of Acts an anachronistic testament to the Lukan church, but he has by careful design placed it at the turning point[198] of Paul's career—when he embarks on the journey that will end in arrest and imprisonment. No doubt with a nod to his contemporaries, Luke lays great stress on the integrity of the church's founder in remaining true to the gospel message (a point that is made in verse 20 and repeated for emphasis in verse 27). The dialectical context of this assertion, of course, is the spread of Gnostic teaching in the period after Paul's death, a development that called Luke's normative Christianity into question. Here Paul himself is invoked against them: Foreseeing the future challenge, he offered a preemptive safeguard of the Lukan norms. No doubt the "deceivers" attacked in verses 29–30 offered a counter interpretation of Paul, a secret "Pauline teaching available only to the initiated. Note that both verses 20 and 27 specifically oppose such an esoteric doctrine, a "heresy" that since the presbyters of Ephesus are addressed, appears to have emerged in and/or around that city. Seen thus, the speech epitomizes he evangelist's understanding of Paul.

Although the speech proper ends with verse 32, Luke has added an exhortatory exhortation in which he sets forth his own good example of financial self-sufficiency and support for the weak—apparently to drive home the point that the weak can get little help from those who cannot support themselves. Thus Paul's living by his own exertions exemplifies the obligations of the elders to the poor and sick of their community, a responsibility based on a purported saying of Jesus: "It is more blessed to give than to receive." Here Luke is surely creating an echo of 2:45 and 4:34, and even more to Jesus' gospel injunctions to charitable works. Luke is thus vicariously insisting that his community must take the ethics of the gospel to heart.[199]

THE TRADITIONS REWORKED BY LUKE

At this point two separate questions arise: (a) To what degree is the Miletus speech rooted in tradition; (b) Did tradition provide the story of Paul's meeting with Ephesian elders in Miletus and the inclusion of this event in Paul's journey?

(a) The basis of the speech in tradition

Verse 28: Elsewhere in the New Testament, the term "church of God" (in Greek, *ekklesia tou theou*) is found only in Paul's letters and in those from the Pauline tradition.[200] The second half of the verse contains a major ambiguity: Whose blood is involved in the expression "with his own blood" (or, "with the blood of his Own")? Does "his" refer to God or Christ? That is, shall "own" (in Greek, *idiou*) be understood as an adjective or as a substantive? If it is the latter, then God is the referent, who has obtained the church through the blood of his Own (son). If the former reading be adopted, then God has bought the church with his own blood. At all events, since the blood of Jesus plays no role in the Lukan concept of salvation, Luke is here (as in the first part of the verse) being deliberately Pauline. The problem may arise simply because Luke is combining two formulas in a single verse.[201] The other possibility is that the verse reflects individual elements of the Pauline mission tradition, and not a concept derived from Paul's letters.

Verses 29–31: This piece may reflect Mark 13:21–23.

Verse 34: The statement that Paul worked for his daily bread could have come either from Luke's knowledge of Paul's letters (see 1 Thess. 2:9; 1 Cor. 4:12) or from oral tradition about Paul (see Acts 18:3). The latter suggestion is to be preferred, if only because Paul's practice of manual labor was no doubt widely known in the Christian churches. It is, of course, possible that this information came to Luke from both these sources.

Verse 35: Jesus' purported axiom, "It is more blessed to give than to receive," appears in this or similar form nowhere in the canonical Gospels.[202] It resembles a Persian maxim that underlies Thucydides 2.97.4, "It is better to give than to get."[203] This so-called saying of Jesus probably reflects a Christian adaptation of an originally secular proverb, and likely can be attributed to Luke or his community. If that is so, the Christian "more blessed" has replaced an original "better."[204]

(b) The basis in tradition of a meeting between Paul and the presbyters of Ephesus in Miletus

It is probably safest to assume that Paul's stay in Miletus (possibly en route) comes from the tradition. Roloff, however, suspects "that the account of the journey in the tradition contained the report of a meeting between Paul and delegates from the community in Ephesus."[205] Conzelmann believes that Luke knew of an account of a meeting in Miletus.[206]

HISTORICAL ELEMENTS

Paul's speech is nonhistorical.

We may also be very skeptical as to whether Paul met in Miletus with delegates from Ephesus, since this has no basis in the tradition. For while Paul's journeys may have taken him to Miletus, we cannot discover a precise historical setting for such a stop. Either Paul did pause in that city on his last journey to Jerusalem (as Luke would have it), or it was a stop on his journey to Palestine/Syria (18:22) to attend the Jerusalem conference.

THE HISTORICAL VALUE OF LUKE'S ACCOUNT

According to Luke, it is Paul who warns that wolves in sheep's clothing will appear within the community promoting false doctrines (verses 29–30). As noted earlier, these teachers probably advanced their own interpretation of Paul and offered a secret formula for the attainment of perfection. Clearly this is what verses 20 and verse 27 oppose in stating that the gospel expounded by Paul did not lack in any way.[207] This indicates that a Pauline Christian community in Asia Minor must have fallen into schism. Luke champions the Pauline party in its mortal struggle with the heretical group he calls "wolves." In short, Paul is at the center of a dispute now being played out in communities the apostle himself served—and may indeed have founded. The authenticity of Luke's vicarious report can be understood to be confirmed by the use of first person plural in the account leading up to the Miletus speech (verses 13–15), since the "we" implies that an actual Pauline address is being passed on, that from one of the apostle's disciples they are gaining precise knowledge of what Paul *really* said in Miletus to the elders of Ephesus. But since critical research into Acts has established the fictitious nature of the authorial "we," so too is shown the impossibility that this is an eyewitness account by a companion of Paul (16:10–17; 20:5–15; 21:1–18; 27:1–28:16).[208] This "smoke and mirrors" approach to historical narrative corresponds all too well to the long tradition of accepting the inaccurate attribution of a number of letters to Paul (2 Thessalonians, Ephesians, and Colossians, inter alia)—a pious pretence also in urgent need of correction in the interest of historical accuracy.

It is from Mark and the earliest Christian tradition that Luke has learned the device of letting the hero deal in advance with the problems of the later church by putting solutions on his lips.[209] Thus Luke sought to edify his own churches at the expense of what really happened. It must be stressed that we have incontrovertible knowledge of why Paul went to Jerusalem. And we know not only that his purpose was to deliver the collection, but also that afterward he planned to take his missionary work in Spain. Indeed, he had asked the Christian congregation in Rome for help in this matter (Rom. 15:24) and would surely have been both astonished and incensed at what Luke dared to put on his lips. Paul certainly did not journey to Jerusalem in order to be arrested and to die in Rome.[210]

[49]
ACTS 21:1–36
PAUL'S TRIP TO JERUSALEM; VISIT WITH JAMES; ARREST IN THE TEMPLE

(1) And when we had parted from them and *put out to sea*, we came by a *straight course* to Cos, and the next day to Rhodes, and from there to Patara. (2) And

having found a ship crossing to Phoenicia, we went aboard and *put out to sea*. (3) When we had come in sight of Cyprus, leaving it on the left we sailed to Syria and landed at Tyre, for there the ship was to unload its cargo. (4) And having sought out the *disciples*, we stayed there for seven days. *And through the Spirit they were telling Paul not to go on to Jerusalem.* (5) *When our days there were ended, we departed and went on our journey, and they all, with wives and children, escorted us until we were outside the city. And kneeling down on the beach, we prayed* (6) *and said farewell to one another.* Then we went on board the ship, and they *returned* home.

(7) When we had finished the voyage from Tyre, we arrived at Ptolemais, and we *greeted the brothers* and stayed with them for one day. (8) Departing on the next day we came to Caesarea, and we entered the house of Philip the evangelist, who was one of the seven, and stayed with him. (9) He had four unmarried daughters, who *prophesied.* (10) During the course of the several days we stayed there, a prophet *named* Agabus came down from Judea. (11) Approaching us, he took Paul's belt and bound his own feet and hands and said, "Thus says the Holy Spirit, 'This is how the Jews at Jerusalem will bind the man who owns this belt and deliver him into the hands of the Gentiles.'" (12) *When we heard this, we and the people there urged him not to go up to Jerusalem.* (13) *Then Paul answered, "What are you doing, weeping and breaking my heart? For I am ready not only to be imprisoned but even to die in Jerusalem for the name of the Lord Jesus."* (14) *And since he would not be persuaded, we ceased and said, "Let the will of the Lord be done."*

(15) After these days we got ready and went up to Jerusalem. (16) And some of the disciples from Caesarea went with us, bringing us to the house of Mnason of Cyprus, an early disciple, with whom we were *to lodge.*

(17) *When we arrived in Jerusalem, the brothers received us gladly.* (18) *On the following day* Paul went with us to James, *and all the elders were present.* (19) *After greeting them, he related one by one the things that God had done among the Gentiles through his ministry.* (20a) *And when they heard it, they glorified God.* (20b) And they said to him, "You see, brother, many thousands among the Jews are believers, and they are all zealous for the law. (21) They have been told that you teach all the Jews who are among the Gentiles to forsake Moses, telling them neither to circumcise their children nor to follow our way of life. (22) What then is to be done? They will certainly hear that you have come. (23) Therefore do as we suggest. We have four men who are under a vow; (24a) take these men and purify yourself along with them and pay for the shaving of their heads. (24b) *That way everyone will know that there is nothing in what they have been told about you, but that you yourself also live in observance of the law.*

(25) *But as for the Gentiles who have believed, we have sent a letter with our judgment that they should abstain from what has been sacrificed to idols, and from blood, and from what has been strangled, and from fornication."*

(26) Then Paul took the men, and the next day he purified himself along with them and went into the Temple, giving notice of when the days of purification would be fulfilled and the offering would be presented for each of them.

(27) *When the seven days were almost completed,* the Jews from Asia, seeing him in the Temple, stirred up the whole crowd *and seized him,* (28) crying out, "Men of Israel, help! This is the man who is teaching everyone everywhere against our people, our law, and this place. Moreover, he even brought Greeks into the Temple and has defiled this holy place." (29) For they had previously seen Trophimus the Ephesian with him in the city, and they supposed that Paul had brought him into the Temple.

(30) *Then the entire city was stirred up, and the people rushed together. They seized Paul and dragged him out of the Temple, and at once the gates were shut.* (31) *And even as they were trying to kill him, word came to the tribune of the cohort that all Jerusalem was in an uproar.* (32) *He at once took soldiers and centurions and ran down to them. When they saw the tribune and the soldiers, they stopped beating Paul.* (33) *Then the tribune came up and arrested him and ordered him to be bound with two chains. He inquired who he was and what he had done.* (34) *Some in the crowd were shouting one thing, some another. And as he could not learn the facts because of the uproar, he ordered him to be brought into the barracks.* (35) *And when he came to the steps, the violence of the crowd was so great that he soldiers had to carry him,* (36) *for the mob pressed close behind, crying out, "Away with him!"*

Outline

1–16: Journey from Miletus via Rhodes and Patara to Jerusalem

- 1–3a: From Miletus to Tyre
- 3b–6: <u>Lodging with disciples in Tyrus.</u> Their warnings not to go to Jerusalem. Farewell scene
- 7a: From Tyre to Ptolemais
- 7b: <u>One-day lodging with the brothers in Ptolemais</u>
- 8a: From Ptolemais to Caesarea
- 8b–9: <u>Lodging in Caesarea with Philip</u>, the father of four daughters endowed with the gift of prophecy

> 10–14: Prophecy of Agabus and reaction of Paul and his
> companions ("we")
> 15: From Caesarea to Jerusalem
> 16: <u>Lodging in the house of Mnason</u>

17–36: Paul in Jerusalem until his arrest

> 17–19: Paul and his companions received by the brothers;
> next day Paul reports to James and the elders the suc-
> cess of the Gentiles mission
> 20–21: The Christian zealots and the rumors about Paul that
> have come to them
> 22–26: The advice given to Paul about the Nazirate and
> about paying for four Nazirites to fulfill their vows.
> Readers are reminded (verse 25) of the Apostolic
> Decree

27–36: Riot in the Temple at the instigation of Jews from Asia; Paul
arrested

LUKE'S PURPOSE

Verses 1–16: Because this section alternately describes itinerary and lodging
with Christian brothers (see the outline—notes of lodging are underlined), Luke
most likely edited it. Yet the accounts of lodging may ultimately derive from tradition (see below, p. 280). Luke deliberately points out that the Palestinian congregations were involved in and contributed to Paul's trip to the mother church
in Jerusalem.

Typically Lukan expressions—indicated in the translation by italics—
appear throughout. Luke's shaping of the content is especially clear in verses 4
and 12, the warnings by the Spirit not to go to Jerusalem (on the latter see the following analysis of the tradition reflected in verses 10–14) and in verse 5, the dramatic farewell scene and the theme of prayer (cf. 20:36). Identifying Philip as
one of the Seven harks back to events in Acts 6. The repeated warnings to Paul
not to proceed to Jerusalem (verses 4b and 12) are Lukan redaction that both provide dramatic foreboding and yet again introduce the theme of the Spirit. Para-
doxically, they are attributed to the same Holy Spirit that has ordained the
apostle's journey to Jerusalem (cf. 20:22; 19:21). Like Jesus, Paul proclaims
(verse 13) his readiness to die in Jerusalem;[211] dying for Jesus' name recalls
20:23, in which Paul reports being warned by the Spirit of having to suffer. The
lodging motif (verses 15–16) is a Lukan favorite.[212]

Verses 17–19: Luke's editorial work is made clear by the obvious seam in this verse: Although Paul and his companions have already arrived in Jerusalem and are lodged with Mnason (verse 16), verse 17 has them arriving once again. This verse also seems to clash with verse 22, for it reports that the whole community ("the brothers") greets the apostle, whereas verse 22 implies that many are unaware of his presence in the city. If verse 22 reflects tradition (see below, p. 281), then verse 17 is likely a Lukan creation. Verse 18 mentions the same leaders of the Jerusalem community who appeared in chapter 15: the presbyters. Verse 19 is a clear echo of 15:12. In these unambiguously redactional verses (17–19), Luke is at pains to portray a mutually respectful relationship between Paul and the Jerusalem community. The apologetic pressure of this view causes him to overlook the clumsiness of Paul's double entry into Jerusalem (verses 16, 17), and the "unanimous" greeting by many who will hear of Paul's arrival only later.

Verses 20–26: Here Luke's editorial intervention can be found in a number of places. Verse 20a notes the reaction to Paul's report of his missionary success (verse 19), which is itself redactional (cf. 11:18). The number "many thousands" (lit. tens of thousands)[213] at verse 20b reflects Luke's love of exaggeration.[214] The information about Paul's performance of a Jewish ritual (verses 23–24b, 26) is inconsistent. As it stands, the story reports that Paul makes a Nazirate vow (verses 24a, 26) and also pays for four others to undertake the same vows (verse 24b; cf. verse 27). But the term of such a vow is at least thirty days, not the seven that Luke seems to assume (verse 27). Accordingly one may well suspect that Paul's Nazirate is wholly attributable to Luke, while the commitment reported in verse 24a reflects tradition. When he wrote verse 24a, Luke may have been thinking of the vow Paul undertook when he had his head shaved in Cenchrae (see 18:18)—a vow that he presumably would have kept throughout his journey. Verse 25 is so out of place in this context that it can only be the author's ill-conceived way of reminding the reader of 15:20.

Reading this section (verses 20–26) as Luke intends it to be read, we get the following scenario: The presence of numerous Jewish-Christian zealots and the existence of rumors that Paul is teaching the Jews in the Diaspora to apostatize from the law cause James and the presbyters to advise Paul to make a show of his own fidelity to the law. He is to sanctify himself along with four Nazirites and to pay the cost of cutting their hair; thus all will recognize that he is faithfully fulfilling the law. Paul follows this advice, as the leaders of the Jerusalem community knew from the beginning that he would—for they had never doubted his loyal observance of the law. The significance of the section thus becomes clear: Luke's Paul remains completely within Judaism to the very end. Far from ever transgressing the law, he circumcised Timothy (16:3), freely and of his own volition made a vow (18:18), and during his last visit to Jerusalem was scrupulous in his ritual observance.

Verses 27–29: The verb "to seize" (verse 27) appears also in 4:3; 5:18; 12:1. Verse 28 derives from Luke, though the substance of the charge likely comes from tradition: Here Paul's preaching, like that of Stephen before him (6:13–14), is misinterpreted by the Jews, who take it to be directed against the law and the Temple. Verse 29 explains how the Jews came to so mistaken a conclusion.

Verses 30–36: In verse 30 Luke once again describes a riot.[215] The depiction of the Roman intervention in the melee between Jews and Christians is true to Luke's well-known pattern. The detail of binding in verse 33 picks up the prophecy in verse 11 that Paul will be bound by (on account of) the Jews taken into custody by the Gentiles. Verse 35 adds the detail that the Roman soldiers had to carry Paul up the steps because the Jewish mob was so violent. This section is important for Luke because it fulfills Agabus's prophecy in verse 11 that Jews will hand Paul over to the Gentiles. And thus he furnishes the setting for Paul's apologetic speech (22:1–21), makes the Jews responsible for the conflict between them and the Christians, and concludes by implicitly commending Christianity to the Romans (22:21b).

THE TRADITIONS REWORKED BY LUKE

The itinerary in verses 1–16 derives from a source that reported a journey of Paul from Miletus to Jerusalem. As to whether this was the conference journey or the collection journey, see pages 282–83 below. In either case, the detailed nature of the report (rather than its contrived "we style") validates the above conclusion.

Another issue is the degree to which the reports other than the itinerary can be assigned to tradition and whether any such data were elements of the source that included Paul's journey from Miletus to Jerusalem.

Verses 8b–9: The details of the Caesarea sojourn may come from this source, especially the note about Philip's four prophetic daughters, since its report of spirit-filled activity fits well with the traditions of the Hellenists (see above, pp. 94–96, 117–19) and is both noteworthy and free of prejudice. Still, it cannot be certainly attributed to the source.[216]

Verses 10–14: The story of Agabus may also have been found in Luke's tradition source. To be sure it displays redactional features (see above), but the name Agabus and his specific prophecy are clearly tradition-based. Whether Luke has placed Agabus in the correct historical context is less sure, for the same figure appears in 11:27–28 during another journey by Paul to Jerusalem. But since this latter is a Lukan artifact created from individual traditions about Paul traveling to Jerusalem, the Agabus episode could well derive from the source I have mentioned.

Verse 16b: That the hospitality afforded by Mnason derives from tradition is multiply attested: First, we have the redactional nature of verses 17–19 (see above, p. 279); second, the uncommon name Mnason; and third, the interesting datum that Christians from Caesarea escorted Paul to his lodging in Jerusalem. This also strongly suggests that verse 16b came from the source material.

Verses 17–19: The report that James was the leader of the Jerusalem community during this visit by Paul is clearly an element of tradition.

Verses 20–27: The following are identifiable elements of tradition:

1. Many zealously observant Jews belong to the Jerusalem community (see the tension noted at p. 279 above between verse 22 and the redactional verse 17).

2. Rumors have accused Paul of teaching Jewish Christians to forsake the law of Moses and circumcision (verse 21). In view of Luke's thoroughly Jewish portrait of the apostle, these rumors seem out of place in Acts; accordingly, they probably come from a tradition. As Ferdinand Christian Baur observed, "We can only wonder how a writer who has hitherto taken the greatest pains to conceal, as much as possible, the true relation in which the Apostle stood to the Jewish-Christians, should have here come forward for once with the bare naked truth."[217]

3. Paul enters into a Jewish ceremony and assumes the costs that allow four Nazirites to fulfill their vows. Such a pious act[218] has no necessary connection with Paul's purported entering upon a Nazirite vow. In addition, the "seven days" is probably a datum taken from tradition. At the traditional level this information was connected with Paul's visit to the Temple: Paul must have undertaken an agreement with one of the priests; he not only had to disburse money to defray expenses, but as a new arrival from abroad, he would also need to regain ritual purity. Paul, then, took the four Nazirites to the Temple and went with them to the Temple to report his own purification and to give notice of when the purification of the four would be fulfilled. "The date could then be fixed on which the appropriate sacrifices—for which Paul paid—were to be presented: it was the seventh day, on which he himself was to be cleared from guilt."[219]

Verses 28–29: For Trophimus, the name of Paul's Gentile companion, as clearly an element of the tradition underlying this section, see 20:4. The account of hostile Jews charging Paul with taking Trophimus into the Temple is probably from tradition, inasmuch as Luke brands this report, as he did the accusation against Stephen in 6:13, as false witness.

The outline of Luke's source

Paul and his companions travel from Miletus via Caesarea to Jerusalem. He receives hospitality from two Hellenists: in Caesarea from Philip, and in Jerusalem from Mnason. The Jerusalem community, highly devoted to the law under James's leadership, perceives Paul as controversial because of widespread rumors of his antinomianism and his repudiation of circumcision. In an attempt to buy favor, Paul assumes the expense of four men who are taking Nazirite vows. The likely conclusion of the source reported Paul's presence in the Temple to receive purification. Its content (especially James's position of leadership) renders it appropriate only to Paul's third and final visit to Jerusalem.

Although their relationship to the rest of the material is no longer clear, Trophimus and the charges his presence elicited ("Paul has brought Gentiles into the temple") doubtless belong to that source (see below, p. 312), as may also the description of Paul's arrest, but the specifics of this inclusion remain uncertain.

The foregoing analysis constitutes the best argument for assuming a *continuous* source, for the resulting report exhibits a straightforward narrative line with no tensions or discontinuities.

HISTORICAL ELEMENTS

Verses 1–15: The historical reliability of the source outlined above is to be affirmed, since its individual parts are either verified or rendered probable by authentic knowledge independent of Acts 21.

Verse 8–9: Paul's lodging at Caesarea with the Hellenist Philip and the prophetic activity of his daughters are both credible data; the latter element comports with the pneumatic-eschatological character of Hellenist preaching.[220]

Verse 16b: That Paul found lodging with the Hellenist Mnason seems reasonable in view of his previous connection with Hellenist circles: Note that Mnason, like Barnabas, is a Cypriot.

Verse 18: Independent sources confirm both James's leadership and the strongly observant practices of the Jerusalem community in the 50s.[221]

Verse 21: The charges here invoked against Paul are undoubtedly historical, since they accurately reflect the objections of the Jerusalem Christians to his teaching and practice. As Ferdinand Christian Baur long ago recognized, the testimony of Acts to this effect "is of all the more value, as it must be looked on as wrung from him against his will by the might of historical truth. The result then is that, according to the statement of the author of the Acts of the Apostles himself, the Jewish Christians saw in the Apostle Paul an apostate from the law, and a preacher of this apostasy among both Jews and Gentiles."[222]

In any case, the accusation in verse 21 corresponds to what clearly had become common practice in at least some Pauline communities. To be sure, the extant letters of Paul do not point to anything like the specifications in verse 21, but those accusations described the possible if not likely consequences for Jewish Christians living in Pauline communities. If Torah observance was at best provisional in view of Christ's new creation (1 Cor. 7:19; Gal. 6:15), Jewish Christians would inevitably be alienated from the law, and would no longer observe dietary and purity regulations or circumcise their children. Certainly Paul suffered in Jerusalem for a cause which was not his own, namely the total detachment of Christianity from Judaism. But the Jewish Christians were right: *In the last resort Paul's activity destroyed the Jewish customs and put an end to the law of Moses.* At the very least, then, verse 21 offers a reliable historical reflection not only of the possible results of introducing the teachings and practices fundamental to Pauline Christianity among Jews, but also of the Jerusalem community's fundamental disapproval of Paul's missionary work.

Verse 26: Finally, in view of Paul's self-proclaimed readiness and skill in the matter of adapting preaching and praxis to the circumstances present (see above, p. 230), and because of the crucial importance to his personal and institutional status of a favorable reception in Jerusalem, his participation in cultic ritual should be regarded as historically probable.

THE HISTORICAL VALUE OF LUKE'S ACCOUNT

We know from Paul's own testimony that the central purpose of his last journey to Jerusalem was to deliver the collection from the Pauline communities; the question is whether that understanding was contained in the source worked over in Acts 21. In view of the remarks made above on the historical reliability of Acts 21, it seems impossible that the source contained no reference to the collection. This raises in turn another question: Why did Luke *delete* from that chapter all references to the collection that appeared in his source? The only possible answer is that the source he used reported a failure to deliver it, or reported that it was rejected,[223] and Luke's idealized portrait of a universal church is so powerful an article of faith that he cannot bring himself to report that Paul's attempt to achieve unity was a failure.[224] And, of course, he does not dare to tell the truth that the leadership of the Jerusalem church contributed to the distrust of Paul.[225] Unfortunately, Luke could not face up to historical truth; fortunately, he left enough traditional elements in the narrative to afford us a pretty clear picture of what really happened.

NOTES

1. See Hans Conzelmann, *Acts of the Apostles: A Commentary of the Acts of the Apostles* (Philadelphia: Fortress Press, 1987), p. 125.

2. Joseph A. Fitzmyer, *The Acts of the Apostles: A New Translation with Introduction and Commentary* (New York: Doubleday, 1998), p. 576. According to Fitzmyer "Paul is obviously not contravening the decision of the 'Council' (15:10–12)" (ibid.). *Rebuttal:* For pragmatic reasons, the council did *not* suggest circumcision of Gentiles.

3. Ernst Haenchen, *The Acts of the Apostles: A Commentary* (Philadelphia: Westminster Press, 1971), p. 482.

4. The clause "the churches were strengthened in the faith" contains an echo of the formula "firmness/steadfastness of faith" that is employed in Col. 2:5 and 1 Pet. 5:9.

5. 2 Tim. 1:5 and 3:15 attest the fact that personal traditions about Timothy were in circulation.

6. Differently Shaye J. D. Cohen, *The Beginnings of Jewishness: Boundaries, Varieties, Uncertainties* (Berkeley: University of California Press, 1999), pp. 264–73, 377.

7. For details see Lawrence H. Schiffman, "At the Crossroads: Tannaitic Perspectives on the Jewish-Christian Schism," in *Jewish and Christian Self-Definition*, vol. 2, *Aspects of Judaism in the Greco-Roman Period*, ed. E. P. Sanders with A. I. Baumgarten and Alan Mendelson (Philadelphia: Fortress Press, 1981), p. 121, who points out that the narrative parts of the books of Ezra/Nehemiah (Ezra 9:2; 10:2,10; cf. Neh. 13:23) are concerned only negatively with the instances of the marriage of a Jew with a non-Jewish woman, whereas the legal texts (Ezra 10:11; Neh. 10:31; cf. Neh. 13:23) prohibit intermarriage regardless of which partner is Jewish. "Further we are told that marriage with a non-Jewish wife leads to the diluting of the 'holy seed among the people of the land' (Ezra 9.2)" (ibid.).

8. Haenchen, *Acts of the Apostles*, p. 482.

9. Here is Paul's report of the incident at Antioch, Gal. 2:11–14: (11) "But when Cephas [Peter] came to Antioch I opposed him to his face, because he stood condemned. (12) For until certain persons came from James, he was taking his meals with the Gentiles; but when they came, he drew back and separated himself, because he was afraid of the advocates of circumcision. (13) And with him the rest of the Jews acted **hypocritically**, so that even Barnabas was carried away by their **hypocrisy**. (14) But when I saw that they were not straightforward about the truth of the gospel, I said to Cephas in front of them all, 'If you though a Jew, live like a Gentile and not like a Jew, how can you force the Gentiles to live like Jews?'" For the question of what really happened at Antioch see my *Paul: The Founder of Christianity* (Amherst, NY: Prometheus Books, 2002), pp. 45–46.

10. See my *Paul, Apostle to the Gentiles: Studies in Chronology* (Philadelphia: Fortress Press, 1984), p. 153.

11. For the identity of Silas and Silvanus see Walter Bauer, William F. Arndt, and F. Wilbur Gingrich, *A Greek-English Lexicon of the New Testament and Other Early Christian Literature*, 2nd ed. (Chicago: University of Chicago Press, 1979), p. 750. Cf. 1 Pet. 5:12.

12. See 2 Cor. 1:19.

13. Acts 14:6.

14. Gal. 2:3; 5:2–3, 6.

15. Paul's theological stance with respect to the act of circumcising a Jewish Christian is another matter. The apostle expresses it in 1 Cor. 7:19: "Circumcision is nothing and the foreskin is nothing." Later he takes part in a Jewish ceremony in Jerusalem with a similar attitude (Acts 21).

16. In passing let me quote a recent evaluation based on the hypothesis that Luke fabricated the section on Timothy's circumcision by using Paul's Letter to the Galatians. Heikki Leppä writes, Luke "knew that Paul had said that Titus was not circumcised and also that Paul had several conflicts with Jewish Christians. This did not fit his picture of Paul. So he was silent about this occasion. Instead he created a story which is not directly against any writing of Paul, the story of the circumcision of Timothy" (*Luke's Critical Use of Galatians,* theological diss., University of Helsinki [Vantaa, 2002], p. 140). Unfortunately, this proposal is too simplistic and fails to pay sufficient attention to the different layers of the text. For another case of imagining how Luke could create stories on the sole basis of Paul's letters see my *Early Christianity According to the Traditions in Acts: A Commentary* (Minneapolis: Fortress Press, 1989), pp. 181–82. There I deal—concerning Acts 16:11–12—with Wolfgang Schenk, *Die Philipperbriefe des Paulus. Ein Kommentar* (Stuttgart: Kohlhammer, 1984), p. 339.

17. Haenchen, *Acts of the Apostles*, p. 491.

18. Acts 9:10; 10:3, 17, 19; 11:5; 12:9; 18:9; 22:17–18; 23:11; 27:23.

19. See Martin Dibelius, *Studies in the Acts of the Apostles* (London: SCM Press, 1956), pp. 12, 129, 176, 197–98.

20. Similarly and—in my view—correctly, *The New English Bible* (New York: Oxford University Press, 1976), "In the early days of my mission."

21. For a detailed substantiation of this thesis see my *Paul, the Apostle to the Gentiles: Studies in Chronology* (Philadelphia: Fortress Press, 1984), pp. 104–107, 135–37.

22. See Herodotus 4.42 for the division of the world into Europe, Asia, and Libya.

23. See the "Chronological Chart" below, pp. 357–60.

24. Luke 8:22; Acts 13:13; 18:21; 20:3, 13; 27:2, etc.

25. See Conzelmann, *Acts of the Apostles*, p. 99.

26. Two recent monographs on Philippi are Lukas Bormann, *Philippi. Stadt und Christengenmeinde zur Zeit des Paulus* (Leiden: Brill, 1995), and Peter Pilhofer, *Philippi, Band I. Die erste christliche Gemeinde Europas. Band II. Katalog der Inschriften von Philippi* (Tübingen: J. C. B. Mohr/Paul Siebeck, 1995–2000). See the evaluation in my *Primitive Christianity: A Survey of Recent Studies and Some New Proposals* (London and New York: T & T Clark, 2003), pp. 125–28. Cf. Richard S. Ascough, *Paul's Macedonian Associations: The Social Context of Philippians and 1 Thessalonians* (Tübingen: J. C. B. Mohr/Paul Siebeck, 2003), pp. 110–61.

27. But by way of qualification, see Jacob Jervell, *The Unknown Paul* (Minneapolis: Augsburg Publishing House, 1984), pp. 146–57.

28. Haenchen, *Acts of the Apostles*, p. 502.

29. Note the wordplay with the verb "to go out" in verses 19 and 18. I have tried to imitate it in the translation and have written the verb in boldfaced type.

30. For the question see Acts 3:37; Luke 3:10, 12, 14.

31. See Martin Hengel, *Judaism and Hellenism* (Philadelphia: Fortress Press, 1974), pp. 240–41.

32. Cf. 13:6; 19:13–16.

33. See Gottfried Schille, *Die Apostelgeschichte des Lukas* (Berlin: Evangelische Verlagsanstalt, 1983), p. 370: "The true Romans of the story are the missionaries who were initially calumniated as Jews. They not only take heed of Roman law but see that it is observed."

34. Henry J. Cadbury, *The Book of Acts in History* (New York: Harper & Brothers Publishers, 1955) notes "this strange expression" but opines that its meaning is no longer available to us.

35. See below, pp. 238–39, on Acts 18:8.

36. Richard I. Pervo, *Profit with Delight: The Literary Genre of the Acts of the Apostles* (Philadelphia: Fortress Press, 1987), pp. 21–22.

37. See below, pp. 301–304.

38. See Irena Levinskaya, *The Book of Acts in Its Diaspora Setting*, vol. 5 of *The Book of Acts in Its First Century Setting* (Grand Rapids, MI: Wm. B. Eerdmans, 1996), pp. 213–25. However, Ascough, *Paul's Macedonian Associations*, pp. 208–12, argues that there was no Jewish community in Philippi and that *proseuchê* does not necessarily mean "place of prayer for the Jews."

39. Conzelmann, *Acts of the Apostles*, p. 130.

40. See above, p. 214.

41. I. Howard Marshall, *The Acts of the Apostles: An Introduction and Commentary* (Grand Rapids, MI: Wm. B. Eerdmans, 1980), p. 265.

42. As a blatant example see Luke 3:10–14.

43. Haenchen, *Acts of the Apostles*, p. 500.

44. Ibid., p. 501.

45. Ibid.

46. Ibid., p. 504.

47. Christoph vom Brocke has published a new, comprehensive monograph in German on Thessalonica, *Thessalonike—Stadt des Kassander und Gemeinde des Paulus. Eine frühe christliche Gemeinde in ihrer heidnischen Umwelt* (Tübingen: J. C. B. Mohr/Paul Siebeck, 2001). See the report in my *Primitive Christianity*, pp. 128–29.

48. Cf. Luke 24:25–27, 44–46; Acts 2:22–36; 3:18; 8:32–35; 13:27, 29.

49. See Hans Conzelmann, *The Theology of St. Luke* (New York: Harper & Brothers, 1960), pp. 141–49.

50. Cf. Luke 8:13; Acts 8:14; 11:1, but cf. also 1 Thess. 1:6; 2:13.

51. Cf. Acts 7:1; 24:9.

52. In that case the remark about the conversion of a multitude (in Greek, *plethos*—note Luke's language) of god-fearing Gentiles would highlight the contrast with the conversion of only a few Jews.

53. Cf. Conzelmann, *Acts of the Apostles*, p. 135. Cf. Acts 25:26.

54. Harry W. Tajra, *The Trial of St. Paul: A Juridical Exegesis of the Second Half of the Acts of the Apostles* (Tübingen: J. C. B. Mohr/Paul Siebeck, 1989), p. 34. See further G. H. R. Horsley, "The Politarchs," in *The Book of Acts in Its Graeco-Roman Setting*, ed. David G. Gill and Conrad Gempf, vol. 2 of *The Book of Acts in Its First Century Setting* (Grand Rapids, MI: Wm. B. Eerdmans, 1994), pp. 419–31; Heike Omerzu, *Der Prozess des Paulus*. Eine exegetische und rechtshistorische Untersuchung der Apostelgeschichte (Berlin: Walter de Gruyter, 2002), pp. 184–87 (bibliog.).

55. 2 Thessalonians is a forgery. See my *Die Intoleranz des Evangeliums. Erläutert an ausgewählten Schriften des Neuen Testaments* (Springe: zu Klampen, 2004), pp. 67–95. This improves and expands the section on 2 Thessalonians in my *Heretics: The Other Side of Early Christianity* (Louisville, KY: Westminster John Knox Press, 1996), pp. 108–119.

56. See my *Paul, Apostle to the Gentiles*, p. 97.

57. Conzelmann, *Acts of the Apostles*, p. 253.

58. Let me hasten to add that in all likelihood there was no synagogue at Thessalonica or at Beroea. "Luke's shift back to the term *synagôgê* in Acts 17 is due to the much more schematic nature of his sources for the remainder of Macedonia" (Ascough, *Paul's Macedonian Associations*, p. 210n104).

59. See my *Paul: The Founder of Christianity*, pp. 151–54.

60. Klaus Wengst, *Pax Romana and the Peace of Jesus Christ* (London: SCM Press, 1987), pp. 99–100.

61. See the survey by Haenchen, *Acts of the Apostles*, p. 518n1.

62. Plato *Apology* 24c.

63. Cf. Acts 8:26; 16:12; 23:8. For a study of these and other asides in Luke-Acts see Steven M. Sheeley, *Narrative Asides in Luke-Acts* (Sheffield: Sheffield Academic Press, 1992). On 17:21 he writes, "On the one hand the reader is distanced from the Athenians, since the inhabitants of Athens have been portrayed in a bad light. On the other hand, the reader is involved in much the same activity ('hearing something new') and is cautioned to examine his or her motives and priorities" (p. 171). That interpretation seems far-fetched, since the readers are Christians with little or no interest in hearing new messages.

64. Demosthenes *Philippics* 1.43.

65. See my *Early Christianity According to the Traditions in Acts*, pp. 192–93.

66. Cf. 1 Thess. 2:2; 3:1, 6.

67. Rom 1:20: "Ever since the creation of this world his (God's) invisible nature, namely, his eternal power and deity, has been clearly perceived in the things that have been made. So they are without excuse."

68. Rom. 1:21–22: "Although they (the Gentiles) know God, they did not honor him as God or give thanks to him, but their thoughts became directed to worthless things and their confused minds were darkened. (22) Claiming to be wise, they became fools."

69. Cf. 1 Cor. 9:19–22: (19) "For though I am free from all men, I have made myself a slave to all, that I might win the more. (20) To the Jews I became as a Jew, in order to win

Jews; to those under the law, I became as one under the law—though not being myself under the law—that I might win those under the law. (21) To those outside the law I became as one outside the law—not being without law toward God but under the law of Christ—that I might win those outside the law. (22) To the weak I became weak, that I might win the weak. I have become all things to all men, that I might by all means save some."

70. That record comes from the church father Eusebius (fourth century), who writes in his *Ecclesiastical History* 4.23.2–3 about a letter of Bishop Dionysios of Corinth to the community of Athens. (It should be noted, though, that the letter's assertion that Dionysius the Areopagite had been the first bishop of Athens belongs in the realm of legend.)

71. See 1 Thess. 2:14.

72. 1 Cor. 15:32; 2 Cor. 1:8; Acts 19.

73. Gilbert Murray, *Four Stages of Greek Religion* (London: Watts & Company, 1935), p. xiii.

74. For the exegesis of Acts 17:16–34 I have used material from my *Paul: The Founder of Christianity*, pp. 114–30, which in part is based on my *Early Christianity According to the Traditions in Acts*, pp. 189–95.

75. Cf. Luke 2:1; Acts 8:1; 11:28; 21:30, etc.

76. See Luke 1:5; 2:1–2; 3:1; Acts 11:28.

77. See Acts 9:22; 17:3; 18:28.

78. See Acts 13:51.

79. Josh. 2:19; Judg. 9:24; 2 Sam. 1:16; 1 Kings 2:32; Ezek. 33:4. Cf. Herodotus 2.39: "They pray that if any evil is impending either over those who sacrifice, or over universal Egypt, it may be made to fall upon that head [of the sacrificed animal]. These practices, the imprecations upon the heads, and the libations of wine, prevail all over Egypt, and extend to victims of all sorts."

80. See on Acts 16:9. See in addition Rick Strelan, *Strange Acts: Studies in the Cultural World of the Acts of the Apostles* (Berlin and New York: Walter de Gruyter, 2004), pp. 131–90 ("Seeing Things").

81. Acts 21:21, 24, 28; cf. 22:3; 24:14; 25:8; 28:17.

82. Cf. Acts 23:29; 25:18. Omerzu claims that Gallio meant to tell the Jews that they have a juridical system of their own to deal with Paul's case (*Der Prozess des Paulus*, p. 269). Unfortunately, that historicizing comment pays too little attention to the text.

83. Suetonius *Life of the Caesars. Claudius* 25.

84. See my essay "Das Judenedikt des Claudius (Apg 18,2)," in *Der Treue Gottes trauen. Beiträge zum Werk des Lukas*, ed. Claus Bussmann and Walter Radl (Freiburg, Basel, and Wien: Herder, 1991), pp. 289–98.

85. Dio Cassius *Roman History* 60.6.6.

86. Dio Cassius *Roman History* 57.18.5.

87. See my *Primitive Christianity*, pp. 122–24 for a critical update of recent work on the edict of Claudius. In addition see Levinskaya, *The Book of Acts in Its Diaspora Setting*, pp. 171–80.

88. See my *Paul, Apostle to the Gentiles*, pp. 163–64.

89. Rom. 16:5 should certainly be understood in this sense.

90. 1 Cor. 4:12; cf. 1 Thess. 2:9.

91. Differently my *Early Christianity according to the Traditions in Acts,* p. 201. In any case, if Paul did convert them, he did not consider them the first Christians in Corinth but rather "the house of Stephanas" (1 Cor. 16:15).

92. See 1 Cor. 15:32; 2 Cor. 1:8–9.

93. Cf. also Phil 4:17.

94. See my *Paul, Apostle to the Gentiles,* pp. 163–64.

95. See Barrett, *Acts of the Apostles,* 1:629.

96. Rainer Riesner, *Paul's Early Period: Chronology, Mission, Strategy* (Grand Rapids, MI: Wm. B. Eerdmans, 1998), p. 209.

97. Conzelmann, *Acts of the Apostles,* p. 155.

98. See the remarks above about "Syria" in verse 17.

99. Cf. the all too free translation of the Jerusalem Bible: "When they reached Ephesus, he left them, but first he went alone to the synagogue." Here the synagogue clearly *is* in Ephesus.

100. Conzelmann, *Acts of the Apostles,* p. 155.

101. Ibid., p. 156.

102. Ibid.

103. Ibid., pp. 152–56.

104. That being the case, a journey to Antioch between the conference visit and the last journey to Jerusalem is as improbable as one to Jerusalem. On various attempts to find in Acts 18:22 a historical journey to Antioch (without a visit to Jerusalem) see my *Primitive Christianity,* p. 117.

105. See my *Paul, Apostle to the Gentiles,* pp. 152–57.

106. Ibid., pp. 75–76.

107. See 2 Cor. 2:1; 12:21; 13:2.

108. See Étienne Trocmé, *The Childhood of Christianity* (London: SCM Press, 1997), p. 59: The move to Jerusalem "is reported in five words and by all accounts was fruitless, doubtless because the Jerusalemites were not ready to make the least concession to the schismatic who was trying to regain their favour. Paul then went to Antioch, apparently by land. Did he get a better reception there than in Jerusalem? That is not certain, although according to Acts 18.23 Paul 'spent some time there.'" For a similar view see Jacob Jervell, *Die Apostelgeschichte* (Göttingen: Vandenhoeck & Ruprecht, 1998), pp. 467–68. Both—rightly famous—scholars here and elsewhere display a credulous attitude with respect to Acts that will not wash.

109. Paul W. Walaskay, *Acts* (Louisville, KY: Westminster John Knox Press, 1998), p. 173.

110. Fitzmyer, *Acts of the Apostles,* p. 633.

111. James D. G. Dunn, *The Acts of the Apostles* (Valley Forge, PA: Trinity Press International, 1996), pp. 247–48.

112. Haenchen has Gal. 2:11–14 in mind.

113. Haenchen, *Acts of the Apostles,* p. 548.

114. Luke Timothy Johnson, *The Acts of the Apostles* (Collegeville, MN: Liturgical Press, 1992), pp. 334–35.

115. Gerhard Krodel, *Acts* (Minneapolis: Augsburg, 1986), pp. 352–53.

116. Cf. Luke 24:19.

117. The suggestion is sometimes made that the tradition spoke of a *non-Christian Jew*, later converted by Aquila and Priscilla, who taught with enthusiasm in the synagogue. Yet this is improbable. The pre-Pauline existence of Christianity in Ephesus also tells against that.

118. See Matthias Günther, *Die Frühgeschichte des Christentums in Ephesus,* 2nd ed., enl. (Frankfurt: Peter Lang, 1998), pp. 32–37; on Acts 18:24–28 see ibid., pp. 54–59.

119. See my *Paul, Apostle to the Gentiles*, pp. 80–100.

120. For this see my *Opposition to Paul*, pp. 65–71.

121. Haenchen, *Acts of the Apostles*, p. 555.

122. Ben Witherington III, *The Acts of the Apostles: A Socio-Rhetorical Commentary* (Grand Rapids, MI: Wm. B. Eerdmans, 1998), p. 567.

123. Rom. 6:3–4: (3) "Do you not know that all of us who have been baptized into Christ Jesus were baptized into his death? (4) We were buried therefore with him by baptism into death, so that as Christ was raised from the dead by the glory of the Father, we too might walk in newness of life."

124. Ernst Käsemann, *Essays on New Testament Themes* (Naperville, IL: Alec R. Allenson, 1964), p. 136.

125. Conzelmann, *Acts of the Apostles*, p. 159.

126. Parr. Mark 1:7–8/Matt. 3:11–12.

127. Cf. the earlier cases in Acts 8:14–25; 11:1, 22.

128. See further Hermann Lichtenberger, "Täufergemeinden und frühchristliche Täuferpolemik im letzten Drittel des 1. Jahrhunderts," *Zeitschrift für Theologie und Kirche* 84 (1987): 36–57.

129. Cf. John 1:35–42.

130. See John 1:20; 3:28.

131. See F. Stanley Jones, *An Ancient Jewish Christian Source on the History of Christianity: Pseudo-Clementine Recognitions 1.27–71* (Atlanta: Scholars Press, 1995).

132. Steve Mason, *Josephus and the New Testament*, 2nd ed. (Peabody, MA: Hendrickson Publishers, 2003), p. 220.

133. Ibid.

134. Haenchen, *Acts of the Apostles*, p. 557.

135. Ibid., p. 148.

136. Cf. Acts 5:12–16.

137. Conzelmann, *Acts of the Apostles*, p. 163.

138. See its synoptic parallel, Mark 9:38–40/Luke 9:49–50.

139. Luke 1:1; Acts 9:29.

140. Luke 7:21; 8:2; 11:26.

141. See also Luke 20:12.

142. Dibelius, *Studies in the Acts of the Apostles*, p. 19.

143. Cf. Rom. 16:23; 2 Tim. 4:20.

144. See my *Paul, Apostle to the Gentiles*, pp. 178–79.

145. Luke 7:18 (Matthew differs); Acts 9:38; 10:7, 20.

146. Haenchen, *Acts of the Apostles*, p. 565.

147. Ibid., pp. 567–68.

148. Cf. Acts 9:2; 19:9; 22:4; 24:14, 22.

149. Klaus Wengst, *Pax Romana and the Peace of Jesus Christ* (London: SCM Press, 1987), p. 102.

150. "So Paul is victorious, without himself setting foot on the field of battle. Politically exonerated, he can as victor leave the shattered paganism of Ephesus to itself" (Haenchen, *Acts of the Apostles*, p. 579).

151. For whom see Lily Ross Taylor, "The Asiarchs," in *The Beginnings of Christianity*, 5:256–62, and more recently R. A. Kearsley, "Appendix: The Asiarchs," in Gill and Gempf, *The Book of Acts in Its Graeco-Roman Setting*, pp. 363–76. Kearsley challenges the identification of the Asiarchs with the high priests in Asia.

152. Yet cf. Acts 27:3.

153. In Greek, *ekklesia*.

154. In Greek, *demos*.

155. In Greek, *ochlos*.

156. In Greek, *tarachos*.

157. In Greek, *sygchysis*.

158. In Greek, *stasis*.

159. In Greek, *systrophê*.

160. Haenchen, *Acts of the Apostles*, p. 577.

161. "Guardian" or "temple keeper" (in Greek, *neôkoros*) was a title assumed by cities in Asia Minor in connection with the rise of the emperor cult. In a few cases the construction and the maintenance of these temples was extended to other deities such as Artemis. Yet "the phrase 'neokoros of Artemis' probably does not date to the days of Paul, although it was likely known by the time of the writing of Acts, nearer the turn of the second century" (L. Michael White, "Urban Development and Social Change in Imperial Ephesus," in *Ephesos: Metropolis of Asia. An Interdisciplinary Approach to its Archaeology, Religion, and Culture*, ed. Helmut Koester [Valley Forge, PA: Trinity Press International, 1995], p. 37).

162. "Finally a respected person appears, the 'town clerk,' who stills the crowd and makes a speech counter to that of Demetrius, at which, however, he was not present. With the statement that everyone knows Ephesus as *neôkoros* of Artemis the reproaches against the Christians are finished with—as if the success of the Christian mission were made good again by this vague assurance. But the crowd goes quietly home and at the same time has the anxious prospect of being prosecuted for *stasis*. The Christians do not blaspheme the goddess—they only deny her divinity. But this the town clerk as well as his listeners has forgotten" (Haenchen, *Acts of the Apostles*, p. 577).

163. In Greek, *ennomos ekklesia*.

164. In Greek, *ekklesia*.

165. White, "Urban Development and Social Change in Imperial Ephesus," p. 37.

166. For an evaluation of recent works on Ephesus see my *Primitive Christianity*, pp. 129–36.

167. Richard I. Pervo, *Profit with Delight: The Literary Genre of the Acts of the Apostles* (Philadelphia: Fortress Press, 1987), p. 37.

168. Cf. Günther, *Die Frühgeschichte des Christentums in Ephesus*, pp. 59–63.

169. Alfons Weiser, *Die Apostelgeschichte*, 2 vols. (Gütersloh: Gütersloher Verlagshaus, 1981–85), 2: 543–44.

170. Against Jervell, *Die Apostelgeschichte*, pp. 494–96.

171. Haenchen, *Acts of the Apostles*, p. 577.

172. Aristarchus also appears in Acts 20:4; 27:2.

173. See Helmut Koester, "Ephesos in Early Christian Literature," in *Ephesos: Metropolis of Asia: An Interdisciplinary Approach to Its Archaeology, Religion, and Culture*, ed. Helmut Koester (Valley Forge, PA: Trinity Press International, 1995): The narrative is "related to the actual situation at Luke's own time" (p. 131). Luke may have known about Christian threats—analogous to the ones reported by Pliny *Epistles* 10.96—"to the normal performance of the cult of Artemis in Ephesos and to the sale of religious paraphernalia. This may have been the basis for the development of this narrative" (ibid., pp. 130–31).

174. Pervo, *Profit with Delight*, p. 37.

175. Haenchen, *Acts of the Apostles*, p. 576.

176. Fitzmyer, *Acts of the Apostles*, p. 660, referring to Haenchen, Acts of the Apostles, p. 574n1.

177. Haenchen, ibid.

178. On Peter's power to raise somebody from the dead see above Acts 9:36–43.

179. Conzelmann, *Acts of the Apostles*, p. 171.

180. Dibelius, *Studies in the Acts of the Apostles*, pp. 17–18.

181. Ibid., pp. 18–19.

182. Thus Dibelius, ibid.

183. Roloff, *Apostelgeschichte*, p. 297.

184. Conzelmann, *Acts of the Apostles*, p. 170.

185. Schille, *Apostelgeschichte*, p. 399.

186. For an imitation of the story of the youth Eutychus by the *Acts of Paul* (Martyrdom of the Holy Apostle Paul) see *New Testament Apocrypha,* revised edition of the Collection initiated by Edgar Hennecke and ed. Wilhelm Schneemelcher, English translation ed. R. McL. Wilson, vol. 2, *Writings Related to the Apostles, Apocalypses, and Related Subjects* (Louisville, KY: Westminster John Knox Press, 1992), p. 261: "But a certain Patroclus, Caesar's cup-bearer, came late to the barn and, being unable because of the crowd to go in to Paul, sat at a high window and listened to him teaching the word of God. But since the wicked devil was envious of the love of the brethren, Patroclus fell from the window and died, and the news was quickly brought to Nero. But Paul, perceiving it in the spirit, said: 'Brethren, the evil one has gained an opportunity to tempt you. Go out, and you will find a youth fallen from a height and already on the point of death. Lift him up, and bring him here to me!' So they went out and brought him. And when the crowd saw (him), they were troubled. Paul said to them: 'Now, brethren, let your faith be manifest. Come, all of you, let us mourn to our Lord Jesus Christ, that this

youth may live and we remain unmolested.' But as they all lamented the youth drew breath again, and setting him upon a beast they sent him back alive with the others who were of Caesar's house."

187. Dibelius, *Studies in the Acts of the Apostles*, p. 197.

188. Conzelmann, *Acts of the Apostles*, p. 171.

189. Against Günther Bornkamm, *Paul* (New York: Harper & Row, 1971), p. 92.

190. Cf. 1 Cor. 16:2; Rev. 1:10; Did. 14:1.

191. Cf. Haenchen, *Acts of the Apostles*, p. 588.

192. Ibid., p. 586.

193. Cf. Acts 14:23; 15:2, 4, 6, 22–23; 21:18.

194. Luke 22:28.

195. See my *Paul, Apostle to the Gentiles*, pp. 13–14.

196. Cf. Luke 8:1; Acts 8:12; 19:8, 28:23, 31. See Conzelmann, *Theology of St. Luke*, pp. 113–19.

197. See my *Primitive Christianity*, pp. 129–30.

198. Cf. Dibelius, *Studies in the Acts of the Apostles*, p. 158.

199. See Friedrich Wilhelm Horn, *Glaube und Handeln in der Theologie des Lukas* (Göttingen: Vandenhoeck & Ruprecht, 1983), pp. 50–53.

200. 1 Cor. 1:2; 10:32; 11:16, 22; 15:9; 2 Cor. 1:1; Gal. 1:13; 1 Thess. 2:14; 2 Thess. 1:4; 1 Tim. 3:5, 15.

201. See Conzelmann, *Acts of the Apostles*, p. 175.

202. It has an interesting counterpart in 1 Clem. 2:1: *hêdion didontes ê lambanontes* (giving is more pleasurable than getting). The author is praising the Corinthian community.

203. In Greek, *hêdion didonai mallon ê lambanein*.

204. For the comparative *mallon* see Acts 5:29.

205. Roloff, *Apostelgeschichte*, p. 301.

206. Conzelmann, *Acts of the Apostles*, p. 173.

207. Cf. Haenchen, *Acts of the Apostles*, p. 596: "The assurance that Paul has omitted nothing, that he bears no guilt if anyone goes astray, is repeated and delivered with such emphasis that we cannot make do with the information offered by Dibelius that this trait belongs to the style of such farewell speeches. . . . W. Bauer, pp. 235ff., has called attention to the fact that the congregations founded by Paul in Asia Minor were largely lost to the Gnostic heresy. . . . The Lucan apology of Paul . . . corresponds to the situation at the end of the first century. Paul (whom Luke considers the representative of the apostolic, legitimate Church) bears no guilt for the catastrophe which after his death began to loom up in the Church of *Asia*: he has done everything a man could possibly ask, indeed more." Haenchen refers to Bauer's book, *Orthodoxy and Heresy in Earliest Christianity* (Philadelphia: Fortress Press, 1971). See the evaluation of this excellent book in my *Primitive Christianity*, passim, and the survey on the reception of Bauer's book in my *Heretics: The Other Side of Early Christianity* (Louisville, KY: Westminster John Knox Press, 1996), pp. 242–45.

208. For details see Jürgen Wehnert, *Die Wir-Passagen der Apostelgeschichte. Ein lukanisches Stilmittel aus jüdischer Tradition* (Göttingen: Vandenhoeck & Ruprecht, 1989).

209. Mark 13:1–37.

210. Nonetheless, the analogy to Jesus' journey to Jerusalem and its subsequent Christian interpretation should be noted.

211. Haenchen, *Acts of the Apostles*, p. 602.

212. Acts 10:6, 18, 23, 32; 28:7.

213. Cf. Philo *Special Laws* 2.253: "There are thousands who are zealots for the laws, strictest guardians of the ancestral customs, merciless to those who do anything to subvert them."

214. See Acts 1:15; 2:41; 4:4.

215. Cf. similarly Acts 19:27, 32–34.

216. Polycrates of Ephesus (in Eusebius *Church History* 3.31.3) reports on Philip and his three (and not four) virgin daughters in Hierapolis (or Ephesus). Although he includes Philip among the twelve apostles, the mention of the prophetic daughters may be evidence that the tradition here originally meant the evangelist Philip (cf. perhaps in this sense the Montanist Proclus in Eusebius *Church History* 3.31.4). See also the narrative of Papias (in Eusebius *Church History* 3.39.9) about the stay of Philip with his daughters in Hierapolis. However, he confuses the evangelist with the apostle Philip just as Polycrates does.

217. Ferdinand Christian Baur, *Paul, the Apostle of Jesus Christ,* 2 vols. (London/Edinburgh: Williams & Norgate, 1875, 1876), 2:203.

218. Cf. Josephus *Jewish Antiquities* 19.294.

219. Haenchen, *Acts of the Apostles*, p. 612.

220. Cf. in *Testament of Job* 48–50 the description of the prophetic activity of the three daughters of Job.

221. See my *Opposition to Paul*, p. 58.

222. Baur, *Paul, Apostle of Jesus Christ*, 1:204.

223. Dieter Georgi, though, suggests an informal delivery of the collected assets: "There would have been no need to suppress any subsequent memorandum concerning the celebration that accompanied the conveyance of the collection, because none existed. Had Luke learnt of such an announcement, he would certainly have made use of it. But as things turned out, the collection . . . was received as if 'on the side,' accompanied by whispers; quite a blow to the congregation. Hence, Luke, the first historian of Christianity, had good reason to pass over the whole episode in silence" (Dieter Georgi, *Remembering the Poor: The History of Paul's Collection for Jerusalem* [Nashville: Abingdon Press, 1992], p. 126). That is quite speculative.

224. For details see my *Opposition to Paul*, pp. 59–62; *Heretics*, pp. 48–49.

225. See Stanley E. Porter, *The Paul of Acts: Essays in Literary Criticism, Rhetoric, and Theology* (Tübingen: J.C.B. Mohr/Paul Siebeck, 1999), pp. 172–86.

chapter IV
Acts 21:37–28:31
PAUL, THE PRISONER
AND DEFENDER OF THE
GOSPEL FROM
JERUSALEM TO ROME

The motto of this section is apology, the defense of Christianity against accusations raised especially by the Jews.[1]

In these chapters, then, Luke wishes to present first of all not what has taken place but what is taking place.[2]

[50]

ACTS 21:37–22:21
PAUL'S ADDRESS TO THE PEOPLE

*(21:37) As Paul was about to be brought into the barracks, he said to the tribune, "May I say something to you?" And he said, "Do you know Greek? (38) Then aren't you the Egyptian who a little while ago stirred up a revolt and led four thousand terrorists out into the desert?" (39a) Paul replied, "I am a Jew, from Tarsus in Cilicia, a citizen of no insignificant city. (39b) I beg you, permit me to speak to the people." (40) And when he had given him permission, Paul, standing on the steps, motioned with his hand to the people. And a great hush having fallen over the crowd, he addressed them **in the Hebrew language**, saying: (22:1) "Brothers and fathers, hear the defense that I now make before you." (2) And when they heard that he was addressing them **in the Hebrew lan-***

guage, they became even quieter. And he said: (3a) "I am a Jew, born in Tarsus in Cilicia, but brought up in this city, (3b) educated at the feet of Gamaliel *according to the strict manner of the law of our fathers, being zealous for God as all of you are this day.* (4) *I persecuted this Way to the death, binding and delivering to prison men and women,* (5) *as the high priest and the whole council of elders can bear me witness. From them I received letters to the brothers, and* I journeyed toward Damascus *to take those who were there and bring them in bonds to Jerusalem to be punished.*

(6) As I was on my way and drew near to Damascus, about noon a great light from heaven suddenly shone around me. (7) And I fell to the ground and heard a voice saying to me, 'Saul, Saul, why are you persecuting me?' (8) And I answered, 'Who are you, Lord?' And he said to me, 'I am Jesus of Nazareth, whom you are persecuting.' (9) Now those who were with me saw the light but did not hear the voice of him who was speaking to me. (10) And I said, 'What shall I do, Lord?' And the Lord said to me, 'Rise, and go into Damascus, and there you will be told all that is appointed for you to do.' (11) And since I was unable to see because of the brightness of that light, those who were with me led me by the hand until we came to Damascus. (12) And one Ananias, a devout man according to the law, well spoken of by all the Jews who lived there, (13) came to me, and standing by me said to me, 'Brother Saul, recover your sight.' And at that very hour I recovered my sight and looked him. (14) And he said, 'The God of our fathers appointed you to know his will, to see the Righteous One and to hear a voice from his mouth; (15) for you will be his witness to all the world of what you have seen and heard. (16) And now why do you wait? Rise and be baptized and wash away your sins, calling on his name.'

(17) "When I had *returned* to Jerusalem and was praying in the Temple, I fell into a *trance* (18a) and saw him there speaking to me, '*Hurry* and get out of Jerusalem *quickly,* (18b) because they will not accept your testimony about me.' (19) And I said, 'Lord, they themselves *know* that in one synagogue after another I imprisoned and beat those who believed in you. (20) *And when the blood of Stephen your witness was being shed, I myself was standing by and approving and watching over the garments of those who killed him.'* (21) And he said to me, 'Go, for I shall *send you far away* to the Gentiles.'"

OUTLINE

1–3: Address; Paul speaks in Aramaic

3–16: Paul's conversion near Damascus

17–21: Paul's subsequent vision in the Temple

Luke's Purpose

Verses [21:] 37–40: Luke has shaped this section throughout. From the moment of Paul's first contact with the Roman officer it is made clear that the charge of insurrection is totally false: he is not, as the tribune assumed, the Egyptian leader of a previous revolt (verse 38).[3] Since the tribune obviously expected a positive answer, it is all the more amazing that his suspicion is so quickly allayed,[4] the more so since like Paul, Egyptian Jews spoke Greek. Furthermore, "the crowd which had just been shouting, 'Kill him!' simply would not think of becoming quiet just because the man was preparing himself to speak."[5] Note the clearly Lukan use of litotes in verse 39: "no insignificant city," as well as the typical rhetorical gesture (verse 40, cf. 12:17; 13:16; 26:1) that signals the beginning of the speech.

Verses [22:] 1–2: The beginning of Paul's address (verse 1a) corresponds to the introduction to Stephen's speech (7:2); the second part of the verse announces his purpose: "a defense . . . before you." Verse 2 echoes 21:40b: Paul, who had spoken Greek to the tribune, now speaks to the people in Aramaic, the demotic form of Hebrew spoken at that time.

Verses 3–5: Verse 3a picks up 21:39a. Luke puts in Paul's mouth a threefold biographical formula:[6] born in Tarsus, brought up in Jerusalem, educated at the feet of Gamaliel. In Hellenistic literature such a pattern was a customary way of describing someone's upbringing;[7] Luke's Paul (like the author of Acts) is shown to be a member of the educated elite. Verses 4–5 once again attest Paul's activity as a persecutor (cf. 7:58; 8:1–2; 9:1).

Verses 6–16: Here Luke treats us to a different depiction of Paul's conversion experience, though the same basic story also underlies chapter 9—for details see above, page 125. Verse 15 differs from 9:15 in directing Paul's witness not only to Gentiles, kings, and Israelites, but to all people everywhere. What he had portrayed as a conversion, Luke now defines as a call to universal apostleship.

Verses 17–21: The same shift is made clear by the Temple vision, which also reinterprets the conversion: note especially verse 21, "Go, for I shall send you far away to the Gentiles." Lukan language in verses 17–21 is indicated in the translation by italics. Verse 20, which alludes to 7:58, is in tension with the present context, since the preceding verse refers to Christian persecutions outside Jerusalem, an activity that in fact followed the killing of Stephen. This gross

anachronism seems inexplicable except on the assumption that Luke was somewhat hastily editing existing material.

THE TRADITIONS REWORKED BY LUKE

Verse [21:] 39: For the traditional association of Paul's origins and citizenship
with the city of Tarsus, see page 303 below.

Verses [23:] 3–16: For Paul as persecutor and the Damascus event, see
above, pages 123–30, on chapter 9. Whether the reports of Paul's rearing and
education in Jerusalem reflect tradition—setting aside for now Luke's positive
bias in his inclusion of the remark in verse 3—must wait until historical decisions
can be made (see below).

Verses 17–21: Despite linguistic elements indicating Luke's pen, the basic
content of this section, excluding verse 20, likely reflects tradition. Unlike 9:28
and 26:20, the tradition does not report that Paul had preached in Jerusalem;
indeed, note verse 18b: "They [the people in Jerusalem] will not accept your testimony about me." Thus the tradition is unique in locating Paul's call to the Gentile apostolate not in Damascus, but in the Temple (verse 21). Furthermore, Luke
here contradicts Paul's own testimonies by justifying the Gentile mission on the
grounds of divinely attested resistance of the Jerusalem Jews.

HISTORICAL ELEMENTS

On the matters of Paul as persecutor and the Damascus event, see above, pages
122–28, on Acts 9.

Verse 3: Since no existing evidence points to Pharisaic training outside
Jerusalem, the information that Paul was raised as a Pharisee in Jerusalem may
be from tradition and therefore historical.[8] Of course he could have attended a
school in Tarsus before that (cf. 21:39). The duration of his residence and/or
study in Jerusalem cannot be determined.

Verses 17–21: That Paul was called to be apostle to the Gentiles in the course
of a vision in the Temple is patently unhistorical, not the least because in Gal.
1:17 he implies that call took place near Damascus. Where, when, and why this
tradition was formed must remain moot, unless one were to connect it with Paul's
report in 2 Cor. 12:1–5, which likewise speaks of (a) an ecstatic experience, (b)
a vision,[9] and (c) an audition.[10]

THE HISTORICAL VALUE OF LUKE'S ACCOUNT

Some scholars have shown a remarkable willingness to accept the historicity of Paul's speech. Dunn writes,

> Did Paul deliver this speech in these circumstances? The dramatic context sketched out by Luke is not at all so far-fetched as many assume. In a day when public oratory was the principal means of disseminating information and canvassing public support for policy, the tradition of crowds giving a hearing to speeches would be well established. As usual, Luke would feel no obligation either to provide a transcript of what Paul actually said, or to refrain from recording any speech. In accordance with the conventions of historical writing of the day, it was enough for Luke and his readers that he could represent what Paul could or would have said on the occasion in question. The variation in the three accounts of Paul's conversion, reproduced by one and the same author, is a reminder both of the liberty an author felt in retelling the same story and that this was quite acceptable historiographical technique for the time.[11]

And Hengel opines,

> The event as a whole and the setting for the scene correspond amazingly to what we know from Josephus and must have a basis in history. In my view, at this point Luke was not just working over an outside source, but may be drawing on his own memories.[12]

Yet, as Hengel himself points out "critical scholarship has long and rightly demonstrated that it is historically unlikely [that] Paul, mistreated (Acts 21.31f) and in fetters (Acts 21.33), guarded by soldiers could have quieted the raging crowd (Acts 21.34; 22.22) with one of those gestures of the hand so beloved of Luke and by his speech 'in Hebrew' (Acts 21.40; 22.2)."[13] Therefore claiming a basis in history for "the event as a whole" and the specific action of calming the raging storm of Jewish protest becomes by his own admission little more than foggy, and is ultimately self-contradictory. The same objection applies to Dunn's opinion. As for Hengel's claim of Luke's eyewitness status to back up the trustworthiness of the event and the scene,[14] this seems to be refuted by the very arguments that Hengel himself levels against its historicity. It is at the very least disheartening to observe the contortions that otherwise reputable scholars will perform in their attempts to provide safe havens for vessels that by any measure are no longer seaworthy.

[51]
ACTS 22:22–29
PAUL'S APPEAL TO HIS ROMAN CITIZENSHIP

(22) Up to this word they listened to him. Then they raised their voices and said, "Away with such a fellow; he should not be allowed to live!" (23) And since they were shouting and throwing off their cloaks and flinging dust into the air, (24) the commander ordered him (Paul) to be brought into the barracks, and gave instructions to examine him by <u>scourging</u>, to find out what reason there was for such an outcry against him. (25) But when they had tied him up for the lash, Paul said to the centurion, who was standing there, "Is it lawful for you to <u>scourge</u> a man who is a Roman citizen, and moreover has not been found guilty?" (26) When the centurion heard this, he went and reported it to the commander and said to him, "What are you about to do? For this man is a Roman citizen." (27) So the commander came and said to him, "Tell me, are you a Roman citizen?" And he said, "Yes." (28) The commander answered, "I bought this citizenship for a large sum." Paul said, "But I was born a Roman citizen." (29) So those who were about to examine him withdrew from him hastily; and the commander also was alarmed, for he realized that Paul was a Roman citizen and that he had chained him.

OUTLINE

22–23: The Jews react with furor

24–29: Paul brought into the Roman barracks and preparations for flogging. Paul appeals to his Roman citizenship

LUKE'S PURPOSE

Verses 22: The phrase "to raise the voice" occurs in the New Testament only in Luke-Acts.[15] The details of the violent expressions of rage shown by the Jews are Lukan touches used to accentuate the dramatic intensity of the scene. The demand for Paul's death—that he be utterly removed from the earth—recalls the animus of the Jews as in 21:30 (and accordingly 25:24 can be seen as referring to the present scene). Two points are noteworthy: Paul's speech was a failure, and this failure can be directly assigned to his claim that God had called him to take his mission to the Gentiles.

Verse 23: Luke describes "symbolic acts of protests against Paul and what he has been saying."[16]

Verses 24–29: This section reports Paul's appeal to his Roman citizenship, an affirmation that fits well with the apologetic bias of Luke-Acts. The first real Gentile convert to Christianity is a Roman centurion.[17] Further, the way that Roman officials treat Christians who have been denounced by Jews is exemplary.[18] These apologetic tendencies shed light on less-well-known passages that also deserve to be classified as apologetic:

> Jesus' parents demonstrate loyalty to the Roman state when they undertake the difficult journey (moreover Mary is pregnant) from Nazareth to Bethlehem to be enrolled.[19]
>
> John the Baptist's sermon on the responsibilities of people of various ranks,[20] a Lukan compendium,[21] ends with a prescription for tax collectors and soldiers. Though neither are in the least concerned about the baptism of John, the ethical advice, "Collect no more than is prescribed for you. . . . Do violence or injustice to no one, and be content with your wages,"[22] indicates that they should be loyal to the Roman Empire.
>
> Luke's passion narrative[23] portrays Jesus' death as that of a martyr and thereby wards off any possible political interpretation of this event—especially one along the lines of Jewish messianism. When the Roman governor cross-examines Jesus, he is unable to find anything that warrants condemnation[24] and is completely cleared of guilt for Jesus' death.

Though the information that Paul is a Roman citizen fits well with the apologetic predisposition of Luke-Acts, the author's intention and the testimony of the tradition are not necessarily incompatible. The parallel relationship between this scene and 16:16–39 is instructive. In both passages the appeal to Roman citizenship is delayed (cf. 22:25 with 16:37), and accordingly Paul is either subjected to or threatened with physical punishment by the Roman authorities (cf. 22:24 with 16:22–23). On each occasion the casual cruelty of the Roman authorities is contrasted with their fear when they discover that Paul is a Roman citizen (cf. 22:29 with 16:38). The probable narrative intent of all this is to stress Paul's Roman citizenship and to emphasize the apostle's safety from Jewish violence under the protection of the Roman state.

THE TRADITIONS REWORKED BY LUKE

There are no elements of tradition in this scene except for the detail of Paul's Roman citizenship, which Luke apparently knew about and effectively worked into various stories in order to disparage the Jews.

HISTORICAL ELEMENTS

In the following I shall make a case in favor of the historicity of Paul's Roman citizenship[25] by first listing various arguments against it and then offering a rebuttal.

(a) At no point does Paul mention his Roman citizenship.

   Rebuttal: It must be recognized that he had no particular occasion to—not even in a situation like that of 2 Cor. 11:25. He simply may not have attached any great importance to it.[26] Besides, on the basis of 1 Cor. 9:12 we may conclude Paul "was not in the habit of insisting on all his rights." [27]

(b) Paul was beaten with the rods three times (2 Cor. 11:25).

   Rebuttal: While indeed the beating of a Roman citizen with rods as a punishment was forbidden, this rule was often violated.

(c) The contradiction between Paul's manual labor (suggesting that he came from the lower middle class) and his Roman citizenship (indicating that he belonged to the upper class) tells against the latter, as the former is indisputable.

   Rebuttal: In the early empire bestowal of citizenship was in no way restricted to prominent citizens. Moreover, since his rabbinical training probably motivated Paul's manual labor, it is hardly to be used as conclusive evidence of his social status. To be sure, the rabbinical texts about the study of the Torah and manual labor come only from the middle of the second century CE, but this does not exclude an earlier provenance. There *are* no rabbinical texts before the middle of the second century in general, though quite a few go back to earlier material.

I shall now offer arguments in favor of Paul's Roman citizenship:

   1. The apostle bears a Roman name, Paul, that *against* the information of 13:9 he had had, together with the Semitic name Saul, since his childhood. (There are many examples from Roman Judaism that Jews had dual names.) Paul is a *cognomen* or *praenomen*. The name is rare in the East and suggests high birth. Its adoption can be explained in two ways: For one thing, it could reflect an attempted assimilation, a way of facilitating social contacts or even dealings with the Roman authorities. Paul may have been chosen as a phonetic equivalent of Saul. Or perhaps it indicates that the apostle was a Roman citizen. Since Roman citizens had the right and often felt the duty to bear a Roman name, Jews who became citizens commonly adopted appropriate names. Here it

seems worth considering the possibility that Paul had citizenship as the descendant of a freedman, for the legal freeing of a slave by a Roman citizen secured him citizenship without further ado, and without the need for any state consent. However, the freedman and his children did not get unlimited citizenship immediately. Therefore in fact they could be regarded as second-class citizens.

2. If the apostle's imprisonment in Jerusalem is a fact, his transportation to Rome can best be explained by an appeal to the Roman emperor by the Roman citizen Paul (25:10–11). One should not argue the other way around that Luke concluded from Paul's transportation to Rome that Paul had appealed to the emperor, since that would beg the question of why he was transported to Rome in the first place.

3. The fact that while a prisoner Paul could write to Philemon and carry on his work (see Philemon 24) is strong evidence that he was kept not in harsh confinement but in liberal detention. This may well have been due to his citizenship, for as a rule Roman citizens were not allowed to be subjected to harsh confinement.

4. Paul traveled frequently, widely, and freely through Roman colonial territories (Pisidian Antioch [Acts 13:14], Philippi, Corinth) and regularly uses the names of the Roman provinces when writing about his travel plans and his missionary activity: cf. Syria-Cilicia (Gal. 1:21); Asia (2 Cor. 1:8); Macedonia (Phil. 4:15; 2 Cor. 7:5; 8:1); Achaia (2 Cor. 9:2); Galatia (1 Cor. 16:1; Gal. 1:2). One explanation of his plan to go to Spain (Rom. 15:28) would be that he could be sure of finding Roman colonies there. For along with Gaul, Spain was at the center of a deliberate policy of Romanization. And Roman citizenship was both his passport and his shield on these wide-ranging missionary journeys.

5. Paul's admonitions in Rom. 13:1–7 that Christians give to the governing authorities of the Roman Empire what they demand—taxes, duties, revenue, and respect—fit in with Paul's Roman citizenship—though one must, of course, grant that noncitizens could have given the same exhortation.

Thus, in all probability Paul was a Roman citizen. Whether at the same time he was also a citizen of Tarsus (21:39) is not so easy to decide. At all events, being a citizen of Tarsus did not rule out being a Roman citizen, for the rule that Roman citizenship was incompatible with citizenship of another city had already been relaxed at the end of the Republic and in the early Principate.[28]

THE HISTORICAL VALUE OF LUKE'S ACCOUNT

Any attempt to envision the episode as a record of actual events must bring with it a reasonable answer to an obvious question: Why did "Paul not immediately divulge his Roman citizenship to the tribune when he asked about his identity?"[29]

It is apparent that the scene Luke has constructed does not reflect the actual course of events, the more so since to achieve the maximum literary effect by heightening the tension the author has his hero "speak the liberating word only at the last moment."[30] This is neither to condemn all employment of literary skill nor to deny that last-minute deliverances sometimes occur; however it does suggest once again that we must be sufficiently circumspect in reading Luke's accounts to be willing take them with a grain of salt—particularly when he is pushing an agenda item or gilding a hero, and when common sense enjoins a skeptical attitude.

[52]
ACTS 22:30–23:11
PAUL BEFORE THE HIGH COUNCIL

(22:30) *But on the next day, desiring to know the real reason why he* (Paul) *was being accused by the Jews, he* (the tribune) *unbound him and commanded the chief priests and all the High Council to meet, and he brought Paul down and set him before them.* (23:1) And gazing at the High Council, Paul said, "Brothers, I have led my life before God in all good conscience up to this day." (2) And the high priest Ananias commanded those who stood by him to strike him on the mouth. (3) Then Paul said to him, "God is going to strike you, you whitewashed wall! Are you sitting to judge me according to the law, and yet contrary to the law you order me to be struck?" (4) Those who stood by said, "Would you revile the high priest of God?" (5) And Paul said, "I did not know, brothers, that he was the high priest, for it is written, 'Of the ruler of your people you shall not speak evil.'"

(6) *But when Paul perceived that one part were Sadducees and the other Pharisees, he cried out in the high council, "Brothers, I am a Pharisee, a son of Pharisees. It is with respect to the hope and the resurrection of the dead that I am on trial."* (7) *And when he had said this, a dissension arose between the Pharisees and the Sadducees, and the assembly was divided.* (8) *For the Sadducees say that there is no resurrection, either as an* **angel** *or as a* <u>spirit</u>, *but the Pharisees acknowledge them both.* (9) *Then a great clamor arose, and some of the scribes of the Pharisees' party stood up and contended sharply, "We find nothing wrong in this man. What if a* <u>spirit</u> *or an* **angel** *spoke to him?"*

(10) *And such a great uproar arose that the tribune, afraid that they would tear Paul to pieces, commanded the soldiers to go down and seize him from their midst and take him into the barracks.*

(11) *The following night the Lord stood by him and said, "Take courage, for as you have testified about me in Jerusalem, so you must testify also in Rome."*

OUTLINE

22:30: The tribune summons the high council
23:1–9: Paul before the high council and the reaction of the Pharisees and Sadducees
   10: Paul taken to the barracks
   11: That night Paul hears the Lord tell him that he will also bear witness in Rome

LUKE'S PURPOSE

Verse [22:] 30: This verse prepares for Paul's speech before the high council.

Verses [23:]1–9: This scene has several peculiar features. The tribune's presence is neither implied nor asserted as in 22:30 and 23:10. Paul appears to have been remanded without guard or protection to the Sanhedrin's jurisdiction (verse 2). Then Paul begins speaking several times without giving a real speech: The dialogue in verses 2–5, involving three speakers, is unusual for Luke. Paul's unintentional insult and apology to the high priest (verse 5) is as awkward as it is unusual: Luke makes the apostle seem as abashed over his transgression as if he had knowingly violated correct usage. Last of all, an obvious narrative discontinuity between verses 5 and 6 indicates that Luke is stitching together various pieces. These several striking peculiarities suggest that Luke formulated the scene on the basis of tradition—particularly the first part—but has, as the following will show, colored it with his theology.

Verse 1: Here we have yet another declaration of innocence: "Brothers, I have lived before God in all good conscience up to this day." Paul assures the council that contrary to the charges made against him (see 21:21, 27–29) he has remained a faithful Jew. How this affirmation fits with his role in the lynching of Stephen, one should better not ask, for this would subvert Luke's argument.

Verses 2–3: The action of the high priest Ananias is quite unmotivated. Luke has created this physical chastisement so that Paul can in turn chastise "Judaism through its representatives—its relation to the Law is broken and hypocritical (cf. 7:50–53)."[31]

Verses 4–5: By quoting Exod. 22:28 (LXX 22:27) the Lukan Paul assures the council of his respect for the law; had he known Ananias to be the high priest, he would not have rebuked him.

Verses 6–9: Now Luke's hero goes on the offensive, and pits the two Jewish parties against each other with the result that the council is paralyzed. Clearly this set piece is a "scene arranged by the author of the Acts."[32] Paul's claim that as a Pharisee he is being condemned for his belief in the resurrection of the dead (verse 6), clearly a Lukan ploy since it will not bear close scrutiny, immediately results in the opposing parties becoming deadlocked. The phrase "when he had said this" (verse 7a) exemplifies the literary technique of interruption (cf. 10:44), and in this case it leads to uproar between the Sadducees and Pharisees. The remark attributed to several Pharisees, "We find nothing wrong in this man. What if a spirit or an angel spoke to him?" (verse 9) is highly reminiscent of Gamaliel's advice in 5:38–39—a passage that also derives from Luke. Absent proof to the contrary, Paul has been established as an "orthodox" Jew.

Verse 10: This verse closely parallels 22:30 and effects a transition to the episode in verses 12–35.

Verse 11: Between the above-mentioned passages, Luke introduces a fictitious appearance of Christ:[33] the heavenly figure assures Paul that he as he has borne witness in Jerusalem, so he must now do in Rome. This is Luke's way both of anticipating Paul's journey to and incarceration in Rome, and of once again establishing the wider context of the Christian mission. Paul's activity will, of course, comport with his commission (22:15), for his way is determined by divine necessity.

THE TRADITIONS REWORKED BY LUKE

Verses [23:] 1–9: We have noted above (p. 305) the reasons for suggesting that in verses 1–5 Luke has been influenced by tradition. Now it is possible to be more specific: Luke was familiar with a report that Paul insulted the high priest, and in verse 3 he reproduced this correctly; but in verse 5 he reworked the tradition to accommodate it to his own theology. In the traditional version, Paul may have been remanded to the high priest for possible punishment.

HISTORICAL ELEMENTS

Verses 1–5: In this reconstructed tradition Paul, after being turned over to the penal jurisdiction of the high priest, had insulted him. Since it seems all but impossible to imagine a reason for creating such a tradition, the likelihood of a historical kernel is great. Yet we do not know who had handed Paul over to the high priest—though it was almost surely the Romans—or why, and how he gained release from that jurisdiction. I hesitate to base an attestation of historicity on such an isolated tradition.

THE HISTORICAL VALUE OF LUKE'S ACCOUNT

Verse [22:] 30: The summoning of the Jewish high court *by a Roman officer* is clearly unhistorical,[34] as is his participation in the session (23:10).[35]

Verses [23:] 1–9: It is quite remarkable that Dunn regards the setting and content of the scene as likely to be historical. He writes,

> As ever, we cannot be sure that such a confrontation did take place in just these terms. Luke could well have had good first-hand reports to draw on here, and the events described, though surprising, are hardly implausible. Paul's identification of himself as a Pharisee accords with Phil. 3.5, and he shared Luke's conviction that the resurrection of Jesus was absolutely central to Christian faith (e.g. Rom. 10.9; I Cor. 15.14, 17). Perhaps more to the point, whatever the finer points in detail, Luke's portrayal has certainly hit the nerve of Jewish factionalism of the period, and of earliest Christianity's role within that factionalism.[36]

Rebuttal: Blaming the Jews for factionalism smacks of an argument from the arsenal of anti-Judaism. Furthermore, Dunn (like Luke) seems to cast doubt on the integrity and character of the historical Paul. The comment of Ferdinand Christian Baur on this episode is worth recalling:

> [I]t was only very superficially true that he stood for judgment as a Pharisee, on account of a belief which he held in common with the Pharisees. Even in this assertion we have a shifty and ambiguous way of evading the question at issue. And the same applies to the statement that the whole difference between the Apostle and his opponents could be reduced to the doctrine of the resurrection. The Apostle must have known perfectly well that the doctrine of the resurrection was not in dispute here at all; in regard to it he was in exactly the same case as the Jewish Christians of Jerusalem who believed in the resurrection of Jesus and were not molested on that account.[37]

It is surprising how soon Dunn has forgotten the tried and tested insights of the nineteenth-century critical school. But even if he were as unfamiliar with this important body of scholarship as he seems to be, one could wish that he would be more cautious than to base his conclusions on what amounts to wishful thinking about Luke's sources and on Paul's self-serving claim to be (not even "to have been") a Pharisee—even though his preaching and practice both indicate a somewhat less than strict observance of Jewish law. Historical judgments should be made of stronger stuff than this.

[53]
ACTS 23:12–35
THE PLOT ON PAUL'S LIFE; HIS TRANSPORT TO CAESAREA

(12) *Early the next morning the Jews made a plot and BOUND THEMSELVES BY AN OATH TO NEITHER EAT NOR DRINK TILL THEY HAD KILLED PAUL.* (13) *More than forty of them joined this conspiracy.* (14) *They went to the high priests and elders and said, "We have BOUND OURSELVES BY AN OATH TO TASTE NO FOOD TILL WE HAVE KILLED PAUL.* (15) *Now then, you and the high council must request the tribune to bring him down to you on the pretext that you wish to reexamine his case. And we are ready to kill him before he comes near."* (16) *Now the son of Paul's sister heard of their ambush, so he went to the barracks and told Paul.* (17) *Paul called one of the centurions and said, "Take this young man to the tribune, for he has something to tell him."* (18) *So he took him to the tribune, saying, "Paul the prisoner called me and asked me to bring this young man to you, as he has something to say to you."* (19) *The tribune took him by the hand, and going aside asked him privately, "What is it that you have to tell me?"* (20) *And he said, "The Jews have agreed to ask you to bring Paul down to the High Council tomorrow, as though they were going to look into his case more closely.* (21) *But do not be persuaded by them, for more than forty of their men are lying in ambush for him, and have BOUND THEMSELVES BY AN OATH TO NEITHER EAT NOR DRINK TILL THEY HAVE KILLED HIM. And now they are ready, waiting for your consent."* (22) *So the tribune dismissed the young man, charging him, "Tell no one that you have informed me of these things."*

(23) *Then he called two of the centurions and said, "Get ready two hundred soldiers, with seventy horsemen and two hundred spearmen to go as far as Caesarea at the third hour of the night.* (24) *Also provide mounts for Paul to ride and escort him safely to Felix the governor."*

(25) *And he wrote a letter to this effect:* (26) *"Claudius Lysias, to his Excellency the governor Felix, greetings.* (27) *This man was arrested by the Jews and was about to be killed by them when, having learned that he was a Roman citizen, I came with the guard and rescued him.* (28) *And desiring to know the charge with which they were accusing him, I brought him down to their High Council.* (29) *I found that he was being accused concerning matters of their law,*

but charged with nothing deserving death or imprisonment. (30) And when it was disclosed to me that there would be a plot against the man, I sent him to you at once, ordering his accusers also to state before you what they have against him."

(31) So following their instructions, the soldiers took Paul under cover of night to Antipatris. (32) The next day they returned to the barracks, letting the horsemen go on with him. (33) When they had come to Caesarea, they delivered the letter to the governor and presented Paul before him. (34) On reading the letter, he asked [Paul] what province he was from. And when he learned that he was from Cilicia, (35) he said, "I will give you a hearing when your accusers arrive." And he commanded him to be guarded in Herod's praetorium.

OUTLINE

12–15: Jewish conspiracy against Paul

16–22: Report of the conspiracy to Felix by Paul's nephew

23–35: Transport of Paul to Caesarea with a letter from the tribune Claudius Lysias to Felix

> 23–24: Two centurions receive the order to take Paul to Felix
>
> 25–30: The content of the letter with an introduction in verse 25
>
> 31–35: Paul's transport to Felix overnight and short hearing before Felix

LUKE'S PURPOSE

Luke has developed this scene to extraordinary breadth. Its compass far surpasses its significance. The Jewish conspiracy is narrated precisely and with emphatic repetition.[38]

This is a timeless tale of high adventure which, in any other work, would be called pure entertainment.[39]

Verses 12–15: The plot against Paul is described vividly. Note that the council's assent to the conspiracy is mentioned only in verse 20.

Verses 16–22: The report by Paul's nephew in verses 20–21 repeats the account of verses 12–15. (Similarly 10:30–32 is taken up in 11:4–17.) But the reader is not told how Paul's nephew learned about the planned ambush. The author's customary inventiveness seems to have deserted him at this point. The transition into direct speech (verse 24) is a Lukan touch, as likewise in 1:4; 17:3, etc.

Verses 23–24: The large size of the escort (two hundred foot soldiers, seventy cavalry, and two hundred spearmen) is obviously in conflict with the desire to carry out a *secret* mission. As he does elsewhere, Luke exaggerates to the point that the resulting contradictions betray him.[40] The troops are ordered to leave at 9 PM ("at the third hour of the night").

Verses 25–30: Clearly, the author has invented the letter of the tribune Claudius Lysias to Felix: As Barrett observes, it "is hard to imagine how Luke could have obtained access to Roman archives whether in Jerusalem or in Caesarea."[41] Besides the letter is Lukan in both language and content. It "serves to illumine the situation from the Roman standpoint (as Luke understands it). Legal innocence is acknowledged by the first Roman functionary who dealt with the matter. The view is the same as in the Gallio scene: The Roman does not state that Christianity is identical with Judaism, but rather that the whole matter is of no concern to Rome."[42] The form of verse 26, the prescript of the letter, matches the prescript of the letter in 15:23–29. Verse 27 contains the same Lukan use of "to arrest" that we find in Luke 22:54; Acts 1:16; 12:3. Claudius's report of Paul's arrest does not entirely parallel the account in 21:30–38; 22:22–29. According to his letter, he has rescued a Roman citizen from a Jewish mob; according to Luke's account in 21:33, 38 he first took the apostle to be a foreign terrorist, only to discover afterward that he was a Roman citizen. Furthermore, Claudius claims to have directed Paul's accusers to present their charges before the governor in Caesarea, a detail totally absent from the previous narrative. These tensions should not be used to argue for the existence of tradition at this point; rather, Luke is simply employing his customary authorial freedom to repeat a narrative while modifying its content (cf. the similar relationship between 11:14 and 10:5, 32 and between 11:15 and 10:44). Note also that he allows the tribune (no doubt realistically) to present the situation on the basis of his "present" knowledge and to conveniently forget his illegal order to scourge Paul (22:24). The phrase "questions of the law" that appears in verse 29 is also to be found in 18:15. Another Lukan inconsistency is evident in verse 30: The Jewish accusers cannot very well be advised to present their charges before Felix until Claudius knows that Paul has been safely delivered to him.

Haenchen aptly sums up Luke's perspective in the composition of the scene:

> Now Rome is saving the Apostle's life for the third time already [21:32–33, in the Temple, 23:10 in the High Court]. . . . How favourable [sic] it judges him comes out in the tribune's accompanying letter: he explains the proceedings before the council exactly as Luke wants it: Paul—the Roman citizen!—has done nothing which merited death or prison. His conflict with the Jews is rooted solely in inner-Jewish differences such as those between the Pharisees and Sad-

ducees. Accordingly Paul is exonerated by the highest representative of Rome who has as yet anything to do with his trial.[43]

Verse 31: The orders issued by the tribune (verse 23) are carried out. "By night" (verse 31) recalls "at the third hour of the night" (verse 23). Here Luke would have the reader imagine a troop of soldiers traveling forty-odd miles in about nine hours—a feat of miraculous proportions.

Verse 32: Since from Antipatris to Caesarea the heavy escort would pass through a largely Gentile area it was no longer needed.[44]

Verse 33: Here both the letter (verses 26–30) and Paul (as ordered in verse 24) are delivered to Felix.

Verses 34–35: These verses prepare for the next scene. Felix's question about Paul's home province recalls Pilate's query in the Lukan account of Jesus' trial whether "this man is a Galilean."[45] Felix's question, however, has no bearing on future proceedings against Paul and the subject is not picked up again.

THE TRADITIONS REWORKED BY LUKE

Verses 12–35: This account stands in sharp contrast to verses 1–9 both in its broad chronological and geographical setting and in its dramatic detail: a plot to assassinate Paul, his nephew's discovery and reporting of the cabal, the night-time removal of Paul from Jerusalem, the route through Antipatris to Caesarea, and the names Claudius Lysias and Felix.

Although the redactional verse 15 makes a trial before Felix seem a continuation of the pseudo-hearing begun in verse 1, the tradition clearly has no idea of any previous judicial action. Note also that the high council played no part in the plot against Paul: Only in verse 20 is this Lukan detail added. One may well doubt that the conspiracy and its discovery were elements of the tradition; in all likelihood Luke has composed a vivid scene on the basis of fragmentary traditional elements.

Hengel has asserted that Acts 23 reflects accurate geographical knowledge on Luke's part (the citadel Antonia, Antipatris, Caesarea) and that given the first-century context the events are generally plausible. He opines, "Josephus could hardly have depicted the event more appropriately. In other words . . . the account must ultimately derive from an eyewitness."[46] But such a judgment borders on the grotesque. Luke must have had a seriously distorted notion of the distance between Jerusalem and Antipatris, since he has what would be a rigorous forced march of two full days accomplished in less than a single night. It requires more than a few random elements of local color to demonstrate the historicity of a complex action—especially one marred by a patently impossible performance.

Hengel's easy credulity in accepting this as an eyewitness report exactly matches Luke's intent, but in fact the situation renders this all but impossible; indeed, nearly every important action—the plot, its revelation, moving Paul by night—takes place in secret. It is by means of this motif of secrecy, of course, that Luke ingenuously suggests to the reader the reason why this episode is only now being revealed.

HISTORICAL ELEMENTS

The following historical events can be hypothetically assumed to have provided the basis of the tradition in this section.

1. The transfer of Paul by Claudius Lysias from Jerusalem to the governor Felix in Caesarea is likely historical, even though the details are no doubt largely imaginative.

2. Transporting Paul was necessary, since the trial would as a matter of course take place in Caesarea, the residence of the governor, who was the ranking judicial authority of the province. Another likely historical factor was the plot by Paul's Jewish enemies to assassinate him. This narrative element comes from the tradition, and is confirmed by the tense situation that existed during the apostle's last visit to Jerusalem: As a result of his being attacked by a Jewish mob charging him with defiling the Temple, Paul was either arrested or taken into protective custody. Eduard Schwartz is likely correct in assigning his arrest to the charge of bringing Gentiles into the Temple (21:28; 24:6): "The non-Jew who entered the inner area of the [T]emple was an outlaw. If the Jews put up with it, the Romans authorities did not of course intervene; but if a born Jew caused a Gentile to transgress the commandment (which is what Paul was accused of) and if this incited the Jews to a rebellion, he could be prosecuted for *seditio* and condemned to death."[47] It is highly unlikely that the Jewish charge was true, for not only did Paul respect Jewish customs that had no negative effect on Gentile Christianity, but having arrived with the collection, a sort of peace offering, he was surely eager to do all he could to earn the good will of the Jerusalem community. In light of the distrust and even enmity of many Jerusalem Jews, however (see the commentary on 21:21), it is not difficult to imagine that the charge was a slanderous attack on Paul by disaffected Jewish Christians.

3. The accuracy of the tradition in depicting the plot and its discovery by Paul's nephew cannot be determined. The Sanhedrin's involvement undoubtedly comes from Luke, since it so effectively suits his purpose. Throughout the episode, key scenes are given fictive elaboration: For example, it is hard to imagine that an otherwise unknown individual like Paul's nephew gain imme-

diate access to a Roman tribune. Still, that Paul had a sister and nephew in Jerusalem is likely historical.

THE HISTORICAL VALUE OF LUKE'S ACCOUNT

Verses 14–15, 20–21: Note the conflict between this scene and the preceding one that showed sharp dissent between the Sadducees and Pharisees. While then they could not agree, now they even consent in a murder plot against Paul. On this point, note Haenchen's apt remark:

> In reality the contradiction to the previous scene is easily explained if we remember how independently the several scenes stand side by side in Luke. He and his readers set store by attractive single pictures; they had not the slightest inclination for their critical evaluation. Hence Luke can employ a technique which is denied the modern historian and which is shunned even by modern narrators.[48]

Verses 34–35: In preparation for the future trial Felix briefly interrogates Paul. Taking cognizance of the documents "after a brief cross-examination [he] decides to take over the trial for himself. Paul is shown to his quarters—he cannot ask for more."[49] Yet, the portrait of Felix painted by Tacitus and Josephus contradicts this Lukan picture of a correctly acting Roman proconsul and proves that its historical value is nil.[50]

Tacitus on Felix: *Annals* 12.54: "He believed that he could commit all kinds of enormities with impunity." *Histories* 5.9: "Practicing every kind of cruelty and lust, he wielded royal power with the instincts of a slave."

Josephus's view of Felix agrees with that of Tacitus. See *Jewish Antiquities* 20.160–64: (160) "In Judea matters were constantly going from bad to worse. For the country was again infested with bands of brigands and impostors who deceived the mob. (161) Not a day passed, however, that Felix captured and put to death many of these impostors and brigands. He also, by a ruse, took alive Eleazar the son of Dinaeus, who had organized the company of brigands; for by offering a pledge that he would suffer no harm, Felix induced him to appear before him. Felix then imprisoned him and dispatched him to Rome. (162) Felix also bore a grudge against Jonathan the high priest because of his frequent admonition to improve the administration of the affairs in Judea. For Jonathan feared that he himself might incur the censure of the multitude in that he had requested Caesar to dispatch Felix as procurator of Judea. Felix accordingly devised that would remove from his presence one who was a constant nuisance to him; for incessant rebukes are annoying to those who choose to do wrong. (163) It was such reasons that moved Felix to bribe Jonathan's most trusted friend, a native of Jerusalem named Doras, with a promise to pay a great sum, to bring in brigands to attack Jonathan and kill him. Doras agreed and contrived to get him murdered by the brigands in the following way. (164) Certain of these brigands went up to the city as if they intended to worship God. With daggers concealed under their clothes, they mingled with the people about Jonathan and assassinated him."[51]

Antiquities 20.182: "When Porcius Festus was sent by Nero as successor to Felix, the leaders of the Jewish community of Caesarea went up to Rome to accuse Felix. He would undoubtedly have paid the penalty for his misdeeds against the Jews had not Nero yielded to the urgent entreaty of Felix's brother Pallas, whom at that time he held in the highest honor."[52]

Henry Thoreau once observed, "circumstantial evidence can be very strong—as when you find a trout in the milk." Anyone who steps forward to defend the historicity of the foregoing bit of Lukan romance must be prepared to demonstrate the invalidity of Haenchen's analysis and the falsity of the reports of Tacitus and Josephus. As things stand, Luke's account looks pretty "fishy" to any critical reader.

[54]
ACTS 24:1–27
PAUL BEFORE GOVERNOR FELIX AT CAESAREA

(1a) And after five days the high priest Ananias *came down with some elders and* an advocate, Tertullus. *(1b)* They laid before the governor their case against Paul. *(2a) And when he [Paul] had been summoned, Tertullus began the charge, saying:* (2b) *"Since through you we enjoy* MUCH *peace, and since by your foresight, most excellent Felix, reforms are being made for this nation,* (3) *in every way and everywhere we accept this with all gratitude.* (4) *But, to detain you no further, I beg you to hear us briefly with your customary graciousness.* (5) *For we have found this man a plague, one who stirs up riots among all the Jews throughout the world and is a ringleader of the sect of the Nazarenes.* (6a) He even tried to profane the Temple, *but we seized him.*[53] (8b) *By examining him yourself you can* **ascertain** *from him about everything of which we accuse him."* (9) *The Jews also joined in the charge, affirming that all these things were so.* (10a) *And Paul replied when the governor had nodded to him to speak:*

(10b) *"Knowing that for MANY years you have been a judge for this nation, I cheerfully make my defense.* (11) *You can **ascertain** that it is not more than twelve days since I went up to worship in Jerusalem,* (12) *and neither in the Temple did they find me disputing with anyone or causing the onset of a **crowd**, nor in the synagogues nor in the city.* (13) *Neither can they prove to you what they now bring up against me.* (14) *But this I confess to you, that according to the Way, which they call a sect, I worship the God of our fathers, believing everything written down according to the law and in the prophets,* (15) *having a hope in God, which these men themselves accept, that there will be a resurrection of both the just and the unjust.* (16) *So I always take pains to have a clear conscience toward God and toward men in all things.* (17) *Now after several years I came to bring alms for my people and to offerings.* (18) *While I was doing this, they found me purified in the Temple, without any **crowd** or tumult. But some Jews from Asia—*(19) *they ought to be here before you and to make an accusation, should they have anything against me.* (20) *Or else let these men themselves say what wrongdoing they found when I stood before the high council,* (21) *other than this one thing that I cried out while standing among them: 'It is with respect to the resurrection of the dead that I am on trial before you this day.'"*

(22) *But Felix, having a rather accurate knowledge of the Way, put them off,* saying, *"When Lysias the tribune comes down, I shall decide your case."* (23) Then he gave orders to the centurion that he should be kept in custody but have some liberty, and that none of his friends should be prevented from attending to his needs.

(24) *After some days Felix came with his wife Drusilla, who was Jewish, and he sent for Paul and heard him speak about faith in Christ Jesus.* (25) *But when he began to discuss righteousness and self-control and the coming judgment, Felix was alarmed and said, "That will do for now. When I get an opportunity I will summon you."* (26) *At the same time he hoped that Paul would offer him a bribe; so he sent for him often and conversed with him.* (27) When two years had passed, Felix was succeeded by Porcius Festus, *and desiring to do the Jews a favor, Felix left Paul in prison.*

OUTLINE

24–27: Paul in Caesarea
   24–26: Repeated conversations between Felix and Paul
   27: Replacement of Felix by Festus two years later

LUKE'S PURPOSE

Verse 1: The verse goes back to 23:30 and continues the narrative thread that was interrupted by the account of Paul's transportation to Caesarea. Following the instructions of the tribune Claudius Lysias, the Jews have sent a prosecutor and witnesses against Paul to press their case before Felix.

Verses 2–6a, 8b: The orator Tertullus opens the prosecution in verses 2–4 with the customary *captatio benevolentiae*—an attempt to gain the listener's favor. (Paul will similarly compliment the governor in verse 10b.) The two charges against Paul reported in previous episodes are reiterated: (a) Paul foments unrest and rebellion among Jews everywhere (verse 5); (b) Paul attempted to profane the temple (verse 6). The first charge echoes 17:6, which contained Jewish charges against Paul; the second is a rehearsal of 21:28.

Verse 9: By their support of the accusations, the Jewish witnesses heighten the drama: "All these things are so" (in Greek, *houtôs echein*) is a Lukan phrase (cf. 7:1; 17:11).

Paul's defense speech in verses 10–21 is closely related to the charge.

Verse 10: "Paul" is currying favor (cf. verses 2–4) by noting the long and honorable service of Felix: He "for many years"[54] had been "judge for this people," i.e., procurator in Judea. This represents either shameless flattery or Lukan ignorance, since Felix had been in office for no more than a short period.[55]

Verse 11: "You can ascertain," recalls the same phrase in verse 8. Luke places Paul's arrival in Jerusalem twelve days earlier by adding the seven days mentioned in 21:27 to the five days specified in 24:1.

Verse 12–13: These verses refute the charge of verse 5 that Paul has been stirring up discussions among Jews in every place.

Verses 14–15: As usual Luke presents a positive picture of Paul's Christianity, including his belief in the scriptures (verse 14) and his trust (like that of the Pharisees) that God will bring about the resurrection of both the just and the unjust (verse 15).

Verse 16: Luke has Paul offer yet another indication of his innocence: "So I always take pains to have a clear conscience toward God and toward men in all things."[56]

Verse 17: It comes as a surprise to hear Paul say that the purpose of this visit to Jerusalem was to bring "alms and offerings for my people" (see below, p. 318).

Verses 18–19: These verses paraphrase 21:27, once more defending Paul against the accusation of causing a tumult ("crowd" in verse 18 recalls "crowd" in verse 12).

Verses 20–21: This stresses Paul's innocence yet again: It should be noted that like the Asiatic Jews of chapter 21, his present accusers cannot demonstrate any wrongdoing. Verse 21 alludes to the (first) hearing before the Sanhedrin when Paul claimed (23:6) that the charges resulted from his belief in resurrection.

Verses 22–23: These verses prepare for the next section (verses 24–26). The information that Felix knows about the Christian way (verse 22)[57] is narratively developed in verse 24b. Felix's continuation of the hearing until the Lysias's arrival provides the necessary opportunity for the forthcoming encounters between Paul and Felix and Paul and Festus. Felix's order to ease the terms of Paul's confinement (verse 23) is Luke's creation (cf. 27:3).

Verses 24–26: The content clearly indicates Luke's apologetic interest, since it reports that Felix and Drusilla were initially interested in Paul's discourse (verse 24). "The interest in Christianity shown by those in high places is a Lukan theme."[58] Moreover, the reported list of Paul's topics—justice, self-control, and the coming judgment (verse 25)—is in effect an outline of Lukan Christianity adapted to the situation, for Felix was widely known for his licentiousness. Verse 26 corresponds to what such authors as Josephus and Tacitus tell us about Felix (see above, pp. 313–14). His negative characterization, and in particular his widely reputed venality, obviously conflicts with the positive portrait in verses 22–23; but if nothing else, the information that he hopes Paul will offer a bribe to gain his freedom, explains why, despite his obvious innocence, the apostle is not set free. Such a payment is, of course, out of the question in view of Paul's sermon (see verse 25). Once again Luke has invoked a favorite theme: the incompatibility of wealth and the gospel.[59]

Verse 27: Concerning "two years" as the reported duration of Paul's imprisonment, it is worth noting that the reason given in verse 27b (that by holding Paul Felix was doing the Jews a favor) is reminiscent of 12:3. And though in some tension with verse 26, this may indicate Luke's desire to provide a further reason for an extended incarceration. Note also that by now the reason given in verse 22—to await the arrival of Claudius Lyias—has been conveniently forgotten.

THE TRADITIONS REWORKED BY LUKE

Verse 1a: The lawyer Tertullus and the high priest Ananias reflect tradition; it is possible that their joint presenting of the case (verse 1b) is also traditional; for this possibility, see below on verses 22–23.

Verse 17: Luke knew the tradition about the collection, but suppressed it in chapter 21. Either he let it slip in here, or he is aware of custom for Jewish pilgrims to bring alms to Jerusalem when visiting the city. Since such a gesture would appeal to Luke, this report cannot be unambiguously related to the collection.

Verses 22–23: To be sure, these two verses are eminently at home in the present context, since they prepare for the next scene in verses 24–26; nevertheless, Eduard Schwartz suggests a basis in tradition: In the phrase, "he put them off" and, "I shall decide your case," Schwartz writes, "the pronouns cannot cover the two parties but only denote those who want something from Felix, the plaintiffs; and they were the Jews."[60] Yet in the Lukan context the pronouns may refer both to the Jews and to Paul—for Paul had been the speaker since verse 10. That in turn suggests that the tradition Luke is using told of the Jewish authorities (Ananias and Tertullus) making accusations against Paul before Felix in Caesarea (cf. verse 1b). (Actually the charges were presented to Festus; see below, pp. 320–23.) Originally, no doubt, the substance of the charge was desecrating the Temple (cf. verse 6a). Cf. the general comments on page 312. (As to whether the characterization of Felix [verses 24–26] reflects the tradition, see above, pp. 313–14.)

Verse 27: That Festus replaced Felix in office came to Luke from a tradition that reported Paul's imprisonment in Caesarea when the change took place. (In this connection note also the tradition in 18:12–17 about Paul's stay in Corinth in the time of Claudius.) The datum "two years" also derives from tradition.[61]

For historical reasons, then, the "two years" may refer to the duration of Felix's term of office; for more on this see below. "What Luke actually learnt about Paul's trial under Felix can only be conjectured. The most natural assumption is that a Jewish delegation with the lawyer Tertullus presented itself at Caesarea, but had to be satisfied with an adjournment. That Luke from such a notice could have created so colorful a story is the secret of his great art."[62]

HISTORICAL ELEMENTS

All the elements of tradition that have been reconstructed have a high claim to historical probability:

Verse 1: The names of the high priest Ananias (whose term ran from about

47 to 59 CE)[63] and the attorney-at-law Tertullus (nowhere else attested) are factual. Their presentation of formal charges before Felix after Paul's arrival in Caesarea (cf. verses 22–24) is likewise historical. But these events must have occurred when Festus, Felix's successor, was in office.

Verse 17: While the report about the "collection" may well be historical, it is only through the evidence of Paul's letters that we are able to identify this element as factual.

Verse 27: Combining statements by Tacitus and Josephus can corroborate that Felix was procurator for two years. In the former we read that at the end of 55 CE Nero removed Felix's brother Pallas from administrative control of the empire's finances and stripped him of all political influence.[64] In the latter source we learn that upon being replaced by Festus, Felix was accused before Nero by the leaders of the Jews of Caesarea; only through the influence of Pallas, whom Nero prized highly *at that time* was the charge dropped.[65] Josephus's report is not to be seen as exclusively gossip[66] but as authentic in its representation of Pallas's fraternal intervention when he was (temporarily) in the emperor's good graces. That situation did not obtain, of course, after his dismissal.[67]

A Note on the Historical Course of Events

When we combine the reliable elements of tradition, the following historical sequence becomes clear: While Paul was a Roman prisoner in Caesarea, Jewish authorities under the high priest Ananias traveled to that city to participate in a trial of Paul under Felix. With them came Tertullus, an attorney knowledgeable in both Roman and Jewish law. Although these Jewish notables appeared before Felix, no trial was held during his two-year term—either because Paul arrived in Caesarea shortly before Felix's tenure ended (in 55 CE), or because for one reason or another Felix temporized.

THE HISTORICAL VALUE OF LUKE'S ACCOUNT

Verses 24–26: Scholars to this day amazingly consider the scene of Paul before Felix and Drusilla as historical. Two examples may suffice:

> Paul also had a personal encounter with the procurator and his wife Drusilla in which he did not fail to talk to them of what he thought they needed to hear— of righteousness, chastity and future judgment (Acts 24:25).[68]

Another scholar writes similarly,

> But what he (Felix) heard from Paul was nothing superficial. Paul did not spare him as he spoke about *justice*, *self-control* and the coming *judgment*, the very things that Felix and his wife needed to hear about. He had sufficient of a conscience left to feel some alarm at the Christian message, but he very quickly had as much as he could take, and he dismissed Paul until he had further time available. He had no intention of repenting.[69]

Yet Felix's "governorship was marked by a disregard for the Jewish religion and for Jewish customs, provoking in turn an ever-increasing hostility to the Roman rule."[70] Moreover, what Tacitus and Josephus write about Felix (see above, pp. 313–14) render a supposed meeting between him and Paul on his own request impossible. Luke again turns out to be a swindler in the interest of theology and religious propaganda. Indeed, throughout "his captivity in Caesarea, Paul functioned like the chief attraction in a fashionable salon"[71]—a clear indication of propagandist fiction.

One should also exclude Felix's wife, Drusilla, as the real driving force for the meeting. "By the fact that she broke off her marriage to king Aziz of Emesa and married the heathen Felix, who had a brilliant career in prospect, she revealed how little Jewish religion bound her. But if we make curiosity the motive which impelled her, then we miss the tenor of the narrative."[72] Moreover, it is an intellectual impudence on Luke's side to make us believe that "Paul almost succeeded in converting the procurator Felix, as he converted the procurator Sergius Paulus and as he will almost succeed in converting King Agrippa II (26.28)."[73]

Once again a pretty piece of wishful thinking—however edifying it may seem at first blush—must be assigned to a genre other than that of history. To pick up a previous analogy: However disinclined to "carp" on the point, one must insist that this episode, like the preceding one, has a distinctly piscine aroma.

[55]

ACTS 25:1–12

PAUL'S APPEAL TO CAESAR BEFORE GOVERNOR FESTUS

(1) Now *three* days after Festus had arrived in the province, he went up to Jerusalem from Caesarea. (2) And the chief priests and the principal men of the Jews laid out their case against Paul, *and they urged him* (3) *that as a favor to them he summon* Paul *to Jerusalem—because they were planning an ambush to*

kill him on the way. (4) Festus replied that Paul was being kept at Caesarea and that he himself intended to go there shortly. (5) "So," said he, "let the men of authority among you go down with me, and if the man has done anything wrong, let them bring charges against him." (6) After he stayed among them not more than eight or ten days, he went down to Caesarea. And the next day he took his seat on the tribunal and ordered Paul to be brought. (7) When he had *arrived*, the Jews who had come down from Jerusalem stood around him, *bringing against* him many serious charges that they could not *prove*. (8) *In his own defense Paul argued, "Neither against the law of the Jews, nor against the Temple, nor against Caesar have I committed any offense." (9) But Festus, wishing to grant the Jews a favor, said to Paul, "Do you wish to go up to Jerusalem and there be tried on these charges before me?"* (10) *Paul said,* "I am standing before Caesar's tribunal, where I ought to be tried. To the Jews I have done no wrong, as you yourselves know very well. (11) If then I am a wrongdoer and have *committed anything for which I deserve to die,* I do not seek to escape death. But if there is nothing to their charges against me, no one can hand me over to them. I appeal to Caesar." (12) Then Festus, when he had *conferred with* his council, answered, "To Caesar you have appealed; to Caesar you shall go."

OUTLINE

1–5: The charges of the Jewish leaders in Jerusalem against Paul before the new procurator Festus

6–12: Paul's appeal to Caesar before procurator Festus in Caesarea

LUKE'S PURPOSE

For the most part, Acts 25:1–22 is transitional, providing the impetus to move Paul from custody in the praetorium to Rome. At the same time, this section of Acts reiterates the unrelenting opposition of the Jewish leadership from Jerusalem and the image of Paul as fully competent to navigate his circumstances and dictate their outcome. . . . In light also of Jesus' words in Acts 23:11 to Paul in the Roman barracks, Paul's boldness and adroit handling of his case are not the only factors at work in his ability to impact his circumstances. They are only the *human* ones. Paul can be so bold within his setting because of his confidence in God's promises and ability.[74]

Verses 1–5: Verses 2–3 amount to a reprise of 23:15: the Jews seek to expose Paul to an assassination attempt. In this version of the plot, they appeal to Festus to have

Paul sent to Jerusalem. And although Festus's refusal conflicts with the favorable inclination reported in with verse 9, the expected answer to the clearly fictitious question in verse 9 would have the same results as the refusal reported in verses 4–5. Therefore the tension can be attributed to less-than-perfect Lukan editing, and should not lead to source-critical analysis. This appears to be a doublet of the corresponding portions of chapter 24. In both cases Jewish leaders approach the Roman procurator (first in Caesarea, then in Jerusalem) to accuse Paul of wrongdoing. Luke cannot have been unaware of the close parallel. For what this suggests about Luke's intention—and an evaluation of this observation—see below, page 323.

Verses 6–8: This section is a yet clearer doublet of material in chapter 24. Verse 7 summarizes 24:2–8—though unlike the earlier passage it does not report the content of the Jewish charges for the simple reason that the reader already knows them. We also find a similarity in this report of Paul's defense (verse 8) and that found in 24:10–21. Although verse 7 merely states that the Jews made accusations and verse 8 is hardly a full response, the latter nonetheless presents a succinct and dramatically effective summary of the apostle's defense: "Neither against the law of the Jews, nor against the Temple, nor against Caesar have I committed any offense."[75]

Verses 9–12: Although verse 9 reasserts the procurator's desire to grant the Jews a favor, that inclination is now enlisted to serve Luke's narrative ends in a very different way. Here Festus is made to ask Paul an obviously fictitious rhetorical question: Would the apostle prefer to have himself and his trial moved back to Jerusalem? (The notion and the question derive from Luke. See the above commentary on verse 4 concerning the tension between verses 4 and 9). The expected negative answer is a necessary preparation for verses 10–11 and verse 12, where Paul's long-anticipated journey to Rome (see 19:21; 23:11), can be arranged for at the narrative level. Verse 10 is Luke's dramatic preparation for the subsequent appeal to the emperor: "I am standing before Caesar's tribunal, where I ought to be tried" (verse 10a)," stands in ironic contrast to the tersely stated, climactic appeal (end of verse 11) that is Paul's last resort: "I appeal to Caesar"— an appeal that Festus accepts (verse 12).

Wellhausen attempted to find a conflict between verse 10 and verses 11–12 by proposing that verse 10 referred to the judgment of the procurator and verses 11–12 to that of the emperor. He writes: "But in that case how can he (Paul) . . . at the end appeal from the procurator to the emperor, and in the same breath, as if the one did not contradict the other, but followed from it."[76] As suggested above, however, this apparent difficulty is resolved if we see verse 10 as a Lukan prologue that gives dramatic emphasis to the laconic insistence of Paul's appeal to the emperor (verse 11) and Festus's acceptance in verse 12. "To Caesar you have appealed; to Caesar you shall go," is no doubt another literary flourish by the author.

THE TRADITIONS REWORKED BY LUKE

Taking into account the results of the analysis of chapter 24, we can now evaluate the hypothesis that chapters 24 and 25 are duplications. In chapter 25 Luke presents the account of a trial before Festus. For theological reasons he has already employed it as the basis of chapter 24 and decorated it with speeches by both parties, but the tradition behind chapter 25 does not seem to allow for a previous public hearing—"whether before the Sanhedrin in Jerusalem or before the Roman procurator in Caesarea in the presence of members of the Sanhedrin."[77]

It is possible that the tradition mentioned the appeal to the emperor, and inasmuch as such an appeal was usually the prerogative only of Roman citizens, Paul's appeal to the emperor may have been used to indicate his Roman citizenship. Yet Luke does not always apply this criterion in describing appeals to the emperor (cf. 25:10–11; 28:18–19). It seems likely, then, that here he has redactionally severed an original connection—as he earlier did when in chapter 16 his explanation for Timothy's circumcision conflicted with the tradition (see above, pp. 207–208).

HISTORICAL ELEMENTS

We may safely grant historical authenticity to the overall scenario: Paul's trial before Festus in Caesarea, the involvement of prominent Jews from Jerusalem, and Paul's appeal to the emperor, citing his Roman citizenship.[78] The specific reason for this appeal is unclear: Had the apostle been falsely condemned for incitement to riot, did he anticipate such a sentence, or did he fear for his life if freed in Palestine? Or was this a safe and expedient way of fulfilling his plan to visit Rome after delivering the collection?

THE HISTORICAL VALUE OF LUKE'S ACCOUNT

The account evokes the following unanswerable questions, posed by Haenchen, "1. why after the close of the proceedings no verdict follows, but a transference of the trial is proposed, 2. why Paul does not simply insist on a continuation of the trial in Caesarea, but appeals to Caesar, 3. why Festus does not himself try a man charged with *laesae maiestatis* (or send him to Rome). These contradictions are immediately resolved if we consider the Lucan narrative no longer as a court minute but rather as suspense-laden narrative created by the author."[79] The solution is that we must regard the Lukan narrative not as the transcription of a hearing "but rather as suspense-laden narrative created by the author."[80] Its historical value is nil. An ambivalent reaction is appropriate: We may properly be dismayed to find yet another example of historical legerdemain, but at the same time grateful for the palpable improbabilities that allow us to see what Luke is doing.

[56]
ACTS 25:13–27
PAUL BEFORE AGRIPPA II AND BERNICE

(13) *Now after an interval of some days Agrippa the king and Bernice arrived at Caesarea and greeted Festus.* (14) *And as they were staying there for many days, Festus laid Paul's case before the king, saying, "There is a man left prisoner by Felix,* (15) *and when I was at Jerusalem, the chief priests and the elders of the Jews laid out their case against him, asking for a sentence of condemnation against him.* (16) *I answered them that it was not the custom of the Romans to give up anyone before the accused has met the accusers face to face and had opportunity to make his defense concerning the charge against him.* (17) *So when they came together here, I made no delay, but on the next day took my seat on the tribunal and ordered the man to be brought.* (18) *When the accusers stood up, they brought no charge in his case of such evils as I supposed.* (19) *Rather they had certain points of dispute with him about their own religion and about a certain Jesus, who is dead, but whom Paul asserted to be alive.* (20) *Being at a loss how to investigate these questions, I asked whether he wanted to go to Jerusalem and be tried there regarding them.* (21) *But when Paul had appealed to be kept in custody for the decision of the emperor, I ordered him to be held until I could send him to Caesar."* (22) *Then Agrippa said to Festus, "I would like to hear the man myself." "Tomorrow," said he, "you will hear him."* (23) *So on the next day Agrippa and Bernice came with great pomp, and they entered the audience hall with the military tribunes and the prominent men of the city. Then, at the command of Festus, Paul was brought in.* (24) *And Festus said, "King Agrippa and all who are present with us, you see this man about whom the whole Jewish people petitioned me, both in Jerusalem and here, shouting that he ought not to live any longer.* (25) *But I found that he had done nothing deserving death. And as he himself appealed to the emperor, I decided to go ahead and send him.* (26) *But I have nothing definite to write to my lord about him. Therefore I have brought him before you all, and especially before you, King Agrippa, so that, after we have examined him, I may have something to write.* (27) *For it seems to me unreasonable, in sending a prisoner, not to indicate the charges against him."*

OUTLINE

13–22: Festus's conversation with Agrippa about Paul; Agrippa's desire to hear Paul.
23–27: (The next day:) Solemn entry by Agrippa and Bernice. Festus introduces Paul to Agrippa.

LUKE'S PURPOSE

Verses 13–15: Festus presents Paul's case to Agrippa II and Bernice (his sister and sexual partner) who came with him to welcome Festus to Caesarea.

Verse 16: This verse formulates the basic guidelines of Roman jurisdiction. The accused has a right both to be heard and to defend himself.

Verse 17: The promptness of Festus's procedure stands in stark contrast to that of Felix (24:22).

Verses 18–19: The situation matches that in 18:15. The conflict is among Jews and has no political relevance. "Here the apologetic aim becomes quite clear: the goal is not to achieve the recognition of Christianity by the state, but to urge Rome's withdrawal from the legal proceedings."[81]

Verses 20–21: For verse 20 see verse 9; for verse 21 see verse 11.

Verse 22: Agrippa's wish to make Paul's acquaintance is a literary transition to the next section. (Luke had read at Mark 6:20 that another Jewish king—Herod Antipas—enjoyed hearing John the Baptist. However, he omitted that passage in his gospel.)

Verses 23–27: Paul's meeting with Agrippa and Bernice (cf. verse 13) results from Agrippa's decision (verse 22) to hear the case in person. In verses 24–27 Paul is presented by Festus, who reiterates (verse 25) that Paul has done nothing to warrant his condemnation. Note that this hearing before Agrippa and Bernice is a doublet of that before Felix and Drusilla (24:24–26). Luke's clear purpose is to establish Paul's important place in world history. The appearance before king Agrippa also serves the important role of fulfilling the visionary prophecy of 9:15.

THE TRADITIONS REWORKED BY LUKE

The only traditions available to Luke for the composition of this scene were the names of King Agrippa and his sister Bernice as well as general knowledge about their incestuous relationship.[82] Though it is plausible that they went to Caesarea to greet the newly appointed governor, that seems not to be a traditional element, especially since any such report should have included Paul. That, however, is not the case.

Historical Elements

There are no historical elements in the tradition or elsewhere that support this patently fictitious account.

The Historical Value of Luke's Account

Though occasionally the encounter between Paul with Agrippa II and Bernice is even today regarded by some as factual,[83] the totally fictitious nature of this episode helps to reveal its exclusively literary purpose: that of preparing the reader for the next chapter in which Luke's hero will receive the endorsement of both Festus and the last Jewish king, Agrippa II.

[57]
Acts 26:1–32
Paul's Speech before Agrippa II

(1) *Then Agrippa said to Paul, "You have permission to speak for yourself." And Paul stretched out his hand and made his defense:* (2) *"I consider myself fortunate that it is before you, King Agrippa, that I am to make my defense today against all the accusations of the Jews,* (3) *especially because you are familiar with all the customs and controversies of the Jews. Therefore I beg you to listen to me patiently.* (4) *My manner of life from youth onward, spent from the beginning among my own nation and in Jerusalem, is known by all the Jews.* (5) *They have known for a long time, if they are willing to acknowledge it, that as a Pharisee, I have lived according to the strictest sect of our religion.* (6) *And now I stand here on trial because of my hope in the promise made by God to our fathers,* (7) *to which our twelve tribes hope to attain, as they earnestly worship night and day. And for this hope I am accused by Jews, O king!* (8) *Why is it thought incredible by any of you that God raises the dead?*

(9) *I myself was convinced that I ought to do many things in opposing the name of Jesus of Nazareth.* (10) *And I did so in Jerusalem. I not only locked up many of the saints in prison after receiving authority from the high priests, but when they were on trial for their lives I cast my vote against them.* (11) *And I*

punished them often in all the synagogues and tried to force them to blaspheme, and in my raging fury I persecuted them even in foreign cities.

(12) *In this connection I journeyed to Damascus with the authority and commission of the high priests.* (13) *At midday, O king, I saw on the way a light from heaven, brighter than the sun that shone around me and those who journeyed with me.* (14a) *And when we had all fallen to the ground, I heard a voice saying to me in the Hebrew language, 'Saul, Saul, why are you persecuting me?* (14b) *It is hard for you to kick against the goads.'* (15) *And I said, 'Who are you, Lord?' And the Lord said, 'I am Jesus whom you are persecuting.* (16) *But rise and stand upon your feet, for I have appeared to you for this purpose, to appoint you as a servant and witness, to testify both to what you have seen and to what you will see;* (17a) *and I will protect you from your own people and from* the Gentiles (17b) to whom I am sending you (18) *to open their eyes, so that they may turn from darkness to light and from the power of Satan to God, and thus may receive forgiveness of sins and a place among those who are sanctified by faith in me.'* (19) *Therefore, O King Agrippa, I was not disobedient to the heavenly vision,* (20) *but proclaimed first to those in Damascus, then in Jerusalem and throughout all the region of Judea, and also to the Gentiles, that they should repent and turn to God, performing deeds in keeping with their repentance.* (21) *For this reason the Jews— having seized me in the Temple—tried to kill me.* (22) *To this day I have had the help that comes from God, and so I stand here testifying both to small and great, saying nothing but what the prophets and Moses foretold would come to pass:* (23) *that the Christ must suffer and that he first would, on the basis of the resurrection of the dead, proclaim light both to the people and to the Gentiles."*

(24) *And as he was saying these things in his defense, Festus said with a loud voice, "Paul, you are mad; your great learning is driving you into madness."* (25) *But Paul said, "I am not mad, most excellent Festus, but I am declaring words of truth and self-control.* (26) *For the king knows about these things, and to him I speak boldly. For I am persuaded that none of these things has escaped his notice, for this has not been done in a corner.* (27) *King Agrippa, do you believe the prophets? I know that you do."* (28) *And Agrippa said to Paul, "Do you expect to make a Christian of me in that short a time?"* (29) *And Paul replied, "I wish to God that, whether short or long, not only you but also all who hear me this day should become such as I am—except for these chains."*

(30) *Then the king rose, and the governor and Bernice and those who were sitting with them.* (31) *And when they had withdrawn, they said to one another, "This man is doing nothing to deserve death or imprisonment."* (32) *And Agrippa said to Festus, "This man could have been set free if he had not appealed to Caesar."*

OUTLINE

1: Introduction
2–23: Paul's speech
24–29: Dialogue of Paul with Festus and Agrippa
30–32: Agrippa, Bernice, and Festus agree among themselves: Paul is innocent

LUKE'S PURPOSE

It seems clear that Luke has created this whole section—except for verse 17b—in order to reiterate—with minor variations—what we already know, and to establish once more that Christianity has a valid claim to public status. It should be noted that this moving oration (verses 2–23) makes no sense whatever in this narrative context: Festus having accepted his appeal to the emperor, he must go to Rome.

Verses 2–8: After currying favor in verses 2–3 (cf. 24:20), verses 4–8 sketch Paul's life and summarize the accusations against him. Luke's Paul is on trial because of Israel's hope (verses 6–7; cf. 28:20; 23:6). Verse 8, like 24:15 before, emphasizes Paul's loyalty to Judaism and its promise (he somewhat misleadingly claims) that God raises the dead (see verse 23).

Verses 9–23: This section is a third telling of the conversion story found in chapters 9 and 22, with "appropriate" variations that indicate Luke's intent. The purpose of verse 11 is not clear. As Dunn writes,

> "Blasphemy" properly speaking was insult to the divine majesty. Luke can hardly mean that Saul tried to force Jewish believers to blaspheme God as such. But he could mean that Saul sought from them a confession which he would then have regarded as blaspheming God, that is, as making claims for Jesus, which detracted from the honour due to God alone (cf. Luke 5.21; Mark 14:62–64). Or, less likely, he tried to force them to deny Jesus as their Lord, and thus to blaspheme against his God-given status and glory, that is, blaspheme in Paul's (but not Saul's) ears. The reference to persecution "even to foreign cities" is equally hyperbolic.[84]

Verse 14b contains the statement, "It is hard for you to kick against the goads." It is a widely used Greek proverb.[85] "Before his conversion he was 'kicking against the goads' and hence he was ruled by madness, whereas after his conversion he speaks the truth and self-controlled wisdom (v. 25)."[86] At the same time, of course, Luke is making the theological point that one struggles in vain against God. In 5:38–39 a similar statement was put into the mouth of Gamaliel. In speaking of an appearance of Jesus to Paul, verse 16b recalls the christophany reported in 9:4–6.[87] Verses 16–18 define Paul's mission to the Gentiles after grounding it in the christophany. In verse 17b the tradition of a call story surfaces. Verse 20 is not so much an appeal to Agrippa as a thinly veiled exhortation to the reader to repent and turn to God.[88] In verse 21 the participle "having seized" is a clear echo of 23:27. Verses 22–23 present a formally developed proclamation about Christ: Paul's teaching contains nothing more than "what the prophets and Moses said would come to pass: that the Christ must suffer, and that, by being the first to rise from the dead, he would proclaim light both to the people and to the Gentiles" (cf. verses 6–7).

Verse 24: It is not by chance that upon hearing the mention of resurrection, the Gentile Festus breaks in on Paul's speech.[89] "Madness is used as a foil for Paul's ready answers in the speech just delivered."[90] It does not refer to Festus's attempt to find a way of freeing Paul for reason of insanity.[91]

Verse 25: For Luke, Paul's preaching is the very paradigm of self-possession (that is, self-control, a completely un-Pauline term). Thus the madness of which Paul is accused by Festus is artistically set in contrast with self-control (in Greek, *sôphrôsynê*), a virtue that Paul embodies.[92]

> Like the proverb in verse 14, the opposition of madness with self-control or sobriety in verse 25 has not gone unnoticed. Indeed, the explicit juxtaposition of *mania* and *sophrosyne* in Xenophon's *Memorabilia* (1.1.16) is often noted. . . . Xenophon is describing Socrates' teaching about self-control and madness in this context of a larger discussion about the moral virtues in general and how the knowledge of these things makes for a gentleman. Luke seems to be offering a similar argument, although in not quite the same systematic way as Xenophon's description of Socrates' teaching. Before Paul's conversion he is 'beside himself' and therefore not a man of virtue. After Paul's conversion he has self-control and is sober and therefore has become virtuous.[93]

Verse 26: Luke's Paul argues that Christianity is not a furtive or underground movement ("This has not been done in a corner"),[94] but open to public scrutiny. "These words light up Luke's presentation in Acts from beginning to end. . . . The entire history of Christianity—it is no secret society!—is enacted publicly and before high and exalted personages."[95]

Verse 27: Agrippa, a loyal Jew, is pictured in the following verse as one all but ready for conversion.

Verses 30–32: When both Agrippa and Festus declare that Paul is not guilty,

Luke's apologetic program has reached its narrative climax. "Paul is explicitly pronounced innocent by the highest authorities he has yet encountered. How Luke could be aware of what the king and the governor said to each other is not explained."[96]

THE TRADITIONS REWORKED BY LUKE

Verses 16–18: In these verses and more specifically at verse 17b an element of a traditional call story surfaces that Luke in Acts 9 has changed into a conversion story (see above, pp. 127–30 for details).

HISTORICAL ELEMENTS

Luke has composed the foregoing narrative on the basis of his theological views. This verdict must be defended against claims of historicity like that of Hemer:

Verses 30–32: Hemer recognizes that "there is no apparent source for the private consultation of Festus with Agrippa," yet still holds, "presumably a verdict in some such terms must in any case have been known to Paul after the *consilium* of the judges."[97] Barrett retorts, "But Festus and Agrippa were not acting as judges; Festus was gathering information for his dossier and Agrippa was indulging a curious whim. Of course, if kindly disposed they may have passed on to Paul the essence of the report that would be sent to the higher court."[98]

> *Rebuttal:* That is a very shaky edifice. To conclude that two people who (contrary to the text) are merely assumed to have consulted together then arrived at a verdict that was totally unnecessary represents a kind of folly rather the opposite of tilting at windmills: Here the windmills are created out of thin air—that is, the desire to believe—and then recommended to us as real.

THE HISTORICAL VALUE OF LUKE'S ACCOUNT

Eventually there remains a trial without prosecutor or witnesses; only the defendant speaks. Both Paul's alleged defilement of the Temple and the charge of being an apostate are forgotten. Still, I. Howard Marshall assumes the historicity of verses 27–28:

> In any case, Paul attempts to call on Agrippa as a witness not only to the facts, but also to the prophetic oracles that Christians interpreted as pointing to Jesus.

If Agrippa was a worshipping Jew he must surely have believed what *the prophets* said—and surely also accept what seemed to Christians to be the only possible identification of the fulfilments of their words. It is not quite clear what led Paul to say "*I know that you believe.*" . . . At most he must be suggesting that Agrippa believed that the prophets foretold the coming of the Messiah. . . . So he answers: "*In a short time you think to make me a Christian!*" The reply is light-hearted, but not ironic. It is Agrippa's attempt to get out of the logical trap in which he is in danger of being caught.[99]

Shall we next be called upon to view the artfully constructed verbal thrusts and parries of Lear and Shylock and assent to their historicity? Moreover, Agrippa was a worldly man and the law of Moses was irrelevant to him where his relationship with his sister Bernice was concerned. Agrippa was certainly not a worshipping Jew. We are dealing with drama, not history.

[58]
ACTS 27:1–44
SEA VOYAGE, SHIPWRECK, RESCUE

(1) And when it was determined that we should sail for Italy, they handed over Paul and some other prisoners to a centurion of the Augustan Cohort *named* Julius. (2) And *embarking* in a ship of Adramyttium, which was about *to sail* to the places along the coast of Asia, we put to sea, Aristarchus, a Macedonian from Thessalonica, being with us. (3) The next day we *put in* at Sidon. *And Julius treated Paul kindly and allowed him to go to his friends to receive their attention.* (4) And putting out to sea from there we sailed under the lee of Cyprus, because the winds were against us. (5) And when we had sailed across the open sea along the coast of Cilicia and Pamphylia, we *came* to Myra in Lycia. (6) There the centurion found a ship of Alexandria sailing for Italy and put us on board. (7) We sailed slowly for a number of days and arrived with difficulty off Cnidus, and as the wind did not allow us to go farther, we sailed under the lee of Crete off Salmone. (8) Coasting along it with difficulty, we came to a place called Fair Havens, near which was the city of Lasea. (9) *Since much time had passed, and the voyage was now dangerous because the Fast had already gone by, Paul* **urged** *them,* (10) *saying, "Sirs, I perceive that the voyage will be with injury and much loss, not only of the cargo and the ship, but also of our lives."* (11) *But the centurion paid more attention to the pilot and to the owner of the ship than to what Paul said.* (12) And because the harbor was not a suitable for wintering, the majority

formed the plan to put out to sea on the chance that somehow they could reach Phoenix, a harbor of Crete that faced both southwest and northwest, and spend the winter there.

(13) Now when a gentle south wind began to blow, they thought it would suit their purpose, and so they weighed anchor and sailed along Crete, close to the shore. (14) But soon a tempestuous wind that was called the northeaster swept down from the land. (15) And when the ship was caught and could not face the wind, we gave way to it and were driven along. (16) Running under the lee of a small island called Cauda, we managed with difficulty to secure the ship's boat. (17) After getting it hoisted up, they used cables to undergird the ship. Then, fearing that they would run aground on the Syrtis, they took in the sail and drifted with the wind. (18) Since we were violently storm-tossed, they began the next day to jettison the cargo. (19) And on the third day they threw the ship's tackle overboard with their own hands. (20) When neither sun nor stars appeared for many days, and no small tempest lay on us, all hope of our being saved was at last abandoned.

(21) *Since they had been without food for a long time, Paul stood up among them and said, "Men, you should have listened*[100] *to me and not set sail from Crete and incurred this injury and loss. (22) Yet now I **urge** you to take heart, for there will be no loss of life among you, but only of the ship. (23) For this very night there stood before me an angel of the God to whom I belong and whom I worship, (24) and he said, 'Do not be afraid, Paul; you must stand before Caesar. And look, God has granted you the lives of all those who sail with you.' (25) So take heart, men, for I have faith in God that it will be exactly as I have been told. (26) But we must run aground on some island."*

(27) But when the fourteenth night came, as we were being driven across the Adriatic Sea, in the midst of the night the sailors suspected that they were nearing land. (28) So they took a sounding and found twenty fathoms. A little farther on they took a sounding again and found fifteen fathoms. (29) And fearing that we might run on the rocks, they let down four anchors from the stern and prayed for day to come. (30) Now the sailors planned to abandon ship, and had lowered the ship's boat into the sea under pretense of laying out anchors from the bow, (31) *but Paul said to the centurion and the soldiers, "Unless these men stay in the ship, you cannot be saved."* (32) Then the soldiers cut the ropes of the ship's boat and let it go.

(33) *As day was about to dawn, Paul exhorted them all to take some **food**, saying, "Today is the fourteenth day that you have continued in suspense and without **food**, having taken nothing. (34) Therefore I exhort you to take some **food**. It is for your health, for not a hair is to perish from the head of any of you."*

(35) *And when he had said these things, he took bread, and giving thanks to God in the presence of all he broke it and began to eat.* (36) *Then they all were encouraged and ate some food themselves.* (37) All together there were 276 persons in the ship. (38a) And when they had eaten enough, (38b) they lightened the ship, throwing the wheat into the sea.

(39) Now when it was day, they did not recognize the land, but they noticed a bay with a beach, on which they planned if possible to run the ship ashore. (40) So they cast off the anchors and left them in the sea, at the same time loosening the ropes that tied the rudders, and hoisting the foresail they made for the beach. (41) But striking a reef, they ran the vessel aground. The bow stuck and remained immovable, and the stern began to break up from the surf. (42) The soldiers' plan was to kill the prisoners, lest any should swim away and escape. (43) But the centurion, *wishing to save Paul,* kept them from carrying out their plan. He ordered those who could swim to jump overboard first and make for the land, (44) and the rest clung to planks or other pieces of the ship. And so it was that all were brought safely to land.

OUTLINE

1–5: Voyage from Caesarea to Myra
6–44: The shipwreck on the voyage from Myra to Malta
      6–8: From Myra to Fair Havens
      9–12: Voyage continued despite Paul's warning of danger
      13–20: Shipwreck
      21–26: Paul encourages those on board
      27–32: Sighting of land; Paul prevents the crew's attempt to flee
      33–38: The meal at sea and the jettisoning of remaining cargo
      39–44: The ship is beached and all are saved

LUKE'S PURPOSE

The voyage to Rome, of course, is much more than an adventure starring Paul the apostle and Roman gentleman. It is also an aretalogy, for protection of those in peril on the sea was an important responsibility of ancient gods, and the voyage gave Paul a chance to show how the new faith could compete. The entire story is a "miracle," but no less interesting for all that. This is one of Luke's major efforts, as style, structure, and length demonstrate. It is therefore legitimate to look to Acts 27 for an intimation of the writer's intentions. They are glorification of the faith, exaltation of its leading exponent, and narration of high adventure. Formally, chapter 27 is a typical episode of a religious novel. Any diary of these events appears to have been drowned in the shipwreck, as it were. Luke has shaped this material. Once again, there is the dilemma of a historian who fails to behave like one.[101]

Verses 1–5: "Italy" in verse 1 stands for Rome (cf. 18:2; 27:6). The special treatment accorded Paul by the centurion Julius recalls 24:23. The theme of Roman respect and friendly treatment for Paul similarly appears in 19:31 and 28:2.

Verses 6–44: Any analysis must deal with the fact that the use of technical nautical expressions is so extensive that we easily lose track of its central concern: the journey of Paul and his companions to Rome. In retrospect, one notes with surprise that Paul is mentioned in only four places—and that "these seem to have been added later to the account of the voyage. Truly literary criticism will lead us to suppose that the nautical description is taken from the numerous accounts of sea-voyages in literature and not from experience."[102]

The four incidents showcasing the apostle are limited to the following verses: (a) 9–11; (b) 21–26; (c) 31, 33–36; (d) 43. In the translation they appear in italics.

(a) + (b) Verses 9–11, 21–26: These two passages portray Paul as a prophet of disaster whose warnings are blithely ignored (verses 9–11) and a foreteller of rescue (verses 21–26) that is assured by divine plan: since Paul is fated to appear before the emperor in Rome (cf. 25:11–12; 21:25–27; 26:32), both he and all his fellow-voyagers have been granted safe conduct (verse 24; cf. verse 44b). Indeed, verses 21 and 26 make specific reference to the earlier warning in verse 10: "You should have listened to me, and should not have set sail from Crete and incurred this injury and loss" (verse 21b). Note also that "to urge" (verse 9) is picked up in verse 22; "life" (verse 10) in verse 22b; and that verse 26 points forward to 28:1.

(c) Verses 31, 33–36: After thwarting the crew's plan to flee the doomed vessel (verse 31), Paul invites all those on board to take food (verses 33–36)—after an incredible fast of two weeks. The awkward parenthesis of verse 37 is apparently an attempt to provide narrative continuity between the taking of food and the improved spirits and renewed activity that resulted. The reported number on board, 276, is an utterly incredible figure; it evidently represents a remnant of whatever stirring saga has been pressed into service as a vehicle for Paul's fateful journey to Rome. Perhaps a report in the original tale about taking sustenance (here in verse 38a) provided Luke with the occasion to include a cameo appear-

ance by his hero (verses 31, 33–36). For a similar literary ploy, see verse 12, a bit of expository narrative that may well have provided the context for Paul's advice in verse 9–11. "Some assume that the sequence, 'took bread, gave thanks to God, and broke it,' must describe a eucharistic act. This is most unlikely. The actions are simply those of a normal Jewish meal, with the blessing and breaking of the bread and its distribution (not mentioned here) as the first act of the meal by means of which all present can share in the blessing of the bread."[103]

(d) Verse 43: After the ship runs aground, the soldiers want to kill the prisoners to prevent their escape (verse 42).[104] But the centurion's concern for Paul (recall his friendliness, reported as early as verse 3) leads him to order that all hands either swim to land or paddle ashore clinging to wreckage. Since the author does not trouble himself to tell us how the intended beneficiary of the centurion's orders managed to get ashore, we are no doubt entitled to conclude with Dibelius that the "story of the centurion's apt decision thus, obviously, has nothing to do with Paul; it belongs to the description of the voyage, and, by the introduction of four words, has been made into an account concerning Paul."[105]

From these four insertions we can derive Luke's underlying agendas:

1. Although a prisoner, Paul is the one person who remains calm, and thereby he in effect has control of the situation. While his first two exhortations (verses 10 and 21–26) were ignored, the third (verses 31, 33–34) gets both a positive reaction (verses 32, 36) and positive results. In Luke's portrait, Paul has become an inspiration to all, and the offering of thanks to God (verse 35) is clearly the climax of the narrative.

2. Luke employs the perils of storm and shipwreck to impress upon the reader his contention that the journey to Rome is part of God's plan: Not even natural disaster can thwart divine providence.

3. That Paul (and all those sailing with him) survive storm and shipwreck is yet another Lukan corroboration of the apostle's innocence of any wrongdoing. The "hero being saved from shipwreck does not surprise the reader of the Greek novel where the rescue from the anger of the waters had become, since the Odyssey, a classic metaphor of divine protection of the righteous."[106] Furthermore, assuming the correctness of my subsequent delineation of the original source material, Acts 27 once again attests to Luke's reliance on Hellenistic literature, an adoptive process no doubt intended to earn the approbation of his Hellenistic readers.

In sum: "With all the clarity one could wish, Luke has prepared his readers for the apostle's appearance before Caesar. But when the moment is approaching, the author of Acts devotes fifty-nine verses (21.1–28.15) to narrating the commotions of the trip to Rome with abundant details on the navigational manœuvres to

which there is no equivalent in Greek literature. Considering the strategic position of the narrative (just a few lines from the end!), the voyage to Rome has a
delaying effect, which must have a specific function with regard to the reader's
expectation."[107] Luke's purpose in this narrative was to give honor to his star and
to Christian worship. "The bright light upon Paul pierces even the condition of
chains and the presence of a storm, and his companions are so minor as to be
anonymous."[108]

THE TRADITIONS REWORKED BY LUKE

Verses 1–5: The names of Julius (the centurion of the Augustan cohort) and
Aristarchus (the Thessalonian Christian) in verses 1 and 2 may have a basis in
tradition. Especially noteworthy is the appearance of the latter at the outset of
this journey, for he was earlier reported (19:29; 20:4) to have accompanied Paul
on the apostle's last journey to Jerusalem. Paul's route from Caesarea via Sidon
and Cyprus to Myra—in which city the Acts of Paul places the apostle as a missionary miracle worker[109]—may also go back to tradition, for unlike the free-
flowing narrative style of the subsequent episode, the report in verse 5 is brief
and to the point. It could equally well derive from Luke, however, and represent
his authorial preparation for the impending journey.

Verses 6–44: With Luke's additions removed, the account of the ill-fated
journey is a coherent whole. Verse 8 (". . . we came to a place called Fair Havens,
near which was the city of Lasea") has such a natural continuation in verse 12
("and because the harbor was not suitable for wintering in, the majority formed
the plan to put to sea from there. . . .") that one may well suggest the temporary
removal of verses 9–11 in order to recognize the original connection. Verse 20
("And when neither sun nor stars appeared for many days, and no small tempest
lay on us, all hope of our being saved was at last abandoned") is picked up by
verse 27 ("But when the fourteenth night came . . . the sailors suspected that they
were nearing land"). For verse 43 see page 335 above.

Although verses 31, 33–36 cannot be neatly detached from the tradition in
the interest of creating a coherent narrative, one should bear in mind the all but
habitual use of the theme of escape (verse 30) in romances. At any rate, the continuity and sequence of the action reported by the tradition is clear: In anticipation of shallow waters as the ship nears land, all hands join in lightening the ship
by jettisoning the remaining cargo that had been retained as ballast.

Whatever Luke's source for this tale of adventure, the present episode is strikingly different from the accounts of voyages in Acts 20:1–21:16 in its detail and
the use of technical nautical terms.[110] The narrative is highly reminiscent of any

number of ancient stories of ocean voyages—which like the present one begin with a first person plural narrative that in places gives way to the third person plural (cf. 27:17).[111] It is unlikely that the account Luke has used bore any relation to the journey from Caesarea to Myra, nor can it be considered an eyewitness account (especially since the "we" is an element of genre in sea-voyage accounts). What we have is rather a literary entity derived from Luke's reading, into which he inserted the person of Paul in the places noted above.[112] Lucian, *De mercede*, 1–2, offers a particularly interesting possibility for a *Sitz im Leben* of this narrative type: The author notes that people sometimes invent stories of deliverance from shipwreck so as to appear favored by the gods and thus to gain people's favor. The only real question is whether Luke appropriated a story wholesale or inventively recast elements garnered from a number of Hellenistic models.[113]

HISTORICAL ELEMENTS

Verses 1–5: If the itinerary here delineated goes back to tradition, it may derive from a report by Aristarchus, and therefore include historically reliable data about Paul's last journey. But considerations noted above, page 336, must lead to nagging doubts. If the stages specified do not reflect tradition, one must necessarily question whether Luke has given the elements of tradition (Aristarchus, Julius of the Augustan cohort) their correct historical setting.

Verses 6–44: Setting aside redactional additions, the contents of these verses come from Luke's reading and therefore are devoid of historical content. Therefore, while one cannot claim total certainty, it seems at the very least unnecessary to join Dibelius in assuming that "whether through Luke's being an eyewitness, or whether by means of someone else's tradition in his possession, the recollection of Paul's stormy journey to Italy"[114] was the occasion for the composition of this voyage. It is highly unlikely that Paul was shipwrecked on Malta while on the way to Rome, but it may well have been a port of call, inasmuch as the account in 28:11–12 is eminently reasonable and may reflect a reliable tradition concerning a journey from Malta to Rome.

THE HISTORICAL VALUE OF LUKE'S ACCOUNT

Haenchen has rightly denied any historical value to Luke's account. He writes,

> Paul was no noble traveler with special authority, but a prisoner accused of inciting to riot. He therefore had no say in any of the decisions. Just those edifying supplements which extol Paul are additions by the author to a journal of

reminiscences which could not report anything special about Paul, but only described the voyage, the danger and the rescue. . . . The unreality of the scene is most easily seen at vv. 21–6: Paul delivers a speech on a pounding ship in a howling storm as if he stood on the Areopagus.[115]

Later, Haenchen aptly points out that the "scenes inserted correspond exactly to the Lucan image of Paul. Paul always stands in the limelight. He is never at a loss for advice. He never despairs. . . . Luke . . . knows only the strong, unshaken favorite of God who strides from triumph to triumph."[116]

Dunn's overall assessment differs,

If the details of the storm and of the desperate measures taken, vivid as they are, do not settle the question of the chapter's historical value, there are others which do suggest that through the storyteller's artistry there are clear historical reminiscences to be detected. We may mention, in sequence: the names of the centurion and his cohort and of Paul's companions (27.1–2); the details of the itinerary, including lesser known place names like Cnidus, Salmone and Cauda (27.7, 16); the name of the "typhonic wind," "Eurakylon (Northeaster)" (27.14); and the numbers involved (27.37). Notable also is the restraint of the storyteller. We read of no overtly supernatural intervention beyond the reassurance provided by an angel in a dream or vision (27.23–24): Luke, who elsewhere delights to draw parallels between Paul and Jesus . . . ignores the opportunity suggested by Luke 8.22–25. No miracle is attributed to Paul beyond the prediction of 27.26; otherwise his advice is simply good sense born of experience (27.10, 31). He is indomitable, but not divine (contrast 28.6).

Dunn continues,

Above all there is the appearance of the storyteller in first person terms ("we"), beginning at 27.1. Some suggest that this too is simply a feature taken over from the genre of sea voyages; but much the most obvious conclusion to draw from the "we" form is that the writer intended his readers to understand that he himself had been present, an eyewitness of and participant in the events described. In fact, therefore, the simplest and most obvious conclusion to draw is that the chapter, as indeed the rest of the book, was written by one who had been a companion of Paul throughout this particular journey, and indeed, all the way to Rome (the final "we" is at 28.16). Where so much remains unclear, the simplest and most obvious solution is probably the best.[117]

Rebuttal: Dunn is much too easily impressed with lists of geographic and meteorological names if on the basis of such he is willing to infer the historicity of an account. And he places altogether too much trust in the verisimilitude created by "the details of the storm and the desperate measures taken." This is especially obvious when we are asked to suppose that practiced seamen who are being driven south-southwest toward Syrtis (verse 17) are apparently oblivious to a wind shift that subsequently drives them almost due west some six hundred miles. One must also suspend a great deal of disbelief to imagine that after fourteen days of drifting helplessly before a raging gale they hit a target not more than ten or twelve miles wide. Even more surprising is his blithe credulity in accepting the report of a sudden burst of energy (verse 38) on the part of men who have had nothing at all to eat for two weeks (verse 33). It appears that he is equally adept at raising the forensic value of equivocal data (or the absence thereof) to near certainty, while at the same time ignoring—or overlooking—obvious details that make a mockery of the claim of historicity. Once again an apparent compulsion to hold fast to an untenable hope subverts the search for truth.

[59]
ACTS 28:1–10
PAUL ON MALTA

(1) Having been brought safely through, we then learned that the island was called Malta. (2) The natives showed us unusual *kindness*, for they kindled a fire *and welcomed us all*, because it had begun to rain and was cold. (3) When Paul had gathered a bundle of sticks and put them on the fire, a viper came out because of the heat and fastened on his hand. (4) At the sight of the snake hanging from his hand, the natives said to one another, "No doubt this man is a murderer. Though he has escaped from the sea, Justice has not allowed him to live." (5) He, however, shook off the creature into the fire and suffered no harm. (6) They were waiting for him to swell up or suddenly fall down dead. But when they had waited a long time and saw no misfortune come to him, they changed their minds and said that he was a god. (7) Nearby were lands belonging to the chief man of the island, named Publius, *who received us and entertained us hospitably for three days*. (8) *Now the father of Publius happened to lay sick with fever* and dysentery. *And Paul visited him and prayed, and putting his hands on him, healed him.* (9) *And when this happened, the rest of the people on the island who had diseases also came and were cured.* (10) *They also honored us greatly, and when we were about to sail, they put on board whatever we needed.*

Outline

1–2:   Safe arrival and friendly reception on Malta
3–6:   Paul suffers no harm despite the poisonous snake bite
7–9:   Paul the miracle worker
  10:   The people of Malta honor Paul and provide for the continuation of the voyage

Luke's Purpose

Theologically, one of the most important features of the Malta episode is what does *not* happen, since nothing is said of Paul preaching and teaching there.[118]

Verses 1–2: Since a hospitable welcome to those who have suffered shipwreck is a common theme in travel accounts, Luke may have taken a literary model for guidance in creating this scene. The kindness shown by the barbarians recalls Paul's favorable treatment by the centurion Julius (27:3). Note that the further fate of the non-Christian shipwreck victims merits no authorial concern: They have suddenly become superfluous bystanders.

Verses 3–6: Here Luke employs a miracle story (with no reference to Jesus) to remind the reader once again of Paul's extraordinary endowments. In significant contrast to 14:11–18, Paul does not trouble himself to repudiate the proclamation of his divinity. The ultimate purpose of this incident is to show yet again that nothing—not even a lethal snake bite—can thwart the divine plan to have Paul bear personal witness to the gospel in Rome.

Verse 7: This introduces the miracle story that is to follow. It reflects the oft-repeated theme of showing Paul in contact with persons from the higher classes. This time it is the "chief man" from the island, Publius. Paul's status as a prisoner does not enter the picture.

> The hospitality accords with the traditions of hospitality of the time, though we should also note that it was limited to three days. Despite the further round of healings (28.8–9), Luke makes no attempt to suggest that Publius continued to entertain Paul for the remainder of their time on the island (three months— 28.11). Luke also continues to focus on Paul, or rather on "us"; the reader is led to assume that the rest of the 276 survivors were given hospitality for an initial period too. Thereafter, presumably, they had to pay for their lodgings.[119]

Verses 8–9: When composing these verses, Luke obviously drew on the incident reported in his gospel, Luke 4:38–41: Note the close correspondences in Luke 4:38/Acts 28:8; Luke 4:40a/Acts 28:9; Luke 4:40b/Acts 28:8.[120] Further, the gospel account reports the healing of a mother, that in Acts, that of a father. The causal nature of the relationship adduced above is further supported by the similar order of events in the two cases: the miracle (Luke 4:38–39/Acts 28:8) followed by a summary and further healings of witnesses and others (Luke 4:40–41/Acts 28:9), following the pattern provided by Mark in 1:29–34. Acts 28:8–9 is therefore to be understood as a composition by the author based on his earlier report in Luke 4:38–41. "A scene from the beginning of Jesus' ministry is echoed in the last description of healing in Acts."[121]

While it may be considerably overstating the case to describe the illness of Publius's father as remarkably detailed, it must be agreed that to the generic expression "fever" (cf. Luke 4:38–39) the author here adds "dysentery." This term, found nowhere else in biblical Greek, is a detail that would normally signal reliance on a tradition, and in this case an eyewitness recollection. Nevertheless it is noteworthy that here, contrary to what one would expect from a traditional source, demonic possession is not adduced, and that Paul's methodology, while it reflects standard practice (prayed and laid on hands; cf. 6:6; 8:15, 17; 13:3), omits any invoking of the name of Jesus (as opposed to 3:6, 16; 4:10, 30; 16:18). Indeed it is Paul himself who performs the healing (note the contrast to 9:34). Can it be that Luke has created a redactional echo of the godlike status Paul and Barnabas achieved (14:11) in the eyes of the people of Lystra?

In Luke's scheme the significance of verses 7–9 is the same as that of verses 3–6: Both showcase Paul's power as a "divine man."

Verse 10: "Honors" do not mean gifts or doctor's fees for the healing but paying respect. "Luke has not suggested that Paul and his colleagues were working in the ordinary sense as doctors, and material needs are seen in the next clause."[122]

The Traditions Reworked by Luke

Verses 3–6: Paul's immunity to the bite of a poisonous snake—and, indeed, the whole story—comes either from Luke's reading[123] (and thus has a basis in secular miracle stories) or from a personal legend about Paul that arose after the events portrayed.[124]

Verse 7: The name Poplius (the Greek form of the Roman *praenomen* Publius) and his identification as the "chief man of the island" may come from a tradition, since that particular title is elsewhere connected with Malta.[125] If Luke was here working from a source, it no doubt related Publius, identified as the chief man of the island, with Paul's stay on Malta.[126] Although this judgment may seem optimistic to those who would assign to Luke's general knowledge elements that have the stamp of tradition about them, such objectors would be hard pressed to explain how Luke could identify Publius as "leading man of the island." Yet, since Luke likes to associate Paul with leading persons in general this argument is not very strong.

HISTORICAL ELEMENTS

Not only might Paul's stay on Malta reflect historically reliable tradition, but since it reportedly occurred during his trip to Rome as a prisoner and no other visit to Malta is possible, the included chronological setting could also be correct. But note that Paul's situation as a prisoner is forgotten. Indeed, this may cast doubt on the historicity of the whole episode.

THE HISTORICAL VALUE OF LUKE'S ACCOUNT

The historicity of the two miracle stories must be rejected. The second is patterned on the first and the first, like many such products of a religious environment, is based solely on the hopes of the first Christians.

Nonetheless Dunn insists,

> The episode with the viper has a circumstantial plausibility, and though Luke uses it to make his own point, his account is very sparse and he makes no attempt to elaborate it (28.3–6). The sequel (28.7–10) recalls the name of the island's leading citizen (Publius) and the detail of the initial illness cured ("dysentry"), and otherwise could well reflect the enthusiasm which reports of Paul's double deliverance and initial healing occasioned; it is told as a rounded out tale complete in itself.[127]

Rebuttal: Thus one far-fetched "incident" is judged credible because it has been succinctly reported and another is promoted via circumlocution to the level of distinct possibility on the basis of a rare medical term and the likelihood that Paul's arrival in Italy was a source of rejoicing to Christians. To elevate such unsubstantiated speculation to the realm of the possible—let alone the probable or certain—is a disservice to historical research.

[60]
ACTS 28:11–31
PAUL'S ARRIVAL IN ROME AND HIS PREACHING IN THE CAPITAL OF THE WORLD

(11) After *three* months we set sail in a ship that had wintered in the island, a ship of Alexandria, with the Twin Brothers as a figurehead. (12) And when we landed at Syracuse we stayed there for *three* days, (13) and from there sailing round arrived at Rhegium. A day later, a south wind sprang up, and on the second day we came to Puteoli. (14a) There we found **BROTHERS** and were invited to stay with them for seven days. (14b) And so we came to Rome. (15) And the brothers there, when they heard about us, came as far as the Forum of Appius and Three Taverns to meet us. On seeing them, Paul thanked God and took courage. (16a) *And when we came into Rome,* (16b) Paul was allowed to stay by himself, with only a soldier to guard him. (17) *After **three** days he called together the local leaders of the Jews, and when they had gathered, he said to them, "**BROTHERS**, though I had done nothing against the people or the customs of **our fathers**, yet I was delivered as a prisoner from Jerusalem into the hands of the Romans. (18) When they had examined me, they wished to set me at liberty, because there was no reason for the death penalty in my case. (19) But because the Jews objected, I was compelled to appeal to Caesar—not that I mean to lay the blame on the (whole) nation." (20) For this reason, therefore, I have asked to see you and speak with you, since it is because of the hope of Israel that I am wearing this chain." (21) And they said to him, "We have received no letters from Judea about you, and none of the **BROTHERS** coming here has reported or spoken any evil about you. (22) But we desire to hear from you what your views are, for with regard to this sect we know that everywhere it is spoken against." (23) So they agreed on a day, and a large number of them visited him at his lodging. From morning till evening he explained and testified to **the kingdom of God**, appealing to both the law of Moses and the prophets in an effort to convince them about Jesus. (24) And some were convinced by what he said, but others would disbelieve. (25) And so they disagreed among themselves, and as they departed, Paul offered one final statement: "The Holy Spirit was right in saying to **your fathers** through Isaiah the prophet: (26) 'Go to this people, and say, You will indeed hear but never understand, and you will indeed see but never perceive. (27) For this people's heart has grown dull, and with their ears they can barely hear, and their eyes they have closed; lest they should see with their eyes and hear with their ears and understand with their heart and turn, and I would heal them.' (28)*

Therefore let it be known to you that this salvation of God has been sent to the Gentiles; and they will listen to it."[128] (30) He lived there two whole years at his own expense, *and welcomed all who came to him,* (31) *proclaiming* **the kingdom of God** *and teaching about the Lord Jesus Christ openly and without hindrance.*

OUTLINE

11–16: Journey from Malta via Syracuse, Rhegium, and Puteoli to Rome. Welcome by the Christian brothers there. Paul's privileges in his Roman captivity: private quarters watched over by a single guard

17–28: Paul meets with the Jews of Rome and proclaims the kingdom of God

30–31: Living at his own expense, Paul preaches unhindered for two years

LUKE'S PURPOSE

Verse 11: The Twin Brothers are the twin sons of Zeus, Castor and Pollux, who were expected to deliver people from distress at sea.[129]

Verses 12–13: "The ship docked in Syracuse for three days, then in Rhegium, and from there it sailed about 230 miles in only two days, with a south wind blowing, to Puteoli, the chief Italian port for overseas shipping at that time."[130]

Verses 14–16: This section is not without tensions, for while verse 14b reports that Paul and his companions have reached Rome ("and so we came to Rome"), verse 16a seems to depict a second arrival. In keeping with verse 16a but clashing with verse 14b, verse 15a reports that representatives of the Christian community met Paul at both the Forum Appii, some forty-three miles from Rome, and Tres Tabernae, about thirty-three miles from the city.

Conzelmann[131] explains the tension by saying that in verse 14b Luke anticipates the arrival in Rome, but he gives no reason for this, and indeed none seems evident. A more likely proposal offered by Haenchen[132] is that verse 14b is part of the travel account and verse 15 is a redactional expansion by means of which Luke intended a parallel to Paul's reception by the Jerusalem church in 21:17. The trouble with this is that Luke makes no further use of the incident, since further contact with the Christian community would have intruded on Paul's conversations with the Jews. (Note the corresponding neglect of the Jerusalem community in Acts 22–26). Verse 16 once again exemplifies Luke's scheme of showing Romans to be generally well disposed to Paul (cf. 27:3 to verse 16 and recall the deferential attitude of the tribune in 21:40a and the centurion's concern in 22:26). Of course, we must not assume that Luke's purpose and the content of the tradition he reworked were always in conflict.

Verses 17–20: In this brief apologia Paul repeats earlier protestations: He has traduced neither his people or his ancestral customs (verse 17; cf. 25:8; 21:21). It was some of his fellow Jews who compelled him to seek safety in an appeal to the emperor rather that be set free by the Romans and be vulnerable to assassination plots (verses 18–19; cf. 25:9–12). It is to secure the future hope of Israel that Paul is in prison.[133]

Verse 21: Although this verse presents the picture of a major split between Roman Jews and Christians as well as a serious difference of opinion between the Jews of Rome and those in Jerusalem, neither of these situations can claim evidentiary or even inferential support. We can, however, see another of Luke's many portraits of Paul as both triumphant missionary to the Gentiles and interpreter of Christianity to the Jews.[134]

Verse 22: That the Jews knew nothing of Paul and only by hearsay of Christianity is all but incredible in view of seemingly unassailable reports that during the reign of Claudius Jewish-Christian riots—instigated by "Christ"—led to an expulsion of Jews from Jerusalem (cf. 18:2). Here Luke may well be redacting tradition so as to portray Paul as the putative founder of the Roman church, but he may be equally interested in establishing that Paul is making a fresh start with a clean slate in relation with the Jews of Rome.[135]

Verse 23: The author is the one who has forged a connection between "kingdom of God" and verbs of testimony and proclamation (cf. on 19:8 and below verse 31). Paul's preaching to Roman Jews is one last recapitulation of the Lukan kerygma. His listeners' reaction is so described as to convey the impression that by and large they are a lost cause.

Verse 24: It may at first seem that the statement, "And some were convinced by his words but others would disbelieve," fails to accord with the subsequent conclusion in verse 28: "Know then that this salvation of God has been sent to the Gentiles: they will listen"—and that verse 24 therefore reflects a tradition. Indeed, verse 24 seems to show a result which does not match the cursing of the Isaiah quotation. On the other hand, 17:4 and 19:9 show similar redactionally created Jewish responses to Paul's preaching. Moreover, the verse stresses the divisive effect of Paul's preaching. It is thus eminently reasonable to understand verse 24 as redactional preparation for the subsequent action.

Verse 25: The Jews demonstrate one more time that they are at variance among themselves. Note the contrast to verse 17: Paul no longer speaks of "our fathers" but of "your fathers." Thus Luke distances Paul from the Jewish people. (Cf. the use of the same technique in the speech of Stephen above, pp. 99–102.)

Verses 26–28: This citation of Isa. 6:9-10[136] is the last of repeated assurances that the gospel will hereafter be preached only to the Gentiles (see 13:46–47; 18:6). Verse 28 is a summary that employs an unmistakably Lukan vocabulary. Conzelmann[137] is correct in saying that as much as we may deplore the historical consequences, the Lukan church is thoroughly Gentile Christian. A different note is struck by J. D. G. Dunn:

> The turn to the Gentiles is *simply* part of God's larger scheme of salvation: the turn to the Gentiles does not imply a rejection of Israel (see also on 13.46–47). In other words, the Lukan Paul is no different than the Paul of Rom. 9–11: the mixed and largely negative response of the Jews to the gospel of Messiah Jesus and the positive response of the Gentiles is *simply* a phase in the larger purposes of God to include all, Jews and Gentiles, within his saving concern.[138]

Similarly, Gerhard Krodel remarks,

> Since Luke did not write "all Gentiles," we must assume that the meaning of all is inclusive of Jews rather than exclusive. In the epilogue Luke did not establish a new Gentile particularism at the expense of the Jews—something that would run counter to his whole narrative.[139]

Yet Joseph B. Tyson observes wisely,

> We must seriously consider the significance of the fact that the third Pauline announcement about going to the Gentiles comes at the very end of the book. Narrative endings carry special weight and often supply just the ingredient that is necessary for a full understanding of the text. In the present case we have a motif that has appeared twice before (Acts 13:46–47; 18:6), with some confusion about its implications. At the end it comes again (Acts 28:28), but now with a sense of finality. On principle, there is no reason to reject the supposition that a text may refer to an event that is beyond the temporal scope of its narrative world. But here the only clear reference is to the reception of the gospel by Gentiles: "they will listen" (Acts 28:28), and nothing further is said about Jewish reception.[140]

Verse 30: The statement that Paul remained two whole years in his quarters seems to presuppose Luke's knowledge "(1) that a change then occurred, and (2) in what it consisted. But Luke does not divulge a thing."[141] The phrase "living at his own expense" may recall 20:33–34. "Luke wants it known that Paul does not take advantage of others."[142] The visitors whom Paul welcomed included "all"— according to codex D also the Jews—but that latter proposal must be excluded.

Verse 31: This verse gives a description of Paul's missionary activity in Rome. As elsewhere, the object of his preaching is the kingdom of God (see above, verse 23). Significantly, the last word in Acts is "without hindrance."[143]

In short, Luke's purpose shines through here. He pictures the people of Rome as at least tolerant of Paul's ministry as well as the Christian message, and seems thus to be advising the Roman state to leave things alone. For Rome to continue its "hands-off" policy toward Christianity is no doubt among Luke's chief desires, and perhaps the central aim of the book's final chapters is to promote this end. Indeed, it is this motive, together with the many echoes we hear from the opening pages of the book, that alerts us to the great care with which Luke has shaped his ending. Further support for this conclusion appears in clearly purposeful omission of any mention of the impending judicial crisis or its outcome. We are told that Paul's imprisonment dragged on for another two years (28:30); but his trial—to say nothing of the possibility of his being found guilty—must be expunged from the record to allow for a properly heroic ending.

By not telling the story of Paul's martyrdom Luke avoided introducing the reader to the ugly side of it. So he did not have to highlight any involvement of false Christian brothers in it or that of Jews.[144] Last but not least, he could also spare the Roman state, whose favor in the present he was constantly currying. "Luke had stressed the church's unity in the power of the Spirit from the beginning, and he had shown that when problems arose they were solved in a spirit of unanimity (cf. 6:1–6; 15:5, 22–29). He would not possibly mar this story at its conclusion."[145]

THE TRADITIONS REWORKED BY LUKE

The final itinerary—from Malta to Rome via Syracuse, Rhegium, and Puteoli—may be part of the tradition.

Verse 15: The note about the reception of Paul by representatives of the Roman Christian community was either part of the traditional report of the journey or an isolated piece. Be that as it may, Luke obviously knew of the existence of the Roman community.

Verses 16b, 30: Descriptions of Paul's imprisonment in Rome likely reflect tradition if only because Luke would seem to have no reason to create this specific information. The datum "two years" is often used to argue for the author's knowledge of later events such as Paul's martyrdom and his apologetic silence on such matters. From hints contained in 20:18–38, one can conclude only that Luke knew of Paul's martyrdom but preferred not to report it. Neither elements of tradition discoverable in the text nor the redactional content indicate when this occurred.

Historical Elements

The tradition is historically accurate in reporting that Paul was transported from Malta via Syracuse, Rhegium, and Puteoli to Rome.

Details of Paul's imprisonment found in the tradition are probably authentic. In accordance with the most lenient sort of detention,[146] the accused was commonly guarded by two soldiers, but in Paul's case, one. Since this form of custody could conceivably allow the prisoner to go about his business, Paul could have practiced his craft and thus paid rent and underwritten the expense of his guard. It should be noted that *enemeinen . . . en idiô misthomati* is almost always translated "in his own rented dwelling," but this translation lacks specific evidential support; the phrase could equally well be translated "at his own expense"[147] or "on his own earnings."[148]

1 Clem. 5:4–7—composed in the late nineties of the first century in Rome and sent to the church in Corinth—allows us to conclude that Paul died as a martyr in Rome:

> (4) Let us set before our eyes the good apostles. Peter, who because of unrighteous jealousy suffered not one or two but many trials, and having given his testimony, went to the glorious place which was his due. (5) Because of jealousy and strife Paul showed the way to win the price of endurance. (6) Seven times he was in bonds, he was exiled, he was stoned, he was a herald both in the East and in the West, he won the noble glory of his faith. (7) He taught righteousness to all the world, and when he had reached the limit of the West he gave his testimony before rulers, and thus passed from the world and was taken up into the Holy Place, the greatest example of endurance.

Clearly this passage displays features of a "rhetorical panegyric modeled on the classical motif of the truly wise man battling in the arena of the spirit."[149] The expression "limits of the West" either stems from the fact that the author concluded from Rom. 15:24–25, 28 that Paul had conducted a mission in Spain (cf. also the use of 2 Cor. 11:23–26 in 1 Clem. 5:6), or it understands Rome as the farthest limit of the West (for the author the westernmost point and the place of Paul's martyrdom are the same).[150] Despite the above rhetorical features and a lack of any description of the circumstances of Paul's death, that he died a violent death in Rome is certain (1 Clement is a letter from the Roman community), since the sentence "he gave his testimony before rulers" refers to his martyrdom[151]—an interpretation that is further confirmed by the clause "he passed from the world," which follows immediately.[152]

The precise date of Paul's martyrdom is unknown. Many propose Nero's actions against the Christians in Rome in 64 CE.[153] But an earlier time cannot be ruled out. Indeed, Paul's appeal to the emperor may have led to a verdict that Paul is guilty; i.e., "his words and deeds were judged to have directly and indubitably diminished and injured the Emperor's person, station and sovereign authority."[154]

If Paul composed Philemon and Philippians in Rome, then these writings could serve as windows to his activity there and the latter would shed light on his local Christian opponents (see Phil. 1:15–17).[155] Unfortunately, it is far from certain that the two letters were written in Rome.[156]

THE HISTORICAL VALUE OF LUKE'S ACCOUNT

> How could he [Luke] have gone on to tell of his [Paul's] execution, having earlier stressed to such a degree the legal correctness of the Roman authorities and their assertion of Paul's innocence?[157]
>
> The fact that Paul was sent as a prisoner to Rome and not set free was historically solely the result of Roman actions; Luke, however, has turned this into a tragic complex of circumstances. In his account Romans often appear as those who save Paul's life; in reality Romans eventually executed him. The most amazing thing is the elimination of the violent expression of Roman rule in the report on the death of Jesus, which in view of the existing tradition can only be said to have been a violent one. Luke could not simply pass over the death of Jesus as he did that of Paul. As he wanted to write a Gospel he had to portray this death. In literary terms, the way which he relieves the Roman authorities of responsibility for the execution of Jesus and the carrying out of the crucifixion, using others instead, is a *tour de force*; in historical and theological terms it is **a monstrosity**.[158]

The ending of Acts is bizarre. Although Luke knows that the Roman state executed Paul, he not only fails to report it but also instead stresses that Paul was privileged by the Romans to preach the gospel without hindrance. (Note that the presence of a Roman guard is mentioned only once in verse 16, while succeeding verses make no reference to him.) These details are interrelated. For one thing, Luke omits the end of the story of Paul, "because it was not edifying,"[159] and for the other, he is eager to underline Paul's freedom to engage in unhindered preaching. Thus he creates a theologically grounded (but deliberately unhistorical) picture of the Roman state in order to secure present and future privileges of unhindered preaching. While this is entirely understandable, it casts serious doubt on Luke's veracity in general and on the credibility of this account. Luke again turns out to be a cunning propagandist with a theological bias.

NOTES

1. Ernst Haenchen, *The Acts of the Apostles: A Commentary* (Philadelphia: Westminster Press, 1971), p. 259.

2. Martin Dibelius, *Studies in the Acts of the Apostles* (London: SCM Press, 1956), p. 134.

3. The reference to the Egyptian cannot be used directly for chronological calculations. Cf. the anachronism 5:36. Against Robert Jewett, *A Chronology of Paul's Life* (Philadelphia: Fortress Press, 1982), pp. 43, 102.

4. "That the tribune voices this suspicion and then lets it drop constitutes the first acquittal of Christendom: the suspicion that Paul belongs in this company is immediately dropped" (Haenchen, *Acts of the Apostles*, p. 622).

5. Ibid., p. 621.

6. Cf. Acts 7:20–22 (of Moses).

7. See my *Paul, Apostle to the Gentiles: Studies in Chronology* (Philadelphia: Fortress Press, 1984), p. 39n72 (bibliog.).

8. See my *Paul: The Founder of Christianity* (Amherst, NY: Prometheus Books, 2002), pp. 91–94.

9. Cf. *idein*, Acts 22:18, with *optasia*, 2 Cor. 12:1.

10. Cf. *auton legonta*, Acts 22:18 [,21], with *arrheta rhemata*, 2 Cor. 12:4.

11. James D. G. Dunn, *The Acts of the Apostles* (Valley Forge, PA: Trinity Press International, 1996), pp. 292–93.

12. Martin Hengel, *Between Jesus and Paul: Studies in the Earliest History of Christianity* (Philadelphia: Fortress Press, 1983), p. 106.

13. Ibid., p. 198n71.

14. Hengel claims that Luke "travelled up to Jerusalem from Caesarea with a party, could stay there for only a few days because of unfavourable conditions and then returned to Caesarea (21.15ff.; 24.11). Chapters 21–24, a vividly written continuous passage, indicates Luke's own view: together with the continuation in chs. 25–28 this is the climax of the whole work which Luke wants to attain in his two volumes and which he hints at a long time before, in the *en hêmin* of the prologue. Whether as a travelling companion of Paul he stayed in Caesarea for the whole of the two years that the apostle was imprisoned there is in my view improbable. . . . Luke then again accompanied the apostle on the journey to Rome (27.1ff.). He may have written his two-volume work some twenty to twenty-five years later, perhaps referring back in the so-called 'source' to earlier notes which he had written himself" (ibid., p. 127).

15. Luke 11:27; Acts 14:11.

16. Joseph A. Fitzmyer, *The Acts of the Apostles: A New Translation with Introduction and Commentary* (New York: Doubleday, 1998), p. 711.

17. Acts 10:1–48.

18. Cf. the portrayals of Gallio in Acts 18:12–17, Felix in 22:24–26, and Festus in 26:24–29.

19. Luke 2:1–5.

20. Luke 3:10–14.

21. For exegetical details see my *Jesus After 2000 Years: What He Really Said and Did* (Amherst, NY: Prometheus Books, 2001), pp. 276–78.

22. Luke 3:13–14.

23. Luke 22–23.

24. See also Acts 3:13.

25. For what follows cf. my *Paul: The Founder of Christianity*, pp. 133–35, which is based on my *Early Christianity According to the Traditions in Acts*, pp. 240–41.

26. Cf. Klaus Wengst, *Pax Romana and the Peace of Jesus Christ* (Philadelphia: SCM Press, 1987), pp. 74–75, 102.

27. C. K. Barrett, The *Acts of the Apostles,* 2 vols. (T & T Clark: Edinburgh, 1994–98), 2:802.

28. On Paul's Roman citizenship see Harry W. Tajra, *The Trial of St. Paul: A Juridical Exegesis of the Second Half of the Acts of the Apostles* (Tübingen: J. C. B. Mohr/Paul Siebeck, 1989), pp. 76–89; Heike Omerzu, *Der Prozess des Paulus. Eine exegetische und rechtshistorische Untersuchung der Apostelgeschichte* (Berlin and New York: Walter de Gruyter, 2002), pp. 17–52 (bibliog.).

29. Haenchen, *Acts of the Apostles*, p. 635.

30. Ibid.

31. Conzelmann, *Acts of the Apostles*, p. 192.

32. Ferdinand Christian Baur, *Paul: The Apostle of Jesus Christ*, 2 vols. (London and Edinburgh: Williams & Norgate, 1875–76), 1:209.

33. Luke employs the same technique in Acts 16:9; 18:9–10; 27:23–24.

34. Cf. Matt. 2:4.

35. A different view is found in Emil Schürer, *The History of the Jewish People in the Age of Jesus Christ (175 B.C.–A.D. 135),* 3 vols., rev. and ed. Geza Vermes, Fergus Millar, and Matthew Black (Edinburgh: T & T Clark, 1973–87), 2:223. The evidence for this claim outside of Acts is missing. "It would be naive to conclude from Jos. *Antt.* 20.202 on the basis of our passage that the commander of a Roman guard had the authority to convene the Sanhedrin" (Haenchen, *Acts of the Apostles*, p. 640).

36. Dunn, *Acts of the Apostles*, p. 202. A generation before Dunn, Haenchen could still write, "No proof should really be necessary that here it is not the historical Paul who speaks. That he 'was circumcised on the eighth day, from the *genos Israel*, of the tribe of Benjamin, according to the law a Pharisee . . . and according to the righteousness of the law blameless,' all that he 'considered a dung' that he might win Christ (Phil. 3.5–9). . . . [Luke] is concerned about . . . the truth that the bridges between Jews and Christians have not been broken. It is Luke's honest conviction that fellowship between Pharisaism and Christianity is in the end possible: the Pharisees also hope for the Messiah, await the resurrection of the dead. In this they are at one with the Christians. Their mistake is only that in this their hope and faith they are not consistent where Jesus is concerned. The resurrection of Jesus, and his Messiahship thereby attested, are not contrary to the Jewish faith" (Haenchen, *Acts of the Apostles*, p. 643).

37. Baur, *Paul: The Apostle of Jesus Christ,* 1:206. Later Baur writes, "All this is in the highest degree improbable, and shows clearly that this whole trial before the Sanhedrim is, in the form in which we have it, a scene arranged by the author of the Acts, in which he does not even take pains to sustain the dignity of the Apostle's character" (p. 209).

38. Haenchen, *Acts of the Apostles,* p. 649.

39. Richard I. Pervo, *Profit with Delight: The Literary Genre of the Acts of the Apostles* (Philadelphia: Fortress Press, 1987), p. 32.

40. Cf. Acts 11:27–30.

41. Barrett, *Acts of the Apostles,* 2:1071.

42. Conzelmann, *Acts of the Apostles,* p. 195.

43. Haenchen, *Acts of the Apostles,* p. 650.

44. Cf. Fitzmyer, *Acts of the Apostles,* p. 729.

45. Luke 23:6. For the juridical background of Felix's question—the question of *forum domicilii* (home province)—see Tajra, *The Trial of St. Paul,* pp. 116–17.

46. Hengel, *Between Jesus and Paul,* p. 120. Though Hengel does not say that Luke—which he takes to be the real name of the author—was the eyewitness, he reasons that Luke was close to the events because he had gone with Paul from Caesarea to Jerusalem (ibid., p. 121).

47. Eduard Schwartz, *Zum Neuen Testament und zum frühen Christentum. Gesammelte Schriften,* vol. 5 (Berlin: Walter de Gruyter, 1963), pp. 165–66.

48. Haenchen, *Acts of the Apostles,* p. 649.

49. Ibid., p. 650.

50. On the historical Felix see Schürer, *History of the Jewish People,* 1:460–66; Omerzu, *Der Prozess des Paulus,* pp. 404–406.

51. Translation from Josephus, *Jewish Antiquities,* Books XVIII–XX with an English translation by Louis H. Feldman, Loeb Classical Library (Cambridge, MA: Harvard University Press, 1969), pp. 477–79.

52. Ibid., p. 487.

53. Verses 6b–8a read: "And we would have judged him according to our law. (7) But the tribune Lysias came and with great violence took him out of our hands, (8a) commanding his accusers to come before you." These verses are clearly inauthentic, however, for the earliest manuscripts do not include them.

54. In Greek, *ek pollôn etôn.* This picks up "much peace" (in Greek, *pollês eirênês*) from verse 2.

55. See Lake/Cadbury, *Beginnings of Christianity,* 4:300 for a parallel instance.

56. Cf. Acts 13:46; 18:6; 20:26; 23:1.

57. For "Way" as a designation of Christianity cf. Acts 9:2; 19:9, 23; 22:6, etc.

58. Conzelmann, *Acts of the Apostles,* p. 201.

59. Cf. Acts 3:6; 5:1–11; 8:18–20; 16:16–24; 19:23–27.

60. Schwartz, *Zum Neuen Testament und frühen Christentum,* p. 161n2.

61. See Haenchen, *Acts of the Apostles,* p. 68.

62. Ibid., p. 659.

63. See Schürer, *History of the Jewish People,* 2:231.

64. Tacitus *Annals* 13.14

65. Josephus *Jewish Antiquities* 20.182.

66. Thus Conzelmann, *Acts of the Apostles*, p. 195.

67. Jewett, *Chronology*, pp. 42–44, on dubious grounds, puts forward another view of the Pallas problem.

68. Schürer, *History of the Jewish People*, 1:465. At least, the editors of Schürer saw no reason to retract his untenable statement as in other cases such as the infamous § 28 "Life and the Law" (ibid., 2:464–87).

69. I. Howard Marshall, *The Acts of the Apostles: An Introduction and Commentary* (Grand Rapids, MI: Wm. B. Eerdmans, 1980), p. 381.

70. Tajra, *Trial of St. Paul*, p. 110.

71. Pervo, *Profit with Delight*, p. 79. See also Pervo's apt general comments: Throughout Acts Paul moved "with equal facility among the ruling class of both Jewish and Roman worlds. He could impress the Areopagus, manipulate the Sanhedrin, and fill the leisure time of Festus and Agrippa (Acts 17; 24; 26). His friends included the most wealthy and snobbish inhabitants of the Roman province Asia (19:31). He was able to convert Sergius Paulus, a senatorial governor, and came near to adding the names of Felix and Agrippa to the baptismal register of the church at Caesarea. His manner of teaching was also dignified. No fees were charged, nor would he resort to use of the streetcorner or marketplace (except at Athens). Magicians despised him. He could stop rioters in their tracks. The style of his life and the circle of his friends qualified Paul as the kind of person one would read about in a letter of the younger Pliny, a sort of Dio of Prusa. Even in custody he shone. The leaders of Philippi hastened to correct their mistreatment. Felix ascertained that his confinement was not too rigorous. The chief citizens of Malta received him and his colleagues as honored guests, their status notwithstanding. Roman officials kept him in a mild form of house arrest (Acts 28). Lesser types all but abased themselves in his interest. The concern displayed by his jailer at Philippi, by Lysias, the tribune who arrested him, and by Julius, his centurion escort to Rome, is touching. . . . The viewpoint of Acts is snobbish and aristocratic: workers are despised, the crowds of unemployed scorned, and only the well-to-do given prominence. . . . The upward mobility of many new religions encourages fictional propaganda about their adherents' social status" (ibid., pp. 78–79).

72. Haenchen, *Acts of the Apostles*, p. 662.

73. Ibid., p. 663.

74. Matthew L. Skinner, *Locating Paul: Places of Custody as Narrative Settings in Acts 21–28* (Leiden and Boston: Brill, 2003), pp. 143–44.

75. For the Lukan significance see Conzelmann, *Theology of St. Luke*, pp. 142–43.

76. Julius Wellhausen, "Kritische Analyse der Apostelgeschichte," *Abhandlungen der Gesellschaft der Wissenschaften zu Göttingen—Philologisch-historische Klasse* n.s. 15, no. 2 (1914), p. 52.

77. Ibid., p. 51.

78. For the legal questions see Henry J. Cadbury, "Roman Law and the Trial of Paul," in *Beginnings of Christianity*, 5:297–338.

79. Haenchen, *Acts of the Apostles*, pp. 668–69.

80. Ibid., p. 669.

81. Conzelmann, *Acts of the Apostles*, p. 206.

82. On the historical Agrippa II see Schürer, *History of the Jewish People,* 1:471–83.

83. Amazingly, Schürer, ibid., p. 475, regards the encounter between Paul and Agrippa with Bernice as historical. He writes, "Although, according to the Acts of the Apostles, Agrippa and Bernice were curious to see and hear Paul (Acts 25:22ff.), to the Apostle's fervent testimony, the king would only reply, 'You think it will not take much to make a Christian of me!' (Acts 26:28); from which it is clear that he was admittedly free from fanaticism, but also from any real involvement in religious questions."

84. Dunn, *The Acts of the Apostles*, pp. 327–28.

85. See Dibelius, *Studies in the Acts of the Apostles*, pp. 188–91; John Clayton Lentz, *Luke's Portrait of Paul* (Cambridge and New York: Cambridge University Press, 1993), pp. 84–86.

86. Lentz, *Luke's Portrait of Paul*, p. 85.

87. Cf. 1 Cor. 15:8 and Acts 9:17. Yet in the latter case the recollection is not an ingredient of Paul's conversion narrative but a part of Ananias's speech.

88. See Conzelmann, *Theology of St. Luke*, pp. 99–101.

89. Cf. Acts 17:31–32.

90. Fitzmyer, *Acts of the Apostles*, p. 763.

91. Against Paul W. Walaskay, *Acts* (Louisville, KY: Westminster John Knox Press, 1998), p. 230. He refers to ancient Roman law that prescribed not only the punishment of rash persons but also their excuse as possibly insane. Walaskay obviously does not think that the historical Festus wanted to excuse Paul but that it was Luke who had the ancient Roman law in mind.

92. At least, that is what Luke says. *Sôphrôsynê* should *never* be attributed to Paul. Paul is a *fanatic*—a character trait that is quite the opposite of *sôphrôsynê* as used in a millennium of Greek literature.

93. Lentz, *Luke's Portrait of Paul*, p. 87.

94. See Wengst, *Pax Romana*, pp. 89–104.

95. Haenchen, *Acts of the Apostles*, pp. 691–92.

96. Barrett, *Acts of the Apostles*, 2:1173.

97. Colin J. Hemer, *The Book of Acts in the Setting of Hellenistic Historiography* (Tübingen: J. C. B. Mohr [Paul Siebeck], 1989), p. 349.

98. Barrett, *Acts of the Apostles,* 2:1173.

99. Marshall, *The Acts of the Apostles*, pp. 369–70.

100. The Greek verb is *peitharchein*, cf. Acts 5:21, 32, where it must be translated "obey."

101. Daniel Marguerat, *The First Christian Historian: Writing the "Acts of the Apostles"* (Cambridge and New York: University Press, 2002), p. 216.

102. Dibelius, *Studies in the Acts of the Apostles*, p. 107.

103. Dunn, *Acts of the Apostles*, p. 341.

104. "The soldiers' plan to kill the prisoners (27.1) was the natural reaction of the

escort; they would be held responsible should the prisoners have escaped (cf. 12.19; 16.27) in the confusion" (Dunn, *Acts of the Apostles*, p. 342).

105. Dibelius, *Studies in the Acts of the Apostles*, p. 205.

106. Marguerat, *First Christian Historian*, p. 72.

107. Marguerat, ibid., p. 216.

108. Pervo, *Profit with Delight*, p. 53.

109. See *New Testament Apocrypha*, revised edition of the Collection initiated by Edgar Hennecke and ed. Wilhelm Schneemelcher, English translation ed. R. McL. Wilson, vol. 2, *Writings Related to the Apostles, Apocalypses, and Related Subjects* (Louisville, KY: Westminster John Knox Press, 1992), pp. 220–23, 248–49.

110. Only in two passages in Acts 20:1–21:16 are there nautical terms: 21:1, *euthydromein* and 21:3, *anaphainein*; *apophortizesthai*.

111. A large number of these, as may be expected, were inspired by the voyages of Odysseus (*Od* 11–12).

112. Given the wealth of instances that Alfons Weiser, *Die Apostelgeschichte*, 2 vols. (Gütersloh: Gütersloher Verlagshaus, 1981–85), 2:660, has adduced, there should no longer be any dispute here. See also B. E. Perry, *The Ancient Romances* (Berkeley: University of California Press, 1967), pp. 326–27.

113. See the massive study by Weiser's student Peter Seul, *Rettung für alle. Die Romreise des Paulus nach Apg 27,1–28,16* (Berlin and Vienna: Philo Verlagsgesellschaft, 2003), pp. 437–59. According to Seul, Luke has composed the whole scene and included the passages about Paul from the outset.

114. Dibelius, *Studies in the Acts of the Apostles*, pp. 7–8.

115. Haenchen, *Acts of the Apostles*, p. 709.

116. Ibid., p. 711.

117. Dunn, *Acts of the Apostles*, p. 335.

118. Beverly Roberts Gaventa, *The Acts of the Apostles* (Nashville, TN: Abingdon Press, 2003), p. 362.

119. Dunn, *Acts of the Apostles*, p. 348. This is a pointless speculation. Besides, "three" is a typically Lukan number.

120. Note that each of the three passages from Luke's Gospel differs from Mark's Gospel that "Luke" had in front of him.

121. Robert Tannehill, *The Narrative Unity of Luke-Acts: A Literary Approach*, 2 vols. (Philadelphia: Fortress Press, 1986–90), 2:342.

122. Barrett, *Acts of the Apostles*, 2:1226.

123. See Dibelius, *Studies in the Acts of the Apostles*, p. 8n16.

124. Cf. the commentaries on Acts.

125. Alfred Wikenhauser, *Die Apostelgeschichte und ihr Geschichtswert* (Münster: Aschendorff, 1921), pp. 343–46.

126. As an analogy cf. Acts 18:12–17.

127. Dunn, *Acts of the Apostles*, p. 345.

128. Verse 29 ("And when he had said these words, the Jews departed, holding much dispute among themselves") does not belong to the original text; it is a later addition.

129. See Lucian *Navig.* 9; Epictetus 2.18.29.

130. Krodel, *Acts*, p. 482.

131. Conzelmann, *Acts of the Apostles*, p. 224.

132. Haenchen, *Acts of the Apostles*, p. 719.

133. See Acts 23:6; 24:15.; 26:6.

134. See Barrett, *Acts of the Apostles*, 2:241–42.

135. Ibid., p. 1242. Roloff, *Apostelgeschichte*, p. 372, differs: Luke is silent about the community because he knows that its relationship to Paul was not clear.

136. In Luke 8:10 the Third Evangelist omitted the quotation from Isa. 6:10 which he read in Mark 4:11.

137. Conzelmann, *Theology of St. Luke*, pp. 145–50.

138. Dunn, *Acts of the Apostles*, p. 356. Italics added.

139. Krodel, *Acts*, p. 507.

140. Joseph B. Tyson, *Luke, Judaism, and the Scholars: Critical Approaches to Luke-Acts* (Columbia: University of South Carolina Press, 1999), p. 145.

141. Haenchen, *Acts of the Apostles*, p. 726.

142. Gaventa, *Acts*, p. 368.

143. In Greek, *akôlytôs*.

144. See Tajra, *Martyrdom of St. Paul*, p. 84.

145. Krodel, *Acts*, p. 487.

146. Tajra, *Trial of St. Paul*, p. 181.

147. Ibid., pp. 191–92.

148. Lake and Cadbury, *Beginnings of Christianity,* 4:348

149. Günther Bornkamm, *Paul* (New York: Harper & Row, 1971), p. 105.

150. See Andreas Lindemann, *Die Clemensbriefe* (J. C. B. Mohr/Paul Siebeck, 1992), p. 39.

151. Cf. 1 Tim. 6:13.

152. See Bornkamm, *Paul*, pp. 105–106.

153. See Tacitus *Annals* 15.44; Suetonius *Caesars. Nero* 16.

154. Harry W. Tajra, *The Martyrdom of St. Paul* (Tübingen: J. C. B. Mohr/Paul Siebeck, 1994), p. 4.

155. See my *Opposition to Paul*, pp. 103–109.

156. The majority of scholars today favors Ephesus as the place where Paul wrote Philippians (or parts of it) and Philemon, and so do I.

157. Wengst, *Pax Romana*, p. 95.

158. Ibid., p. 97. My emphasis in boldface.

159. Barrett, *Acts of the Apostles*, 2:1249. Haenchen, *Acts of the Apostles*, p. 732, suggests that Luke has chosen not to relate Paul's execution because he did not want to enhance devotion to Christian martyrs. Other possibilities are listed by Barrett, ibid.

chapter V
CHRONOLOGICAL CHART OF PAUL'S LIFE AND OF PRIMITIVE CHRISTIANITY FROM 30 TO 70 CE

*P*reliminary note: At the beginning a word of caution is necessary. For reasons that will immediately become clear we must be ready to take into account chronological uncertainties ranging between two and four years. The chronology outlined below presupposes the absolute priority in chronological matters of Paul's authentic letters over the book of Acts. It assumes 30 CE as the date of Jesus' death, three years as a probable interval between Jesus' death and Paul's conversion and a one-year stay of Paul in Arabia. Furthermore, it is based on the assumption that Paul's mission in Greece preceded the Jerusalem conference.[1] The main reasons for this far-reaching thesis are as follows:

(a) In Phil. 4:15 Paul explicitly states that the mission in Macedonia and Achaia was the (real) beginning of his preaching;[2]

(b) Acts 18 contains the tradition of two visits of Paul, one of which can be dated to 41 CE and the other to 51 CE.[3]

(c) After the removal of their incorrect chronological settings, the stations in Acts can be related to Paul's journeys, since they follow from a critical reading of Paul's letters.

(d) At the Jerusalem conference in 48 CE Paul promises to organize a collection for the Jerusalem congregation. Since we can follow the progress of a collection for the Jerusalem congregation in the Pauline letters Romans, 1

Corinthians, 2 Corinthians, and Galatians,[4] the conclusion may be drawn that these refer to one and the same collection and that indeed Paul embarked on a collection journey in his churches so as to live up to his commitment. In that case he must have founded these congregations prior to the conference of Jerusalem in 48 CE, for otherwise his promise to collect money from them does not make sense. The only way to avoid such a conclusion would be to assume that a previous collection had come to a halt and was then—after the founding of the above congregations—started again. But that introduces quite a few unknown factors.[5]

30	Crucifixion of Jesus. Visions of the risen Jesus by Cephas (1 Cor. 15:5), the Twelve (1 Cor. 15:5), more than five hundred brothers (1 Cor. 15:6; Acts 2), James (1 Cor. 15:7), all the apostles (1 Cor. 15:7)
31	Killing of the Hellenist Stephen. Expulsion of his followers from Jerusalem. They found congregations as far distant as Damascus.
33	Conversion of Paul in or near Damascus; one-year stay in Arabia; return to Damascus (for one year)
35	Paul's first visit ("Cephas-visit") to Jerusalem (Gal. 1:18). Journey to Syria and Cilicia (Gal. 1:21); mission there and in South Galatia together with Barnabas (Acts 13–14). Conversion and circumcision of Timothy (Acts 16:1–3)
38	Independent mission in Europe: Philippi (1 Thess. 2:2; Acts 16:12–40), Thessalonica (Phil. 4:16; Acts 17:1–9); failure in Athens (Acts 17:16–34; 1 Thess. 3:1)
39–40	*Emperor Caligula plans to have his statue erected in the Jerusalem temple.*
41	*The decree of Emperor Claudius regarding the Jews*
41	In Corinth Paul meets the couple Aquila and Priscilla and works with them. He stays in Corinth for eighteen months (Acts 18:11): Composition of 1 Thessalonians
43	*Persecution of the church in Jerusalem by Herod Agrippa I.* Death of James son of Zebedee (Acts 12:2). Peter escapes from prison and leaves Jerusalem (Acts 12:17)
Circa 44	Founding of Galatian congregations in the north of the Roman province (Gal. 3:1; Acts 16:2),[6] due to an illness (Gal. 4:13)
48	Incident at Antioch (Gal. 2:11–14; Acts 15:1–2)—or immediately after the Jerusalem conference

48	Paul's second visit to Jerusalem ("conference-visit"): the Jerusalem conference (Gal. 2:1–10/Acts 15:6–29), followed by the journey to the Pauline congregations for the organization of the collection
49	Paul for the second time in Galatia; organization of the collection there (1 Cor. 16:1)
49–53	Paul in Ephesus (1 Cor. 15:32; 16:8; Acts 19)
49	Sending of Timothy to Macedonia and Corinth (1 Cor. 4:17); the previous letter to the Corinthians (1 Cor. 5:9–10) with instructions about the collection (or else the instructions were sent by messenger)
50–51	Timothy in Macedonia
51–52	*Gallio proconsul of Achaia*
51	(spring): Letter from the Corinthians with questions regarding the collection (or else the questions were delivered orally) (1 Cor. 16:1)
51	(around Easter): Composition of the First Letter to the Corinthians
51	(between Easter and summer): Timothy in Corinth
51	(summer): After Timothy's bad news about Corinth upon his return to Paul in Ephesus, short intervening visit of Paul to Corinth (cf. 2 Cor. 2:1; 12:21; 13:2); "Paul before Gallio" (Acts 18:12–17); precipitate return to Ephesus; "letter of tears" (2 Cor. 2:3–9; 7:8–12); sending of Titus to Corinth
51–52	(winter): Paul in danger of his life (imprisonment in Ephesus, 2 Cor. 1:8); composition of Philemon and of Philippians (or else composition of both letters in Rome between 58 and 60 CE)
52	(spring): Paul's journey with Timothy from Ephesus to Troas (2 Cor. 2:12); further journey to Macedonia
52	(summer): Arrival of Titus in Macedonia from Corinth (2 Cor. 7:6–7); bad news from Galatia; composition of 2 Corinthians 1–9; 10–13 and Galatians; sending of Titus with parts of 2 Corinthians to Corinth in order to complete the collection
52–53	(winter) Paul in Macedonia; completion of the collection there
53	(spring/summer): Journey of Paul with Macedonian escorts to Corinth; completion of the collection there (Rom. 15:26)
53–54	(winter): Paul in Corinth; composition of Romans
53–55	*Felix procurator in Judea* ("two years": possibly in Acts 24:27)
54	(spring): third Journey of Paul to Jerusalem in order to deliver the collection ("collection visit," Rom. 15:25; Acts 21:17–19)

55–62	*Festus procurator in Judea*
55–57	Imprisonment of Paul in Caesarea (possibly in Acts 24:27)
57	Journey as a prisoner to Rome (Acts 27)
58–60	Paul a prisoner in Rome (Acts 28:14–31)
60	Paul's execution by the Romans (or else during the general persecution of Christians in Rome under Nero in 64 CE (Tacitus *Annals* 15.44.2–5); cf. 1 Clement 5
62	Execution of James, the leader of the Jerusalem church, upon the order of the High Priest Ananus (Josephus *Jewish Antiquities* 20. 197–203)
70	Destruction of Jerusalem by the Romans

NOTES

1. See my *Paul: The Founder of Christianity* (Amherst, NY: Prometheus Books, 2002), pp. 23–64. This thesis—though still a minority view—has found increasing support in recent years. Apart from the references given in the aforementioned book, see now the explicit assent by Karl Paul Donfried, *Paul, Thessalonica, and Early Christianity* (Grand Rapids, MI: Wm. B. Eerdmans, 2002), p. xxvii. I hasten to add that the American scholar John Knox (1900–1990) was the first to place Paul's mission in Greece before the Jerusalem conference. See John Knox, *Chapters in the Life of Paul*, ed. Douglas A. Hare, rev. ed. (Macon, GA: Mercer University Press, 1987); Knox, "Reflection," in *Cadbury, Knox, and Talbert: American Contributions to the Study of Acts*, ed. Mikeal C. Parsons and Joseph B. Tyson (Atlanta: Scholars Press, 1992), pp. 107–13. John Knox was so kind as to write a foreword to my *Paul, Apostle to the Gentiles: Studies in Chronology* (Philadelphia: Fortress Press, 1984), pp. xiii–xiv. Knox regards the book as "the first full-length, full-bodied, and fully documented study of Paul's apostolic career which is based solely on the letters" (ibid., p. xiii).

2. See above, p. 211.

3. See above, pp. 236–37.

4. Philippians, 1 Thessalonians, and Philemon do not mention the collection.

5. On the "temporary cessation" of the collection, Georgi reasons, "Paul's interest had probably declined in the wake of the frictions within the Antiochene congregation, his separation from Barnabas, and, possibly, the temporary break-up with Antioch as a whole" (Dieter Georgi, *Remembering the Poor: The History of Paul's Collection for Jerusalem* [Nashville, TN: Abingdon Press, 1992], p. 46).

6. Indeed, similarities of Galatians to 2 Cor. 10–13 and Romans render the "north Galatia hypothesis" likelier than the "south Galatia hypothesis." See my *Paul, Apostle to the Gentiles*, pp. 85–86.

chapter VI
THE REAL VALUE OF LUKE'S ACCOUNT IN ACTS FOR PRIMITIVE CHRISTIANITY BETWEEN 30 AND 70 CE

I have linked Eusebius of Caesarea with Acts because he follows essentially the same kind of method. Just as Luke writes an account of the triumph of the gospel through the figures he selects, so Eusebius writes a history of the divine truth, as it meets resistance, conflict and persecution. There are good guys and bad guys: the good are bishops, Christian teachers and martyrs; the bad are heretics, evil emperors and—of course, sadly and horrifically an inevitable development—the Jews. Again, the ground plan is straight-line and simple. And of course straight-line and simple ground plans can be communicated very well. They are easily remembered and are extremely influential. But they have their victims. The first and main victim, of course, is the truth. The simple approach fails to represent the complexity of events as they were.[1]

LUKE'S THEOLOGICAL PRESUPPOSITIONS

(a) The Holy Spirit is instrumental in salvation history.

(b) All things are predetermined by the will of God.

(c) The spread of the Primitive Christian mission is unstoppable.

(d) Roman power is sympathetic to Christianity. (A corollary of this is that any pro-Roman traits or characterizations in Acts and the third Gospel are open to historical doubt.)

(e) The unbelieving Jews will go to any lengths to thwart Christian goals and purposes. (As with the previous statement, any negative statement about them is likewise open to historical doubt.)

WHERE LUKE WAS RIGHT

(a) At the beginning of Primitive Christianity, the Jerusalem community played an important role.[2]

(b) Paul was a key figure for the mission, expansion and shaping of Primitive Christianity. Luke rightly devotes more than half of Acts to him.

WHERE LUKE WAS WRONG

(a) Luke has misrepresented Paul's relationship to the Jerusalem community.

(b) Luke has misrepresented Paul's theology.

(c) Luke's description of Paul's actions is in part miraculous, in part false, and deceptively incomplete.

(d) Luke makes Peter appear Pauline and Paul appear Petrine.

(e) Luke places Paul's major mission immediately after the Jerusalem conference (Acts 15). In reality it had started long before the Jerusalem conference—indeed at least a decade earlier.[3]

(f) Since the inner and outer growth of the communities is divinely assured, Luke presumes that strong affirmations of extraordinary growth do not demand sources

WHAT IS MISSING IN ACTS

(a) Granted that Luke's narrative on the various missionary places is unbalanced, it is a strikingly obvious omission that he fails to say anything about the real beginnings of Christianity in Galilee, Northern Galatia, Rome, and Egypt. Instead he spends sixty verses—most of them the purest fiction—on the sea voyage to Rome.

(b) "Acts is full of loose ends, the existence of which even its author cannot disguise, and raises questions which he does not seek to answer. There are troublesome figures like Apollos, and the disciples in Ephesus who had never heard about the Holy Spirit."[4]

WHY ACTS CANNOT PROFITABLY BE READ WITHOUT THE AUTHENTIC LETTERS OF PAUL

(a) Acts presents an inaccurate chronology of Primitive Christianity between 30 and 70 CE.

(b) The routes reported in Acts are partly inventions, partly duplications, and commonly misplaced in time. Paul's letters allow us to reconstruct the real chronological place of his missionary journeys and to rightly integrate the valuable itineraries of Acts into a chronology that is solely based on the Pauline letters.

(c) In many cases Acts not only fails to provide solutions to the enigmas of the letters, but further complicates these enigmas.

RESULT

By interweaving history and legend, Luke confused facts, fiction, and faith. He blended historical and suprahistorical fact, thereby falsifying history for the sake of piety, politics, and power. This was clearly an offense against the rules of critical historiography even in his day. This evaluation is neither intended as denunciation nor rooted in skepticism. After all, the issue before us is a matter not of taste, but of truth. Indeed, it is my close and critical inquiry into the details of Acts that has, as it were, obliged me to formulate such a harsh verdict—one which I hereby present for the process of verification and criticism that is inherent in public discourse.[5]

NOTES

1. John Bowden, "Appendix: Ideologies, Text and Tradition," in Gerd Lüdemann, *The Unholy in Holy Scripture: The Dark Side of the Bible* (Louisville, KY: Westminster John Knox Press, 1996), pp. 159–60.

2. Unfortunately, in some quarters the criticism of Acts has turned into a total neglect of it as a source. See Burton L. Mack, *The Christian Myth: Origins, Logic, and*

Legacy (New York and London: Continuum, 2001). Reporting about meetings of a seminar of North American scholars, Mack writes, "The notion of a 'first Church in Jerusalem' was thoroughly analyzed and found wanting. . . . The 'reports' of Paul and the narratives of Luke both use the diaspora perspective to great rhetorical advantage. . . . Thus the emergence of a Christian congregation in Jerusalem in the immediate wake of the gospel story of Jesus needs to be deleted from the traditional imagination of Christian origins. There is absolutely no evidence for it" (pp. 209–10).

3. If this thesis should turn out to be incorrect, most of my objections to Luke's historical work would nonetheless remain intact.

4. Bowden, "Appendix," p. 159.

5. Thus I have arrived at a result that differs—as far as Acts is concerned—from that of Barbara E. Organ, *Is the Bible Fact or Fiction? An Introduction to Biblical Historiography* (New York and Mahwah, NJ: Paulist Press, 2004). After dealing with Acts, 1 and 2 Maccabees, Deuteronomistic History, and Joshua/Judges, she concludes her volume with the following assessment: "As historiography, the biblical books cannot be assessed against modern standards of accuracy, evidence, and impartiality, but they can be assessed against the standards of their own eras. In that context, the biblical histories stand up well. The more we read them in their own literary and historical contexts, the more we realize their creativity and integrity, their complexity and richness" (p. 170). Note that the last sentence smacks not of critical discourse, but of confessional or even devotional rhetoric.

chapter VII
A BRIEF NARRATIVE OF PRIMITIVE CHRISTIANITY FROM 30 TO 70 CE

IN RETROSPECT: JESUS' PROCLAMATION OF THE KINGDOM OF GOD AND THE CIRCUM- STANCES OF HIS DEATH

Under the Roman prefect Pontius Pilate[1] Jesus was crucified on a Friday in the spring of about 30 CE. At or just after his arrest, the male disci- ples who had traveled with him from Galilee to Jerusalem—apparently to share a never-to-be-forgotten Passover—abandoned him and fled in fear back to their native Galilee. Several women who were part of that same entourage were more tenacious. They remained as near as possible, though of course they could not prevent his fate. Among them, we may be sure, was a woman named Mary from the Galilean fishing village of Magdala.

The reason why the Roman authorities executed Jesus is clear. He was one of many troublemakers—and one with apparent royal pretensions—who must be permanently put out of action. Besides, members of the Jerusalem priesthood appear to have lodged false political charges against him as a result of perceived eschatological and messianic aspirations that may have included a claim to be the long-awaited Son of Man and certainly involved his teaching or even proclama- tion of something he called the kingdom of God.

Although Jesus and his disciples rejected the radical theocratic program of Judas the Galilean,[2] their advocacy of a form of ethical radicalism was influenced by Judas's message of an in-breaking of God's kingdom leading to God's exclusive rule. To be sure, Jesus never proposes an explicit choice between God and the emperor; but then, he rarely makes political statements. Any teaching that might impinge on political realities was expressed in terms of symbolic action. We need think only of his assignment of twelve fishermen to rule over Israel, the contrast between the report of his humble approach to Jerusalem and the typical entry of the Roman governor surrounded by the pomp and panoply of power, or his use of the image on a coin to comment the fiscal rights of the empire. However subtle the political import of these token performances, the clear subtext of the proclamation of God's kingdom is the presentation of a stark ultimatum: God or the emperor. If God indeed rules, any apportionment of authority must be at best provisional; no other power can pretend to reign beside him.[3]

Moreover, Jesus' cleansing of the Temple[4] must have alerted the Jerusalem priesthood. As such it may have been a symbolic deed referring to something beyond. Jesus intended a symbolic overthrow of the Temple. His deed had in view neither reform nor the prevention of further pollution. Rather, he wanted to make room for a completely new Temple, one that was eschatological and thus granted by God. Yet, anything that could be interpreted as a threat against the present Temple outraged the Jerusalem priesthood and afforded them a pretense to take action against a possible offender.

The condemnation and death of Jesus occurred on a single day. Next day was the Sabbath, which that year fell on the first day of the Passover feast. This raised the problem of what to do with the body of Jesus, for Jewish law and custom forbade leaving a corpse on the cross overnight. Even more offensive to Jewish sensibilities, of course, would be its remaining there on a Sabbath, especially when that was also the first day of Passover. For whatever reason, the Roman authorities apparently gave permission for Jesus' body to be taken down from the cross. Perhaps the Jewish leadership entrusted Joseph of Arimathea to place the body in a tomb; perhaps persons unknown to us buried the corpse elsewhere. At any rate, as far as the Roman and Jewish authorities were concerned, that ended the matter.

Completely unknown are Jesus' thoughts and feelings in his last hours. The words attributed to him during the trial and on the cross are certainly creations of the Christian community, since none of his followers were present to hear and pass them on; moreover, they are variously reported and clearly reflect the agendas of the several evangelists. Of these it is Luke who puts the most daring words into Jesus' mouth—promising the criminal on his right side a place with him in paradise on the very same day, asking God to forgive his enemies, and finally commending his own spirit into his Father's hands. The theology of glory and the sovereignty of Jesus expressed in his last sayings on the cross can be followed like a scarlet thread throughout Acts. Indeed, Luke will create many parallels between Jesus and the heroes we meet throughout Acts.

HOW THE DISCIPLES MANAGED TO OVERCOME THE DISASTER OF GOOD FRIDAY

For Jesus' disciples his death was so severe a shock that it required an explanation proportionate to their devastation. The process of reconceptualization began in Galilee and was marked by visions that involved admonitions and interpretations. The disciples' propensity toward phantoms is backed by several reports in the Gospel tradition.[5] Not long after Good Friday, Peter experienced a vision of Jesus that included auditory features, and this event led to an extraordinary chain reaction. Peter reconstituted the circle of the Twelve in Galilee, apparently modeling the fellowship on that founded by Jesus. This regathering reflected the hope—which may also have been Jesus'—that at the imminent arrival of the kingdom of God, the twelve tribes of Israel would be fully represented.

The disciples had, after all, followed Jesus to Jerusalem yearning for and perhaps half expecting the advent of that "kingdom," the arrival of which was somehow intertwined in their minds with the message and example of their Master. At first his crucifixion and death had destroyed their hope, but these appearances rekindled, then fulfilled, and at last even surpassed it. The kingdom of God had begun, though differently from the way the disciples had originally expected it.

Peter experienced Jesus' appearance to him as reacceptance by the one whom he had thrice repudiated; the other disciples experienced it as forgiveness for their desertion. Peter had seen and heard Jesus. Naturally the content of the vision and the attendant audition was passed on to others, and the news swiftly spread that far from abandoning Jesus in death, God had indeed taken Jesus to himself. To this may well have been added—at first, perhaps as a merely speculative notion—the report that Jesus would soon be appearing as the Son of Man on the clouds of heaven. That created a new situation, and the circle around Jesus embarked on a tremendous new venture. Now the women and men who had attached themselves to Jesus could return to Jerusalem and there take up the work their master had left unfinished: to call on both the people and the authorities to undergo a change of heart and mind. (This may well have been seen and proclaimed as the very last reprieve that God would offer.) The first vision of Peter proved formally infectious, and was reportedly followed by others—one to the Twelve, and another to more than five hundred at one time. At this point, at least, any non-ecstatic interpretation comes to grief.

We must fully take into account the dynamic power of such a beginning. It was so compelling that the natural brothers of Jesus were caught up in the excitement, and went to Jerusalem; James even received an individual vision[6]—the same James who had shown little if any affinity with his brother during Jesus' lifetime, and seems likely to have participated in Mark's reported attempt to have his "crazy" brother put away.[7]

A number of concurrent and mutually supporting elements can be identified in the earliest Christian experience. In addition to the personal visionary encounters with the "Risen One," we find the recurrence of three powerful historical themes galvanizing the community's faith: (1) the act of breaking bread together enabled the members to recapture the presence of the Master who had been so cruelly killed but was now so wonderfully restored; (2) recalling his words and works at table and in worship set him again in their midst; and (3) the messianic promise of scripture, and especially the familiar Psalter hymns, now took on new meaning as expressions of the present reality of the exalted Son of Man.

THE RISE OF THE HELLENIST FACTION OF PRIMITIVE CHRISTIANITY IN JERUSALEM AND ITS EXPULSION

Even at this earliest stage, the movement took on new dimensions when Greek-speaking Jews in Jerusalem joined, perhaps in the aftermath of Christ's appearance to the more than 500 brothers at one time at the feast of the weeks (Pentecost).[8] Bilingual disciples may have talked to and converted them.[9] They in turn newly interpreted the words of Jesus in the context of the experience of the Spirit and an imminent expectation that led them to break through the intense traditional link with Torah and cult.[10] Yet the hostile reaction of the Temple priests was only a matter of time, and in one resulting altercation one of the Hellenist leaders was killed. Thus the Hellenists were forced out of Jerusalem and began to spread the message about Jesus—as their inclusion of Gentiles caused it to be interpreted and practiced—to cities like Damascus, Antioch, and Caesarea. As Luke indicates, they were the first to transfer Primitive Christianity from the village to the city and to change the new faith "from a basically rural and rustic sect whose founders were Galilean 'backwoodsmen' into an active and successful city religion."[11]

THE ITINERANT MISSIONARIES AND THE FORMATION OF THE SOURCE Q

The itinerant activists—another group of followers of Jesus—who did not make it into the book of Acts remained within the rural areas.[12] Indeed, Jesus' ethical radicalism found a welcome home in their ranks. In matters economic, his radical message is explicit in the choice he offers between God and mammon.[13] Jesus' deprecation of wealth and the wealthy is harsh to the point of exaggeration: no rich person can find salvation;[14] anyone who aspires to be his follower must first sell all his possessions.[15] Those who in effect had nothing might understandably bid farewell to home and family, and aspire to the spiritual exaltation of life without employment, possessions, or even means of defense. The demand for asceticism marks earliest Christianity as a movement recruited from among the dispossessed and having a strongly countercultural ethos. Yet since the ideal of an exalted and universal ethic was inherent from the outset, Primitive Christianity may be said to have had a dual spirit: while seeking to exit or overthrow a corrupt society, it strove to establish the highest ethical principles. The faithful must overthrow one set of values and conform to another.

In the ethical stance of Jesus and his immediate followers, then, we see both implicit resistance to political power and an explicit moral rebuke to their own people. And this ethical radicalism may have been resurrected and reformulated by political struggle as early as the first generation after Jesus' death; for Q seems clearly to reflect a sharp challenge to the itinerant radical ethos. At three points it departs from the relatively formulaic presentation of sayings to narrate Jesus' temptation,[16] the healing of the centurion's servant,[17] and the cure of the mute demoniac that is followed by Jesus' explanatory remarks about Beelzebub.[18] A number of scholars believe these accounts to be related, and to reflect editing of Q.

The mountaintop climax of the temptation story can easily be imagined to constitute an allusion to Caligula's attempt in 39/40 CE to place his statue in the Temple.[19] This crisis could well have challenged the fledgling movement both to reassess its radical ethic and to compile a written collection of its traditions. In short, this important introductory narrative suggests the historical provenance of this early collection of prophetic sayings. The story about the centurion whose trust amazed Jesus would then offset the antiestablishment screed by portraying the acknowledgment of Jesus' authority by a ranking representative of the empire. The saying about Beelzebub can then be seen as yet another counter-march to highlight the imperial conflict between Satan God, and the exorcism as a vivid example of Jesus' dominion over the world. Where Jesus confronted those in power with symbolic deeds, the writers who are formulating the con-science of the early movement deal in myth. Thus Roman imperial power was seemingly parodied in the mountaintop posturing of Satan.[20]

HOW PAUL, A PERSECUTOR OF THE CHURCH, TURNED INTO A MISSIONARY OF THE GOSPEL

Paul, from the great city of Tarsus in Cilicia, is rightly regarded as one of the most influential figures in the Christian West. He was at once a Jew, a Roman, and a Christian. Above all, he saw himself as an apostle called personally by the risen Jesus to take the Gospel to the Gentile world. He was born around the same time as Jesus, but some four hundred road miles north of his master's native Galilee. He was a Diaspora Jew and had inherited Roman citizenship from his father. As a result, he had a share in both the Jewish and the Greco-Roman worlds. Certainly some restrictions were imposed on contact with Greeks, and we cannot be sure that Paul studied the Greek classics. However, he did receive a basic education, mediated through Hellenistic Judaism, which included instruc-tion in the Greek language and rhetoric. At the same time, elements of his ances-tral culture remained, and were reflected many years later in his letters. Paul went to the theater, followed the contests in the arena, and witnessed philosophical dis-putations in the market place. In other words, he was imbued with the breadth and beauty of the Hellenistic world and its innate rational temper as well. Even as a child, Paul may have been prompted to wish that one day he might become part of this great cosmos.

Nonetheless, from his ancestral religion he gained both a sense of belonging and the knowledge of its exclusiveness. He learned by heart large parts of the Holy Scripture in Greek (the Septuagint). He was no average member of his ancestral religion, but someone who took seriously the God who had chosen Israel and given it the commandments by which to live. No wonder, then, that sooner or later Paul left his ancestral home for Jerusalem. He had to go and study at the place where his heavenly Father had had the Temple built and where—by divine grace—daily sacrifice was offered for the sins of his people. Here was to be found the center of the world for all true Jews. Here, the young zealot completed his education as a Pharisee, and here—where God had placed him—was where he wanted to work. It seemed to have been pre-ordained that his would be a scholar's career.

However, as a result of his zeal—or should we say fanaticism?—things turned out otherwise. In Damascus, Paul got to know a group of Greek-speaking Jews who named themselves after a crucified Jew named Jesus and even confessed that he was Messiah. Not only that, they claimed that he had been elevated by God and to this added criticism of the Law: as if the proclamation of the crucified Jesus as Messiah were not enough! It was too much for Paul. As had often happened to the elect of Israel, he was driven to act out of zeal for the ancestral law, to the glory of God. He attempted to nip this new movement in the bud by the use of physical force. Other fellow countrymen thought that as yet there was no reason to intervene—at any rate not in such a draconian way. But the young zealot took a completely different view, and the subsequent burgeoning of this group of Jesus' followers, originally from the Diaspora, was to prove him right. It was the beginning of a movement that would soon be a deadly threat to Jews; the notion that he was to play a key role in its dissemination would have taken his breath away.

Still, the inconceivable happened: in the midst of a bloody persecution near Damascus, the very one whose followers he was pursuing appeared to Paul in heavenly form. Seeing him in his glory, Paul had no doubts. It was imperative to enter into his service, for surely this was the Son of God, and all that his followers had said of him was true. All this happened so suddenly and overwhelmingly that Paul had no choice, no alternative course of action. He had to seek to join the community that previously he had been persecuting. Since all this took place at a deeply emotional level, Paul temporarily lost his sight immediately after this heavenly vision. But one of his new brothers in the faith, Ananias, healed him, of course in the name of Jesus: Ananias welcomed Paul and instructed him in the new faith which the persecutor so far had known only in a rudimentary way.

HOW PAUL DISCOVERED HIS SPECIAL ROLE IN THE DRAMA OF SALVATION

Paul had time to reflect on how Jesus had appeared to him and what it meant. He recalled all those passages in scripture in which a future Messiah had been prophesied. But how could he reconcile with this the fact that the Christian Messiah had died on the cross—in other words, that he had suffered? In his previous studies, Paul had never learned of a suffering Messiah. However, since his encounter with the heavenly Lord unmistakably proved to him that this was none other than the crucified Jesus, the ex-Pharisee who was so knowledgeable about the Bible did not find it difficult to give an answer. In a bold leap of thought, he combined the Jewish ideal of the Messiah with the Suffering Servant from the book of Isaiah. This was made easier by the fact that the suffering of Jesus was in any case only a transitional stage before his entrance into the heavenly glory. And this must be true not only for Jesus but also for all other Christians. They would all suffer tribulation before the great Day.

In scripture Paul also discovered a special role for himself in the heavenly drama. He eagerly appropriated those passages in which the prophets Isaiah and Jeremiah said that God himself[21] had set them aside from their mothers' wombs and applied them directly to himself and fantasized that, like the two great prophets of the past, he had been called from his mother's womb to be a preacher—of course by God himself. So a tremendous self-confidence developed in Paul that exceeded even that of his pre-Christian period. This becomes all the more remarkable the more one considers that this man from Tarsus never knew Jesus of Nazareth personally.

How could Paul derive his own authority immediately and directly from the heavenly Lord himself without learning from those whom he had persecuted? What had he experienced to claim this immediacy from heaven that allowed him later to set himself on the same footing as the personal followers of Jesus? Indeed, Paul attributes the words of institution at the Lord's supper, which he must have learned in teaching from the community, to a direct intervention and report by the Lord himself: "I received from the Lord what I also handed on to you. . . ."[22] He similarly accounted for everything else that had been communicated to him about the Lord. The authority of the Lord, who had personally commissioned Paul to be his apostle, automatically hallowed it. Believing himself in direct contact with the Lord, Paul received the special indications he needed—he called them revelations or mysteries—and immediately followed them.

Thus, while for Paul heaven was almost always open, an angel of Satan could also castigate him if the Lord so willed and if the abundance of revelations went to his head. At the same time, he was strong enough to invoke the power of Satan where grievous sinners had to be condemned to a just death[23] in order to preserve the community from uncleanness and to save the spirit of the sinner— imagined in a bodily form made incorruptible through baptism—on the day of judgment. Furthermore, Paul recognized the spirit of Satan where life was made difficult for him in the communities in the persons of false apostles. Still, whatever adversity they gave rise to, Satan and his angels functioned only as predetermined by God and never had power over Paul and his communities. Their real power could in no way oppose that of God, who had sent his Son into the world to save men and women from sin. Paul felt that he was the agent of God and the Lord Jesus, who was bound up in this cosmic drama of redemption. Here the key point for Paul was that salvation would and should include Gentiles: They did not have to become Jews first, but were to belong to the church of Jesus Christ on the same footing as the Jews who believed in Jesus. Such a view was repugnant to many Jewish Christians.

HOW THE NEW EXPERIENCE DEVELOPED IN PAUL AND AMONG OTHER CHRISTIANS

From the beginning, Paul had experienced in an almost intoxicating way the reality and the praxis of the unity of the church made up of Jews and Gentiles. We see this in two passages in which he quotes the liturgy for the baptism of converts: "There is neither Greek nor Jew, male nor female, slave nor free, but all are one in Jesus Christ."[24] In this formula, which was repeated time and again in worship, all the barriers that the Torah had erected around Israel were demolished: "If anyone is in Christ there is a new creation; the old has passed away, look, the new has come."[25] That was Paul's cry of jubilation. But this new element could be introduced only through the atoning death of the Son of God himself, as the continuation of this cry of jubilation indicates: "All this (is) from God, who has reconciled us to himself through Christ."[26] Paul constantly finds new descriptions to explain the liberation brought about in this way: "If God is for us, who can be against us? For he did not spare even his only-begotten son, but has given him up for all of us."[27]

This new experience called for rites to keep it alive. Already Paul had received instruction about the two chief ones—baptism and Eucharist—from the congregation he had persecuted. They were the major rituals also of other developing communities, for thus we read in the Gospel of Mark whose anonymous author, a younger contemporary of Paul, provides the basis for the two new rites of the first Christians. That his gospel is framed by Jesus' baptism and his institution of the Eucharist is an unmistakable indication that the evangelist is consciously involved in both the narrative creation of a new community of faith and the narrative inclusion of both Jews and Gentiles in that body. In Mark's account not only do the effects of Jesus' preaching spill over into the Gentile areas of Galilee, but his fame precedes him on a trip to Syro-Phoenecia,[28] and Mark's Jesus repeatedly nullifies the purity and dietary codes that had long divided those two populations. Most notable is the fact that Mark invokes no lesser an authority than Isaiah to put into Jesus' mouth the assurance that God's house must be open to all peoples.[29] It cannot be imagined that what amounts to an open-door policy for Gentiles is an unintended feature of the first gospel.

Luke offers a somewhat different scenario: for him the Jews' rejection of the new preaching triggered the Gentile mission. In all likelihood it worked the other way around—that is, dispensing with Jewish traditions and practices to facilitate the conversion of Gentiles so diluted Judaism as to provoke Jewish outrage. Be that as it may, the Markan and Lukan models agree in picturing an ever-increasing withdrawal and alienation of Christianity from its Jewish roots.[30]

THE ESTRANGEMENT OF PAUL AND HIS COMMUNITIES FROM THE JEWISH MOTHER RELIGION: REASONS, RESULTS, CONSEQUENCES

Experiences of Christ in the early community were experiences of the Spirit. But the Spirit pointed to an even greater event, namely the consummation of the kingdom with the coming of Jesus on the clouds of heaven. Now Paul faced a problem. To those who had known Jesus himself and who in Jerusalem were awaiting the future glory and the rewards of the coming kingdom, how was he to explain experiences that he had had time and again in his home community? Moreover, how could he persuade them that his authority was equal to theirs and that he could provide the story of Jesus with an independent interpretation that was of at least equivalent value?

The history of Paul's relationship to the Jerusalem community is a conclusive indication that all this was far from being a matter of course. The first visit, around three years after Paul's vision of Christ, lasted two weeks and enabled him to make cautious contact with the leader of that community, Cephas, Jesus' first disciple. During the visit, the mission to the Gentiles was already a topic of discussion, along with issues involving Jesus of Nazareth and the Easter events. Paul was glad to have this meeting and the resulting agreement over the Gentile mission as validation for his preaching activity that shortly followed. Then events came thick and fast. The mission to the Gentiles, which Cephas had agreed was Paul's task, proved extraordinarily successful, but Jewish-Christian communities also came into being: Lydda, Joppa, Caesarea, Sidon, etc. Moreover, the "Holy Spirit," imagined as a mysterious and miraculous being, found acceptance and favor everywhere: first of all in Syria and then under the influence of Paul in Galatia, Macedonia, and Achaia. A movement was born and really first called to life by a man who, though he had never known Jesus personally, was all the more in contact with the heavenly Jesus.

We will perhaps understand this event better if we compare it and its antecedents with a gigantic closed container of water that is coming to a boil. The growing number of disciples who invoked the risen Christ had brought Judaism to the boiling point. The water could no longer be kept in the container. It burst, and the water poured out hissing everywhere until, still steaming, it made different ways for itself into somewhat calmer channels. In this manner, numerous new communities composed of both Jews and Gentiles suddenly came into being. But this inevitably generated later conflict, for strict Jewish Christians were scandalized by nonobservant activity in the mixed communities, and they attempted to put a stop to it. While they did not mind what Gentile Christians did, it was important to them that ecumenical mixing did not erode the unique identity and practice of Jewish Christians.

Understandably, the demand for strict segregation of the Jewish Christians from their pagan brothers was only a matter of time. The inevitable happened: In Paul's presence delegates from Jerusalem fomented a bitter dispute over the purity of the Jewish Christians in the mixed community of Antioch. This put in question all that had been achieved. Thereupon, fourteen years after his first visit, Paul received a revelation from his heavenly Lord to go to Jerusalem. No doubt he traveled with a proud and unbowed heart, for he took the uncircumcised Greek Titus with him to establish a precedent. It is no coincidence that Paul's former partner in the mission, Barnabas, was also a member of the party, but so too were those strict Jewish Christians who, as Paul put it, had crept into the (mixed) community and provoked a bitter dispute.

The initial situation was completely different from that of the first visit. In Jerusalem, power had shifted. Now ont only Cephas, but also Jesus' biological brother James, had a say. James stood at the head of a group of three consisting of himself, Cephas, and John. Here it is illuminating that Cephas and John, two immediate disciples, were junior to someone who had not followed Jesus in his lifetime but, along with the rest of the family, including Jesus' mother Mary, was at least skeptical about him.

After vigorous clashes in Jerusalem, an agreement was sealed with a formal handshake. In spreading the Good News, the Jerusalem church was to be responsible for the Jews, Paul and Barnabas for the Gentiles. More important than this rule, which needed interpretation, was the very fact of the meeting, for it provisionally rescued the unity of the church, and that was Paul's main concern. The agreement was, like so many treaties, a kind of elastic statement that allowed both parties to read their own understandings into it. In the case of the Jews, for example, one had to consider both those living in the mother country of Palestine and also those in the Diaspora.

It should also be noted that the most burning problem of all, how people were from then on to live together in mixed communities, was not discussed at all. At any rate, the agreement did not rule out an interpretation in favor of a strict segregation of Jewish Christians and Gentile Christians; in fact, the agreement was about conditions for separation. However, despite all the problems of the "formula of union,"[31] there was agreement on the collection;[32] no dispute was possible over the terms of the collection—a project that, ironically, was soon enough to become an acid test for the relationship between the Gentile-Christian and the Jewish-Christian churches.

The Gentile-Christian communities, represented by Paul and Barnabas, were to bring it—Barnabas from the church of Antioch and Paul from the churches in Greece and Galatia that he had founded as early as the late 30s CE. Since this gave Paul the possibility of holding the Jerusalem people to their agreement by expeditiously collecting from his mission churches an offering to sustain the Jerusalem community, it also served as an instrument in church politics; at the same time, this was confirmation of his own hope that his apostolate to the Gentiles was based on the unity of the church made up of Jews and Gentiles. Paul's own assessment was that without this unity of the church, his apostolate to the Gentiles was null and void.

To be sure, Paul had already envisaged a great plan to carry out a mission in Spain. In this way, the apostle wanted to conquer the last part of the world for his Lord; it was urgent for him to reach his destination, because the Lord's return was near. But for now the agreement had to be safeguarded. Paul first undertook a journey among his communities to secure the collection and to cement the bond of unity between his churches and the church in Jerusalem.

Accompanied by a staff of colleagues, Paul traveled through Galatia, where he passed on detailed instructions about how the collection was to be made; he gave his other communities in Macedonia and Achaia instructions to do likewise. On the first day of every week, the members of the community were to put something aside in order to guarantee a handsome sum when Paul traveled through to collect it and deliver it to the delegation that would take it to Jerusalem. Of course, the journey for the collection did not serve only financial and political ends; Paul naturally initiated missions among new believers when occasion arose, as in Ephesus. Furthermore, there was constant need to advise and to exhort the existing communities personally or to strengthen them through delegates like Titus or Timothy.

Then disaster struck. Suddenly delegates from Jerusalem began to invade Paul's communities; they threatened to destroy all that he had laboriously built up and steadfastly defended in Jerusalem. The "false brethren" whom Paul had defeated in Jerusalem now attacked him in his own communities. They put his apostolic authority in question, introduced additional precepts of the law, and thus destroyed any fellowship between Paul and Jerusalem. So the battle for the unity of the church became the battle for the collection, or rather the battle for the collection also became the battle for the unity of the church. To make sure that the collection was still welcome to the people in Jerusalem, Paul changed his plan to have others take it to Jerusalem. By appearing in person, he would be fighting for the third time a battle in which he had previously prevailed.

At the height of this conflict, shortly before he set off to Jerusalem, Paul wrote the letter to the Romans, an intended destination of which must also have been the Jerusalem community. In this memorable document, the apostle proclaims his message of righteousness by faith, which is to be grasped in faith as free grace on the basis of the atoning death of Jesus and which is available to both Jews and Gentiles. But he does not seem to notice that in Romans 9–11 he in part takes back everything that he has written previously. Suddenly, an ethnocentric attitude that Paul thought he had overcome draws him under its spell, for now he rather explicitly suggests that after the fullness of the Gentiles has entered in, all Israel will be saved without any ifs, ands, or buts—in other words, even without believing in Christ.[33] Thus, belonging to the chosen people suddenly seems more valuable than one might have expected after reading the first eight chapters of Romans.

Paul indicates the special reason for this about-face in his introductory remarks at the beginning of chapter 9. On account of his Jewish brothers, the vast majority of whom have not accepted salvation in Christ, he suffers deeply and personally, and goes so far as to express the wish that if it would effect their deliverance, he might be accursed by Christ for their sake. Here we see another side of Paul. After the sharp attacks on the law in Galatians and in the first part of Romans, this sounds strange; yet at the same time it attests the ultimate priority of feeling over thought—in Paul as in nearly all humans.

However, none of this was of any use to the Jews in the subsequent era. In the Gentile-Christian church founded by Paul, the invention of a special way for Israel to attain salvation could not prevent unbelieving Israel from being damned to eternity, any more than a like provision could save the unbelieving Gentiles in a yet later period from divine wrath. The statement by the risen Jesus from the secondary ending to Mark, in fact, applies to both of them: "Who believes and is baptized will be saved, but who does not believe will be condemned."[34]

THE OLDEST EVANGELIST AS AN EXAMPLE OF ALIENATION FROM JUDAISM[35]

In Mark's gospel, the historical Jesus appears as a heavenly being miraculously given earthly form. Long before the resurrection, a divine glory illuminates the life of the human teacher and healer. To signal this transformation Mark places epiphany scenes at the beginning, middle, and end of his account. In the baptismal vision, a heavenly voice identifies Jesus as God's son;[36] in the transfiguration story the same heavenly voice accords him once again the same title[37] and at the foot of the cross a Roman centurion—a Gentile—is the first person to confess his divine sonship.[38] The first of these proclamations is addressed only to Jesus. The second commands the disciples—in the presence of Moses, Elijah, and Jesus himself—to "listen to" Jesus who, standing in the presence of Moses and Elijah, thus symbolically supersedes the Torah and the Prophets they represent. In both cases we have heavenly figures and speakers; but at the cross Mark has put into the centurion's mouth a message that is to be passed on to others. The intrusion of heaven into the real space-time of this world becomes at each step more dramatic until the demand that the message be spread implicitly includes all mankind. As the divine mystery is gradually unveiled, the reader comes to see the full significance of his adoption, his presentation to the disciples, and his recognition by a representative of the very power that has sought to eliminate him. Jesus has not claimed divinity; it has been assigned to him—and at last by one of those least likely to be moved by divine promptings.

A first step in distancing Christianity from Judaism—I use the term "Christianity" anachronistically—came with Paul's view of Jesus as a divine being on the basis of his resurrection, and the resulting conviction that it was God's action alone that had conferred divinity upon him. By reflecting what might be called Jesus' Easter sovereignty in the account of his life, Mark has endowed the earthly Jesus with a divine aura, and thereby continually betokens the divine nature of the one who multiplies loaves and walks on the water. Mark's derogation of the disciples, poignantly dramatized in Jesus' plaintive "Do you not yet understand?"[39] stems from what he sees as their inability to bridge the conceptual gap between the Jesus they know and the Eternal Son. And it is his divinization of Jesus (a step that comports with—if it does not derive from—Paul) by which Mark steers the gospel tradition onto a path that led inexorably away from the strict monotheism of Judaism.

That separation is evident in Mark's theme of recurring conflicts with Jewish opponents over Sabbath observance, purity regulations, and the value of sacrifice. But nowhere is it as striking as in his employment of the Temple as a symbol. It is no longer enough—as it was with Paul—that Jesus fulfils prophesy; now he is the prophet who invokes the destruction of the indispensable structure that in its provision of the locus of sacrifice embodies Judaism itself. And at the end Jesus' death symbolically rings the death knell of that tradition and of the Temple that is its central artifact; for his last cry, Mark reports, is accompanied by the rending of the veil that represents the exclusivity and sanctity of the cult.[40] Not only that, but the concurrence of that cataclysm and the centurion's confession (clearly a Markan contrivance, for the soldier at the cross could not have seen the Temple) makes unmistakably clear the evangelist's use of symbolism to assert both Christianity's substitution for Judaism and the inclusion of deserving Gentiles in God's plan for the salvation of mankind.

PAUL AS AN EXAMPLE OF ALIENATION FROM JUDAISM

Paul himself was to experience how the Jewish-Christian church repudiated its bond with the Gentile-Christian church. The collection from his own communities was rejected, and the Christian "brothers" who were hostile toward him even denounced him to the Roman authorities in order to get rid of him. He was said to have taken a Gentile Christian into the Temple. In order to save his life, Paul appealed to the emperor and only thus reached his destination, Rome. Alas, he was executed there under Nero. He never traveled to Spain.

Tragic though all that was, it is only fair to say that the charges made against Paul by his opponents in Jerusalem were based on facts. They had claimed that Paul was now teaching in the Diaspora that Jews should no longer circumcise their sons and was alienating them from the Jewish law. Granted, we do not find anything of this sort said explicitly in Paul's letters—Paul emphatically calls on Jews not to go back on their circumcision—but it has to be conceded that the consequences of Paul's preaching were similar to those expressed in the accusation.

In practice, Jewish Christians who lived in Pauline communities were alienated from their mother religion, and as a result, the minority of Jewish Christians ceased to circumcise their male descendants. In other words, sooner or later Jewish Christians lost their identity in the Pauline communities. And there was another thing. The apostle's doctrine of justification, according to which grace is attained only through faith without the Law, left the ethical question unanswered[41] and could easily be misconstrued as libertinism.

Finally, Paul's way of dealing theologically with the law was anything but clear. In fact, Paul no longer stood on the ground of the law but made mutually exclusive, i.e., contradictory, statements about the Torah; because he had already found an answer in the light of Christ or in the light of that answer he equivocated about the law. The Jewish side could no longer come to an understanding with such a man.

PAUL AND GREEK ENLIGHTENMENT

One last point must be made: the Jewish theologian Paul had become a Gentile to the Gentiles, a Jew to the Jews, and thus in effect neither a Gentile nor a Jew. Where then was his commitment? Throughout his activity there was not only a dash of arrogance but also a tendency to vacillation which must have been perplexing to honest spirits. But as his great life's work attests, this openness on all sides was a good way to succeed. Only in Athens did it cause him to run into a brick wall on the occasion when he attempted to convince the intellectual elite, the Stoic and Epicurean philosophers, who showed him his limits when he tried to impress them by speaking of the future judgment through Christ and the bodily resurrection.[42]

Despite his repeated—if sometimes deceptive—advocacy of the right use of reason, his religion, grounded in mystical experiences, was not up to the intellectual challenge of Greece. The fact that Paul founded no community in Athens speaks volumes here. At the same time, it suggests that his remarks in the First Letter to the Corinthians about human wisdom being folly before God were at least in part an evasion and a way of coping with the defeat in Athens.[43]

Here some general remarks about Paul's relationship to the Greek enlightenment may be appropriate. Paul did not come to a knowledge of the truth through a mind trained in logic—one that examines strictly the content and viability of all concepts and views, and that defiantly fights against the phantasms of the imagination and acknowledges no authority over itself, whether that of a god or of a human being. By contrast, the mysticism that Hellenistic Christianity and its leading figure Paul represent is of a supernatural kind. It calls for mindless sub-jection to authority and surrender to divine guidance: The norm is not the mind but the feelings and the mystical exaltation of the self seized by the Spirit. In this way, the pneumatics are elevated high above people with everyday minds (the psychics), and thus to them alone is disclosed the vision of the mysterious truth which can never be grasped by reason.

But the deepest reason for the victory of the Christianity of Paul and his pupils lay in the spirit of the time. The world had become weary of thought. Large numbers of people sought a more convenient way to secure their immor-tality—through initiation into mysteries, of which baptism and the Lord's Supper were only two of many. The public had become completely credulous and the power of the human intellect had suffered total defeat.

Thus, in Paul and his Christian brothers, a reaction against the Greek Enlightenment occurred in the sphere of spiritual and religious life in the same period in which state and law and customs, even forms of greeting, came to be dominated by authoritarianism. The quintessential freedom of ancient Greece was throttled just as much as the constitutional spirit of the Roman state. Authority replaced untrammeled research; faith substituted for knowledge; the humble subordination of the human spirit to the deity above the world took the place of its independence; and slavish observance of the commandments imposed by God on human beings supplanted the moral law recognized as morally free life. This was the world that Paul entered. As a result, the downfall of the ancient state, along with its worldview and culture that had grown up out of Hellenism, was complete.

THE RESULT OF PAUL'S ACTIVITY

What did Paul's life yield? First of all, it has become clear that the Christian church owes almost everything to this Jewish man from Tarsus, and Luke rightly devotes more than half of Acts to him whom we may call the real founder of Christianity. Paul was right when he said that he worked harder than all the rest,[44] because he created the foundations for all future developments in the church. He transplanted his misunderstanding of the religion of Jesus to Gentile territory and, without really wanting to, formulated the permanent separation of the church from Israel.

This in turn occasioned the tragic outcome of his activity. Christian anti-Judaism on pagan soil was given decisive stimulus by Paul along with others, and had a devastating effect. The New Testament authors thrashed the unbelieving Jews with anti-Jewish language for not accepting Jesus as the savior. At any rate, without Paul and his brothers in Christ, Judaism would never have been led into the abyss.

In addition, the Primitive Christians and Paul find themselves facing insuperable arguments from the side of critical reason. These extend to almost all the details of their beliefs: (a) the notion that God's Son had to atone for the sins of the world; (b) the nonsensical identification of Jesus and the Christ, and with it the arrogant claims of Paul and of other Christian authors to serve as the mouthpieces of someone whom they had never known personally; (c) the view that human beings can derive a serious expectation of decisive help from mystical wishes; (d) the confused statements about the Law which persistently conceal their presuppositions, including the assumption that a solution—"Christ"—has already been found before a question can be put; (e) the claim that a historical event can bring about the salvation of the world.

One can perhaps understand a man of the first century along with anonymous worshippers of Jesus making such foolish assertions, but we see how dangerous such claims can finally become when we see how they are still advocated by the Christian churches and even by academic theologians. To cite only one example, this means that the resurrection of Jesus has an objective significance for the history of the world: Indeed, that together with the death of Jesus, the resurrection becomes the turning point of that history and at the same time also an event of cosmic significance.[45]

THE DISASTROUS EFFECT OF CHRISTIAN "MONOTHEISM" ALONG WITH ITS POLITICAL THEOLOGY

To narrate the story of Primitive Christianity means to make at the same time a critical judgment about Paul and his brothers in Christ. True, the apostle to the Gentiles was certainly a great figure in Primitive Christianity, indeed the real founder of the Church. But the view that his letters and the rest of the New Testament scriptures represented God's word is a crime against reason and against humanity. Studying them today may make us realize that no real pointer to the future can be expected from his way of thinking. Because of the image of God it purveys, such "logic" cannot respect the "unbelievers," but only summon them to be obedient so as to avoid the eternal punishment of hell. With Primitive Christianity, monotheism—shaped by Christology—was on the brink of turning into totalitarianism with no respect for dissenters within or nonbelievers such as

Jews and pagans outside the church catholic. It took only three centuries until these dissenting or merely different groups became the target of a joint action of the true believers along with the political forces of the Roman Empire and were destroyed or at least neutralized. The burning of books that in Acts 19 Luke had reported as a voluntary measure of former pagans who were now Christians was henceforth to be an act of violence directed against the opponents of orthodox Christianity. Thus willy-nilly Luke's overtures to the Roman Empire paid off and indeed bore rich fruit.

Yet despite the historical results of Primitive Christian apologetics, one can neither deny the human accomplishments of the earliest churches nor doubt that these derived in large measure from their members' conscious commitment to God. At the same time, the religious zeal of its representatives remains suspiciously close to a fanaticism of faith, the kind of fanaticism that, once it had found an ally in political power, over the course of the succeeding two millennia has cost the lives of at least a million people per century. Unfortunately, as history shows, conflict inevitably turns such a commitment against human beings, mere mortal men and women that they are.

NOTES

1. Let me hasten to add that Jesus was not tried before Pilate; the simple and obvious reason is that the verdict is lacking. In the chaotic situation of an approaching Passah, when thousands of Jews were flocking to Jerusalem, the Roman authorities, among others, grabbed Jesus and crucified him in order to deter others from rebelling. At that time Pilate was prefect in Judea and present in Jerusalem.

2. On Judas the Galilean see above, p. 88.

3. For the last paragraph see Gerd Theissen, *A Theory of Primitive Christian Religion* (London: SCM Press, 1999), pp. 240–41.

4. Mark 11:15–19.

5. Mark 6:49; Matt. 14:26.

6. 1 Cor. 15:7.

7. Mark 3:21. Because this information was so embarrassing, Matthew and Luke (who obviously had Mark's gospel in front of them) left it out.

8. 1 Cor. 15:6.

9. See Martin Hengel, *Between Jesus and Paul: Studies in the Earliest History of Christianity* (Philadelphia: Fortress Press, 1983), p. 14.

10. Ibid., pp. 25–26.

11. Ibid., p. 26.

12. Luke has included traditions about them in his gospel, thus restricting their activity to the life of Jesus; see Luke 10.

13. Matt. 6:24.

14. Mark 10:25.

15. Mark 10:21.

16. Matt. 4:1–11/Luke 4:1–13.

17. Matt. 8:5–13/Luke 7:1–10.

18. Matt. 12:22–29/Luke 11:14–22.

19. Note the depiction of one who rules over all and demands to be worshipped.

20. For the above see Theissen, *Theory of Primitive Christian Religion*, pp. 241–42.

21. See Gal. 1:15–16.

22. 1 Cor. 11:23.

23. 1 Cor. 5:1–5.

24. Gal. 3:26–28, repeated in 1 Cor. 12:13 without "male and female."

25. 2 Cor. 5:17.

26. 2 Cor. 5:18.

27. Rom. 8:31–32.

28. Mark 7:24–30.

29. Mark 11:17 (Isa. 56:7).

30. See Theissen, *Theory of Primitive Christian Religion*, p. 182.

31. Gal. 2:9.

32. Gal. 2:10.

33. Rom 11:26a.

34. Mark 16:16.

35. For what follows cf. Theissen, *Theory of Primitive Christian Religion*, pp. 171–75.

36. Mark 1:11.

37. Mark 9:7.

38. Mark 15:39.

39. Mark 8:21.

40. Mark 15:38.

41. See Rom. 3:8.

42. Acts 17:16–34.

43. 1 Cor. 1:17–25.

44. 1 Cor. 15:10b.

45. See one of Germany's leading theologians, Joachim Ringleben, *Wahrhaft aufer-standen. Zur Begründung der Theologie des lebendigen Gottes* (Tübingen: J. C. B. Mohr/Paul Siebeck, 1998), p. 47n93.

APPENDIX
ACTS OF THE APOSTLES AS A HISTORICAL SOURCE[1]

In 1897 Adolf von Harnack wrote a sentence that has ever since evoked a great deal of discussion. "With respect to the evaluation of the sources of earliest Christianity," Harnack wrote, "we are at present caught up in a movement back to ecclesial tradition about these sources."[2] This situation was especially applicable to a source that Harnack considered to stand alongside Paul's letters and Eusebius's church history as a pillar for historical knowledge about early Christianity, namely, the *Acts of the Apostles*. In three brilliant monographs, Harnack presented proof for his statement and its relevance to Acts. These were *Luke the Physician* (1907), *The Acts of the Apostles* (1909), and *The Date of the Acts and the Synoptic Gospels* (1911).[3] These volumes mark the end of nineteenth-century critical research into *Acts*,[4] research that had begun in the work of Ferdinand Christian Baur. After a hesitant start, Baur examined the historical information in Paul's letters alongside that of Acts and came to the conclusion that a "comparison of these two sources [necessarily] leads to the opinion that, in the light of the great differences between the two presentations, historical truth can reside only on one side or the other."[5] This keynote, struck in the introduction to his book on Paul from the year 1845, is then applied to, or argued for, in each chapter on Acts in part 1 of the book.[6] This is where Baur treats the "life and work of the apostle Paul." Since he follows the sequence of Acts in this part of his study, there results a sort of commentary about Acts that has the main purpose of ferreting out its historical elements. The methodological criteria for determining them are comparison with the letters of Paul, the history of religion, literary criticism, and tendency criticism. The comparison between the historical parts of Acts and the Pauline letters especially led Baur to conclude that only a few sections in Acts have positive historical value. On the other hand, the history of religions and tendency criticism reveal the value of Acts to be great indeed:[7] with them he concludes that Acts was written in the second century to reconcile the opposing parties of Paulinists and Judaists.[8] Albert Schwegler[9] and Eduard Zeller,[10] two of Baur's students who later achieved renown as classical philologists, then adopted this thesis. Both Schwegler and Zeller set a large and firm question mark behind Acts as a historical source. Furthermore, Baur's type of criticism of Acts was brilliantly displayed in 1870 when Franz Overbeck, a member of the Tübingen school in the allegorical sense, revised W. M. L. de Wette's commentary.[11] Overbeck does differ from Baur with respect to the purpose of Acts: according to him the author was almost completely unaffected by the old parties and wrote as a gentile Christian who freely transferred the ecclesial situation of his own time into the primitive apostolic period.[12] In the actual historical work on the text of Acts, however, and in the conviction that early Christianity must be investigated on a purely historical basis, Overbeck and Baur see eye to eye.[13] Overbeck surpasses Baur in refining—or introducing—source criticism,[14] but his opinion of the historical value of Luke's presentation is a low as that of his predecessor.[15]

It would be wrong, however, to give the impression that the type of criticism of Acts presented by Baur and Overbeck was generally acclaimed in the nineteenth century. Rather, the opposite was the case. Their position became the object of recurrent critique from both the learned and the unlearned.[16] Nevertheless, it must be admitted that for decades the Tübingen approach, and particularly its detailed exegesis, formed the generally acknowledged point of departure for liberal critical analysis of Acts[17]—that is, until precisely from among this circle Harnack delivered the forceful counterstroke. After pronouncing the verdict cited earlier that early ecclesiastical tradition was enjoying a growing assessment of reliability in the eyes of research, Harnack published his brilliant three-volume apology of Luke in 1906–11 and there asserted the opposite of virtually everything that the Tübingen scholars and the liberal theologians following them had said about the historical value of Acts.[18] First of all—as one might expect— ancient Christian tradition[19] is right in saying that Luke, the companion of Paul, is the author of both the Gospel of Luke and Acts. He announces himself as such in the "we" passages, which, together with all the other parts of the second half of Acts, present historically correct reports of what he himself has witnessed. The report of events in Acts 1–12, to which Luke naturally was not an eyewitness, derives from various sources of diverse quality.

Thus the difference between Harnack and Baur's school in evaluating the historical value of Acts could hardly be greater, and we may describe the Tübingen school and Harnack as the two major poles in research into Acts, between which, of course, at the turn of the century there were many variations. Baur, Overbeck, and Harnack seem to me still to be the great antipodes, as a short glance at the study of Acts after Harnack reveals.

Alfred Wikenhauser and no less than Eduard Meyer continued Harnack's line.[20] For Meyer the authorship of Luke, the companion of Paul, had been definitely established, and Acts is "one of the most important historical works preserved from antiquity."[21] (Volume 3 of his work *Ursprung and Anfänge des Christentums* basically offers a "history" of early Christianity on the basis of Acts.)[22] Strong support for Harnack's evaluation of Acts is found to the present day, especially in the Anglo-Saxon sphere.[23] Finally, sections of contemporary German research manifest that the evaluation of the historicity of Acts is in an upward trend, and the most recent statements of Martin Hengel reveal that Harnack's analysis of Acts is indeed a resource for current research.[24]

The line of Baur and Overbeck continues mainly in literary critical work such as the studies of Julius Wellhausen,[25] which leave Acts behind in bits and pieces, almost losing sight of the question of the historical value of the traditions and sources recovered from Acts. Here, too, belong the studies by Martin Dibelius,[26] which successfully tested style criticism on Acts, and large stretches of North American research, which under the direction of Henry Cadbury, Kirsopp Lake, and F. J. Foakes Jackson established a milestone in the critical investigation of Acts with the five-volume work *The Beginnings of Christianity* and in which the secondary character of Acts was emphasized by such scholars as John Knox and Donald Riddle.[27] Redaction-critical investigation of Luke's two-volume work, especially Acts, should also be mentioned here.[28] While the concern of this type of study was, above all, to become Luke's reader, it needs to be critically remarked that, contrary to the intention of the founders of such investigation, the currently thriving redaction criticism has not seldom led to an almost total neglect of the question of the historicity of the reports in Acts.

This neglect is due, on the one hand, to an overgrown skepticism about everything that Luke wrote and, on the other hand, to the conviction that reconstructing history is theologically questionable because only the kerygma is truly of importance. Contrary to this neglect of history, I would emphasize that since the advent of historical thinking, reconstruction of early Christian history is necessary in order to understand early Christian writings. Since Luke himself regards Acts as a historical report about early Christianity (see Luke 1:1–4), we have to address systematically the question of the historical value of this document.

In that respect, the first question to be asked, "Was the author of Acts an eyewitness?" is of such importance that it must be treated here once again. If it is answered positively, the acts should be placed next to the letters of Paul and should be considered virtually a primary source. If the author was not an eyewitness, then Acts should be regarded as a secondary source and its historical value considered much lower that that of the primary source, the Pauline letters.[29]

But what criteria can lead us to a clear-cut decision on this question? One possible approach would be to compare the theologies of Paul and Acts and especially of Paul in Acts.[30] If there prove to be major differences, then it could be concluded that the author of Acts could not have been a companion of Paul. This approach must be left to one side, however, for theological differences between Luke and Paul are likely to be very unreliable criteria for the resolution of our question. Furthermore, one must take into account that even Paul's contemporaries understood his theology in very divergent ways[31] and that in the following period his theology was only superficially apprehended.[32] For these reason, we cannot rule out the possibility that a companion of the historical Paul is responsible for the so very non-Pauline theology of the two Lukan volumes.[33]

Viable approaches to the solution of the problem should be sought solely in historical considerations. Along this line, one argument that has been brought against the thesis that Luke was an eyewitness refers to the fact that Luke has omitted some conflicts that Paul's letters reveal to have been decisive. It is said, for example, that Luke mentions neither the gentile Christian Titus, whose circumcision was a disputed point at the Jerusalem Conference, nor the crises in the Pauline congregations that are documented in the letters. Such arguments, however, are not likely to be convincing. The author of Acts did not write *sine ira et studio*. An impartial reading of Acts readily reveals that Luke knew more than he reported. That is to say, it is certain that Luke left out certain details—for example, the execution of the apostle, or the delivery of the collection during Paul's last visit to Jerusalem—owing to the particular intentions. The absence of such details cannot be used as a persuasive argument against the thesis that Luke was an eyewitness. Satisfactory arguments against that thesis are most likely to be based only on historical statements that disclose total personal ignorance of Paul on the part of the author of Acts.

Let us test this criterion. Among the happy coincidences for Pauline research is that the extant sources allow certainty with regard to the number of times that the apostle traveled to Jerusalem as a Christian. Gal. 1:15–24 excludes any additional journey between the first visit (verses 15–16) and the second trip, to the Jerusalem conference (2:1–10). The report of the agreement for the collection (Gal. 2:10) and the history of the collection in the Pauline congregations give convincing force to the thesis that Paul was in Jerusalem only one other time, namely, to deliver the collection. That is, it is virtually certain that Paul was in Jerusalem only three times as a Christian.[34] Acts, in contrast, reports no fewer than five trips to Jerusalem.[35] It seems impossible that Luke could have been a companion of Paul and simultaneously susceptible to such a mistake. This inaccuracy rather proves Luke to be an author who evidently had no personal knowledge of the life of the apostle. One should also expect that in case of a companionship with Paul, Luke would have told us more about the early Paul.

But there is also another passage that leads to the conclusion that the author of Acts belongs to a later era. In the prologue of the Gospel—a prologue that should be taken to apply to both volumes—Luke differentiates three separate groups of witnesses: the eyewitnesses; those who have composed written reports of the events; and himself as author of the two volume work dedicated to Theophilus. Two things are clear from the prologue: (a) Luke had predecessors and employed their reports in his work; that is, he is using tradition(s) as he writes. Thus, in the Gospel he employs at least Mark and the sayings source Q. (b) Luke probably belongs to the third generation. This last point also speaks against the thesis that Luke was a companion of Paul. The thesis that Luke was an eyewitness will therefore have to be left to one side, even though one must acknowledge that research has too quickly dismissed this assumption.

I have already briefly indicated above that Luke knew more than he reported and that he employed traditions in the composition of his two-volume work. Where did these traditions come from? Who passed them on to Luke? How can they be reconstructed? With regard to the origin of the traditions in the Pauline part of Acts, we are faced with three possibilities:

1. Luke knew and used only the letters of Paul.
2. Luke had access only to traditions other than the Pauline letters.
3. Luke used both the letters and the traditions.

To aid in accomplishing the task we have set for ourselves, each possibility needs to be evaluated. We shall begin with the first and ask, did the author of Acts know and use Paul's letters?

The assumption that Luke knew the letters of Paul is a well-founded hypothesis, which becomes all the more persuasive the later Luke's two-volume work is dated. If Luke belongs to the third Christian generation, as I suggested above, then in light of the fact that he understands himself as a student of Paul or—expressed more carefully—that he stands within the sphere of Pauline tradition (for otherwise I cannot explain the extensive portrayal of Paul), his awareness of the existence of Paul's letters is almost certain.[36] The question, then, is not whether Luke knew the letters of Paul, but whether he used them in composing his work.

This question can be answered only if traces of the use of Paul's letters can be established with certitude.[37] In short, we must search for agreements between Acts and the letters and then ask whether these agreements are best explained by the assumption that the letters were employed in writing Acts. In what follows we shall list the most important reasons supporting the assumption that Luke uses Paul's letters:[38] (a) Most of the places in areas mentioned in Acts as stations of Paul's activity also recur in the corpus Paulinum.[39] (b) The agreement of 2 Cor. 11 with Acts 9 regarding Paul's daring flight from Damascus is even more striking because both reports break off at the same point, with Paul being let down in a basket through the city wall. (c) The stations in Paul's journeys in Acts disclose surprising coincidence with the stations that can be reconstructed on the basis of the letters. In each case Paul travels from Philippi through Thessalonica and Athens to Corinth (cf. Acts 17 and 1 Thessalonians 2–3). (d) The names of Paul's co-workers in Acts generally agree with similar information in Paul's letters.

Each of these points draws attention to considerable agreement, but not a single one of them brings convincing proof that Luke used Paul's letters, and the question arises whether these observations are more adequately explained by the assumption that Luke used traditions deriving from the area missionized by Paul, traditions the age, origin, and place of which remain to be determined.

In order to avoid biasing the results, it is best to use the word "tradition" in a broad sense. In the remainder of this article, "tradition" means both written sources and oral information.[40] Thus, our question about the historical value of Acts must be reformulated. We must ask not about the value of Acts itself but about the value of the traditions Luke has reworked. If Luke himself does not have any personal knowledge of the events he describes, then it would be nonsensical to determine the historical value of Acts by analyzing the story level of the text. Luke's activity as an author—this we can already say—consists of coupling traditions with one another. For us this means that our first task must be the separation of redaction and tradition. The second task will then be the determination of the historical value of the recovered tradition.

The isolation of tradition in Acts, however, entails considerable difficulty. The reasons for this difficulty lie in the literary character of Acts and in the fact that, in contrast to the situation with Luke's Gospel, almost none of the materials used in Acts have been preserved elsewhere. The literary character of Acts often prevents the classical methods of literary criticism from attaining reliable results. Word statistics are only partially useful, for Luke has transformed—or at least tried to transform—all of the material into his own language. Observation of tensions in the text does not necessarily direct us to pre-Lukan material, for such tensions might be attributed to the author's conscious attempt at varying his style.[41] Although I do not want to question the value of these two methodological steps, the limitations just mentioned as well as the fact of Luke's editorial reworking of the traditions should be emphasized once more. But on the other hand, Lukan language and style cannot be taken as proof that Luke did not use traditions.

In this article we will, of course, be able to analyze only a few selected texts. It is not without reason that the passages have been taken from the part of Acts that deals with Paul, for here there is relatively often the possibility of advancing redaction-critical and historical analysis by comparison with the Pauline letters. The following texts will be examined:

(a) Acts 18 (Paul in Corinth)
(b) Acts 17–18; 18–19; 27 (the routes of Paul's journeys)
(c) Acts 21 (Paul in Jerusalem)

We shall proceed by determining first the meaning of each text at the redactional level, then the content of its traditional character, and finally the historical value of the individual traditions.

PAUL IN CORINTH (ACTS 18:1–17)

The passage reports Paul's mission in Corinth, which is first carried out weekly in the synagogue and then later in the neighboring house of Titius Justus. Silas and Timothy arrive from Macedonia and find Paul, who during his stay in Corinth has been working with the couple Aquila and Priscilla. (The couple had been forced to leave Rome because of the edict of Claudius and had come to Corinth.) It is here in Corinth that the famous "trial" of Paul before the proconsul Gallio, who dismisses the accusations of the Jews against Paul (Acts 18:10–17), takes place.

Redactional features are quite obvious in this section: Paul's preaching in the synagogue every Sabbath (the connection with the Jews) and the positive portrayal of Gallio, the Roman proconsul, whose attitude is presented as an example of how the Romans (in contrast to the Jews) behave—or should behave—toward Christians. The fact that these themes find numerous parallels in Acts reveals that these aspects derive from Luke.

Otherwise, the report seems to reflect tradition. This is the case with Paul's employment by Aquila and Priscilla in Corinth shortly after Claudius's edict against the Jews, with the arrival of Silas and Timothy from Macedonia, with Paul's Preaching in the house of Titius Justus, with the conversion of Crispus (the ruler of the synagogue), with a "trial" before Gallio, and with the activity of Sosthenes as ruler of the synagogue. Not linguistic considerations but rather the concreteness of these reports leads to the conclusion that this material is traditional.

The question now arises whether Acts had chronologically located these traditions correctly and whether the traditions all derive from one and the same visit by Paul to Corinth. This twofold question should probably be answered in the negative for the following three reasons:

1. The passage discloses a break between verse 11 and verse 12. Verse 11 concludes with a temporal reference: Paul remained in Corinth for eighteen months. Then the new material is introduced with the words, "When Gallio was proconsul of Achaia. . . ." Thus, even on a purely external showing, the two units are disparate.
2. Verse 8 knows a Crispus as ruler of the synagogue. Verse 17, in contrast, has Sosthenes in this position. Since it is highly probable that only one person exercised the office of a ruler of the synagogue, each unit probably refers to a different period of time.
3. The chronological references contained in the traditions belong to periods separated from each other by approximately ten years. The expulsion of Jews from Rome, mentioned in verse 2, took place in the year 41. An increasing part of recent scholarship is in agreement as to that. Gallio, however, was in office in the years 51–52.

At this point and in confirmation of the above analysis, it should be noted that Luke habitually reports on Paul's mission by grouping together into one narrative all the pieces of information known to him. If Paul visits the same place more than once, Luke reports it only summarily.[42] This observation makes it necessary to locate chronologically anew each of the traditions that can be recovered. It is also in accord with the earlier analysis of Acts 18, where we concluded that this passage contains traditions that derives from the year 41, since Paul worked with Aquila and Priscilla during his initial mission in Corinth. The other unit reflects the years 51–52 CE, when Gallio was proconsul of Achaia.

If we evaluate the historical veracity of the traditions, we can ascertain that they have a high historical value. Paul's connection with Aquila and Priscilla during the founding visit in Corinth, which is also evident from the letters (1 Cor. 16:19b) is confirmed by the report in Acts, as is the fact that Silas and Timothy reached Paul during the initial mission in Corinth. This is the case because Silas and Timothy were probably closely connected with the Macedonian brethren who, according to 2 Cor. 11:9, brought Paul financial aid when he was in Corinth (see 1 Thess. 3:6). With regard to the years 51–52, a stay in Corinth different from the founding mission may also be determined from the letters. This visit belongs in the period of the great collection which the apostle undertook in accordance with the agreement at the Jerusalem conference. If what has been said already indicates that the traditions of Acts 18 are of high historical value, then this index would increase even more if John Knox's and my own proposed early dating of the initial Pauline mission should prove to be correct. For in that case a traditional part of Acts 18 would preserve chronologically correct information about Paul's arrival in Corinth. His arrival would indeed have taken place during the year in which Claudius expelled Jews—including Aquila and Priscilla—from Rome, that is, the year 41. The same historical value to which the traditions in Acts 18 attain could not, of course, be acknowledged for the Lukan redaction. Insofar as Luke would have transferred the initial mission in Corinth to the period after the Jerusalem conference and would have unified into one narrative, events that were actually separated by more than ten years, he would be responsible for dating the Pauline mission to Greece about a decade too late.

TRAVEL ROUTES

Luke presents Paul's mission as a journey that achieves its goal in Rome. The journey leads Paul from the place of his conversion near Damascus to Damascus itself (Acts 9:8), from there to Jerusalem (9:26), then to Cilicia (9:30, "Tarsus"), then to Antioch (11:26) and Jerusalem (11:30), and thereafter on to the so-called first missionary journey (chaps. 13–14) through Cyprus and South Galatia back to Antioch. Next comes the third trip to Jerusalem (15:3–4), followed by the so-called second missionary journey (15:40–18:22) from Antioch through Asia Minor and Greece back to Jerusalem. Finally, the same stations are visited on the so-called third missionary journey (18:22–21:15). At the end occurs the dangerous voyage to Rome (chaps. 27–28).

On the one hand, the journeys of Paul are a Lukan mode of presentation to illustrate the spread of the gospel from Jerusalem to Rome. They are paralleled by the journey of Jesus (the Lukan travel narrative, Luke 9:51–19:28), the redactional character of which may be demonstrated by a comparison with Mark. On the other hand, traditions can be recovered at the following three points:

First, we recall that the order of stations in 1 Thess. 2–3 and Acts 17 (Philippi, Thessalonica, Athens, Corinth) has sometimes led to the conclusion that Luke made use of the letters of Paul. Even though this thesis proved unsatisfactory for the known reason, the fact that called forth this thesis, namely the remarkable correspondence in the list of stations, nevertheless deserves to be explained. In my judgment, the best explanation is that Acts 17 is based on a traditional list of stations (an itinerary).

Second, Acts 18 presents a trip from Ephesus to Caesarea, then to Jerusalem, and from there to Antioch, Phrygia, the region of Galatia, and Ephesus. Julius Wellhausen once described the peculiar character of this journey in these words: "From Ephesus, to Caesarea, up to greet the brethren, down to Antioch, back through Galatia and Phrygia. With plans made at a moment's notice and reported in telegraphic style, no American could have done it better."[43] In my judgment, the epitomic character of this report, which covers a journey of more than a thousand miles, speaks for the assumption that our passage indeed contains traditional material at this point, for otherwise it is "not apparent why the author would have invented this entire list and then have treated it so cursorily."[44]

Third, Acts 27 presents a dangerous voyage. Verses 9–11, 21–26, 31, and 33–36, which are concerned with Paul as a prophet of misfortune and a savior in time of need, may be separated out. There remains the report of a shipwreck and the successful escape from it. Wellhausen's conclusion seems irrefutable: In Acts 27, Luke has employed a non-Christian source and has expanded it by adding the figure of Paul.[45]

We can now formulate a historical judgment of the three traditions about the journeys, which we have isolated:

(a) With regard to the journey in Acts 17–18: The tradition here can claim historical value insofar as the order of the stations agrees with the one given in the letters. 1 Thess. 2–3 makes it likely that when Paul missionized Greece, he came from Philippi through Thessalonica and Athens to Corinth. But one must again be critical with respect to Luke's chronological placement of this journey. On the basis of Paul's own witness and—as may already be said here—owing to the chronological correspondence of the expulsion of Jews from Rome and the initial mission in Corinth (Acts 18:2), it is probable that this initial journey took place ten years earlier than Acts reports. It would have to be placed—if one wanted to maintain the order of Acts—between Acts 10 and 11.

(b) With regard to the journey in Acts 18–19: Our results on Acts 18–19 will be similar to those on Acts 17–18. Paul's own witness makes it likely that the apostle undertook a journey from Greece to Jerusalem that agrees with the order of stations in Acts 18.[46] To this extent the tradition is historically valuable. There are, however, serious reasons to doubt the accuracy of the journey's chronological placement. Its present placement assumes that in the middle of his journey to organize the collection, Paul undertook a trip to Palestine—which being a distance of over a thousand miles, would have been an exasperating detour. In agreement with many others, I consider this impossible. Nevertheless, the historical value of this tradition becomes apparent when one transfers the journey to its historical place as that can be reconstructed from Paul's letters. The tradition then accurately reports the journey from Greece to Palestine that Paul undertook in order to participate in the Jerusalem conference.[47]

(c) With regard to the journey in Acts 27: Compared with the trips already discussed, a different picture emerges for the voyage in Acts 27. Although it is certain that Paul traveled to Rome after his last visit in Jerusalem,[48] the report of the voyage does not stand in any genetic relationship with Paul's trip to Rome. Luke himself probably adapted the report of this voyage from a literary model. It should thus be designated a product of his reading and be considered nonhistorical.

PAUL IN JERUSALEM (ACTS 21)

Acts 21 reports Paul's arrival in Jerusalem. Here he finds lodging in the house of the Hellenist Mnason and receives a warm welcome from James and the elders, to whom he relates the success of the mission to the Gentiles. James nevertheless advises Paul to manifest his loyalty to the law by assuming responsibility for a Jewish ritual, because Christians who are zealous for the law have heard that the apostle to the Gentiles teaches Jews who dwell among the Gentiles to forsake Moses, telling them not to circumcise their children or live according to the Jewish customs. Paul follows this advice.

The section just described bears clear marks of Lukan redaction: Paul maintains good relations with the congregation in Jerusalem and with James, its leader. Similarly, Paul transgresses the law in not a single point up to the end. By his participation in a Jewish ritual, Paul even openly documents that he upholds the law.

There are two things that call for attention: (a) In verse 17 the entire congregation greets Paul and his companions. But in the following the many zealous brethren who have heard the hostile rumors are distinguished from the entire congregation. (Do they not belong to the congregation?) (b) It is strange that there are any rumors at all about Paul's criticism of the law, especially since the portrayal of Paul in Acts provides absolutely no foundation for such rumors. Thus the inference seems likely that both the mention of Christians who harbor reservations about Paul and the report of Paul's proclamation about the law are pieces of tradition that the author of Acts has transformed in accordance with his theology but was unable to eliminate completely.

What about the historical value of such a tradition? In my judgment it should definitely be estimated as high, for the witness of Paul's letters confirms the content of Acts 21:21. Admittedly, his proclamation concerning the law does not correspond with the principles outlined in Acts 21:21. Paul wanted all, both Jews and Gentiles, to remain in their own states.[49] But in practice, the predominately gentile Christian Pauline congregations had left this noble principle behind. The minority of Jewish Christians and their children in the Pauline congregations seem to have actually been estranged from the Mosaic Law. Acts 21:21 is thus definitely a historically reliable statement about what was really occurring in the Pauline congregations.

The other part of the tradition in Acts 21, the existence of many anti-Pauline Jewish Christians in Jerusalem, should also be considered definitely historical. In Rom. 15:31, Paul himself indicates that the Christians in Jerusalem might not be receptive to him. Furthermore, we know from the letters that the anti-Pauline opposition in the Pauline congregations originated in Jerusalem.[50] We can thus say that the Lukan report of Paul's arrival in Jerusalem in Acts 21 contains traditional material that should be considered both old and historical.

By way of conclusion we may review the course of the argument and formulate a few provisional perspectives on the historical value of the Acts of the Apostles.

We began with a survey of the turbulent history of research into the historical value of Acts. At the beginning stood the radical criticism of F. C. Baur; in the middle, the reversion toward tradition by Adolf von Harnack; and at the end, a polarity—on the one hand, redaction criticism with diminished interest in the historical question, and on the other hand, a rising tide of research that defends the historical reliability of Acts. In retrospect it can be said that on the question of the historicity of Acts, Baur and Harnack have remained the classic antipodes even to the present. It thus seemed best to make some decisions about the mutually exclusive positions of Baur and Harnack. For that purpose we critically addressed the alternative theses that the author of Acts was an eyewitness and that he employed the Pauline letters. The first thesis would imply that Acts is of very little historical value. Both theses proved unacceptable, and instead we postulated that Luke in his composition had reworked other traditions to a larger degree than had been assumed. That meant that the question of the historicity of Acts should be adequately addressed only as the question of the historical value of the traditions that have been reworked therein. In accordance with this task we selected three different textual units and in each case posed questions regarding redaction, tradition, and historical veracity. Though only a small portion of Acts was analyzed, the results that we achieved seem to provide a basis for the following general inferences:

(1) Acts remains an important source for the history of early Christianity alongside the letters of Paul.

(2) This is because much of its content is historically reliable and provides information about Primitive Christianity that goes beyond that contained in Paul's letters.

(3) Of course, it must be added immediately that this judgment applies only for the traditions that have been reworked in Acts, the chronological framework of which must furthermore be reconstructed from the letters.

(4) To this extent, a chronology developed solely on the basis of the primary source, the letters, is a necessary prerequisite for the isolation of traditions in Acts.

(5) The recovered traditions often cannot be form-critically classified and furthermore can be reconstructed only in their basic outlines.

(6) In reconstructing the traditions, one could in general give more consideration than has been customary to the effect of Luke's reading of extra-Christian material. Such effects are found in Acts 27 and were probably the influence elsewhere too.

(7) A special problem is posed by the parts of Acts which were not treated in this article and which are not paralleled by a historical witness in Paul's letters. Their analysis is yet to be undertaken, but the manner in which traditions have been reworked in the Gospel and in the parts covered by the Pauline letters should provide valuable guidelines for this task. Owing to the thorough nature of Lukan redaction, it does admittedly seem to be a hopeless undertaking to try to reconstruct sources of a continuous nature for these parts. Here too only individual traditions are recoverable. In not a few cases judgments about their historicity will have a low degree of reliability because of the dearth of material for verification.

(8) A critical analysis of Acts, with attention given to the question of the traditions it contains and the historicity of those traditions, has become an important task following the flood of redaction-historical studies of Acts. This is not a hopeless undertaking, as the examples above have shown. Thus, the type of research that I have described is a necessary preliminary task for a long-overdue history of Primitive Christianity.

NOTES

1. Reprinted from *The Social World of Formative Christianity and Judaism*, ed. Jacob Neusner, Peder Borgen, Ernest Frerichs, and Richard Horsley (Philadelphia: Fortress Press, 1988), pp. 109–25 (slightly revised). Copyright © 1988 Fortress Press. Used by permission of Augsburg Fortress. The essay goes back to my inaugural address as Professor of New Testament given February 1, 1984, at the Auditorium of Georg-August-University of Göttingen and was first printed in German in my *Das frühe Christentum nach den Traditionen der Apostelgeschichte. Ein Kommentar* (Göttingen: Vandenhoeck & Ruprecht, 1987), pp. 9–24. From there John Bowden translated it as part of the English version of the volume *Early Christianity according to the Traditions in Acts* (Minneapolis: Fortress Press, 1989), pp. 1–18 ("The Historical Value of the Acts of the Apostles"). I include the 1988 version here in order to document my ongoing occupation with Acts and to make up for giving short shrift to the history of research in the present book—though some overlaps between the book and the essay were unavoidable. In some cases I have added material on the history of research and indicated where English editions of the books cited are available.

2. Adolf von Harnack, *Geschichte der altchristlichen Literatur bis Eusebius*, pt. 2, vol. 1, *Die Chronologie der Literatur bis Irenäus* (Leipzig: J. C. Hinrichs, 1897), p. x.

3. Adolf von Harnack, *New Testament Studies*, vol. 1, *Luke the Physician, the Author of the Third Gospel, and the Acts of the Apostles* (New York: G. P. Putnam's Sons, 1907); Harnack, *New Testament Studies*, vol. 3, *The Acts of the Apostles* (New York: G. P. Putnam's Sons, 1909); Harnack, *New Testament Studies*, vol. 4, *The Date of the Acts and the Synoptic Gospels* (New York: G. P. Putnam's Sons, 1911).

4. See Arthur Cushman McGiffert, "The Historical Criticism of Acts in Germany," in *The Beginnings of Christianity*, pt. 1, *The Acts of the Apostles*, 5 vols., ed. F. J. Foakes Jackson and Kirsopp Lake (London and New York: Macmillan, 1920–33), 2:363–95; Andrew Jacob Mattill, "Luke as a Historian in Criticism since 1840" (PhD diss., Vanderbilt University, 1959), pp. 20–206; Emmeram Kränkl, *Jesus, der Knecht Gottes: Die heilsgeschichtliche Stellung Jesu in den Reden der Apostelgeschichte* (Regensburg: Friedrich Pustet, 1972); and W. Ward Gasque, *A History of Criticism of the Acts of the Apostles* (Grand Rapids, MI: Wm. B. Eerdmans, 1975), pp. 21–106.

5. Ferdinand Christian Baur, *Paulus, der Apostel Jesu Christi—Sein Leben und Wirken, seine Briefe und seine Lehre: Ein Beitrag zu einer kritischen Geschichte des Urchristentums* (Stuttgart: Becher & Müller, 1845), p. 5. My translation.

6. Ibid., pp. 15–243; ibid., 2nd ed., ed. Eduard Zeller, 2 vols. (Leipzig: Fues's Verlag, L. W. Reisland, 1866–67), 1:19–272.

7. Ibid. (1845), p. 13; (1866), 1:17.

8. Ibid. (1845), pp. 5–6; (1866), 1:8–9.

9. On Schwegler see my *Opposition to Paul in Jewish Christianity* (Minneapolis, MN: Fortress Press, 1989), pp. 7–9.

10. Albert Schwegler, *Das nachapostolische Zeitalter in den Hauptmomenten seiner Entwicklung*, 2 pts. in one vol. (Tübingen: L. F. Fues, 1846), 2:73–123; and Eduard Zeller,

Die Apostelgeschichte nach ihrem Inhalt und Ursprung kritisch untersucht (Stuttgart: Carl Macken, 1854), p. 318. ET: Eduard Zeller, *The contents and origin of the Acts of the apostles, critically investigated. To which is prefixed, F. Overbeck's Introduction to the Acts, from De Wette's handbook*, 2 vols. (London and Edinburgh: Williams & Norgate, 1875–76).

11. W. M. L. de Wette, *Kurze Erklärung der Apostelgeschichte*, 4th ed., rev. and enl. Franz Overbeck, *Kurzgefasstes exegetisches Handbuch* (Leipzig: S. Hirzel, 1870).

12. Ibid., p. xxxi; see also Franz Overbeck, "Über das Verhältnis Justins des Märtyrers zur Apostelgeschichte," *Zeitschrift für wissenschaftliche Theologie* 15 (1872): 305–49; and Paul Wilhelm Schmidt, "De Wette-Overbecks Werk zur Apostelgeschichte und dessen jüngste Bestreitung," in *Festschrift zum 500-jährigen Bestehen der Universität Basel* (Basel, 1910), pp. 32–33 (pp. 274–75).

13. Franz Overbeck, *Über die Christlichkeit unserer heutigen Theologie*, 2nd ed., rev. and enl. (Leipzig: C. G. Naumann, 1903), p. 4. ET: *On the Christianity* [sic!] *of Theology*, translated with an introduction and notes by John Elbert Wilson (San José, CA: Pickwick Publications, 2002).

14. See Overbeck's remarks about the "we"-passages in Wette, *Kurze Erklärung der Apostelgeschichte* (1870), pp. xxxvii–lii.

15. For Overbeck's criticism of Acts, see also Johann-Christoph Emmelius, *Tendenzkritik und Formengeschichte: Der Beitrag Overbecks zur Auslegung der Apostelgeschichte im 19. Jahrhundert* (Göttingen: Vandenhoeck & Ruprecht, 1975).

16. For examples, see my *Opposition to Paul,* pp. 9–12.

17. See Otto Pfleiderer, *Das Urchristentum: Seine Schriften und Lehren im geschichtlichen Zusammenhang*, 2nd enl. and rev. ed., 2 vols. (Berlin: G. Reimer, 1902); Heinrich Julius Holtzmann, *Die Apostelgeschichte*, 3rd ed., completely rev. (Tübingen: J. C. B. Mohr [Paul Siebeck], 1901); Carl Heinrich von Weizsäcker, *The Apostolic Age of the Christian Church*, 3rd ed., 2 vols. (New York: G. P. Putnam's Sons, 1899–1907).

18. For a criticism of Harnack, see Emil Schürer's review of *Lukas der Arzt* by A. von Harnack, in *Theologische Literaturzeitung* 31 (1906): 405–408; and Heinrich Julius Holtzmann, "Harnacks Untersuchungen zur Apostelgeschichte," *Deutsche Literaturzeitung* 29 (1908): 1093–99.

19. Oldest text about 180 CE: Irenaeus *Haer.* 3.1.1; 3.14.1.

20. Alfred Wikenhauser, *Die Apostelgeschichte und ihr Geschichtswert* (Münster: Aschendorff, 1921); and Eduard Meyer, *Ursprung und Anfänge des Christentums*, 3 vols., 1st–3rd eds. (Stuttgart and Berlin: J. G. Cotta, 1921–23).

21. Ibid., 1:xiii.

22. For a criticism, see Martin Dibelius's review of *Ursprung und Anfänge des Christentums* by Eduard Meyer, in *Deutsche Literaturzeitung* 45 (1924): 1635–43.

23. For an overview, see Gasque, *History of Criticism*, pp. 251–66.

24. Representative of this movement are Martin Hengel, *Acts and the History of Earliest Christianity* (Philadelphia: Fortress Press, 1983); and Jürgen Roloff, *Die Apostelgeschichte* (Göttingen: Vandenhoeck & Ruprecht, 1981).

25. Julius Wellhausen, "Noten zur Apostelgeschichte," *Nachrichten der*

Gesellschaft der Wissenschaften in Göttingen—philologisch-historische Klasse (1907): 1–21; Wellhausen, "Kritische Analyse der Apostelgeschichte," *Abhandlungen der Gesellschaft der Wissenschaften zu Göttingen—Philologisch-historische Klasse* n.s. 15, no. 2 (1914).

26. Martin Dibelius, *Studies in the Acts of the Apostles* (London: SCM Press, 1956).

27. F. J. Foakes Jackson and Kirsopp Lake, eds., *The Beginnings of Christianity*, pt. 1, 5 vols. (London and New York: Macmillan, 1920–33); John Knox, "'Fourteen Years Later': A Note on the Pauline Chronology," *Journal of Religion* 16 (1936): 341–49; John Knox, "The Pauline Chronology," *Journal of Biblical Literature* 58 (1939): 15–29; John Knox, *Chapters in a Life of Paul* (Nashville, TN, and New York: Abingdon-Cokesbury Press, 1950; London: A. & C. Black, 1954); and Donald Wayne Riddle, *Paul, Man of Conflict: A Modern Biographical Sketch* (Nashville, TN: Abingdon-Cokesbury Press, 1940).

28. See Hans Conzelmann, *The Theology of St. Luke* (New York: Harper & Row, 1960); Conzelmann, *Acts of the Apostles: A Commentary on the Acts of the Apostles* (Philadelphia: Fortress Press, 1987); and Ernst Haenchen, *The Acts of the Apostles: A Commentary* (Philadelphia: Westminster Press, 1971).

29. For historical method see Ernst Bernheim, *Lehrbuch der historischen Methode und der Geschichtsphilosophie: Mit Nachweis der wichtigsten Quellen und Hilfsmittel zum Studium der Geschichte*, 5th and 6th ed., rev. and enl. (Leipzig: Duncker & Humblot, 1908), pp. 179–251. See also Gilbert J. Garraghan, S.J., *A Guide to Historical Method* (New York: Fordham University Press, 1946). Unfortunately, Bernheim's classic has never been translated into English.

30. See Philipp Vielhauer, "On the 'Paulinism' of Acts," in *Studies in Luke-Acts*, ed. Leander E. Keck and J. Louis Martyn (Philadelphia: Fortress Press, 1980), pp. 33–50.

31. Cf. Rom. 3:8 and, on the other hand, 1 Cor. 6:12a; 8:1.

32. 2 Pet. 3:14.

33. See, correctly, Gerhard Schneider, *Das Evangelium nach Lukas*, 2 vols. (Gütersloh: Gerd Mohn; Würzburg: Echter Verlag, 1977), 1:33.

34. See my *Paul, Apostle to the Gentiles: Studies in Chronology* (Philadelphia Fortress Press, 1984), pp. 37, 51, 147–48; and Robert Jewett, *A Chronology of Paul's Life* (Philadelphia: Fortress Press, 1979), pp. 85–86, 95–96, and elsewhere.

35. Acts 9; 11; 15; 18:22; 21.

36. See John Knox, "Acts and the Pauline Letter Corpus," in *Studies in Luke-Acts*, pp. 279–87.

37. See Andreas Lindemann, *Paulus im ältesten Christentum: Das Bild des Apostels und die Rezeption der paulinischen Theologie in der frühchristlichen Literatur bis Marcion* (Tübingen: J. C. B. Mohr/Paul Siebeck, 1979), p. 156.

38. For an overview, see William O. Walker, "Acts and the Pauline Corpus, Reconsidered," *Journal of the Study of the New Testament* 24 (1986): 3–23, esp. 8–9.

39. See Lindemann, *Paulus im ältesten Christentum*, p. 165.

40. For the difficulties with using the term "tradition" in Acts, see Jacob Jervell, *The*

Unknown Paul: Essays on Luke-Acts and Early Christian History (Minneapolis, MN: Augsburg Publishing House, 1984), p. 69.

41. See James Hardy Ropes, "An Observation on the Style of S. Luke," *Harvard Studies in Classical Philology* 12 (1901): 299–305.

42. See above, p. 235.

43. Wellhausen, "Noten," p. 14.

44. Pfleiderer, *Das Urchristentum*, pp. 514–15.

45. Wellhausen, "Noten," pp. 18–19.

46. See my *Paul, Apostle to the Gentiles*, pp. 152–56.

47. That Paul himself reports that he and Barnabas went to Jerusalem (Gal. 2:1a) is no conclusive argument against this thesis. Gal. 2:1a neither mentions the place from which Paul and Barnabas left for Jerusalem, nor presupposes that they have worked together immediately before the conference. Note that it was Titus whom Paul took along with him to Jerusalem (Gal. 2:1b), a detail that seems to indicate an independent Pauline mission.

48. 1 Clem. 5:7 shows that Paul dies as a martyr in Rome. On this text see above, p. 348.

49. 1 Cor. 7:17–20.

50. See my *Opposition to Paul*, pp. 64–115.

SELECT
BIBLIOGRAPHY

Alexander, Loveday. *The Preface to Luke's Gospel: Literary Convention and Social Context in Luke 1.1–4 and Acts 1.1.* New York: Cambridge University Press, 1993.

Ascough, Richard S. *Paul's Macedonian Associations: The Social Context of Philippians and 1 Thessalonians.* Tübingen: J. C. B. Mohr/Paul Siebeck, 2003.

Barrett, C. K. *Luke the Historian in Recent Study.* London: Epworth Press, 1961.

———. *The Acts of the Apostles.* 2 vols. Edinburgh: T & T Clark, 1994–98.

Bauer, Walter, William F. Arndt, and F. Wilbur Gingrich. *A Greek-English Lexicon of the New Testament and Other Early Christian Literature.* 2nd ed. Chicago: University of Chicago Press, 1979.

Baur, Ferdinand Christian. *Paul: The Apostle of Jesus Christ.* 2 vols. London/Edinburgh: Williams & Norgate, 1875–76.

Bormann, Lukas. *Philippi. Stadt und Christengenmeinde zur Zeit des Paulus.* Leiden: Brill, 1995.

Bornkamm, Günther. *Paul.* New York: Harper & Row, 1971.

Bovon, François. *Studies in Early Christianity.* Tübingen: J. C. B. Mohr/Paul Siebeck, 2003.

Bowden, John. "Appendix: Ideologies, Text and Tradition." In *The Unholy in Holy Scripture: The Dark Side of the Bible,* by Gerd Lüdemann, 146–61. Louisville, KY: Westminster John Knox Press, 1996.

Brocke, Christoph vom. *Thessalonike—Stadt des Kassander und Gemeinde des Paulus. Eine frühe christliche Gemeinde in ihrer heidnischen Umwelt.* Tübingen: J. C. B. Mohr/Paul Siebeck, 2001.

Cadbury, Henry J. *The Book of Acts in History.* New York: Harper & Brothers Publishers, 1955.

Charlesworth, James H., ed. *The Old Testament Pseudepigrapha.* Vol. 1, *Apocalyptic Literature and Testaments.* New York: Doubleday, 1983.

———. *The Old Testament Pseudepigrapha.* Vol. 2, *Expansions of the "Old Testament" and Legends, Wisdom and Philosophical Literature, Prayers, Psalms, and Odes, Fragments of Lost Judeo-Hellenistic Works.* New York: Doubleday & Company, 1985.

Cohen, Shaye J. D. *The Beginnings of Jewishness: Boundaries, Varieties, Uncertainties.* Berkeley: University of California Press, 1999.

Conzelmann, Hans. *The Theology of St. Luke.* New York: Harper & Brothers, 1960.

———. *Acts of the Apostles: A Commentary of the Acts of the Apostles.* Philadelphia: Fortress Press, 1987.

Crossan, John Dominic. *The Birth of Christianity: Discovering What Happened in the Years Immediately After the Execution of Jesus.* San Francisco: HarperSanFrancisco, 1998.

Dibelius, Martin. *From Tradition to Gospel.* New York: Charles Scribner's Sons, 1934.

———. *Studies in the Acts of the Apostles.* London: SCM Press, 1956.

Donfried, Karl Paul. *Paul, Thessalonica, and Early Christianity.* Grand Rapids, MI: Wm. B. Eerdmans, 2002.

Dunn, James D. G. *The Acts of the Apostles.* Valley Forge, PA: Trinity Press International, 1996.

Fitzmyer, Joseph A. *The Acts of the Apostles: A New Translation with Introduction and Commentary.* New York: Doubleday, 1998.

Fornara, Charles William. *The Nature of History in Ancient Greece and Rome.* Berkeley: University of California Press, 1983.

Gasque, W. Ward. *A History of Criticism of the Acts of the Apostles.* Grand Rapids, MI: Wm. B. Eerdmans, 1975

Gaventa, Beverly Roberts. *The Acts of the Apostles.* Nashville, TN: Abingdon Press, 2003.

Georgi, Dieter. *Remembering the Poor: The History of Paul's Collection for Jerusalem.* Nashville, TN: Abingdon Press, 1992.

Grant, Robert M. *Gnosticism and Early Christianity.* Rev. ed. New York: Harper & Row, Torchbooks, 1966.

Günther, Matthias. *Die Frühgeschichte des Christentums in Ephesus.* 2nd ed., rev. Frankfurt: Peter Lang 1998.

Haar, Stephen. *Simon Magus: The First Gnostic?* Berlin: Walter de Gruyter, 2003.

Haenchen, Ernst. *The Acts of the Apostles: A Commentary.* Philadelphia: Westminster Press, 1971.

———. "The Book of Acts as Source Material for the History of Early Christianity." In *Studies in Luke-Acts,* edited by Leander E. Keck and J. Louis Martyn, 258–78. Philadelphia: Fortress Press, 1980.

Harvey, Van A. *The Historian and the Believer: The Morality of Historical Knowledge and Christian Belief.* Urbana and Chicago: University of Illinois Press, 1996.

Hemer, Colin J. *The Book of Acts in the Setting of Hellenistic History.* Tübingen: J. C. B. Mohr/Paul Siebeck, 1989.

Hengel, Martin. *Judaism and Hellenism.* Philadelphia: Fortress Press, 1974.

——. *Between Jesus and Paul: Studies in the Earliest History of Christianity.* Philadelphia: Fortress Press, 1983.

Hengel, Martin, and Anna Maria Schwemer. *Paul Between Damascus and Antioch: The Unknown Years.* Louisville, KY: Westminster John Knox Press, 1997.

Gaventa, Beverly Roberts. *The Acts of the Apostles.* Nashville, TN: Abingdon Press, 2003.

Jackson, F. J. Foakes, and Kirsopp Lake, eds. *The Beginnings of Christianity.* Part 1, *The Acts of the Apostles.* 5 vols. London and New York: Macmillan, 1920–33.

Janssen, Martina. *Unter falschem Namen. Eine kritische Forschungsbilanz frühchristlicher Pseudepigraphie.* Frankfurt: Peter Lang, 2003.

Jeremias, Joachim. *Jerusalem in the Time of Jesus: An Investigation into Economic and Social Conditions during the New Testament Period.* Philadelphia: Fortress Press, 1969.

——. *New Testament Theology.* Vol 1, *The Proclamation of Jesus.* Philadelphia: Fortress Press, 1971.

Jervell, Jacob. *The Unknown Paul.* Minneapolis, MN: Augsburg Publishing House, 1984.

——. *Die Apostelgeschichte.* Göttingen: Vandenhoeck & Ruprecht, 1998.

Jewett, Robert. *A Chronology of Paul's Life.* Philadelphia: Fortress Press, 1982.

Johnson, Luke Timothy. *The Acts of the Apostles.* Collegeville, MN: Liturgical Press, 1992.

Käsemann, Ernst. *Essays on New Testament Themes.* Naperville, IL: Alec R. Allenson, 1964.

——. *New Testament Questions of Today.* London: SCM Press, 1969.

Keck, Leander E., and J. Louis Martyn, eds. *Studies in Luke-Acts.* Philadelphia: Fortress Press, 1980.

Klauck, Hans-Josef. *Magic and Paganism in Early Christianity: The World of the Acts of the Apostles.* Edinburgh: T & T Clark, 2000.

Knox, John. *Chapters in the Life of Paul,* rev. ed., edited by Douglas A. Hare. Macon, GA: Mercer University Press, 1987.

——. "Reflection," in *Cadbury, Knox, and Talbert: American Contributions to the Study of Acts,* edited by Mikeal C. Parsons and Joseph A. Tyson, 107–13. Atlanta, GA: Scholars Press, 1992.

Koester, Helmut, ed. *Ephesos: Metropolis of Asia. An Interdisciplinary Approach to Its Archaeology, Religion, and Culture.* Valley Forge, PA: Trinity Press International, 1995.

Krodel, Gerhard. *Acts.* Minneapolis, MN: Augsburg, 1986.

Lentz, John Clayton. *Luke's Portrait of Paul.* Cambridge and New York: Cambridge University Press, 1993.

Levinskaya, Irena. *The Book of Acts in Its First Century Setting.* Vol. 5, *The Book of Acts in Its Diaspora Setting.* Grand Rapids, MI: Wm. B. Eerdmans, 1996.

Lindemann, Andreas. *Paulus im ältesten Christentum. Das Bild des Apostels und die Rezeption paulinischer Theologie bis Marcion.* Tübingen: J. C. B. Mohr/Paul Siebeck, 1979.

Lohfink, Gerhard. *Die Himmelfahrt Jesu: Untersuchungen zu den Himmelfahrts- und Erhöhungstexten bei Lukas.* Munich: Kösel Verlag, 1971.

Lüdemann, Gerd. *Untersuchungen zur simonianischen Gnosis.* Göttingen: Vandenhoeck & Ruprecht, 1975.

——. *Paul, Apostle to the Gentiles: Studies in Chronology.* Philadelphia: Fortress Press, 1984.

——. *Early Christianity According to the Traditions in Acts: A Commentary.* Minneapolis, MN: Fortress Press, 1989.

——. *Opposition to Paul in Jewish Christianity.* Minneapolis, MN: Fortress Press, 1989.

——. *Heretics: The Other Side of Early Christianity.* Louisville, KY: Westminster John Knox Press, 1996.

——. *Virgin Birth? The Real Story of Mary and Her Son Jesus.* Harrisburg, PA: Trinity Press International, 1998.

——. *Jesus After 2000 Years: What He Really Said and Did.* Amherst, NY: Prometheus Books, 2001.

——. *Paul: The Founder of Christianity.* Amherst, NY: Prometheus Books, 2002.

——. *Primitive Christianity: A Survey of Recent Studies and Some New Proposals.* London and New York: T & T Clark, 2003.

——. *Die Intoleranz des Evangeliums. Erläutert an ausgewählten Schriften des Neuen Testaments.* Springe: zu Klampen, 2004.

Marguerat, Daniel. *The First Christian Historian: Writing the "Acts of the Apostles."* Cambridge: Cambridge University Press, 2002.

Marshall, I. Howard. *The Acts of the Apostles: An Introduction and Commentary.* Grand Rapids, MI: Wm. B. Eerdmans, 1980.

Murray, Gilbert. *Four Stages of Greek Religion.* London: Watts & Company, 1935.

Omerzu, Heike. *Der Prozess des Paulus. Eine exegetische und rechtshistorische Untersuchung der Apostelgeschichte.* Berlin: Walter de Gruyter, 2002.

Organ, Barbara E. *Is the Bible Fact or Fiction? An Introduction to Biblical Historiography.* New York and Mahwah, NJ: Paulist Press, 2004.

Parsons, C., and Richard I. Pervo. *Rethinking the Unity of Luke and Acts.* Minneapolis, MN: Fortress Press, 1993.

Pervo, Richard I. *Profit with Delight: The Literary Genre of the Acts of the Apostles.* Philadelphia: Fortress Press, 1987.

Pilhofer, Peter. *Philippi,* Band I. *Die erste christliche Gemeinde Europas.* Band II. *Katalog der Inschriften von Philippi.* Tübingen: J. C. B. Mohr/Paul Siebeck, 1995–2000.

Porter, Stanley E. *The Paul of Acts: Essays in Literary Criticism, Rhetoric, and Theology.* Tübingen: J. C. B. Mohr/Paul Siebeck, 1999.

Reimer, Andy M. *Miracle and Magic: A Study in the Acts of the Apostles and the Life of Apollonius of Tyana.* Sheffield: Sheffield Academic Press, 2002.

Riesner, Rainer. *Paul's Early Period: Chronology, Mission, Strategy.* Grand Rapids, MI: Wm. B. Eerdmans, 1998.

Roloff, Jürgen. *Die Apostelgeschichte.* Göttingen: Vandenhoeck & Ruprecht, 1981.

Schiffman, Lawrence H. "At the Crossroads: Tannaitic Perspectives on the Jewish-Christian Schism." In *Jewish and Christian Self-Definition.* Vol. 2, *Aspects of Judaism in the Greco-Roman Period,* edited by E. P. Sanders with A. I. Baumgarten and Alan Mendelson, 115–56. Philadelphia: Fortress Press, 1981.

Schille, Gottfried. *Die Apostelgeschichte des Lukas.* Berlin: Evangelische Verlagsanstalt, 1983.

Schottroff, Luise, and Wolfgang Stegemann. *Jesus and the Hope of the Poor.* Maryknoll, NY: Orbis Books, 1986.

Schürer, Emil. *The History of the Jewish People in the Age of Jesus Christ (175 B.C.–A.D. 135).* 3 vols. Revised and edited by Geza Vermes, Fergus Millar, and Matthew Black. Edinburgh: T & T Clark, 1973–87.

Schwartz, Daniel R. *Agrippa I: The Last King of Judaea.* Tübingen: J. C. B. Mohr/Paul Siebeck, 1990.

Schwartz, Eduard. *Gesammelte Schriften.* Vol. 5, *Zum Neuen Testament und zum frühen Christentum.* Berlin: Walter de Gruyter, 1963.

Sheeley, Steven M. *Narrative Asides in Luke-Acts.* Sheffield: Sheffield Academic Press, 1992.

Skinner, Matthew L. *Locating Paul: Places of Custody as Narrative Settings in Acts 21–28.* Leiden and Boston: Brill, 2003.

Sterling, Gregory E. *Historiography and Self-Definition: Josephos, Luke-Acts and Apologetic Historiography.* Leiden: E. J. Brill, 1992.

Strelan, Rick. *Strange Acts: Studies in the Cultural World of the Acts of the Apostles.* Berlin: Walter de Gruyter, 2004.

Tajra, Harry W. *The Trial of St. Paul: A Juridical Exegesis of the Second Half of the Acts of the Apostles.* Tübingen: J. C. B. Mohr/Paul Siebeck, 1989.

———. *The Martyrdom of St. Paul.* Tübingen: J. C. B. Mohr/Paul Siebeck, 1994.

Talbert, Charles H. *Reading Luke-Acts in Its Mediterranean Milieu.* Leiden and Boston: Brill, 2003.

Theissen, Gerd. *The Miracle Stories of the Early Christian Tradition.* Edinburgh: T & T Clark, 1983.

———. *A Theory of Primitive Christian Religion.* London: SCM Press, 1999. (US edition published as *The Religion of the Earliest Churches: Creating a Symbolic World.* Minneapolis, MN: Fortress Press, 1999.)

Trocmé, Étienne. *The Childhood of Christianity.* London: SCM Press, 1997.

Tyson, Joseph B. *Luke, Judaism, and the Scholars: Critical Approaches to Luke-Acts.* Columbia: University of South Carolina Press, 1999.

Vielhauer, Philipp. "On the 'Paulinism' of Acts." In *Studies in Luke-Acts,* edited by Leander E. Keck and J. Louis Martyn, 33–50. Philadelphia: Fortress Press, 1980.

Walaskay, Paul W. *Acts.* Louisville, KY: Westminster John Knox Press, 1998.

Wehnert, Jürgen. *Die Wir-Passagen der Apostelgeschichte. Ein lukanisches Stilmittel aus jüdischer Tradition.* Göttingen: Vandenhoeck & Ruprecht, 1989.

———. "Das Markus-Evangelium als Quelle der Apostelgeschichte." In *Historische Wahrheit und theologische Wissenschaft,* edited by Alf Özen, 21–40. Frankfurt: Peter Lang, 1996.

———. *Die Reinheit des "christlichen Gottesvolkes" aus Juden und Heiden. Studien zum historischen und theologischen Hintergrund des sogenannten Aposteldekrets.* Göttingen: Vandenhoeck & Ruprecht, 1997.

Welborn, Laurence L. "Paul's Flight from Damascus: Sources and Evidence for an Historical Evaluation." In *Historische Wahrheit und theologische Wissenschaft,* edited by Alf Özen, 41–60. Frankfurt: Peter Lang, 1996.

Wellhausen, Julius. "Kritische Analyse der Apostelgeschichte." Abhandlungen der Gesellschaft der Wissenschaften zu Göttingen—Philologisch-historische Klasse n.s. 15/2 (1914).

Wengst, Klaus. *Pax Romana and the Peace of Jesus Christ.* London: SCM Press, 1987.

Wikenhauser, Alfred. *Die Apostelgeschichte und ihr Geschichtswert.* Münster: Aschendorff, 1921.

Wilken, Robert L. *The Myth of Christian Beginnings; History's Impact on Belief.* Garden City, NY: Doubleday, Anchor Books, 1972.

Williams, C. S. C. *The Acts of the Apostles.* London: Adam & Charles Black, 1957.

Witherington, Ben III, ed. *History, Literature, and Society in the Book of Acts.* Cambridge and New York: Cambridge University Press, 1996.

———. *The Acts of the Apostles: A Socio-Rhetorical Commentary.* Grand Rapids, MI: William B. Eerdmans, 1998.

INDEX OF
NEW TESTAMENT
PASSAGES

INDEX OF
MODERN AUTHORS